Goal Directed Behavior

Originally published in 1985, this book was an attempt at a comprehensive review of the psychology of action in various areas of psychology. It is also an attempt to bridge two languages and traditions in psychology: German and Anglo-American. Although Anglo-American psychology had had an enormous influence on German psychology, the influence had not gone the other way around – at least not in recent years. Therefore, this book attempts to get the two traditions to speak with each other. The main article, from one language area, and the following discussion, from the other language area, together result in an extensive treatment of an action-theoretic approach in the respective psychological area; thus, both the main article and "discussion" should be read together.

Goal Directed Behavior

The Concept of Action in Psychology

Edited by
Michael Frese and John Sabini

Routledge
Taylor & Francis Group

LONDON AND NEW YORK

First published in 1985
by Lawrence Erlbaum Associates, Inc

This edition first published in 2021 by Routledge
2 Park Square, Milton Park, Abingdon, Oxon OX14 4RN

and by Routledge
52 Vanderbilt Avenue, New York, NY 10017

Routledge is an imprint of the Taylor & Francis Group, an informa business

A Library of Congress record exists under ISBN: 0898595290

ISBN: 978-0-367-71398-0 (hbk)
ISBN: 978-1-003-15074-9 (ebk)
ISBN: 978-0-367-71416-1 (pbk)

GOAL DIRECTED BEHAVIOR:

The Concept of Action in Psychology

Edited By

MICHAEL FRESE
University of Pennsylvania

JOHN SABINI
University of Pennsylvania

IEA LAWRENCE ERLBAUM ASSOCIATES, PUBLISHERS
1985   Hillsdale, New Jersey   London

Lawrence Erlbaum Associates, Inc., Publishers
365 Broadway
Hillsdale, New Jersey 07642

Library of Congress Cataloging in Publication Data
Main entry under title:

Goal directed behavior.

  Includes bibliographies and index.
  1. Intentionalism.   2. Goal (Psychology)   I. Frese,
Michael.   II. Sabini, John, 1947–
BF619.5.G63   1985   153.8   84-24722
ISBN 0-89859-529-0

Printed in the United States of America
10 9 8 7 6 5 4 3 2 1

Contributors

Michael Athay, School of Law, New York University, New York, New York, United States

Jonathan Baron, Department of Psychology, University of Pennsylvania, Philadelphia, Pennsylvania, United States

Lee Roy Beach, Graduate School of Business, University of Chicago, Chicago, Illinois, United States

Virginia Blankenship, Oakland University, Rochester, Michigan, United States

Donald E. Broadbent, Department of Experimental Psychology, University of Oxford, Oxford, England

Michael Chapman, Max Planck Institut für Psychologische Forschung, München, West Germany

John M. Darley, Department of Psychology, Princeton University, Princeton, New Jersey, United States

Kim G. Dolan, Institute of Child Development, University of Minnesota, Minneapolis, Minnesota, United States

Michael Frese, Institut für Psychologie, München, West Germany

Charles R. Gallistel, Department of Psychology, University of Pennsylvania, Philadelphia, Pennsylvania, United States

Winfried Hacker, Technische Universität, Dresden, German Democratic Republic

Heinz Heckhausen, Max Planck Institut für Psychologische Forschung, Berlin, West Germany

Claes von Hofsten, Department of Psychology, Uppsala University, Uppsala, Sweden

Eric Klinger, Department of Psychology, University of Minnesota, Minneapolis, Minnesota, United States

Debra A. Kossman, Department of Psychology, University of Pennsylvania, Philadelphia, Pennsylvania, United States

Julius Kuhl, Max Planck Institut für Psychologische Forschung, Berlin, West Germany

Richard S. Lazarus, Department of Psychology, University of California, Berkeley, California, United States

Ulric Neisser, Department of Psychology, Emory University, Atlanta, Georgia, United States

Franz Reither, Studiengang Psychologie, Universität Bamberg, Bamberg, West Germany

John Sabini, Department of Psychology, University of Pennsylvania, Philadelphia, Pennsylvania, United States

Wolfgang Schnotz, Deutsches Institut für Fernstudien, Universität Tubingen, Tubingen, West Germany

Wolfgang Schönpflug, Institut für Psychologie der Freien Universität, Berlin, West Germany

Volker Schurig, Interdisziplinares Zentrum für Hocjschuldidaktik der Universität, Hamburg, West Germany

Norbert Semmer, Bundesgesundheitsamt, Berlin, West Germany

Rainer K. Silbereisen, Institut für Psychologie, Berlin, West Germany

Maury Silver, Baltimore, Maryland, United States

Ellen A. Skinner, Max Planck Institut für Psychologische Forschung, Berlin, West Germany

Michael Stadler, Studiengang Psychologie Universität Bremen, Bremen, West Germany

Thea Staüdel, Studiengang Psychologie, Universität Bamberg, Bamberg, West Germany

Walter Volpert, Technische Universität, Berlin, West Germany

Theo Wehner, Studiengang Psychologie Universität Bremen, Bremen, West Germany

Contents

Preface xv

Action Theory: An Introduction   **xvii**
Michael Frese and John Sabini
   Introduction xvii
   Basic Concepts of Action Theory xvii
   What Kind of Theory Is Action Theory? xxiii
   Methodological Implications xxiv

I.   HISTORICAL TRADITIONS AND PHYLOGENESIS OF ACTION

1.   **"Purposive Behavior" in Psychology and Philosophy: A History**   **3**
   Maury Silver
      Introduction 3
      Explaining Purpose and Explaining It Away 5
      How Goals Influence Behavior 12
      Psychology Finds a Respectable Teleology 15

2.   **Stages in the Development of Tool Behavior in the Chimpanzee (Pan troglodytes)**   **20**
   Volker Schurig
      Introduction 20

Levels of Language and Abstraction Within the Term *Tool Behavior* 21

Instinctive Tool Use$_2$ in Chimpanzees: The Construction of Sleeping Nests 23

Learned Tool Use$_3$ Under Natural-Habitat Conditions 25

The Action Aspect in Chimpanzee Tool Use 27

The Societal Level of Functioning: Tool Use$_5$ as *Activity (Taetigkeit)* 30

3. An Action-Theory Perspective of the Tool-Using Capacities of Chimpanzees and Human Infants   **35**
Kim G. Dolgin
Introduction 35
A Discussion of Schurig's Model 36
The Piagetian Perspective 40
Chimpanzee Language Studies and Tool Use 42

II. FUNDAMENTALS OF ACTION THEORY

4. Motivation, Intention, and Emotion: Goal Directed Behavior from a Cognitive-Neuroethological Perspective   **48**
Charles R. Gallistel
Introduction 48
The Framework 49
Motivation and the Principle of Selective Potentiation and Depotentiation 52
Representations and Intentionality 55
Representations and Emotion 61
What Function Do Act-Outcome and Motivational Representations Serve and What Is the Behavioral Evidence of Their Existence? 62
Summary 64

5. Anticipation as a Basic Principle in Goal Directed Action   **67**
Michael Stadler and Theo Wehner
Introduction: Representation and Anticipation 67
A Model for Representation: The Functional System 69
Levels of Anticipation 73
Conclusions 77

6. Perception and Action   **80**
Claes von Hofsten
Introduction 80
Gibson's Ecological Approach to Perception 81

Control of Balance and Locomotion—The Basis for Action 85
Timing 87
Exploratory Actions 92
Concluding Comments 95

7. **The Role of Invariant Structures in the Control of Movement**   **97**
Ulric Neisser
Introduction 97
Theories of Perception 97
Invariants of Stimulus Information 99
Invariants of Motor Organization 101
Schemata, Images, and Mental Practice 103
Anticipations and the Perceptual Cycle 104
von Hofsten's Critique 106

8. **Thinking and Action**   **110**
Franz Reither and Thea Stäudel
Introduction 110
Characteristics and Demands of Complex Problems 111
Complex Problem-Solving Processes 112
Modifications in Thinking and Action 117
Relations Between Thinking and Action 119
Summary 121

9. **Action: Decision Implementation Strategies and Tactics**   **123**
Lee Roy Beach
Introduction 123
Goals 123
Implementation Strategies and Tactics 124
Monitoring Progress Toward the Goal 125
Failure to Progress Toward the Goal 126
Attractive Goals, Aversive Tactics—A Special, but Instructive,
    Case 127
Teaching Implementation Skills 128
Implementation and the Reither and Stäudel Results 130

10. **From Wishes to Action: The Dead Ends and Short Cuts on the
    Long Way to Action**   **134**
Heinz Heckhausen and Julius Kuhl
Introduction 134
An Extended Taxonomy of Motivational Variables 135
Different Goal Levels and Their Interrelations 137
From Wishes to Intentions: A Process Oriented Analysis 140
Developmental Path of Wishes at the Different Goal Levels 143

Empirical Support for the Wish-Related Section of the Model 145
Pre- and Postcommitment Processes: Motivation versus Volition 150
From Intentions to Action: Self-Regulatory Processes 152
Defective and Degenerated Intentions 154
Impairing Effects of Defective and Degenerated Intentions 155
Outlook 158

11. The Dynamics of Intention   **161**
Virginia Blankenship
Introduction 161
The Dynamics of Action Model 162
Thought and Action in the Dynamic Model 165
Dynamic Aspects of Intention 167
Unconscious Motivation 169
Conclusions 170

**12. Goal Directed Behavior as a Source of Stress: Psychological Origins
and Consequences of Inefficiency**   **172**
Wolfgang Schönpflug
Efficiency of Action 172
Origins of Inefficiency 176
Deliberate Disengagement: An Option in the Face of Inefficiency 186
Summary and Concluding Remarks 187

**13. Toward an Understanding of Efficiency and Inefficiency in Human
Affairs: Discussion of Schönpflug's Theory**   **189**
Richard S. Lazarus
Introduction 189
Some History 190
The Work of Schönpflug 192
Some Nagging Concerns 194
The Dual Perspectives on Human Functioning 197

14. Action in Development—Development in Action   **200**
Michael Chapman and Ellen A. Skinner
Introduction 200
Fundamentals of Action and Development 201
Action in Personality and Cognitive Development 204
Conclusion 212

15. Action-Theory Perspective in Research on Social Cognition   **215**
Rainer K. Silbereisen
Introduction 215
Research on Social Cognition in an Action-Theory Format 216
Action for Development: A Summary of Potential Contributions 225

16. **The Role of Power in Social-Exchange Relationships**   **230**
Michael Athay and John M. Darley
Introduction 230
Social Action as a Process of Treatment Production 231
Social Exchange and Rational Choice 232
Positional Power and the Organization of "Social Production" 233
Illustrations: Roles in a University Department 236
Positional Power versus Rational Choice 240
Domains of Application for Positional Power and Social Exchange
   243
Modes of Social Exchange 245
Concluding Comments 247

17. **Some Contributions of Action Theory to Social Psychology: Social Action and Social Actors in the Context of Institutions and an Objective World**   **249**
John Sabini, Michael Frese, and Debra Kossman
Introduction 249
Positional Power and Expectancy Value Theory 249
Action Theory and Person Perception: Action versus Perception 253

III. APPLICATIONS OF ACTION THEORY

18. **Activity: A Fruitful Concept in Industrial Psychology**   **262**
Winfried Hacker
Introduction: The Roots of the Concept 262
The Design of "Activities" and the Mental Processes: Regulating
   Them as the Subject Matters of Industrial Psychology 263
Work as a Special Class of Goal Oriented Activities 267
The Concept of Complete versus Partialized Structure of Activity—A
   Useful Guide 272
Mental Representations of Goals and Plans in the Regulation of
   Activities 276

19. **Multiple Goals and Flexible Procedures in the Design of Work**   **285**
Donald E. Broadbent
The Importance of Activity 285
Problems of Empirical Findings 287
Some Conceptual Suggestions 290
Some Directions for the Future 292

20. **Action Theory in Clinical Psychology**   **296**
    Norbert Semmer and Michael Frese
      Cognition and Action 296
      Abnormal Behavior as Ineffective Actions 300
      Therapeutic Implications of Action Theory 305
      Summary and Conclusion 309

21. **Missing Links in Action Theory**   **311**
    Eric Klinger
      Introduction 311
      An Action Theory Still Lost in Thought 311
      Applications to Psychopathology 315
      Applications to Treatment 317
      Summary 318

22. **Rational Plans, Achievement, and Education**   **322**
    Jonathan Baron
      Introduction 322
      Descriptive, Normative, and Prescriptive Models 323
      Rawls' Theory as a Normative Theory of Action 324
      The Rationality of Achievement Related Action Styles 328
      Training in Action Styles 336
      Multiattribute Utility Theory (MAUT) 339
      Conclusion 342

23. **On Problems of Rationality in Education**   **345**
    Wolfgang Schnotz
      The Problem of Norms in Education and Educational Psychology 345
      On Deduction of Educational Objectives from Normative Models 346
      How Can We Achieve More Rationality? 350
      Are Normative Theories Appropriate for Deriving Educational
          Objectives? 351

IV. **POSTSCRIPT**

Epilogue   **357**
    Walter Volpert
      Looking Through Facets to a Whole 357
      System Models and Process Models 358
      Schemata—The Invariants with Limited Variability 360
      Sequentiality in Process Models: No Algorithm, but Internal Logic
          362
      Concluding Comments 364

References 367

Author Index 397

Subject Index 407

PREFACE

This book is an attempt at a comprehensive review of the psychology of action in various areas of psychology. It is also an attempt to bridge two languages and traditions in psychology: German and Anglo-American. Although Anglo-American psychology has had an enormous influence on German psychology, the influence has not gone the other way around—at least not in recent years. Therefore, this book attempts to get the two traditions to speak with each other. We tried to assure this by having, in each section, a person of one language area write the main article (e.g., the psychology of work) and a person from the other language area discuss it. Because these responses are supposed to complement the approach of the main article, it is a little misleading to call them discussions. They are meant to be more than that. In each case the main article and the discussion *together* result in an extensive treatment of an action-theoretic approach in the respective psychological area; thus, both the main article and "discussion" should be read together. Sometimes the discussion consists of a peer critique of the article. Sometimes, on the other hand, the article is a jumping-off point for the discussant to raise issues that seem to be particularly important in the other language area. And sometimes, there is a mixture of these two.

We want to thank various people who have helped us in the rather complicated task of orchestrating a book like this. Mike Feeley helped us in some of the translations from German. Fran Clifford typed many of the manuscripts, even in cases in which the editors decided for the fourth time that the manuscript should be revised one more time. Most important was the help that we got from Peggy Ovington, who read all the manuscripts, corrected the English, spelling mistakes, missing references, and so on. Furthermore, she made us aware when things just did not "sound right." Finally, she was the one, in the end, who really knew on which side of the Atlantic which manuscript happened to be, at the moment, and what work still had to be done on it.

Action Theory: An Introduction

Michael Frese
John Sabini
University of Pennsylvania

INTRODUCTION

This book is an international endeavor to use the concept of action in various areas of psychology. Psychologists from two language communities—German speaking and English speaking—and traditions have participated in this book. These two language communities have had a long tradition of mutual exchange which stopped when barbarism destroyed the science of psychology in Germany. Now there is a burst of interest in the concept of action on both sides of the Atlantic; so it seemed time to renew the dialogue around the concept of action.

In this introduction, we pursue three topics. First, we discuss the basic concepts of action theory; second, we make clear the sense in which action theory is a theory; and finally, we mention some of the methodological (in a broad sense of the term) implications of an action-theoretic approach.

BASIC CONCEPTS OF ACTION THEORY

The concept of goal oriented action (*Handlung* in German) is as old as psychology, and has been particularly prevalent in German psychology. Wundt (1907), Ach (1910), Lewin (1935), and Tolman (1932) all conceived of action as the fundamental unit of psychology. But behaviorism displaced the notion of action with the much less precise term *behavior*. But the notion that we and other organisms engage, for the most part, in goal directed action has had a resurgence both in the English-speaking and German-speaking countries. With this return to an earlier conception of what psychology must explain comes a series of problems—conceptual and empirical—that behaviorism avoided. This book is a progress report about the current state of thinking about these new and old problems.

One old problem intimately associated with the notion of action is the concept of *will*. For example, Ach (1910, p. 256) defines action as the material realization of an object oriented act of the will. This notion contains many facets of action theory, facets discussed in this book: Action is related to an anticipated result (the goal), to an intention (will), which implies effort (will-act), and to a plan to reach the goal (object oriented content).

Modern action theory starts where Tolman (1932) left off: There is a goal, and there is a map. But are the map and the goal related to behavior? How is the gap between cognition and action to be bridged? How is the gap from a vague wish to an actual intention to be bridged? And finally, how can one bridge the gap between the real world outside and cognition inside? Thus, three gaps must be filled with conceptual and empirical advance: (1) from the objective environment to cognition; (2) from an opportunity to pursue a goal to the intention to pursue a goal; and (3) from an intention to behavior. Finally, there is a somewhat broader issue: What are the phylogenetic and ontogenetic courses of development of the abilities that must be present for an organism to be able to manage intentional action?

The Gap from the Objective Environment to Cognition

In contrast to Lewin's (1936) emphasis on the organism's life space as its subjective environment, the emphasis of action theory is on the objective environment. The epistemology of action theory, like Pragmatism, its American cousin, is captured by the phrase: In acting you get to know the world because in action one gets feedback from the objects acted upon. Through feedback cycles (Neisser, 1976, this volume; von Hofsten, this volume) one approaches the true state of affairs in the world. This notion is in sharp contrast to the more constructivistic notion of much of cognitive psychology (for a critique compare Neisser, 1976).

One reason for the constructivistic orientation of much of modern cognitive psychology stems from its reliance on experiments that do not allow the person to engage in a complete perceptual cycle (looking—expectancy—looking to see whether the object of perception meets one's expectations—changing expectations—looking again, etc.) or to act. Experiments that do not allow the person to act upon the objects of perception truncate the processes by which we normally come to know the world, and in this way build a misleading model of cognition. The distortion is most prominent in the research tradition relying on tachistoscopes. Tachistoscopes show us to be error-prone creatures, but when a subject is able to act upon an object, when he or she is able to get feedback from the environment, illusions are replaced by better and better approximations of reality.

This distortion crops up in the perceptions of relatively static objects, but it is even more severe in the perception of social events, which are, in some sense at least, more complicated (cf. Lazarus, this volume; Sabini, Frese, & Kossman, this volume). Not only are social situations more complicated, but they also change without input from the actor/observer (cf. Reither & Stäudel, this volume, for research on subjects' responses to complex problems). From an action theory point of view, however, perceiving social situations is not qualitatively different from perceiving objects. It is just more difficult. A longer perceptual cycle is needed to approximate realistic perception; more action on the social environment is needed before one can grasp what it is about. This view that an objective world is apprehended by action is in contrast to much of social and clinical psychology. In particular, it contrasts with research guided by attribution theory, which often gives the impression that people have no business dealing with the real world at all, that it is adequate for them just to deal with their constructions of the world. (Sabini & Silver, 1982; Hacker, Schönpflug, Semmer & Frese, Sabini et al., and particularly von Hofsten and Neisser, all this volume, present evidence and arguments for this more objective conceptualization of acting and perceiving the real world.)

The Gap between Wish and Intention

Obviously, we do not act on all of our wishes: The mind recoils from the chaotic world constructed by the fantasies stimulated during a single boring colloquium. But classical expectancy × valence (or value) theories have difficulty explaining how a wish with a positive valence is transformed into an intention, because, equally obviously, our wishes sometimes do become our acts. Heckhausen and Kuhl (this volume) flesh out the processes that might take place between a wish and an intention.

One needs, first, the notion of opportunity: The extent to which a wish is transformed into an intent is regulated by the opportunities and affordances that one perceives one will have in the future. Even when one intends to do something, one does not act immediately—again, one must often wait for opportunity to knock. I may, in the midst of typing, notice that I need a new ribbon, but the middle of a sentence is a poor moment to replenish stationery; better I should wait until I am passing an appropriate store.

A further theoretical problem for expectancy × valence theory arises when people do not act even though expectancies and valences have recently become high. At first blush we might explain this failure to act by claiming that the actor did not notice that circumstances have changed. But this account leads to a snare of theoretical questions. For example: How are calculations of expectancy and value initiated? To solve this problem Heckhausen and Kuhl introduce the metaphor of a spinning top: In their view, a wish, once entertained but dismissed as unrealistic, does not just vanish, but persists as an element of mental life, as a top set spinning persists in its motion. The "top" guides attention and cognition in the direction of finding opportunities, circumstances in which to form an intention and to formulate a plan.

The opposite of an opportunity is an obstacle; an obstacle can have an effect similar to an opportunity's on the relation between a wish and an intention. Obstacles hinder the development of an intention, decrease desire, and lead to a variety of emotional reactions. Schönpflug (this volume) takes up this point, though with different terminology, in his discussion of model and goal construction.

Baron (this volume) is concerned with values and desires as well, but he approaches the problem from a different angle. He asks what values and wishes one *ought* to have. Thus, instead of offering a descriptive model of the formation of desires and plans, he argues for a prescriptive theory specifying the values and desires education ought to inculcate. The values that turn out to be important in education, on his account, are intimately related to action theory; for example, Baron argues that the desire to contribute to the social order is intrinsically desirable, whereas the desire to gain information about the world is only contingently desirable.

The Gap between Intention and Action

Guthrie complained that Tolman's theory left his rats buried in thought. A similar problem has beset decision theory (Beach, this volume). Miller, Galanter, and Pribram (1960) can be credited with the first attempt to give a coherent framework within which the regulation of action through cognition could be described. They argued that there is an interlocked hierarchy of feedback units (the so-called Test–Operate–Test–Exit units) that relate a cognition to action. Plans for the course of action are made up of these units. A hierarchical structure is necessary, according to Carver & Scheier, 1982, because it:

> allows one to account successfully for the fact that exceedingly restricted and concrete behavioral acts (i.e., changes in levels of muscle tension) are used to create behavioral events that are often so abstract as to seem completely unrelated to those concrete acts (e.g., writing an article, winning a tennis tournament, faithfully executing the office of president) [p. 117].

A similar argument has been made in more concrete physiological terms by Gallistel (1980a, this volume). The notion of hierarchy also allows one to describe different levels of regulation within the same theoretical framework (cf. Hacker and Semmer & Frese, this volume). Of course, a plan of action does not have to be completed before initiating an act; the plan may be completed while acting (Volpert, 1976). But according to action theory, there must be at least a general notion of a goal and a general plan before one is able to act at all. Acts and their outcomes are fed back into the system, allowing for adjustment of the plan. Furthermore, action theory posits that practicing a certain plan of action leads to automatization of this plan (Shiffrin & Dumais, 1981). Automatization means that fewer decisions have to be made, less effort need go into the particular action, and less central processing capacity is needed in developing the outline of the action. These advantages of automatization also give rise to institutions in social settings (cf. Athay & Darley, this volume). In contrast to Shiffrin and Dumais (1981), however, action theory does not posit two distinct processing systems, but one that goes from a high degree of automatization to one that is marked by deliberate control of action (cf. Hacker and Semmer & Frese, this volume). Automatization develops when there is redundancy in the environment and action plans are well practiced. The idea that there is hierarchical regulation of action also solves a dilemma of classical learning theory: It had to postulate an essentially limitless memory capacity and an impossible amount of practice before one could carry out even the simplest actions. In the action-theory view, on the other hand, plan development is accomplished with a limited number of heuristics, and lower-level, automatized plans are stored schematically with parameters added depending on the circumstances under which they are used by the plan in the concrete circumstance the actor faces (Schmidt, 1982b). The notion that there is hierarchical control of action, with lower levels subserved by automatized action, sheds some light on the nature of emotion. Several contributors to this volume (Schnotz; Lazarus; Klinger; Semmer & Frese; Reither & Stäudel) mention the impact of emotion on action. Emotion can both facilitate and obstruct action. These two aspects of the effect of emotion can, perhaps, be better understood by seeing emotions as automatized patterns of thinking and acting. One characteristic of emotional experience is the compelling way it fixes our attention on objects (or aspects of objects) in the environment—when really angry with someone we find it difficult not to dwell on the wrongs they have done us. Another aspect of emotional experience is the way that our responses to emotion-laden objects sometimes fail to be integrated with our broader plans and goals: We may respond in a hostile way to the person with whom we are angry, even though our broader goals would be better served by ignoring the insult we think he is guilty of. If emotions are seen as automatized reactions, we can understand why these unfortunate aspects of emotion burden us, but also why, when in an emotional state, our reactions are facilitated.

Phylogenetic and Ontogenetic Development of Action

Ontogenetic development itself may take the form of action (cf. Silbereisen, this volume). For example, we may undertake as intentional actions the development of our careers or abilities, and we may even decide to alter our own values (cf. Baron, this volume). It is necessary to exert effort to reach these developmental goals (cf. Chapman & Skinner, this volume).

Many action theorists[1] have thought of work as the prototype of action (Leontiev, 1971; Hacker and Schurig this volume). Work is theoretically important for action theory in two ways: First, work typically involves a goal, a conception of what the finished product must be before action is begun, and it typically involves a plan, a conception of how to reach that desirable state of affairs. Second, in work, recurrent social plans are objectified and materialized in the form of tools. (Cf. Berger & Luckmann, 1966, on tools as "sedimentations," collective, external records of the ways our lives are led and our problems overcome.) The usual way of thinking about tools is that they have been invented to solve problems. But in addition, tools shape the way we come to see the problems we have, casting the problems our shared biology gives us into the specific cultural form with which we confront them. Scholarly journals, obviously, are a response to a particular problem we have—communicating discoveries to the interested community. In that sense they are tools. But just as obviously because of their substantive and methodological requirements, scientific journals shape the way we approach the problems we face, and even create the problems we are called upon to solve. Less obviously, hammers, too, are more than a solution to a specific problem; they also shape the problems we come to have. In developing culturally and ontogenetically, we have to accommodate to the culturally shared tools; thus the cultural transmission of action plans (and sometimes action goals) is achieved. Because work is the very model of action, Schurig (this volume) developed his phylogenetic account of the evolution of intentional action with regard to work, discussing similarities and differences between chimpanzees and humans in their abilities to use tools, engage in work, and undertake action in the full-blooded sense. Dolgin (this volume), too, distinguishes human work from primate tool use; she emphasizes the human potential to chain together socially dependent actions—something a chimpanzee is not able to do. Furthermore, she focuses on some of the ways that phylogenetic and ontogentic development overlap.

We turn now to our second goal, a consideration of the sort of theory action theory is.

---

[1]Undoubtedly some were influenced by Marx's famous discussion of the differences between a bee and an architect (Marx, 1906/1977):

"We presuppose labour in a form that stamps it as exclusively human. A spider conducts operations that resemble those of a weaver, and a bee puts to shame many an architect in the construction of her cells. But what distinguishes the worst architect from the best of bees is this, that the architect raises his structure in imagination before he erects it in reality. At the end of the labour-process, we get a result that already existed in the imagination of the labourer at its commencement. He not only effects a change of form in the material on which he works, but he also realises a purpose of his own that gives the law to his modus operandi, and to which he must subordinate his will. Besides the exertion of the bodily organs, the process demands that during the whole operation, the workman's will be steadily in consonance with his purpose" [p. 198].

WHAT KIND OF THEORY IS ACTION THEORY?

Theory is a rather diffuse notion. On the one hand there is the virus theory of cancer, a specific claim, perhaps better called a hypothesis, about the cause of something. The virus theory of cancer just might be false. But then too, there is "evolutionary theory." It is hard to imagine what could convince us that natural selection is false. We could find out that natural selection played a more limited role than we had imagined in the emergence of species as we know them; but even if this is so, we would want to say that natural selection is more limited than we had imagined rather than that it is false in the way that the virus theory of cancer might just turn out to be false. Action theory, in this way, is much more like evolutionary theory than it is like the virus theory of cancer.

Action theory begins with a conception of human behavior: that it is directed toward the accomplishment of goals, that it is directed by plans, that those plans are hierarchically arranged, and that feedback from the environment articulates with plans in the guidance of action. Such a view is, no doubt, a poor model to apply to some behaviors—sneezing, for example—but it seems reasonable to apply it to other behaviors—building a cabinet or pursuing a flirtation. Questions about how much of our behavior is captured by an action-theory framework have to do with how useful action theory is, rather than with whether it is true.

There seem to be three kinds of intellectual fun one can have once one has a theory of the action-theory sort. One kind of fun is filling in the details of the picture in cases that clearly fit the theory. Thus, one thing to do with evolutionary theory is to apply it to specific species in specific ecologies; application is a bit of an art, in that perspicacity is exercised in taking a very general framework and seeing how it is made manifest in specific cases. The outcome of such work is a better understanding of the specific species at hand. Some of the articles in this book (for example, Hacker's) illustrate this use of "action theory."

A second kind of filling in of detail involves raising general issues about details that a particular theory is mute about. For example, one might ask about the mechanism of evolution. The "new synthesis" of evolutionary theory with Mendelian genetics well illustrates this sort of fun—and this sort of payoff. Several contributors in this volume illustrate this use of action theory—for example, Heckhausen and Kuhl, who ask about the formation of intentions in the first place, and Reither and Stäudel, who ask about thinking and the ways of getting feedback about the world, or Athay and Darley who ask about the utility of applying expectancy-value notions in the case of role-structured interactions.

There is still another kind of intellectual fun we can derive from a theory: the fun of applying it in places where it does not seem to fit. Dawkins' (1976) application of evolutionary theory to cultural evolution is a nice example of this use of a theory. Schönpflug (this volume) and Semmer and Frese (this volume) take action theory and apply it to domains in which one would not, on the face of it, expect a model of intentional action to shed much light—to problems of psychopathology and emotion.

The reader, then should not expect an answer, or the evidence for an answer, to the question: Is action theory true? Rather, he or she can expect answers to the questions: What is action theory good for? How can it help me understand some particular things? What unsolved questions does it raise? How can it be extended to phenomena different from those that inspired its creation?

Action theory stresses the way we go about creating specific plans in specific environments to reach specific goals. But it also suggests that we have at hand abstract, schematic plans specifying the kinds of information we ought to get from the world to help specify those plans, and heuristics telling us how to proceed once we have that initial information. Action theory is, in its own terms, just such an abstract, schematic guide to information to get and steps to take to reach our goal of understanding human behavior.

METHODOLOGICAL IMPLICATIONS

Action theory embraces some aspects of both the American behaviorist tradition and the modern cognitive view. In keeping with the American behaviorist tradition, action theorists are not content to describe people's cognitive capacities and processes, but ask about how they are deployed in the carrying out of concrete tasks. Like behaviorists, action theorists are responsible to performance data, to what people actually do in the world. Still, action theory retains as a central explanatory concept the notion of a representation, and the cognitive faculties— for example, memory—that must be invoked to explain the development of representations. In the use of such notions action theory displays its strong links to cognitive science; unlike behaviorism, it is hardly content to posit a black-box mind mediating between the world and behavior.

But action theory's approach to cognition has a particular emphasis, one that differs from much of current cognitive science. Action theorists tend to be less interested in the fundamental elements of cognition, whatever they may turn out to be, and more interested in how knowledge is brought to bear on action. Thus, research in this tradition tends to be more concerned with the details of the ecology in which the actor must act; for this reason the research tends to be carried out in natural settings, using natural tasks (cf. Silbereisen, this volume, as an example). And when the research is conducted in the laboratory, it tends toward simulation rather than simplification (cf. von Cranach, 1982; Reither & Stäudel, this volume). Action theory is not, then, a tool with which all of the questions that psychology, or cognitive science, can be explored, but it is a way of thinking that leads to a sharper understanding of how our cognitive equipment is put to use in the service of our projects and in relation to the world we happen to inhabit.

We can illustrate these features of the action-theory approach with three examples drawn from the chapters to follow. In his article on perception and action von Hofsten examines the capacities of the infant perceiver, but his emphasis is not on what the infant can learn about a static display with an extrinsic, if any, connection to its plans, but rather on what knowledge about the world the infant can display when that knowledge is required by its action. Thus, we find the infant perceiver capable of a remarkable capacity to use information about the trajectory of an object, when it puts that information to use in the act of grasping a moving object. Von Hofsten teaches us just how subtle an infant can be when we ask it questions in a form that is natural to it.

Reither and Stäudel ask about people's abilities to solve complex problems. In this way they share a focus with a strong tradition in cognitive psychology. But the traditional approach to this problem offers people information about the world and asks how well they use it to answer questions posed by the experimenter. Reither and Stäudel, in contrast, offer subjects the opportunity to pose their own questions of the world, or at least of a computer world meant to simulate some of the structural relations of the real world. Their approach reveals some of the difficulties people have in developing a strategy of inquiry about that dynamically changing world, difficulties that cannot be seen in research that does not offer subjects the opportunity to have a strategy of inquiry.

Lastly, Schönpflug addresses emotion from the perspective of action theory. He roots his analysis not in the physiological aspects of emotion, but in the relations between a person's emotions and his or her ongoing projects. The aim is to articulate how the structures of projects give rise to emotional experience, and how that emotional experience affects the execution of projects. Thus, emotion is located in the activities of an acting organism. In these ways, the action perspective, then, reorients and enriches our thinking about perception, cognition, and emotion, among other things.

HISTORICAL TRADITIONS AND PHYLOGENESIS OF ACTION

HISTORICAL TRADITION

Silver traces some of the debate over the status of the concept of intentional action in American psychology, and he shows why the concept of action was a problem within the behaviorist tradition. On the one hand, molar behaviorists like Tolman argued that the notion of intentionality was central to our description of much of human behavior, and even of the behavior of rats. On the other hand, molecular behaviorists, like Hull, argued that the notion of intentionality did nothing to specify the mechanism by which the act was accomplished. Hull's behaviorism was an attempt, at least, to specify what was going on inside the organism. Unfortunately, Hull's explanations, in terms of habits, had the effect of showing that the behavior was not intentional after all.

In retrospect, we can appreciate the sense in which both were right. Tolman was right in insisting that organisms, including both humans and rats, do sometimes act intentionally. Hull was right in arguing that we need a mechanistic description of how that intentionality is realized. Hull's problem was that the analytic tools of his day were just not well suited to the job he wanted them to do. The Miller, Galanter, and Pribram model showed how goal directed acts could, in principle, be explained mechanistically without reducing them to habits.

1 "Purposive Behavior" in Psychology and Philosophy: A History

Maury Silver
The Johns Hopkins University

INTRODUCTION

Purpose in the History of Behaviorism

The intent of this chapter is to trace the treatment of the concept of *purpose* by American psychologists and their philosophical allies from J. B. Watson's *Psychology as the Behaviorist Views It* (1913/1948) to Miller, Galanter, and Pribram's *Plans and the Structure of Behavior* (1960), one image of the new cognitive science.[1] Along the way I point out reasons why the concept was so

---

[1] We have chosen to avoid treating Skinner in this history. By its emphasis on discriminative rather than eliciting stimuli, in its hauteur toward physicalistic reductionism, and in its unit of response's being environmental effect rather than a particular sequence of movements, Skinner's system has the possibility of giving a sophisticated behaviorist explanation of purposive behavior. On the other hand, a commitment to associationism and an impoverished set of explanatory constructs undercuts that possibility. I avoid including Skinner's system partly because Skinner intentionally kept aloof from the theoretical controversies of the other behaviorisms, and even more because the problems that Skinner's system throws up are sufficiently distinct that they require a separate treatment.

refractory to its students and occasionally even proffer suggestions as to its appropriate management.

Overview

Watson and his allies and the behaviorism that followed were concerned with two problems and a pseudoproblem in analyzing goal directed action and its central concept "purpose": (1) The pseudoproblem: Purpose (the will) had been conceived of in terms of consciousness by mentalist psychologies prior to behaviorism, and consciousness was an anathema to behaviorists. But, quite sensibly, the behaviorists, as we see, finessed this issue, reserving "consciousness" as rhetoric to insult enemies and rally allies. (2) The behaviorists were torn between giving a behaviorist analysis of purpose and showing that "purpose" was an illusion. (3) The behaviorists were troubled about how having a goal and acting on it could be related. To some of them, purposive notions necessarily involved antiscientific conceptions such as the future acting back on the present—future goals controlling current behavior. A problem related to the notion of having a purpose was that knowledge of our own purposes appears incorrigible; at least, we need special explanations to account for our not being aware of our purposes, explanations which simultaneously invoke the presence and absence of self-knowledge (e.g., bad faith, the unconscious). I examine how the behaviorists dealt with these issues.

After this survey of the behaviorists' account, we understand why behaviorist approaches to purpose faltered before the new cybernetic models. We glance at some of the ways these models circumvented behaviorist difficulties.

The Pseudoproblem of Consciousness

The acceptability of phenomena to behaviorism was never based on the issue of consciousness; instead, it depended on whether the phenomena could succumb to behavioral methods (as opposed to introspection) and be captured by behaviorist categories. Watson, for example, was a pioneer in assessing the perceptual capacities of animals: What could be more mentalistic than psychophysics?

If, for some reason (unrelated to the issue of consciousness), purpose was found not to be a proper explanatory entity or target—if, for example, it was not obviously reducible to physics—then charges of vitalism, mentalism, and animism would ensue. "Consciousness," the mental, was a conceptual trashbag for improper behavioral explanations. (Watson even lumped together the mental and the spiritual in his polemics; cf. J. B. Watson, 1919, p. 1; J. B. Watson & McDougall, 1928.)

EXPLAINING PURPOSE AND EXPLAINING IT AWAY

The Molar, the Purposive, and the Adaptive

Behaviorists used the concept of *purpose* to cover two different sorts of cases: a wasp's building its nest and a person's baking a cake. The language of goal direction describes behavior in terms of an end. In the case of the wasp, however, Tolman (1922b/ 1951) states that it is "not that those ends are necessarily before the organism itself, but rather that they are before us the observer. They are conceptual pegs upon which *we,* for convenience, hang *our* descriptions" [p. 16]. The wasp's behavior might better be called *adaptive*—selected during the life of the species by the happenstance of which genetically based behaviors happened to fit its behavioral niche. The distinctive feature of the evolutionary account is that it shows how apparently purposive design can occur without purpose. Adaptivity and purpose do not necessarily contrast, however; intelligent, purposeful behavior may well be adaptive. One line of fracture among behaviorists was between those who held that all purposes were only apparent— as in the case of the wasp—and those who argued that some behavior was genuinely purposive: the division between molecular and molar behaviorists (cf. Tolman, 1922a/ 1951). Both groups, of course, were attempting to account for the facts of purposive-looking behavior. The molarists wanted to show how such complex behaviors were possible: to show the ways behaviors interacted to become goal directed, to find simpler constructs to capture the phenomenon, and so on. They believed that the concepts necessary to describe purposive behavior would be no more incompatible with our common-sense notion of purpose than is, to use a current example, the belief that cats have edge detectors in their striate cortex incompatible with the belief that they see shapes. Edge detectors are part of an attempt *to explain how* cats perceive shape. The molecularists, on the other hand, attempted to strip purposive behavior of its guise of complexity. They did so by showing how the interaction of very simple units could give the *appearance* of complexity, of purpose, even though once the context was altered the behavior would be revealed as brute and nonpurposive. It is convenient to call the former sort of explanation *explaining* or *explaining how* and the latter sort *explaining away*.

Explaining Away: Clever Hans

Psychology's most celebrated instance of explaining away is the case of Clever Hans. Hans was a horse. He appeared to be both willing and able to do arithmetic problems upon request. When presented with a problem he would paw the ground until he reached the correct answer, and then he would stop. After a celebrated turn as an arithmetic genius, Hans was found out. Unfortunately, the source of his cleverness was a sensitivity to his owner's tension. His owner would inadvertently tense until the horse pawed to the right answer, and then he would relax; when his owner relaxed, Hans would stop pawing. This story explains away the horse's arithmetical inclination by showing how the simple skill of pawing until his owner relaxed conjoined with the unsurprising fact of his owner's knowing how to do sums was sufficient to produce the *appearance* of Hans' doing arithmetic. Of course, there was genuine arithmetic knowledge in this system—the owner's. Wasps, however, build excellent nests, and they do not rely on some concealed intelligence to do so.

Intelligence, Purpose, and the Thorndike Experiments

A major battleground between molar and molecular behaviorists was a famous series of experiments carried out by Thorndike (1898/1948). (Oddly enough, Thorndike wasn't one of the people concerned with whether the beasts in his experiment displayed purposiveness, but he was interested in whether they displayed intelligence, and, as we shall see, these issues are linked.)

Kittens were placed (one at a time) in a box that was arranged to open only if they performed some specific act, say pulling on a ring. Given the kittens' experience, there was no way for them to figure out this connection. Thus, the kittens entered the box, mewed, howled, scratched, pushed at the bars, and in their flailing eventually pulled at the ring and were released. With repeated trials the kittens went straight to the ring and made more graceful exits. Now, were the kittens acting purposively in their *first* entrapment?

Well, they were clearly unhappy about being in the case and they purred when they were released, so we can understand why they would try to get out, if they did try. But the expression of pain at being trapped and subsequent pleasure at being freed isn't enough. Imagine someone's burning himself and moaning in pain until salve is applied. Clearly, the moaning isn't necessarily an attempt to get the salve. Sleeping in the center of the cage, huddling in the corner furthest from the door, and similar behaviors would not strike us as attempts to get out. Why these examples strike us as not being instances of the kittens' trying is that the behavior is not suitable for getting out. If the kitten had inadvertently backed into the ring and had thus gotten free, we would argue that the kitten, on that trial, had not been trying to get out, at least not by that particular movement. The kitten could not have appreciated the relation between its bump and release. This is why we argue that intelligence—that is, a more or less accurate assessment of the possibilities of the situation—is a necessary part of purposive behavior.

Now, once again, were the kittens acting purposively in their first entrapment? Oddly enough, the answer seems to be that in their first success they displayed no purposiveness because they could not have perceived the relation between the act and release. But in some of their previous *failures* they were. In pushing at the bars they were doing something sensible, perhaps based on an appreciation of how pushing or squeezing could get them out of an enclosed space. In another context, a different cage, squeezing might get them free. So the kittens displayed no intelligence, and thus no purposiveness, in their success, but they may have in their more intelligent failures.

We have not distinguished between intelligent behavior based on an assessment of suitability and the suitability of behavior not based on intelligence but evolutionarily built in.

The cat's squeezing looked intelligent because it was the sort of thing that the cat could know would release it. On the other hand, even though a high-pitched yowl of certain frequencies might open a voice-tripped door, we would not, on the first trial, at least, give the cat credit for yowling—it is not the sort of thing the cat could be expected to know. (We might even find that the cat startles when the door opens after a yowl.) In these circumstances we would not find the cat's yowling to be purposive: Successful behavior is not, ipso facto, intended.

One reason that Thorndike's study was so atractive to behaviorists was that it concerned learning, and learning seemed to imply purpose. On Thorndike's learning account the cat's behavior can be neither intelligent nor purposive; on his interpretation the kittens blundered against the release mechanism—some movement accidentally triggered success. On subsequent trials these movements would be more likely to be repeated—that is, successful movements (those followed by pleasure) were "stamped in." These movements thus become more likely, and the cat becomes more likely to be successful. Intelligence plays no role. And if intelligence was precluded, then, according to our argument, purposiveness was too. Unfortunately, the kittens' behavior looks, from a common-sense view, purposive, and the behavior surely is adaptive, so the paradigm became attractive to some molar behaviorists as an exemplar of purpose in animals (e.g., Perry, 1918).

Tolman's Account of Purpose

Necessary Connections between Beliefs, Intelligence, and Purpose. In Tolman's account, beliefs, desires or purposes, and intelligence were interrelated—one of his important differences from Thorndike. As Tolman (1932) stated, "If we conceive behavior as purposive we *pari passu* conceive it also as cognitive" [p. 13]. In "A Behavioristic Theory of Ideas" (1926/1951) Tolman illustrates the relation between purposes and implicitly intelligent beliefs with an imaginary rat experiment: After mastering a maze a rat goes dashing through its zig-zag like a shot. The experimenter shortens the alley between trials and the rat bounces off the new end of the alley. Tolman (1926/1951) asserts: "His behavior postulates, expects, makes a claim for the old length" [p. 52], and "Our evaluation of his claim involves a knowledge also of his purpose" [p. 52]. It is only because we assume that the rat did not want to bump its head that we believe that its behavior shows that he mistakenly thought the alley to be of the old length. We might add that an assumption of rationality is also involved. After all, if the rat were sufficiently stupid or crazy, then it might recognize the length, not want to get bumped, and still find itself caroming into the wall.

Over time Tolman, his colleagues, and students developed and tested on the white rat, of course, an analysis of the central characteristics of purposive behavior. We follow one strand: the features of purposive behavior, in Tolman's account, that distinguish people—and occasionally rats—from wasps.

Persisting until the Goal is Reached.   Tolman, like most of the molar behaviorists, sees *perseverance*—the "persistence until" a particular goal is reached—as central to the notion of purpose. Persistence as used by early molar behaviorists did not distinguish between Thorndike's picture of a kitten howling until released (which we argued was not genuinely purposive) and, say, the purpose embodied in a person's yelling for a friend to come. Tolman, on the other hand, restricts perseverance to something like an intelligent choice of means for ends: If one strategy fails, then try another. In normal circumstances adaptive behavior looks intelligent. One way to tell whether an apparently purposive goal directed behavior is in fact purposive is to see if the animal will select another appropriate means when its primary one is blocked.

Consider the following example: A rat that has learned to run a maze will, with practically no upset, swim it (McFarlane, cited in Tolman, 1959) or roll through it after vestibular damage (Lashly & Ball, cited in Tolman, 1959); rats in a Skinner box interchangeably press the lever with left paw, right paw, and head. Tolman argues that the animal first learns a type of organism–environment rearrangement. The rat already knows how to walk, swim, run, and press, and also knows that maze traversing is the sort of performance that can be done by these antecedently learned skills.

Acting on Beliefs. Beliefs also have a role in Tolman's analysis of purpose. Purposive actions involve intelligently acting on a set of beliefs about the relation of means to ends. We cannot present here a detailed analysis of Tolman's concept of belief, but two examples can help present the nature of his concept and its role in purposive behavior. Consider the phenomenon of "latent learning." Let a rat meander around a maze that does not contain any reward. It might appear that the rat is not learning anything as it meanders. If you then put food (presumably a goal for a hungry rat) into the goal box, the error curve drops abruptly. Tolman argues that the rat could be described as constructing a cognitive map as it wanders (e.g., Tolman, 1959).

A simpler, more compelling example of an animal's acting on belief can be seen in Tinklepaugh's switch (cf. Tinklepaugh, 1928; Tolman, 1932). In front of a monkey an experimenter hides either a banana, a preferred food, or lettuce, under one of two containers. After an imposed delay the animal goes to the food container and eats the hidden food. Next the experimenter places a banana under the container, and then secretly replaces it with lettuce. When the monkey lifts up the container, it discovers the nonpreferred food (food that it previously would eat). Now (Tinklepaugh, 1928):

> She looks at the lettuce but (unless very hungry) does not touch it. She looks under the cup and behind the board. She stands up and looks under and around her. She picks the cup up and examines it thoroughly inside and out. She has on occasion turned toward observers present in the room and shrieked at them in apparent anger [p. 224].

Surely the monkey expected that, believed that, the banana (its preferred end) was underneath the containers—or why would it get upset?

With these examples of Tolman's approach we can appreciate how Tolman attempted to transform a description of the merely molar into a description of genuinely purposive behavior. Hull argued that Tolman's attempt was a failure, that Tolman's system, by its nature, could not *explain* purpose.

Hull's Critique of Purposive Behaviorism. According to Hull's account (1943), although Tolman may have paid lip service to the reducibility of his purposive constructs to physics and physiology, he never clarified just how goal following could be reduced to movements. Furthermore, the possibility of such a reduction was far from self-evident. To explain purposive or intelligent behavior one would have to show how it was made up of elements (e.g., behavior, neural structures) *which were not in themselves purposive or intelligent;* otherwise, there would always be a residual intelligence or purpose to explain. Because Tolman's accounts are always at the purposive, intelligent level, Tolman forfeits the possibility of explaining purpose or intelligence. Any sort of explanation of purpose would have to meet this description, not only a behaviorist one. For instance, an analysis of a computer simulation of an intelligent behavior can end only at the algorithmic level—an unambiguous specification of a procedure (cf. Dennett, 1978, Chapter 4, for a discussion of this point). And Hull appears to be correct about this. Tolman seems to sacrifice an explanation of purpose—in a reductive sense—to provide an intricate description of the sorts of behaviors that constitute purposive behavior.

Hull had a further criticism. He argued (1943) that *anthropomorphism*—the "surreptitious substitution and acceptance of one's knowledge of what needs to be done . . . for a theoretical deduction" [p. 24]—resulted from the use of constructs such as purpose and intelligence. Because Tolman's theory sees rats, for instance, as purposive rational creatures in that sense similar to humans, a purposive behaviorist would ask herself "What would I do in the rat's place?" to predict the rat's behavior. Even if her prediction were correct it could only, according to Hull (1943), "increase the reputation for accurate prophesy of the one making such intuitive judgments, but a prophet is not a principle, much less a scientific theory" [p. 24]. Looking back on his career, Tolman (1959, p. 97), confesses to using intuition and common sense in attempting to extend the application of his concepts.

But Hull's critique misses the point. Tolman's theory was an attempt to describe purposive behavior as rational, as guided by intelligently interrelated purposes and beliefs. If Tolman is right that rats as well as people are purposive, then when accounting for rat behavior, once you have arranged a purpose (say, by food deprivation) and have a good idea about what the rodent could know in the situation, then you are being quite reasonable in "putting yourself in the rat's place." What this amounts to is assuming for the both of you some general principles of rationality. Our beliefs and actions are logically connected because we are rational and intelligent, and if rats are also, to an extent, rational and intelligent, then they should create and structure actions much as we do. This prediction is not a prophesy. A disconfirmation will not only discredit the prophetic power of the predictor, but would show that the assumptions that rats are purposive/rational—like us—did not hold up.

So, Hull was correct in arguing that Tolman did not give a (reductive) explanation of purpose, but he was wrong in believing that the use of nonreductive concepts precluded giving a scientifically informative account.

Hull and the Attempt to Give a Reductive Account of Genuinely Purposive Behavior

Hull attempted to give a genuinely explanatory account of purpose. Like Watson, he believed that only explanatory entities patently reducible to physics should be used in a psychological theory. At the same time, he held that "purpose" was genuine and that any proper psychological system would ultimately have to give an account of it (Hull, 1943):

> An ideally adequate theory even of so-called purposive behavior ought, therefore, to begin with colorless movements and mere receptor impulses as such, and from these build up step by step both adaptive behavior and maladaptive behavior. The present approach does not deny the molar reality of purposive acts (as opposed to movement), of intelligence, of insight, of goals, of intents, of strivings, or of value; on the contrary, we insist upon the genuineness of these forms of behavior. We hope ultimately to show the logical right to the use of such concepts by deducing them as secondary principles from more elementary objective primary principles [p. 2].

Yet, we shall find that in attempting to give an explanation of purposive behavior Hull skids from explaining to explaining away. Hull's most sustained attempt at accounting for purpose—"Goal Attraction and Directing Ideas Conceived as Habit Phenomena" (1931; also cf. 1943)—gives a habit-formation account of goal seeking behavior. Consider a hungry rat eating in the goal box of a maze: Stimuli from the rats' hunger drive as well as from the licks and gulps of the rat's eating responses (r_G) become the associational peg to hold together all sorts of movements that first occurred on the way to getting food in the goal box. Hull uses these stimuli to account for the guidance and control that he argues is the substance of purpose. Regrettably, we cannot follow his argument here, but let us examine, on an unfortunately abstract level, the sort of response Hull might make to the Tinklepaugh study.

Hull might argue that finding lettuce instead of a banana is not disappointing, the dash of an expectation, but rather a transient disruption caused by the interference of lettuce-eating habitual associations with banana-eating associations. On this level, the molarist might answer him that finding bananas in place of lettuce should be equally disruptive, but it is not (Tolman, 1932, p. 76). Further, habit interference might account for a disruption of behavior, but in this view why should the monkey have been emotionally upset—shrieking at observers? Why the apparent searching that is not a part of the typical banana- or lettuce-getting routine? The real point, though, is not that Hull could not explain each of these phenomena piecemeal, but that his account (Hull, 1943) does not "insist on the genuineness of these forms of behavior" [p. 2]; rather, it explains them away.

Standoff

Hull's attempt to demonstrate the logical right to use purpose collapses into explaining purpose away. Tolman's attempt at analyzing purpose was close to the reality of purpose but was not an explanation.

For most behaviorists, Hull's account was more compelling: It was reductive and used the right sort of (physicalistic) concepts. Consider Hilgard's reaction to the Hull-Tolman r_G versus expectation controversy. In what was the most influential text on learning theory (Hilgard, 1956), he argues that expectations *must* be something like r_G's:

> Because r_G's have the [physical] dimensions of ordinary responses they can be treated with quantitative precision. Because cognitions lack such dimensions, similar treatment is not feasible. Critics of the r_G concept do not deny the possibility of precision, but they believe that precision in the use of r_G has not been achieved, and that some of the suggested uses of r_G are faulty [p. 212].

This argument, reducing Tolman's position to a quibble about the appropriate physical parameters for Hull's constructs, is astonishing; yet it would seem to be the dominant view of the times. Because Hull had the right *sort* of constructs, his system *must* win—in reality, had won from the very beginning. Notice that it is a philosophical issue, not empirical evidence, that is responsible for Hull's success. Behaviorists were in the grips of a "picture" of science. They knew that reduction must be attainable (for the unity of science and the exclusion of ectoplasm), and they possessed only one picture of reduction. Thus, an understanding of purpose was blocked until the development of new models of explanation (programs), more specifically, new models of reduction (computer functionalism).

HOW GOALS INFLUENCE BEHAVIOR

The Problems of Prevision and Teleology

We have thus far examined how notions of proper scientific explanation and the models chosen as instances of purpose influenced behaviorism's analysis of action. We have avoided what is perhaps the concept's worst taint—not only to behaviorism but to many of the previous mentalist psychologies: Purpose seems to imply *teleology*—the conception that the future acts back upon the past. The challenge to those who would give a naturalistic account of purpose is to avoid teleology, to give a plausible account of how the anticipation of a goal, *prevision*, can help bring the goal about.

Tolman attempted an analysis of prevision in his "A Behavioristic Theory of Ideas" (1926/1951). He argues (1926/1951) that "a *representation* of results" allows the results to become determiners for or against the act which leads to them [p. 60]. "By virtue of such representation the organism is able to evaluate the result of his act, and to release it or not to release it, as the case may be" [p. 66]. This is a fair statement of the problem of prevision, but it evades the issue of what it is about such a representation that facilitates achieving the goal. Tolman attempts to give evidence for representation by pointing to sharp drops in learning curves or showing that an animal, after hesitating between alternatives, will sometimes quickly take correct action. But why should this supposed representation help the organism to evaluate the results of its act—that is, why is prevision useful? Couldn't an organism have a prevision, say, a mental picture of the task it wants to achieve, and still not know how to make use of it? Tolman argues (1926/1951) that Thorndike's kitten hesitating a moment before clawing the release mechanism probably has "a representation of only the very immediate consequences of the act, a prevision, perhaps of the opening door" [p. 60]. But why would this prevision increase the likelihood of the kittens' clawing. Why doesn't it run to the door to see if its vision is true?[2]

Bertrand Russell: Purpose without Prevision, Teleology, and Incorrigibility

Bertrand Russell attempted an analysis of "purpose" that would eliminate prevision and teleology and solve two related puzzles in our conception of human purpose: (1) the special knowledge that people believe they have about their purposes—that is, the "incorrigibility" of purpose accounts; (2) the apparently special connection between purpose and action: If someone has the opportunity, ability, no other overriding purposes, and the like, but still does not do anything about an avowed purpose, we are likely to question whether the avowal is sincere. Sometimes, however, people act this way, and yet we have other reasons to believe their sincerity. This sort of problem, "weakness of the will," has bothered theorists since Plato.

In *The Analysis of Mind,* Russell (1921) devised a behaviorist account of human purpose that would solve the problems of apparent incorrigibility and the weakness of the will, avoid the notion of prevision and teleology, and be compatible with behaviorist psychology. Russell (1921) first presents the ordinary view of desire and purpose:

> A man's acts are governed by purposes. He decides, let us suppose, to go to a certain place. . . . If the usual route is blocked by an accident, he goes by some other route. All that he does is determined—or so it seems—by the end he has in view, by what lies in front of him, rather than by what lies behind. . . . Further, we can know them [our desires] by an immediate self-knowledge which does not depend upon observation of our actions [p. 30].

Russell ironically comments that such a belief is comforting because we can absolve ourselves of spiteful acts as long as we have not entertained them

---

[2]Tolman's later conception of a cognitive map better captures the inferential nature of the relation between goals and behavior (cf. Tolman, 1959).

consciously. In contrast to this self-deception, Russell presents a simpler model. He starts from the "primitive desire" of animals (Russell, 1921):

> A hungry animal is restless until it finds food; then it becomes quiescent. The thing which will bring a restless condition to an end is said to be what is desired [its purpose, cf. p. 65]. But only experience can show what will have this sedative effect, and it is easy to make mistakes [p. 32].

In order to suit this model to human behavior, Russell adds beliefs about the causes of restlessness. A person acting on a purpose may sometimes have beliefs about what might alleviate her discomfort, but a true or false belief is *not* essential to having a purpose. True beliefs (correct hypotheses) are convenient, but one can achieve sedation without them and miss it despite them.

Virtues of Russell's Model.   By separating the notion of having a "purpose or desire" from a "belief as to what the purpose is about," Russell avoids having to postulate self-deception, repression, or other defenses. If part of the meaning of "having a purpose" involves knowing what the purpose is about, then to account for instances of acting on a purpose when the person sincerely says that he or she did not realize what she was doing involves postulating hidden knowledge. Russell's account is much simpler: People need not have true beliefs about their desires (or any beliefs for that matter). Because to have a desire does not imply that we know we have it, ignorance, even self-serving ignorance (avoiding unpleasant information), is to be expected.

Russell handles the problem of weakness of will in a similar way: There is no reason to think that what we believe to be our aims really are our aims. A typical case of weak will involves not acting to secure a known and attainable greater good in the future because of the temptation of a much lesser good in the present. Although this sort of behavior will not maximize the individual's happiness, it is not conceptually problematic. The lesser immediate good sedates our restlessness. Our beliefs about what would be better or worse are secondary issues: The real problem is why people are not always "weak willed."[3]

But is what sedates us necessarily our purpose? What if I wander into a waterfront bar and am sedated by knockout drops. Does that mean that it was knockout drops that I was desiring—even if I had struggled against swallowing them or tried to spit them out? What if I wander through a red-light district to rent a lover and instead encounter the Bible and am sedated. Does this mean that I really desired the Bible all along, or that I desired the Bible and the lover indifferently?

---

[3]Curiously, Russell's account even captures a piece of the phenomenology of desire—for instance, that restlessness in which we want to do something and yet do not know what (as in some forms of boredom), or the realization that we are ravenously eating despite having believed that we were not hungry at all, or the disappointment with a treat even though it is as we imagined it to be.

A Development of Russell's Critique of Incorrigibility.   Sometimes people do treat the question of what they are wanting, what they are trying to do, as seriously problematic. Someone may be tormented by the question of whether he genuinely liked his boss' jokes, appreciated her pleasantries, or was really a toady, a sycophant. Consider his problem: The sorts of behaviors in which a toady and a sincere person engage—laughing at jokes, showing appreciation, offering compliments at a success, and so on—may be identical. The difference is, roughly, that the sincere person would behave in just the same way to his boss whether she was the boss or not—a counterfactual. Counterfactuals are not introspectable. Here we have a case of someone sincerely perplexed about *what he or she is trying to do.* Notice that we have not needed "unconscious motivation" to describe this case. In contrast, trying to find your wallet when you misplace it is the sort of thing in which we almost must know what we are doing. How is wallet searching different from currying favor? Contrary to Russell, in searching for the missing wallet we typically do not just wander until we happily come across it. We think of probable places for it to be—in yesterday's pants, under the bed, and so on—and look there; we may even decide to call the police to ask if any pickpockets have been arrested. All of these procedures require adjusting what we are doing to the specifications of a wallet (if the wallet were elephant-sized the search would differ), and they make use of our knowledge of the specific vulnerabilities of wallet carrying (pickpockets, etc). Unlike Russell's blind wandering, at each juncture of the search, the individual is using knowledge about wallets and other facts to guide his or her action. Because we presumably have access to our wallet searchings we would know from the beginning what we were doing. This knowledge, like all causal claims, is corrigible, but the evidence is so overwhelming so early—the search provides the tests we need—that to doubt would be a skeptic's game. So the difference between the two cases is that in searching for my wallet the search itself provides immediate evidence as to what is being searched for.[4]

PSYCHOLOGY FINDS A RESPECTABLE TELEOLOGY

Feedback

The concept of negative feedback had been applied specifically to goal directed behavior in the early 1940s (Rosenblueth, Wiener, & Bigelow, 1943). It did not

---

[4]There is another reason why our desires seem transparent: Announcing our desires has a *practical* incorrigibility. Announcing a desire, as Austin (1970) has it, makes a commitment, takes a stand, makes a choice. If you ask me which pastry I want and after I answer, you tell me "No you don't," then you are not trying to match inferences with me, you are trying to override my choice. Announcements of wants are not displays of inference tickets; they make choices and thus bring up questions of power and propriety, not prediction. To doubt an announcement of a want usually undercuts, insults, the person making it; hence, what looks like a belief in incorrigibility is just a tactful refraining from rudeness.

really catch hold until the late 1950s partly because of the weakening of behaviorist presuppositions that associationism was necessary to any scientific explanation of behavior and partly because real embodiments of cybernetic notions were not available until World War II.

Rosenblueth et al. (1943) divide nonpurposeful from purposeful mechanisms (servomechanisms) in terms of feedback. A system using negative feedback is controlled by the difference between the present state of the system and an "intended" state, a goal; this difference is fed back as input, reducing the difference between the actual and the intended state; feedback continues until the difference is eliminated. A thermostat, for instance, turns on a heater whenever the temperature falls below an intended level; this adjustment eventually raises the temperature above the intended level, which then causes the heater to be turned off, the temperature falls, and so forth. In behavior without feedback, on the other hand, no signals from the goal alter the actual state in the course of the activity. Notice how the notion of feedback makes plausible a goal's affecting the behavior designed to achieve it—and without postulating mystical entities. As G. A. Miller et al. (1960) point out, this language was not entirely new to psychology; in fact, it is quite similar to Dewey's (1896/1948) analysis of the relation of stimulus to response; it is comfortable with Tolman's metaphor of a cognitive map and does not need or want a map reader. According to Miller et al. (1960), "Once a teleological mechanism could be built out of metal and glass" [p. 43], it became, by that fact, respectable. Cybernetics showed the relation between prevision and its goal to be technical and not metaphysical. The visual metaphor of prevision, so suggestive of consciousness, now stands out as just one metaphor—feedback can be based on the superimposition of pictures, templates, feature lists, the output of analogue devices, and so on. And insofar as a template, for instance, is a representation of some state of affairs in the world, it can be a misrepresentation. Representations are corrigible in many ways; they are not goals squeezed back in time.

Plans and the Structure of Behavior

Miller et al.'s *Plans and the Structure of Behavior* (1960) is an early example of using the new cybernetic model to explain purpose without explaining it away. A "plan," by their account (Miller et al., 1960) is much like a program; it is "any hierarchical process in the organism that can control the order in which a sequence of operations is to be performed" [p. 16]. The relation of a plan to a goal is embodied in their fundamental unit of behavior, the TOTE. The test–operate–test–exit unit is a feedback loop—that is, the TOTE embodies the fact that the operations an organism performs are constantly guided by the outcomes of various tests. Comparison of test outcomes continues until the incongruity between tested outcome and criteria is 0. The "image" of a goal supplies the criteria that must be met before the test is passed. Miller et al. (1960) suggest that "The compound of TOTE units unravels itself simply enough into a co-ordinated sequence of tests and actions, although the underlying structure that organizes and co-ordinates the behavior is itself hierarchical, not sequential'' [p. 34]. Can this model get around the difficulties the behaviorists faced?

One of Tolman's problems was that he could not trace a plausible causal link between an image of a future result and the action achieving it; Miller et al.'s image—a set of criteria used as a standard of comparison by the operational tests—specifies the link. Because the specification of criteria might not be met by any test outcomes, we can give substance to the concept of the search for the nonexistent.

The Problem of Reduction

Perhaps the major reason why the behaviorists' attempts at explaining purpose slid into explaining it away (or just describing it) was their difficulty in reducing purposive behavior to a simpler set of notions compatible with physics. Because the feedback loop does not call up ghosts and presumably is a simpler notion that purposive behavior, the behaviorists' dilemma appears to be resolved. Unfortunately, there is still a problem in relating concepts expressed in functional terms, say, relating to goals and physicalistic descriptions (cf. Melden, 1961, for an expression of the incompatibilist position and Davidson, 1980, for an attempt at reconciliation). What made purposive explanations a threat to behaviorism is that they seemed to be the sort of things that were not reducible to physicalistic entities. If this were true *and* purposes were real, then it would seem that the existence of purposive activity would require the violation of "materialist monism"—that is, the position that only matter exists. But as Davidson (1980) points out, the possibility of reduction is not necessary to ensure materialism. Consider: *Every* instance of, say, entertaining a desire to visit my father might have a particular material embodiment—for example, a reverberating cell assembly; if so, then the conditions for materialist monism would be met. But, *each* instance of entertaining that desire might have a *different* material embodiment. What would make these entertainings the same, then, would not be that they are reducible to the same physical substrate, but that they are the same at a functional, we might say molar, level. Perhaps this position, *token physicalism,* is not correct. What the *possibility* of such a position's being true demonstrates is that issues of monism, ghost avoidance, and so on, need not trouble the study of purpose. Hence, the discomfort that behaviorists from Watson through Hull (and more recently) felt about using a vocabulary of beliefs, desires, and purposes without immediately tacking them down to physicalistic description was psychosomatic.

ACKNOWLEDGEMENT

My thanks to John Sabini for making me work as hard as I did on this project.

EVOLUTION OF ACTION

Schurig takes up the phylogenetic development of the ability to use tools. He argues that work is one very important instance of action: In work we have a goal, develop plans to reach that goal, and react to feedback from the environment. Schurig argues that the human ability to work—to use and produce tools in a socially organized way—has evolved through five stages, of which the chimpanzee has reached the first four. Stage one of tool use consists of the use of specialized body parts (e.g., beaks) to a specific end; stage two consists of the instinctive use of tools; stage three consists of the learned trial-and-error use of tools; stage four consists of tool use with an appreciation of the means–ends relation that the tool implies; and stage five consists of the use and production of tools in a socially cooperative and differentiated way in the animal's natural habitat. Schurig claims that only humans can use tools in this socially organized way. In this claim Schurig joins a long-standing tradition seeing the special sort of action we call work as the hallmark of human nature.

Dolgin takes a different starting point for the development of tool-using abilities in humans. She attempts to link phylogenetic development with individual development by looking at phylogenetic development of tool use through Piaget's developmental theory. She finds parallels between the ontogenetic development of the ability to act intentionally and the phylogenetic development of the ability to use tools.

Contra Schurig, Dolgin argues that there is evidence for the social coordination of tool use among chimpanzees, and she suggests that what may in fact distinguish human tool use from chimpanzee tool use is the ability to chain together the use of different tools by different individuals. This ability, she suggests, may be linked to our unique ability to use language; she thus links the two traditional views of the hallmark of the human.

2 Stages in the Development of Tool Behavior in the Chimpanzee (Pan troglodytes)

Volker Schurig
University of Hamburg

INTRODUCTION

One way to research the phylogenetic development of actions is through experiments on and observation of the use of tools in animals. Grasping an object in the environment, an action developed in primitive species (e.g., insects), is a species-specific instinctual behavior. In more developed species choice of an object suggests a differentiation between subject and object—that is, a differentiation between one's own behavior and the function of an instrument. A highly developed animal use of tools cannot be explained in terms of simple motor patterns (as, e.g., Hull would have done), because it implies *teleology;* it is this quality that makes the object a tool and the behavior an action. Natural objects have the status of "tool" if their functions are derived from action goals: if they are used as means to accomplish these goals. Animals' tool use can, therefore, be seen as a model of the phylogenetic development of a *means–end–relation* in behavior, which is characteristic of "action." The use of an external object as a tool is, thus, a criterion for experiments on cognitive capabilities in *tool action;* the demonstration of tool use is a methodologically "hard" criterion for the determination of whether or not there are cognitive capacities like "problem solving," "insight," and "intelligence," over and above stimulus–response relations. The specifics of both tool and movement patterns allow for a reconstruction of the internal logic of means–end relations. This potential reconstruction makes tool use a prototype of animal "planned actions" (Rensch, 1973).

Tool use exists in chimpanzees and humans. For chimpanzees, however, tool use is really not essential for survival—phylogenetically and ontogenetically. For human beings, on the other hand, tool use is necessary for individual, collective, and species survival and is the essence of human nature. This difference between chimpanzees and humans is the focus of this chapter.

LEVELS OF LANGUAGE AND ABSTRACTION WITHIN THE TERM *TOOL BEHAVIOR*

The term *tool use* has been not only one of the most important but also one of the most controversial and ambiguous concepts of behavioral research since the experiments of Köhler. Heymer (1977), Immelmann (1982), and others include in the term tool use all of the relevant abilities of animals shown in their use of objects for a purpose; however, they also place the term in quotation marks to avoid "psychologizing" animal behavior. In a narrower interpretation, however, animals do not possess real tools; rather, they merely instrumentalize objects. According to this interpretation, tools are products of societal activities and are, along with language, an important qualitative animal–human difference. The development and use of tools is connected to work, which characterizes human behavior only.

To avoid anthropomorphizing animal behavior vis-a-vis the concept of *tools*, various functional levels of tool-use behavior must be distinguished. The contrast between *instrument* and *tool* can then be used to establish a *qualitative* distinction between animal and human. But the customary association of *tool use* with animal behavior and *tool manufacture* with human work is challenged by evidence of tool manufacture in chimpanzees (van Lawick-Goodall, 1965) and Darwin finches (*Cactospiza pallida*). Because of this evidence, complex ethological classifications of tool use have been developed by Tembrock (1968) and Schurig (1980); these classifications are intended to reduce anthropomorphism of tool use. It is possible to differentiate among: (1) the incidental use of readily available resources; (2) the purposeful use of available resources; (3) the modification of resources for direct use; (4) the modification of resources for future use; (5) the incidental manufacture of tools; and (6) the systematic manufacture of tools. Other classifications of tool use, (e.g., Parker & Gibson, 1982), empha-

size the increasing complexity of object manipulation. They postulate the following developmental stages: (1) single-object manipulations; (2) tool use; (3) simple manufacture; (4) manufacture by construction; and (5) engineering. An
additional way to distinguish levels of tool use is with general behavioral categories. Four levels can be distinguished: instinct, trial-and-error learning, and
"activity" (*Taetigkeit*). The special final activity of using tools is "work,"
which, as we see, is different from animal tool use.

The following brief discussion of the basic characteristics of a general *theory
of tool use* focuses on the special example of chimpanzee tool use. This example
is important for two reasons: First, because human tool use or work came from
phylogenetic precursors, the behavior and the psychology of animal primates—
particularly apes—permits comparisons; chimpanzee tool use represents an
important phylogenetic connection. Second, the most highly developed animal
tool use has a special place because it is exactly at the boundary between human
and animal behavior. It, therefore, cannot be adequately described either with
concepts appropriate to the tool use of other animals, or with concepts appropriate only to human work (*Taetigkeit*).

The most important developmental stages of animal and human tool use are:

Tool use$_1$, body tools (claws, teeth, etc.): These tools are made of special
substances (e.g., chitin, horn, dentin). One of the most universal body tools is
the beak, used as a grasping organ. Birds use beaks for brooding and defense,
and specializations do exist within these areas. Darwin finches, for example,
have different beak forms depending on the main food source available to them.
These body tools constitute, in the evolution of tool behaviors, first-order specializations. In general, these body tools are rigidly connected with the organism.

Tool use$_2$, instinctive tool use: The functional limits of the different body
adaptations of tool use$_1$ constitute the prerequisite for an integration of first or
primary tools into genetically coordinated movement patterns. Closing of the
brood tube of the tomb wasp (*Ammophila*) with pebbles and destruction of eggs
with stones by vultures (*Neophron percnopterus*) have naturally selected, survival advantages compared to the simpler behavior patterns of food competitors.
Instinctive tool use$_2$ arose, therefore, through evolution, independently in different animal types and in different behavioral arenas, such as food acquisition and
brood care. In general, tool use$_2$ is relatively rare. Of approximately 8000 bird
species, only five have instinctive tool use$_2$—that is, tool use consisting of innate
behaviors that have no independent motivational basis.

Tool use$_3$, learned instrumentalization of external tool objects: Tool use$_3$ is
dependent on several biological prerequisites that are met by the chimpanzee:
One of these is the existence of a pentadactyl grasping extremity; another is a
precision grip through the use of the thumb; a third is that the forward extremities
are not used in locomotion. Not only are such implements as combs and brushes

successfully imitated in tool use$_3$, but also true tool use (e.g., drawing) can be learned. Instinctive tool use$_2$ is characterized by great functional specialization, species specificity, and an inflexible coupling of organism, behavior, and tool. In learned tool use$_3$ object instrumentalization can be transferred to other arenas. The prerequisite for transfer is a flexible coupling of behavior patterns to tools with several degrees of freedom.

Tool use$_4$, intelligent tool use: Investigations into this area are carried out in experimental animal psychology. The complexity and goal orientation of instrumentalization of tools is taken to be a measure of intelligence. Here, in contrast to genetically coordinated tool use$_2$, are precursors of "achievement motivation", actions that are not oriented solely toward food reward; successful solution is an incentive in and of itself. Individual steps in tool use$_4$ are a result of a logical and causal understanding. Therefore, stimulus–response terminology is replaced here with the construct *action*. Because of its coherent structure, tool use$_4$ is evidence of *insightful learning;* manipulation of objects in insightful learning are a criterion for the cognitive aspect of "action." Tools become means to achieve goals expediently.

Tool use$_5$, systematic transformation of objects and materials in nature through work: Tool use$_5$ distinguishes the human from the animal in a way not possible by tool use$_4$, which is part of the behavior of the chimpanzee. One important methodological problem in researching tool use of anthropoid apes is avoiding uncritical "psychologizing" of the action chain, while at the same time describing the relevant cognitive abilities displayed. Describing tool use in primates can involve the same inadmissible anthropomorphism that has been criticized by linguists when the term *language* has been used to signify all sorts of communication. In addition to the distinction between tool use and tool manufacture, another distinction separates animal and human tool use: The "action" of lower-animal tool use is less developed than the specifically human action organization of "activity" (*Taetigkeit*). Human activity does not originate simply by connecting atomic action components, but, in addition, contains a societal component that is most precisely rendered by the concept *work*. Some typical criteria of tool use$_5$ are discussed more extensively later in this chapter.

INSTINCTIVE TOOL USE$_2$ IN CHIMPANZEES: THE CONSTRUCTION OF SLEEPING NESTS

Instinctive tool use$_2$ is exemplified in the construction of nests (cf. Figure 2.1). Constructing nests is genetically determined; it is typical for all Pongidae species. Chimpanzees build tree nests some 8 to 10 meters in the air (sometimes as high as 20 meters). Because of daily migrations within their territory, the nest must be rebuilt frequently, which requires a good deal of time. To build the nests the chimpanzees gather or break off branches, which they then weave together, filling gaps with moss or leaves. These nests are quite solid pieces of construction because chimpanzees weigh 40 to 50 kg. The way chimpanzees lay out the nests in natural habitats is one of their most striking behavior peculiarities, and it was one of the first such behaviors to be observed in the wild (Nissen, 1931). The social structure of the chimpanzee group is reflected in the spatial relationship of the nests. Also, within the resting area are individual territories that have a stronger home "valence" than the general area in which the animals roam.

The example of nest-building behavior is frequently missing from lists of tool uses by chimpanzees in their natural habitats. This omission is rather extraordinary because the sleeping nests, which have a diameter of 1 meter, not only take more time, but require much more complicated operations than does the preparation of a blade of grass to be used for fishing termites. According to Parker and Gibson's (1982) classification system of tool use, sleeping nests represent the most complex case of animal tool use: "engineering," or active alteration of the environment by one's own constructions. One reason for this omission of nest building is that many other authors discuss only one of the functional levels of tool use$_{1-5}$. P. Meyer (1976), for example, writes, "Nest construction is to be seen as an instinct action and not as tool manufacture" [p. 233]. An additional reason for the neglect of nest building, even though it is the most frequent type of tool behavior in the chimpanzee, is that the existence of genetically coordinated tool use disturbs the cognitivist picture of intelligent tool use. In completing each of the individual tool actions, as well as following broad goals, the chimpanzee behaves in an "uninsightful" manner: The behavioral tendency to build sleeping nests remains even in captivity. Here, the "intelligence" of the behavioral organization is lost and the behavior appears to observers to be pointless and dysfunctional.

Wazuro (1975) has impressively described how little Pavlov's chimpanzees conformed to anthropomorphic conceptions of a comfortable sleeping environment, but rather instrumentalized their synthetic environment in a way that made sense given their own biology:

> Instead of laying himself on the mattress and covering himself with the blanket, he tore open the mattress cover and spread the insides on the floor in a type of nest. In order to shorten the time the ape needed to make his nightly camp, and to make the work of the support personnel easier, the bedding was replaced with dry hay [p. 94].

The observer was especially irritated because "Rafael" sat or lay naked on the floor surrounded by a wall of hay and other material. Within the nest itself typical sleeping postures such as a half-seated one were assumed.

In contrast to its otherwise intelligent tool use, the chimpanzee is "unteachable" at the instinctive level of tool behavior. Within this "uninsightful" tool use, however, many different objects can be used as instruments to create a nest. Their selection follows their goal even when the function of the nest disappears in captivity. Innate tool use$_2$ is a genetic behavior disposition which, in the natural habitat, has value for species survival. In animals reared in isolation from their species, or in deprivation experiments, this phylogenetic programming nonetheless remains (Reynolds & Reynolds, 1965). At the functional level of tool use$_2$, represented by nest-construction behavior, the specific behavior is typical for *all individuals of a species;* this uniformity does not hold in learned tool use$_3$.

LEARNED TOOL USE$_3$ UNDER NATURAL-HABITAT CONDITIONS

The notion that chimpanzees are tool users is the result of numerous laboratory experiments. Tool experiments have also been done with orangutans (cf. Jantschke, 1972) and gorillas (Rensch & Ducker, 1966). Despite the complexity of tool operations, the animal in such experiments is merely completing something the experimenter has thought through and put into the design of the experimental situation. For this reason, experimental tool use carries an air of *artificiality* and *secondariness* as, for example, when putting two sticks together is stimulated by the way the two sticks have been constructed by the experimenter. Nevertheless, systematic observations carried out in natural habitats since 1960 on the Gombe River in Tanzania and in the Budonga forest in Uganda have demonstrated that tools are not used just in experiments. Longitudinal studies, such those by van Lawick-Goodall (1965), Reynolds and Reynolds (1965), and the Japanese research groups of Itani and Suzuki (1967), have demonstrated, independently of one another, that modifiable tool use$_3$ exists in different populations. This incidence complicates the picture of tool use as a criterion with which to distinguish human from animal. The tool use of the Pongidae is not just a product of artificial laboratory experiments, but also has adaptive value in natural habitats (Hall, 1966).

In contrast to species-specific tool use$_2$ is learned tool use *typical only of specific individuals and regions.* If tool use$_3$ produces a phylogenetic advantage, it must be related to the development of social learning and the development of traditions. This relationship secures a certain stability across time and place for the tool use by several animals; transmission occurs most often from mother to child. The limitations that characterize tool use$_3$ give rise to a methodological problem: Observations are often based on only a few cases and are difficult to verify.

Learned tool use$_3$ can appear in different behavioral arenas such as: (1) comfort behavior (scratching, picking teeth); (2) food acquisition (different hitting movements); (3) drinking (the sponge function of leaves); (4) aggression; and (5) exploration (new and unknown objects are examined with instruments). Tool use in these arenas can be extended to action chains with different degrees of complexity. In drinking behavior water can be sucked directly into the mouth. A functional enhancement is achieved when the forward extremities are used as "biological (scooping) tools." Finally, in tool use$_3$ leaves can be crumpled and used to suck up water. The use of tools lies in every case in the phase of the behavior pattern that is most variable; the development of the motivation and the consumatory behavior (water intake, swallowing) remain endogenously determined.

Fruit gathering can be used to present tool use$_3$ in more detail. This is a complex reaction chain that involves elements of goal oriented action. The gathering and opening of nut-like fruits using hammering instruments (stones) is a type of learned tool use$_3$, which is an important foundation for the development of tool use$_5$ in hominid evolution.

The tool use$_3$ of chimpanzees in opening fruit is interesting because the food is typically neither gathered nor distributed as is common with other primates; exceptions in chimpanzees exist only during a limited period within the mother–child relationship. Especially among the terrestrial primates, there is fierce competition for food. As a rule, everything that is seen is eaten immediately (Kummer, 1975). Thus, gathering fruit does not belong to the typical behavior repertory of the chimpanzee, but is a secondary development, possibly a consequence of using tools to open fruit. The use of a tool becomes, in this case, the cause of a new organization of behavior. When using instruments to open fruits, it is useful to gather several pieces of fruit at one time rather than open each piece at a different time and place. Thus, the original pattern of food gathering and immediate eating is abandoned. Gathering and storing are, along with hunting, the phylogenetic prerequisites of human economies. These factors are considered by several authors (e.g., McGrew, 1982) to be decisive in hominization.

Tool use by chimpanzees in the opening of Gabun nuts was first described by Beatty (1951). As with all types of learned tool use$_3$, it is not a species-specific characteristic, but rather a behavior modification the distribution of which remains limited to special populations. New observations from C. Boesch (1978) in the Tai National Park (Ivory Coast) also showed differential preference for tool use between female and male animals. The complete pattern of learned tool use$_3$ "gathering/opening" contains the following suboperations:

1. Sighting of a tree, either the Coula tree (*Coula edulis*) or the Panda tree (*Panda eleosa*).
2. Climbing the tree or gathering the fruit from the ground. Gathering is only useful when opening of the fruit, using tools, has already been planned; gathering is one of the most elementary forms of optimalization of learned behavior.

3. Opening the nuts through tool use; search for a branch fork or a firmly placed abutment as an "anvil." The pattern of hits has to be coordinated with the amount of force used.

4. Eating the food. Through tool use$_3$, chimpanzee populations develop new food sources which would not be available if only "body tools" were used.

THE ACTION ASPECT IN CHIMPANZEE TOOL USE

Experiments on tool use are empirical indicators of the difference between behavior and action in chimpanzees. Methodologically, there are differences between the reaction chains seen in tool use$_3$ and actions (however, there is a smooth transition from this tool use to tool use$_4$):

1. The *teleological aspect*—that is, the goal of tool use$_4$—is missing from simple behavior. The use and manufacture of tools is a relatively closed, logical, and temporally structured action aimed at the *realization of a goal*.

2. From the teleological structure of tool use$_4$, the animal is known to be an active organism. Thus, stimulus–response terminology, which interprets the organism as a passive receiver of stimulus causes, is replaced by action terminology such as *activity, action,* and *action system*. Description of tool use as "action" assumes another and completely different causal understanding in which the activating cause comes from the animal.

3. The concept of action is connected to the introduction of explicit psychological explanations. Gallup (1977), for example, has performed experiments with mirrors using chimpanzees, gorillas, and several macaque species (e.g., rhesus monkeys to show that there is consciousness in these experimental animals and to determine the extent of this consciousness. The use of the notion of *consciousness*, which follows from using the concepts of action and intelligence, is controversial here.

Historically, this "psychologizing," especially of the chimpanzee, began with the paper "Animal Intelligence" by the English zoologist Romanes (1883), a follower of Darwin. Although Romanes' work was severely criticized on methodological grounds and serves, in the history of animal psychology, as a classic example of anthropomorphization, his system of cognitive psychological constructs has been developed and expanded. Köhler's (1921) tool experiments are important in this controversy, because to explain the special cognitive abilities of the chimpanzee, he introduced the concept of "insight learning," a new category of learning postulating the existence of cognition in addition to stimulus–response connections. Insightful behavior has several cognitive dimensions:

1. "Insight" means spontaneous, immediate solution, which precedes the motor component of the tool use. Compared to a blind attempt, "trial and error," insight involves a new cognitive structure regulating action. Tool use assumes the existence of an "inner model" in the central nervous system, a model used to play motor behavior through in thoughts. Tool use is, then, a criterion through which one can indirectly assess the *intelligence* of an experimental animal.

2. Tool use and tool manufacture are different dimensions of insight. On the one hand, insight is concerned with a *task*. A task has a *defined goal* and a known algorithm for solving the problem. In tool manufacture, on the other hand, the solution to the problem and the exact goal state are not known.

3. Insightful tool use also has characteristics of "foresight," which make it "planned action." The action steps are coordinated in such a way that each step anticipates the results of the next. Tool use often shows directly how many partial steps have been anticipated. Planning foresight is an aspect of problem solving as a Gestalt (*Ganzheit*) that organizes tool use$_4$ via the construction of action goals. Planned actions require an objectivation of the spatial relationships (e.g., of subject and tool object) and time course.

The Stick as a Universal Tool of the Chimpanzee

In both natural observations and in laboratory experiments, chimpanzees' tool use frequently has the same structure: the use of a stick or similar instrument to reach a goal. In contrast to specialized, instinctive tool use$_2$, sticks are used to reach goals in *many* behavioral domains (e.g., comfort behavior, getting nourishment, defense) in a *similar way*. Motorically, tool use corresponds with the ability to strike, but also has finer movement patterns that make, for example, the gathering of fruits possible. In their natural habitat chimpanzees use sticks and branches frequently for poking at bees' nests as well as for investigating unknown but interesting objects. Even tooth picking or fishing for termites contains the principle of using a stick as a tool. Stick-use variations have been the object of many experiments. In one of Köhler's (1921) best-known investigations, a stick was used as an instrument to acquire food that would not be reachable without it. In Kortlandt's (1968) experiments in nature, sticks were used by male chimpanzees against a leopard mock-up. Menzel, Davenport, and Rogers (1970) reported on the use of sticks to overcome barriers. Various attempts to have chimpanzees paint also incorporate the basic motor element of being able to handle a paintbrush as a stick (Rensch, 1961).

Reaching for a stick in tool experiments has a biological predisposition that comes from an aboreal lifestyle. Sticks are constantly available in the natural environment of the chimpanzee and represent a purposeful, functional extension of the forward extremities. Grasping, which has developed through the climbing lifestyle, is a basic operation that helps to manage the tool. An additional step in tool evolution is reached when the ability to manipulate the stick is increased. In laboratory experiments tool use can be expanded by, for example, putting two sticks together. The improved tool use of savanna-bound chimpanzee populations, as demonstrated by Kortlandt (1968), is interesting in evolutionary terms because the selection conditions in the area (which was also the life space of protohominids) accelerate the evolution of tool behavior. The chimpanzees of the jungle hit in an undirected fashion, but the chimpanzees of the savanna have special hitting techniques, such as hitting down from above. In several cases they hit Kortland's leopard mock-up precisely on the head, resulting in decapitation. The cognitive ability to transfer from one variant of stick use to another has an immediate survival value. There is an "internal model" that regulates tool use$_4$; that model permits transfer of the use of tools to other areas. Use of the stick as a multipurpose tool can be compared with the use of the "hand axe" by the hominid. In both cases, a multipurpose tool exists as an "unspecialized" tool.

Despite the evolutionary utility of using tools, in none of these tool examples is there an actual selection pressure that makes achieving the adaptation necessary for survival. The evolutionary preconditions of this behavior remain unclear. There are currently three (equally plausible) explanations for the evolution of tool use:

1. Playful tests and the discovery of new functional uses. Tool use is more likely to develop in areas in which the survival of the species is secured biologically through body adaptation or instinctive reactions. The optional, playful character of chimpanzee tool use is dependent on the experience of specific individuals.

2. Through the application of additional instruments there is an effective increase in self- and species survival. Through increased complexity and expansion, additional ecological niches are developed. An example is the use of stones to open nuts; this renders a new food source for chimpanzees.

3. The use of tools becomes necessary for survival because of an intensification of the selection conditions. This intensification can come about, for example, through a change in the natural habitat; the playfully discovered behavior capacities acquire species-survival function.

Throwing Actions

Zoos often report that chimpanzees throw food and other objects at people they dislike. In natural conditions, throwing stones does occasionally appear, for example at baboons (Goodall, 1974). In Kortlandt's (1968) experiments, aroused chimpanzees threw sticks and other material at predator mock-ups.

The ability of the chimpanzee to instrumentalize objects by throwing them is notable for two reasons. Throwing can be interpreted as a functionally higher form of hitting. Being able to conquer distance, as it were, also assures a long-term increase in action effectiveness as compared to hitting. In aggressive animals, however, throwing is frequently unaimed and occurs in states of increased arousal accompanied by flailing and thrashing about. The tool character of the thrown object is determined primarily by its own physical characteristics, such as the strength it requires (Plooij, 1978).

Success at throwing is, above all, dependent on the existence of clear goals whose development is accompanied by spatial understanding. Compared to hitting, throwing has a higher functional level because it takes place within more complex space–time coordinates. The psychological specialness of throwing consists in movement of the object from one's own body after having been grasped as a tool. Throwing actions, even if they are very elementary, constitute, for that reason, a basic new functional form. In the tool use of Pongidae, they also constitute an obvious model of the first forms of the subject–object separation: The object is separated from the body in terms of space and time.

Throwing is functionally a part of aggressive behavior, which appears in chimpanzees, in natural conditions, in the form of territorial defenses against invaders or in flight. For example, chimpanzees throw stones at baboons not to capture them, but to drive them out of their territory. Throwing in intraspecies fighting or in capturing prey has not been observed; chimpanzees do not have the special hunting techniques evident in predators (e.g., other primates such as young baboons and long-tailed monkeys; Goodall, 1974), because they are primarily fruit gatherers and eat meat only occasionally.

The psychological development of throwing actions as defensive behaviors does not preclude the possibility that in the evolution of the hominids, throwing became a basic part of aggressive behavior because flight and attack contain the same motivational basis. There are numerous functional specializations within human aggression, including throwing at prey as an element of human hunting. The development of throwing actions could, therefore, be interpreted as a model for the phylogenetic development of a special, purely human tool type, the weapon. The development of weapons (i.e., instruments used for aggressive purposes) is a tool area in which animal precursors are not known.

THE SOCIETAL LEVEL OF FUNCTIONING: TOOL USE$_5$ AS *ACTIVITY (TAETIGKEIT)*

The chimpanzee remains a part of nature even in the most complicated experimental design. Its cognitive abilities are adequate to imitate work-like operations on the action level; however, even the most intelligent problem solving in tool use$_4$ will not force the experimenter to the interpretation that the experimental animal is "working." The tool use$_4$ of chimpanzees is limited to several special goals that may also appear as components in human work and that, when simplified, can be simulated in animal experiments.

That animals and humans differ qualitatively in tool use was repeated many times in the nature theory of the 19th century. Because the use and development of work materials characterize the *specifically human work process* (although they may appear in rudimentary form in certain animal species), Benjamin Franklin defined humans as "tool-making animals." Under the influence of Darwin, Engels (1876/1940) compiled the criteria for determining the differences between animals and humans. Despite the close phylogenetic relationships, there is one basic qualitative difference between Pongidae and Hominidae: Only humans have the ability to work, as they not only instrumentalize natural objects as tools for their purposes, but they also change nature itself by tool manufacture.

The difference between tool use in animals and humans is significant for methodological reasons (e.g., avoidance of anthropomorphizing) and theoretical reasons (e.g., differentiating phylogenetic stages of work in the Pongidae and hominid evolution). In soviet psychology (Leontiev, 1980) and German psychology (Holzkamp, 1983; Schurig, 1978), the distinction between the level of tool use in chimpanzees and the specific tool use$_5$ in human work has been elaborated. Tool use$_5$ is related to the term *Taetigkeit*, which is not easily translatable in English (*activity* is the closest term) and signifies planning and goal direction. Two arguments are discussed here.

Activity (*Taetigkeit*) as a Social Endeavor and Development of Tradition

Experiments with chimpanzees have shown that single animals were able to learn to solve problems individually; they were, however, not able to coordinate their tool use with other individuals. Even pulling a box with a cord—which requires two individuals—is very difficult for them to learn. Chimpanzees may use other chimpanzees as passive tools to reach their goals—for example, when they climb another chimpanzee to reach fruit. Here the other chimpanzee is like a box upon which one climbs. Nevertheless, when it is necessary to pile up boxes in cooperation with other individuals, they are not successful because they work agaist each other (Rensch, 1973). Thus, at the level of tool use$_4$, each animal looks for solutions alone. Social cooperation in the use of tools is typical only for human beings.

In paleoanthropology, systematic alteration of natural objects, evidence for tool use$_5$, is taken as an empirical indicator of the existence of human hominids. For that reason, the difference between animal tool use$_4$ on the level of the action concept and activity (*Taetigkeit*) as the specifically human concept of tool use$_5$ approximates a boundary between primatology and anthropology.

The animal–human transition time period may have begun with the Ramapitecus about 10 million years ago and ended with the Australopithecus group. The Australopithecus afarensis "Lucy," 3.5 million years old, is the oldest known human hominid. Lucy is controversial primarily because it is not clear to what extent the Australopithecus afarensis was already using bipedal locomotion. In hominid evolution bipedality is a decisive biological precursor of the ability to manufacture tools. From the manufacture of the first "real" tools, it is possible to determine directly the phylogenetic origin of the specifically human behavior: the origin of activity (*Taetigkeit*) as the socially organized form of natural appropriation. Tool use is, therefore, a criterion of the animal–human difference.

A further difference between human activity and the chimpanzees' individual tool use is the development of *tool traditions*. Various degrees of complexity of tool traditions can be distinguished:

1. In the paleolithic period one can distinguish core tools (such as pebble tools and the chopper tools of the Australopithecines) from the more developed flake tools. These tool traditions were handed down from generation to generation for hundreds of thousands of years.

2. Each technology made it possible to develop other types of tools. For example, typical flake tools were scrapers, scratchers, and blades, which were made in mass in a standard way. These traditions can rightfully be called industries (e.g., the blade manufacture of the Neanderthals).

3. Tool traditions are the most complex form of the development of traditions and lead to a change of the whole lifestyle of the hominids. The discovery of fire as a tool has, for example, changed nourishment, tool manufacture, and dwellings profoundly.

The handing on of information in tool tradition is, of course, not done genetically but externally. In tools there is a kind of stored experience that functions as a "social memory," one that transmits information between generations. Social cooperation in tool manufacture in the forms of division of labor and tool traditions are tool use$_5$ aspects that are specific to the human being and that cannot be seen in animal tool use.

The Activity (*Taetigkeit*) Character of Tool Experiments

The developmental difference in the evolution of tool behavior that is represented by tool use$_4$ for animals and the specifically human use of tools$_5$ becomes clearest by contrasting the activity of the experimenter with the level of tool use of the experimental animal. The tool use of the chimpanzee is, in every case, the calculated consequence of human activity.

Through planning of the tool experiment, the experimenter is completing a "planned action" in which the possibilities of an experimental "action plan" of the chimpanzee are the object of interest. The societal character of the experimental action plan is demonstrated by the fact that the experimenter (as opposed to the experimental animal) does not act in isolation but within the scope of scientific knowledge. This societal memory (i.e., science) is always greater than the knowledge of the individual and has special forms of "objectivation" (e.g., journals, movies). Even constructing the tool experiment is activity (*Taetigkeit*) because work is done to make the chimpanzees' tool use possible. Every rope, box, or plastic plate is not manufactured by the experimenter but is taken from the societal production process and is used in the organization of the experiment. Only by reinterpreting their functional value can they be used in the action of the chimpanzee. Because "character" of work is missing, the tool use can be only partially "humanized": a box or a hammer is only "lent." The experimental animal can at most complete those operations that the experimenter conceived in planning the experiment. The chimpanzee is "insightful" or problem oriented, but does not behave "scientifically" as does the researcher (i.e., does not use the specific form of human work). Experimental animal tool use thus shows not only what the experimental animal can*not* do compared with human activity level but also that the animal can be raised to the level of action, tool use$_4$. In tool experiments, cognitive action goals that are much greater than the adaptation performances forced by natural selection can be simulated. An intelligent performance rests on the complete use of cognitive abilities through *artificial selection*. The brain capacity of the Pongidae has the potential to adapt to artificial demands such as those of tool use. Exploiting this potential, it is possible to stimulate artificially various developmental features of the transition from animal action level to human activity that followed phylogenetically in hominid evolution.

ACKNOWLEDGEMENTS

Translated by M. Feeley and the editors.

3

An Action-Theory Perspective of the Tool-Using Capacities of Chimpanzees and Human Infants

Kim G. Dolgin
University of Minnesota

INTRODUCTION

In the previous chapter, the author presents a model of tool use that he believes reflects the phylogenetic emergence of this important behavioral class. The necessity for such a model, it is suggested, comes from the fact that in the past researchers have evidenced a tendency to make unwarranted attributions of intent and goal direction to nonhumans on the basis of their tool-using abilities; even though he does acknowledge other classification schemes (e.g., Immelmann, 1982), the author finds them inadequate in that they do not successfully distinguish human from nonhuman behavior. Schurig's scheme is such that the most advanced level of tool use (*tool use$_5$*) is solely within the perview of human beings, as it requires a capacity for *Taetigkeiten* (work). In addition to developing his model, Schurig discusses chimpanzees' capacities to manufacture and use tools and attempts to fit their behaviors into his framework.

Although I am in complete agreement that human beings devise and use tools in a more complex fashion than chimpanzees, and that tool use can be used as a yardstick with which to measure goal direction, I disagree with Schurig on several points. It is my view that his model fails to differentiate all of the important grades of tool use. In addition, I disagree with a number of his characterizations of chimpanzee tool-using behavior.

In this chapter, Schurig's model is discussed and chimpanzee tool-using behaviors are reviewed. In this light, laboratory research by investigators who have used artificial languages to study chimpanzees' cognitive and protolinguistic abilities (e.g., Premack, 1976; Rumbaugh & Gill, 1977) is examined. In addition, an ontogenetic description of human children's emerging tool-using behav-

35

ior is presented and their behaviors are matched against the model. In this manner, modifications of Schurig's model of tool use are suggested.

A DISCUSSION OF SCHURIG'S MODEL

Briefly, the model of tool use developed by Schurig entails five stages. The most primitive of these (tool use$_1$) involves the use of *body tools,* or anatomical modifications that permit adaptive responses that would be impossible if they were not present. The second stage (tool use$_2$) is represented by the rigid, instinctive use of objects in very restricted ways. The use of nonprogrammed, learned object manipulations emerges in the third stage (tool use$_3$), but a limitation on these variable behaviors is that they are the result of instrumental learning and are reflexive in nature. "Intelligent" tool use (tool use$_4$) is attained if the tool user can conceptualize his goal and understand the steps he must take— including tool use—in order to attain it. Finally, tool use$_5$, or systematic transformation of objects through work, is characterized by a shared societal understanding of tasks, goals, and instruments, and by actions directed to "higher" causes. At first glance, this scheme appears to track an increasing emergence of purposeful, goal directed behavior. In fact, it does not, as an examination of each of the stages indicates.

Tool Use$_1$, Body Tools

Schurig uses the term *body tools* to describe specialized body parts that are used adaptively to accomplish some basic need. He introduces one arbitrary feature to distinguish these organs: composition of *special substances.* He also suggests that these body tools are typified by rigid attachment. Beaks and claws possess these attributes, but hands (and to a large degree, lips)—primates' primary body tools—do not. Lips are specialized structures that afford suckling (i.e., access to a specialized food source) in the same way that beaks afford pecking; hands, too, are more impressive tools than claws, because they are used in a wide variety of subtle, complex, adaptive ways. Claw use is more circumscribed and inflexible.

More importantly, as described, this most primitive stage of tool use makes no distinction between action oriented and instinctive use of the body part. (This distinction does not cut in the same way as do the special substance and rigidity criteria—for example, the infant chimpanzee's use of lips in suckling is instinctual.) Although my preference would be to exclude use of *any* body part in a scheme of tool use, if any were to be included I would distinguish among reflexive use of the body part, its instrumental use, and its purposive, goal oriented use. Instinctive use should be included only at stage 1, whereas instrumental and goal oriented use would be placed at (separate) higher stages.

Tool Use$_2$, Instinctive Tool Use

This stage is reasonably placed at the lower extreme of the true tool-use continuum and it represents its least developed form of action orientation. Even the instinctive use of objects as tools requires chained response steps, however, and so in a very primitive way can be viewed as future directed. At the very least, animals must be able to recognize appropriate objects; in addition, they frequently must search, at least briefly, to find adequate objects. Another step is added if the selected instrument is modified, as happens, for example, when a chimpanzee shapes a branch to make it more suitable for nest manufacture. A comprehensive review of this kind of tool use is given by Alcock (1972).

Tool Use$_3$, Learned Instrumentalization Of Objects

The placement of instrumental use of objects as the next stage in a scheme of increasingly activity oriented tool use is sensible and valid. However, several of the criteria that Schurig proposes for the capacity to instrumentalize objects are unnecessary. In particular, Schurig claims that possession of a pentadactyl extremity, a precision grip, and the nonuse of the forward extremities in locomotion are "biological prerequisites" for tool use$_3$. These requirements are surely erroneous. Although when coupled with bipedalism the pongid/human five-fingered hand with its opposable thumb is conducive to the development of tool use (at all stages, not only tool use$_3$), other body configurations are also suited for this behavior. Circuses employ elephants, for example, precisely because they can be taught to manipulate objects with their trunks. In addition, the nonhanded rats and pigeons trained in Skinner boxes definitionally learn to use keys, switches, pingpong paddles, and so on instrumentally.

Under natural conditions, young primates typically learn to instrumentalize tools from their mothers (as Schurig states). There is also a second major avenue to learning to use tools: play behavior. Many authors (e.g. Fagan, 1976; Loizos, 1967) believe that play evolved precisely because it served the function of generating novel behaviors. Innovations that begin as accidental outcomes of playful activities often spread first through the young individuals in the social group as they play (e.g., potato washing by Japanese macaques; see Itani & Suzuki, 1967). Whereas established tool-using behaviors are learned by the young from their mothers, innovative tool-using strategies are usually the result of play.

Finally, gathering/opening is cited as an example of instrumental tool use. At the same time it is asserted that gathering is of use only when the using of tools has already been planned, thus indicating the presence of sequenced steps and foresight. By these criteria, gathering/opening seems a better example of the next grade of tool use, *tool use $_4$*.

Tool Use$_4$, Intelligent Tool Use

Again, although the basic concept of a separate stage for intelligent tool use is warranted, and its position as more advanced than instrumental tool use is appropriate, the characteristics of this stage, as outlined by Schurig, are questionable. First, Schurig states that tool use$_4$ can be distinguished from tool use$_2$ because, unlike that more primitive form of tool use, it is not necessarily marked by a food-acquisition goal. However, in a later section in his chapter, he cites nest building, an activity unrelated to food acquisition, as an example of tool use$_2$.

The defining characteristic of tool use$_4$ is that the animal be capable of forming a logical and causal conceptualization of the steps involved in using the tool to solve the task at hand. Yet one example given for tool use at this stage is stick throwing, an activity that does not usually meet this criterion. Sticks are widely used by chimpanzees in a great variety of ways that would fall under the tool use$_4$ category. Sticks are typically *thrown*, however, only when the animal is aroused: Usually there is little concerted aiming (personal observation) and throwing is neither methodical nor goal directed. In natural conditions, chimpanzees throw objects only when they are engaged in agonistic displays; this behavior is better conceived of as instinctive (tool use$_2$) and as a part of display behavior. It is probable that such behavior originated as chance action (the opportunity may have come from sticks held for the purpose of noise making) but became incorporated into the display because it proved successful at driving off or (rarely) wounding opponents. I do not believe that chimpanzee stick throwing is related to weapon use in the hominid line; weapon use more likely evolved from purposive hitting actions by protohominids. Finally, *contra* Schurig's claim, humans and pongids are not the only animals to use objects agonistically. The archer fish, *Toxotes jaculatrix*, for example, shoots jets of water at its insect prey to dislodge them from their perches, causing them to fall within reach.

Another stated characteristic of tool use$_4$ is that it is evidence of *insightful learning*. The term *insight* is traditionally restricted to those solutions that are obtained without trial-and-error groping (see Köhler, 1927). Although an animal might discover a use for an object through insight, it equally might learn through practice to use a tool to produce a desired end. If the other criteria of "action" (*Handlung*) are met, then even slowly learned actions should be included in tool use$_4$.

Finally, it should be noted that tool use$_4$ differs from tool use$_3$ and tool use$_2$ in the amount of evidenced individuality. Because the object manipulations of the kind seen in tool use$_2$ are the result of genetic predisposition, they are characterized by relative uniformity and universality. As Skinner noted (see "superstitious behavior, B. F. Skinner, 1969), even instrumental learning situations sometimes result in idiosyncratic behavioral selections. However, insight (as well as intelligent learning) can result in myriad different solutions to a given problem. This is particularly true as the number of steps used to attain a solution increases.

Tool Use₅, Systematic Transformation, through Work, of Objects and Materials in Nature

Although it is certainly reasonable to call for an avoidance of uncritical anthropomorphizing of primate behavior, Schurig never clearly delineates the criteria for engaging in level-5 tool-using behavior. The several "differences" between stages 4 and 5 cited seem unsupported. For example, one given difference is that whereas humans manufacture tools, chimpanzees merely use them. This contradicts later statements, and is simply untrue: Although the tools constructed by chimpanzees are far simpler than those constructed by humans, this is a matter of degree, not of kind. Other differences include "the ability to change nature" "objectivation," "societal functioning," and "work."

In order to delineate chimpanzees' capacities, it is necessary to integrate information from laboratory and field studies. It is true that in an experimental setting chimpanzee subjects must rely on their human captors for access to tools; because there is a certain dependence to their actions, their abilities seem limited. It is also true, however, that human beings placed in the same situation—in a cage, without means to acquire materials on their own—would evidence the same passivity demonstrated by the chimpanzees. Laboratory settings and field studies differ in the opportunities they offer researchers. In the former, psychologists can train and "stretch" their subjects in order to best determine the upper limits of their abilities; it is certain that some capacities evidenced in the laboratory are never performed in the wild (e.g., symbol use). Field studies are better suited to indicate what typical, naturally occurring behaviors look like. If the issue in question is *capacity,* then it is inappropriate to denegrate laboratory performance. In any case, if a claim is to be substantiated (e.g., chimpanzees do not make tools), then it must hold true in both settings.

Schurig argues that only humans, modern and prehistoric, are/were capable of changing nature through their use of tools. This again appears to be an issue of magnitude rather than of kind, and, in addition, seems irrelevant. There is no basis for claiming that the most primitive hominids "changed nature" to a significantly greater degree than chimpanzees. (Furthermore, an instinct-driven, dam-building beaver, who forms lakes and alters ecosystems, can be credited with this ability to a substantially greater degree than either a chimpanzee or a protohuman.) In a similar vein, humans will societally share their information/inventions through journals, the media, and so on ("objectivation"), whereas chimpanzees cannot. If this criterion is held, then early hominids should be excluded from stage-5 tool use along with chimpanzees.

The term *work* seems to be used to mean "a socially organized activity." It must indicate something other than widespread, commonly performed tool-using behaviors, because if it does not, then chimpanzees' construction and use of leaf sponges for drinking would qualify as work. If, alternatively, work is taken to denote activities that are restricted to particular members of the social group, then the use of sticks in hunting by adult male chimpanzees would qualify. By the same example, it cannot be meant to include only those behaviors in which group members act in a unified, coordinated action, because tool-aided hunting would mean performance by apes. Tool-related work cannot indicate only those activities that are passed along from one generation to the next, because, as noted, different groups of chimpanzees have unique behaviors that are maintained by succeeding generations. Similarly, it cannot exclude activity that is not based on an aggregate societal knowledge—individual discovery of adaptive object manipulations by chimpanzees ensures that the "shared knowledge" of the troop will be greater than the knowledge of its individual members. The only useful definition of work makes it synonymous with *activity (Taetiokeitin)*—that is, goal directed behavior that subsumes individual actions. As I argue later, a good indicator that activity is occurring may be the chained use of tools.

If tool use is to be used as a yardstick with which to measure how advanced nonhuman primates are in their abilities to perform activities and actions (*Handluno*), then what is needed is a scheme that directly concentrates on increasing hierarchical levels of goal orientation. Perhaps the best avenue to that involves isolating, at a more fire-grained level, the precursor abilities that serve as components to goal directed behavior. Parker and Gibson (1979), who contend that flexible tool use evolved in the human line as a specialization to cope with the demands of extractive foraging (the finding and eating of food that must be removed from the inedible covering in which it is embedded), have specified several abilities they believe to be central to tool use for this purpose. They have stated that extractive foraging requires an understanding of: object–object spatial relations, such as above–underneath and inside–outside; the causal relation between force and movement; the use of variable experimentation to determine an object's properties; and goal directed trial-and-error coordination. The emergence of these behaviors in the human infant has been well studied within the framework of the developmental psychologist Jean Piaget.

THE PIAGETIAN PERSPECTIVE

As outlined by Piaget (Piaget, 1952; see also Flavell, 1963), the human infant progresses through six stages of intellectual development during the first 2 years of life. Passage through these stages represents the mastery of *sensorimotor intelligence*. It is during this phase of life that the infant learns about objects, causality, and spatial relations.

From approximately birth through the first month, the infant is capable only of performing unmodified reflexes. The infant reacts to objects if they are placed in her hand (by grasping) or mouth (by sucking), but in a rigid, undifferentiated way. (At the end of this stage, however, the infant does discriminate among objects in the limited sense that only some objects will serve to trigger reflexes—for example, only milk-producing nipples will cause sucking behavior.) If tool use$_1$ is taken to include organs such as lips and hands, then the infant's behavior during this stage is exemplative of this grade of behavior. Object use *proper* is not present, because infants in this stage do not seek out and acquire objects on their own, but only react to them if they come in contact with their bodies.

During stage 2 of the sensorimotor series, which occurs when the infant is between 1 and 4 months of age, *primary circular reactions* develop. These are nonpurposive, body oriented, repetitive behaviors in which the infant maintains a behavior that began reflexively. The primary improvement in object use over the first stage is that objects are, in a rudimentary and limited way, sought—that is, the infant will grasp an object if it and her hand are in her visual field at the same time.

With the appearance of stage 3 behaviors, which usually occurs between the fourth and eighth months, the infant can be said to have made significant progress vis-a-vis her interactions with objects. *Secondary circular reactions* emerge: These differ from stage-2 primary circular reactions in that they are external in focus. They represent the infant's attempt to repeat interesting environmental events: After such an event occurs, the infant acquires the goal of sustaining it. In this way, intentionality and goal directedness make their first, albeit weak, appearance. Piaget believed that the criteria for intent included: the degree of external, outward orientation; the appearance of a number of intermediary means steps prior to goal attainment; the behavioral adaptation to the specific situation. The primitiveness of the intentional actions performed during this stage lies in the fact that the goals are acquired post hoc, only after the means to attain them have already been realized, and that the goal directed behaviors are limited to repetitions of previous actions. Also, in this stage, objects are assimilated to habitual behavior patterns and little accommodation is made to them. The infant's behavior seems closest to Schurig's tool use$_3$, because the behaviors are acquired and used to produce specific environmental results. (There is no equivalent of tool use$_2$ in the human infant, because there are no objects that humans use instinctively to solve specific and narrowly delineated problems.)

It is in the course of stage 4 (typical of 8- to 12-month-old infants) that the first fully intentional actions occur. Infants at this age appropriately juxtapose two or more of their simple action patterns to produce temporally coordinated behavioral sequences. For example, they may use one object as an instrument so as to obtain a second; conversely, they may set aside one object if it impedes their ability to reach another. These sequences demonstrate a grasping of means–end relationships: It is clear that the goal is anticipated from the first action's beginning. It is also during this stage that the infant demonstrates for the first time any ability to externalize causality—that is, the infant behaves as if he or she understands that other persons besides herself can cause actions. Novel objects are actively explored. The stage-4 infant is thus capable of intelligent tool use (tool use$_4$), the first stage to require true intentionality.

From approximately the age of 1 year to 18 months (stage 5 of the sensorimotor period), *tertiary circular reactions* predominate in the infant's behavioral repertoire. These actions consist of varied repetitions, and are important in that they constitute the means to discover items' properties and to find novel ways to solve problems through trial-and-error experimentation. In addition, relationships among objects in space (e.g., "in front of") come to be understood.

Finally, the stage-6 infant, aged 18 to 24 months, comes to be able to internally (mentally) represent objects and thus becomes able to solve problems cognitively, through representation. In other words, insight is attained. At the same time, the infant becomes capable of inferring causes without having perceived the action that resulted in those causes. At this age infants remain, at most, capable of Schurig's tool use$_4$.

The Piagetian perspective has been used to study apes (Chevalier–Skolnikoff, 1977, and Mathieu, 1978, in chimpanzees; Parker & Gibson, 1977, and Redshaw, 1978, in gorillas) as well as other primates (see Parker & Gibson, 1979, for a review). Chimpanzees and gorillas pass through the stages of the sensorimotor period in the same sequence and at almost the same pace as human infants. However, they (nonlanguage-trained apes) fail to complete either the spatial or the causality series: They attain only stage-5 abilities in these areas. These levels are sufficient for attainment of tool use$_4$, however. (Language-trained chimpanzees have demonstrated a more sophisticated comprehension of causality; see Premack, 1978.)

Tool use$_5$ does not occur until after the complete sensorimotor series is attained and the child has become capable of language. Although no other animal species possesses language, experiments have demonstrated that chimpanzees are able to comprehend many concepts that figure among its precursors. The experimental situations into which these chimpanzee subjects were placed can be viewed as instances of tool-using opportunities in addition to language-learning opportunities, and so the results of these studies should be helpful in determining the limitations of chimpanzees' abilities to use tools. This is particularly interesting in light of suggestions that the emergence of language was linked to tool-using capacity (Steklis & Harnad, 1976).

CHIMPANZEE LANGUAGE STUDIES AND TOOL USE

The chimpanzee language studies most cogent to the topic of tool use are those by Premack (1976, 1978) and by the Yerkes group (Rumbaugh & Gill, 1977;

Savage & Rumbaugh, 1977). The subjects in Premack's studies were taught a language whose "words" and grammatical markers consisted of pieces of plastic that were different shapes and colors; Rumbaugh's chimpanzees were taught to punch commands onto a computer keyboard in order to receive food, tickling, company, and so on. The pieces of plastic and the keyboard can be considered tools that the animals used to attain diverse goals; furthermore, the chimpanzee subjects were often required to compose novel "sentences" (rule-following strings) with these symbols. "Writing sentences" in Premack's studies, for example, involved multiple instances of: (1) selection of an appropriate piece; (2) its correct orientation; and (3) correct sequential placement (in relation to the spatial position of the other pieces) on the response board. The chimpanzees' capacities to do this is further evidence that they are capable both of insight— because they are usually correct and do not need to engage in trial-and-error experimentation—and of coordinating multiple actions (*Handlung*) in the service of some larger goal.

The Yerkes chimpanzees were required to engage in "dialogue" with each other so that they could cooperatively solve a problem and receive a reward. Specifically, in order to obtain the goal, one chimpanzee needed to "ask" another, via the computer keyboard, for a tool, and the second chimpanzee had to respond by giving the first a tool to which only it had access. Again, this involved both temporally correct sequencing and coordination of actions (between as well as within individuals, in this case).

Performance in either language-training program also indicates that the animal is capable of rendering an "internal model" through the use of symbolic representation. This is a capacity that Schurig claims is necessary for attainment of tool use$_4$. In addition, another capacity chimpanzees have demonstrated through use of these artificial languages is consciousness/self-awareness: Each of the chimpanzees who has been so trained has learned to use a symbol that represents itself, and can use this symbol appropriately. Language-trained chimpanzees can, for example, distinguish between the sentences "(Chimp) give (trainer) apple" and "(Trainer) give (Chimp) apple" (Premack, 1976). As a last point, chimpanzees who are language trained are, at least in a weak way, capable of objectivation, because they make records as to the state of the world and of their desires.

None of these points directly refutes Schurig's contention that chimpanzees fail to engage in tool use$_5$: Chimpanzee goals and the strategies they use to obtain them are less complex than those of humans. Tool use of any kind by apes is a relatively rare occurrence (see van Lawick-Goodall, 1970; McGrew, 1977; McGrew, Tutin, & Midgett, 1975). Still, the criteria Schurig used to distinguish tool use$_5$ are definitional and teleological, and instead of his characterization I propose one based on a more "quantifiable" measure.

One hard criterion that might serve to distinguish human from nonhuman tool use is chaining, or the use of multiple tools to make or use tools. This is an ability that chimpanzees rarely, if ever, demonstrate (Köhler, 1927; McGrew, 1977;

Redshaw, 1978); similarly, one chimpanzee rarely uses another to manipulate (Bates, 1976; Redshaw, 1978) or to get (Köhler, 1927; Parker & Gibson, 1977) tools for it. The ability to chain tools is one that has been implicated for language (Bates, 1976), and, as mentioned before, the emergence of language has been linked to tool use (Steklis & Harnad, 1976). Because chimpanzees are capable of most sensorimotor skills but do not have language, this lack may be causal for both their communicative limitations and their failure to perform *Taetigkeiten*.

FUNDAMENTALS OF ACTION THEORY

GOAL DIRECTED BEHAVIOR IN
PHYSIOLOGICAL PSYCHOLOGY

The action-theory framework makes use of notions like representation, hierarchical organization, and feedback. To physiological psychologists it is crucial to know just how these abstractions are expressed in the nervous system. Gallistel argues that neurobehavioral research has so far identified three primitive units of behavior (elementary neuromuscular circuits): oscillators, reflexes, and servomechanisms. Having identified these primitives, Gallistel turns to the mechanisms by which they are coordinated so as to produce complex behavior.

The central concept here is the notion of potentiation and depotentiation. In Gallistel's view, biological drives act by altering the threshold for activation of higher order constellations of these primitive units (complex units of behavior). Hunger, for example, lowers the threshold for activation of the complex units subserving eating and food seeking (that is, hunger potentiates these units); satiety raises the thresholds (depotentiates).

Gallistel then turns his attention to the role of representations in the organization of goal directed action, in order to clarify his conception of intentionality and emotionality in behavior. He suggests that goal directed behavior is intentional only if its organization makes essential use of an act-outcome representation. He argues that full-fledged emotionality depends upon an animal's having representations of its own motivational states. This kind of self-referential knowledge, Gallistel argues, is necessary for the kind of emotional experience we humans, and perhaps some other species, have.

Michael Stadler and Theo Wehner take up an issue not addressed directly in the Gallistel chapter. Gallistel argues that for an organism to act intentionally it must have a representation of the consequences of its actions—that is, it must anticipate *the effects of its actions by way of an act-outcome representation. Stadler and Wehner point out that Anokhin, a Soviet physiologist, advanced a notion in the 1930s called the* functional system, *which can embody anticipations. Anticipations can be specified at a variety of levels of abstraction, ranging from the subsensor level through cognitive representations. In the last section of their chapter, Stadler and Wehner give us a feel for the kinds of experiments and evidence that bear on the notion of the functional system.*

4

Motivation, Intention, and Emotion: Goal Directed Behavior from a Cognitive-Neuroethological Perspective

Charles R. Gallistel
University of Pennsylvania

INTRODUCTION

The associationist or sensorimotor approach to the mechanisms underlying behavior attempts to explain behavior with a single structural concept, the concept of a connection by which one element activates another element. In behavioral neurobiology the sensorimotor approach is the attempt to explain behavior in terms of reflexes (whether conditioned or innate). In learning theory, it is the attempt to explain learned behavior in terms of the development of associations between stimuli and stimuli or between stimuli and responses. In his history of 19th-century neuropsychology, Young (1970) notes the failure of sensorimotor behavior theory to offer an explanation of the differences among individuals of a species or among species. This failure is directly traceable to the assumption that the mechanisms underlying all sorts of behavior can be dealt with by a single principle or structural concept.

Ethology and modern cognitive psychology have in common the disposition to posit a more elaborated and differentiated structure for the mechanism that generates behavior. In an earlier work (Gallistel, 1980b), I elaborated a view of the mechanism underlying behavior that derived primarily from ethology and secondarily from cognitive psychology. This view assumed that the structure underlying behavior had many distinct kinds of components and made use of a variety of distinct principles. One might hope that this view would offer insight into the nature of the differences between animals regarding the mechanisms that generate their behavior. The purpose of the earlier work was to lay a clear foundation for the ethological drive theory. It showed how the key concepts in the ethological theory—the hierarchical structure of the system and the coordinative role of selective potentiation and depotentiation within this hierarchical structure—emerge from a consideration of the elementary units of behavior and the manner in which these elementary units are coordinated to form complex units.

Despite the preoccupation with the concept of motivation in behavior, the earlier work said nothing about either intention or emotion, two concepts closely intertwined with motivation in the layperson's explanations of behavior. In this essay, I place an account of intention and an account of emotion within the framework previously elaborated. This approach leads to some suggestions about the nature of the differences between the behavioral mechanisms of animals from disparate phyla (e.g., between sea slugs and humans).

THE FRAMEWORK

Behavior may be decomposed into units; some complex, some elementary. A unit of behavior is a combination of neuronal, glandular, and or muscular elements capable of generating a *naturally occurring* muscular movement or glandular secretion. It must have a muscular or glandular effector, an element, or elements, that conducts signals to the muscular or glandular effector, and an element, or elements, in which neural or endocrine signals arise under natural (nonexperimental) circumstances. The elements in which behavior-initiating and guiding stimuli arise are receptors and pacemakers (endogenously active sources of rhythmic signals). A unit is elementary if it cannot be experimentally broken down into constituents that are units of behavior in their own right. It is complex if it can be so broken down.

We have the beginnings of a taxonomy for the elementary units of behavior, but little as yet in the way of a taxonomy of complex units. Three distinct kinds of elementary units are now known: the reflex, the oscillator, and the servomechanism. The functional structures of these three kinds of elementary units are given in Figure 4.1.

The vestibulo-ocular reflex is a prototype of the reflex category of elementary units. In this reflex the eyes rotate in a direction opposite to the direction in which the head rotates. The neuromuscular circuit underlying this elementary unit of behavior has sensory receptors (the semicircular canals of the vestibular apparatus) activated by angular acceleration and a set of pathways within the central nervous system (CNS) by which the signals from these receptor elements are integrated and passed to the oculomotor effector apparatus. There is no feedback from eye rotation onto the vestibular apparatus, so there is no question of this being a servomechanism. There is no endogenous rhythmicity in the output from this unit (ignoring the saccadic position-restoration component that comes into play only with sustained rotation), so it is not an oscillator.

The optokinetic reaction is a prototype of a servomecahnism. The optokinetic reaction is a rotation of the eyes in the same direction as, and in response to,

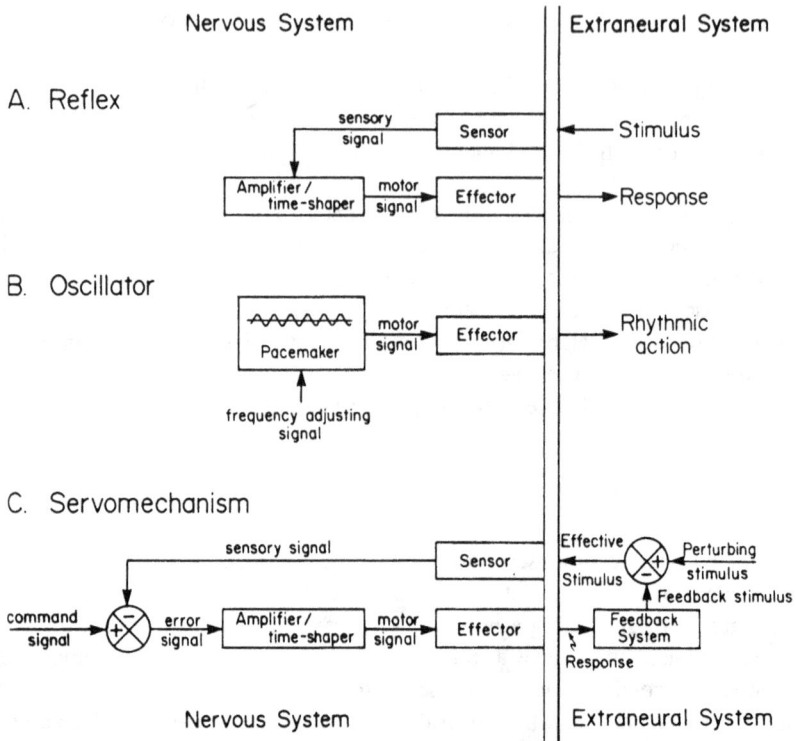

FIG. 4.1. The functional structures of the three most common elementary units of behavior. The arrows represent quantities (magnitudes), either in the external world (on the right), or in the neuroendocrine system. In the neuroendocrine system, the quantities represented are the magnitudes of neural or endocrine signals. The boxes represent transformations of quantities. The circles represent additive combination of quantities, with quantities entering negative wedges being subtracted from quantities entering positive wedges.

movement of the visual image across the retina. The naturally arising signals that initiate this movement come from circuits in the retina designed to extract the velocity of image motion across the retina. The velocity signals coming from the retina are integrated and relayed to the oculomotor apparatus via pathways in the CNS. There is feedback from the eye movement to the input elements, because the angular velocity of the retinal image is the angular velocity of the world relative to the animal minus the angular velocity of the eyes relative to the animal. The latter quantity is the output of the system, whereas the first-named quantity is the input. It can be shown experimentally that this feedback is an integral part of the functioning of the unit. When the feedback is prevented, the output differs radically from that observed under the natural condition (i.e., with feedback present; see Baarsma & Collewijn, 1974; also Gallistel, 1980a, 1981). Tests of the role played by feedback in the ordinary operation of a unit are central in deciding the classification of the unit as a servomechanism: Feedback must not only be shown to exist, it must also be shown to be integral to the normal functioning of the unit.

The beating of the heart is the prototype of an oscillatory unit of behavior. Specialized pacemaker cells in the sino-atrial node undergo rhythmic depolarization due to intrinsic properties of their cell membrane (Noble, 1975). Each regenerative depolarization of these cells triggers action potentials that are conducted to the heart muscle by the Purkinje fibers within the heart. The frequency of the rhythmic output from this oscillator (the heartbeat) may be adjusted by signals arriving over the vagal nerve, but the rhythm is intrinsic and is present after the extrinsic neural input to the heart has been removed.

There is no experimental evidence of which I am aware that suggests that any of the three just-named prototypes can be broken down into constituents that are units of behavior in their own right. By contrast, the scratch reflex, which has often been taken as a prototypical reflex, was long ago shown to be decomposable under anesthesia into two constitutents that themselves satisfy the definition of a unit of behavior (Brown, 1910). One constituent is the reflex raising of the paw to the point that is to be scratched; the other is rhythmic scratching. The first is a reflex; the second, an oscillator. I have urged that the term *reflex* be used only to designate a particular kind of *elementary* unit of behavior. Because the scratch reflex is not an elementary unit of behavior, it should not be called a reflex at all.

In addition to circuitry that mediates the action of elementary units of behavior, the CNS contains circuitry with a different function: the function of coordinating selected ensembles of elementary (or less complex) units in such a way as to form more complex units of behavior. To say that the neurobehavioral system has a hierarchical structure is to say that there exists circuitry whose purpose is to coordinate the combined functioning of units of behavior in such a way as to achieve functions that none of the units being coordinated achieves on its own. It is to say further that the circuitry that imposes a particular coordination is called on by still higher levels when the pattern of behavior coordinated by those higher levels requires that particular lower-level coordination. In other words, higher levels of the nervous system generally gain access to lower units by way of the intermediate circuits that create particular patterns of coordination in the operations of ensembles of lower units.

The neurobehavioral hierarchy is multileveled, as is the somewhat analogous hierarchy of embedment seen in chemical structures. At the lowest level of chemical structure there are the 96 elementary substances. The analogy to the neurobehavioral hierarchy is imprecise because the neurobehavioral taxonomy of elementary units is a taxonomy of types. Different reflexes (the limb-flexion reflex and the oculomotor reflex, for example) are not interchangeable, whereas different instances of the same elementary substance are. Nonetheless, the analogy is useful in seeing what is involved in the often-argued claim that the neurobehavioral system has a hierarchical structure. The first level of chemical structure above the level of the elementary substances is the combination of a few atoms into radicals—carbon rings, the amonia radical, the hydroxyl radical, and so on—the building blocks of the more complex molecules. Similarly, a reflex, an oscillator, and a servomechanism are coordinated in such a way as to form the unit that controls the stepping of an insect leg (see Gallistel, 1980a and 1980b, for elaboration on this and the following examples of ever-more complex neurobehavioral units). Various radicals then combine to form still higher-level chemical building blocks, such as amino acids and nucleotides. Similarly, the stepping circuits for each of an insect's six legs are coordinated by still higher-level circuitry to produce the unit for forward locomotion. (A different circuit coordinates the same lower level units to form the unit for backward locomotion.) The amino acids and nucleotides combine to form still higher-level units—polypeptides, proteins, and nucleic acids—the building blocks of cellular macrostructures. Similarly, the locomotion units are coordinated with orientation units to produce various types of oriented progressions—one of the building blocks of higher behavior.

MOTIVATION AND THE PRINCIPLE OF SELECTIVE POTENTIATION AND DEPOTENTIATION

A fundamental principle in the coordination of lower-level units by higher-level units is the principle of selective potentiation and depotentiation. Potentiation is the raising of a unit's potential for becoming active; depotentiation is the lowering of this potential. This principle is as fundamental and ubiquitous in behavioral neurobiology as the principle of covalent bonding is in chemistry. It is seen in the coordination of small numbers of elementary units to form the first order of complex units and it is seen at the top of the hierarchy, where it constitutes the basic mechanism of motivation.

Higher circuits almost always apply potentiation and depotentiation in tandem, raising the potential of some units while lowering that of others. In cats, for example, the reflex flexion of the leg joints in response to a touch on the dorsum of the paw—a reflex that serves to lift the swinging paw over obstacles that threaten to trip the cat—is potentiated during the swing phase of the step cycle. The opposite reflex, the extension of the leg joints, which serves to unload the paw more quickly when it is in danger of being swept out from under the cat, is depotentiated during the swing phase, when it can serve no useful purpose. During the stance phase of the stepping cycle, the potentiation and depotentiation of these two opposing reflexes is reversed: The flexion reflex is depotentiated and the extension reflex is potentiated (Forssberg, Grillner, & Rossignol, 1975). The potentiating and depotentiating of these reflex pathways by the pacemaker that sets the stepping rhythm of the leg coordinates the operation of the reflexes with the operation of the stepping oscillator. This illustrates the use of selective potentiation and depotentiation to impose coordination in the operation of elementary units of behavior at the lowest level of the hierarchically structured mechanisms of coordination.

Turning now to the highest level, the motivational level of the hierarchy, we find the same principle at work in establishing the flexible coordination among acts that leads us to speak of motivation. Consider, for example, the hungry fly whose behavior and physiology have been described with such wit and care by Dethier (1976), from which the following account derives. The hunger state in the fly is governed by signals that come from stretch receptors in the foregut and abdomen and reach the fly's brain (its supraesophageal ganglion) by way of the recurrent nerve and the ventral nerve cord, respectively. The appetitive aspects of the fly's food-seeking behavior are probably also governed to some extent by blood-borne factors. The nerve signals indicative of an emptied gut and the blood factors indicative of nutritional deficit increase the potential for activity in the following neural circuits:

The reflex whereby a dissolved sugar applied to the sugar receptors on the fly's feet (tarsi) elicits extension of its proboscis (the long hose through which it sucks in food) becomes potentiated. The threshold for the elicitation of this reflex varies by seven orders of magnitude as the fly's state of food deprivation is varied! The reflex opening of the lips at the end of the proboscis in response to sugar stimuli applied to the hairs on these lips is also potentiated by deprivation. The turning on of the peristaltic pumping mechanism in response to sugar stimuli delivered to the hairs inside the lips is also potentiated. These three elementary units function together to produce injestion. No one of them produces injestion if performed in isolation. It does no good to extend the proboscis if the lips do not open and the pump does not run. It does no good to have a hair-trigger lip-opening reflex if the proboscis does not extend in response to sugar stimuli at the feet, because then the lips almost never contact the stimuli that are needed to trigger their opening. It does no good to have a hair-trigger pump if the proboscis won't extend and the lips won't open. In order for these three elementary units of behavior to combine in a way that serves the fly's purposes, they must all become potentiated—ready to operate—under the same conditions. This illustrates again the coordinative function of selective potentiation, but we have hardly begun the list of potentiating effects of the hunger stimuli in the blowfly:

When a front foot of a hungry fly contacts sugar water, the fly stops walking. The satiated fly does not stop, it wades right on through. In other words, the circuit that inhibits the locomotion circuit upon receipt of a sugar signal from the feet is potentiated in the hungry fly and depotentiated in the satiated fly. The next thing the hungry fly does is pivot around the stimulated leg, turning toward the side of sugar stimulation. This turning reaction cannot be elicited in the satiated fly.

When the fly sucks a drop of sugar water dry, it retracts the proboscis, takes one step, and extends the proboscis again (even if its feet don't happen to be in contact with the sugar water). This reaction, a reaction to the offset rather than the onset of a sugar stimulus, also becomes less and less probable as the fly becomes more and more satiated. If several steps and reextensions of the proboscis fail to contact more sugar water, a new and now very complex act occurs: The fly dances! The fly circles first to the right, then to the left, then to the right, and so on, with the radius of its turns getting gradually longer. The result is an expanding series of figure eights, a demonstrably efficient search pattern. The fly dance occurs only in the hungry fly. Removing the sugar stimulus from the feet of a satiated fly does not elicit a fly dance.

The fly locomoting hither and yon while hungry has orientational dispositions that the equally active nonhungry fly does not have. When hungry, the fly will turn into the wind in response to certain food odors and fly up wind until the odors become strong, when it will land. The fly orients toward the source of the wind by flying so that the axis of dispersion of the optic array is aligned with its body axis *and* so that the optic flow is minimal for the effort the fly is expending in propulsion. By flying so that the ground streams longitudinally beneath it rather than diagonally, as it will whenever the fly is not oriented either directly up or directly down wind, the fly gets itself aligned with the wind. By choosing the alignment that maximizes the effort expended for a given rate of longitudinal streaming, it orients up the wind rather than down. Thus, in the hungry fly, an odor releases a complex unit of behavior that has two complex subcomponents, one being the act of flying, and the other being the act of orienting by means of computations on the streaming of the optic array.

The signals from the stretch receptors in the gut and in the abdominal wall of the blowfly and the blood-borne factors do not trigger or guide a single one of the behaviors just reviewed. Each of them has some stimulus or internal condition peculiar to it, which actually throws it into action or guides its action. The signals from the gut merely vary the potential for activation in all of these units. In so doing they make the fly into the effective food-finding and injesting machine it is. The selective potentiating effect of these hunger signals on the circuitry mediating each of the just-reviewed acts is a crucial aspect of the coordinative process by which these acts are made to function together to achieve results that no one act by itself has any substantial probability of achieving.

The signals from the gut and the effects they exert upon the high-level coordinating circuits in the supraesophageal ganglion establish the behavioral disposition we call hunger. The reason we need a concept of hunger is because the different stimuli that play a role in food-seeking behavior have different kinds of behavioral effects: Some elicit an act, some guide an act, and some control the disposition to perform a spectrum of functionally coherent acts. Stimuli that function in this latter, dispositional mode are motivating stimuli, as opposed to triggering stimuli or guiding stimuli.

One cannot tell whether a particular act is motivated or not from any examination of the act itself. The property of being a motivated act is not a property that inheres in the act itself; it is a property that arises by virtue of a relation that the act bears to other acts that the organism performed or was disposed to perform on the occasion in question. The occurrence of a proboscis extension in the blowfly is motivated just in case it can be shown that the fly was disposed to perform a variety of other acts at about that same time. The variety must be a functionally coherent variety. It must be clear that the proboscis extension formed part of a spectrum of acts that were rendered probable at that same general time by a set of neural and hormonal signals acting in the dispositional mode and that these acts together could be expected to produce a result that no one of them would ordinarily produce on its own.

The account of motivation that I have just given is in essence the account offered by most ethologists and many physiological psychologists for the better part of this century. It is backed by an enormous amount of behavioral and physiological data. No one familiar with the multitudinous dispositional effects of estrogen on the acts that together comprise the sexual and maternal behavior of the female rat (see Adler, 1978, for review) could doubt that processes of the kind I have described play a fundamental role in the behavior of animals much more complex than the blowfly. One might object that these processes do not constitute motivation,but that is rather clearly a terminological quarrel. We have no other convenient term to apply to it (I am assuming that *drive* is to be understood as a more technical term for motivation). It has been called motivation by generations of workers. And, in its frankly dispositional character, it accords well with a property that philosophers have generally fastened on in trying to elucidate our conception of motivation.

Motivation, then, is the process of selective potentiation and depotentiation operating at the upper levels of the neurobehavioral hierarchy to give sustained functional coherence to the diverse acts observed in an animal within an extended frame of observation. In calling this motivation, I do not mean to say that we have now a clear notion of what is going on in the motivated behavior of higher vertebrates such as man. Rather, it is designed to lay the groundwork for a discussion of what may be going on in the motivated behavior of higher vertebrates that is not going on in the motivated behavior of the blowfly. Higher vertebrates make use of more sophisticated and extensive forms of representations than do lower organisms, and therein lie the differences between them. Insects and primates are equally motivated, but one kind of organism has a vastly more elaborated intelligence apparatus. This intelligence apparatus (representational apparatus) enriches the manner in which and the mechanisms through which the motivational (dispositional) state finds expression in behavior.

REPRESENTATIONS AND INTENTIONALITY

A representation is a mapping of some attributes of one system onto attributes of another system for the purpose of facilitating interaction between the representation-making system and the represented system. The scale of numerical weights, to take one example, is a mapping from the world of real masses (system one) to the world of numbers (system two) for the purpose of facilitating human interaction with real-world masses. It facilitates, for example, the choice of cables appropriate for suspending the mass of a bridge deck, a choice one would not want to make by trial and error. To take another example, which I make more use of later on, a terrain-recognizing guided missile has placed in the memory of its on-board computer an electromagnetic representation of the topography of selected patches of ground that should appear directly beneath it at specified times in its course toward its target. This representation is a mapping of certain aspects of the earth's surface (system one) into aspects of the electromagnetic configuration of the computer memory (system two). The representation is used in conjunction with radar readings of actual topography taken at specified times during the missile's flight to correct the missile's trajectory.

The making and use of representations by animals is common, even in insects. What distinguishes insects from primates is not the making of representations but rather what gets represented and how the representation is used. What I want to suggest is that humans represent both the consequences of their own acts and their own motivational states, whereas insects may not. Because humans have a representation of their acts and their consequences, the mechanism by which a given motivational state potentiates a given act may make use of this representation—that is, the potentiation for the act in question may reach the neural circuitry that coordinates that act only because the act and its consequences are specified in an "act-outcome" representation (Irwin, 1971). If this guess about the structure of one aspect of higher brain function should prove correct, then I suggest that we follow Irwin (1971) in calling acts potentiated by virtue of act-outcome representations intentional acts. Organisms whose acts can be potentiated by this route would form the class of organisms exhibiting intentional behavior.

Intentional behavior, in this view, is not synonymous with motivated goal directed behavior. Rather, intentional behavior is a proper subset of the set of motivated behaviors. Many examples of motivated behavior—the fly's food-seeking behavior, for example—are not examples of intentional behavior. They are motivated behaviors because they are composed of a number of distinct acts coordinated by means of selective potentiation and depotentiation to achieve results that no constituent act can achieve by itself. They are not intentional behavior, however, unless evidence can be brought forward that the acts that comprise the motivated sequence are potentiated only by virtue of a representation the animal has that those acts produce those outcomes.

The representation whose use leads us to call the resulting behavior intentional must have three distinct components: a component representing the act, a component representing a consequence, and a component representing the fact that this act has this consequence. The representation of an act is a mapping from the animal's behavior to a part of the CNS not involved in coordinating the act itself. The representation of a consequence is a mapping from situations to some part of the CNS. The representation of an act's having a consequence is a mapping to the CNS from a relation between an act and a situation.

Even motivated behavior that makes essential use of a representation is not necessarily intentional behavior. Only if the representation employed has the three components specified, and only if each of those three components is essential to the use made of the representation, can we call behavior intentional.

The maternal behavior of the female digger wasp is an example of a motivated behavior. It makes essential use of two distinct kinds of representations, a spatial representation and a representation of the state of the female's nests; yet it may well not be intentional behavior. The behavior is a good deal more complex than the food-seeking behavior of the fly. It has three interdigitated phases, each composed of many complex acts: the nest-digging phase, the egg-laying phase, and the provisioning phase. The use of the two distinct representations occurs in the provisioning phase. Digger wasps may (depending on the species) tend several different nests at once. Each nest consists of a burrow in the ground containing an egg, or wasp larvum hatched therefrom, and paralyzed caterpillars put there by the mother wasp for the larvum to feed on. Bärends (1941) studied the nest-tending behavior of one such species in detail; the nest-tending parts of the following account derive from his monograph.

Each of the nests is plugged with a small pebble when the mother is not in immediate attendance. The mother begins her day by visiting each of the nests in turn to see whether the larvum it contains has hatched and, if so, whether it requires more caterpillars. Bärends showed experimentally that the observations made during this survey visit to all the nests determine which nest will be provisioned during the rest of the day and the number of caterpillars with which it will be provisioned. He also showed that the number of caterpillars brought to the nest being served was determined entirely by the observations made during the survey visit. If the experimenter added caterpillars while the mother was away hunting for more, she persisted in trying to stuff in the number she had decided on in the initial survey visit. If the experimenter removed the caterpillars, she nonetheless brought only as many as she would have, had the experimenter left the nest alone. Following her survey visit, the wasp took no account of the effect of her acts on the state of the nest.

I do not believe that it is possible to construct a model of process by which the nest to be served is fixed on without positing a mapping from each nest to some variable within the nervous system of the wasp that indicates the provisioning requirement of that nest. Such a mapping constitutes a representation of the provisioning requirement of the nest at the start of the day. This representation controls both which nest the female serves and how many caterpillars she brings to it. This control extends for hours after the survey that establishes the representation is made. Bärends showed that the control persisted through experimentally imposed delays of up to 15 hours. The wasp's indifference to experimentally produced alterations in the state of the nest during her provisioning is evidence that her acts are not controlled by way of an act–outcome representation. The repetition of this provisioning act a suitable number of times has the outcome of bringing the nest being served up to a certain state; however, adjusting the provisions in the nest to as much or more than the level that would ordinarily be achieved (and that the larvum requires) does not terminate the provisioning behavior once the sequence of repeated provisioning acts has begun. So, it does not appear that each act is potentiated by a route that takes account of the outcome the act will have and channels potentiation to the act just in case that outcome is required. It is possible to design a system that uses the representation of the state of the nest during the survey visit to select subsequent behavior without the system's containing a representation of the animal's own acts, or of the outcome those acts will have, or of the fact that those acts have those outcomes—in short, without any of the components that are required of a representation that controls intentional behavior.

The other kind of representation, a spatial representation, is used by the wasp to find the nests, both in her survey visit and when she returns to a nest from many meters away laden with a paralyzed caterpillar. Tinbergen and Kruyt (1938) arranged a circle of pine cones around a female digging a nest. When the nest was finished, the female made a figure-eight survey flight over it, before departing on a hunt for the first caterpillar. While she was absent hunting, Tinbergen and Kruyt moved the circle of cones a meter or so to one side. When the female returned she landed in the middle of the circle and never found her nest. This establishes that the final stages of the approach to the nest are controlled by a representation of some aspect of the spatial relation between the nest and surrounding landmarks. Thorpe (1950) worked with a species that captured caterpillars too big to fly home with. These wasps fly out on their hunting expeditions (thus, cannot leave odor trails), but walk home. Thorpe captured females while they were toiling home and transported them inside an opaque box tens of meters away from the capture point to another point of the compass relative to the home nest. He found that the females nonetheless made it to the nest, usually by quite a straight route (Figure 4.2). This establishes that the females have a representation of the nest's position relative to landmarks that can be perceived from considerable distances and that nestward orientation is established by reference to this "map" (see also van Iersel, 1975).

Experiments designed to test the geometric properties captured by the wasp's map have not yet been done, although recent experiments by van Beusekom (1948), Collet and Cartwright (1983), and van Iersel (1975) are clearly relevant. Cheng and Gallistel (1983) have outlined an experimental program for deciding such questions and have applied this program to the rat. I now suggest a simple model of the kind of representation the wasp makes and how it is used to get the wasp home. The model is advanced not for its own sake but in order to make

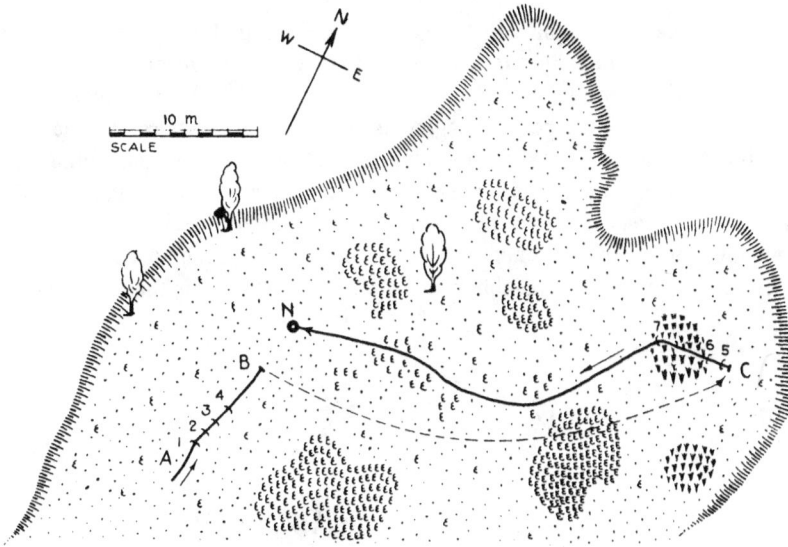

FIG. 4.2. Diagram to show the route taken during detour and displacement experiments by an individual of *A. pubescens* engaged in dragging its prey toward the nest. Heavy line = course of insect. *A* = point at which first observed. Numbers 1 to 4 = points at which metal screen placed in its path for detour test. *B* = point at which insect captured. Broken line = transfer of insect in box to release point *C*. Numbers 5 to 7 = further detour experiments. *N* = nest. Shading = a slight depression in an area of gravelly heath land with small patches and scattered plants of *Erica* and *Calluna* indicated by the symbol E and with small birch trees (*Betula*) about 4 to 6 feet high indicated by the conventional tree symbol. The remaining symbol • = tussocks of *juncus*, and so on. Conditions: Bright sunshine. Noon, 27 July, 1947. Eversley Heath. Berkshire. Time taken by insect: approximately 15 minutes. (From Thorpe, 1950, by permission of E. J. Brill, publisher, and the author.)

clear how a representation could be used in goal directed behavior without the behavior's being intentional in the just-specified sense of intentional:

Suppose what the wasp does during its survey flight is store pairs of retinal snapshots, each pair consisting of two narrow sectors of the horizon lying at opposite ends of a line through the nest. (Evidence that bees store something like a snapshot is found in Collet and Cartwright, 1983, and van Iersel, 1975.) Thus, the representation consists of a list of snapshot pairs, the nest being collinear with each pair. This representation captures only the collinearity properties. It does not represent distance, angle, parallelism, and other higher-level geometric properties related to these. When the wasp has found and paralyzed a caterpillar, the representation is used in the following way: The wasp turns until it finds itself aligned with one of the pairs. At any point away from the nest, the wasp will be able to align itself with one and only one pair on its list, the pair lying on the

unique line that passes through the nest and the wasp. I am assuming that the
wasp can correct for changes in scale, so as to recognize correspondence between
a snapshot of a horizon segment and the view of that same segment from a
different distance. If the horizon segments are distant relative to the distance the
wasp travels from its nest, then the changes in scale will be small. Finding the
unique pair with which it is presently collinear gives the wasp the line along
which it must steer; its only problem now is to determine in which direction
along this line it should steer. To determine the direction to be steered, the
system could examine a neighboring pair in the list, a pair that will make an

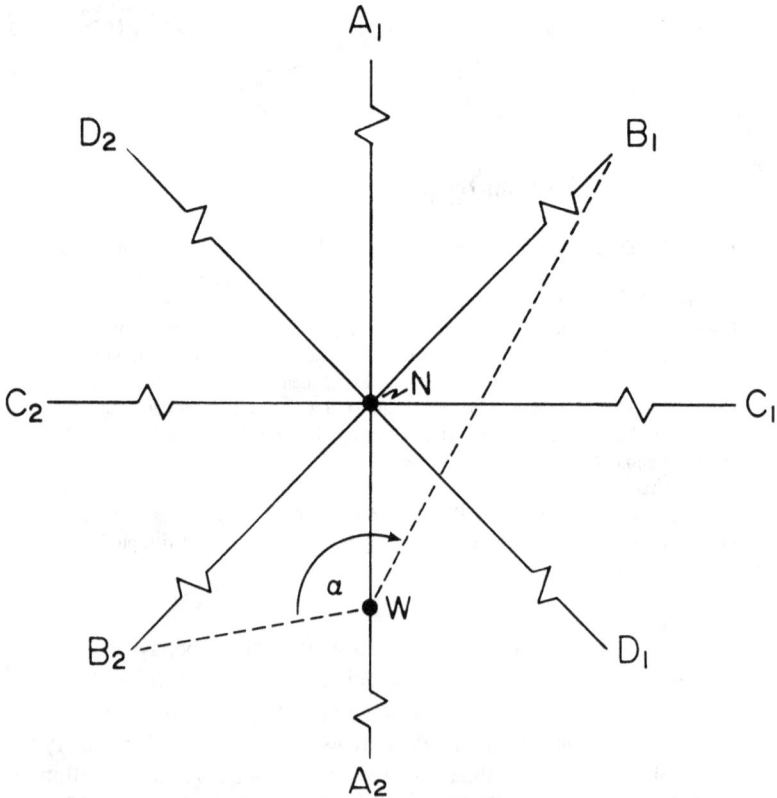

FIG. 4.3.   An illustrative model of navigation with the use of a spatial representation consisting only of a list of pairs of snapshots of horizon segments that are
collinear with the nest (goal). Each pair is designated by a letter of the alphabet,
with the members being distinguished by subscripts. N = the nest. W = the wasp.
The wasp first finds the unique pair that is collinear with the wasp's present
position. It must steer toward one or the other horizon segment in this pair. Which
segment it steers toward is determined by the angle formed by the wasp and
another pair on the list (dashed lines). The wasp steers so as to increase this angle
toward a straight angle.

obtuse visual angle with the wasp, and steer so as to increase rather than decrease this angle (see Figure 4.3).

Whether the preceding model bears any resemblance to what actually goes on in the wasp is not my concern here. The model exhibits a system that makes and uses a primitive spatial representation in order to find its way back to a nest from an arbitrary location within tens of meters distance from the nest. Yet, the model does not contain any representation of the homing act itself. The circuitry that generates the act is not a representation of the act, any more than the concrete and steel that comprise a bridge deck are representations of the mass of the deck. One must distinguish between the representation of something and the embodiment of something. Nor does the model contain a representation of the consequence of the acts—getting to the nest—nor, of course, a representation of the fact that the act will have that consequence. The terrain-recognizing missile mentioned earlier is another instance of a system that uses a representation to help determine a goal directed sequence without satisfying the definition of intentionality.

REPRESENTATIONS AND EMOTION

I now want to suggest that emotion in both its aspects—emotional behavior and experienced emotion—is a representational phenomenon, with motivation being the thing that is represented. Emotional *behavior* represents an animal's motivational state to other animals, usually of the same species. It is, as Darwin (1872) first clearly recognized, a mapping of motivational state onto otherwise pointless observable behavior. This observable representation of an animal's disposition is used by conspecifics in adjusting their own behavior to take account of the displaying animal's probable reactions; or, in some cases, the display may function to elicit a complementary motivational (dispositional) state in a conspecific (Lehrman, 1964). In any case, it enables social organisms to interact at the motivational level. It was Darwin's great insight to realize that a crucial aspect of the environment of a social organism was the reactive *disposition* of its conspecifics and that emotional behavior was the mechanism by which it was possible for one organism to perceive the disposition of another before it came to a substantive manifestation of that disposition.

Emotion in the Darwinian sense—behavior whose function is to indicate disposition to conspecifics—does not distinguish among widely different types of animals (e.g., arthropods and humans). It has been recognized in much of the animal kingdom. It is commonly found in mating behavior, because it is useful for one animal to know in advance how its sexual advances will be met. A dramatic example of this usefulness is furnished by the praying mantis. A suitable display system has apparently not evolved in this predatory insect. Consequently, the male, who is much smaller than the female, approaches her with great stealth. Nonetheless, he often gets captured and eaten. Fortunately for the continuation of the species, the female eats the male's head first. The rest of the male mantis can and often must complete the act of copulation without the aid of the head (Roeder, 1967). Other animals prefer not to place so much reliance on the female's consummatory preferences among male body parts nor upon the resourcefulness of the headless male. They establish one another's disposition by suitable displays before getting within the range where one animal can damage the other.

The ubiquity of display behaviors that communicate something about disposition is documented in any modern text on ethology. The study of these displays forms an important part of the discipline (see, e.g., Smith, 1977). Emotion in this overt sense, far from being the uniquely human characteristic that a layperson may imagine it to be, is found in the fiddler crab, which signals its readiness to defend its mating area to its conspecifics by waving its large claw in a stereotyped way (Salmon, 1967). It is possible, however, that the belief in emotion as a characteristic of the human, or at least higher, animal has some foundation. Humans not only snarl, they know that they are angry—that is, they have a representation of their own motivational states.

It is important to distinguish again between a representation and an embodiment. All animals have embodiments of their motivational states when they have neural and endocrine activities that carry out the function of selectively potentiating functionally coherent sets of acts. But there need not exist a mapping from the dispositional state embodied by a particular pattern of neural and endocrine activity to variables in another part of the nervous system, variables that do not themselves exert potentiating and depotentiating effects. If such a mapping can be demonstrated, and if the mapping serves to facilitate an interaction between another system within the animal and the motivational system that is mapped, then an animal may be said to *have* a representation of its motivational state. Animals that indicate their motivational states to conspecifics by means of suitably stereotyped behavior but do not have any internal CNS mapping of the states may be said to *display* emotions but not to *have* them. In this sense, then, having emotions may be a characteristic peculiar to higher social animals.

WHAT FUNCTION DO ACT–OUTCOME AND MOTIVATIONAL REPRESENTATIONS SERVE AND WHAT IS THE BEHAVIORAL EVIDENCE OF THEIR EXISTENCE?

The suggestions made earlier about the central role of representations in the phenomena of intentionality and experienced emotion are put forward with great tentativeness, because I can offer no clear answer to the two questions posed in the heading. I have been at some pains to show that a representation may be used in the course of goal directed, motivated behavior without the behavior's being intentional. One may well ask, then, what the particular advantages of act–outcome representations are and where in the behavior of higher animals do we find clear evidence for the existence of that sort of representation? The first question is very hard. It does not seem likely that we will be in a position to answer it until we understand better what kinds of representations different kinds of animals have and how they make use of them. Because animal learning is only now beginning to be thought about in representational terms and because explicit theories of these representations are few and poorly developed, we are not in a position to judge the limits of what is possible with representations that do not capture acts and their outcomes. A great deal of experimental and theoretical work must be done on the use of representations in the control of behavior before we can judge the peculiar virtues of act–outcome representations.

The second question—What behavioral evidence is there that such representations exist?—is in one way trivial. Human testimony to the effect that doing such-and-such will have such-and-such result would seem to be as good evidence for the existence of such representations in humans as one could wish. The legal system is predicated on the assumption that humans have such representations and that they play an important role in human behavior. If we stipulate, however, that only nonverbal behavior is relevant to the answer sought, then the question becomes very difficult, for the same reason the first question is: To answer it, we would have to have a clear theory about the behavioral limitations imposed by the lack of act–outcome representations. We would have to be in a position to say that such-and-such a behavior is possible only through the mediation of an act–outcome representation. Our notions of the distinct kinds of representations that animals may have are at present in an exceedingly rudimentary state, as are necessarily our notions about what the limitations are on what can be accomplished through the use of a given kind of representation. Thus, we are not in a position to specify the kind of behavior that is diagnostic of an act–outcome representation.

Very similar observations apply in the case of the suggestion that the peculiarity of emotion in higher animals is that the motivational states are themselves represented. As evidence that this is so in humans, we have everyday testimony to the effect that one is or was angry, etc. If one asks, however, what behavioral capacity is conferred by such representations, then the answer is far from clear. It may have something to do with the fact that many motivational states, particularly social ones, are aroused by external situations. It may happen that one of the acts potentiated by a given motivational state routinely brings about a situation that arouses a more powerful motivational state, a state that takes control of the direction of behavior away from the original state. In this case, the capacity to have an act–outcome representation and to have the animal's own motivational state fall within the domain of representable outcomes may make it possible to plan courses of action that prevent one motivational state's from "tripping over" another.

I resist the temptation to speculate further along these lines, because, as I indicated earlier, I think it is too early in the development of our understanding to address these very deep questions fruitfully.

SUMMARY

The cognitive-neuroethological conception of the structure of the system underlying behavior makes it possible to suggest the nature of intrinsic qualitative differences in the neurobehavioral systems found in widely divergent kinds of animals such as arthropods, mollusks, and humans. It is difficult to elaborate such suggestions within the confines of the sensorimotor-associationist conception, because this conception offers only a single structural concept, the concept of a sensorimotor connection—that is, a reflex. This restriction leaves room only for quantitative differences among different phyla, because reflexes and some capacity to learn are present in them all. The parsimony of the sensorimotor approach—often cited as its most attractive feature—is something of an embarrassment when it comes to saying what differentiates the neurobehavioral system of the sea slug *Aplysia* from the neurobehavioral system of humans. Is it simply that humans have a larger store of reflexes and a greater capacity to form new ones? In the cognitive-neuroethological conception, the system underlying behavior is given a far richer structure, with many different kinds of components that interact in accord with a variety of quite different principles.

The conception here championed recognizes at least three distinct kinds of elementary units of behavior—reflexes, oscillators, and servomechanisms—each with its own peculiar principles of interaction.

The notion that the mechanism underlying the generation of coordinated patterns of action has a hierarchical structure is also central to this view, whereas the hierarchical structure of the system generally receives only lip service within the sensorimotor view. The hierarchical view is that there are elements and whole subdivisions of the nervous system devoted to imposing particular patterns of coordination on thelower-level units of the system. The behavioral expression of these higher-level units is seen only in the pattern of coordination that they impose: The higher levels have little direct control over the muscles themselves.

The principle of selective potentiation and depotentiation, which plays a central role in the neuroethological conception of motivation, is a principle of interaction between levels of the hierarchy. It is one of the means by which higher-level units impose a pattern of coordination on the operation of lower units. Selective potentiation and depotentiation operating at the upper levels of the neurobehavioral hierarchy give behavior the sustained functional cohesiveness that leads us to speak of motivated behavior. An act is motivated just in case it forms a part of a functional cohesive sequence of diverse acts—for example, the sequence seen in the hungry fly.

The structural components summarized so far are found in all the animals that have a central nervous system. They all exhibit the three different kinds of elementary units of behavior. They all make use of a hierarchical structure to coordinate the elementary units into complex units, that increase in complexity as one goes up the levels of the hierarchy. In all the animals, selective potentiation and depotentiation is a fundamental principle of between-level coordination. Because motivation is defined here as the use of selective potentiation and depotentiation at or near the top of the motor hierarchy, all animals exhibit motivated behavior. What sets the phyla apart, it is suggested here, are the *kinds* of representations they form and use in the course of that motivated behavior. The capacity to form and use representations does not itself distinguish between animals as diverse as vertebrates and arthropods. This lack of differentiation is evident from experiments that show that the behavior of the digger wasp depends on representations the wasp makes of the spatial relation between its burrow and the surroundings and also on a representation it makes of the provisioning state of its burrows. The difference must lie in what about the world and its inhabitants a given animal is capable of representing.

I suggest that what may distinguish the representations made and used by vertebrates (or at least some mammals) from the representations made and used by other kinds of animals are self-referential kinds of representations. More specifically, I consider two kinds of self-referential representations: (1) representations of the relation between the animals' own acts and their outcomes; and (2) representations of the animals' own motivational states. I follow Irwin (1971) in calling the first kind of representation act–outcome representations, and, like Irwin, I suggest that this kind of representation is a sine qua non of intentional behavior. An act is intentional just in case it was determined internally by way of processes that made use of a representation of the act and its outcome. Under this definition of intentionality, an animal that lacks an act–outcome kind of representation would not be capable of intentional behavior. The second kind of representation is a representation of the animal's own motivational state, which I call experienced emotion, to distinguish it from expressed emotion. The function of expressed emotion, as Darwin pointed out, is to enable conspecifics to take each other's motivational conditions into account in the determination of their own behavior. The function of experienced emotion may be to enable an animal to anticipate its own motivational state under the circumstances brought about by its own actions. Expressed emotion is very widespread. The capacity to know (represent) one's own motivational state may be much less widespread in the animal kingdom.

ACKNOWLEDGMENTS

The suggestions about emotion and intention made in this chapter derive in some measure from years of collegial interaction with Alan Epstein and Frank Irwin, although, of course, I must ultimately be held responsible for them. The interaction has been most enjoyable and rewarding and is here gratefully acknowledged.

5 Anticipation as a Basic Principle in Goal Directed Action

Michael Stadler
Theo Wehner
University of Bremen

INTRODUCTION: REPRESENTATION AND ANTICIPATION

In 1980 Gallistel published a book entitled *The Organization of Action: A New Synthesis,* which has aroused considerable attention. In this book Gallistel presented three elementary behavior units: *reflex, oscillator,* and *servomechanism.* Behavior, in the organizational form of a complex lattice hierarchy, is composed of these three elementary units. At the top of this hierarchy are cognitive representations of the external world, which regulate actions of primitive animals as well as those of primates and humans. Gallistel substantiates his theoretical synopsis with classical works of Sherrington, von Holst, Wilson, Fraenkel, and Mittelstaedt, and Paul Weiss, which are printed in the original—some in translation—in his book. Gallistel deserves our special thanks for this, as modern jet-set scientists very rarely look back further than 10 years in their bibliographies. In 1981 Gallistel wrote a précis of his theory for open discussion in the journal *Behavioral and Brain Sciences* and discussed the 24 peer reviews.

Now, in this book, Gallistel follows one specific branch of his theoretical synthesis. After briefly discussing the elementary units of behavior, he deals with ethological evidence for motivational, intentional, and emotional processes. We believe that Gallistel's theory of goal directed action has some theoretical and empirical gaps that, in view of psychophysiological findings, can at least be formulated, if not completely explicated. In the following, we therefore devote our attention not only to Gallistel's contribution in this volume, but also to his theory as it is expressed in all three publications just mentioned.

The three elementary units postulated by Gallistel have the advantages of being fairly exactly physiologically definable, not subdivisible, and verifiable—

67

that is, there are methodical rules that lead to the discovery of these units. Each of the three elementary mechanisms in Gallistel's theory represents a unit of an impulse-originating, a signal-conducting, and an energy-converting (contracting) function. Thus, the essential stages of an action are indicated. Only the *goal* directedness of this action is missing. Even a meticulous study of Gallistel's work does not convince the reader that by means of a lattice hierarchy a representation could be constructed out of these elements, a representation that would, in fact, lead to the actual reason for the action—that is, the goal. Since Lewin (1926a), we have known that the distinguishing feature between *action* and *behavior* is that actions are undertaken to obtain goals and that actions are motivated and controlled by their goals. In his theory, Gallistel draws an analogy between the construction of actions from the three elementary units of behavior and the chemical construction of atoms into elements that, in a hierarchical arrangement, produce amino acids, for instance. These amino acids, in turn, produce proteins, and so on. "Elementaristic" thinking has certainly found its most successful object in chemistry. Whether it is just as successful for the construction of a theory of action remains to be proved.

In spite of Gallistel's introduction of intentional action to his theory in the preceding chapter, it seems to us that an important basic prerequisite for intentional and goal directed action—that is, anticipation—is still missing in Gallistel's formulation. His theory does contain a process similar to anticipation— namely, a circular transmission unit, a servomechanism that through negative feedback (as is the case for von Holst's principle of reafference) can balance the movements (*Eigenbewegung*) of the organism and thus present to its actions an invariant external world. Successful goal directed action cannot, however, be explained without a basic *feed-forward* mechanism that makes adaptation to changes in a dynamic external world possible.

Several other commentators (cf. Bolles, 1981; Hollerbach, 1981; Lewis, 1981) have also noted this gap. Although Gallistel admitted the importance of this basic principle, he maintained that no adequate analyses in connection with this subject were known to him.

Nevertheless, we should ask not "what is *possible* with the known fundamental mechanisms" but "what is *necessary* in order to explain goal directed action?"

Today we know that mechanisms of anticipation are by no means specific to goal directed action but are already manifest in primitive organisms as a means of adaptation to their environment. Psychology, in its first consolidated paradigm, set about explaining behavior as the *consequence of a preceding stimulus situation*—that is, as something resulting from the *past*. It thus conflicted with the then prevailing teleologic views, which assumed a goal directedness in biological development and the organization of behavior without being able to explain this goal directedness with other than idealistic constructs. The paradigm of *reaction* was most successful for theories of learning. In 1943, however, Kurt Lewin had already set his concept of "definition of the field at a given time" against the determination of human behavior by the past. According to his scheme, behavior is determined by the *immediate present situation as a whole,* a sectional plane between past and future. The theory of goal directed action goes one step further: Although explaining behavior from the *future* it does not consider the future as an underdetermined agent in the teleological sense but in a concrete sense, as anticipated goals that have their origin in the past via experience. Anticipation is therefore not possible by "clairvoyance"; rather, it requires memory processes by which dynamic processes can be extrapolated from the past into the future. It should be quite possible to operationalize and model the representations psychophysiologically, based on memory processes of the aspects of the external world that are relevant to action (in the sense of a cognitive map). In these representations, goals are integrated in space and time. In the following discussion, we try, therefore, to complement Gallistel's theory with some reflections on physiological models and empirical evidence for the concepts of *representation* and *anticipation.* In doing so we first go back to the work of the Soviet psychophysiologist Anokhin (summarized in 1967, 1969, 1978). Anokhin worked primarily on the *search for the special forms of space–time structures of reality* in different organizational levels of matter and, above all, in living organisms. In the process of adaptation between the time–space relations of animate and inanimate nature, the most important parameter for him is that of "advance *reflection*" or, in psychological terms, *anticipation.*

Anokhin showed that even the very first living beings, which were separated from the external world by simple membranes only, displayed anticipation in the high speed of their chemical processes: Reactions in the protoplasma occurred even before movement across the membrane.

Anokhin elaborated the *functional system* as the basic model of behavior organization containing representations of the environment and anticipations: This model implies that the result of action already existed in this system.

A MODEL FOR REPRESENTATION: THE FUNCTIONAL SYSTEM

The servomechanism is the most differentiated unit in Gallistel's triad: He describes von Holst's principle of reafference as its most elaborate form. The latter implies that for each voluntary movement an efference copy is stored that is negatively switched to the reafferences in order to annul the self-generated movement of the organism and create an invariant environment. Although Gallistel (1981) describes efference copies as "instances of expectations which are neurophysiologically explainable" and as "centrally generated signals which *anticipate* sensory signals" [p. 614], the principle of reafference remains a simple negative feedback mechanism because no hypotheses about *future conditions of environment* are anticipated. Instead, information about *future effector activity* alone is stored (efference copies), information that is precisely known to the organism because it itself just generated it.

The principle of reafference as a basic mechanism may help to explain environmental invariance in perception, but it is not a fundamental unit for explaining the anticipative characteristic of action. Because goal directedness is a criterion for distinguishing between action and behavior, we would like to understand the physiological mechanism that reflects future conditions of the environment (goals) as well as the effector activity that is needed to attain the goal. Because we do not know the precise physiological mechanism yet, we can only develop some metaphysiological concepts, concepts related to the concept of reafference.

Eighteen years prior to the discovery of the principle of reafference by von Holst and Mittelstaedt (1950), Anokhin (1967/1932) modelled the principle of reafference with the feed-forward component postulated previously, and he has since further elaborated on it in many investigations. This fundamental mechanism was called the *functional system* and is characterized by *afferent synthesis* and the *acceptor of effect*. Figure 5.1, which follows Gallistel's representation (p. 71, this volume), may explain the functioning of such a system in its simplest form. A_1 and A_2 are two states of the environment at times t_1 and t_2. These environmental states are perceived through *sensors*, which produce sensory signals transmitted to the central nervous system, where, initially, an *afferent synthesis* takes place. Guided by one dominant motive, all relevant sensory signals—both proprioceptive and exteroceptive—are united, compared, and integrated there. At this point, moreover, memory (i.e., the cumulated experience of the organism) flows in. Afferent synthesis forms a dynamic image of the organism and its environment; motivated by the needs prevailing at that time, it extrapolates a state A_3 of the environment at a future time t_3 from the stimuli received immediately before and from prior experiences in similar situations. Anokhin calls this process the formation of an *advance image*. Such an anticipation of a future state is prerequisite for the *conscious decision to act,* which is experienced as an *intention* to act. When this decision has been made, in Anokhin's model, a *program of action* is produced on the basis of afferent synthesis, which simultaneously results in an *acceptor of effect*. The program of action regulates the motor signals, which activate the *effectors,* and the acceptor of effect produces a matrix of expected *effectory effects* and *external results* of action—that is, the changes of the environment effected through the activity of the organism.[1] In the acceptor of action, effector reafferences (effect control signals) as well as exteroceptive information (result control signals) about the results of action are received and checked for their congruence with the predic-

---

[1]Statements of athletes often contain a subjective correlate of the acceptor of effect. The American high jumper Richard Fosbury reports, for instance, that at the moment of take-off he already knows whether he will get across the bar or not.

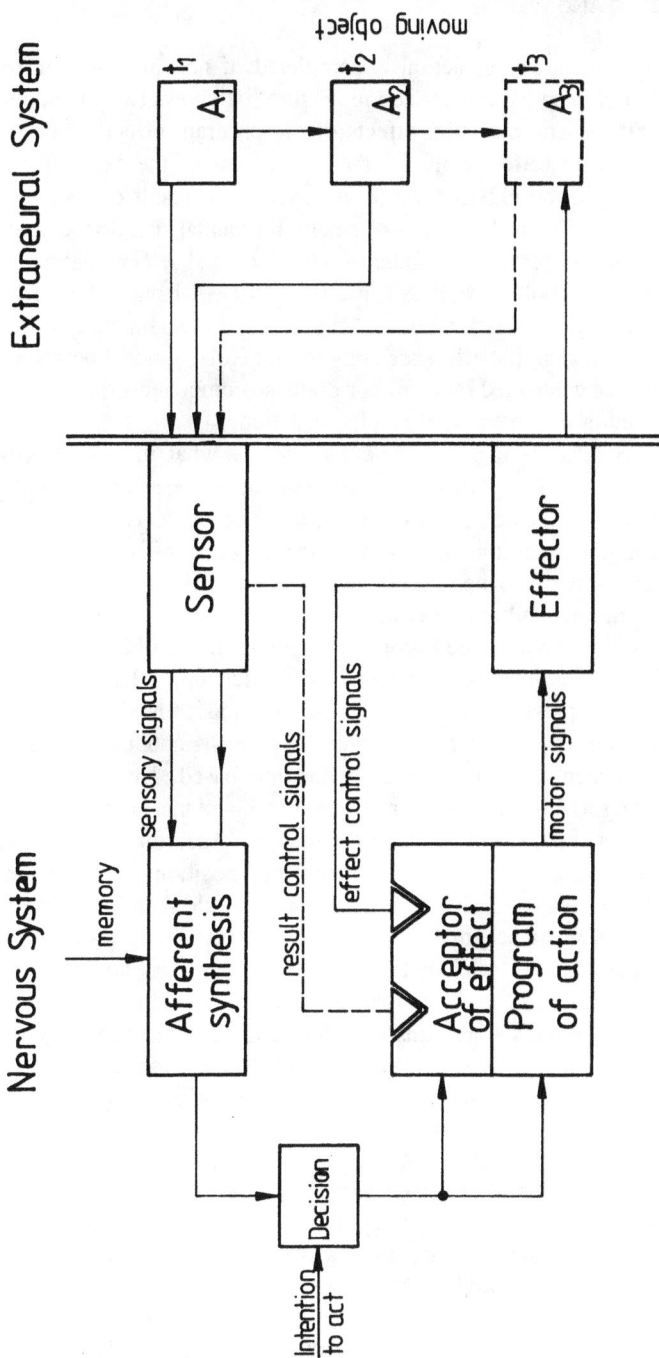

FIG. 5.1. Schema of a functional system; see text.

tion. If there is congruence, action is completed; if not, an *orienting reaction* results and is followed by another action. Figure 5.1 shows two functions of the acceptor of effect: The muscular effects of the program of action are checked within the organism (effect control), and, by means of the exteroceptors, the results of action in the external world are examined (result control = broken line). In our case, this result consists of an environmental situation A_3 at the time t_3. The functional system is the model of a fundamental self-regulating process. Anokhin and his school, as well as Luria (e.g., 1973), have begun to work on proving this through experimentation. Afferent synthesis and acceptor of effect achieve more than a simple efference copy in von Holst's model because neither are the efferences controlled by them nor do these components make possible an afferent prediction of the external results of action.

Afferent synthesis is a physiological model of what in modern cognitive psychology is called a *cognitive map, schema,* or *representation* (cf. Neisser, 1976). Furthermore, the acceptor of effect is a *physiological model of the goal* of action because it includes the anticipated external results of action as well as the anticipated motor performance that is necessary to attain it.

Afferent synthesis and the program of action/acceptor of effect constitute an afferent/efferent unit that in the European cognitive theory of action is called the "system of operative images" (Hacker, 1980; Oschanin, 1966).

What kind of representation may be expected in afferent synthesis? Gallistel (1980b, 1981) advanced a very interesting hypothesis about the physiological processes on which the schemata of action are based. He postulates that a suitably chosen set of oscillations constitutes a complex that contains all essential characteristics of the movement to be carried out. According to Fourier's theorem, any movement can be analyzed as the superposition of simple sinusoidal waves. Sinusoidal waves of different frequencies would therefore constitute the "alphabet of movement schemata." We think that this hypothesis is most attractive for two reasons: The "alphabet of movement schemata" not only allows for a frequency synthesis of simple sinusoidal waves combined into complex movements, but it also suggests that sensory information and memory information is represented cerebrally as a set of sinusoidal waves. Pribram (1971) pointed in this direction with his holography theory of memory. According to such a scheme, complex experiences are analyzed into their basic frequencies of sinusoidal waves, stored relatively economically (e.g., as power spectra), and, at a given moment, are revived as a cognitive image by means of a search or *resonance* oscillator. In the field of perception, too, there have been findings that show that the visual system, for instance, analyzes spatial frequencies (Maffei & Fiorentini, 1973). More recently, frequency-specific analysis of the visual system has been found for temporal processes (Kruse, Stadler, Vogt, & Wehner, 1982). If the complexity of the sensory input of an organism is actually represented in the cortex in frequency-analyzed form and, if necessary, stored in memory in this form, and if the actions of an organism are built up by frequency synthesis, such a cortical alphabet may help us to understand the transition from afferent to efferent processes more fully. Another feature leads us to accept the representation of cerebral processes as frequency analyses and frequency syntheses: The process of afferent synthesis is, as shown earlier, too complex to be described adequately as a sum of individual nervous excitations. If, however, integrative cortical activity exists in the form of superimposed sinusoidal waves, it is possible that cortical and subcortical areas, far apart from one another, simultaneously come together through a *resonance*-resembling process.

On the basis of recent neurophysiological results on the oscillatory activity of the brain, the hypothesis of frequency processing allows for a holistic modelling of psychophysical processes as called for by Köhler, Lashley, and Pribram (cf. Stadler, 1981).

LEVELS OF ANTICIPATION

In the following discussion, we try to indicate and characterize various levels of anticipation in different stages of behavior regulation. For purposes of analysis, behavior and information processing may be divided into cognitive functions and regulative processes.

In 1980, Lomov summarized the results of Soviet research in the field of anticipation and distinguished among five levels of anticipation: (1) subsensor level; (2) sensorimotor level; (3) perceptive level; (4) level of secondary images (representation, imagination); and (5) level of abstract thinking. Anticipations at levels 1 to 3 have more of a *regulative function,* whereas those at levels 4 and 5 constitute *cognitive representations.* Although, for the time being, only regulative levels can be analyzed psychophysiologically, here we briefly characterize all of the levels because the range and viability of the concept of anticipation must not be ignored.

Cognitive Levels of Representation

The level of abstract thinking (5) and the formation and storage of images cannot be adequately described without a concept of anticipation. Information and the rules for the production of new knowledge are stored on these levels of representation. The cumulated experience of the species is integrated into the stock of knowledge. Its rules of production permit the "prolongation" and advance of present knowledge.

Anticipation characteristics of abstract thinking are most convincingly seen in the formation of a model based on pure thinking. A classic example of such anticipations in abstract thinking is Wertheimer's analysis of "Einstein: The Thinking that Led to the Theory of Relativity" (1945).

The entire value of such models lies in the future. The model abstracts from momentary reality. The rules for the formation of such models neither refer to past experiences nor are based on concrete ideas.

Level 4 is characterized by processes of anticipation in the form of fantasy and operations within schemata. Fantasy is also based on anticipations of the external world. It refers to images, changes them, and anticipates future experiences in a world not yet actually existing. Fantasy abstracts from momentary needs and anticipates future forms of satisfaction of these needs. It virtually requires realism behind the illusion. If we describe thinking as trial acting (*Probehandeln*), we can classify imagination (e.g., fantasy) as trial thinking (*Probedenken*). *Imagination* is based on reality, on experiences, and on images of potential alterations of this reality. Because of these mental changes, fantasy activity and imaginative processes are no longer the original concrete experiences; they abstract from existing acceptors of effect and plans. When one develops concrete plans without the opportunity to obtain perceptive information on the goal object, anticipatory phenomena in the sense of *operating with schemata* occur. Afferent synthesis is carried out without momentary sensory input by transforming concrete space–time schemata into images. For instance, when a person is planning to visit a friend on the way home, his or her existing cognitive map is projected in imagination and this representation schema is extended in the direction of the anticipated goal.

Quantification is most difficult in the case of anticipation on levels 4 and 5. Methods of introspection and of thinking aloud or stimulated recall as well as biographical methods (life-event/life span analysis) are adequate for obtaining "soft" data. In the case of levels 4 and 5 anticipation cannot be described with physiological data or terms but only with psychological ones. The abilities involved in solving problems, restructuring, and generalizing, for instance, show anticipation characteristics of these levels. Applied to Figure 5.1, levels of anticipation of cognitive representations constitute phenomenal correlates of the afferent synthesis and the acceptor of effect. If, however, cognitive anticipations are not analyzed in connection with actions to be solved—with a fixed point of reference to the tasks that are to be solved—the danger exists, according to Lomov, that they will be interpreted as "shadows of perception" or as "weakened sensations."

Regulative Functions

The three regulative levels of anticipation—perceptive, sensorimotor, and subsensory levels—characterize the achievement of organized courses of action. According to Lomov (1980), "These are in fact the different levels of receiving and processing manifestations of the mind's cognitive and regulative functions" [p. 155]. If they indeed are, then anticipation plays the part of *regulative* knowledge and serves as the link between the task—the anticipated goal—the accompanying images, and the execution of the action according to the plan.

Anticipation characteristics on the regulative levels can be psychophysiologically measured. It is useful to carry out operationalization via time in the purely physical sense. The duration of anticipation appears as an inverse quantity of reaction time (e.g., central or peripheral precession of electrophysiological activity before the onset of the accompanying performance of movement). The quantity measured depends on the methods chosen and the place of measurement. Eye movements and EMG activity, evoked potentials, cerebral blood-flow values, and other variables can be quantified; however, it is important to choose a parameter that directly reproduces the object transformation, as does, for instance, the myogram. The following measurable effects can be expected:

1. When measuring actions at definite time points, peripheral temporal lead time should be greater than, or least equal to, reaction time.
2. The anticipation amounts should be greater than the almost constant premotor time (8 $+/-$ 2 msec), which is a system constant necessary for prompt energy supply (Botwinick & Thompson, 1966; Inman, Ralston, de Saunders, Feinstein, & Wright, 1952).
3. The variation of anticipation during analog-processual measurement should reflect the complexity of the motor task and, hence, its structure. Constant anticipation values therefore are not expected.

Predictions (1) and (2) have been tested by various researchers in tracking behavior and reaction tasks. Methods of time-series analysis should offer a suitable procedure for examining assumption (3).

In the description of the anticipation processes on the regulative levels, we begin with the *subsensor level* (1). This level concerns unconscious processes on the neuromuscular level as, for example, the previously mentioned premotor time as well as central preprogramming of movements. Assumptions (1) and (2) may be supported by results reported in a study by Eccles (1982). In this study, a morphological correlate, the *Supplementary Motor Area* (SMA) of both hemispheres, is proposed as the place of localization for the regulation of voluntary movements.

Eccles' study provides three lines of experimental evidence using different physiological methods:

1. The earliest discharge of neurons in the Supplementary Motor Area can be registered on average at 450 msec before the onset of movement (Brinkman & Porter, 1979). The wide range of the measured values between 170 msec and 650 msec may be an indication of the variability of the anticipation process as postulated in assumption (3).
2. A large number of SMA neurons were activated about 200 msec before the pyradmidal tract discharge.
3. The readiness potential can be measured up to 800 msec before movement execution (Deeke & Kornhuber, 1978).

Furthermore, Eccles reports increased activity (cerebral blood flow) in the Supplementary Motor Area during the imaging of a movement (i.e., when movement is thought of, but not executed). Eccles' findings meet the necessity of showing exact temporal anticipation effects on a central nervous level. Anticipations should be measured in more complex performances of action at the borderline between the nervous system and the extraneural system (see Figure 5.1).

A man–machine system (tracking behavior) serves the purpose of examining anticipation effects on *sensorimotor* (2) and *perceptive* (3) *levels* best. Poulton (1952), Adams (1961), and Schmidt (1968) reported experimental findings that support assumptions (1) and (2). Next, we report on a series of experiments for measuring anticipation effects in which assumption (3) was also supported.

In the time-serial procedure of our research (Stadler & Wehner, 1982; Wehner, Stadler, Kruse, & Dahlke, 1982), anticipation is defined as a quantity that results from the comparison of two continuous and on-line registered data sets (time series) that are measured on the same time axis. In the man–machine system of such a computer-controlled pursuit-tracking experiment, *perceptive anticipation* is measured during the transmission of information from the machine to the sense organs of the subject. This measurement on the input side is made by temporal comparison of the motion of the target with the peripheral activity of the visual system (horizontal eye movements). The transmission of information from human to machine (output side) is the basis for measuring *operative anticipation* in sensorimotor learning. This measurement is made from temporal comparison of the motor activity of the working muscle with the bebavior at a lever. It is evident that perceptive anticipations at the input side of the human system must be greater than the operative anticipation at its output side because system-inherent processing times must be accounted for. In terms of Figure 5.1, this means that perceptive anticipation is measured by temporal comparison between sensor and extraneural system and operative anticipation by temporal comparison between effector and extraneural system.

The hypotheses derived concerning reactions to cognitively anticipated stimuli were also supported. Both on the perceptive and on the operative sides, anticipation times between 0.3 sec and 1.0 sec were demonstrated, the perceptive anticipation values (between 0.7 sec and 1.0 sec) were always greater than the operative anticipation values (between 0.3 sec and 0.5 sec).

It was also shown that in a sensorimotor learning process the relationship between anticipation times and tracking achievement is contraposed. When a second task is added to the tracking task, perceptive anticipation values grow until the additional task is mastered and integrated. The comparison of untrained and trained Ss showed, moreover, that the operative anticipation values decrease with more training. This relationship indicates a shift of anticipation from lower to higber levels of regulation during sensorimotor training.

We have assumed that anticipations should not be a constant value (for instance, an inverse function of reaction time), but should reflect the external conditions under which the organism acts. Only the variability of anticipation guarantees an adaptational advantage for the organism. When we succeed in detecting, for example, task-specific periodicities (presented by a complex tracking curve) in intraorganismic variables (electromyographic activity) and, moreover, show the existence of a time lag between the two processes, a time lag that varies over time, we may assume that the amount of anticipation is a task-specific quantity. As we carried out an analog-synchronous registration of the parameters and variables in our experiments, we were also able to examine this assumption. Stadler, Wehner, and Hübner (1980) have shown, by calculating gliding cross-correlations, that the time lags, as representatives of anticipation, are not constant but reflect the complexity and difficulty of the tracking course.

CONCLUSIONS

The measurement of anticipation in the sensorimotor process seems to us important not only for theoretical reasons but also because the understanding of such a function may help us better understand movement disorders (such as spastic paralysis) or sensorimotor phenomena (such as rapid error correction). For the latter aspect, see Rabbitt (1966) and Schmidt and Gordon (1977).

In summary, we have argued that;

1. Anticipation and representation are prerequisites for goal directed action.
2. There exists empirical evidence that organisms have, in fact, developed anticipative functions measurable on the behavioral and the physiological levels.
3. The functional system represents a physiological model for representational and anticipational functions.
4. The physiological mechanisms on which such a model may be based have not yet been found and should be the focus of further research.

GOAL DIRECTED BEHAVIOR AND
PERCEPTION

J. J. Gibson's ecological approach to perception roots perception in action; it argues that what we perceive from an environment depends on the actions that environment will support. Von Hofsten reviews recent work in perception developed from this view.

In particular, von Hofsten suggests that for any organism to take advantage of the opportunities the environment offers it will have to engage in action, and its perceptual systems will have to be so constructed as to guide those actions. Thus, our perceptual systems will have to be "tuned," for example, to give us the information we need to carry off the complex task of maintaining balance while locomoting. The timing of our acts in relation to events in the environment is also a basic requirement of much that we do, so we would expect, and the evidence suggests we have, a particular acuity with regard to detecting and producing closely timed acts. Von Hofsten's own work, also reviewed here, has focused on the development of another basic talent we have: exploring the world.

Neisser considers some implications of the Gibson view as developed by von Hofsten. In his earlier work, Neisser proposed that perception is guided by anticipations—that is, what we look for in, for example, a visual display is determined, in part, by what we expect to find there. These anticipations are central in the sense that we can expect to find certain kinds of visual features because of information in the form of sound—hearing a bell ring may lead us to look for a specific visual form. Thus, Neisser has argued that perception is guided by amodal "central representations." In the current chapter Neisser goes on to suggest that these same central representations are also involved in action. Thus, in a sense, the representations we form through perception are representations of action.

To support this view, Neisser discusses some recent research on the effects of "mentally practicing" motor skills, like dart throwing. Subjects profit from imagining themselves performing these motor tasks, suggesting that by "focusing on a mental image" subjects can integrate their motor and perceptual apparatus. This recent work forms a substantial bridge between the psychology of motor movement and the psychology of perception.

6 Perception and Action

Claes von Hofsten
Uppsala University, Sweden

INTRODUCTION

Perception and action are closely interwoven in everyday life. It is indeed difficult to speak of one of these two aspects of biological functioning without referring to the other. Not only are all actions founded on and guided by perception, but perceiving is also in itself an act—an exploratory act. For instance, seeing implies scanning of the optic array by means of eye movements, head movements, and maybe even gross body movements. Exploratory actions are often combined with performatory actions, most obviously in the handling of objects by the manual system. Banging, rubbing, squeezing, and throwing are important means that even infants use in an efficient way for obtaining information about objects.

In the present chapter I deal with the different aspects of perception and action from a functional perspective. I ask in what respects action can be served by perception and what kind of information is needed to guide action. I argue that in this perspective perception and action are inseparable and should be studied in reference to one another.

One of the most remarkable properties of perception is its immediacy. The occurrence of events in the world and our perception of them are almost simultaneous. The powerful machine required for such high performance could only have been evolved in the service of action. If the purpose of perception were just to contemplate the world, immediacy would not be a critical property of perception.

Despite the clear connection between perception and action, perception has traditionally been considered in total isolation from actions, performatory as well as exploratory (von Helmholtz, 1925). Perceiving has not even been considered to be dealing with events (i.e., change over time), but only with static images. So many times a second the impressions of physical energy on the receptor surfaces are said to be read off by the mind, which infers from each of them the status of the outer world at that moment. By comparing several consecutive sense readings, the mind is then thought to be able to infer the goings-on in the world. Perception is not conceived of as devoid of activity, but the activity is thought to be going on in the head only. These ideas still exert considerable influence on theorizing in perception (c.f. Hochberg & Brooks, 1978; Rock, 1977).

The traditional approach not only took perception out of its proper biological context, but perception psychologists could also make the amazing assertion that the senses were not to be trusted. They showed convincingly that the static images with which the senses supplied the mind were ambiguous. Numerous experiments with simple static patterns and drawings confirmed what mathematics had already proven. These pictures were sometimes difficult to perceive, and perception of them was sometimes ambiguous and distorted. The paradox was that in much more complex everyday life situations, ambiguities and distortions almost never occurred. As the senses were apparently failing to give us information about the world, it seemed that the mind had to supply us with that knowledge. Where the mind got the knowledge from in the first place was unclear, but it did not concern perception psychologists very much, as the answer seemed to lie outside their discipline.

There are a few notable exceptions to this rule. First, the interrelatedness between perception and action has always been a central theme in Soviet psychology (Wertsch, 1981); however, this tradition has had little influence outside the USSR. Second, in system-theory approaches, as in the discussion of the reafference principle, perception and action have been considered to be different aspects of a single process (Held & Hein, 1958; von Holst, 1954). These theories, however, were considered as primarily dealing with motor control, and their implications for a general theory of perception were more or less obscure.

GIBSON'S ECOLOGICAL APPROACH TO PERCEPTION

J. J. Gibson (1950) was the first to challenge this established view of perception seriously. He heavily criticized the perceptionists for being too preoccupied with what was going on in the head while neglecting the important questions of how and why the world is explored. For Gibson it was obvious that perception evolved in the service of action and that perception had to be considered in that context (J. J. Gibson, 1966). The task of guiding action is so well accomplished in everyday life that it was a puzzle to Gibson that anyone would believe that the world was inaccessible to the senses. On the contrary, he claimed that there is information available about the environment, and the events within it, in the energy flux at the receptors. There now exists good evidence that Gibson was right in his assumptions, at least concerning the optic array (Lee, 1974; Ullman, 1979). This representation, however, is valid *only* if change over time is taken into account; then there exists an unequivocal relation between the spatial layout of the environment and the optical flow at the receptors.

If the world is going to be accessible to the visual system, then the visual system has to be sensitive to optical change over time. How patterns of optical motion elements are perceived has been studied extensively by Johansson and his associates (Johansson, 1950, 1964, 1975, 1978; Johansson, von Hofsten, & Jansson, 1980). Their research has demonstrated that the visual system is extremely sensitive to structuring over time. Even simple motion patterns consisting of only two or three dots evoke stable perception of motion in depth (Borjesson & von Hofsten, 1972, 1973). Perhaps an even more compelling demonstration of the potency of temporal structuring is those patterns consisting of a few light dots representing the motion of the main joints of a person. They evoke in every perceiver a most vivid percept of a person's performing just the act simulated by the pattern (Johansson, 1973).

That the accessibility of the world is limited to conditions of optical motion and change does not impose a serious constraint on the visual system. The intrinsically ambiguous static image is a limiting case. It does not exist in the real world, only in artificially produced displays. The huge amount of research knowledge about the perception of static displays should be viewed in this perspective. Even if it may prove to be useful in understanding some of the procedures used by the brain in processing visual information, this knowledge will never tell us very much about perception in everyday life. Given the specificity of information and the high performance of the system in natural settings, the important questions are not so much about the processing of information but about the information itself and the way it is picked up.

In his last two books, *The Senses Considered as Perceptual Systems* (1966), and *The Ecological Approach to Visual Perception* (1979), J. J. Gibson attempted a thorough description of the activity of perception and the information upon which it is based. His ideas, which are firmly based in biology, constitute a new approach to the problems of perception. Gibson begins by considering the ecology of the animal, how the species has evolved in its niche and habitat, and how in the long course of evolution the niche and the biological structures have mutually affected one another. The highly specialized means that we possess for extracting information about the world are the result of such a mutual relationship. The perceptual system have adapted so as to enable us to select and extract the information we need for our survival.

Affordances

Not all properties of the world either need, or could, be known by all animals. Perception is by necessity selective, extracting some of the available information and neglecting much more. A particular animal need only know about those properties of the world that have some potential consequences for it—either good or bad. The rabbit, but not the human being, needs to be able to perceive the subtle sound of an approaching fox; the human being, but not the rabbit, needs to be able to perceive the socially important message of the smile. Perceiver-significant properties of the world are called *affordances* by Gibson (1979).

Affordances are real physical properties of the world, but taken in reference to specific animals. Grass affords eating to the cow but to the cat it just affords lying down upon. A tree branch over a creek affords support to the mouse but not to the moose. So, although affordances are descriptions of the physical environment, they are also indirectly descriptions of the perceiver. Or as Gibson (1979) puts it:

> An important fact about the affordances of the environment is that they are in a sense objective, real, and physical, unlike values and meanings, which are often supposed to be subjective, phenomenal, and mental. But, actually, an affordance is neither an objective property nor a subjective property; or it is both if you like. An affordance cuts across the dichotomy of subjective-objective and helps us to understand its inadequacy. It is equally a fact of the environment and a fact of behavior. It is both physical and psychical, yet neither. An affordance points both ways, to the environment and to the observer [p. 129].

Gibson's suggestion is that affordances are the natural units of perception. In other words, we perceive directly what the world offers us in terms meaningful to our actions. Gibson's use of the term *direct* perception has often mistakenly been taken to mean that he asserts that no processing is involved (Michaels & Carello, 1981; Ullman, 1980). In fact, the directness of perceptions has nothing to do with the issue of processing. In this context, "direct" refers to the kind of properties of the world with which perception deals. From a functional perspective it is evident that the units of perception must be action related. It is in our actions that we need that immediate knowledge about the world that is so characteristic of perception.

What do we need to know about the environment in the context of our actions? What environmental properties will provide guidance and support for us? First of all, to be able to move around we need to know about the spatial layout of the environment. We need to perceive the clutteredness of the surface we are stepping on and the obstacles, openings, and drop-offs ahead of us. We need to perceive whether the surfaces around us offer support or not, if they are slippery, spongy, or if we will sink through them, as is so of water. We also, though, need to perceive our own movements relative to ourselves and to the environment.

We may need to alter aspects of the environment to suit our needs and goals. To be able to interact with the environment, we need to perceive detached objects, and to be able to handle and manipulate them we need to perceive their form and substance. It would also be useful to perceive some of the potential functions of objects so they could be picked up and used as tools in the appropriate ways. Finally, we need to perceive the motions of objects, inanimate as well as animate, and to determine whether we want to chase and catch them, move to avoid them, or run away and hide from them.

To be able to interact socially and communicate efficiently with other people, we need to know their intentions and emotions, and to perceive the spoken and written messages used in communication. We also need to perceive our own production of such messages.

Knowledge of the world in the context of our actions implies immediate accessibility of the perceived events to our action systems. We know from our own experiences that many of the properties of the world just described are accessible to us in this way; however, we have yet to determine, through empirical research, exactly the affordances to which we are sensitive or to which we may acquire sensitivity. In a perception-action perspective, this is an important task. Once we know what information is controlling our actions, we can also ask how our actions are controlled. First of all, however, we need to describe our actions and their properties in a systematic way, to get an idea of the kind of information needed to control them.

How to Define Action

Darwin pointed out (cf. Reed, 1982) that actions are functionally and not anatomically or mechanically specific. The catching of a ball, for instance, could be carried out by either the left or right hand, the starting position of the approach and the catching position of the ball might change from one reach to the next, and not two reaching trajectories will look exactly the same. These movements are still classified as the same action, though, because they share the same function.

The functional specificity of an action implies that its properties should vary with the task demands. This variation is even true for the catching of objects by young infants. Von Hofsten (1979) studied the catching of moving objects in infants 15 to 36 weeks of age. One reason to call the reaches of these young infants *actions* and not *reactions* is that the properties of their movements changed with the task demands. When the velocity of the object increased, the reaches improved in several respects. The movements became faster and the trajectories straighter. The infants seemed to adjust their behavior according to some minimum requirement for successful performance.

Darwin's experiments on earthworms (*Lumbricidae*) are another nice example of what is meant by functional specificity (Reed, in press). These worms dig tunnels, which they inhabit; the exposed ends of their burrows are plugged up with suitably sized and shaped materials (leaves, twigs, petiales). Darwin's hypothesis was that the function of this plugging is to maintain a flow of moist, warm air over the worms' epidermis, for they are harmed by cold and dessication. This hypothesis was confirmed by showing that the precision of the worms' plugging varied as a function of experimentally manipulated humidity and temperature. When conditions were warm and humid, plugging was imprecise and "sloppy," but as the temperature and humidity decreased the precision of the behavior increased.

Another important property of actions is that they are always controlled. An action is never just triggered or elicited. According to J. J. Gibson (1979), "They are constrained, guided, or steered and only in this sense are they ruled or governed" [p. 225]. Although triggered movements have commonly been the subject of study in experiments on motor control (Reed, 1982), such movements are probably extremely rare in everyday life.

Early infant reaching has often been described as triggered and ballistic (Bower, 1974; Twitchell, 1970). In my studies on early infant reaching (von Hofsten, 1979; 1980; von Hofsten & Lindhagen, 1979) I found no sign of triggering. On the contrary, the infants seemed to attempt to reach only for objects moving slowly enough to be caught. The proportion of misses was small in all conditions at all ages. Younger infants would reach less often for the fast objects, but when they reached for them they would catch them about as frequently as older infants.

CONTROL OF BALANCE AND LOCOMOTION—THE BASIS FOR ACTION

Bernstein (1967) has pointed out that the relationship between efference and the form of movement is not straightforward: The same impulse may produce different movements, and different impulses may produce the same movement. Because individual muscles and their innervational states do not have fixed consequences, single movements cannot be defined in isolation (Bernstein, 1967). Coordination and regulation of movement is possible only in relation to a stable context—that is, the posture of the body. To be able to act purposefully we must be able to maintain balance and equilibrium of the body and a stable orientation relative to the surroundings. Postural problems lead to motor disturbance. It is no coincidence that children with movement disorders often have problems controlling their postures (Forsstrom & von Hofsten, 1982).

The problem in maintaining posture is the forces acting on the body; this problem becomes most obvious when we move. Every movement we make, however small, induces forces and moments that have to be counterbalanced. This need for counterbalancing holds even for such movements as those controlling respiration, and the inability to compensate for respiration posturally can lead to severe movement disorders (Gurfinkel, Kots, Krinskiy, Palstev, Feldman, Tsetlin, & Shik, 1971).

Maintaining posture while locomoting seems especially difficult—but also extremely important—for skillful actions. A small child who is going to pick up a ball rolling on the floor does not do that while locomoting. Before bending down she stops and stabilizes her posture (Gentile, 1981). The time required for doing so may be so long that the ball rolls out of reach. The task will be mastered only when the child has developed the ability to pick the ball up while locomoting. A similar inability to integrate adaptive action with locomotion may be observed in an inexperienced subject throwing a spear. A novice's momentary stop to stabilize posture just before the throw will make it impossible to use the run-up to increase the power of the throw.

The task of maintaining posture is usually accomplished through small, but continuous, compensatory adjustments. Such adjustment requires information about small changes in position and orientation. The vestibular system has been evolved to serve those needs; however, the visual system also seems to play a very important part in the maintainance of posture. Lee and Lishman (1975) studied the control of body sway in subjects standing in a "swinging room," a large floorless box suspended just above the floor from a high ceiling so that it could swing noiselessly forward and back along a virtually straight arc. The main conclusion drawn from those studies was that vision generally affords the most sensitive and reliable information for balance and is an integral component of the control system. Oscillating the swinging room through as little as 6 mm caused adult subjects to sway approximately in phase with this movement. An interesting aspect of these experiments is that the subject is usually neither aware of the motion of the "swinging room" nor of his or her own sway. If, however, the motion of the "swinging room" is increased, the subject starts to perceive himself moving. That is a very compelling experience. Lishman and Lee (1973) induced various types of conflict between wide-angle visual information and other information about direction of locomotion. The subject either walked or stood still on a platform that could be moved relative to the "swinging room." In all these situations, whether the subject was actively locomoting or not and whether the platform was moving or not, vision always dominated the perceived direction of locomotion.

The peripheral retina seems to play a crucial role in the perception of egomotion (see, e.g., Johansson et al., 1980). Johansson (1977a, 1977b) projected linear motion onto a limited peripheral retinal area of a subject sitting in a fully lighted room; this evoked the paradoxical perception of the whole room and the subject as moving. Motion stimulation of a very small part of the peripheral retina seems to be enough to evoke this effect. In some subjects, even a single dot in oscillatory motion 70° from the fovea evoked perceived egomotion (Johansson, 1977b). Thus, whereas motion patterns in the central part of the retina usually give rise to perception of object motion, the same stimulus' falling on a peripheral area brings about perception of self-motion.

A dramatic demonstration of the importance of peripheral vision in securing essential orientation for performances has been provided by Kreshovnikov (1951; see also Graybiel, Jokl, & Trapp, 1955). Kreshovnikov had athletes performing various activities after the exclusion of either central or peripheral vision. Peripheral vision was eliminated by using goggles from which tubes

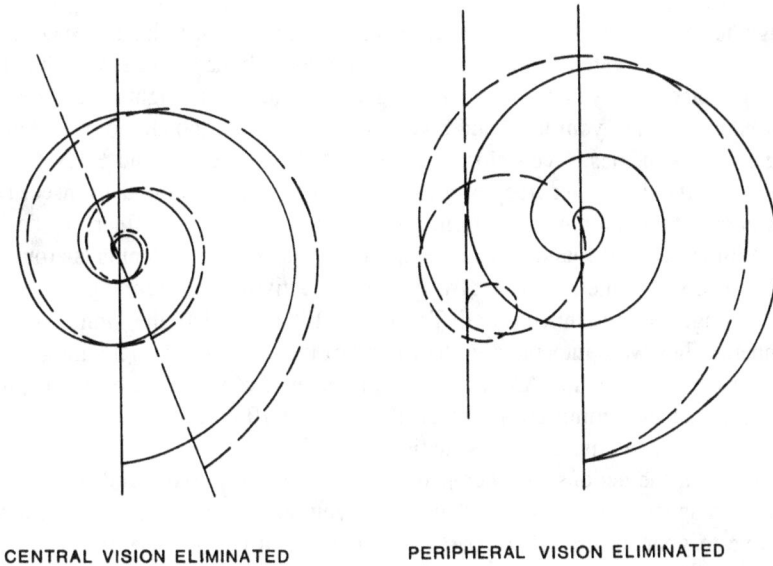

CENTRAL VISION ELIMINATED   PERIPHERAL VISION ELIMINATED

Fig. 6.1.   Effect of eliminating central and peripheral vision in prescribed figure-skating pattern (uninterrupted spiral lines). (From Kreshovnikov, 1951.)

protruded. Central vision was eliminated by using goggles with close-fitting glasses, to the center portions of which black paper circles were glued. Among other things, tests were conducted on expert skiers who ran on a 150-m slalom course. When central vision was excluded, only minor difficulties of action control were encountered, whereas when peripheral vision was excluded much more marked deterioration occurred. In the latter case, the athletes found it exceedingly difficult to follow the course; their ski tracks became uneven and judgment of distance was almost impossible.

Figure skaters were also tested. With the elimination of peripheral vision, there was a dramatic loss of symmetry, precision, and timing of movements; the elimination of central vision caused only minor problems. These effects are illustrated in Figure 6.1.

TIMING

Timing is an essential and integral part of all actions. An act is usually constructed from a number of component movements and these components have to be delicately timed relative to one another if the whole act is to be smooth and balanced. The most important facet, however, is that actions are adapted to the environment. As the environment exists independently of ourselves, adaptive coordination is possible only if we can time our actions relative to properties of the environment. Take, for instance, catching a fast baseball or running over rough terrain. In both these cases, precise timing is essential for successful performance. To catch a ball one-handed you not only need to get your hand to the right place, but you also have to close your fingers at the right time. The ball will hit the palm of your hand and bounce out if you close too late, or it will bang you on the knuckles if you close too soon. Alderson, Sully, and Sully (1974) found that the timing accuracy of grasping action had to be around 14 msec. In a fast game like table tennis the timing precision has to be even finer. Tyldesley and Whiting (1975) found that the temporal precision in table tennis is around 5 msec. The same fine timing is also typical for activities like running, jumping, and skiing. Lee, Lishman, and Thomson (1982) studied the timing of ski jumpers. They were interested in the timing of the explosive straightening of the legs just before the lip. Analyses of films taken close to the lip of the jump revealed that the timing error was on the order of 10 msec.

Timing is also crucial in all situations in which you have to coordinate your actions with the actions of other people or animals. In boxing and fencing, as well as in dancing, your success depends on your ability to time your movements relative to your opponent's or partner's. In riding it is necessary that you time your movements with the movements of your horse. In *Anna Karenina,* Tolstoy (1939) provides a dramatic example of a fatal failure of timing:

> It was only from feeling himself nearer the ground and from the peculiar smooth- ness of his motion that Vronsky knew how greatly the mare had quickened her pace. She flew over the ditch as though not noticing it. She flew over it like a bird; but at the same instant Vronsky, to his horror, felt that he had failed to keep up with the mare's pace, that he had, he did not know how, made a fearful, unpardonable mistake, in recovering his seat in the saddle. All at once his position has shifted and he knew that something awful had happened. . . . The clumsy movement made by Vronsky had broken her back [pp. 238–239].

Finally, in all kinds of communicative actions, timing is crucial. Gestures mean different things depending on when they appear in an interaction. Some authors, like Stern (1977), have characterized human interaction as a kind of a dance in which timing is crucial for the establishment of contact between the participants. Stern studied interactions between mothers and infants and found that in this case also interaction takes place in a split-second world. The ap- pearance of early disturbance in communicative acts has in some cases been traced to the inability of the caretakers to adapt their timing to the rhythms of the infants (Cunningham & Mittler, 1981). Cunningham studied interaction patterns in developmentally matched 4- to 6-month-old normal and Down's syndrome infants. He found significantly fewer types of behavior produced by the Down's syndrome group than by normals and a strong tendency for their mothers to keep up a high rate of reactive behavior, apparently attempting to elicit responses from the infants. The result was opposite to that intended. When the mothers were told to slow their pace and to respond only to behavior emitted by their infants, there was a significant increase in the frequency of the infants' behavior.

Timing always implies some extrapolation to the future. You must be able to anticipate the consequences of your own movements and the consequences of the events with which you are going to time your actions. Obviously, you need very good information about the progression of your own movements and about your relationship to the environment.

One potentially useful variable in the optical flow for a subject who wants to time his behavior relative to some object or landmark that he or she is approaching, or that is approaching him, is the rate of optical expansion at the retina; this specifies time-to-contact with the object (Lee, 1976). This variable has been successfully used by Lee and his associates to predict such diverse timing phenomena as the adjustment of gait in long jumping (Lee et al., 1982) and the folding of the wings by gannets plummeting into the sea (Lee & Reddish, 1981).

In the long-jump study, Lee et al. (1982) found that jumpers had a rather consistent stride pattern up to about the last four strides, when they regulated their gait visually in order to hit the take-off board. The result could most easily be explained by assuming that only one gait parameter was regulated during the run-up—the vertical impulse that was applied to the ground at each step. During the stereotyped phase of the run, the impulse was kept rather constant; then, as the jumpers neared the board, they regulated the impulse—and thereby the durations of their strides—on the basis of visual information about the time-to-reach the board.

Catching a moving object is a somewhat more complicated timing task than those just mentioned. It is true that the subject has to approach the target to catch it. In those animals in which the catching instrument is the mouth, which has a fixed relation to the eye, the expansion pattern of the target on the retina could very well be used in timing the catch. In the human being, however, the catching instrument is the hand, whose relation to the eye changes all the time. The eye may not even approach the target at all, and therefore the optical-expansion pattern will be of less use in timing the catch.

Catching a moving target is more complicated in another respect as well. It is not possible to catch a fast target like a baseball by simply approaching it; the catch must be aimed for some point ahead of the target where the hand and the target would meet. The question is how the subject knows where to aim. There are at least two ways to answer this. First, it is possible that the subject calculates future positions of the object and the time it would take the object to get to those positions. If the subject also knows the time it takes to reach out with his hand, he could choose a position to reach for at which the reaching time matches the motion time of the object. This is the traditional way of conceiving the solution of the problem—by mental calculations. In the light of such complicated procedures, the ability to catch fast-moving targets was considered to develop rather late (Kay, 1969).

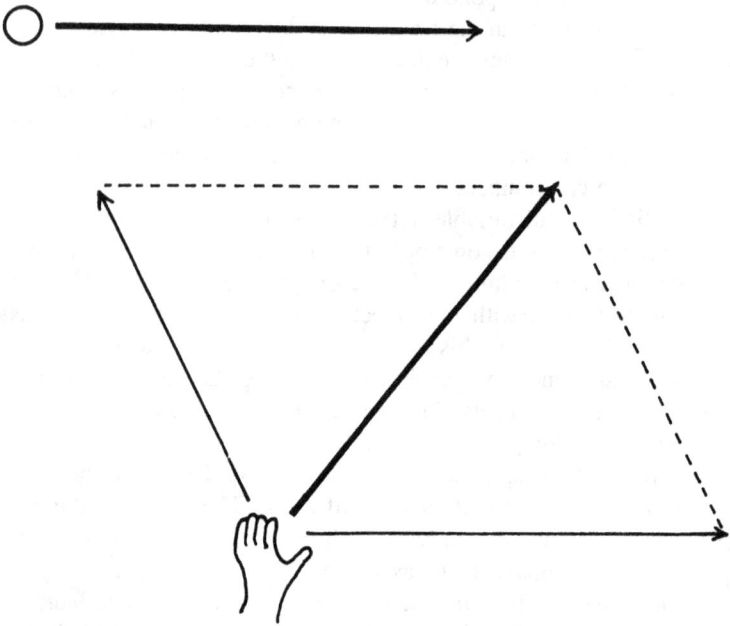

Fig. 6.2.   A movement of the hand directed at the meeting point with the object can also be described as a movement with the object and toward it at the same time.

A second way to explain successful predictive reaching is to regard the reaching act as a combination of an approach and a tracking of the moving target as depicted in Figure 6.2. This approach does not imply that the subject performs two movements at once, but rather that the performed movement has two determinants. The system can be regarded as two servomechanisms coupled together. If the tracking component correctly matches the velocity and direction of the target, the hand is bound to get to the meeting point with it. Such a system offers great flexibility with precision preserved because it allows for continuous control of movement. From a cognitive point of view, this task is also much simpler than the one mentioned previously. Both solutions require precise information about target motion; however, for the approach-tracking solution, the subject does not need to use his knowledge of target motion to calculate future positions of the object, nor does he need to know the time it takes to reach out. A sensorimotor system like this could develop quite early.

It has indeed been found that the ability to catch moving objects is an early achievement (von Hofsten & Lindhagen, 1979). Infants who had just started to reach successfully for stationary objects would also catch moving ones. Four-month-old infants caught objects moving with a speed of 30 cm/sec, and the

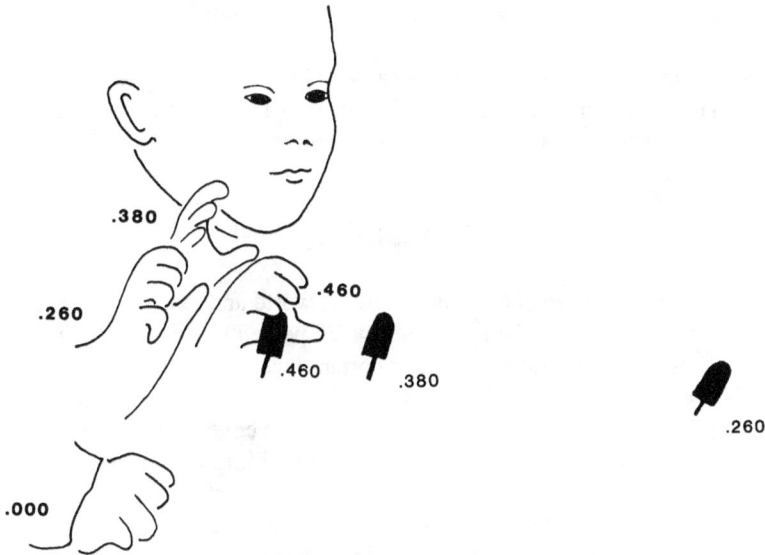

Fig. 6.3. An infant catching an object moving in front of her at 120 cm/sec. The duration of the reach was 460 ms. The object was encountered at 430 ms. The picture shows the position of the hand and the object at different time intervals from the start of the reach. Note that during the movement, the hand first opens and then closes just in time to grasp the object.

reaches were typically aimed at the meeting point ahead of the object (von Hofsten, 1980). In another study, 8-month-old infants were shown to catch fast-moving objects with velocities up to 120 cm/sec (von Hofsten, 1983). Figure 6.3 shows an example of such a reach. In this second study, velocity and starting position of the object were systematically varied. Timing and aiming of individual reaches were measured by a technique that took into consideration their three-dimensional properties. It was found that the reaches in all conditions were aimed close to the meeting point with the object right from the beginning of the approach. The precision in timing was about a twentieth of a second, and the systematic errors were close to zero. In each condition the infants typically reached for the object the first time it passed in front of them, and timing and aiming were just as precise then as later. There was no fixed catching position. Rather, catching positions were distributed over all position within reach of the infant. All these facts speak in favor of a very flexible sensorimotor system that does not rely on fixed catching positions or complicated mental calculations. Its early appearance suggests that it is basic to human functioning. It is not, however, essential only to humans; it is a very basic skill throughout the animal kingdom. For instance, any predator, however simple, needs such flexibility for its survival.

In summary, moving objects, animate as well as inanimate, often have important consequences for us. The ability to deal with such events in our action is crucial; humans have that capacity as early as infancy. The early appearance of timing skills in communication as well as in the catching of moving targets are indications that timing is a very general and basic aspect of behavior.

EXPLORATORY ACTIONS

As pointed out earlier, events occurring in the world and our perception of them are almost simultaneous. The immediacy of perception is a necessity if our actions are to be successful. Another important facet of perception is its flexibility. Flexible perception is also a necessity because different actions require knowledge about different sets of affordances in the environment. Ideally, selection of information from ongoing events and the utility of that information for performance coincide.

How can the requirements for flexibility and immediacy be simultaneously realized? It is clear that the immediacy of perception imposes severe restrictions on the flexibility of procedures used by the perceptual systems in analyzing the energy flow at the receptors.

Flexibility is achieved through scanning, orienting, and focusing activities of the perceptual systems. These exploratory activities are also referred to as attention. Attention does not need to involve overt movements, but in the vast majority of cases it does. The organs that perform these exploratory actions usually have other functions as well. The hand is an obvious case. It is designed to explore as well as to manipulate objects. The tactual sensitivity of the fingertips is extreme, and so is the dexterity of the fingers.

Exploratory actions are performed in the service of perception but, like all other actions, exploratory actions are also supported by perception. This notion of perception as a continuous process in which earlier perceiving guides later perceiving has been extensively discussed by E. J. Gibson (e.g., E. J. Gibson, 1969, and E. J. Gibson & Rader, 1979) and Neisser (1976). Neisser (1976) has called it the perceptual cycle.

Neisser (1976) believes that to be able to perceive the affordances relevant to a certain task, we must have expectancies of what these affordances are. Earlier perception, both near and far away in time, will supply us with the necessary expectancies of what to perceive. These expectances are called *schemas* by Neisser (1976). The existing schema determines what information is picked up, but it does not add to the information. If what we expect to find in tbe world is not there, our schemas will not ordinarily make us misperceive. Perception does not serve merely to confirm preexisting assumptions, but to provide us with new information. As Neisser (1976) has stated: "We cannot perceive *unless* we anticipate, but we must not see *only* what we anticipate [p. 43].

The question is whether in perceiving the world it is really necessary to anticipate what we are going to perceive. Perception seems to be reduced to just a confirmatory–disconfirmatory process. If that is so, and we perceive something we had not expected, how is the correct schema mobilized? Or even more problematic, what happens if we set our eyes on something completely new, something for which we have no schema? Isn't it enough to know how to direct attention to get access to the information we need for a certain task? Such a directed attention seems to make better use of the information available in the energy flow at the receptors. This is also the position of E. J. Gibson (E. J. Gibson, 1969; E. J. Gibson & Rader, 1979). To Gibson, learning to perceive is not a matter of getting more and more specific expectations about what to perceive, but of getting better and better procedures for perceiving, procedures that are efficient and economical.

To me, Gibson's position makes more sense; however, I am not denying that expectancies play an important role in perception. Perceiving events implies perceiving how things are going to change, and that is of great importance for our ability to maintain an efficient strategy of information pick-up. In that sense, the perceptual cycle is a crucial concept. Neither am I denying that knowing what to look for will economize perceiving. There are good demonstrations that it does (e.g., Neisser, 1967). No, it is the conception of schema that gives me difficulties. Knowing what to look for is not the same as expecting what to find. Only the former case describes the activity of perceiving, and only in this case can we talk about economy and efficiency.

Exploratory actions appear quite early in development. Indeed, even the neonate seems to have at his or her disposal several means for exploring the world. The most obvious example is the case of eye movements. From the very first minutes of life the neonate looks around in an active way. These eye movements have been carefully studied by Haith (1980). Haith found that even in the dark, where no external stimuli could have caused the eye to move, eye movements were organized and systematic. They seemed to reflect an intense visual search that would, perhaps, maximize the likelihood of detecting subtle contours and dim stimuli. Thus, newborns seem to be equipped to seek out visible objects on their own, independent of external stimulation. Haith (1980) also studied the eye movements of newborns in the presence of patterned stimuli. When bars or edges were placed in a scannable portion of the visual field, newborns tended to fixate near the contours and make eye movements that crossed them. Those eye movements that crossed the contours were on the average larger than those that did not, indicating that the subjects did not simply happen to cross edges. Haith (1978) concluded that "if we can talk about intention in newborns, it indeed appears that they intend to cross contours" [p. 37].

The newborn infant will follow an attractive moving target with eyes and head (Aslin, 1981; Bullinger, 1977; von Hofsten, 1982). Pursuit eye movements are not smooth, however. They consist of a jerky series of saccadic refixations on the moving target. Smooth-pursuit eye movements do not appear consistently until around 2 months of age (Aslin, 1981).

Although it was subject to some debate earlier, it now seems rather clear that coordinated vergence eye movements (Slater & Finlay, 1975) and accommodation (Banks, 1980) are present in the newborn. Aslin (1977) also showed some convergence and divergence in 1 month olds to approaching and receding targets. Vergence eye movements are further coordinated with accommodation from an early age. Aslin and Jackson (1979) measured binocular eye alignment in 2- to 6-month-old infants under both binocular and monocular viewing conditions. In the monocular condition there was only an accommodative stimulus present. Infants at all ages, including the 8 week olds, showed reliable convergence under both binocular and monocular viewing conditions.

The function of eye movement is not only to direct the eye to interesting events in the environment, but also to enable the eye to maintain fixation irrespective of head and body movements. Such eye movements depend on vestibular function. They are present at birth (Peiper, 1963), even in blind infants.

The visual system as an instrument for explorative actions does not function in isolation at birth. It is coordinated with other information-extracting systems of the neonate, like the auditory system and the exploratory system of the upper limbs. A reasonably complex sound—it may be a human voice (Alegria & Noirot, 1978; Mendelson & Haith, 1976) or a bottle of popcorn shaken (Field, Muir, Pilon, Sinclari, & Dodwell, 1980)—presented to the side of the infant's head will evoke an appropriate movement of the head toward the source of the sound. Von Hofsten (1982) studied the arm movements of newborns in the presence of a slowly and jerkily moving object. As in earlier studies on the topic (DiFranco, Muir, & Dodwell, 1978; Ruff & Halton, 1978), successful reaching was not observed; however, a closer analysis, taking into account the aiming of arm movements in three-dimensional space, revealed that the reaching was not quite uncoordinated (von Hofsten, 1982). Arm movements performed while the infant fixated the object were found to be aimed closer to the object than arm movements performed while the infant looked elsewhere or closed his or her eyes. The effect could not be explained in terms of head–arm coordination or any explanation based on head position and/or object position.

It is evident from these studies that grasping is not an integral part of newborn reaching: The object was rarely touched and never grasped. Newborn reaching, however, has not only latent functions. I like to stress the exploratory nature of these aimed movements. When the neonate looks at an object and reaches out for it, both the reaching and the looking seem to be parts of the same orienting response toward the object. The infant may be said to prepare herself for the encounter with the external event by concurrently pointing his or her feelers toward it.

It can be concluded, therefore, that the sense organs of the newborn infant are preadapted to function as exploratory systems. These exploratory systems are precoordinated for their task of extracting information about the environment.

CONCLUDING COMMENTS

It has been argued in the present chapter that perception and action are functionally inseparable. The function of perception is to guide action in setting goals as well as in supporting movements. This is done by making knowledge about critical task-related properties of the world (i.e., affordances) immediately available to the action system.

It seems probable that the ability to perceive affordances has coevolved with the actions themselves. In lower animals this concordance is rather obvious. Arbib (1981) has pointed out that the frog may be said to possess a number of specific visual systems: one for prey catching, one for threat avoidance, one for barrier negotiation, one for phototactic orientation, and so on. In higher vertebrates perception is no doubt less specialized than that. According to Rozin (1976), this is a general evolutionary trend. Capacities first appear in narrow contexts and later become extended into other domains; however, perception may still be specialized enough to make it more appropriate to speak of a number of perception-action systems than to conceive of perception as a single unitary process separate from action. It is rather obvious that, for instance, the ability to perceive emotional expressions in the human face and to perceive the meaningfulness of human speech are quite specialized capacities. Even in cases like space perception, in which we are used to conceiving of the capacity as a unitary one, it may be partly task specific. Even if perception of space is essential to all actions, it enters into different tasks in different ways.

The close connection between perception and action does not exclude other kinds of control. Actions are hierarchically organized. More global aspects of actions may not need immediate access to the affordances of the world. When I decided to write this chapter, the setting of that goal was influenced very little by immediate perception, but as I move my pen to formulate the last word of this sentence, immediate perception is a necessity for that action. I do not intend to elaborate any more on nonperceptual means of action control; that is the topic of many other chapters in this volume. I would, however, like to note an important intermediate case: The control of perceiving itself may have a highly abstract origin. Memories, expectancies, and reflections about the world enter into the "perceptual cycle" and do affect our exploratory actions. This involvement may help or hinder us in perceiving the affordances we need for a specific tasks. When we know what to look for (which is different from expecting what to find) perceiving becomes more economical and actions more skillful. The importance of directed attention for skillful performance has been discussed by Ulric Neisser in a most thorough way. I would like him to elaborate further on it.

ACKNOWLEDGMENTS

This chapter was prepared while the author was a visiting professor at the Institute of Child Development, University of Minnesota. I am grateful to Herbert Pick, Anne Pick, and Kim Dolgin for helpful discussions of the manuscript.

7 The Role of Invariant Structures in the Control of Movement

Ulric Neisser
Emory University

INTRODUCTION

Under normal circumstances perception and action are simultaneous and well coordinated. The links between them are very close. Indeed, von Hofsten finds them all but inseparable: "It is . . . difficult to speak of one of these two aspects of biological functioning without referring to the other" (p. 80). But unfortunately it is *not* difficult; we have been doing it for a century. By now the distinction between perception and action has become embedded in the institutional framework of science itself. Some scientists (mostly psychologists) study information pick-up and the senses; others (often in entirely different disciplines) study the functioning of joints and muscles. To discuss the relation between perception and action is to cut across deeply established categories. Such a discussion requires a willingness to go beyond existing evidence and consider unusual hypotheses. Because there is little to criticize in von Hofsten's excellent chapter, I will take this opportunity to examine some more speculative possibilities.

THEORIES OF PERCEPTION

The word *perception* refers to the acquisition of information by the sensory systems; the word *action* refers—in the sense I use here—to bodily movement. The first step in a scientific discussion of their relationship, then, must be to describe information pick-up and motor control in compatible terms. Until recently, this requirement could not be met. For over 100 years, theories of perception were formulated in terms that could not possibly apply to action because they made no allowance for movement. Theorists of every persuasion—Helmholtzians who argued that perception moves from sensations to inference as well as Gestalt psychologists who preferred to postulate self-organizing fields—took the motionless observer staring fixedly at a static scene as their prototypical case. The principal theoretical and philosophical problem was to explain how that observer's frozen retinal image could be transformed into the rich world of perceptual experience. The fundamental concepts of classical perceptual theory—field forces, unconscious inference, and all the rest—are all responses to that rather peculiar challenge.

The study of action, in contrast, has always started with movement. Perhaps it would have been possible to begin instead witb the act of standing still, but no one has done so. Moreover, theories of action have typically been more concerned with actual physical structures than with hypothetical mental ones. The fundamental question for the study of movement has been very concrete: How can the activity of muscles and joints be properly orchestrated by neural impulses? This question sounds less like a dilemma for philosophers than a problem in engineering, and it has usually been answered in just that spirit. Given these fundamental differences in the way they are usually conceived, it is little wonder that perception and action have remained theoretically irreconcilable for so long.

The classical theories of vision had another disadvantage: They were incompatible not only with action but with most forms of perception itself. A processing model that begins with a static retinal image cannot easily be stretched to explain phenomena like the haptic perception of shapes or the auditory perception of events. These everyday forms of perception were thought of as fundamentally different from vision, and especially from the prototypical static case. As a result, the simultaneous use of several perceptual systems has always seemed just as mysterious as the relation between perception and action. Although we often look at the objects we are touching (or see the events that make the sounds we hear), relations between the modalities were either ignored completely or relegated to an unimportant category called *intersensory phenomena*. Even today, many information-processing psychologists believe that the sensory modalities have a kind of adversary relationship: A person who is listening must "switch" to vision before he can see, for example (Posner, Nissen, & Klein, 1976).

If these century-old barriers no longer seem unsurmountable, it is primarily because J. J. Gibson (1966, 1979) has given us a new way to think about perceiving. For Gibson, the first step in the study of perception was not to invent mechanisms, but to describe the sorts of things that can be perceived: the environment, objects, events, affordances, and so on. When that had been accomplished, the next and more difficult step was to analyze the information structures that specify those sorts of things and thereby make perception possible. These critical information structures exist objectively, outside the perceiver; in the case of visual perception Gibson liked to say that they were "in the light." The main point is that they are not in the mind. Although the perceiver's nervous system must be appropriately "tuned" if it is to pick up information, Gibson did not encourage speculation about the structures responsible for the tuning. He treated all theories of mental mechanisms as regrettable regressions to the classical theories of perception. My views differ from Gibson's on this point; other theoretical commitments have forced me to take mental structure more seriously than he did. These differences do not diminish my appreciation for what he accomplished, particularly for the way in which his concepts have helped to clarify the relation between perception and action.

Several aspects of Gibson's theory are important for understanding that relationship. The first of these is his account of what kinds of things are actually perceivable: objects and their layout, surfaces, substances, events of various kinds, the perceiver's own body together with its position and movement, and especially *affordances*. As von Hofsten reminds us, affordances are objectively existing possibilities for action by a particular organism. Apples afford eating; tools afford manipulation; a moving object may afford catching, even to a baby. When we perceive, we see these affordances; when we act, we make use of them. Perception and action are organized in terms of the same units.

Another of Gibson's contributions was his focus on change over time. Much of the critical information for perception appears in the form of temporal patterns and structures that do not even exist at any single instant. This was always obviously true of hearing and touch (acoustic information consists of temporal wave forms or frequencies; haptic information is acquired by exploratory movements), but Gibson showed that it applies to vision as well. Flow fields, rate of change, occlusion/disocclusion and looming are examples of the kinds of optical structures that provide information for the visual system. None of them appears in the frozen retinal image that was the basis of the classical perceptual theories. Gibson's analysis of these forms of information has now made it possible to speculate about how the different perceptual and motor systems might be coordinated with one another. In particular, it suggests that they may all be organized in terms of the same temporal structures.

If we are beginning to understand *what* is perceived and *when*, it is natural to ask *how* as well. But "how" is ambiguous: An answer to "How are affordances perceived?" could either offer a more detailed account of the information that is used or suggest hypotheses about the mechanisms that use it. I begin by considering the first of these two interpretations; the second comes up almost of its own accord.

INVARIANTS OF STIMULUS INFORMATION

Any attempt to describe the information for perception at a fundamental level must come to grips with Gibson's most difficult concept: *invariant structure.*

Von Hofsten says little about invariants in his otherwise thorough chapter; he may have felt that the introduction of such an obscure idea would only confuse the reader. If that was his view, I cannot blame him, because I once held essentially the same opinion. (Invariants got rather short shrift in my 1976 book, *Cognition and Reality.*) It seems to me now, however, that several types of invariants play central roles in mediating the relation between perception and action,

One type of invariant, perhaps the most familiar, appears when some significant aspect of stimulus structure remains fixed while many other things change. However far away a given object may be, for instance, it always occludes the same number of texture elements on a regularly textured ground. A more dynamic example appears whenever an observer moves directly toward a surface: The center of expansion of the optical flow field specifies the precise point toward which the motion is directed. Such a flow field actually provides a great deal of useful information to the perceiver, not all of it in the form of invariants. For example, Lee (1980) has defined an important flow parameter that he calls *tau:* the ratio of the distance r which separates any projected point from the center of expansion to the velocity v with which that point is moving. Lee has shown that *tau* directly specifies how long it will be until the observer hits the surface (or vice versa), assuming constant velocities. Because *tau, r,* and v are all changing functions of time (tau $(t) = r$ (t) $/v$ (t)), *tau* is not invariant except in the sense that its meaning remains unaltered; nevertheless, it is a significant and informative parameter of the optic array. Such parameters make smooth and effective movement possible.

These optical invariants and parameters are not the only information structures relevant to the control of movement. Equally important are the "amodal invariants," which have been studied intensively by E. J. Gibson, E. Spelke, and others. An amodal invariant is an underlying structure that is not specifically visual or acoustic or haptic; it is defined by spatio-temporal patterns that can be expressed in various modalities. Because it is not modal, the invariant may make the same information available to several different perceptual systems at the same time. (On many occasions, of course, the information will be available to only a single modality. What makes it "amodal" is not the presence of several kinds of information but the abstract level of structure at which it is defined.) It is just this highly abstract kind of information that can best specify the real nature of many kinds of events, including bodily movements. Indeed, I believe that the descrption of movements in terms of amodal invariants is not relevant only to how they are perceived; it is also essential to understanding how they are executed.

The best-established class of amodal invariants are those that govern event perception in infancy. Their existence can be most easily demonstrated with a paradigm first devised by Spelke (1976). When infants are given the opportunity to look at either of two interesting films (projected side by side) while the sound track of one of the films is being played (through a central loudspeaker), they generally look toward the sound-relevant film rather than the silent one. The effect does not seem to depend on previous experience with the events depicted in the films. Spelke concluded—correctly, I believe—that it occurs because something about the sound of the event is *the same* as something about how it looks.

Subsequent work by Spelke (1979) and others has isolated a number of different invariants in this situation. Tempo, rhythm, and abruptness of onset (Bahrick, 1980) can all be picked up by infants from both optical and acoustic information. Moreover, amodal invariants are not restricted to vision and hearing. Using a similar paradigm, E. J. Gibson and Walker (in press) have shown that 1–month–olds distinguish between rigid and soft objects placed in their mouths; the babies demonstrate that they have made the distinction later, by looking preferentially at one of two visible objects that are undergoing rigid or deforming movements. Human beings are apparently born with the ability to perceive the basic structures of events on the basis of abstract information that is available to a number of different modalities.

INVARIANTS OF MOTOR ORGANIZATION

That several sensory systems can yield essentially the same perceptual experience is reminiscent of a similar equivalence among different motor systems. It has often been pointed out that a skilled movement learned with one set of muscles or in one attitude immediately becomes available to a wide range of other motor systems with little loss. Having once learned to sign my name with a pencil held in my right hand, I can also sign it vertically with chalk on a blackboard, and maybe even with a crayon held in my teeth. Something must remain unchanged over all these bodily transformations. Could this "invariance" across motor systems be related to the amodal invariants of perception?

One argument for an affirmative answer to that question comes from considering a special case of the relation between perception and action: the case of *imitation*. It is surprisingly easy to imitate the observed actions of other people. Although imitation is rarely perfect, we can almost always make a stab at it. Suppose, for example, that we watch someone throw a ball through a basket and then try it ourselves. Our first try may not succeed, but the throw will probably go in the general direction of the basket. Or suppose we try to imitate another person's facial expression: We won't get it quite right, but we will usually achieve at least some kind of similarity to our model. It would be rash to attribute all such accomplishments to "past experience;" how did we imitate throwing on the first occasion? Indeed, how do young children manage to imitate so many activities as successfully as they do? The work of Meltzoff and Moore (1977) suggests that some such ability may even be present from birth: The newborn babies in their experiments seem to imitate other people's facial expressions to some extent. At first glance this is an astonishing result. How could a baby know what muscle movements will create an expression like the one at which it is looking? The puzzle will remain even if infant imitation turns out to be an artifact, because we do not know how older children or adults manage to mimic facial expressions either. Any form of imitation or observational learning is evidence of a functional link between actions *seen* and actions *performed*. What is the basis of that link?

The concept of amodal invariants offers a possible solution to this problem. In observing another person's movements, we see not only the superficial features and positions of their limbs but the deep structure of the entire action: its timing, its use of certain degrees of freedom, its path through the environment, its smooth or abrupt flow of action. This underlying structure is invariant, appearing not only in how the movement looks but in how it sounds. It can even be perceived by the haptic system, if we happen to be in physical contact with the individual executing the movement. It is only one more step—though a very speculative one—to assume that the mental structures that organize the movements of our own limbs are represented internally in the same format. On that assumption, imitation would only require us to repeat what we have just done: to tune ourselves to a particular invariant structure.

This is not an entirely original proposal. The structures I have in mind are certainly related to the *coordinative structures* postulated by the Connecticut group of ecological psychologists (e.g., Fitch, Tuller, & Turvey, 1982), although their concept describes the actual organization of motor systems more explicitly. What I am emphasizing here is that the basic form of those structures may also be the abstract, basic form of our perceptual experience: Amodal invariants underlie what we do as well as what we see, hear, and touch. That is why motor skills transfer so readily from one posture or one starting point to another, and even to entirely different effector systems. Actions are organized by structures that remain invariant across such changes, just as they remain invariant across different sensory modalities.

This hypothesis does not apply only to the special case of imitation; it addresses every form of action in a perceivable environment. The very fact that we can see affordances and act on them, documented so thoroughly by von Hofsten, also suggests that movements must be organized in terms of perceptual invariants. To catch a ball, for example, "you not only need to get your hand to the right place, but you also have to close your fingers at the right time" (von Hofsten, p. 88). The beginning of the finger-closing movement must be under visual control if the ball is to be caught (otherwise it would not begin soon enough), but its subsequent course must be responsive to haptic information from the arm and hand if the ball is not to be dropped before it has been properly grasped. I do not believe that there can be a shift from one control system to another in the course of such a smoothly coordinated action. The entire movement must be organized in a way that is indifferent to the particular sensory modality through which information arrives—that is, in terms of amodal invariants. To act on a perceived affordance, then, is to align one abstract invariant structure with another.

SCHEMATA, IMAGES, AND MENTAL PRACTICE

In the course of examining the first sense of "How are affordances perceived?"—the kind of information that is used—we have now stumbled upon the second: the mechanisms that use it. Detailed consideration of the information on which motion perception is based have suggested the existence of "internal representations" for movements—abstract, amodal, temporally extended representations that have the same form as the invariant structures of perception itself. Although the last of those claims may still be speculative, there can be no doubt that some kind of control structures—*mechanisms,* in the broad sense of that word—are responsible for the coordination of action.

To claim that the mechanisms or *schemata* of action are amodal is to say that no single kind of environmental information is essential to their operation, and that no uniquely defined muscle movement invariabley results from it. We may plausibly go one step further: Perhaps they can operate without *any* sensory information and without producing any overt response at all. A system that can run on the basis of several forms of information and govern several different sorts of action can probably run independently as well. In such a case the internal representation unfolds more or less as if the action were really going on, but (by definition), no actual movement results. When this happens, I believe we are *imagining* the action in question. To imagine an action is to run part of the temporally extended system that would normally govern it. Such images may be at various levels of abstractness; they may be amodal, but they can also be specific to particular movements or definite modes of experience.

Imagined movements are important for several reasons. First, they certainly occur in everyday life. Second, they are obviously related to the imagined *perceptions* (often simply called *images*), which are the subject of a great deal of current theoretical interest among cognitive psychologists. Third and perhaps most surprisingly, they have a real effect on subsequent overt behavior. Indeed, imagined movement is often carried out deliberately in an effort to improve proficiency in a skill. Many athletes are convinced that "mental practice" of this kind improves their performance, and a number of experimental studies substantiate that opinion. (For reviews see Corbin, 1972; Richardson, 1967a, 1967b). In recent experiments at Cornell, Nigro (1983) has demonstrated that mental practice can lead to substantial improvement in the accuracy of throwing darts or bean bags at a target. Nigro's experimental subjects made 24 real throws, then 24 imaginary throws, and finally 24 more real throws. The amount of improvement between the first and third blocks was substantially greater in these subjects than in controls who received no imagining trials.

At present we have no good theory of mental practice, and cannot say exactly how and why it benefits subsequent performance. MacKay (1981) reviews several obvious possibilities—for example, that it works by producing tiny unobservable movements—but finds them all unsatisfactory. He proposes a very general associative theory of practice that does not consider the relation between perception and action at all. It seems to me, however, that mental practice must be based on the same invariant structures that are responsible for perceiving and for overt activity.

Those structures may take various forms, and they are not always amodal. Subjects in mental-practice experiments often imagine the consequences of their actions in the environment as well as the bodily motions themselves, and they do so in various ways. Some people "see" the flight of the dart to the target, some visualize their own bodies in motion, some have little or no visual imagery but are able to imagine the kinesthetic feelings that accompany throwing. We know very little about these differences, but they may be important. Nigro (1983) showed, for example, that dart throwers who imagine seeing themselves from an observer's perspective—in profile, as it were—benefit less from mental practice than those who try to reinstate the perspective that one has in the act of throwing. This superiority of the "field" over the "observer" perspective may not hold for all skills or all stages of training, but it demonstrates that the effectiveness of mental practice can depend very specifically on what is being imagined. One rehearses not only the coordination *of* movement but the coordination of perception *with* movement.

ANTICIPATIONS AND THE PERCEPTUAL CYCLE

Although action cannot take place and apparently can hardly even be imagined without a perceptual component, the converse is not true. Perception can and does occur without action: One can stand still and see the layout of a stationary environment, for example. (As I pointed our earlier, this was the prototypical case of perceiving for the classical theories.) One can also stand quite still while observing the movements of objects or other people. By the same token, it is possible to *imagine* layouts and movements without imagining any action of one's own. Indeed, theories of mental imagery have been primarily concerned with images of this kind. What role could these "stationary" perceptions and images play in a theory of action?

From a functional point of view, the answer is obvious. It is useful to perceive or imagine the layout of the environment even when no action is in progress because some *future* action may depend on it. The future in question may be either immediate or remote. Having seen where the door of the room is, you can make your exit right away or wait until later; you will know how to proceed in either case. If the lights fail and the room is plunged into darkness, you can still imagine the door in its proper location and head for it. It is plausible to describe these forms of perception and imagery as "anticipatory," because they serve to prepare the individual for something that may be done at a later time.

In *Cognition and Reality* (1976) I went further than this, using the term *anticipation* in a somewhat unorthodox way. I suggested that perception itself depends on cognitive structures—*anticipatory schemata*—that actively direct perceptual exploration because they are prepared for certain types of information. Perceiving is a cyclic activity in which the schemata are changed by the information they have picked up; this results in new exploration, more information, further changes in the schema, and so on. This model had several attractive characteristics: It offered a way of thinking about the mental structures that must be involved in perception; it portrayed perceiving as a temporally extended and continuous process, and it proposed a sensible relation between perception and mental imagery. Imagery consists of the activity of the anticipatory schemata when they are detached from the perceptual cycle—that is, when there is no objectively existing information to be picked up.

I now believe that at least one aspect of this theory must be modified. The critical aspect is not the relation between perception and imagery, which seems to me better established than ever, nor the concept of *schema,* which especially disturbs von Hofsten; it concerns the particular kinds of information for which the schemata are prepared. Before considering this difficulty, however, I review some aspects of the theory that still seem valid.

The effectiveness of mental practice suggests that images resemble real actions in at least one respect: Both must be "anticipatory." Any coordinated action is a temporal unit. The early stages are carried out in a way that prepares for the later ones, and the ending follows smoothly from what has gone before. (That is why athletes insist on the importance of "follow through" in actions such as swinging a bat.) This principle must also apply to imagined actions, if they are to benefit subsequent execution. Images, like movements, have their ends prefigured in their beginnings. This hypothesis is consistent with the interpretation of stationary imagery that I presented in *Cognition and Reality:* To imagine a scene is to prepare the process of looking at it, by activating the appropriate schemata.

The schemata that produce mental images may be just as amodal as the ones that control our actions. Although mental representations of spatial arrangements are usually called *visual images,* they need not be visual in a modality-specific sense. Kerr and I (1983) have found it useful to distinguish between two forms of imagery: *mental seeing* and *spatial knowing.* Our research indicates that people can imagine arrangements that include fully concealed objects, even though such objects cannot be "mentally seen." This form of spatial knowing creates mnemonically useful associations, just as other images do. Moreover, Kerr

(1983) has found that congenitally blind individuals can carry out most of the tasks that cognitive psychologists once regarded as clear-cut demonstrations of visual imagery. These findings suggest that many kinds of imagining, like many aspects of perceiving and acting, are based on deep and amodal structures.

VON HOFSTEN'S CRITIQUE

To describe images as perceptual anticipations is not very useful unless the role of anticipation in perceiving itself is understood. I agree with von Hofsten that some clarification of this issue is necessary. Three points demand particular consideration: (1) the generality of perceptual anticipations; (2) the term *schema* and its implications; (3) the kind of information that is actually anticipated.

Von Hofsten aruges that perception is too flexible to depend on specific expectancies. "The questions is whether . . . it is really necessary to anticipate what we are going to perceive. . . . What happens if we set our eyes on something completely new, something for which we have no schema?" (p. 93). He argues that "Knowing what to look for is not the same as expecting what to find" (p. 93). In fact, however, I never suggested that perceptual anticipations must be specific. On the contrary (Neisser, 1976): "The advance specification need not be sharply limited. . . . Schemata can operate at various levels of generality. You may be ready to see 'something over there,' or 'somebody,' or your brother-in-law George, or a smile on George's face, or even a cynical smile on George's face" [p. 55]. But we can never encounter what von Hofsten calls "something completely new, for which we have no schema": We are equipped from the beginning with something like a schema for perceiving objects, just as we are born with the ability to detect amodal invariants. Every specific anticipation of an object is a particularization of that general schema, which always remains available. Having a general schema is essentially equivalent to what von Hofsten calls "knowing what to look for." I have even used the same turn of phrase (Neisser, 1976): "Because we can see only what we know how to look for, it is these schemata (together with the information actually available) that determine what will be perceived" [p. 20].

Von Hofsten is particularly critical of the concept of *schema*. To say that perception depends on schemata is to postulate hypothetical mechanisms of the sort that Gibson rejected so decisively. Why not just say that we perceive? But I believe that perception requires a properly tuned nervous system, and that the specific structures responsible for different forms of tuning must be acknowledged. It is only by thinking of them as distinct that we can understand how perceptual learning may be restricted to particular domains, or how mental images may be related to the act of perceiving. To deny the existence of internal structures entirely would be a serious mistake; it would eliminate any hope of linking the theory of perception with the rest of cognitive psychology.

To be sure, my (1976) choice of the term *schema* for those structures may have been problematic. That term has become surprisingly popular in recent years: Cognitive psychology is now enduring a virtual deluge of story schemata, social schemata, person schemata, and the like. There are even schema theories of movement itself (Schmidt, 1982a, 1982b), quite different from the proposals I am making here. The schemata in such theories are usually rigid and specific: They have fixed structures, with just a few open "slots" for new information. Whatever their relevance in their own domains, such schemata are quite different from the abstract and open structures that (I believe) control perception. Nevertheless, I am reluctant to introduce yet another theoretical term. For the present I continue to use *schema,* despite the differences among the kinds of structures to which it may refer, and hope that the necessary distinctions can be conveyed by context.

The most serious difficulty facing the theory of the perceptual cycle lies elsewhere. What kind of information do the schemata anticipate? My original proposals were ambiguous on this point. Although I did suggest (Neisser, 1976) that schemata could be "temporal in their very nature" [p. 22], I often treated them as if they were static cross-sections of the perceptual cycle—cross-sections that could then turn into equally static mental images. Such an interpretation tends to suggest that perceiving consists of a succession of separate still "frames," somehow strung together by anticipations. That would be a mistake: As we have seen, normal perception depends heavily on flow parameters and invariants that extend over time.

Anticipations are sometimes established by the same type of information that will subsequently confirm them. As an object approaches, for example, perceivers who pick up Lee's *tau* (or some similar parameter) can see directly how much time remains before it will reach them. If they continue to watch it, the same kind of information will be continuously available. In such a case perception is not so much "cyclic" as continuous and direct. Note, however, that the schemata which are tuned to that information may also run independently of it. Good outfielders can actually turn their backs on the ball while they run to the deepest part of the outfield to catch it, because their amodal representation of its flight will continue on the same "trajectory" as they run. It is that representation which enables them to turn around again at the last moment, ready with the right anticipations for the current values of *tau.* The notion that internal representations have trajctories was first elaborated by Shepard (1975), in connection with his well-known studies of mental rotation. It has important implications for the coordination of perception and action.

In summary, I have argued that we cannot hope to understand the relation between perception and action unless we first describe them in compatible terms. Gibson's concept of amodal invariants has made this possible for the first time. An amodal invariant is an abstract spatio-temporal structure that can be embodied in more than one kind of stimulation. The characteristics of the invariant specify objective properties of the real events that give rise to it, and thus provide a basis for veridical perception.

Perceivers pick up invariants by tuning certain internal structures to them: *schemata,* for want of a better word. I have suggested that very similar schemata are responsible for the control of movement during action. Perceiving and doing are coordinated by aligning two abstract structures with one another. Moreover, schemata can sometimes operate without picking up any stimulus information and without producing any overt action at all—they may ''anticipate'' information that never arrives and movements that are never executed. On such occasions we say that we are imagining the objects, events, or actions in question. Thus the hypotheses proposed here make it possible to describe imagery and mental practice in the same terms as perception and movement: All of them depend on the same class of abstract structures.

GOAL DIRECTED BEHAVIOR AND
THINKING

Cognitive psychology, particularly the psychology of thinking, has traditionally been concerned with relatively simple problems: problems that have clear goals, for which plans can be delineated rather easily. Thus, the questions of action theory—namely, how to weigh different alternative goals, how to decide among them, how to develop a plan, how to execute the plan, at what point one should stop and reconsider, how one should monitor the plan and the action process—have not been asked in such a framework. This tradition changed with work by Reither and Stäudel (together with Dörner at the University of Bamberg). Complex situations— such as the situation of a development-aid specialist or a (powerful) mayor of a town—were simulated on a computer, and subjects were asked to prevent a famine or run a city (the experiment lasted several days). In such a situation, goals, plans, and relevant feedback parameters are all unknown at first. In addition the situation is dynamic: It changes even without doing anything. Thus, inaction becomes action. One of the results is a nonresult: Intelligence tests (i.e., IQ) do not predict performance in such a situation. Much more important predictors are emotional stability and self-confidence. Similarly, training programs to increase performance via knowledge accumulation are not sufficient; rather, it seems that training in metacognition is more important.

Beach compares an action-theory orientation to the psychology of thinking with the theoretical orientation of decision theory. Decision theory has not been interested in dynamic situations of the same complexity as was simulated in Reither and Stäudel's computer experiments. Furthermore, implementation of decisions has not been the central focus of decision theory; nevertheless, there are remarkable similarities between these two systems of thoughts. The decision maker must have a goal, must decide which strategies and tactics to use, and must monitor progress. Complications arise when one does not reach the goal and particularly when the goal is attractive but the tactics are aversive (Beach spells out several different strategies that may help in such a case).

8 Thinking and Action

Franz Reither
Thea Stäudel
University of Bamberg

INTRODUCTION

Action in general means goal directed behavior. It serves to satisfy human needs or to guarantee their satisfaction in the long run. In many cases, one knows how to reach a desired goal intuitively: To achieve it one may either use automatisms or knowledge from experience about a certain part of reality. One has knowledge about the structure of this part of reality, about the operations necessary to influence it, and also of the sequence of steps necessary to achieve it—epistemic knowledge as we call it. Parts of this thoroughly detailed plan, however, may be missing. One may not know how to combine the available operations (a problem of synthesis), or one may not yet know the operations themselves (a problem of analysis). One may even be unaware of the exact criteria for the desired goal state (a dialectical problem; see Dörner, 1976). In all of these cases one is confronted with a problem and must use heuristics to find a solution. The least complicated heuristic is trial-and-error behavior; a more complex heuristic is, for example, "planning backward." The demands imposed upon the actor by the problem are dependent on the characteristics of the field of reality itself and on the characteristics of the problem solver.

In the following sections we first describe characteristics of complex problems and the demands they make on cognition and action. Second, we present a general model of complex problem solving as an action-oriented process. We present the model in a theoretical form from which we make deductions to compare it with corresponding empirical results. After this, we describe conditions that can modify otherwise very stable and resistant problem-solving processes. Finally, we offer some integrative ideas, which show the indispensable interaction of cognitive and emotional processes in this context.

110

CHARACTERISTICS AND DEMANDS OF COMPLEX
PROBLEMS

Real, everyday problems differ in several ways from those that commonly confront subjects in psychological research. An actor in a political situation, for example, must deal with complex circumstances and with relations partially hidden from view. The actor in our example must take into consideration many different aspects of the situation, such as financial constraints, "varied group interests," and so on. Furthermore, needed information is inaccessible. Indeed, some information may be false or totally missing, when, for example, important features of the situation are hidden. In addition, many variables relevant to the situation may be interdependent; one cannot influence one without changing others. Also, things may change on their own, because of their own dynamics. If the actor in our example misses the deadline for his intended moves, the whole situation is changed with regard to his intentions.

Such a complex, partly hidden network of active and passive elements causes uncertainty, under which the problem solver has to act. In a series of investigations we examined the problem-solving behavior of people confronted with such complex problems. To observe subjects' behavior, especially thought verbalization, and to make the problems as realistic as possible in the ways just mentioned, we, for the most part, used computer simulation and gaming. We constructed computer realities in which subjects could gather information, make decisions, and get feedback about the effects of their actions on the system.

We constructed, for example, a model of a third-world country called *Tanaland* and put our subjects in the positions of development aid volunteers (Dörner & Reither, 1978); simulated a small town called *Lohhausen* with subjects acting as mayor (Dörner, Kreuzig, Reither, & Stäudel, 1983); and built different versions of the ecological, climatic, and ethnic conditions in the Sahel region, asking our subjects to help the simulated inhabitants improve their living conditions.

At the beginning of one simulation subjects were introduced to *Dagu*, an area inhabited by about 300 nomads with their herds of cattle. The Dagu had a relatively high birth rate, but poor living conditions and a short life expectancy caused a nearly constant total population over the long run. The cattle were also in poor physical condition; they suffered from sleeping sickness communicated by tsetse flies. This disease, coupled with poor pasture land and a lack of medical care, resulted in a subsistence-level existence for the human inhabitants.

The subjects' task was to help the Dagu to improve their living conditions and to increase the population, but to avoid extreme population growth. Subjects had several different ways to affect the food supply of the inhabitants: They could influence birth and death rates by introducing birth control and other kinds of medical care; they could affect the size of the cattle population by taking action against the tsetse flies; or they could improve irrigation. They might also arrange for the natives to sell products to raise money for further projects.

The subjects were presented with this initial situation, and they had to decide what to do: They had to decide what measures to take, how long they wanted their programs to last, and how long they wanted to wait before getting feedback about the effects their programs were having. The computer simulated 20 years of development.

In all of these attempts subjects had to deal with what were, on a structural level, similar problems. The complexity of all of these tasks produced a flood of information. If the subjects did not want to drown, they had to apply information-reducing techniques such as abstraction, condensation, and reduction. The high degree of interdependency among the problem variables caused side effects, which subjects could grasp only if they had a good cognitive map of the situation. Here outlines of flow and block-diagrams were helpful and, sometimes, necessary. Concealed structural relations were additional impediments that were difficult to overcome. Subjects had to search for symptoms of the invisible connections and relations in the problem, and this analysis required developing analogies and carrying out experiments. Finally, the internal dynamic of the problem situation produced time pressures for the subjects, so that some kind of trend analysis and careful consideration of what were important and unimportant aspects of the problem was needed.

The advantage of experiments with simulations like ours is that subjects can decide on concrete operations that they can subsequently carry out; subjects can also discover all of the effects of their actions. Furthermore, they have to continue their planning and action on the basis of the specific new situation they help to create. Such a simulation is more realistic than a static situation and also has certain effects on subjects' behavior. They are forced to think about the concrete realization of their decisions and not just to formulate goals, as they did in an earlier series of experiments in which they had to plan one-time-only interventions divorced from this dynamic structure.

Problems that have the just-mentioned attributes and demand specified activities and abilities call for certain kinds of behavior in thinking and acting. To show this is the task of the following section.

COMPLEX PROBLEM-SOLVING PROCESSES

What kind of problem solving is necessary to master such complex problems? In this section we address this question and report real subjects' behavior.

Goal Finding

First of all, most everyday problems have an open goal state—that is, the goal criteria are vague: the goal "an adequate living standard for everyone," for example. Such global goals are insufficient to lend concrete guidance to a course of action. One should specify one's goals as clearly as possible when confronting complex problems. One must, therefore, decompose the global goal state and define precise criteria. In many cases this decomposition leads to several partial goals, so the goal state is polytelic. Further, some of the partial goals may contradict others. To reach a satisfactory compromise, it is necessary to balance partial goals. Generally, people dislike analyzing and even formulating their goals, especially defining them in a precise manner; often, therefore, they are unaware of contradictions. Reither (1980, 1981, 1983a) showed this under a variety of experimental conditions. In all cases subjects preferred to leave their goals unformulated or only poorly defined, although—or because—no exact test could be made of the degree to which the goal had been achieved later on.

Situation Analysis

Faced with a complex problem, people need knowledge about the structure of the situation as well as about relevant variables and ways to affect them. In complex systems, however, many elements and their relations are invisible. One has to observe "symptoms" to be able to infer the underlying structure. One must, therefore, seek relevant information at the right level of decomposition—that is, at the right level of abstraction. This level must be neither too concrete nor too abstract if it is to catch the critical variables connected with the desired goals (Dörner, 1980a). Accordingly, in the Lohhausen experiment, successful subjects analyzed the system on a more abstract level than did unsuccessful ones, who asked for extremely detailed information; one subject went so far as to ask for the names of some of the inhabitants of Lohhausen (Dörner, Kreuzig, Reither, & Stäudel, 1983)!

Research on information gathering had been restricted to comparatively simple situations. For example, Piaget's impressive investigations, restricted for the most part to children, illustrate this tendency to use simplified situations. Information seeking in complex situations seems to be a rather difficult form of action and quite different from Piaget's tasks. Subjects often simply try to avoid it, and, perhaps for that reason too, research has paid only a little attention to it. A first attempt at a theory of asking questions has been offered by Flammer (1980) who, however, stresses the difficulty involved in using adequate methods of information gathering. Several investigations (e.g., Dörner & Reither, 1978; Reither, 1983b) have shown that subjects are often quite unwilling to ask for information, even if it is urgently needed.

Cognitive operations that build up knowledge about unknown situations include, to mention two, the use of analogies and the application of abstract, structured schemata. These operations require not only a great deal of knowledge about a wide range of matters but also an understanding of the appropriate conditions for their successful application. This is probably one reason that these techniques are often replaced by simple opinions and untested hypotheses about an unknown reality.

Another way to uncover the hidden relations and structure of a complex system is to use the method of isolated variation of conditions. Such manipulation holds only a small chance of success in this case, however. It serves only to give the actor an illusion of a definite connection between his or her action and the reaction of the system. The adequate way to approach this problem is to combine suitable and connected variables in a bundle that must be varied as a whole and related to a set of effects in order to gain an image of the whole causal network and its linkages. In the Lohhausen experiment, successful subjects asked more questions, especially more "why" questions, than did unsuccessful ones and thus tried to build up such causal networks. Furthermore, they used strategies to fix new information in their memories and to compare it with existing data. Thus, they detected more discrepancies than did the unsuccessful subjects and achieved a more adequate picture of the situation more quickly (Dörner, Kreuzig, Reither, & Stäudel, 1983).

Setting up Priorities

If the situation is spontaneously dynamic, time pressure may arise, which, together with the complexity of the situation and restricted human information-processing capacity, requires one to choose the points at which to devote most of one's effort. One has to concentrate on certain goals and certain aspects of the system.

In the Lohhausen experiment (Dörner, Kreuzig, Reither, & Stäudel, 1983), successful subjects worked at the central aspects of the system right from the beginning, whereas unsuccessful subjects dealt first with secondary aspects, such as the organization of people's leisure time, even though there were severe problems of unemployment due to an economic recession. Successful subjects also concentrated on the relevant themes when necessary and then spread their activities as soon as the central variables were in the desired states. Even as one is occupied with the main points of effort, though, one must simultaneously control background variables to avoid overlooking crucial changes in the rest of the system.

Often, subjects set up priorities about what should be done immediately and what could wait, based on the probability of success of affecting one particular aspect of the problem, instead of using the more rational strategy of searching for essential criteria of urgency for choosing priorities. This simpler procedure provides agreeable results initially, but leads to erroneous judgments about the real state of affairs, which can become dangerous in the course of time. On the other hand, once subjects had chosen one aspect of the problem on which to focus, they often persisted in concentrating their efforts on that feature alone. This irreversibility of priorities results in one-sidedness and inadequate decision making.

Action Planning and Decision Making

If the system does not change in the desired direction by its own dynamics, it is necessary to influence the critical variables in order to reach the desired goal state. Sometimes people ignore the internal dynamics and "try to push the river, though it flows on its own." To manipulate the system actively, adequate operations must be found and the dosage of the operations must be defined. Doses that are too small usually do not cause much trouble, but excessive doses disturb, and sometimes even destroy, the system, especially systems with many interactions and positive feedback, such as ecological ones. Our subjects in the simulations of the Sahel region (as well as real development aids) often overreacted this way, for example by drilling so many wells that the water resources of the region were totally exploited.

They also overlooked side effects and long-range effects and made linear (as opposed to exponential) extrapolations of trends in determining population growth (cf. Dörner & Reither, 1978; Stäudel, 1983b). It seems to be especially difficult for the human imagination to envision other than the desired effects of an action and to take into account acceleration. This neglect leads to an underestimation of the explosiveness of the development of essential variables. Hence, one or another type of reactive planning is often seen in which no long-range planning takes place. Subjects are content to wait passively for emergencies and then try to correct the defects as soon as possible. When emergencies accumulate, this kind of action fails completely, and the actor either tries to escape from the situation or resorts to some kind of violence (Dörner, 1980b). So, for example, some of our Lohhausen mayors, after having tried several unsuitable techniques to overcome unemployment, bound the "obstinate" unemployed workers and apprentices to forced labor. To enforce this decision, they engaged a great number of additional police officers, a move that cost much more than had previously been paid to the unemployed workers.

The number of decisions made is indicative of the quality of problem solving. In several investigations successful subjects came to more decisions than did unsuccessful ones. They used a broader bundle of operations to realize their intentions, found the relevant operations more quickly, and continued to use them as long as necessary. Because of this perseverance, they showed a greater consistency in their actions; the negative side of such consistency is that it can result in a certain "narrowness of the expert" (Dörner, Kreuzig, Reither, & Stäudel, 1983; Reither, 1980; Stäudel, 1983b). Experts, because of their success in situations in which they have specialized, often do not appreciate the need to change their ways of acting and thinking, even when such change is urgently needed.

The processes described so far make sense only in a superordinate plan that regulates the organization of action. In Lohhausen successful subjects structured their interventions more actively than did unsuccessful ones. They verbalized their strategic intentions more often and followed through on their ideas until they terminated the specific themes. They were more likely to organize their approaches hierarchically—that is, they went into detail, but came back to the superordinate level afterward. In general, they exhibited a rather clear pattern of concatenation of the elements of information processing that can be characterized by the sequence: "general orientation—specific orientation—depth analysis-decision" (Dörner & Stäudel, 1980). In contrast, unsuccessful subjects exhibited a less organized way of proceeding with "thematic vagabonding" (i.e., frequent changes of themes), "encapsulation" (i.e., working with an irrelevant theme for a long time), and "escape tendencies" (Dörner, 1980b). In cases of failure, they described what they had done, whereas successful subjects analyzed their interventions and tried to change them by self-reflection (Dörner, Kreuzig, Reither, & Stäudel, 1983), a more effective way of improving problem solving in complex situations (Hesse, 1979; Reither, 1980).

Control of Results

At the end of each action sequence there should be an assessment of the extent to which the desired goals have been reached, a determination of which aims are fulfilled, of what remains to be done, and of which new problems exist. Using this systematic approach, it is possible to estimate the suitability of specific actions to corresponding goals; such testing also provides feedback about the adequacy of the actor's conception of the situation.

Ability to control the effects of intervention depends on the concreteness of the criteria defining the goal and the adequacy of the hypotheses about the effects of the interventions. Only successful and experienced subjects were willing to formulate and to test hypotheses in a systematic way (Dörner, Kreuzig, Reither, & Stäudel, 1983; Reither, 1981).

Solutions Through Force

It has often been found (e.g., Dörner, 1980b; Reither, 1980) that subjects acting in complex situations tend to resort to solutions through force when difficulties accumulate or failures continuously recur. Solutions through force, however, not only neglect the real situational demands, but they also fail to take into account the consequences of the use of force: Often solution attempts of this kind destroy essential parts of the problem field so that later help comes too late. For example, when first starting their work several of our "development-aid volunteers" were alarmed about a few starving inhabitants. Very anxious to avoid disasters like this, they ordered wagon loads of food from abroad and installed medical care and hospitals (all of which cost a great deal of money) out of their senses of their "social duties." A couple of years later—after money had become short and after the population had grown significantly through faulty decisions—the same subjects let several hundred inhabitants starve as a result of selling their cattle to provide money to realize the "aid workers'" plans. The hospitals were then torn down, because they only waste money, and without them population growth would, of course, slow down. When this obvious discrepancy from their "social duties" was pointed out to subjects, they curtly referred to their difficult situations, which did not allow for such expansive "gadgets!"

Because the threshold of tolerance for failure differs among individuals, it is difficult to formulate universal criteria for the occurrence of solutions through force; however, the present results make it likely that the tendency to choose drastic means to escape difficult situations is widespread, and subjects to not hesitate very long in giving way to it. One should rely only with great caution on the effectiveness of social rules, norms, and values to inhibit the use of force by those attempting to solve complex problems. With enough pressure from the situation, we found decidedly brutal and antisocial actions, all of which were "justified" by the unfavorable circumstances.

MODIFICATIONS IN THINKING AND ACTION

Investigations concerning thinking and action in complex situations often show remarkable deficits in problem-solving techniques and abilities (e.g., Dörner, 1980b; Dörner & Reither, 1978; Reither, 1981). Even when subjects are given explicit training in better problem-solving approaches,, they still show persistent resistance (e.g., Dörner, Kreuzig, Reither, & Stäudel, 1983). On the other hand, most of the trained subjects *reported* improvements in their problem-solving behavior, improvements that could not be found in their real actions.

Modifications by Self-Reflection

So far we have found one successful approach to improving problem-solving ability, one that involves "self-reflective" cognitions (Hesse, 1979; Reither, 1980). In this context self-reflection means cognitive activity that may be characterized as "thinking about one's own thinking." We have seen that systematically induced self-reflection improves subjects' performance with elementary heuristics and procedures and enhances their ability to combine them into broader patterns in the solution of analytical problems.

Let us first look at the elements of problem-solving processes that changed under the influence of enforced self-reflection. Trial-and-error behavior, an important resource for analyzing new situations, changed from incidental occurrences in situations of boredom and general helplessness into systematic application in difficult phases of the problem solution. Also, subjects were not only increasingly systematic in their search for differences when analyzing relations among variables, but also more perceptive in terms of dimensional abstraction. The result was that subjects trained to self-reflect became increasingly better at considering a larger number of components of the situation simultaneously. Subjects also became more willing—and better able—to formulate their hypotheses about what would happen in a manner that could be falsified—a rather rare, but nevertheless fruitful activity under normal conditions. Finally, subjects under the influence of induced self-reflection became more likely to formulate their goals concretely, so that it became more possible for them to determine the extent to which they had achieved their goals.

In addition to improving subjects' use of elementary heuristics, self-reflection also improved their abilities to combine those elementary procedures into problem-solving strategies; it has also been found (Reither, 1980) that subjects under self-reflection became more flexible in providing and using strategies as measured by the increased number of changes in their applied strategies. Further, the quality of planning improved in that more long-range effects and side effects of interventions were taken into consideration.

Modifications by Guided Experience

Encouraged by the results achieved with systematically induced self-reflection and keeping in mind the frequent finding that subjects offered resistance to attempts to change their failures in problem solving by training (e.g., Dörner, Kreuzig, Reither, & Stäudel, 1983), we tried a broader approach. Up to this point we had given subjects more or less cognitively oriented advice, which they were quite able to understand but nevertheless failed to practice when the situations demanded it. This lack of transfer seems to be caused by an absence of experience. Only by practical application did subjects gain the necessary emotional and motivational background in addition to the cognitive instructions. We have therefore begun to use computer simulation not only as a tool to analyze complex problem solving, but also as a field of guided experience (Reither, 1983b).

Reither (1983b) gave his subjects, four-person groups with job experience in a variety of professions, the task of managing a computer-simulated firm. Actions, decisions, plans, and the corresponding solution processes were analyzed with the subjects after the exercise; this discussion generally produced various kinds of insights and "aha" experiences. Nearly all the subjects thought that they had learned something about their important failures at problem solving and believed that this same task would no longer pose a severe problem for them. They were, therefore, quite astonished to discover that the same problem situation given once more appeared to be very difficult again. Having discovered through experience that problem-solving failures, even when analyzed and well known once, can continue to have their confusing effects, subjects became modest enough not only to hear and understand the training advice, but to take it into consideration when really required. Both thinking and acting were significantly modified by this kind of treatment.

We found that there was an increase in information gathering after the subjects saw that the simple intent to raise more and more detailed questions does not suffice. Typically, untrained subjects in comparable situations declare that they already know all of the relevant information and that there is nothing more of value to be asked. Similar results were found with regard to the subjects' analyses. For the most part, the subjects revealed only meager abilities to carry out systematic analyses of the given situations and their underlying relations, especially with the small amount of data they had gathered. Even with clear negative feedback, untrained subjects believe they have the situations wholly under control. They avoid testing their hypotheses and prefer to believe both that they have considered the appropriate variables and that they have analyzed them sufficiently. If they are forced by the situations to recognize the inadequacy of their assumptions, they simply change the variables and analyze them further in the same restricted way. Trained subjects, in contrast, make use of the guidance to do a trend analysis in a systematic way and to include more variables in their analyses. It is important to note that these differences exist even though the unguided subjects had the same knowledge of the relevant techniques as did the guided subjects.

Guided subjects differ from those who got only informational advice with regard to their problem-solving abilities in their actions as well as their thinking. The very slight extent to which the unguided subjects controlled the situations was significantly increased for the trained ones. Untrained subjects typically confined themselves to isolated variations to avoid tbe uncertainties connected with an increasing number of parts of the systems that must be directed if they are to get control over the whole developments. These self-imposed restrictions are very hard to overcome; they are similar to the tendency of untrained subjects not to change their actions, but rather to concentrate their thoughts and action on very few elements in rigid and conservative ways. The guided subjects, on the other hand, slowly went on to exert a greater range of control over the situations in addition to using more flexible strategies to influence them.

This list of results concerning improved aspects of a complex problem-solving process could be continued; nevertheless, we conclude it, but with two remarks. All changes in thinking and acting are worthless if there are no concrete improvements in performance. Reither (1983b) showed that subjects who were trained in the described way with guided experience with complex problems were significantly better problem solvers than were untrained ones—but the behavioral and cognitive changes achieved were by no means spectacular; the differences seem to be very small.

RELATIONS BETWEEN THINKING AND ACTION

In the preceding sections many differences between successful and unsuccessful problem solvers were explicated, differences having to do with the elements of their thinking and the way those elements were structured when dealing with complex problems. What are the reasons for these differences?

As many investigations have shown, intelligence is not the only predictor of the quality of problem solving, as long as the subject's intelligence quotient is within the range of average intelligence (Putz-Osterloh, 1981). Correlations are found only if the problem is similar to the items of intelligence tests—that is, if the structure of the system is transparent or if the problem is presented without a semantic context (Hesse, 1982).

We assume that individual differences in complex problem solving are largely determined by specific interactions between cognitive and emotional processes. Accordingly, we found relatively high correlations between the quality of problem solving and personality characteristics such as self-confidence, extroversion, neuroticism, and emotional lability, all of which are closely connected with perceived competence (Dörner, Kreuzig, Reither, & Stäudel, 1983). By "perceived competence" we mean the extent of control over one's surroundings that an individual believes he or she is able to exert. We assume that a need for control exists in human beings, and that whenever an individual is confronted with situations of uncertainty, that person checks to see whether he or she will be able to control them, to avoid endangering his or her own needs and goals (Dörner, Reither, & Stäudel, 1983). Österreich (1981) postulates the need for control as an autonomous, basic motive that is always aroused when there are irregularities in an individual's surroundings.

The assessment of a situation as controllable is subjective and is based on the individual's experience with situations of this type. This situational dependence means that resolution depends, on one hand, on knowledge of the structure of this part of reality and, on the other, on the available operations with which to influence it. This is epistemic competence, the competence of a specialist. But human beings are also able to acquire knowledge and to find new operations by using metaoperations, heuristics. Heuristic competence is the assessment by an individual of whether he or she will be able to master a new situation (Stäudel, 1983a). Both components together determine the assessment of the actual competence in the actual situation.

If competence is low, the individual is in a state of uncontrollability, of unspecifiable danger. We assume that this increases readiness to act. The internal processes of thinking and planning diminish and become more simple; control of behavior becomes more dependent on external cues. A tendency arises to show quick and diffuse reactions, which we call "intellectual emergency reactions" (Dörner, 1982). Like Lazarus (1966, 1968), we distinguish three basic forms of behavior during those threatening situations: attack (together with feelings of anger), avoidance (together with anxiety), and resignation (together with feelings of hopelessness and depression).

What does this imply with regard to problem-solving behavior? If the situation is important or urgent, an individual with high actual competence will be in a state of positive tension and feel motivated. He or she will be at a mean level of activation and show adequate, planned, and reflective problem-solving behavior. If difficulties arise, he or she will react with more attention, perhaps with agitation; but it is more probable that he or she will adapt his or her behavior to the demands of the situation by self-reflective processes rather than use undifferentiated methods. As already shown, our successful subjects did exactly this.

Low actual competence, on the other hand, goes along with feelings of uncertainty, anxiety, and excessive arousal. There are differences at the individual level between individuals with high and low actual competence even before they get feedback about the effects of their actions. Corresponding findings were obtained in a simulation and a concept-formation experiment (Stäudel, 1982; Stäudel & Thumser, 1983).

As these experiments also showed, subjects with low competence, especially those with low heuristic competence, continue to feel tension and uncertainty. They also describe themselves in a questionnaire as feeling stress and interfering emotions more often. Their problem-solving behavior is less planned. They seem to have no clear idea of the relevance of partial goals. They often begin to deal with a theme ad hoc, then shift to another one via association, also let it go, and so on, until they are forced to return to it later on. We interpret this "thematic vagabonding" as a tendency to leave a situation because of decreasing competence in the face of increasing difficulties. Another indicator of this competence reduction is their tendency to delegate responsibility, although in a simulated world, there is nobody else to whom to delegate (Dörner, Kreuzig, Reither, & Stäudel, 1983). In addition to the tendency to escape, we observed aggressive behavior (e.g., inadequately high doses of operations) and direct attacks. Resignation, finally, shows itself when subjects stop trying to influence anything any longer.

The type of problem-solving behavior exhibited by subjects with low self-assessments is not very rational and results in the occurrence of fatal mistakes, such as not considering side effects and long-range effects. Thus, in the Sahel zone simulation, subjects with low heuristic competence produced a famine significantly more often than did subjects with a high self-assessment (Stäudel, 1983b). The failures incompetent individuals experience recurrently sustain low self-assessment in a positive feedback loop and this makes change nearly impossible.

SUMMARY

This contribution is intended to give a report of recent findings and theoretical reflections about thinking and action, especially in complex situations. Having described the characteristics and demands of complex problems, we followed the general problem-solving process in order to show its components and their necessary contributions to thinking and acting. Because these requirements are usually only poorly fulfilled and a change of this state is difficult to achieve, attempts at modification of thinking and acting and the results of those attempts were described. Finally, we tried to give some theoretical framework that considers the relations between thinking and action and their interactions with emotional processes.

9 Action: Decision-Implementation Strategies and Tactics

Lee Roy Beach
University of Chicago

INTRODUCTION

My area of scholarly interest is judgment and decision making. A couple of years ago I wrote an overview of the literature in this area (L. R. Beach, 1982). It had three major components: *judgment* (diagnosis of the state of the world and the degree to which it presents a decision problem), *decision* (evaluation of alternative remedial courses of action and selection of one course as most desirable), and *decision implementation* (adoption of a strategy, and its component tactics, for implementing the selected course of action). One of the conclusions of the article was that, even though there still is much to be done, judgment and decision have received a great deal of attention, but decision implementation has, for the most part, been ignored. After reading the chapter by Reither and Stäudel, however, I find that I must recant that conclusion; clearly, research by these authors, and related research by those dealing with the psychology of action, speaks to the question of decision implementation—that is, to postdecisional action.

The purpose of the present remarks is to outline the nature of decision implementation and to tie it to some of the experimental results presented by Reither and Stäudel. The point is to illustrate that the sort of thinking current in some areas of decision research parallels, in important ways, current thinking in the psychology of action.

GOALS

It is becoming increasingly clear that decision making consists of setting a goal toward which a series of actions is directed. Of interest, after the question of how

123

the decision itself is made, is the way in which these actions are planned and executed and how progress toward the goal is monitored.

Defining what is meant by a goal is very difficult. In some sense, the endpoint of every action, however minute, is a goal. But there is also a sense in which we are able to think of some sort of hierarchy of goals and to understand that at the time of decision, and during the implementation of that decision, there is a desirable and often fairly well-defined state of affairs that is regarded as the endpoint of our endeavors: This state is the goal in question. The decision itself marks the proximal cognitive boundary of an action sequence, and the goal in question (endpoint of the action sequence) marks the distal cognitive boundary. Together, these boundaries define an *action unit* that can be described as "trying to do (achieve, acquire, accomplish, complete, etc.)" such and such. Examples of action units are "earning my degree," "buying a Rolls," "getting promoted," and "completing my book."

Clearly, the goal that defines an action unit is itself subordinate to a goal that is higher in the hierarchy (perhaps with Maslow's, 1970, Self Actualization being the ultimate goal, at least for many Westerners). Similarly, at the moment of execution, actions that are components of the action unit are very much focused upon the achievement of their own goals, which are subordinate to the goal of the action unit itself. So, we see that goals are subgoals for higher-order goals and that subgoals momentarily can receive full attention during their execution. There is, however, a goal at some level in the hierarchy that the decision maker regards as the distal boundary of the action unit that is being considered when the decision is made to pursue a particular course of action.

It is likely that the distal boundary of an action unit, its goal, is defined by the way the decision maker specifies the decision problem in the first place, or by the way the problem is specified by the person or agency that presents it to the decision maker. At any rate, inquiry will reveal that the decision maker is aware that the goal is, in fact, subordinate to higher-level goals and that constituent actions are themselves lower-level goals—but behavior and discourse are focused on the action unit goal as the principle goal of interest and other goals, though of interest and importance in the overall scheme of things, are peripheral or secondary to the action unit goal.

IMPLEMENTATION STRATEGIES AND TACTICS

Having selected a distal endpoint for an action unit, a goal, the first step in implementation is to adopt an overall *strategy* and to consider specific *tactics* for carrying out that strategy. Let us suppose that you decided to become the mayor of your city. That decision defines the goal and leaves you with several alternative strategies for achieving it: You could work your way up through elective offices, through the city council, and so on, to the mayor's office. You could become a well-known newspaper or TV commentator on local politics and there-

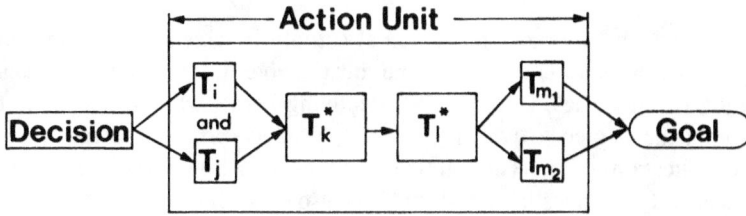

Fig. 9.1.   A diagrammatic illustration of a strategy's component tactics within a hypothetical action unit, as seen by the decision maker at the time that the decision is made.

by establish your credentials as a well-informed and interested person who could use this knowledge to advantage as mayor of the city. You could become a public-spirited business leader and, when well enough known, make a bid for election to the office. In some cities, you might even decide that bribery and strong-arm techniques would constitute the best strategy for attaining the position as mayor. In short, you must select a guiding strategy before you attempt to implement your decision to become mayor. The same is true, of course, for the implementation of any decision.

Having selected a strategy (while, perhaps, keeping other strategy options open, just in case the selected one proves not to work), it is necessary to begin to "flesh out" the action sequence that will implement the strategy and, one hopes, result in achievement of the goal. That is, tactics must be devised and their sequencing must be considered.

Figure 9.1 shows how I think of tactics within an action unit—at least how I think they might look to the decision maker at the time of decision. Tactics are actions resulting in subgoals that facilitate progress toward the goal of the action unit. Some tactics are fairly well defined at the time of decision, designated T. Some are less defined at the time and will become better defined as time for their execution approaches ("I'll cross that bridge when I come to it"), designated T^*. Some tactics are dependent on each other or must be executed simultaneously, designated T_i and T_j. Some tactics, designated T_{m_1} or T_{m_2}, are alternative ways to produce progress, and local circumstances will dictate which will be used when the time comes. Of course, some action units will contain more or fewer tactics than illustrated in Figure 9.1, and there may be various degrees of clarity about them at the time of decision, as well as various degrees of contingency among them (and between them and environmental conditions) as the tactical sequence unfolds in time.

MONITORING PROGRESS TOWARD THE GOAL

As suggested previously, execution of tactics can often be an all-absorbing activity. Getting a quality education may be the goal, but the tactic of studying hard to achieve good grades is the actual activity in which the decision maker engages. The problem is that often one must devote full attention to successful execution (good grades) of the tactics (studying hard), while at the same time monitoring the degree to which the tactics produce progress toward the goal (quality education). We do not know exactly how such monitoring takes place, but it is clear that it does in fact occur. It is also clear, however, that monitoring can fail. If getting good grades requires tactics that do not promote quality education (when the latter includes creative thought and varied intellectual experiences), failure to recognize that the study-hard tactic is counterproductive can preclude goal achievement and leave the decision maker caught in a tactical short circuit with the result that the tactic becomes an end in itself; it becomes autonomous, disconnected from the goal it was to serve. This problem is particuarly likely to arise when the goal is not well defined or is very abstract—the comfortable clarity of a concrete tactic may usurp the guiding function of the ill-defined goal. Often the aim of counseling and formalized implementation programs (which are discussed shortly) is to help decision makers monitor their progress toward their goals and to help them avoid getting caught up in tactics to the exclusion of goals.

FAILURE TO PROGRESS TOWARD THE GOAL

Many things can lead to failure to progress toward the goal. Environmental conditions may have changed since the strategy and its component tactics were adopted, resulting in their failure to be effective in the new conditions. Evaluations of the efficacy of the strategy and its tactics may have been in error when they were adopted (e.g., because of wishful thinking or ignorance). Desires and motives may have changed over time, the once-attractive goal may have lost its attractiveness, and progress toward it may be irrelevant or even counterproductive.

When progress toward a goal is found to be too slow, nonexistent, or irrelevant, decision makers tend to react in a fairly limited number of ways. One way is to work harder in executing the preselected tactics: to force things to work through application of sheer energy or effort. This approach is often accompanied by expressions of renewed determination (when hope for progress exists) or of frustration (when hope is slight). Another way of reacting is to reevaluate the efficacy of the preselected tactics or of the entire strategy and to make changes that hold promise of better results. Yet another reaction is to "kid oneself": to affirm that progress is being made but that it is slow or halting. An example of this reaction is to affirm that the goal of losing weight is being slowly achieved by dieting (the tactic), but that a temporary setback has occurred and "I'll start again on Monday," when, in fact, no progress is being made, and Monday will see just another excuse.

ATTRACTIVE GOALS, AVERSIVE TACTICS: A SPECIAL, BUT INSTRUCTIVE, CASE

Many important decisions involve the pursuit of a very attractive long-term goal that requires employment of very unpleasant short-term tactics to achieve it. Frequently, these goals require tactics for suppression or control of appetites (e.g., for food, alcohol, smoking, or gambling) or for participation in inconvenient or unpleasant activities (e.g., taking medication for hypertension, exercise programs for prevention of or recovery from a heart attack). Although the decision maker may, in his or her better moments, realize that the goal of the action unit (slimness, abstinence, reduced blood pressure, a healthy heart) is extremely desirable, at other times, when attention is narrowly focused on the unpleasantness of the tactics selected for that goal, it may be difficult to execute the tactic—in short, the unpleasantness of the tactic usurps the guiding function of the desirable goal.

In an effort to help people monitor progress, as well as to help them maintain progress toward desirable goals that require aversive tactics, numerous formalized implementation programs have been established. Examples are Alcoholics Anonymous, Weight Watchers, Gamblers Anonymous, smoking-cessation programs, and various health-maintainance programs that promote health-related activities. Although these and similar programs are unique in that they address implementation of decisions for different kinds of goals, they tend to share common elements in the form of the tactics they prescribe. It is instructive to examine these common elements to broaden our understanding of decision implementation, if only because these programs arise from need rather than theory, and the tactics they use are based on experience of what works and what does not. Admittedly, implementation of attractive-goal/aversive-tactics decisions is a special case of implementation in general. It is, however, a very important special case and may prove instructive in understanding the broader problem of decision implementation.

The first common element in many formalized implementation programs is the at least partial externalization of monitoring. The decision maker retains moment-to-moment monitoring, but is accountable to others in the program for success in doing it. In addition, the program often provides for monitoring checks—for example, "weighing in" at Weight Watchers and increased stamina in exercise programs. In some sense, the program monitors the decision maker's monitoring and makes it difficult for him or her to fool himself or herself or to shirk responsibility for monitoring.

The second common element is that the programs teach tactics. Often this instruction consists of tips on how to identify conditions that may trigger relapse or recidivism. For example, Alcoholics Anonymous warns that hunger, anger, loneliness, and tiredness promote relapse. (The mnemonic HALT helps identify these danger conditions.) In addition, programs typically offer advice about what to do as an alternative—have a soft drink, eat, and so on. One frequently prescribed tactic is to "live one day at a time." It can be very discouraging for the decision maker to look down the long road to the goal and focus on all the activities that must be completed before that goal is achieved. If only today's goals and today's tasks are considered, the job does not appear to be unmanageable.

A third common element is social support, in both its positive and negative forms. Positive social support by other program members can encourage the decision maker to stick with the aversive tactics; the threat of social censure, however kindly and nonaggressive, can provide the same encouragement. The negative utility of having to admit to your friendly supporters that you have slipped, that you have failed in your progress toward your goal, coupled with your expectations (accurate or not) about their scorn, is a strong goad to keeping on the right track, however aversive the tactics may be.

A fourth common element is instruction about how to keep the goal in mind when circumstances threaten to lead to abandonment of the already-adopted aversive tactics. For example, decision makers who are trying to control their intake of alcohol or food are often adivsed to stop for a moment and mentally focus their attention on the goal before entering a situation in which drink or food are freely available. This "mental innoculation" seems to aid in adherence to the aversive tactics that promote the goal.

The final common element that we consider (and there are probably many that I have overlooked) is that programs of this sort often provide additional reasons for attaining the goal, or they strengthen existing reasons. For example, the joys of sobriety, slimness, and good health can be witnessed to by those members of the program who have attained them or who are making progress in doing so. If these joys had not been anticipated by the decision maker, they add to the attractiveness of the goal. If they were anticipated, knowledge that they indeed are attainable reduces uncertainty about the expected benefits of attaining the goal, thereby enhancing the goal's attractiveness. Increased goal attractiveness motivates and increases the decision maker's ability to deal with aversive tactics in the service of attaining the goal.

TEACHING IMPLEMENTATION SKILLS

Whenever one teaches a course or delivers a public lecture on the topic of decision making, the question inevitably arises whether people can be taught to be good decision makers. I do not know the answer to that question because I suspect that the question itself means different things to the person of whom it is asked and the person who asks it. Decision theorists are interested in helping people make decisions correctly (i.e., in accordance with the so-called optimal methods that they have devised), whereas decision makers are interested in making correct decisions (i.e., decisions that subsequently prove to work). Given these different interpretations, the question is difficult to answer simply.

Be that as it may, the question has yet another difficulty: Even if a decision is made correctly (i.e., according to the prescriptions of decision theory), it may well prove to be an incorrect decision (it may fail to work). This failure may result from just bad luck—one takes one's chances and sometimes loses. Yet, even for a correctly made decision to eventuate in the goal, which makes it a correct decision if the goal lives up to expectations, the decision maker has to be more than just a good decision maker; he or she must also be able to implement the decision successfully. Thus, in part, the original question about teaching decision making involves an additional question about whether people can be taught to be good decision implementers as well.

What skills should improve implementation? First is the ability to generate and clarify strategies. Second, closely related to the first, is the ability to judge, perhaps from past experience or from advice, which strategies are more or less suitable under the circumstances. Many decision makers appear to be deficient in these skills—they know what they want to achieve, but they do not know how to go about achieving it. In many cases they rely on advice from persons of equal inability in selecting strategies and arraying their tactics, and the results are no better than if they had relied on their own poor skills. Again, counseling often consists of giving good advice (one hopes) about strategies and tactics.

Third, the decision maker needs the ability to modify strategies and tactics that exist in his or her repertory so that they will provide progress toward the goal in question. When this modification cannot be carried out, it is necessary to have the ability to generate new strategies and tactics that will further the goal.

Fourth, the decision maker needs the ability to monitor progress and to detect backsliding and stagnation. This requires keeping the focus on tactic success subordinate to the focus on progress toward the goal. Success of a tactic that does not aid progress is a hollow victory. Consider an analogy to a long-distance swimmer: When the swimmer's head is in the water, the focus is on execution of the appropriate swimming stroke, but from time to time she must lift her head to see if all the exertion is resulting in progress toward the goal, the finish line.

Finally, the decision maker needs the ability to detect conditions in the environment that make the preselected strategy and its tactics obsolete. Obsolescence may result from unforeseen events, from changes in the environment, or from errors in evaluation of the environment or the attractiveness of the goal at the time the decision was made. It is here that the problem of sunk costs arises: Just because the decision maker has invested energy in this strategy is no reason to continue its pursuit if it fails to promote progress toward the goal. This is the "pouring good money after bad" argument, an argument that many decision makers fail to appreciate.

IMPLEMENTATION AND THE REITHER AND STÄUDEL RESULTS

The kind of tasks used in the Reither and Stäudel (R & S) studies are not precisely analogous to the kind that gave rise to the foregoing analysis of decision implementation. They are, however, quite realistic in their complexity and demands; therefore, any light they can cast on this analysis is doubly beneficial.

First, R & S stress that goal seeking in complex decision tasks requires dealing with many hidden interrelationships among variables that define the environment that supports (or fails to support) progress toward the goal. Monitoring progress toward a goal is, therefore, especially difficult when the decision maker is ignorant about how execution of one tactic influences the applicability and chances of success of other tactics. In short, tactics may help each other or hinder each other for reasons that the decision maker can only guess. In such circumstances, the decision maker may be reduced to sheer trial and error until a causal map can be formed to guide subsequent strategy implementation or strategy revision. R & S state that successful decision makers ask why questions in an effort to form such causal maps (knowledge structures) to guide subsequent action.

When ignorance abounds, monitoring of progress is particularly difficult because feedback about progress is not very informative. This lack can be complicated even further if the goal itself is not clearly defined. R & S observed a tendency for decision makers to leave their goals rather vague and ill defined, but, with experience, the successful decision makers began to make their goals more concrete. By the same token, successful decision makers sought information about the task that was more abstract than that sought by the unsuccessful decision makers. I am not sure what ''abstract'' means in this context, but if it means that the information is relevant to the success of tactics vis-a-vis the goal, then such action seems quite reasonable.

R & S found that decision makers often focus on dealing with one feature of complex problems, ignoring the others. This, of course, is much like letting tactics become autonomous and ignoring the larger picture. Also, when failure is experienced by the R & S decision makers, there is a strong tendency for them to attempt to force a solution, as was suggested in the present analysis. This same approach, force, may be used when progress is positive but too slow for the decision maker's taste—another result obtained by R & S.

The characterization of a successful decision maker that emerges from the R & S results is one of a self-confident, orderly, thoughtful ''winner.'' Experience with the task, coupled with some experience at failure, leads these decision makers to reflect upon what they are doing and to modify it in light of what they have learned. This sort of reflection leads to concrete formulation of the goal, crisper delineation of the strategy and tactics, and greater flexibility in discarding and adopting strategies and tactics. These decision makers appear to feel in control and competent to do the task. They work efficiently, with purpose, and they persevere. They appear to have broad vision. They execute orderly, well-structured tactics (interventions), and they do not get lost in detail. Most of all, they profit from training about the task, integrating the training into their behavior by reflection upon what they are doing and how they can improve—thinking about thinking about the task.

In contrast, unsuccessful decision makers seem to lack confidence, to keep things vague, to approach the problem in a rather diffuse manner, and to jump about in a manner R & S describe as "thematic vagabonding." These differences between successful and unsuccessful decision makers naturally raise the question of whether they represent traits of the persons involved, or whether they result from the way these persons initially specify the task for themselves and the strategies they adopt for achieving the goal of that task. Moreover, there is the question of motivation; as L. R. Beach and Mitchell (1978) have pointed out, decision makers may have a large repertory of strategies for making decisions (and for implementing them), but they do not use costly, complex strategies for nonessential problems. This problem of differentiating between *whether* decision makers have the skills necessary to succeed at a task and *when* they will bother to exhibit those skills is a major one. Until we come to grips with it, the whole issue of whether people are, or can be, good decision makers remains very vague. Until it is clarified, the question of the efficacy of training in decision making and decision-implementation skills remains unsettled.

Space limitations prevent further examination of the parallels between action and decision implementation views of postdecision behavior. I trust, however, that the foregoing makes a reasonable argument that such parallels exist. It is to be hoped that future research will draw from both viewpoints in an effort to lead us to a better understanding of purposeful, goal directed behavior.

GOAL DIRECTED BEHAVIOR AND
MOTIVATION

Many theories of action begin their discussion after an intention (goal) has been formed. It has been the task of expectancy-value theories to suggest an understanding of what we intend to do. None of these theories, however, has attempted to explain how a wish is transformed into an intention (which leads to an action). This is the task that Heckhausen and Kuhl set for themselves. A wish is first transformed into a want. Depending on opportunity, time, importance, urgency, and the available means, this want is transformed into an intention that eventually leads to an action. Wishes, wants, and intentions can be analyzed into three levels, depending on whether they refer to the action level (fun in the doing), the outcome level (a positively valued result of an action), or the consequences level (some later outcomes of an action that are related to earlier outcomes). The process of development from wish to action may be short cut (i.e., an action is started prematurely). Or, lack of opportunities in the environment may stop its development and produce a "top spin" in which, for example, a wish is continuously transformed into a want, but is stopped before it is realized, then goes back to become a wish again, which is again transformed into a want, and so on. When such a top spin occurs, the person is geared toward taking the opportunity to develop an intention and to act. (Thus top spins may explain current concerns that we actually do not act upon.)

Blankenship contrasts this theory with the dynamic theory of action (by Atkinson & Birch, 1970). This theory is concerned with the continuous stream of behavior—that is, with the effects of earlier behaviors on later ones in the temporal flow of actions. Thus, the effects of earlier actions on the development of later intentions can be analyzed (e.g., through the concept of consummatory effects). Similarly, Freud's notions of displacement and substitution (being again dependent on possibly unconscious intentions) are taken up within this action-theory framework. Blankenship points out that these two models of action theory— one by Heckhausen and Kuhl and one by Atkinson and Birch—do not contradict each other but can be integrated.

10

From Wishes to Action: The Dead Ends and Short Cuts on the Long Way to Action

Heinz Heckhausen
Julius Kuhl
The Max Planck Institute for Psychological Research, Munich

INTRODUCTION

We know very little about the cognitive processes that transform wishes into intentions. Value-expectancy models of motivation only tell us what will be the most preferred goal once an individual is committed to an action, but they do not tell us why people intend to act in the first place or why they harbor many wishes that are never transformed into intentions. Nor do they tell us how wishes develop, what it is that transforms wishes into intentions and intentions into actions.

The shortcomings of value-expectancy models have been discussed elsewhere (Heckhausen, 1982; Kuhl, 1982b). We use their strength to propose a model of how wishes develop, are transformed into intentions, and how intentions are translated into action. The path from wishes to action is a long one. We start at the very beginning—that is, with the origin of values (see Klinger, 1977, Chapter 4), at the point at which something has acquired a value that exceeds some critical magnitude. This is the point at which the wish-related section of the pathway begins. It ends with the emergence of an intention. The intention-related portion extends to the onset of an action, leading to the realization of the goal.

We ask what happens to wishes that do not become intentions because, for instance, people believe that their wishes cannot be satisfied by any action or that their fulfillment would produce aversive side effects. Furthermore, what is the functional significance of unsatisfied motivational tendencies that never reach behavioral execution, of intentions waiting to be acted upon, of wishes that find a short cut to intentions—and thereby eventually to action—even though they do not meet expectancy-related and value-related criteria? The purpose of the present chapter is to outline some initial steps toward a theory of motivation and volition that provides a more detailed account of the developmental stages of motivations on their way to becoming executable intentions.

We limit our discussion to approach tendencies related to positively valued goals, leaving aside wishes to avoid or prevent aversive events. We do so for the sake of brevity because there is considerable, though not complete, correspondence between these two classes.

AN EXTENDED TAXONOMY OF MOTIVATIONAL VARIABLES

Before discussing the processes that presumably intervene between the emergence of the earliest form of a wish and its transformation into an intention, we would like to define some terms. An extension of the model proposed by Kuhl (1983, Chapter 5), our analysis includes four categories of variables: value, expectancy, relevance, and activation (including control of action tendencies). In addition, we focus on the elaborate logic of the value-expectancy approach as outlined in the Extended Cognitive Model of Motivation (Heckhausen, 1977).

The *value* category consists of valences of anticipated goals. A valence captures the subjective value of a goal and encompasses the specific emotions that will be experienced upon attaining that goal. A similar, frequently used term is *incentive*. As a tribute to Lewin we prefer to use the term *valence* (V).

For the same reason we use the Lewinian term *potency* (P) to specify the expectancy category. Potency variables refer to the unconditional, subjective probabilities of attaining the respective goal (Lewin, Dembo, Festinger, & Sears, 1944). They refer to a general conviction that a certain goal can, or cannot, be attained. In other words, the potency of a goal is assumed to be a function of the subjective likelihood of being able to attain the goal in some way (i.e., without specifying the particular acts or outcomes). Potency is replaced by the term *expectancy* (E) as soon as the probabilities for attaining the goal have become conditional—that is, as the outcome(o) is seen as being dependent on a certain action (a): aEo. A third type of variable within the expectancy category is the *instrumentality* (I) of action outcomes for desired or feared consequences. Instrumentality is the extent to which the presence of an outcome facilitates or impedes the occurrence of a consequence (c): oIc. The instrumentality of an outcome delimits the conditional probability of a consequence and may vary from $+1$ to -1 (negative instrumentality implies that the occurrence of the consequence is improbable if the outcome is present).

In our terminology, wishes are not yet endowed with the critical potency (or, more specifically, with sufficient expectancy and instrumentality). In Lewinian terms, they do not make the transition from the plane of fantasy, or irreality, to the plane of reality (Lewin, 1935); however, when subjective probability variables (conditional or unconditional) for attaining a goal or consequence exceed the critical magnitude, a wish assumes a reality-oriented status on the basis of its valence: The wish is transformed into a *want*. This distinction between *wish* and *want* is based on a conceptual claim made by Peters (1958).

In addition to being realistic, wants must also have relevance for the individual before they can result in commitment to achieve a goal. The relevance category determines whether or not a want is transformed into an intention. An intention, however, is more than the mere contemplation of a goal; it includes the search for appropriate goal oriented action. In terms of Klinger's (1971) theory of current concerns, the transformation of a want into an intention corresponds to a commitment that creates a current concern that persists until a goal has been achieved or abandoned. It is possible, however, that this process may be initiated earlier, at the point at which a wish is transformed into a want.

It is not yet completely clear what it is that initiates a commitment. The transformation of a want—however tempting, urgent, and realistic—into an intention appears to require a brief volitional act, at least when the realization of a want is accompanied by undesirable and irreversible side effects (e.g., one cannot find any, or at least no easy way back). For instance, once an intention has been publicly communicated, there are side effects that make it difficult, if not impossible, to revoke it. This insight became the major focus of the research on cognitive dissonance, once it was discovered that commitment is a necessary condition for reducing dissonance (Brehm & Cohen, 1962).

Commitment, however, does not appear to be a necessary result of the belief that attainment of a goal is desirable. Even a high product of value and expectancy may not be sufficient to produce a commitment. A unique opportunity or increased urgency—in the face of an approaching deadline—may represent an additional requirement for a commitment to future action (i.e., for generating an intention). Hence, in addition to value and expectancy there are other requirements that can be subsumed under the heading of "practicality." An additional purpose or an approaching occasion may make it practical and opportune to become committed. For instance, some individuals easily make up their minds if the goal serves two or more purposes at the same time, whereas others favor objectives that can be achieved by alternate means.

"Setting-related relevance" is yet another determinant. It implies that a want may or may not fit into the current concerns that dominate at the time or social setting. For instance, wants that involve diverting and relaxing activities are more appropriate for leisure or holiday periods, whereas action tendencies directed at long-term consequences become comparatively stronger in vocational settings.

The transition from wants to intentions require a *relevance* check that incorporates both of these features, as well as the promise that a valued goal can be attained at some future point. We tentatively propose the following criteria for the transition of a want into an intention: *opportunity, time, importance, urgency,* and *means.* By combining the initial letters of these five criteria we obtain *OTIUM,* which is our term for the relevance variable.

The five criteria of the *OTIUM-future* check can be easily partitioned into either the value term (importance, urgency) or the expectancy term (opportunity, time, means). Our formulation, however, is not just a restatement of the two

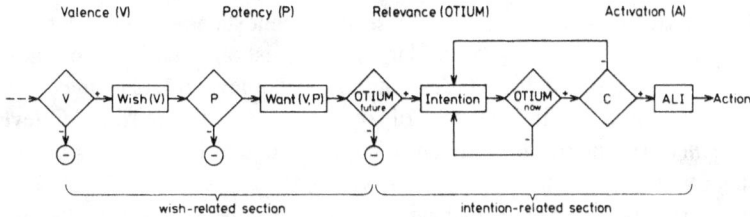

Fig. 10.1 Flow chart of the pathway from emergent wishes to intentions, and from intentions to actions.

terms. It introduces additional, as yet unknown factors, such as practicality requirements and setting-related relevance. At present we do not make any claims about the completeness of our list of criteria or about the differential weights to be assigned to them. We are saying that the probability of a want's being transformed into an intention increases as an *opportunity* for achieving the desired goals arises, as enough *time* is made available for its pursuit, as the goal appears to have personal *importance,* as there is an increasing *urgency* for attaining the goal (e.g., because of an approaching deadline), and as there are currently available *means* for attaining the goal (e.g., money and support from others).

In our model (Figure 10.1) the OTIUM check is executed in two different stages. The first stage, OTIUM future, refers to what is possible and likely in the future. If the prospects exceed a certain magnitude with respect to at least some of the criteria, the relevant want will be transformed into an intention. The second stage, OTIUM now, examines whether the criteria are present at a particular point in time. If they are, it facilitates action appropriate to the intention.

If it is positive, the second OTIUM check will lead to the activation phase, the final stage in the metamorphosis of a wish into an action. A further checkpoint is self-control (*C*), a check to determine whether the intention-related action program is complete and whether it can be maintained despite pressures from competing action tendencies. If these conditions hold, we are finally ready to initiate action. The actual initiator of an action is an action-launching impulse (*ALI*). Note that the competition for dominance among the tendencies and its implied cumulative effects—that is, the extent to which the strength of each waxes when nondominant and wanes when dominant—are the main problems addressed by *The Dynamics of Action* (Atkinson & Birch, 1970). Figure 10.1 summarizes our taxonomy of motivational variables along the pathway from wishes to actions.

DIFFERENT GOAL LEVELS AND THEIR INTERRELATIONS

So far, the object of wishes, wants, and intentions (i.e., the aim of actions) has been termed *goal;* however, goal is a notoriously ill-defined term in motivation theory. We define goal as the molar endstate whose attainment requires actions by the individual pursuing it. But these molar endstates of one's actions can mean quite different things. By and large, goals rest on three levels of endstates with an ascending hierarchical order. The first-order level refers to an *action*, the second-order level to the *outcome* of an action, and the third-order level to *consequences* of that outcome. Each of these three goal levels has its own focus of attention as well as its own types of valence.

On the first-order level the endstates are the activities themselves: the interest in, or the enjoyment of, doing something repetitively or continuously, because it provides excitement. Paradoxically, the endstate may result in an endless flux, in the experience of "flow," as Csikszentmihalyi (1975) termed it. On a second-order level the endstate is an action outcome with characteristics that are required or preset and that are inherently valuable. Finally, at the third-order level, the endstate refers to desirable consequences that might arise from an achieved outcome.

Kuhl (1983) designed a valence-potency-activation (*VPA*) model that distinguishes between the three goal levels in terms of planes of control. Before we discuss the interrelationships of the goal levels as control planes, let us add *relevance* as the fourth category to the *VPA* model. Figure 10.2 illustrates the basic skeleton of the model, which describes, in a shorthand version, the pathway stages leading from wishes to wants and intentions and then to actions, along with their various motivational variables and the three goal levels.

The model implies that processes at higher levels presuppose the structuring of the lower level(s). For instance, if wants are aimed at a third-order goal level

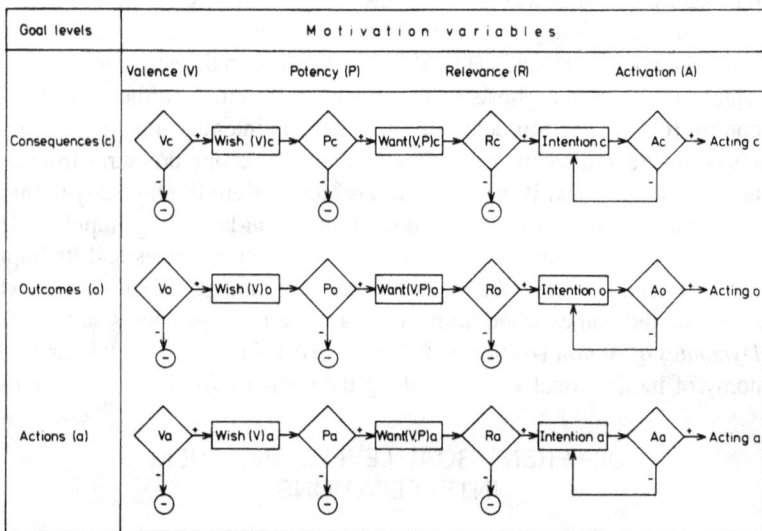

Fig. 10.2.   Skeleton model combining the three goal levels with the motivational variables on the pathway from wishes to action. (After Kuhl, 1983.)

(i.e., a particular consequence of an action outcome), complex motivational processes that include lower-level variables are implied. We call such a top-to-bottom elaboration *lower-level inclusion*. A considerable number of these processes through which wants are eventually transformed into intentions require the inclusion of lower-level variables of potency or expectancy and instrumentality.

Conversely, in the bottom-to-top direction, a lower-level goal can be enhanced by features of a higher-level endstate. Here we find a "higher-level overlap," a temporary overlap of various endstates. Lewin (1938) described this state as two "overlapping situations." For instance, an individual may enjoy a particular action as an end in itself, but may also perceive the action to be an instrumental step toward a desired goal: There is an inclusion of higher-order goal states. These higher-level overlaps may result in different kinds of motivation, such as: (1) an added incentive for attaining the initially pursued lower-level endstate; (2) a fluctuation of attention between the various attractions of two endstates at different goal levels; (3) rivalry between two endstates; (4) the overpowering of the initial (lower-level) endstate by a higher-level endstate, resulting in a qualitative change of motivation that Greene and Lepper (1977) described as undermining intrinsic pursuit by "overjustifying" consequences that diminish the originally intrinsic interest.

In the case of *higher-level overlap*, the actor focuses on a lower-level endstate (e.g., the joy of surfing), and includes, in addition to the valence of that endstate, the valence of the higher-level goal (e.g., winning a surfing competition). The associated expectancies are implicated. Otherwise, there would be no apparent contingency associated with the higher-level goal and, hence, no additional valence anticipated. Given the conditional probabilities, the additional valence of a higher-level overlap can be represented as expectancy or instrumentality in the form of two subscripts, which indicate which lower level leads to which higher level. For example, *Vao* represents the overlapping valence of outcome (*o*), when the lower-level endstate of action (*a*) is the primary object pursued but is also a determinant of that outcome.

In the case of *lower level inclusion*, the lower-level goals usually have no valence of their own. What intrinsic values they do have can be considered incidental to the higher-level overlap and should be treated in the manner previously suggested. Normally, lower level goals receive their valences from the higher-level goals to the extent to which the former influence the occurrence of the latter. One may therefore speak of "borrowed valences." They are borrowed on the basis of the particular expectancy (*E*) or instrumentality (*I*) variables. For instance, the valence of a successful examination (valence of an outcome, *Vo*) is determined by the instrumentality (*I*) associated with the desired admission to a higher level of education (consequence, *c*) and the valence of this consequence (*Vc*):

$$Vo \text{ (if a consequence is intended)} = f(o/c, Vc).$$

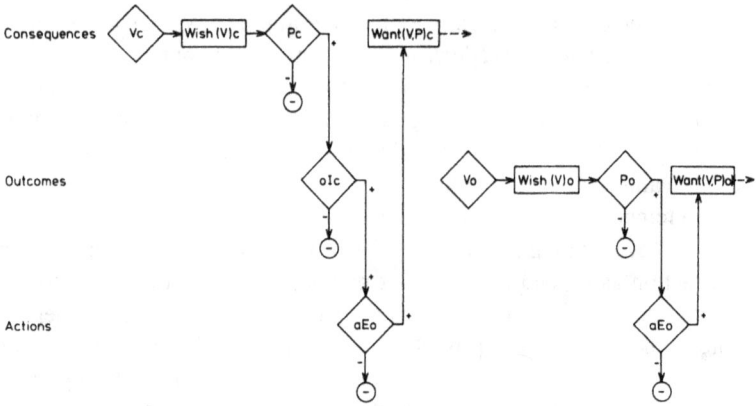

Fig. 10.3.   The two cases of *lower-level inclusion* in order to take account of the conditional subjective probabilities of the underlying instrumentality (*oIc*) and action-outcome expectancy (*aEo*).

Correspondingly, the valence of an action (e.g., to study for passing an exam) is a joint function of its subjective probability to success (*aEo*) in achieving the desired outcome and the valence of this outcome (passing the exam):

$$Va \text{ (if an outcome is intended)} = f\,(aEo,\ Vo).$$

Because lower-level goals borrow their valences from the higher level goals, and because their own contribution only consists of an expectancy variable (*aEo* or *oIc*), in lower level inclusion it suffices to consider the instrumentality or expectancy components of the lower level goals. Figure 10.3 outlines the two cases of lower level inclusion. The left side shows a two-step inclusion, descending from the goal level of consequences to the levels of outcomes and actions. The right side shows a one-step inclusion from the outcome level to the action level. Both cases correspond to the two examples given (i.e., admission to a higher level of education and passing an exam).

We can now better specify how wishes might evolve into intentions.

FROM WISHES TO INTENTIONS: PROCESS ORIENTED ANALYSIS

The evolution of a wish may be initiated at any one of the three goal levels postulated by our model (see Figure 10.2): at the level of perceived consequences, at the level of anticipated outcomes, or at the level of actions.

Top Spins

The first and most undifferentiated stage in the development of a motivational tendency consists merely of the valence associated with a goal; this is a first-order wish. As a rule, the development of a motivational tendency is stopped before it is transformed into a want or an intention if the next checkpoint has not (yet) been passed. At this stage, the motivational tendency has reached an impasse; the process is trapped in an "endless" loop, moving back and forth between the first stage of its development and the checkpoint that it cannot pass. We call this loop "top spin" (i.e., like a spinning top) and contend that top spins have an adaptive motivational function. They initiate and "nourish" preattentive processes such as those postulated by Neisser (1967). They work unobtrusively, usually unconsciously, and are peripheral to the focus of attention. In a way, a top spin functions like a vigilant lookout spotting all of the information that might be helpful in overcoming the obstacles in the developmental path of the wish. Once such information is encountered through perception, thinking, or imagination, there is an increased tendency to redirect attention and awareness to the impasse. Atkinson & Birch (1970) postulated similar effects for the latent-action tendencies. Moreover, top spins capture one's attention even if nothing else of importance is being done. They appear to determine how much of an individual's thinking time (including day dreaming) is devoted to the particular concern. Evidence for this assumption comes from the recent work of Klinger, Barta, and Maxeiner (1980) who report, among other findings, that frequency of thought content is more often associated with a threatened (as opposed to a secure) relationship and with unexpected difficulties in the presence of a special challenge.

This evidence suggests that top spins represent two kinds of states concurrently: a blocking of action and a preparation for action. Top spins may come to an end in the long run, but in the meantime, they provide each wish or want with a chance to survive. An unfulfilled motivational tendency is kept alive at precisely that checkpoint at which its worthwhileness and feasibility are questioned. Top-spinning wishes continue over time; hence, they are placeholders of hope. They prevent us from giving up too early on something that may come true some day.

Even in a top-spinning state, the *motivational function of a tendency* remains alive and is directed toward eventually attaining the goal. This need not be the only motivating function of wishes or wants, however. Individuals frequently indulge in wishful thinking for its own sake. There are motivational tendencies that provide considerable enjoyment while they are caught in a top spin. Care must be taken to prevent their further development, because if they do evolve into intentions, the source of the self-procured enjoyment is depleted. An example of this situation is the ardent wish of a middle-aged man to cross the Sahara

Desert on a motorcycle. He greatly enjoys imagining himself riding through the wild Sahara landscape; but he deliberately avoids moving toward the expectancy checkpoints because—as he frankly confesses—such scrutiny might confront him with a dilemma. The undertaking may turn out to be either too easy or too difficult to carry out. In the first case his wish will lose its thrill, and in the second case it will become dangerous because the wish will be transformed into an intention, leading to real behavior, which in turn might result in undesirable side effects. Normally, wishes are attracted to their anticipated endstates and proceed toward them accordingly.

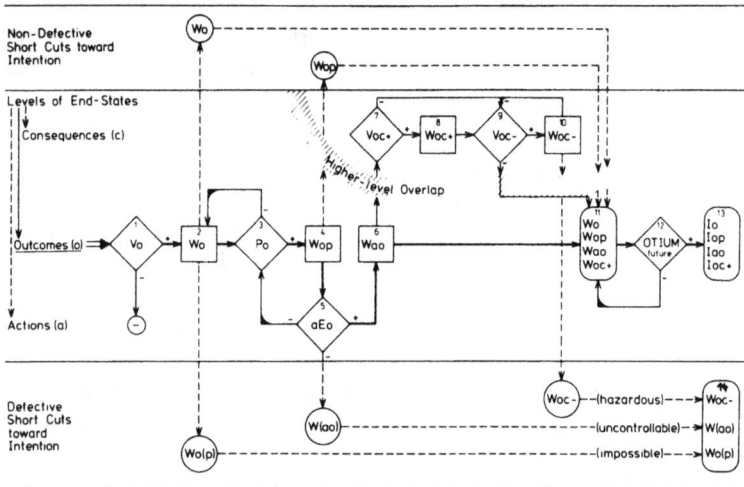

Fig. 10.4.   Flow chart of wish careers for outcome oriented goals.

Abbreviations frm left to right:

Vo = Valence of outcome

Wo = Wish, outcome oriented

Wo(p) = Outcome oriented wish with defective potency

Po = Potency, outcome oriented

Wop = Outcome oriented want, potency checked with positive result

aEo = Expectancy that action leads to outcome

W(ao) = Defective want, with defective action-outcome expectancy

Wao = Outcome oriented want, nondefective

Voc+ = Valence of a positive consequence, contingent on the desired outcome

Woc+ = Want referring to Voc+

Voc− = Valence of a negative consequence, contingent on the desired outcome

Woc− = Want referring to Voc−

Io, Iop, Iao, Ioc+ = Intention referring to Wo, Wop, Wao, Woc+, respectively

Short Cuts

We are not assuming that all newly emerging wishes proceed regularly along the path toward becoming wants and intentions—that is, that they are elaborated with respect to each aspect of valence, expectancy, and relevance. Such an expenditure will often appear unnecessary, particularly in the case of recurrent wishes with which the individual is already familiar. Here a "normal short cut" will be taken. The original wish proceeds nonelaborated and bypasses all remaining gatekeepers along the pathway toward intention (see dashed lines in the upper section of Figure 10.4).

As a rule, such "nondefective" short cuts lead to nonelaborated intentions. Later on, it may well turn out that the short cut was premature, because the requirement of a certain check en route could not have been met. Under such a condition the "normal" short cut is abandoned in favor of a more careful probing of the respective checks before the want proceeds on its path toward an intention. An elaboration is undertaken step by step from the beginning, where decisions of great importance have to be made, or where some aspects of value or expectancy have become more salient, or where one's self-confidence has just been undermined, particularly when the individual experiences self-doubts.

In contrast to "normal" short cuts are "defective" short cuts. Once the motivational process has been caught in a top spin, the longer such circuitry perseverates, the more likely it is that it will take a defective short cut en route to an intention. In other words, although the want is elaborated and perceived as unrealistic, hazardous, or, more generally, immature, it takes a short cut to the "store of defective wants," where it may become transformed into a defective (although elaborated) intention (see dashed lines in the lower section of Figure 10.4). This entails dysfunctional effects—that is, it creates top spins within the intention related section of the pathway to action, which we discuss later.

DEVELOPMENTAL PATH OF WISHES AT THE DIFFERENT GOAL LEVELS

Let us trace the developmental path of a wish in greater detail. We start with the intermediate level of outcome oriented goals before turning to the lower level of action goals and the higher level of consequence goals. The development of wishes at the goal level of *outcomes* is the only one that entails the elaborations of both lower-level inclusion and higher-level overlap, as can be seen in Figure 10.4. Let us trace the pathway in detail. (In the following discussion we use the numbers referring to the boxes in Figure 10.4.) The motivational process starts, as always, with a positive evaluation of the valence of the desired endstate, in this case the desired outcome. If the valence Vo of that outcome exceeds a critical magnitude, a first-order wish that is conceived of as a remote, fantasy-like wish has been generated (see Box 2).

Depending on conditions that are unspecified in the outline of our flow chart (Figure 10.4), this first-order wish (Wo) may be quickly transformed into an intentional format—that is, it may assume the self-committing quality of an intention after it has passed the checkpoint of OTIUM future (12). There may be several reasons for such a nondefective short cut (see dashed lines in Figure 10.4)—for example, an extremely high level of motivation to attain the desired outcome. Other factors that facilitate circumventing the typical path include situational (including social) pressure to produce the goal state in question, time pressure, and suddenly arising opportunity.

If the first-order wish does not follow a short cut, the next step is an assessment of the potency of the desired outcome (Po)—that is, the (unconditional) probability that one will be able to perform an action that will produce the outcome (3). If this subjective probability exceeds a critical magnitude, the first-order wish is transformed from its fantasy-like state to a reality oriented want. At all goal levels of wish development, the model accounts for the possibility that wants may take a (nondefective) short-cut route toward this point. If Po is below the critical probability, the model assumes a regression to assessment of the valence of the outcome. If this assessment results in a positive evaluation of the valence of the desired outcome (as it did before), assessment of Po is repeated; if it has the same negative result, the motivational process is caught in an "end-less" loop. A top spin (3–2–3) has arisen. Eventually, this top spin may "free" itself by taking a defective short cut toward an intention, becoming a rather crude and fantasy-ridden wish, pressing to be transformed into the "intentional for-mat" (discussed next) and to be given access to action $(Wo\ (p))$.

In the event that the potency of the outcome Po has been positively evaluated (4), the last chance to make a nondefective short cut toward intention (Wop) is encountered. Note that such a short cut, following a positive potency check, is quite natural provided nothing else about the want is perceived as unclear or unusual. Otherwise, the analysis proceeds to the lower level, including a check of the (conditional) probability that one is able to achieve the desired outcome by some action (aEo). An unsatisfactory outcome may give rise to another top spin (4–5–3–4); again, the wish may eventually break out of its spin, taking another defective short cut toward an intention, $(W(ao)$, a somewhat hopeless pursuit, because the desired outcome is perceived to be beyond reach.

If action-outcome expectancy (5) has also been evaluated, the first-order want reaches a more focused state, that of advanced wants (Wao). There is no longer any doubt that the desirable outcome can be achieved if one is determined to achieve it. There may, however, still be some uncertainty about potential conse-quences (positive and negative) of the desired outcome. The motivational pro-cess may therefore enter into a higher-level-overlap analysis—that is, analysis moves from the outcome level to the level of consequences. In addition to a standard desire to reduce uncertainty about outcome consequences, some indi-viduals have a high utility orientation. They tend to justify every intention and action by seeking additional payoffs—that is, they usually engage in higher-level overlap to seek additional valence.

It is either this utility orientation or desire for a reduction of uncertainty that motivates an examination of positive ($Voc+$) and negative ($Voc-$) consequences. The valence of each consequence is considered—that is, the conditional probability (instrumentality) that the outcome will lead to the desired consequence is assessed (Boxes 7 and 9). If these checks result in a positive evaluation, an advanced want, with a valence increment ($Woc+$), develops. In contrast, the anticipation of a negative side effect decreases the resulting valence (e.g., when the violation of a moral norm is felt in advance as a qualm). In such a case, the advanced want ($Woc-$), blocked from its natural career, enters a top spin (10–9–10), unless it seeks access to action via a defective short cut toward a somewhat hazardous intention. Note that this last defective short cut appears to be generally more commendable or feasible than the two earlier ones.

Finally, the various routes taken by these wishes lead to a "store for developed wants." For the sake of clarity, we have distinguished two substores, one for nondefective wants (11), and the other for defective ones (14), which have not been blocked by top spin. Note that the "developed" wants in both substores differ considerably in their developmental maturity. Among the nondefective wants, two incorporate short cuts and may turn out to be premature (Wo more so than Wop). The other two advanced wants (Wao, Woc+) are fully developed and should be able to stand the test of reality. Similar distinctions can be made for the three defective short-cut wants.

The eventual fate of the defective wants are discussed in a later section. Nondefective wants, on the other hand, are transformed into intentions of the appropriate types (13) provided they withstand the test of the OTIUM-future assessments (12). If not, they are caught in a top spin from which they cannot escape unless the perceived opportunity to establish the desired outcome (OTIUM future) becomes more advantageous. To complicate matters, it is also possible to change the OTIUM conditions to better meet their demands. For instance, one may seek out situations that offer additional opportunities: One may rearrange one's schedule, look for more appropriate means to attain the goal, or enhance the perceived importance and urgency of the desired goal by self-persuasion (or even self-deception). In a later section we present a more detailed discussion of such self-control activities, which facilitate the enactment of intentions.

EMPIRICAL SUPPORT FOR THE WISH RELATED SECTION OF THE MODEL

So far we have constructed a wish-career model without basing it on direct empirical evidence concerning short cuts and top spins. To some extent, however, it is based on the distinction between the three goal levels, which can hardly be dismissed as a phenomenological fact. Moreover, we based our model on an expanded logic of the value-expectancy approach as detailed in an extended model of motivation (Heckhausen, 1977).

The most significant, though indirect, empirical support comes from Klinger's recent work on the covariation between motivational variables (such as incentive value, expectancy and imminence of the goal) and frequency of daily thought content (Klinger et al., 1980). Klinger et al. found that people spend most of their thinking time on those "things" (goals) that have high incentive values or a high likelihood of success (without an interaction effect of both variables). At first glance this finding suggests that thoughts are focused more on the goals of smoothly progressing wishes—that is, on those without any top spins. Because, however, the authors have not specified when and under what conditions individuals become committed to their goals (onset of a current concern), we do not know the extent to which the reported correlations refer to concerns that are no longer wants, concerns that have already attained the status of intentions. It is easy to imagine that intentions for imminent actions, in pursuit of valuable and probable goals, consume a relatively large portion of an individual's thinking time, because the action is mentally prepared or because the affective state of goal attainment is already being anticipated.

More direct evidence has been found in support of top-spinning wants. As already mentioned, threatened relationships, unexpected difficulties, and special challenges are thought about most often, whereas routine activities—although requiring steady coping—do not demand much thought.

Among the motivational attributes of the current concerns, the authors identify three variables that are close to some of the criteria for our OTIUM check: nearness in time (to attaining the goal), time available (within which it is still possible to attain the goal), and means (uncertain or in need of change). Nearness in time as well as time available (a sort of urgency) correlated significantly with thinking time spent on concerns (whereas uncertain means correlated only slightly). This relationship confirms that the OTIUM criteria of imminence of opportunity, time, and urgency make a difference. When it has attained the status of an intention, goal striving provokes more (conscious) thought than do the precursory stages of wish development.

Interview Data

As these findings demonstrate, thought-sampling studies are undoubtedly an appropriate method to validate our wish-career model. Primarily, we regard it as a heuristic and experiment-provoking tool. In a first attempt we simply used the model as a basis for a semistructured interview about "wishes" in everyday language (without defining the term *wish*). Our subjects of different ages and occupations enjoyed being interviewed about some of their long-standing wishes. Here we use some selected materials for descriptive purposes only, before we go on to extend our model to cover the developmental career of intentions as initiators of appropriate actions.

Let us take the case of a 33-year-old woman. One of her main wishes is "to read." Her goal is not the joy of reading itself, but the benefits to be derived from reading (outcomes): gaining more knowledge, having more education, and becoming more informed, particularly about politics. The expected consequence of such desired outcomes is a general improvement in her lifestyle by knowing what to think and how to act. This goal structure clearly reveals a higher level overlap. Because, however, knowledge and level of education are not only instrumental for improving one's lifestyle, but are also ends in themselves, outcome orientation is the goal level of wish development, even though the outcome facilitates the attainment of valued higher level goals.

The woman buys several books and subscribes to a newspaper. All of these efforts are futile, however, because she has difficulty concentrating on the material and recalling what she has read. She feels tired and stressed after her daily work. She would like to have more free time. When the wish is only 6 months old, it undergoes a rather dramatic development. Applying the interview data to our model, the wish proceeds rapidly to the state of a want (*Wop*), makes a short cut toward intention, passes the OTIUM-future check, is transformed into an intention, and gains access to action. What appears to have been transferred into performance, however, degenerates to the wish-developing stage, where it begins a premature short cut toward an intention. The premature short cut results in a "degenerated want." This phenomenon is discussed later.

Action Centered Wish Development

Before discussing the next example from our interview data, we have to consider a case that differs from the one described in Figure 10.4 in that wish development is initiated at the goal level of *action*. At this level the developmental path from a wish to an intention is rather straightforward. There are only two steps, valence and potency, before a wish reaches the maturity check of OTIUM future and is transformed into an intentional format. (Only a negative potency check might result in a top spin.) For example, suppose someone likes to go skiing on nearby mountains, but there is a lack of snow. If the person does not consider weather conditions, he may just take his skis and drive to the mountain site. In this case he would be acting on the basis of a nondefective short cut to intention, but he would find, after his arrival, that he should have checked the potency variables at home. His wish to ski may be so strong, however, that a defective short cut toward intention ensues. He might not give up, but might stay at the mountain site.

Because action oriented goals belong to the lowest level within the functional hierarchy of goal strivings, considerable higher-level overlap may accrue and intervene before the want store or OTIUM future is reached. On the outcome level, a positive or negative outcome may attach itself to the positive valence of the action. If the attached outcome valence is also positive, one may wonder whether one's interest in the activity itself is genuine and not "overjustified." It has been assumed that a self-attribution of overjustification reduces interest in the activity per se and undermines intrinsic motivation for it (cf. Greene & Lepper, 1977).

To illustrate the course of a developing wish on the goal level of action, we report material from a 25-year-old woman. Since childhood this woman has found extraordinary enjoyment in dancing. After much practice, she has developed considerable skill. All music evokes her desire to dance. She feels the wish to dance nearly every day. The valence of dancing is in a deeply felt harmony with her body, as it expresses her feelings. But now that she is in college, she has no partner. Her boyfriends do not dance. She feels that she is too old and too advanced in her dancing to seek a partner by enrolling in a dancing class. To avoid limiting herself to the substitute activity of singing, she must find a partner who is an excellent dancer and sympathetic to her need, but who does not misunderstand her intentions as seeking a love relationship. She expects such a misunderstanding to be a nearly unavoidable negative consequence of having the opportunity to satisfy her wish. She has already had two such negative experiences. She hopes to be approached by a male amateur dancer who has the same problem. Because this hope is rather vague, she has halfway resolved to use the next opportunity to approach a potential partner, although she feels quite uneasy about doing so. That is the present situation. According to the model, the top spin has stopped at the goal level of consequences in favor of a defective short cut toward a hazardous intention. Whether this intention will ever be executed is questionable.

Consequence Centered Wish Development

The next examples from our interview data illustrate the case in which wish development is initiated on the goal level of *consequences*. Goals at this level represent purposive striving, which works over longer periods of time. Moreover, such goals are prototypically human and require some ontogenetic development to unfold. Goals at the level of consequence cannot be achieved as direct action outcomes. At best, they can be induced by appropriate action outcomes.

Pursuing goals at the consequence level, one, therefore, faces a twofold problem. First, one has to make sure which outcomes of potential actions induce the desired consequence with the highest probability. This question relates to instrumentality. As a rule, several outcomes can eventually lead to the desired consequence. Beyond selecting the action outcome that, in terms of its consequences, has the highest instrumentality (and that is sufficiently under one's command), there is the second problem of ascertaining which secondary consequences each alternative outcome might have and whether such side effects could prove detrimental. In summary, to select the best strategy, various outcome options have to be elaborated and suspended, in terms of their instrumentalities as well as their side effects. This process requires the elaboration of partial solutions, their suspension, a reversal in viewing the problem, and the selection of the outcome best able to induce the desired consequence.

Let us again give some examples from our interviews. Consequence oriented wishes and wants can be simple or rather complex. We first discuss a simple one—namely, a wish pursued by a 35-year-old man who has a handicapped son. For 8 years the man has wanted to obtain an additional source of income to provide greater security for his handicapped son. The expensive hotels at the sea site where he and his family usually vacation inspired him to build a house that he can rent out. His main interest is the payoff of having an investment to provide an additional source of income—that is, the instrumentality of the house, not its intrinsic value.

The man does not see any negative instrumentalities. The only barrier is that he does not yet have enough money to build the house; therefore, an insufficient expectancy to attain the action outcome throws his wish into a top spin. That circularity, however, does not limit his wish related preparatory activities, such as looking for suitable property. Asked what must happen in order to attain his goal, he points to winning a prize in the lottery.

Our interview data showed that, next to lack of time, lack of money was the most frequent reason given for the blockage of wish development. Surprisingly, people did not feel that lack of funds or time represented an ultimate barrier to attaining the goal. Lack of money or time does not appear to be a sufficient reason to abandon wishes involving demands on money or time. Obviously, the social function of lotteries is to provide a chance to win—even if one may be reluctant ever to try. Perhaps that opportunity is why lotteries are so important in the lives of so many people. They prevent innumerable wishes from going bankrupt, because lack of money only makes wishes top spin; it does not starve them. In the case of lack of time, people are confident that getting older will provide them with plenty of time, so that wishes blocked by scarcity of time also top spin rather than disappear.

Another example is the somewhat more complex case of a 35-year-old civil servant in the national railway system. His main goal is to be promoted because, on the next level of the administrative hierarchy, he will be assigned managerial duties, instead of his present clerical work. In addition, he will get a higher salary. But he has to wait longer than usual—5 years—for the next promotion because of an austere savings policy instituted by the railway.

What can this man do to attain the promotion earlier rather than simply wait for the preordained consequence associated with becoming 40 years old? He envisions three actions that might lead him to his goal earlier: First, use strategies to stand out positively and thus have an advantage over his colleagues; second, apply for a transfer to another region with chances for earlier promotion; third, look for a management job in a private firm. He rejects the last option because he thinks the likelihood of getting hired during the present recession is too low. He can achieve the other two outcome options, standing out among his colleagues and transferring to another region, without encountering serious obstacles. Also, their instrumentalities for a promotion in less than 5 years cannot be questioned. But each of these outcomes, viewed from the perspective of its achieved state, is associated with additional consequences in the form of undesirable side effects. Excelling among his colleagues will arouse their anger and envy and will disturb good working relationships. Transferring to another region will separate him from his family and his home and will create many other inconveniences.

Therefore, he abstains from any intention to engage in action directed toward attaining the desired promotion before reaching the age at which it becomes fairly automatic. He just waits. His original wish has developed into a want (because he knows that he *could* make it come true), but this want is being blocked in the case of two options by the check for negative side effects (see stage 10 in Figure 10.4), and in the case of a third option by an insufficient action-outcome expectancy (see stage 5 in Figure 10.4). In other words, the dead-end paths of this "abandoned" want keep in motion three different top spins, which render the man more cognitively responsive to cues associated with these dead-end paths.

PRE- AND POST COMMITMENT PROCESSES: MOTIVATION VERSUS VOLITION

Let us now trace the intention related section of the pathway to action along which self-regulatory processes mediate the enactment of intentions. The first part of the pathway in Figure 10.5 departs from that of wish development as shown for the outcome related goal level in Figure 10.4. Nondefective and

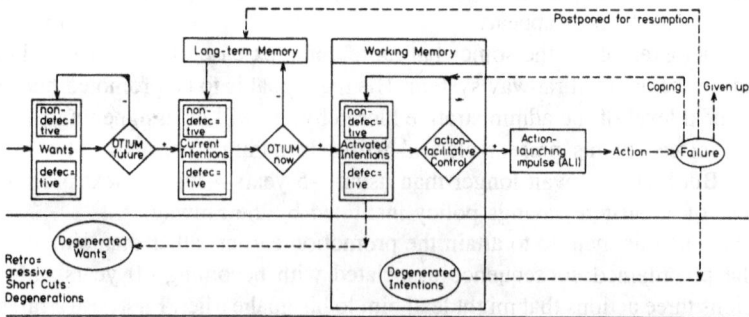

Fig. 10.5.   Flow chart of want careers within the intention related section of the pathway of wishes to action.

defective wants that have passed the check of OTIUM future are transformed into the respective intentions that assume the quality of a current self-commitment. We may therefore speak of "current intentions."

Self-commitment is the demarcation line that separates wants from intentions. In the following we want to show that this demarcation sets apart two distinct processes—namely *motivation* and *volition* (cf. Kuhl, in press). Motivation refers to all elaborations of values and expectancies and their integration. Once the elaborating processes of motivation have run their course or have ceased, leaving behind an invitation to action, self-commitment initiates the volition process that leads to an eventual enactment of the resulting intention in due time and at the appropriate occasion.

A quality that distinguishes intentions from wants is their fixedness as opposed to the fluid state of wants. Intentions represent the final stage after their associated goals have undergone multiple expectancy-value checks and weightings. We should mention that Lewin (1951) acknowledged a process in decision making that mediates between motivation and action, and that, at the same time, freezes a formerly fluid state.

Furthermore, there are puzzling contradictions to well-founded motivational rules or "facts." We list three such contradictions that will lose their puzzling character once the distinction between motivation and volition has been made.

First, according to Atkinson's (1957) Risk-Taking Model, tasks of intermediate difficulty evoke a maximal strength of motivation and should therefore also be performed with the highest degree of effort and persistence, producing top performance. However, Locke's (1968) data indicate that raising the level of aspiration—that is, choosing tasks of higher than intermediate difficulty—resulted in increased performance levels. (It should be added that Locke preferably used speeded tasks.) This apparent deviation from the Risk-Taking Model led Locke (1975) to conclude that "expectancy theories" of motivation cannot be reconciled with "goal oriented theories." However, they can be reconciled. Atkinson's model was designed to predict choice of task difficulty—that is, the outcome of predecisional motivation processes. In contrast, Locke assigned tasks of high difficulty levels to some of his subjects, or enticed them to choose high risks. Thereby, he induced postdecisional processes of volition that mobilized effort and persistence in order to cope with the difficulties of mastering the intended task. This increase in the strength of volition proportionate to an encountered increase of task difficulty was identified by Ach as early as 1910. He called it the "Difficulty Law of Motivation."

Second, Unzner and Schneider (1984) presented preschool children with boxes of increasing weights. The smallest of these could be easily lifted, the biggest one was too heavy to lift. When these children had to predict whether they would be able to lift the various boxes, their mean decision time was longest for the box of intermediate weight. Here they also displayed the most changes in fixation as they scanned from box to box. However, when they were asked to lift each box, their latency in starting locomotion and the speed of the approach toward the respective box increased with the weight of the box (and the perceived inability to lift it). Again, predecisional motivation and postdecisional volition follow different laws. In the motivational case of expectancy, latency is an inverted U function of task difficulty, indicating uncertainty about the possible outcomes of alternative choices. In the volitional case of the initiation of an assigned action, latency is an increasing monotonous function with respect to task difficulty, indicating one's confidence of success in pursuing the set goal.

Third, indirect support for the distinction between motivation and volition comes from the differential effects of imagining "behavioral scripts" (C. A. Anderson, 1983). Imagining that one performs, or does not perform, a certain target behavior produces corresponding intentions to act or not to act (volitional process), but does not (!) change the perceived value of the consequences of that target behavior (motivational process).

FROM INTENTIONS TO ACTION: SELF-REGULATORY PROCESSES

A current intention has to meet the check of OTIUM now. If it does not, the current intention is transferred to long-term memory. Stored in long-term memory, it keeps the characteristic of a "current concern" (Klinger, 1971) and is activated whenever a situation is encountered in which the criteria of OTIUM now (i.e., for performing the intended action) are met. A current intention has then acquired the status of an "activated" intention. At this stage an intention presumably elicits control processes that are likely to facilitate action based on the activated intention.

Several types of control processes have to be distinguished. First, if two or more intentions have been activated, a decision has to be made as to which alternative has priority in access to behavior and how the execution of two or more intentions should be combined or scheduled in a sequential order.

Setting-related relevance is a case in which, simply because of a change in setting, an originally nondominant action tendency of an intention may gain priority. This change can be brought about intentionally either by modifying the present situation or by seeking another setting with relevant opportunities. In both cases, appropriate goal levels are changed and the corresponding strength in tendencies reverses. For instance, an individual may turn a nondominant tendency to work into a dominant one by entering into, or by generating, a work setting.

A second class of control processes consists of sticking to a goal once it has been chosen for imminent action. The activated intention is shielded from competing intentions or action tendencies. For instance, when competing options or inhibitory concerns are to be warded off, the anticipated incentive value of the intended goal may be increased by reflecting on the positive aspects of goal attainment. Kuhl (in press) has presented a detailed theoretical analysis of various action-control processes of this sort, the so-called "action orientation."

A special case in point is the postdecisional conflict discussed by Festinger (1964). Festinger assumed that the "spreading" in the attractiveness of choice alternatives results in dissonance reduction that is preceded by "regret" (the opposite of spreading). Individuals who have made a difficult decision start to reduce a postdecisional conflict by focusing attention on negative properties of the chosen alternative and on the positive properties of the rejected alternative. This initial reappraisal is associated with "regret." After sufficient consideration has been given, however, dissonance reduction takes over, producing a preponderance of subjective values for the chosen alternative (Brehm & Wicklund, 1970; Walster, 1964). In traditional cognitive-dissonance theory, this shift is explained by a tendency for cognitive consistency. An alternative explanation, however, employs a volitional principle that facilitates the continuation of the present course of action. Beckmann and Irle (in press) have reinterpreted these findings from cognitive-dissonance research as evidence for behaviors that are motivated by action control—that is, facilitating the continuation of the chosen course of action.

Third, individuals may possess knowedge about the nature and the effects of some types of control processes. If, in addition, they are able to apply their knowledge in the form of self-motivating strategies, they make use of what has been called "metavolitions" (Heckhausen, in press). Metavolitions represent a rather sophisticated form of self-regulatory processes.

Another function of these control processes, beyond facilitation of action, is their scrutiny of defective components of the activated intention. Remember that activated intentions may have arisen from short cuts to intention (cf. Figure 10.4). Whether these short cuts have been perceived as nondefective or as defective, their effect may be so serious that the imminent beginning of action appears to be undesirable unless the impairment is removed—or at least alleviated. When this removal does not appear possible, the activated intention is blocked from access to behavior. It starts a top spin within working memory, taking up some of its capacity and thereby reducing the efficiency of intellectual activities. Eventually, the impairment resulting from a top-spinning control process may be overcome by the defective, activated intention's regressing to an earlier stage of intention development—namely to a degenerated want. This retrogression means, among other things, that the "frozen" state of an intention has returned to a fluid state.

The retrogressive relapse of an intention into a degenerated want after being activated for performance is not a rare event. Consider how many intentions to perform an action melt away as soon as one approaches the moment of their execution. One begins to discover uncertainties, negative prospects, and prohibitive aspects. Apparently, this had repeatedly happened to our young woman respondent who looked for a dancing partner but was afraid that her intentions might be misunderstood as seeking a love relationship.

If the control processes are successful, an "action-launching impulse" (*ALI*) is activated that initiates the intended action. *ALI* is an activation process that has been identified by early motivation theorists. Ach (1910) spoke of it as the "*aktuelle Moment*" and William James (1890) called it the "*Fiat*."

Finally, the initiated action may result in failure, preventing attainment of the intended goal. As a consequence, the respective intention is either abandoned or maintained. In the latter case there are several options: Either the resumption of the intention is postponed until a later, still unknown, time (i.e., the intention is transferred to long-term memory); or the individual immediately begins to cope with the failure by reinitiating action-facilitating processes before pursuing the goal again. Another possibility is maintaining the intention but avoiding the scrutiny of control processes: The intention regresses to the stage of an activated intention and maintains its defective structure without attempt at improvement. In the case of such a retrogressive short cut, we may speak of a "degenerated intention," analogous to the degenerated want. In contrast to the latter, however, a degenerated intention occupies some space in the working memory, as does a top-spinning, activated intention. As we discuss shortly, there are certain experiences (particularly a depressing string of failures) and certain personality dispositions that lead to degenerated intentions (see Kuhl, 1983; Kuhl, in press).

DEFECTIVE AND DEGENERATED INTENTIONS

We have already seen that the control processes (Figure 10.5) will eventually identify defects that stem from progressive short cuts along the developmental pathway to action. A potency component may be insufficient, a value component aversive, whether this has already been identified (defective short cuts) or ignored (nondefective short cuts). If the defect cannot be removed, a retrogressive short cut eventually ensues. Therefore, we speak of a *degeneration* on the way to action.

In contrast, a *defect* arises wittingly or unwittingly only from progressive short cuts. When a want assumes the status of the current or activated intention it may be defective, but it cannot be degenerated. As we have seen, a degenerated intention is a later stage that presupposes the test of reality—that is, the repeated failure of one's actions. Defective wishes and wants, however, are eliminated at an earlier point on the way to action. They then belong to the final dregs of wishful thinking, the residual garbage of motivational life.

When, after failure, some part of the activated intention becomes ill defined or is lost altogether, the intention degenerates. The temporal determination for OTIUM now, for instance, may degenerate if someone intends to mow the lawn "each Saturday" and repeatedly fails to do so ("I will do it some time").

After repeatedly failing to succeed in a task, all action alternatives available may have proven unsuccessful. The intention to solve the task may be given up or may degenerate. If the actor retains the intention even though it cannot be carried out, it may impair the enactment of future intentions.

The debilitating effect of degenerating intentions is to be expected because of the high priority that they presumably have for accessing the working memory. As a result, degenerated intentions take up memory capacity that may be needed for the processing of new (nondegenerated) intentions. Phenomenologically, this demand for memory capacity may result in ruminating thoughts about a nonattainable goal state, about past failures, or about currently experienced (e.g., emotional) consequences of past failures (cf. Heckhausen, 1982a). Attention is focused on past, present, or future *states* rather than on actions that may bring about a change. This process has been called *state orientation* as opposed to *action orientation* (Kuhl, 1982a).

The woman who wants to educate herself by reading political-science literature serves to exemplify such a degenerated intention. She has failed repeatedly to devote her evenings to her self-assigned readings. She has tried hard to schedule herself, even declining evening invitations. Although this did not help, she maintains her intention. Thus, she struggles in vain every evening. Regular reading of the newly subscribed newspaper is her substitute activity for the unsatisfied outcome goal of improving her educational level.

IMPAIRING EFFECTS OF DEFECTIVE AND DEGENERATED INTENTIONS

A series of experiments has been conducted to test various implications of a theory of action control that has been incorporated in the present model (Kuhl, in press). Although these experiments were designed to investigate intention related pathways (Figure 10.1), they also revealed some information bearing on wish development during the preintentional stages.

In one recent experiment (Kuhl & Helle, in preparation), the assumption was tested that depression may be associated with frequent degenerated intentions claiming access to working memory. Specifically, it was assumed that depressives are more likely to encode action related memory structures in an intentional format; that is, depressives frequently use defective or nondefective short cuts to intentions rather than develop want related top spins. In other words, for depressives, any want may quickly assume the self-committing quality that characterizes the transition from want to intention.

To test this assumption, depressives and nondepressive control subjects were confronted individually with an instruction designed to increase the likelihood that a top spin of an activated intention (a defective intention) would develop. Subjects were told that they should clean up a desk on which things such as files, computer cards, manuscripts, and pencils were scattered. In addition, subjects were told that they could not start this task immediately because several tests would have to be done first. It would be up to them to decide when they had an opportunity to clean up the desk during the course of the experiment. This part of the instructions was designed to leave the realization of the intention (when to clean up the desk) unspecified. It was expected that under these circumstances, nondepressive subjects would not develop full-blown self-committing intentions or—if they did so during the first part of the instruction—they would transform these intentions back into less committing wish related formats (''I may want to do it whenever an opportunity arises.''). In contrast, depressives were expected to hold onto the intentional format even though the context node was ill defined. As a result, depressives should show more reduction in memory capacity because of the high priority assigned to the clean-up intention that, as a top spin, continuously occupied some mental space in the working memory.

The results lent strong support to this proposition. Various measures of short-term memory capacity that were obtained following the clean-up instruction indicated a significant drop in memory capacity for subjects with depressive symptoms assigned to the experimental condition (compared to depressives assigned to a control condition in which they were confronted with the desk without being told to clean it up). This difference in short-term memory capacity between the experimental and the control condition was not found in any of the nondepressive control groups (which had scored below the median on Beck's Depression Inventory; Beck, 1979). Postexperimental self-reports revealed that depressive subjects assigned to the experimental condition thought more often about cleaning up the desk than nondepressive subjects.

Interestingly enough, several studies yielded substantial correlations between depression scores and the score on a questionnaire constructed to assess a personal disposition to become state oriented (Kuhl, in press). These results suggest that the passivity, characteristic of many forms of depression, may be in part attributable to the fact that depressives find it more difficult to clear their working memories of intentions that cannot be carried out. Hence, the development and enactment of new intentions that could be carried out is rendered more and more difficult.

That depressives are unable to carry out intended actions and become preoccupied with the desired goal states does not imply that they are persistent in their behavior. Recent experimental evidence suggests that depressives, although they are more concerned about failure, are less persistent than nondepressives in maintaining their goal estimates following experimentally induced failure (Kanfer, Hagerman, & Smith, 1983). In terms of the extended valence-potency-activation model (Figure 10.2), depressives seem to be characterized by a discrepancy between their rather low persistence on the specific action related level and their extremely high persistence on the rather general consequence related goal level. Although they give up behaviorally, after only one or two failures, they may retain the desired consequences even after experiencing numerous failures that show those consequences to be virtually unattainable. Such a discrepancy of persistence between the goal levels of action and consequence is, of course, prone to produce degenerated intentions.

The study by Kanfer et al. (1983) also yielded some evidence that suggests that the typical depressive's pattern of responding to failure cannot be generalized across all behavioral categories. Their results showed that depressives' responses to failure (e.g., giving up at the behavioral level) occurred only in an experimental condition in which the task was described as being related to some personally relevant current concerns (which were assessed in advance). The depressives' tendency to short cut steps of wish development and to develop defective or degenerated intentions may be restricted to those actions that are related to personally relevant concerns (e.g., social interaction, achievement).

In personally *irrelevant* areas, depressives may be characterized by an excessive degree of wish production, but many of these wishes are never actually transformed into behavioral intentions and carried out. Wants that are blocked at some stage of wish development should, according to our model, create top spins that, because of their low priority value, enter into consciousness only when the working memory is not occupied by some current intention that is to be enacted.

Another series of experiments yielded support for the assumption that an excessive perseveration of cognitions relates to unattainable goals, interfering with task performance especially when the task at hand is rather complex and requires a considerable amount of processing capacity (Kuhl, 1982b; Kuhl & Weiss, 1983). In one experiment, performance deficits on a "test task" in state oriented subjects, following repeated, experimentally produced failures on a "training task," could be reversed when subjects were asked to verbalize their hypotheses regarding the solution to the problem throughout the training phase.

On the basis of our model of wish development, this result may be interpreted as follows: Explicitly verbalizing the problem-solving process may encourage subjects to avoid short cuts in processing task related wants. A more elaborate processing of task related wants increases the likelihood that uncontrollable wants are identified and prevented from being transformed into the attention-demanding format of activated intentions. As a result, one would expect a decrease of the performance deficits caused by the persistent intentions to solve (unsolvable) tasks that were failed in the past.

OUTLOOK

The empirical evidence of the effects of defective and degenerated intentions confirms the way we have conceptualized fluctuations in the development of wishes, wants, and intentions before they evolve into action. We have not restricted our discussion to the selection between tendencies that already exist; we have traced the gradual development until selection can take place.

But what happens once an activated intention has finally gained access to action? Our approach can be extended to encompass the questions of how ongoing action is sequenced, monitored, and guided. Not only must the ongoing action be shielded from competing intentions, it must also be maintained at an appropriate pace. The self-regulatory processes for an appropriate course of action require standards of execution for each subsequent action unit and its intermediate outcome until the main outcome has been attained. In achievement-motivation research, standards of excellence, or levels of aspiration, are concepts with a long-standing tradition. They have been used to explain task choice before the initiation of action and self-evaluation once action has been completed. It is surprising that continuous monitoring and evaluation of an ongoing action has rarely been explained in terms of the notion of a standard of excellence (but see Kanfer & Hagermann, 1981). As semantic network theory appears to yield an adequate representation for developing motivational tendencies, it might also provide an adequate code for standards that monitor ongoing action.

Our theoretical speculation also leads us to suspect that the individual represents a system with an extensive but limited capacity for converting wishes and intentions into action. Perhaps even the number of top spins that can be harbored without negative effects is limited.

Several questions relate to these issues. Are there mismatches between the (daily, weekly) production rate of wishes and wants, and their transformation into intentions, as well as between the production rate of intentions and their transition into action? If there are, under what conditions do they occur? Does the overproduction of wishes, wants, or intentions lead to a blocking by the OTIUM check, or conversely, does underproduction lead to lowered control thresholds along the path to action? Or is, perhaps in addition, the frequency of action correspondingly changed? Is there such a thing as motivational under- or overload for an individual's capacity for action? Is the over- or underproduction of wishes, wants, and intentions—or the overproduction of top spins, of degenerated wishes, wants, and intentions—associated with psychopathological states? Do changes in the processing capacity of wishes, wants, intentions, and actions relate in a normative way to segments of the life span?

These are intriguing questions. The circuitous route to action presumably obscures some possible insights that can only be gained if one considers the individual as a continuous processor of motivational information, if one conceptualizes the base rate of the production of wishes, wants, and intentions, as well as their transferral into action, as a comprehensive system with, among other features, some constraints on its processing capacities.

ACKNOWLEDGMENTS

The authors acknowledge helpful comments on an earlier version of the manuscript by David Birch, Eric Klinger, Peter Leppmann, and the two editors of this volume.

11 The Dynamics of Intention

Virginia Blankenship
Oakland University

INTRODUCTION

The Heckhausen and Kuhl model outlines a complex relationship between thought and action. A great amount of time spent thinking about doing something does not always indicate a great amount of time spent actually doing that activity. Top spins, perseverations in thought, are indicative of inaction. The relationship between thought and action has particular importance in research on motivation in which projective techniques are used for measuring individual differences in motives. Research that led to the development of the Thematic Apperception Test (TAT) for measurement of motives demonstrated a direct relationship between thoughts and actions, that the more a person thinks about achievement the more that person writes about achievement and the more his or her actions reflect achievement interests (cf. McClelland, Atkinson, Clark, & Lowell, 1953). I wish to focus on the importance of this question of the relationship between thoughts and actions in this discussion chapter by outlining the dynamics of action theory of Atkinson and Birch (1970), the most fully developed theory of action that has originated in the United States, and by contrasting the treatment of thought-to-action in this theory with the cognitive model outlined by Heckhausen and Kuhl. It should be pointed out in the beginning that these two models focus on different points in the sequence from wish (or motive) to action. The Heckhausen and Kuhl model brings the person up to action, and the Atkinson and Birch model has the person engaged in continuous action. Despite this difference, the relationship between thought and action is explicitly developed in both theories, and I believe that it will be beneficial to explore the extent to which these two theories of action can accommodate each other.

THE DYNAMICS OF ACTION MODEL

In the Atkinson and Birch (1970) dynamic model of action, the person is viewed as being engaged in a stream of behavior that is characterized by changes in activity determined by the relative underlying tendency levels of the alternatives available in the environment. If the activity is intrinsically satisfying or has been rewarded in the past, the environment (stimulus situation) results in an instigating force that causes an increase in the tendency level to perform the satisfying activity. If the activity is painful or has been punished in the past, the stimulus situation will produce an inhibitory force that serves to block the expression of the activity (Atkinson, 1977). The metaphor "stream" of behavior is intended to suggest that behavior flows from one moment to the next and that an occurrence upstream has an effect on subsequent behavior downstream. Behaviors are therefore not independent phenomena; rather, behaviors (responses) exert consummatory effects that decrease the underlying tendencies responsible for their expression. Changes in behavior most often occur when the ongoing (currently expressed) behavior has stabilized because of its consummatory effect and the subsequent behavior gains ascendence through direct instigation from the environment. To provide an example, we view a student whose tendency to study has stabilized after an hour of intensive reading. Suddenly the tendency to talk with dormmates rises through exposure to (instigation from) the sounds of talking and laughter coming from across the hall. Our student would not stop studying without this outside instigation (i.e., would not leave his or her books to seek out companionship in a quiet dorm), nor would the outside instigation have been so compelling 45 minutes earlier when he or she had just started studying. This example illustrates the importance of time in the dynamic model. The instigation to action (talking and laughter overheard) is conceptualized as a force to engage in a certain activity that causes an increase in the strength of tendency to perform the corresponding action (join the bull session) over time. Tendencies are not stable but fluctuate in time as the result of instigating forces, which cause them to become stronger, and inhibitory forces, which cause them to become weaker. If an activity has a strong inhibitory force associated with it, the activity will be delayed—that is, it will be initiated later. If our student has been punished in the past for joining friends and not studying sufficiently for an upcoming exam (i.e., the feeling of panic when faced with the examination), the sound of talking and laughter would simultaneously instigate the student to join the group and inhibit the student from joining the group. Let us assume that we can view two students simultaneously. One student has never experienced panic in the past because he or she stopped studying and socialized with friends; the second student has. These two students are in adjoining rooms equidistant from the talking and laughter, and their ongoing (studying) tendency levels have stabilized at the same level. Who will leave his or her books sooner and join the conversation? The interaction of environmental stimuli and personality variables will cause our second student with a high inhibitory force to delay initiating the talking behavior. This effect, lower inhibition for the first student, leads to the prediction that the first student will leave his or her books after about 55 time units and that the second student will leave after 130 time units (see Figure 11.1, upper two panels).

Let's examine another way the situational and personality variables might differ. A third student with high instigation and low inhibition for affiliating (like the first) might have a high inertial tendency to affiliate because he or she had not had a chance to visit with friends for a long time. During a particularly busy schedule this student had passed his or her friends in the hallway and had been instigated to talk, but pressing appointments had kept him or her from expressing the tendency. The inertial tendency to talk had not been reduced through consummation (directly or indirectly) so that the night before the examination the instigation from across the hall causes the talking tendency, which is already well above zero, to rise further (see panel 3) and initiation of talking behavior to occur after only 18 time units. The comparison situation would be our first student who had just this very afternoon taken time out to visit with friends, and the instigation from across the hall is increasing a tendency that had fallen to zero because of the satisfaction derived from talking earlier in the day (see panel 1). Our socially sated first student would stay at his or her books longer than the similar third student, who had not had a chance to express an inertial tendency to talk. This inertial tendency represents the wishes that persist until satisfied (expressed directly or indirectly in behavior) that Freud identified. While the stimulus situation (including thought) is a source of instigation and inhibition, tendency levels that are once aroused persist at a high level until they are consummated directly or through substitute activity.

The Atkinson and Birch model differs from the Heckhausen and Kuhl model in that by postulating consummatory effects, the Atkinson and Birch (dynamic) model follows behavior beyond the initiation (or choice) or an action and incorporates the functional significance of the action itself, the turning off of the action that results from engaging in it. The consummatory value of an activity, associated with its satisfaction value and leading to its termination, is not considered an all-or-nothing principle, as emphasized in the cognitive (Heckhausen & Kuhl) model, in which the attainment of the goal is the only source of decrease in the tendency to action. In the dynamic model the action itself has tendency-reducing qualities and the action can be stopped (interrupted) and another activity engaged in before the goal is reached with no extraordinary explanation required. A common assumption that is made when the dynamic model is applied in the achievement domain is that success has a higher consummatory value than failure (cf. Kuhl & Blankenship, 1979a, 1979b; Revelle & Michaels, 1976), but that the consummatory value of failure is greater than zero. Empirical evidence is available from a recent study in which subjects were allowed to divide their time between an achievement oriented target-shooting game and a nonachievement

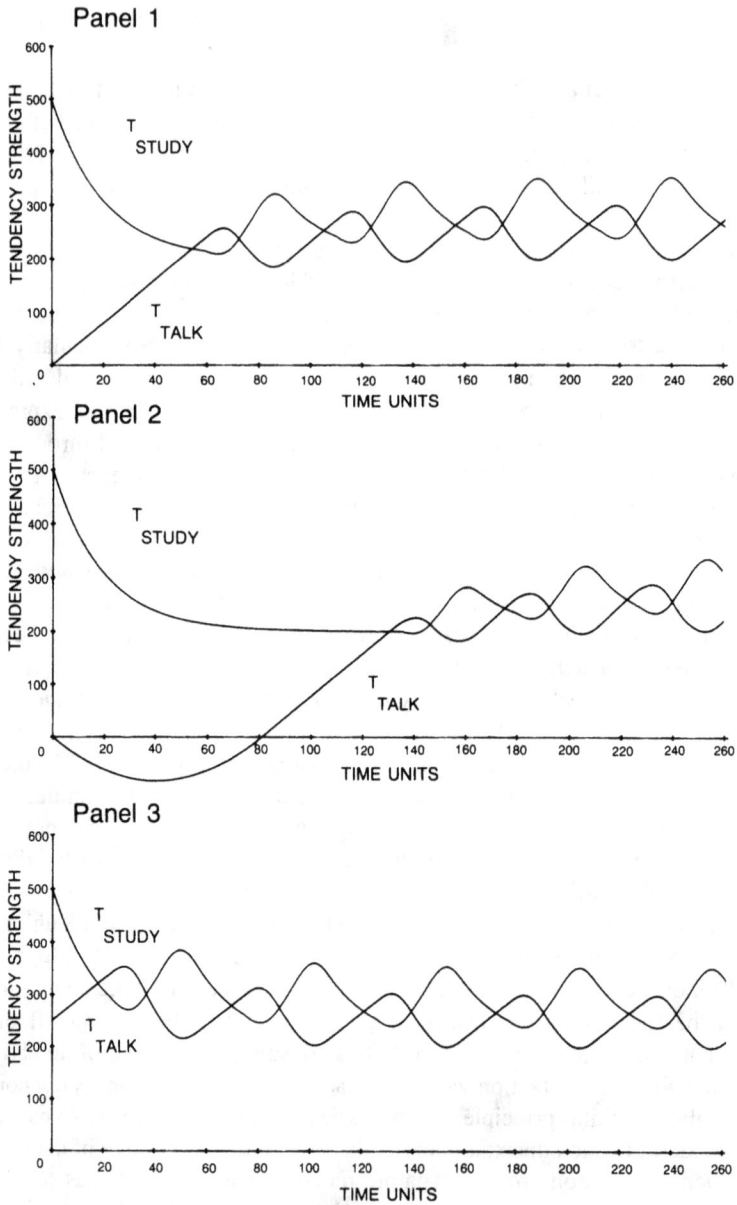

Fig. 11.1. A comparison of studying and talking behavior under three personality × environment interactions. Panel 1: High force to affiliate, no inhibition, no inertial tendency. Panel 2: High force to affiliate, high inhibition, no inertial tendency. Panel 3: High force to affiliate, no inhibition, high inertial tendency.

opinion task presented on a microcomputer (Blankenship, 1982). Sixty-six per-
cent of the subjects, all with strong positive achievement motivation, returned to
the nonachievement task immediately following a failure outcome (goal nonat-
tainment) at the target-shooting game. This result argues against an all-or-nothing interpretation of consummation.

Concepts of displacement and substitution are also fully developed in the
dynamics of action model. Activities are assumed to belong to related families
that share instigation (displacement) and that share consummation (substitution).
When a substitute activity is performed, substitute consummatory (tendency-
reducing) effect is applied to the original underlying tendency. The tendency to
travel may be blocked from expression because of lack of money; however, the
instigation to travel, resulting from seeing travel ads in the Sunday newspaper,
will be displaced to watching travel films (the substitute activity), and the tendency to travel will be thus reduced through the substitute satisfaction (consummatory effect) derived from watching the films. The principles of displacement
and substitution as formalized in the dynamics of action allow the treatment of
this most important psychological phenomenon that was recognized by Freud
(cf. *Civilization and Its Discontents,* 1961) and by Lewin (cf. *A Dynamic Theory
of Personality,* 1935).

THOUGHT AND ACTION IN THE DYNAMIC MODEL

The relationship between thought and action has been developed within the
dynamic model by Birch, Atkinson, and Bongort (1974). They propose that
"products of an individual's cognitive processes can enter equally with the
environment as inputs to the total configuration of forces operative at any particular moment in time" [p. 80]. They describe a situation in which a professor is in
a stimulus-poor environment and is instigated to write a letter to his brother
because earlier he had seen a letter from his brother and that stimulus triggered
thinking about writing a reply. During the time the professor is thinking about
various activities, each time he thinks about writing a letter, the tendency to
perform that activity is increased until it becomes dominant over all other incompatible activities. Figure 11.2 is a diagram of this thought-to-action sequence.
The four intertwined lines in the lower part of the figure represent thinking about
doing various activities, including thinking about writing (dark line). The four
lines in the upper part are action tendencies; the dark line represents the action
tendency to write a letter. Notice that the tendency to write increases (the dark
line rises) only when thought about writing is dominant over thought about other
possible activities. The action tendency is expressed in behavior when the tendency to write becomes stronger than the three alternative action tendencies,
represented in the graph by the point at which the upper dark line crosses the
highest of the other lines. Birch et al. (1974) conclude:

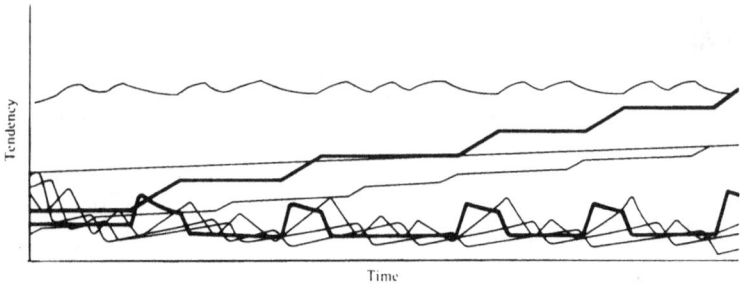

Fig. 11.2.   An example of cognitive control of action simulated from the dynamics of action. (From Birch, Atkinson, & Bongort, 1974).

This analysis of an instance of cognitive control of action derives out of the dynamics of action in a very straightforward fashion. No new principles of motivation need be entertained. All that need be done is to allow instigation and inhibition (though the latter was not a factor in our example) to originate in the content of thought as well as in the external environment [p. 83].

In this discussion I maintain that new principles are required in the sense that the dynamics of action is a general model that requires further specification, and that the Heckhausen and Kuhl cognitive theory of action control can provide that further specification. Atkinson and Birch (1974, 1978) appreciate the necessity of specification as they have provided coordinating definitions between the dynamic theory of action and classic achievement-motivation theory (Atkinson, 1957). By equating the instigating force with the product of motive to succeed, the subjective probability of success, and the incentive value of success, and by equating the inhibitory force with the product of the motive to avoid failure, the subjective probability of failure, and the incentive value of failure, they laid the groundwork for the application and testing of the dynamic model within the achievement domain. Revelle and Michaels (1976), Kuhl & Blankenship (1979a, 1979b), Blankenship (1982), and Reuman (1982) have further specified the relationship between achievement outcomes and dynamic parameters. These specifications have allowed a change in focus in achievement research from actions isolated in time to a sequential analysis of activity choices and amount of time spent in what von Cranach and Kalbermatten (1982a, 1982b) term manifest behavior. It is within von Cranach and Kalbermatten's analysis that the importance of both the dynamic model and the cognitive model is most apparent. The dynamic model describes manifest behavior, but the further specification of an achievement model or a cognitive model is necessary to give the behavior social meaning. Further, with so many degrees of freedom within the parameters of the dynamic model, further specification is necessary so that independent measures of the parameters in a particular domain (such as the measurement of motive to achieve success by use of the TAT and measurement of subjective probability by use of a questionnaire) can impose constraints upon the model when it is empirically tested.

DYNAMIC ASPECTS OF INTENTION

Let us attempt an analysis of thought to action combining the cognitive and dynamic models. For the time being we continue to follow the Birch et al. (1974) model in which thoughts are independent of action in that thought content can be unrelated to the activity in which the individual is currently engaged. Their letter-writing example allowed for an increase in the tendency to write when the activity was being thought about, even though the professor was riding a bicycle at the time. In the analysis of resistance in decision making, Atkinson and Birch (1970), outlined the inhibitory effect of a "covertly expressed expectation of a negative consequence" [p. 257]. They provided the example of a person who resists flying not because of previous painful experience but because of cognitive content (thoughts about possible crashes). These expectations about consequences that exert an inhibitory effect on the action tendency are the result of exposure to information. They conclude (Birch et al., 1974), "Whether this information is not only sufficient but also necessary to establish instigating and inhibitory forces is one of the unsolved questions left for future study" [p. 258].

To accommodate the Heckhausen and Kuhl model, thoughts must have the ability to inhibit (decrease) the action tendency. If the OTIUM check reveals the absence of a crucial element, the OTIUM thoughts would cause a lowering of action tendency to engage in the goal directed behavior. This suppression would be temporary because the negation tendency stabilizes through time due to the force of resistance. The force of resistance uses up the negaction tendency when a strong instigating force continues to exert its positive influence. A strong instigating force to dance, to use Heckhausen and Kuhl's example, is met with the inhibitory force the young woman associates with having to deal with misunderstanding of the relationship between herself and a potential partner. This inhibitory force and its resulting negaction tendency, which keeps the dancing activity from becoming dominant, stabilizes in time from the force of resistance, and the tendency to dance rises again, even though its strength is being displaced to the substitute activity, singing.

To extend this thought-to-action model to cover intentional behavior would require thought about the activity as a necessary but not sufficient condition for its initiation. A computer model could easily handle this requirement, but imposing it within the dynamics of action model could change the nature of the model by reinstituting an episodic focus. As Kuhl and Blankenship (1979a, 1979b) have emphasized, the replacement of episodic thinking in motivational research with a dynamic approach is one of the strengths of the Atkinson and Birch model. The dynamic emphasis would not be lost if some activities in the behavioral repertoire (those activities deemed to be under intentional control) were conceptualized as being capable of dominating thought when their relative tendency strengths were very nearly as strong as the dominant, ongoing tendency. The model would require a minimal period of related thought before intentional activity initiation, a period that would then have an instigating, inhibiting, or consummatory effect, as evidenced by research using the Heckhausen and Kuhl model. In other words, immediately before intentional activity initiation, when an action tendency had reached a critical level, intentional thoughts would be dominant and those thoughts would in turn serve to instigate, inhibit, or consume the corresponding action tendency. The delineation of which conditions would lead to which dynamic effects (i.e., the further specification linking OTIUM checks to dynamic parameters) would proceed from research integrating the cognitive model with the dynamic model.

The dynamic model could also be applied to intentional actions with the condition that thought and action are correlated. The initial activities associated with the dominance of an intentional action tendency would be characterized as the OTIUM checks that would either result in the repeated inhibition and immediate decrease of the ongoing action tendency, if OTIUM criteria were not met, or result in the additional instigation of the action tendency and withdrawal of previous inhibitory force, if the OTIUM criteria were met. The application or withdrawal of inhibition or instigation at the point of the OTIUM check would represent a stimulus change arising from the content of thought. Stimulus changes are an assumption of the dynamic model and serve to model changes in the overt and covert environment (see Atkinson & Birch, 1970, p. 225). A stimulus change can have a dramatic effect on behavior, especially when the change involves the withdrawal of an inhibitory force that has been exerting a dampening effect on an action tendency. This "champagne cork effect" has been demonstrated by Kuhl and Geiger (in preparation) and can be understood more clearly within the dynamic model, with the specifications of the cognitive model, than with the cognitive model alone. When an inhibitory force is suddenly withdrawn, the action tendency rises quickly and percentage of time spent is increased dramatically. (Imagine that our dancer finds a graceful and cooperative eunuch to be her partner!)

When thoughts and actions are correlated, it is no longer necessary to separate their effects and to conceptualize thoughts as intertwined tendencies separate from actions. Just one set of tendencies can serve to represent overt behavior (cf. Reuman, 1982), with thoughts providing additional instigation, inhibition, and consummation when the action tendency is dominant. It may be useful to reexamine James' (1892/1962) observation that "habit diminishes the conscious attention with which our acts are performed" [p. 154]. Our professor riding his bicycle is engaged in habitual behavior, so that his thoughts can range to other topics not concerning the action expressed. During this time other activities can be instigated through thoughts, a situation not possible with less practiced behaviors, such as composing articles and typing them at the same time. For most of us, this very complex task requires constant monitoring, and thoughts cannot range over unrelated topics without disruption of the ongoing behavior.

UNCONSCIOUS MOTIVATION

The dynamics of action model differs most markedly from the Heckhausen and Kuhl model, and from other action theories, in that it deals with both intentional and unconscious motivations. The emphasis, even the complete domination, of intention in action theory (cf. von Cranach, 1982) is unsatisfactory when one considers all the rich and varied behaviors people engage in that are not the result of considered thought and conscious intent. Symbolic behaviors that seem to achieve no declared goal for the individual can only be understood as substitute behaviors that derive their power indirectly from blocked activities—the man who watches endless hours of football, not because he is interested in the outcomes, but because he was unable to play football when he was a boy, or the woman who buys clothing she does not need because this expresses her power motivation, which is blocked from expression in her home and workplace. Harris (1983) has also criticized action theory for ignoring unconscious motivations. She gives examples from psychotherapy of people who intend to refrain from compulsive behaviors but return to therapy the next week to report that they have behaved in ways they intended not to. She argues that intentionality is a multilayered concept and that little is to be gained by narrowing the focus of action theory to include only actions under conscious control. As Nisbett and Wilson (1977) have demonstrated, people have little direct access to "higher order cognitive processes."

But even apart from unconscious motivations, the setting of goals does not necessitate that one operate in the intentional mode. Parents, teachers, and nurses, for example, may have set goals to provide the most responsive care to those under their supervision. To meet those goals and to avoid the frustration of having their intentional goal strivings outside the care-giving domain (house cleaning, lesson preparation, medical record keeping) interrupted, the most functional mode of operation is a respondent mode, a mode in which plans are not articulated but action is initiated in response to the needs and demands of others. An intentional explanation of action ignores this important class of behaviors, behaviors that are controlled by outside demands more than by inside wishes. The wish involved, and its derivative intentions, are so abstract that they cannot guide daily action. People whose jobs require that they manage the work of others must also adopt a respondent mode if they are to avoid frustration. Many people in management have risen from task oriented jobs and do not recognize this important change in the nature of their work. They continue to set task goals when their time is spent mainly in the respondent mode of solving interpersonal problems. They come to the end of each day feeling a sense of failure because their task goals have not been attained, when in fact they have performed well the job they were supposed to perform—responding to the crises around them.

CONCLUSIONS

The cognitive model proposed by Heckhausen and Kuhl and the dynamic model developed by Atkinson and Birch are not antagonistic. The cognitive model provides specification of dynamic parameters, and the dynamic model provides a temporal focus for intentional behaviors. Conceptualization combining the two models followed by empirical testing will lead to important advances in understanding goal directed behavior. The relationship between thoughts and actions requires further clarification before projective measurement of individual differences in motive strength can attain its maximum validity and reliability. The refinement of OTIUM criteria will help specify the action potential of individual achievement concerns. Strengthening these important links in achievement research will accrue benefits for researchers on both sides of the Atlantic.

ACKNOWLEDGMENTS

I would like to thank Professor J. W. Atkinson for his comments on an earlier draft of this chapter.

GOAL DIRECTED BEHAVIOR AND
STRESS

Schönpflug discusses an idea that follows from an action-theoretic treatment of stress research: the notion that actions may contribute to greater stress. All too often stress research assumed that attempts to change stressful conditions lead directly to stress reduction. Schönpflug's chapter is a corrective to this standard approach. He does not deny that coping can be successful, but he asks the questions: What happens when attempts to cope with stress are not successful, and what are the conditions that produce unsuccessful coping attempts? This latter is the question of inefficiency that he treats in detail in the various stages of action: model construction, goal setting, strategy formation and execution, and the use of feedback. When such unsuccessful coping attempts ensue, one can disengage from the goal; disengagement under such circumstances may be functional if it involves appealing to other people to help. Schönpflug's approach is an example of the "objectivistic" character of an action-theoretic approach—Lazarus criticizes just this approach. Lazarus, in commenting on Schönpflug's chapter, gives a broad view of the issues in stress research that he thinks are important to tackle. Some of the issues that he sees as problematic in an action-theory approach are the action theory's reliance on a problem-solving model without orientation to more emotional coping attempts and the problems that arise with a notion of inefficiency.

12
Goal Directed Behavior as a Source of Stress: Psychological Origins and Consequences of Inefficiency

Wolfgang Schönpflug
The Free University of Berlin

EFFICIENCY OF ACTION

Problem Solving, Failure, and Problem Generation

Individuals prepare and execute actions in order to terminate specific problem states (Lewin, 1926a; Tolman, 1932). Many psychological theories have adopted this perspective. Theories of action and of achievement motivation treat the strategies and calculations designed to guarantee subsequent success (Hacker, 1980; Heckhausen, 1977). Some theories of stress describe stressors as problems and coping procedures as adaptive problem-solving activities (Folkman, Schaefer, & Lazarus, 1979; Meichenbaum, Henshaw, & Himel, 1982). Not all actions, however, succeed in eliminating problems. Some actions partially or totally miss their goals and leave the original problems unchanged (failure). Some actions even create new difficulties (problem generation). In the case of failure or problem generation, actions will induce rather than reduce stress.

Because goals can be conceptualized both as immediate results of actions and as consequences, for which immediate results are instrumental (Nuttin, 1953; Vroom, 1964), there are two kinds of failures to be distinguished:

1. Outcomes that fall below intended results (e.g., missing a qualifying score in an athletic contest), and
2. Consequences of intended results that fall below expectations (e.g., a family prepares an excellent dinner for guests, but the guests do not appear).

Further, new problems may arise as:

3. Unintended results of actions (e.g., stabbing an opponent during a fencing championship) or as

172

4. Unexpected consequences of intended results (e.g., winning Jack as a friend surprisingly makes Bill jealous).

Some problem states may not follow from, but rather accumulate during, the course of an action:

5. Preparation and execution of actions consume external resources (e.g., money, tools, social credit), thereby creating a state of scarcity or even indebtedness, and
6. Preparation and execution of actions consume internal resources (physical health, energy, capacities), thereby creating states of impaired physical ability, of psychophysiological exhaustion, and of mental satiation.

If confrontation with problems constitutes a load, activity provides an opportunity to reduce the load; the original load, though, can also be augmented by activity. In general, the efficiency of an action can be defined as its power to reduce a problem state and the load associated with it; an action is inefficient if it augments an original problem state and the load associated with it.

The Behavior Economics Approach

It is the general presupposition of this chapter that individuals strive toward efficiency and economy. This striving is assumed to be not just a product of modern commercial life, but a principle of biological evolution, governing the choice of habitat and prey (Rapport & Turner, 1977). The model of economy or efficiency represented in this chapter does, however, have a restricted scope. The model is described as operating toward minimizing problems, load, and activity and makes no provisions for creative problem search (Getzels & Csikszentmihalyi, 1975), sensation seeking (Zuckerman, 1979), and other types of hedonistic involvement (cf. Scitovsky, 1976). Although the restriction of the model is obvious, it can be advocated for high-load situations and limited-capacity individuals. Thus, it is adequate for the analysis to follow, which deals with the relation of dysfunctional action to stress.

For many actions, efficiency cannot easily be determined, because single actions may produce several effects simultaneously, and therefore have both a positive and negative impact on load. In particular, there is no activity that does not consume resources. Moreover, adverse side and after effects frequently occur. Often relief from eliminating the original problem outweighs the discomfort induced by the new problems; but the new problems caused by an action may also turn out to be a greater burden than the original problems would have been (cf. Schönpflug, 1982, 1983). Only in the case of blatant failure is a straightforward evaluation possible: Because failure does not alter the original problem state but does consume resources and runs the risk of additional unintended negative effects, it almost inevitably increases load.

Following this rationale, the efficiency of an action must be estimated by a procedure that makes use of intended positive results (*IPR*) and their usefulness for expected positive consequences (*EPC*), unintended negative results (*UNR*), and their unexpected negative consequences (*UNC*), as well as their consumption of external resources (*CER*), and of internal resources (*CIR*). (For the sake of simplicity cases in which negative consequences are expected or positive consequences are originally not intended have not been considered separately.) Efficiency scores can then be calculated as a ratio or as a difference measure—that is,

$$\text{Equation 1: Efficiency Ratio } ER = f \left(\frac{IPR + EPC}{UNR + UNC + CER + CIR} \right)$$

or

$$\text{Equation 2: Net Efficiency } NE = f$$
$$((IPR + EPC) - (UNR + UNC + CER + CIR)).$$

Such models are fundamental to the theory of microeconomics (cf. Weise, 1982) and have been used in decision theory and its most popular psychological branch, the expectancy-value theory of achievement motivation (cf. Atkinson & Birch, 1978).

Efficiency models such as those underlying Equations 1 and 2 can be successfully operationalized if terms in the equations are estimated as financial costs and profits, and thereby made comparable on a monetary scale. Estimates and comparisons on a monetary scale have been applied to noncommercial matters (e.g., financial compensations for loss of personal health, marital relations, public reputation) as well, but these attempts appear unsatisfactory from a psychological standpoint. Although a monetary scale can probably not be universally applied, the notion of a general scale of subjective valence need not be abandoned.

Evidence for a universal valence dimension in the minds of individuals can be inferred from subjective ratings (Osgood, May, & Miron, 1975) and equity judgments (Mikula, 1980). Using these figures, estimates of subjective valence can be entered in Equations 1 and 2 for the purpose of detailed psychological analysis. They can then be the basis for determining the subjective tradeoff relations between different effects of actions, especially the tradeoff between effort and achievement (cf. Kukla, 1972) and positive and negative results of decisions (cf. von Winterfeld & Fischer, 1975). Such subjective tradeoffs determine the payoffs of actions, upon which decisions about these actions are based.

It is also important to take time into account. It is efficiency over time that should be maximized, rather than efficiency at any single moment of time. Thus, individuals typically begin an action expecting to reduce their original set of problems, but during the course of this action problems may accumulate because difficulties arise in the course of acting while the original problems still resist resolution. (For instance, a beginner at a job may suffer from many errors in her work, and therefore try to avoid errors by acquiring new skills; for a while she will have to engage in learning efforts, and may still not observe a reduction of her errors). This phase of resistance and accumulating load, however, may last only for a short time. (For example, after a week's training the error rate may drop gradually.) If the original problems are then eliminated, and the coping activity can be terminated without lasting adverse after effects, the total load over time (or, mathematically speaking, the integral of Equations 1 and 2) will be lower than if the original problems had persisted.

Of course, accounting can only be extended over time as long as indispensable internal and external resources are maintained above a critical level; below this level the action system would collapse immediately, for reasons like physical exhaustion or lack of material.

Cognitive and Behavioral Correlates of Inefficiency

Studies of actual behavior in achievement situations have frequently dealt with reactions to failure (cf. Atkinson & Birch, 1978), but not with reactions to problem generation. Some information on reactions to harmful actions and other problems can, however, be drawn from research on moral judgment (cf. Kohlberg, 1976). Both failure and problem generation may have an impact on self-evaluation. Inefficient actions often lower subjective estimates of one's own competence and of self-esteem in general. These changes in self-concept influence aspiration level for subsequent tasks (Heckhausen, 1977). Changes in self-esteem and of aspiration level are evaluated by many individuals with reference to personal or cultural standards of efficiency. If these standards are not met, a personal problem will ensue. Typical emotions going along with the belief that one has failed are guilt, shame, anger, regret, and disappointment (Weiner, Russell, & Lerman, 1978). Similar emotions can be observed when problems are generated in everyday situations. Emotional reactions are experienced as problem states per se.

These cognitions, evaluations, and emotions give evidence for the operation of economic principles; they do not elucidate, however, the origin of the need for economy underlying these principles. As has been argued in the last section, striving for economy and efficiency may trace back to early stages of evolution and reflect constraints of both organismic potentials and of the life space. The crucial function to be optimized under these conditions should be the relation between the degree of mental and motor effort expended and effects achieved. Indeed, valences of objects and states can be shown to be highly correlated with activities directed toward these objects and states; the number of responses performed to attain an object seems to be highly related to both the availability of, and the demand for, the object (Lea, 1978; Rachlin, Green, Kagel, & Battalio, 1976). Because there is a limited number of actions possible within any time period, a person must decide how to spend that time if he is to derive the greatest profit possible.

From this perspective, a problem state is characterized by a set of repeated demands for mental and motor operations (e.g., worrying, monitoring of risks, defensive acts), whereas effective problem solving removes the demand for active concern. Mental and motor operations related to problems can be treated as psychic costs. Efficiency can then be estimated by the relation of psychic costs invested in old and new problems, on the one hand, and costs that are saved after the solution of old problems, on the other. We do not attempt here to define the rules for maximizing efficiency. It is, however, easy to demonstrate that inefficiency will always counteract the objective of minimizing operational costs. At least five cases demonstrate such inefficiency (Schönpflug, 1983):

1. Failure calls for repetition and modification of a former activity (e.g., repeating a class after failing the finals).
2. Problem generation calls for new actions, especially eliminative (e.g., cleaning up a mess), substitutive (e.g., replacing spoiled material), or compensatory (e.g., giving excuses).
3. Orienting activity is initiated to determine the origins of, and responsibilities for, failures and new problems (e.g., investigations of road accidents).
4. Feelings of incompetence may lead to an emotional crisis, in which self-regulation must be used to reduce the level of emotional responses (palliative coping; see Lazarus & Launier, 1978).
5. To make up for failure, or to cope with a newly created problem, it may be necessary to improve one's skills.

Prolonged load resulting from failure and augmented load following from newly generated problems, therefore, result in prolongations and augmentations of mental and motor operations. The number, difficulty, and duration of these operations can be used as estimates of the psychic costs of specific problem states; these costs can be entered in Equations 1 and 2 (Schönpflug, in press). For instance, one can attempt to estimate the impact of fatigue by seeing how long it takes to recover from fatigue (e.g., comparing recovery by a night's sleep to recovery by medical treatment in a hospital).

The number of operations seems to correlate well with stressors and induced stress. In an experimental study, Schulz and Schönpflug (1982) demonstrated that the number of repetitive and irrelevant operations due to failure (repeated calls for relevant and irrelevant information after partial forgetting) increased with the intensity of noise, an external stressor; increased activity corresponded with increased subjective and physiological indices of stress.

ORIGINS OF INEFFICIENCY

Critical Components in the Action Chain

Different versions of action theory converge in the assumption of at least five components of the process of action: (1) model construction: the establishment of a representational model of the actor's world, including functional relationships (Tolman's ''means-end-relations'') and temporal changes (historical and future developments); (2) goal setting: incorporation of alternative states into the model, decisions on priority, urgency, and timing of attempts to transform existing states to preferred alternative states (i.e., decisions about what to do and when to do it); (3) strategy formation: activation or construction of plans or action schemata that represent the desired transformation; (4) execution: motor and verbal performance guided by the selected plans or schemata; and (5) feedback: incorporation of results and consequences of actions into the actor's representational models, including comparison of outcomes and goals.

These five components are organized in sequential structures or chains, and the efficiency of the whole chain is affected by every component (cf. Schönpflug, 1979). In the following sections the five components are analyzed for their contributions to inefficiency and stress (compare Table 12.1). Three aspects are emphasized:

1. Critical defects produced: If misregulated, each component will contribute its own share to unintended outcomes (failures and new problems). The specific defects produced by misregulation will be pointed out.

2. Misregulation in the organization of actions: Each component involves a set of mental and motor operations. The payoff of single operations may be questionable, or either the organization of larger series of operations or the strategy may be suboptimal.

3. Waste of resources: Misregulation increases the risk of lavish consumption of resources, especially the risk of fatigue caused by increased effort.

Before further detail is explored, a basic theme must be stated: There is a parallel and repetitive structure of human actions. In most cases human activity can realistically be described only as a bundle of parallel actions serving a multiplicity of goals. These goals relate to the actor's social environment, her geographical and technical environment, and her own personality. Studies of stress in everyday life and work show that high demands result from the accumulation of problems from several areas simultaneously—from, for example, one's job, health, and family (de Longis, Coyne, Folkman, & Lazarus, 1982; Semmer, 1982). Deficits in dealing with one problem area may spread to other areas (Wilensky, 1981). Further, actions are frequently repeated, and such repetitions may lead to habitualization of suboptimal actions (Schulz, 1981). Suboptimal work strategies, once acquired in a state of stress, may also be transferred to nonstress periods. A demonstration of this last issue has been provided by Wieland (1982): Subjects under noisy conditions adopted less efficient work strategies than did subjects under quiet conditions; when they were permitted to continue their work under quiet conditions, they stuck with their defective strategies and their efficiency remained below the level of the subjects who profited from quiet conditions from the beginning.

TABLE 12.1
Inefficiency in the Action Chain: Defects Produced
and Uneconomical Procedures Performed

Component	Defects Produced	Uneconomical involvement
Model construction	Gaps of attention Inadequate identification/ confusions/illusions Temporal and spatial displacements Selection of inadequate sources of information Retrieval failures/erroneous recollections/conservation errors Erroneous inferences/inap- propriate images/confu- sions of images and perceptions undifferentiated representa- tional models	Uneconomical search strategies Search for and processing of irrelevant information Uneconomical modes of thinking and remembering
Goal setting	Unrealistic aspiration level Delays and omissions of in- terventions to unfavorable proceedings "insulation," i.e., concern for isolated problems dis- regarding the complexity of a task system inadequate priorities/unclear priorities insufficient specification of goals	Criteria for evaluating the process of goal setting unclear

Inefficiency Attributed to Misregulation in Model Construction

Actions often fail to produce intended results or produce unintended ones because the action space is not well represented in the actor's model. Inadequate
model construction may refer not only to the actor's environment (e.g., his car or
family), but also to his own person (e.g., his competences). Accident research
(Halsey, 1961; Reason, 1977) has collected many cases of perceptual deficits
during model construction. Construction deficits include gaps of attention (e.g.,
missing danger signals), inadequate object identification (e.g., failure to recognize instruments), perceptual and functional confusions (e.g., of levers in a
cockpit), and even illusions (e.g., of nonexisting resources). Also temporal and
spatial displacements have to be mentioned.

TABLE 12.1 (Continued)

Component	Defects Produced	Uneconomical involvement
	neglect of temporal perspective (optimization for the time being/ "groupthink," i.e., undue concern for social agreement	
Strategy formation/execution	Unrealistic plans and actions	Excessive planning
	Assembly failures: Confusions between currently active programs and between ongoing and stored programs	Detours in actions Excess of auxiliary and preventive acts
	Subroutine failures: Insertions/omissions/ misorderings	
	Storage and retrieval failures for plans and motor programs	
Feedback	Lack of feedback (open-loop mode)	Excessive involvement in search and evaluation of feedback
	Unrealistic/erroneous feedback	Undue concern for distant consequences of results
	Insufficient elaboration of feedback	Monitoring erroneous feedback
	Stop rule undershoots	
	Branching errors	

Inadequate models may originate from defects in the process of perception as well as from the selection of inadequate sources of information. Some sources are external (e.g., printed instructions, maps), but one source is internal: the person's memory. There are three ways that memory can contribute to defects in model construction: failure to retrieve valid information stored in memory within the time constraints, retrieval of invalid information, and conservation errors. The third type of error needs explanation. Conservation errors are originally correct recollections that miss changes between memorization and reproduction (e.g., a driver's violation of the right of way at a familiar crossroad when he does not pay attention to a recent change of traffic signs).

Improper inferences and unrealistic images may add inappropriate details to representational models or eliminate appropriate details. If reality testing (Johnson & Raye, 1981)—distinguishing the origin of information and checking its reliability—does not work efficiently, the hypothetical nature of inferences and the subjective nature of images are disregarded. In this case invalid inferences and images interfere with accurate perceptions and memories.

Clearly, unrealistic representational models are not a proper basis for efficient activity. Thus, knowledge of conditions and functional relations within the action space become potent factors for efficient performance (Hacker, 1980, 1982a; cf. also Hacker, this volume). In the literature on problem solving (Dörner, Kreuzig, Reither, & Stäudel, 1983; Duncker, 1935) still another variable is mentioned: the vagueness of representational models. Some models may be realistic but rather undifferentiated (e.g., "foreign armament becomes a hazard to our national security"). Undifferentiated models raise the same difficulties as incomplete ones: Goal setting, planning, and execution run a heightened risk of neglecting crucial conditions and producing unintended results. This difficulty can be observed when individuals operate on the basis of abstract and unspecified principles (e.g., in states of religious frenzy).

Constructing a model may necessitate enormous involvement; it may include a variety of mental and overt attempts to search for information (e.g., traveling, microscopy, interrogation of experts), storage and retrieval (e.g., taking photographs, ordering from an archive), and inferential activities (e.g., computer simulation). These activities may consume a considerable portion of the available external resources and require time and effort. Whether the expenses pay off at all will depend on the importance of the task to be accomplished.

Misregulation of the construction process may increase load without contributing to the solution of the problem. One source of deterioration of efficiency is a choice of uneconomical search strategies. An example from everyday life is a scientist walking to a distant library to borrow a book while an identical copy is on his desk. More subtle cases of uneconomical search strategies have been observed by Schulz (1980) and Wieland (1982) in experimental simulations of clerical work. They gave subjects a series of decision tasks such as checking bills, replying to customer complaints, and answering applications for credit or social services. The subjects were seated at computer terminals and had to search for additional information (e.g., personal data about applicants, regulations to be applied) in order to decide the case in question. For orientation to the information available, they could expose directories on the display. A highly effective strategy for blocks of similar tasks was to memorize the directory before starting the tasks. Unless they memorized the list in advance, subjects had to expose it frequently thereafter, interrupting their decision-making process. The frequency with which subjects consulted the directory correlated with their subjective and physiological indices of stress.

Another mode of uneconomical behavior during model construction is the search for and processing of irrelevant information. For instance, in the experimental setup just described, calls for information occurred that were irrelevant to the task at hand (e.g., for regulations on credit while subjects were supposed to be checking bills). The frequency of such calls correlated with indices of stress as well (Schulz, 1979; Wieland, 1982). There are, however, remarkable differences in people's conceptions of what information is relevant. Individuals classified as highly anxious or highly reactive show a greater need for elaboration and certainty than those low in anxiety or reactivity; they collect more information before making a decision, and also engage in more checking before they rely on that information. In more complicated tasks their increased involvement may pay off, but they run the risk of wasting resources in simpler tasks (Mündelein & Schönpflug, 1983; Schulz, 1979; Strelau, 1975).

Costs of model construction are further inflated by errors and inconsistencies. It is well known from everyday experience that mistakes during knowledge acquisition, if noticed, instigate repetitions and checks. This self-checking is associated with greater load and negative feelings. In the experiments by Schulz (1979, 1980) and Wieland (1982), this effect was replicated in the laboratory: If subjects forgot information that they had obtained for solving mental problems, they had to resume their search for the lost pieces of information, and this compensatory activity contributed to stress.

Inefficiency Attributed to Misregulation in Goal Setting

Any failure can be regarded as an unintended outcome, and when accomplishments fall below expectations, it may be because of unrealistic intentions. In general, individuals try to match their aspirations to their competences and to the difficulties of their work (Hoppe, 1931), thereby maximizing both their probability of success and the utility of the outcome. Aspiration levels that are much higher than competences in relation to task difficulties will not only inflate the risk of ultimate failure, but also call for activities that overburden individual resources. Excessive aspirations are, therefore, likely to induce stress (Reykowski, 1972), and individuals experiencing or expecting stressful demands tend to lower their aspirations (Frankenhaeuser & Lundberg, 1977; Krenauer & Schönpflug, 1980; Künstler & Zimmer, 1982).

In static situations—those remaining constant unless a focal person initiates a change—failures because of unrealistic goal setting result when activities miss their aims. In dynamic situations, in which the focal person is also confronted with changes initiated by other agents, undesired results may as well be attributed to omissions or delays of intervening in inappropriate activity. These omissions and delays may be traceable to gaps in goal setting. Dörner and his collaborators (Dörner & Reither, 1978; Reither & Stäudel, this volume) have described subjects in experiments with complex problem solving who show a remarkable lack of interest in perilous trends that were obvious to the majority of observers. For instance, in a simulated task on aiding a developing country, subjects did not guard against the spread of lethal diseases; when attempting to administer a middle-sized town, they allowed the budget to go into deficit to the point at which the town collapsed. A phenomenon Dörner calls "insulation" typically occurred in these cases: The subjects encountered a series of problems that had to be tackled in close succession, but they committed themselves to one problem at the expense of the others. In addition to complete neglect, they also showed inadequate modes of concern, such as general intentions (e.g., "We really must do *something* about it"). After the breakdown of the system, the conditions for working—even on the problem that is being attended—are lost (e.g., a subject who organizes a municipal pop festival until a serious financial crisis, to which the subject only reluctantly reacts, ruins the budget; given these conditions the pop festival has to be cancelled).

Shifts in priorities may also have negative consequences. This is particularly true if goals lose weight after effort has been invested to attain them; then the realization of the goal produces regret instead of pride and joy. This phenomenon is well illustrated in fairy tales of peasants and scientists who barter their souls to the devil. During their life times, they enjoy fulfillment of all their desires and give high priority to this state of satisfaction. When the ends of their lives approach, however, the prospect of eternal condemnation gains priority, and they regret the trade.

Another type of interrelated goal setting is analyzed by Janis (1972) for social-decision situations. In such situations two problem areas are dominant: the matter to be decided and the coherence of the decision group. Janis describes the phenomenon of "group think" in situations in which suboptimal decisions satisfy the majority of the decision group. In such situations, group coherence may be given high priority during the decision phase, to the detriment of the matter to be decided; deficits in decision making show up during or after execution, when failures and new problems result. For example, Janis (1972) presents an analysis of the newly established Kennedy administration's decision making that led to the debacle in the Bay of Pigs in 1961. Military risks of an invasion of Cuba were obviously underrated, and political alternatives were disregarded, because the prospect of taking military actions against Castro's regime solidified the decision group.

Goal setting sometimes places great demands on the individuals involved. The specification of goals and the making of decisions about conflicting goals are especially likely to produce heavy mental load and negative emotions. The participation of other individuals and consideration of social norms sometimes facilitates goal setting, but it can also accentuate conflicts (cf. Brandstätter, Davis, & Stocker-Kreichgauer, 1982). Criteria for optimizing the process of goal setting remain unclear; therefore, it is difficult to evaluate this process apart from an evaluation of the final outcome. There is evidence, however, that the decision-making process stimulates a continuation of information search, focusing on evaluative information and decision rules (e.g., calls for expert judgments, search for rational selection procedures). If control is transferred to information search, the problems of inefficient search strategies recur.

Inefficiency Attributed to Misregulation of Strategy Formation and Execution of Actions

In complex situations a person cannot realize his or her goals, unless he or she develops or activates appropriate plans. Execution of these plans in motor and verbal performance may not satisfy the plans because of shortcomings in verbal and motor skills, but execution frequently suffers from omissions and errors that do not derive from deficits in skills. To a large degree, such lapses can be traced to gaps and inadequacies in plans (Skell, 1976). Inadequate plans are often caused by inadequate representational models (e.g., unrealistic representation of task conditions). If the information upon which the planning process is based is suboptimal, thinking with that information may nonetheless be adequate. If, however, conclusions are drawn that lead to inadequate representations of steps to be taken or to illusions of effects to be achieved, the process of planning or strategy formation itself can be called misregulated.

Plans or action schemata are regarded in action theory as cognitive hierarchies with general principles at the top and motor subroutines at the bottom (Hacker, 1980). Misregulation can be expected on any level of the hierarchy. Psychological research has thus far focused on misregulation at lower levels as exhibited in short-term action slips. Reason (1979) distinguishes between program assembly failures and subroutine failures. Assembly failures include confusions between currently active programs (e.g., calling ''come in'' into the telephone receiver) and confusions between ongoing and stored programs (e.g., getting matches to light an electric fire). Subroutine failures consist of insertions (e.g., turning the light on during daytime), omissions, and misorderings of correct actions (e.g., releasing the handbrake of a car before starting the engine). Norman (1981) describes action slips as confusions or improper triggerings of ''child schemata'' within hierarchies. He also takes into account multiple intentions pursued simultaneously, situations that often favor intrusions from different schemata.

Potent factors producing misregulation of activity seem to be storage and retrieval failures. Reason (1979) lists three such failures: forgetting previous actions, forgetting discrete items in a plan, and reverting to earlier plans. Thus, highly practiced plans and action programs may improperly replace more suitable new plans and programs. Omissions and confusions, on the other hand, can be explained as results of forgetting or of inadequate retrieval of plans. Retraining after changes in procedure illustrates a special case. Experiments in this area have been reported by Schwarz (1927, 1933). In these experiments, subjects were first trained on an apparatus on which pressing a lever released a ball; in later trials the same subjects had to learn that lifting the lever released the ball. During retraining old procedures interfere with new ones. This relationship holds especially for subroutines—like operating a lever within a larger action sequence—if the subject's attention is directed toward higher levels of work organization.

Planning is a cognitively demanding process (Hayes–Roth & Hayes–Roth, 1979), but appropriately elaborated plans may also reduce load during execution (Hacker, 1980; Sperandio, 1971). In this way a tradeoff between planning load and stress reduction is established. New experimental data from a simulated management task (Battmann, in press) demonstrate that heavy involvement in long-perspective planning is not equally effective for all individuals. Whereas highly competent individuals can tolerate the load of planning more easily and enjoy the advantages of effective preparation thereafter, less competent individuals combine the load of planning with the shortcomings of incomplete preparation.

A major point to be considered in evaluating planning is the extent of strategy formation. Some strategies are restricted to the task as explicitly defined (e.g., driving a car to the next town). Some strategies also include preventive and monitoring activities (e.g., checking the pressure in the tires, getting extra gasoline for reserve). Tomaszewski (1967) distinguishes these activities as two classes: productive and auxiliary actions. Depending on one's insight into a task and beliefs about control, the scope of auxiliary activities may be almost indefinitely extended. In this way, both planning and executing auxiliary activities may become a high load. Carrying the load may pay off as long as auxiliary actions, in fact, reduce risks and stressors. In the face of very low probability risks, the load from auxiliary strategies will outweigh its profits (Mündelein & Schönpflug, 1983).

Among the costs of motor actions, the expense of physiological resources— with effort as its subjective correlate—is most prominent in psychological studies. The tradeoff between effort and goal attainment is well documented. Individuals calculate certain degrees of effort as equivalent to success, and they tend to reduce their efforts if they do not expect action outcomes to balance their efforts (Kuhl, in press). High degrees of stress, however, are observed if great effort is maintained despite repetitive, negative results (Schulz, 1979, 1980).

The Contribution of Feedback to Faulty Regulation

Norman (1981) and Reason (1977, 1979) pay a great deal of attention to the role of feedback. Feedback typically operates to control higher levels of the hierarchy. Subordinate motor programs typically are automatized and operate in an open-loop mode. In Norman's and Reason's analyses, therefore, routine motor sequences are assigned a greater risk of misregulation. In Read's material, on the other hand, there is also evidence of feedback failures on a higher level, especially stop-rule undershoots (e.g., going to bathe with underwear on) and branching errors (e.g., going the wrong route by successively choosing the wrong directions). Feedback can also be lacking for larger behavioral units such as work periods or life phases and may then contribute to uncertainty and dissatisfaction (cf. Semmer, 1982).

Whereas realistic and detailed feedback can be used to correct and optimize models, goals, strategies, and executed actions, corrections place additional demands on the individual. For example, feedback makes operation time for easy tasks faster but for difficult tasks slower. The load of reacting to feedback pays off if it is compensated by a reduction of frustrations, failures, and negative results in general. If attempts at optimizing fail, however, their load adds to the load of negative outcomes; in this case, individuals tend to avoid feedback in order to maintain the illusion of a reasonable performance (Schulz, 1980, 1981).

One must also consider cases in which feedback is erroneous. As long as erroneous feedback leads to the illusion of optimal performance, no stress will occur; on the other hand, if erroneous feedback during correct performance induces changes, only suboptimal performance can result. Suboptimal performance, as a consequence, is likely to be followed by negative feedback, realistic or unrealistic. This process creates a high expediture, frustration situation (cf. Dembo, 1931).

It must be emphasized that elaborated and realistic feedback is not always easy to obtain. Whenever reliable feedback is not offered automatically, subjects have to engage in search, inference, and evaluation procedures to determine the results of their activities (e.g., inquiring about customer satisfaction, calculating personal income). The evaluation of the results and consequences of one's own activity may become a social process in which many individuals and institutions are involved (e.g., in the evaluation of academic achievement). In such cases, feedback and performance evaluation may require time, skill, and effort. This need for increased involvement obviously holds for conscious and voluntary modes of monitoring more than for automatic control (cf. Schneider & Shiffrin, 1977).

It is self-evident that the costs of feedback are spent in vain if the feedback actually obtained is insufficient or, worse, erroneous. On the other hand, there is also evidence that complete and realistic feedback does not justify every effort. Monitoring and evaluating feedback information may use so many capacities of an individual that executive skills are blocked (cf. Schulz, 1981).

In addition to the dangers of inadequate and erroneous feedback, there is the risk of excessive monitoring of feedback. Monitoring of feedback can be called excessive if it does not contribute to action control. A general rule is that monitoring the immediate feedback from action (e.g., in the process of a painting) contributes directly to action control, whereas paying attention to further consequences (e.g., the price of the painting) diverts attention from the activity itself and may even corrupt intrinsic motivation for it (Lepper & Greene, 1978). Thus feedback, although essential to control actions, may sometimes impair efficiency.

DELIBERATE DISENGAGEMENT: AN OPTION IN THE
FACE OF INEFFICIENCY

With the prospect of costs or detrimental consequences outweighing the profits of actions, disengagement from these actions becomes a rational alternative. Disengagement can be regarded as adaptive and rational if it avoids increasing strain, when active involvement would make the situation worse. Two patterns of deliberate disengagement are elaborated in the next sections: "disengagement as giving up" and "disengagement as an instrumental act."

Disengagement as Giving Up

Disengagement as giving up is an avoidance strategy that comes about when negative expectations concerning the outcomes and consequences of actions, abilities, and resources outweigh the positive ones. It appears in situations with unsolved tasks and adverse working conditions. If such situations continue, overt activity may drop to complete passivity; motivation, effort, and their physiological correlates, such as heart rate, decrease (Schulz & Schönpflug, 1982; Wortman & Brehm, 1975). During phases of disengagement, emotional reactions range from anger to shame, depending on the causal attributions of difficulties to external sources, such as hostile experimenters and unfair regulations, or to internal sources such as one's incompetence (cf. Dembo, 1931; Klein, Fencil-Morse, & Seligman, 1976). The lack of overt engagement in tasks must not be seen as a total lack of involvement. In states of disengagement, attention may be turned away from the pursuit of action to environmental and personal states that are seen as sources of frustration (cf. Brockner, 1979; Kuhl, 1981). Becoming self-absorbed can make a person worried and miserable. More typically, however, disengagement provides relief from the stress induced by coping with the task (Fuhrer, 1982; Rothbaum, Weisz, & Snyder, 1982).

Disengagement as an Instrumental Act

In social systems, disengagement may be a strategy to engage other people's help for one's own problems, thus transferring the task to somebody else. It operates in groups with shared standards, including solidarity rules. The helplessness of one partner obliges the other partners to lend support. With reference to this obligation, instrumental disengagement may become a means of gaining social support and even of provoking social change. At least three phenomena contribute to the usefulness of this type of disengagement:

1. Calculations of relative efficiency: If one calculates one's own efficiency and compares it to those of one's partners, one may find that one's own efficien-

cy is low in relation to others'. Thus, transferring the task to a more efficient partner makes sense (e.g., "Let him do the work, it is much easier for him."). Related phenomena have been documented in studies of coalition formation (cf. Komorita & Moore, 1976; C. E. Miller, 1980).

2. Persuasive communications of disengagement: Individual disengagement can be communicated for the purpose of getting help. To intensify its persuasive value, disabling features and difficulties can be accentuated or even feigned (e.g., simulating physical ills to escape school or work obligations).

3. Actual generation of inefficiency: Disabilities and difficulties are sometimes purposively produced to provide the conditions for disengagement. Examples are self-mutilation by soldiers to escape combat and sabotage in schools and industry.

Shifting the responsibility for, and the load of, coping to a smaller portion of a group may also be a strategy to alter social procedures and the social values backing them. Nowadays, for instance, a substantial group of physicians and nurses refuses to participate in trainings for nuclear catastrophic aid and, instead, declares the futility of catastrophic aid plans. They support the strategy of decreasing the dangers by eliminating the causes of potential nuclear catastrophies, such as atomic weapons and nuclear power plants.

Deliberate disengagement can be an effective social strategy. If it cannot be justified by social norms, however, it conflicts with solidarity rules. In such a conflict disengagement is suspected as exploitative and illegitimate and will fail to achieve its purpose (J. P. Meyer & Mulherin, 1980; Schwartz, 1977).

There are individual differences in the tendency to disengage. Some people devote a disproportionate amount of their energies, skills, and external resources to coping with relatively minor threats and challenges; they pay too much attention to warnings with low predictive values and uncertain impacts. This misdirected attention can be interpreted as hypersensitivity to loads and dangers and can be contrasted with the notion of *repression*. Repression would then be interpreted either as recognition of harmlessness or as wise detachment from troublesome or even unmanageable tasks (cf. Breznitz, 1982; S. M. Miller, 1981).

SUMMARY AND CONCLUDING REMARKS

We started with the notion that actions, although committed to the improvement of the environment, health, and well-being, may actually yield disadvantages, uncompensated loss of resources, and an augmented experience of stress. These unintended effects have been explained by various processes of misregulation. We have ended with the argument that disengagement from inefficient activities turns out to be a wise decision because it sets limits to the loss of resources and self-inflicted problems, transfers control to other potentially beneficial agents, and does not interfere with their support and help.

This approach assumes that the person who suffers from stress is responsible for it. Although this view agrees that "stress is in the mind of the beholder" (S. Cohen, 1980), it introduces principles of economics that are taken to govern people's behavior and evaluations and to determine their state of stress. The economic principles advocated define a cognitive framework that should receive its detailed structure from concrete appraisals of safety, welfare, and their prerequisites.

This chapter is not devoted to special stressors such as noise, heat, role conflict, or physical disability. It must be acknowledged that environmental and physical factors are essential because they tax human capacities and determine the utilities of human actions. From the theoretical point of view presented here, however, there is no straightforward functional relationship between these factors and human stress or well-being. Rather, the relation is mediated by interactions among the factors, and these interactions, in turn, are shaped by human intentionality and human potential. Thus, the approach is nested in general action theory, because in the landscape of theoretical systems, general action theory is the homeland of the concepts of human intentionality and human potential. The specific point raised in this chapter was the treatment of limitations in human potential and the inadequacy of actions for serving prior intentions. It is hoped that taking a new look at the field of stress from the standpoint of action theory opens new perspectives for both stress theory and action theory. By incorporating and elaborating the core assumptions of action theory, stress theory may gain sophistication and explanatory strength. Through application to phenomena of inefficiency, distress, and disengagement, action theory may gain extension, corroboration, and refinement.

13

Toward an Understanding of Efficiency and Inefficiency in Human Affairs: Discussion of Schönpflug's Theory

Richard S. Lazarus
University of California at Berkeley

INTRODUCTION

The interesting, thoughtful, and sophisticated chapter that Schönpflug presents expands the scope of an old problem, that of how stress affects human functioning. This issue has been analyzed in diverse ways over 75 years or so. Included in this diversity is the Freudian conceptualization of the pathogenic consequences of anxiety, the Hull–Spence treatment of anxiety as drive in the 1940s and 1950s, and the transitions in the 1960s to cognitive views of anxiety and stress, which now appear to dominate thinking in psychology.

Three concerns especially distinguish Schönpflug's work. The first is efficiency in problem solving. The second is an effort to extend the focus from task performance in the narrow, laboratory sense to solving the problems of living, including winning friends, handling disappointments, and achieving long-term goals. Third, adopting a German action-theory view, Schönpflug's emphasis is not strictly on behavior (what "action theory" means to many), but on subjective cognitive and goal directed activities that are not readily accessible to direct observation.

Schönpflug's system of thought communicates readily with a cognitive-phenomenological analysis of emotion as illustrated by my own work, which I assume is why I was invited to discuss this chapter. Before we look at Schönpflug's theory more closely, let us first backtrack by attempting to place this work in the historical context of research and theory on stress and human performance.

SOME HISTORY

Scientific psychology has had to juggle two somewhat different perspectives, each with its own interconnected set of values and methods. There is, on the one hand, the search for principles about people in general and the effort to reduce human diversity to a manageable set of variables. The broad agenda of this perspective is to determine how the environment affects us, and it does so within a Darwinian tradition of survival and natural selection. The emphasis is on biological adaptation, and a core value is how to survive and flourish with maximum effectiveness, which fits well within the traditional values of the Western industrial world in which an abiding goal is mastery over the environment. This perspective is a venerable and important tradition in modern psychology, probably the dominant one, and it might be referred to by the term *psychobiological adaptation*.

The alternative tradition is *personalistic*, and it is distrustful of efforts to reduce human diversity to a few general principles located mainly in environmental regularities. Personalistic psychology emphasizes individual differences and their origins in genetic endowment and experience. Developmentally, these differences create the psychological structures that have as much to do with behavior as does the environment. Personality psychologists and clinicians argue that individual differences encompass a very large share of the variance in human behavior. They align themselves with current models that are interactional or transactional and often cast their analyses in subjective terms.

The reader might recognize that the preceding is a portrait in large measure parallel with Cronbach's (1957) presidential address to the American Psychological Association in which he spoke of two "scientific disciplines of psychology," the experimental and correlational, and bemoaned the failure of psychology to integrate them in research. "Experimental" in Cronbach's discussion referred to manipulation of environmental conditions (e.g., social structures), whereas "correlational" referred to individual differences and their correlates.

The contrast between the two perspectives can be illustrated with the contrast between classical perception theory and research and the "New Look" movement of the 1950s. Classical perception theory asked the question: "How do people manage to perceive accurately what is in the environmental display?"; the New Look asked: "How is it that people perceive the same environmental display differently?" The former emphasized normative responses (of people in general) to the environment and adaptiveness through realistic perception; the latter sought rules about individual differences that explained the selectivity of perception and deviance from reality. These rules focused on personal needs and motives as determinants of how we perceive the world. The two broad perspectives have never been integrated, and the same separate agendas operate today in the contrast between social psychology and personality. Cognitive psychology mainly follows the earlier normative tradition of classical perception theory and ignores the individual-differences issue on which the topic of emotion depends.

If we turn back the clock for a moment also on the history of theory and research on anxiety and stress, we can see that it too reflects these two divergent epistemological traditions, one normative and adaptational, the other individualistic and subjective. The earliest major interest was how skilled performance was impaired by environmental load, or by the increased arousal it generated within the person. This interest drew many researchers to a modest piece of research by Yerkes and Dodson (1908) that reported that the relationship between arousal (or drive) and performance could be expressed as an inverted U-shaped curve; as arousal rose from a minimum, performance improved to a peak and then, with continued increases of arousal, fell. The so-called Yerkes–Dodson Law became a prototype for much thinking about the relations between stress, arousal, and performance effectiveness.

World War II had a tremendously stimulating effect on research on stress, anxiety, and drive (or arousal) for two reasons. First, during combat, soldiers could become ineffective at vital tasks (e.g., when soldiers hunkered down and failed to fire their weapons or when precision bomb-sight calculations could be disrupted while bombadiers flew a fixed course, unable to take evasive action against enemy flak). Second, many soldiers developed emotional breakdowns that required their withdrawal from combat and subsequent treatment. Ways of selecting soldiers who were not vulnerable to impairment were sought, a variant of the individual-differences emphasis. In addition, researchers sought ways of managing stress either by training or, when possible, by modifying the conditions of performance, both variants of the experimental or normative emphasis. Psychologists and psychiatrists in great numbers entered the arena of stress, anxiety, and human functioning and drew upon their theories of human adaptation in the interests of understanding and intervention.

With the end of the war, it became apparent that the arena of stress, anxiety, and human functioning was a very broad and important one, encompassing diverse forms of ordinary life stress such as school examinations, work, and social relationships. Nearly every aspect of human functioning engendered the potential for stress-induced performance impairment.

There have been several basic conceptions of how stress affects performance. In the 1950s, for example, and flowing from the Hull–Spence learning-theory tradition, *drive interpretations* that bore some resemblance to the Yerkes–Dodson analysis took on importance. The concept of stress as *interference* provided an alternative view in which heavy demand, anxiety, threat, or arousal was said to get in the way of the concentration required for task performance or, as in Easterbrook's (1959) influential version, stress narrowed the focus of attention. This latter view seemed to imply a motivational interpretation because the focus of attention was shifted counterproductively by the added dangers generated by stressful demands or threats. In this connection, Schönpflug (1983) has recently reexamined the Yerkes–Dodson Law in motivational terms, suggesting that the downward leg of the inverted U-shaped curve reflects a withdrawal of effort to cope with a high-cost, low-gain condition that results when demands get too heavy.

By the end of the 1950s, interest in the classic problem of stress and performance waned, in large part because it was becoming obvious that simple stimulus response models involving drive or interference were not working. The ubiquitous problem of individual differences was not well understood, which meant examining what was going on in people with divergent goals, styles of thinking, and patterns of coping. A number of analytic reviews of research on stress and performance (e.g., Easterbrook, 1959; Holtzman & Bitterman, 1956; and Horvath, 1959) emphasized the individual-differences theme. One widely read analysis by Lazarus, Deese, and Osler (1952) focused on the role of motivation and personality-based ways of handling stress in the effort to predict the effects of stress on skilled performance. Lazarus and Eriksen (1952) demonstrated that stress could sometimes merely increase the variance of performance—that is, it might have no effect, impair performance in some, or facilitate it in others. To predict which effect would occur required knowledge of the properties of persons that mediated the effects of stress conditions. For example, as a result of different motivations either to achieve academically or to be accepted by others, failure on an exam could be more stressful for some but social rejection could be more stressful for others (Vogel, Raymond, & Lazarus, 1959).

During this period psychology was beginning to abandon mechanistic drive concepts and was turning to cognitive models; the concept of coping was also achieving theoretical and research significance (Lazarus, 1966). With the reformulation of the problem of stress in terms of cognitive appraisal and coping, research interest shifted from performance itself toward what it is in people's makeup that makes them vulnerable to stress and the role of coping in this vulnerability. With the exception of a few scholars (e.g., Broadbent, 1971a; Welford, 1973; see also Corlett & Richardson, 1981; V. Hamilton & Warburton, 1979), the issue of stress and performance, once central, has now taken a back seat. Reinforcing this shift in interest was the resurgence of psychosomatic (or behavioral) medicine, with its focus on the somatic and psychological health outcomes of stress in place of performance or social functioning.

THE WORK OF SCHÖNPFLUG

Schönpflug, therefore, seems to have entered a field that lost its momentum in the early 1960s, bringing to it a conceptual approach—German action theory— that is far more complex and introspective than the dominant formulations preceding him. He has no hesitancy in speculating about internal variables, states, and processes, including goals and goal setting, cognitive activity, and coping processes. These functions are organized by a theoretical framework of value and expectancy that is prominent in behavior economics and social learning theory. What Schönpflug is attempting is the creative fusion of phenomenological theory with the rigorous tradition of experimental research.

This fusion produces an unexpected blend of two styles of explanation, cognitivism, on the one hand and the mathematical equations of the deductive-nomological style of classical mechanics in physics (cf. Haugeland, 1978) on the other. In the chapter we have before us the emphasis is strictly theoretical; in the earlier work I cited previously (Schönpflug, 1983), there is much more attention to experimental findings in which the variables are familiar and relatively simple environmental demands such as noise and time pressure.

The guiding premise of Schönpflug's analysis is that individuals strive toward efficiency and economy, which is offered as a principle of biological evolution. This orientation provides the assumptive base from which emerges the body of the chapter, which centers on what can go wrong—that is, on what creates inefficiency. The detailed conceptual analysis of efficiency and inefficiency is what makes this chapter distinctive and important. The calculation of efficiency depends on several variables, including the intended positive results of action and their consequences, unexpected negative results, and the extent to which available resources (both internal and external) are used up in the preparation and execution of actions to solve the problem. Some achievements fall short of what is intended, or the consequences of such achievements miss the mark, resulting in unintended or unexpected negative consequences. Coping can thus make matters worse rather than better, a situation that itself produces stress, a very important theme in Schönpflug's analysis.

The devotion of systematic attention to sources of inefficiency in problem solving also strikes me as important and instructive. I am aware of no other attempt at a systematic classification of failures in problem solving, their cost, and the additional problems they generate. Failure forces the person to turn attention again toward identification and control of the problem, increasing the effort expended and hence the cost. This view is reminiscent of the earlier idea that thoughts generated by stress or anxiety can interfere with performance effectiveness by deflecting attention and effort from task-relevant activities. It also reintroduces the notion that we are most efficient when we do not have to attend closely to what we do, as when we can perform tasks automatically because of well-practiced skills. Automatization releases energy for other tasks.

I like Schönpflug's extended discussion of the origins of inefficiency in the various stages or components of the action chain, beginning with modeling and proceeding through goal setting, strategy formation, execution, and feedback. I am uncertain, however, about the implication that these stages are necessarily organized sequentially. Stage theories are risky and are rarely confirmed empirically (Krau, 1982). Schönpflug, however, examines what can go wrong at each stage, which is worthwhile even if their sequencing were to prove variable.

Another valuable feature of the analysis is its process orientation—the recognition of the flow of cognitive-behavioral events—in contrast to the traditionally static approach of most analyses of stress and coping (see Folkman & Lazarus, in press). I believe we will not progress very far in our understanding of stress, coping, and adaptation if we do not look at how they change over time and across situations. Although most theories of coping—for example, those stemming from the psychoanalytic ego-psychology framework—are stated in process terms, the research and measurement that has emerged from them is almost exclusively structural. Such research compares, say, avoiders (or repressors) and vigilant persons (or sensitizers), using a single measurement of this trait, with respect to how they react to a single stressful encounter. The assumption is made and rarely checked that a stable trait or style of coping is being measured and that this trait transcends the variable coping demands and requirements of diverse stressful encounters. In contrast, Schönpflug is a dedicated process theorist, which is a refreshing feature of his work.

SOME NAGGING CONCERNS

Schönpflug's central premise that individuals strive toward efficiency and economy presents some difficulties that I think need more attention. In much of his analysis, coping is characterized as highly rational and deliberate, in the tradition of decision theory, and inefficiency is a consequence of a failure of reason. Yet many sources of stress involve problems that cannot be solved. Sometimes the difficulties underlying such stress are not amenable to "efficient" solutions because they entail conflicts having strong emotional significance, or because the environment is refractory. Moreover, people also entertain idiosyncratic and sometimes counterproductive or false premises on which faulty decisions are based; the faulty decisions may occur because hidden assumptions and agendas guide the reasoning process (cf. Henle, 1962, 1971), rather than because of interfering emotions or conflict.

Schönpflug acknowledges something like this in his discussion of deliberate disengagement, and in his assertion, undoubtedly correct, that people differ in the tendency to disengage. He would obviously agree with me that goals are not immutable and that one solution to their blockage or excessive cost is to give them up (Lazarus & DeLongis, 1983). He notes that the process of disengagement can involve emotional reactions ranging from anger to shame. Yet it seems difficult for him to move away from a conception of coping as deliberate and reasoned, as when he later characterizes disengagement and the display of emotions as a useful social manuever. It can be—but need not be—a manipulative tactic. I would have welcomed more emphasis on the variety of cognitive coping devices people commonly use—without deliberation—to regulate distressing feelings when problem solving is laden with conflicts—for example, attentional avoidance, denial, distancing, and redefinition or reappraisal: in short, the remarkably rich and varied ways people manage feelings when they are in situations over which they have limited control or in which they are powerless to act forcefully and efficiently in light of other personal agendas and social constraints. We need to know the factors in the person and in the environment that influence the choice of coping. I would also have welcomed more attention to the unsettled issue of the relative importance of these self-protective and often compulsive devices compared with the problem-solving variety.

Moreover, defining efficiency itself is not as easy as Schönpflug implies, because the definition depends on which of several competing values one adopts. Consider, for example, the person who is uneasy about the need to be somewhere distant for an appointment—for example, to catch a plane at the airport. Anticipating the possibility of a traffic jam, difficulties in parking the car, and other unforeseen sources of delay, he or she copes by leaving for the airport long in advance of the scheduled flight. This means that he or she must wait for an extra hour or two before flight time. Is this inefficient? In one sense yes, but in another sense, the solution succeeds in overcoming fears of missing the plane, or calming distressing fear. Put differently, the person has sacrificed one kind of efficiency, not wasting time, for another—namely, the control of distress. The theoretical problem, then, is to be able to specify what efficiency means in each case, and I think this is a more difficult task than Schönpflug implies. Human agendas include a host of emotional needs and goals, including ego-related ones, that shape the economics of coping. To submerge the problem of competing values under the rubric of biological adaptation is perhaps too glib.

Consider, too, the distressing decision to place one's aged, ailing parent in an institution. The decision may represent efficient coping in Schönpflug's or Janis and Mann's (1977) criteria of good decision making or problem solving, yet the average son or daughter responsible is left with feelings of loss, guilt, and despair. There is no way to win. Effective coping in this case includes the management of these negative feelings. Schönpflug would consider these feelings part of the cost of coping, yet the failure is not in the problem-focused coping decision (i.e., required by events), but in the handling of feelings. Schönpflug's analysis of efficiency is too pat, I think, for such dilemmas.

Another difficulty in the concept of efficiency, one that has not achieved significant research attention, is that not every stressful encounter carries the potential for effective individual coping, because many are bound up in institutional patterns that inevitably defeat individual coping processes and require institutional solutions. This point is, I think, one with which Schönpflug would agree, but it suggests that efficiency must be examined more fully in the context of the social structure as well as the individual's psychological economy. To combine these distinct levels of analysis requires a transactional or relational formulation, and progress along these lines has been slow. The observations of Hay and Oken (1972) on the stresses of intensive-care nursing provide one example in which changes in institutional patterns are necessary to manage destructive work stresses, though these changes will have differing significance for the individuals involved. This issue has been noted by others, including Mechanic (1974). Pearlin and Schooler (1978) have also commented on it, as follows:

> There are important human problems, such as those that we have seen in occupation, that are not responsive to individual coping responses. Coping with these may require interventions by collectivities rather than by individuals. Many of the problems stemming from arrangements deeply rooted in social and economic organizations may exert a powerful effect on personal life but be impervious to personal efforts to change them. . . . Coping failures, therefore, do not necessarily reflect the shortcomings of individuals; in a real sense they may represent the failure of social systems in which individuals are enmeshed [p. 18].

Schönpflug's analysis does not as yet provide us with ways to operationalize the variables in the system. This gap is particularly serious if action theory is to eventuate in research that tests its propositions. It is equally serious in theories of stress and emotion, such as mine, which hinge on concepts of cognitive appraisal and coping. The search for understanding properly begins with a theoretical framework for what is observed anecdotally or intuitively. Nevertheless, ways of measuring the variables and processes of a theoretical system must be sought to put it to empirical test. This is a well-recognized problem, one that I believe Schönpflug also would acknowledge.

The logical positivist movement of the early 1900s, which extended well into the 1950s and still finds expression in what might be called neopositivism, has shied away from the kind of frank subjectivism that characterizes Schönpflug's analysis and German action theory. Its conservatism has probably curtailed the creative development of theories of adaptation and emotion that could successfully capture the cognitive, emotional, and motivational complexity of human functioning. The more complex the theory and the more it turns to process variables, the more difficult it is to connect the theory to observables. Making this connection is not an easy task, though it is by no means insurmountable, as I believe my colleagues and I have recently begun to show (Folkman & Lazarus, in press). We must await publication of programmatic efforts by Schönpflug and his students to advance from the relatively simple empirical research on problem solving that he has reported (cf. Schönpflug, 1983) to the more complex and sophisticated variety mandated by the rich and insightful conceptualization offered here.

THE DUAL PERSPECTIVES ON HUMAN FUNCTIONING

I should return now to the contrast between the two perspectives I described at the outset, *psychobiological adaptation* and the *personalistic* orientation, with a view to locating Schönpflug's formulations.

With respect to the normative individual-differences issue, Schönpflug is a well-known general psychologist who has emphasized motivation, and he is indeed seeking general, normative principles. Yet he clearly sees the sources of behavior as residing not only in the environment but also in the person, having addressed individual-difference variables such as introversion–extroversion, anxiety, level of arousal, and especially achievement motivation under the influence of Heinz Heckhausen. In the theoretical analysis he offers us here, expectations, values and goals, attributions, coping resources, and consequences are central themes. We must wait to see how these individual-difference variables are exploited when this complex theory is put to work in subsequent research. I thus expect that Schönpflug will find Lewin's (1946) statement about these perspectives highly compatible:

> A law is expressed in an equation which relates certain variables. Individual differences have to be conceived of as various specific values which these variables have in a particular case. In other words, general laws and individual differences are merely two aspects of one problem: they are mutually dependent on each other and the study of the one cannot proceed without the study of the other [p. 794].

With respect to the second issue concerning the match between goal directed thought and behavior and the environment, I think Schönpflug comes down on the side of what I have called veridicality as a key to adaptation. Anything else is maladaptive. Put all the variables together in Schönpflug's formulation and one has an equation for inefficiency, a metric of what is maladaptive. The assumptive influence is Darwinian; to survive and flourish one must be good at maximizing efficiency and minimizing inefficiency. There is no room for values other than this maximization, or for variations in what the person should do. Once we have taken into account the agendas (goals) that direct expectations, plans, strategies, and behavioral efforts, what is defined as inefficient is purely mechanical. If information is not used correctly or the efforts at problem solving are too costly, and when there are insufficient resources, these efforts will fail or produce unintended harmful consequences and lead to costly further efforts and preoccupations. Nevertheless, the muddy issue of what is real and how real it is (cf. Watzlawick, 1976) is never examined. I miss in Schönpflug's analysis, for example, any acknowledgment of the widespread ambiguity so characteristic of human social events, ambiguities that often make it so difficult to assess what is happening accurately, its significance for one's well-being, what is about to happen, and what can be done about it.

On the third issue of cold versus hot cognition, I find a dissonance I have difficulty articulating. On the one hand, what is striking about Schönpflug's analysis is his willingness to expand the treatment of problem solving from the experimental analog problems usually examined in the laboratory to the meaningful problems of living in which people have large investments. Meaningful problems generate strong emotions when these investments are challenged. Yet the feel of what Schönpflug offers is mostly cool decision making. Emotions do not seem to play a very important role and are mainly regarded as the cost of poor coping, perhaps merely an epiphenomenon rather than a central, functional process. In contrast, however, I sense a major resurgence of interest in the topic of emotion in psychology, and in the processes of emotion-generation and regulation. Schönpflug is not quite a part of this contemporary movement.

Perhaps this impression stems from the difference in the objectives and cognitive style of someone devoted entirely to generalizing and the artist or clinician who attains satisfaction from recognizable descriptions of people struggling with life, experiencing distress, sadness, and joy. When I read Schönpflug's thoughtful analyses, I miss somehow the latter experience, in which a unique and whole individual is described through some synthetic process in contrast to the analysis and reduction of persons into variables or elements. I suppose the question is: Will we recognize the individual who is drawn by this form of analysis, or will we be unable to reconstruct him or her?

There is, in me, something of an ambivalence between the two cognitive styles or perspectives. The part of me that resonates to careful, precise analysis and the search for generalization greatly admires and respects Schönpflug's efforts; the part of me that resonates to literary, artistic, and wholistic clinical description of people struggling with their lives in the world is left with the feeling of something missing. Nevertheless, I am very glad that participating in this compilation has introduced me to Schönpflug's ideas, which provide much food for thought. He has tackled creatively and thoughtfully what few scholars have had the courage and wit to confront, and the issues addressed are of the utmost importance in human adaptation.

DEVELOPMENT OF GOAL
DIRECTED BEHAVIOR

Chapman and Skinner argue that it is useful for action theory to take developmental patterns into consideration as well as for developmental psychology to use an action-theory framework. Many of the assumptions that characterize action theory are shared by developmental psychologists (e.g., contextualism). Also, aspects of the process of action have been considered, under different names, in the developmental literature (like delay of gratification).

Chapman and Skinner are particularly concerned with two notions: personal control and effort. Beliefs in personal control have an impact on how much effort a person exerts in executing an action plan. Only when one believes that one is able to do something about the situation is one liable to actually execute a plan. Moreover, if one exerts little effort, one will become more helpless.

Effort must be distinguished from ability. Chapman and Skinner argue that only when this distinction is drawn does one develop personal helplessness and that the differentiation of the notions of ability and effort is a relatively late developmental phenomenon (8 to 10 years). Only after children develop this differentiation should beliefs about ability influence effort and children become able to develop a generalized pattern of helplessness. Furthermore, effortful performance has to be distinguished from automatized performance. Only in the former case do control beliefs play a role.

Whereas Chapman and Skinner concentrate on the role of control beliefs and effort, Silbereisen gives additional substance to the claim that an action-theory framework is useful in developmental psychology in the area of social cognitions. He argues that an action-theory approach implies that the notion of social cognition has to be changed and that experiments on social cognition have to be done in a natural environment so that everyday behavior can be studied. The notion of social cognition is related to the intentionality of the object of cognition. Cognitions that treat another person as a nonintentional object are nonsocial. Thus, one can talk about social cognition only when people have mental representations about other people's representations. Representing other people's representations is a quite complicated task; although people are able to do it, there is a tendency to reduce this complexity. In a series of experiments, Silbereisen shows that people reduce this complexity in their everyday behavior in contrast to experimental situations, in which they show their maximal capacity. For example, children and adults show surprisingly little perspective taking in routine and nonroutine everyday situations. Furthermore, master crafts-people reduce complexity by assigning less action and representational complexity to their pupils than to themselves.

14 Action in Development— Development in Action

Michael Chapman
Ellen A. Skinner
Max Planck Institute for Human Development and Education, Berlin

INTRODUCTION

This chapter addresses two interrelated questions: (1) Does action theory have anything to offer developmental psychology? (2) Does a developmental perspective have anything to offer action theory? Both action theorists and developmental psychologists have answered these questions in the affirmative (E. Boesch, 1983; Brandtstädter, 1984; Eckensberger & Silbereisen, 1980; Edelstein & Keller, 1982; Frese & Stewart, 1984; Meacham, 1984; H. N. Mischel, 1984; Oppenheimer, 1981; E. A. Skinner & Chapman, 1984), although some problems remain: Developmentalists may reasonably wonder what the action-theoretical emphasis on intentionality and goal directedness adds to research and theory on development that was not already provided by existing approaches, such as cognitive developmental theory. Similarly, action theorists may wonder how age-related changes are relevant to the basic principles underlying the organization of action.

The present approach to these problems is based on the following propositions:

1. Action theory can contribute to developmental psychology by alerting researchers to the ways in which agents reflexively interpret their own (and others') actions. According to this view, action is in part determined by such

reflexive interpretations, which typically make use of concepts such as goals, plans, intentions, regulations, and beliefs

2. Developmental psychology can contribute to action theory by emphasizing that the components of action and the relationships between them may show developmental change. Given the potential reflexivity of action, developmental change in agents' understanding of their own (and others') action also becomes important.

3. The fruitfulness of any attempted synthesis between developmental and action perspectives will be manifest in the generation of new hypotheses that would not have been generated within each perspective taken separately.

The organization of the chapter reflects these propositions. It begins with a discussion of basic assumptions underlying both action and development, then turns to a consideration of new hypotheses generated by the synthesis of action and developmental perspectives in an area of particular interest to the present authors: the relationship between (1) beliefs about control and (2) action, especially cognitive performance. The new hypotheses are based on the following notions: first, that beliefs about control may be differentiated according to the means–ends structure of action; second, that effort may be an important developmental link between beliefs and performance in general; and third, that current conceptions of "mental effort" provide a means of operationalizing this relationship in the area of cognitive performance. The chapter closes with a discussion of the relationship between individual action and interpersonal interaction.

FUNDAMENTALS OF ACTION AND DEVELOPMENT

The basic premise of action theory is that human beings interpret their own and others' behavior in terms of action-related concepts such as goals, plans, intentions, and beliefs and that their actions are in part determined by those reflexive interpretations. Psychological action theories attempt to give psychological substance to these interpretive action constructs. Perhaps the most central of these interpretive constructs is intentionality or reflexive goal directedness, and for this reason psychological theories of action have generally taken intentionality or reflexivity as their starting point (Eckensberger & Silbereisen, 1980): "Under action theory, we understand in general all those theories that have as their model *human beings (themselves), as potentially reflexive* (able to think of themselves as being in a situation) *and as acting intentionally with reference to the environment"* [p. 24] (see also E. E. Boesch, 1976; von Cranach, Kalbermatten, Indermühle, & Gugler, 1982).

The intentionality of action implies a differentiation of ends and means. The action is performed *in order* to bring about a certain goal. Intentionality entails specific expectations or *beliefs* regarding the various outcomes that are expected to follow from different actions (Goldman, 1970). The hierarchical organization of means within a given action is often referred to as a *plan* (Miller, Galanter, & Pribram, 1960). The role of plans in determining actions has been extensively investigated from a developmental perspective with regard to delay of gratification (see H. N. Mischel, 1984; Mischel & Mischel, 1983; W. Mischel & Patterson, 1978).

Another conceptual constituent of action is voluntary *effort*. Intention in itself is not sufficient for action; one may intend a given outcome without making an effort to bring it about. In attempting to realize an intention by executing a plan, the agent will encounter resistance from external conditions. Effort is the energy exerted by the agent in overcoming such external resistance (Macmurray, 1962). In addition to the effort employed in physical movement, psychological research suggests that there is also a quantifiable *effort of attention* expended in cognitive operations (James, 1892/1961; Kahneman, 1973). As argued later, effort is an important link between subjective constructs (such as beliefs) and observable performances.

Finally, action also takes place in time. Eckensberger and Silbereisen (1980) distinguish among three phases in an action cycle: the initiation phase, the execution phase, and the end phase. These phases may be further differentiated according to the specific processes involved:

1. The action is initiated with the related processes of *goal setting* and *plan selection*. According to value-expectancy theories, the intrinsic value of a goal must be weighted by the subjective probability of success before one goal is selected from the rest (Heckhausen, 1977). Because the subjective probability of success is likely to vary as a function of available plans, goal setting and plan selection will function concurrently.

2. Once a goal is set and a plan selected, the *execution* of the plan becomes possible. In the transition from goal setting and plan selection to execution, *effort* is expended; it is this transition that is referred to in the common expression "making an effort." Accompanying execution is a more or less continuous process of *evaluation* and *regulation* in which outcomes are monitored and discrepancies between these outcomes and the original plan are minimized through appropriate adjustments. These adjustments can have both cognitive and affective aspects and may include regulation of any of the other component processes.

3. Evaluation and regulation continue into the end phase as well. When an acceptable approximation to the goal has been achieved or the goal has been abandoned, this final outcome is evaluated in terms of degree of success or failure. Depending on the outcome, longer-term regulations in the agent's values, beliefs, competencies, and standards may be effected. In this way, each of the components of the whole action process may be subject to development

across time. This potential effect brings us to a consideration of the concept of development itself.

It has been argued in recent decades that models of development may be distinguished by their characterization of the relation between individual and environment (Overton & Reese, 1973; Reese & Overton, 1970). For example, the *mechanistic* model views the individual as essentially passive, with development effected through efficient or material causes in the form of accumulating environmental stimulation or an unfolding biological program, respectively. In contrast, the *organismic* model views the organism as essentially active, with development responsive to both formal and final causes in terms of structure and directionality. According to a third, as yet somewhat less well-articulated model, variously labeled the *contextual* or *dialectical* paradigm, the individual is construed as active and changing and embedded within an equally active and changing environmental context (Dixon & Lerner, 1983). Development is the product of a reciprocal interaction between individual and environment in which each modifies and is modified by the other. Differences in contexts, in the modifiability of individuals, and in the competence of individuals for modifying their environment are all responsible for the multiple developmental pathways observed across the life span (Baltes, Reese, & Lipsitt, 1980; Baltes & Schaie, 1976).

It is the dialectical and contextual perspective on development that is most closely related to action theory. In both orientations, individuals are depicted as modifying the environment at the same time that they are modified by it, and variation in both individuals and contexts is considered to be important (Bronfenbrenner, 1979; Dixon & Lerner, 1983). Action theory emphasizes the immediate interaction between individual and context in terms of specific situational demands and the agent's current states or dispositions. Developmental theory focuses on longer-term individual–context interactions, including the individual's development status as well as developmental tasks involving changes of context (such as entering school). The regulations occurring within a single short-term action sequence might be called microdevelopmental in nature, whereas cumulative regulations or other changes across longer time intervals constitute development as such. A life-span perspective forces the researcher to consider shorter-term and longer-term developmental processes in relation to each other. The intentions that guide a single action may be significantly influenced by the individual's long-term goals, expectations, and beliefs, which in turn are the products of many individual action sequences. Finally, the actual course of long-term development may be influenced by the individual's goals, expectations, and beliefs *with regard to* his or her own development (Brandtstädter, 1984). These two themes, context and change, are the focus of the next sections, which consider specific examples of the relationship between action and developmental theories.

ACTION IN PERSONALITY AND COGNITIVE
DEVELOPMENT

Action theory can enrich the study of the relation between personality and cognitive development in several ways, as represented in the following sections. First, an action model may be used to sharpen or further differentiate existing constructs. An example of such differentiation in the case of personal control beliefs is presented in the next section. Second, the reflexive character of action means that the development of action is influenced by the development of the understanding of action. Thus, the development of beliefs regarding the efficacy of effort and other causes of action outcomes is seen as influencing the mobilization of effort in actual performances. Third, a model of action can be used to integrate constructs that have previously been studied primarily in isolation from each other. Such an integration of control beliefs and effort in the context of cognitive performance and development is also attempted.

Beliefs Regarding Personal Control

The term *personal control beliefs* is used in this chapter to refer to generalized beliefs regarding the causal relationship between an individual and desired outcomes. So defined, control beliefs have been studied extensively under the rubric of "locus of control" and have focused primarily on a single dimension: the extent to which the causes of important events are perceived as "internal" or "external" with reference to the agent of the action (Lefcourt, 1976; Rotter, 1975; Zuroff, 1980).

The action-theory perspective suggests several ways in which personal control beliefs may be further differentiated. The fundamental action-theoretical distinction between ends and means itself implies at least two other conceptually distinct categories of beliefs (E. A. Skinner & Chapman, 1984). The term *causality beliefs* refers to beliefs regarding the relation between potential means and ends: what kinds of conditions or causes are likely to result in different kinds of outcomes. In contrast, the term *agency beliefs* refers to beliefs regarding the relation between the agent and potential means: what causes are available to the person as agent. The control belief that one can bring about desired outcomes can accordingly be analyzed into two components: the causality belief that there exist causes leading to the desired outcomes, and the agency belief that one has or can produce those causes oneself. Conversely, the belief that one cannot produce desired outcomes oneself can result in two ways: either from the agency belief that one does not have access to the necessary causes, or from the causality belief that there are no causes leading to the desired outcomes. There are some suggestions in the literature that these two ways of lacking control over outcomes, similar to what is known in the learned-helplessness literature as personal versus universal helplessness, have different empirical consequences and may therefore need to be treated differently (Abramson, Seligman, & Teasdale, 1978; Garber & Hollon, 1980; Gurin & Brim, in press).

Given this distinction between agency and causality beliefs, control beliefs may be further differentiated according to the types of causes or conditions involved. In most internal–external locus of control scales, both individual effort and personal attributes such as ability or other stable characteristics of the personality have been indiscriminately considered as "internal" causes. Likewise, determinate environmental forces such as chance or luck have often been indiscriminately considered "external." There is reason to believe, however, that beliefs involving these different subcategories of "internal" or "external" causes may contribute in very different ways to the determination of action. For example, persons who believe that certain desired outcomes result primarily from chance or luck may still think that they can "get lucky," whereas persons believing that the same outcomes are wholly under the control of environmental (personal or impersonal) forces may recognize fewer possibilities for successful action. As far as the distinction between effort and ability is concerned, there is evidence (described later) that beliefs involving these two "internal" causes can also affect action in different ways under some circumstances.

Once the importance of the distinction between effort and ability (or other personal attributes) is acknowledged, one may inquire further as to the extent of their interaction. Some personal attributes such as skills are generally recognized as relatively stable, but nevertheless modifiable in the long term through repeated effort. Although beliefs regarding the modifiability of personality characteristics have not received much attention in psychological research, they might well have important consequences, especially in the context of life-span development (Ryff, 1982).

In order to investigate such a differentiated conception of control beliefs in children, the "Causality, Agency, and Control Interview" has been developed by the present authors (E. A. Skinner, Chapman, & Baltes, 1983). As the name implies, control beliefs are analyzed in terms of causality and agency beliefs as previously defined. Causality beliefs are further differentiated by causes or conditions (effort, personal attributes, environmental forces, and chance or other indeterminate factors), by outcome valences (positive or negative), and by domain (general, school, and social). For each of the four causes, agency beliefs are differentiated into two dimensions: the extent to which different causes are available to the agent, and the degree to which that availability is itself modifiable over time. The development of these differentiated control beliefs and their contribution to selected types of action is being investigated in current research.

This investigation of the development of the differentiation of control beliefs illustrates the fruitfulness of the integration of developmental and action perspectives for differentiating existing concepts. Action theory suggests the conceptual distinction between control, causality, and agency beliefs, whereas developmental theory suggests that these categories and their interrelationships may change with age. To be sure, similar categorizations have been made without the benefit of action theory (Bandura, 1977; Weisz & Stipek, 1982), and the development of control beliefs has received a reasonable amount of empirical attention (Steitz, 1982); however, the integration of action and developmental theories expands on these conclusions. As illustrated in the following sections, the use of an action model for understanding the relationship between control beliefs and performance suggests that effort is an important mediator between the two. Further, a consideration of the development of control beliefs within this model suggests a kind of "sensitive period" in children's development during which they may be especially vulnerable to experiences generating certain self-perpetuating developmental trajectories.

Control Beliefs, Effort, and Learned Helplessness

Much research on personal control beliefs has found them to be important predictors of individual functioning (Lefcourt, 1976). To consider only a few examples: Attribution regarding the internality, stability, and globality of the control over negative events have been found to be correlated with depression in both children and adults (Seligman, 1975, 1982); perceptions of internal control for positive (but not negative) events predicted self-imposed delay of gratification for preschoolers (W. Mischel, Zeiss, & Zeiss, 1974); training in effort attributions improved children's arithmetic performance compared to baseline levels (Dweck, 1975). In summarizing research on the psychological effects of internal versus external locus of control, Phares (1976) remarked, "the most basic characteristic of internal individuals appears to be their greater effort at coping with or attaining mastery over their environments" [p. 78]. The research of Dweck and others suggests further that performance depends in part on the type of control beliefs held by the individuals in question. In Dweck's (1975) study, performance levels were affected by changing children's beliefs regarding the efficacy of effort as a cause.

From an action-theoretical perspective, effort is therefore likely to be one of the most important links between control beliefs and performance. Beliefs about control in general (and effort in particular) will facilitate the mobilization of effort, which in turn will facilitate the performance. From a developmental perspective this relationship may be viewed as one that changes with age. Specifically, developmental changes in control beliefs should result in developmental changes in performance through the mobilization of effort. This connection is now illustrated in the context of learned helplessness.

According to the reformulated learned-helplessness theory (Abramson et al., 1978; Miller & Norman, 1979), the beliefs relevant to learned helplessness are perceptions, attributions, or expectations of noncontingency, understood as the absence of a connection between one's actions and desired outcomes. Performance deficits as described by Zuroff (1980) are typically divided into motivational deficits in the form of lowered response initiation and cognitive deficits involving problems in learning contingencies between responses and outcomes. Learned helplessness is considered to be generalized to the extent that such deficits appear across a range of tasks and persist over time (Abramson et al., 1978).

So defined, learned helplessness may be considered one example of the relation between control beliefs and effortful performance. The action-theoretical model outlined earlier suggests further that the feedback loop between effort and belief introduces a certain asymmetry between them that may result in self-perpetuating developmental trajectories. Persons who make efforts because they believe in the efficacy of their actions are open to the possibility that their beliefs will be contradicted by experience. In contrast, persons who do not act because they believe that action will be ineffective will never have their beliefs tested. A noncontingent environment may lead to a "fall into helplessness" (Seligman, 1975), but a contingent environment will not be sufficient in itself to lift the person out of that state. Because experience is in part a product of action (E. A. Skinner, in press), beliefs in the inefficacy of action can not only depress effortful activity, but also close off experiences that might lead to modification of those beliefs. This phenomenon might be called the "passivity paradox" by analogy to the so-called "neurotic paradox," according to which persons who have come to expect a certain situation to be painful avoid it even when the expected aversive consequences no longer follow (cf. Dollard & Miller, 1950).

The passivity paradox introduces a self-perpetuating quality into the "fall into helplessness." Once the process is initiated, it will be difficult to reverse. From a developmental perspective, one can ask whether there are developmental parameters governing the initiation of this process, and whether individuals become more or less vulnerable to the phenomenon at different points in their development. Even infants can perceive the environmental contingencies of their actions (J. S. Watson, 1966), and research has found both motivational and cognitive deficits in infants as the result of noncontingency (J. S. Watson, 1971; J. S. Watson & Ramey, 1972). For the most part, these effects have been demonstrated in specific situations and over short time periods. More important, perhaps, are the parameters governing the development of generalized learned helplessness, especially when noncontingency is attributed to a stable self. It is this kind of *personal helplessness* that is most likely to be most resistant to disconfirmation.

In this connection, the distinction between beliefs involving effort and beliefs about personal attributes such as ability becomes important. In a review of the development of action-outcome attributions in childhood, Heckhausen (1984) cites evidence to the effect that the compensatory relation between ability and effort becomes understood roughly between 8 to 10 years. Only around this age do children begin to understand that effort can compensate for lack of ability as well as the reverse (see also Nicholls, 1978; Nicholls & Miller, 1983). Before then, there is a "linkage" between effort and ability in the sense that extent of ability is inferred from degree of effort. Heckhausen believes that this "linkage" protects children against depressing estimates of their own abilities, because failure cannot be attributed to a stable lack of ability independent of effort. Young children who fail a given task can always prove themselves more "able" by trying harder the next time. From this relationship it might be predicted that children would also become vulnerable to generalized personal helplessness between 8 and 10 years of age, concurrent with the development of the effort–ability compensation.

It is significant that a developmental trend in the susceptibility to learned helplessness has indeed been reported (Rholes, Blackwell, Jordan, & Walters, 1981). In this study, persistence and success in finding hidden figures following initial failure were depressed to a statistically significant extent for fifth graders, but not for kindergartners, first, or third graders. Task persistence was positively correlated with ability attributions for fifth graders but negatively for the other groups. Correlations between effort and ability attributions were negative for the fifth graders and positive for the other groups, suggesting that perhaps only the former understood the inverse compensatory relation between effort and ability. These results tentatively suggest that children begin to become vulnerable to learned helplessness as a generalized phenomenon sometime between third and fifth grade (roughly 8 to 10 years) and that this vulnerability is indeed related to the progressive differentiation of effort and ability attributions. This effect has been subsequently replicated by A. T. Miller (1982), who assessed the development of the effort–ability compensation through direct interviews.

Given the relation between control beliefs and action hypothesized earlier, the differentiation of effort and ability attributions in late childhood might well constitute a "sensitive period" in the development of action control and the self-concept, one that is mediated by cognitive-developmental, rather than maturational factors. Children who begin to attribute failure to a stable lack of ability may become susceptible to a self-perpetuating pattern of passivity and depression. Not only could this passivity itself tend to prevent disconfirming experience, but disconfirming experience, when it does occur, could be interpreted in terms of beliefs already formed. In Dweck's (1975) study, for example, the success experiences of 8 to 13 year olds were not in themselves effective in increasing subsequent performance; only a series of successes accompanied by training in effort attributions led to improvements. Without such training, these helpless children would presumably have continued attributing success to external causes consistent with their helpless self-images.

If development stopped with the conception of substantive personality traits as causes of success and failure, the outlook for helpless individuals would be hopeless indeed. Lacking a belief in the efficacy of effort, they would act less.

With less action, they would seldom test their beliefs. Without testing their beliefs, they would remain helpless. This bleak picture is fortunately contradicted by the results of intervention studies like Dweck's (1975). One reason why victims of learned helplessness are able to overcome their conditions under favorable circumstances might be because personal attributes are recognized as only relatively stable and themselves capable of modification in the long term through appropriate applications of effort. Thus, persons who attribute failure to stable attributes of the self may nevertheless come to believe that those attributes can themselves be modified over time. Just as the belief in the efficacy of action has been found to be an important determinant of the mobilization of effort in actual performance, so the belief in the modifiability of the personality might influence the actual modifiability or plasticity of personality. Such modifiability beliefs might therefore provide a means of escape from the self-perpetuating patterns of personal helplessness. Such considerations underscore the importance of beliefs regarding the modifiability of personal agency as described previously. The developmental parameters of such modifiability beliefs are also under investigation in current research with the "Control, Agency, and Causality Interview" described earlier.

Control Beliefs, Mental Effort, and Cognitive Performance

In the preceding section we have argued from an action perspective that effort is an important factor linking control beliefs and the generalized performance deficits associated with personal helplessness. A consideration of the development of the understanding of the compensatory relation between effort and ability led to an additional hypothesis that children should become vulnerable to generalized effects of personal helplessness roughly between the ages of 8 and 10. We now apply these hypotheses to the specific case of cognitive performance. Previous research has found control beliefs to be associated with deficits in cognitive performance (reviewed by Findley & Cooper, 1983; Lefcourt, 1976; Stipek & Weisz, 1981). Our previous considerations suggest that effort is likely to be one of the most important mediating variables in this relationship and, accordingly, that certain changes in the relationship may be expected concurrent with the development of the effort–ability compensation.

Cognitive performance would seem to be an especially appropriate area for testing the effort-mediation hypothesis because of its importance in education and because the means for operationalizing the construct of effort in this area already exist in the form of "mental effort" (Kahneman, 1973). As summarized by Hasher and Zacks (1979), *effortful* cognitive processes involve access to a limited pool of central processing capacity and therefore interfere with concurrent cognitive processes. In contrast, *automatic* processes do not require capacity and therefore show no interference. Examples of effortful processes include imagery, rehearsal, organization, and some mnemonic techniques, whereas automatic processes typically include the encoding of spatial location, time, frequency of occurrence, and word meaning. These two kinds of processes are conceived of as continuous rather than dichotomous, and effortful processes can themselves be automatized through practice and repetition. A further important difference between them is that effortful processes show marked developmental changes at both ends of the life span, whereas automatic processes tend to be fixed at an early age with little subsequent development.

The mere classification of cognitive processes as effortful or automatic does not in itself explain what underlies this distinction. Many cognitive processes are likely to involve effort in some sense, and in attempting to operationalize this construct it becomes important to specify those processes that are likely to be more central to a wide range of cognitive tasks. In this connection, the concept of *active memory* may be useful (Hunt, 1978)). As we understand this term, the contents of active memory include the representations and/or operations currently active in ongoing cognitive processing. Given the limited capacity of active memory, there is a tradeoff between the capacity used for representation and that used for operations; the more capacity that is used for representing information, the less available for operations, and vice versa. In this respect, active memory may be compared to current conceptions of "working memory" as work space that can be used either for storage or for computation (Baddeley & Hitch, 1974). In contrast to some conceptions of working memory (e.g., Stankov, 1983), information is viewed as being actively represented, not merely "stored" in active memory; thus, both representation and operation are viewed as effortful. According to this view, the effortful process of "rehearsal" is the representation of information in active memory in the context of a memory task. Likewise, active memory is likely to be used for "assembling" new plans or strategies, so that it also provides the basis for what Meacham (1978, 1982) has called "memory for planned action." This hypothetical relationship between mental effort and active memory is supported by research showing that objective measures of mental effort such as pupillary dilation vary with memory load (Kahneman, 1973; Kahneman & Beatty, 1966). Indeed, active memory is proposed as the primary (though perhaps not the only) source of limited-capacity effects in research on effortful cognitive processes. Performances requiring little active memory capacity will also require little effort, but the effort expended will increase sharply as the limits of active memory are reached. This operationalization of effort in terms of active memory is theoretically important for two reasons. First, it provides a connection to a wide range of intellectual abilities. Measures of short-term memory (such as digit span) are known to correlate highly with intelligence scores (Dempster, 1981; Hunt, 1978). The fact that other factors besides active memory capacity can be shown to affect forward digit-span performance (Klapp, Marchburn, & Lester, 1983) does not disprove the common assumption that standard measures of short-term memory are affected to a great extent by limitations in active memory capacity (Burtis, 1982). It is significant in this connection that backward digit span is generally found to correlate more highly with intelligence than forward digit span (Matarazzo, 1972); because grouping and chunking strategies are more difficult in backward as opposed to forward digit span, the former is thought to be a more valid measure of active memory capacity (Case & Globerson, 1974). Active or working memory is believed by some to be a major component of fluid intelligence (Horn, 1982; Stankov, 1983). The second reason why the connection between effort and active memory is important is that it explains why effortful processes show strong developmental effects (Hasher & Zacks, 1979). The functional capacity of active memory increases with age and is believed to affect both short-term memory performance and problem solving, although the mechanisms underlying increase in functional capacity as well as those responsible for these effects are interpreted differently by different investigators (Brainerd, 1981; Case, 1978; Chapman, 1981b; Pascual-Leone, 1970).

The operationalization of effort in the context of cognitive performance makes possible specific action-theoretical hypotheses regarding the relationships between control beliefs and cognitive performance:

1. If effort is the link between control beliefs and performance, then control beliefs should affect effortful, but not automatic, processes. In particular, control beliefs should affect performances in which the limits of active memory capacity are approached or exceeded.

2. As children begin to understand the compensatory relation between effort and ability, they should begin to acquire more stable conceptions of their own abilities, and as a result, these conceptions of their own abilities should begin to correlate more highly with actual performance. In particular, children who tend to attribute failure to lack of ability *and* have developed the conception of ability as a stable attribute of the self should be less likely than other children to persist following initial failure.

3. This latter effect should also be more pronounced for effortful as opposed to automatic performances.

4. As effortful performances become automatized through repetition, children who believe they have greater control should eventually be able to perform those same tasks with *less* effort than children who believe they have less control. The former group's initial capacity for exerting more sustained effort will result in more automatization such that less effort will subsequently be necessary. These hypotheses are currently under investigation by the authors in ongoing research.

In summary, an action-theoretical model has made it possible to differentiate control beliefs according to the means–ends structure of action, to predict the specific effects of these differentiated control beliefs on performance in general, and to specify what types of cognitive performances in particular are likely to be affected. In addition, a developmental perspective has made it possible to indicate a particular point in children's development when these relationships should begin to assume a new form. During this vulnerable period in development, children will be more susceptible to influences affecting their conceptions of self than they will later, when those conceptions are already formed.

CONCLUSION

This chapter has provided a few concrete illustrations of the ways in which an integration of action theory and a developmental perspective can be useful in generating new hypotheses. Examples were taken from research on the contribution of control beliefs to learned helplessness in general and to cognitive performance in particular. An action-theoretical model suggested the *effort-mediation hypothesis*: that effort is a primary mediating factor in the relationship between control beliefs and performance. A developmental perspective on the differentiation of effort and ability beliefs suggested the *vulnerability hypothesis*: that there is a predictable period in development when children will become more vulnerable to the effects of personal helplessness. A consideration of current conceptions of effortful versus automatic cognitive processes suggested ways in which these hypotheses could be operationalized in the study of cognitive performance and development.

The present examples do not exhaust the utility of an integration between action theory and developmental psychology. For one thing, these examples were limited to the instrumental actions of individuals. But the actions of individuals bring them into contact with other individuals, and the resulting interactions are significant phenomena in their own right (Chapman, 1982; Edelstein & Keller, 1982; Meacham, 1984; Youniss, 1984). Such interpersonal interactions may involve either shared or conflicting goals, or they may take on a communicative, rather than an instrumental character (Habermas, 1982). The very terms in which individual agents reflexively understand their own actions and others, are derived from the shared meanings of ordinary language discourse (Winch, 1958; von Wright, 1980).

Examples of interpersonal interaction can also be viewed in a developmental perspective, and in this case the close relation between action theory and a contextual model of development becomes even more obvious. Individual development is viewed as occurring in a social context also subject to change. It is to be assumed that action theory can also contribute to hypotheses regarding development in a social context. One very important social context for child development is obviously the family. In this connection, Chapman (1981a) argued that interpretations of parent–child interaction need to consider the plans, intentions, and expectations of both participants. The finding that children's behavior has a causal effect on their parents' behavior is consistent with at least two interpretations: that parents are passively responding to their children's behavior, or that they are intentionally and planfully adapting to it. One might also expect that the form of parent–child interaction would change with children's cognitive development and with other factors leading to changes in parents' and children's mutual expectations.

Another important social context for children is the peer group (Youniss, 1980). Peer interaction, for example, has been found to be an important contributor to the development of children's self-concepts (Mannarino, 1978; Volpe, 1981). Children's conceptions of their own abilities gradually come to depend more on social comparisons than on personal success experiences alone (Nicholls & Miller, 1983). For this reason, it becomes important to consider the particular reference group to which the self is compared—for example, changes in reference groups following the transition from one type of school to another have been found to result in significant changes in self-concept (Schwarzer, Lange, & Jerusalem, 1982; Schwarzer & Schwarzer, 1982).

In summary, the integration of action and developmental perspectives can prove fruitful with regard to both individual action and interpersonal interaction. In each case, action theory specifies relationships among various determinants or constituents of action, and the developmental perspective describes the temporal evolution of those relationships together with the resulting changes in action outcomes.

15 Action-Theory Perspective in Research on Social Cognition

Rainer K. Silbereisen
The Technical University of Berlin

INTRODUCTION

Chapman and Skinner describe the contribution of action theory to developmental psychology, and vice versa. Similarly, I wish to give empirical examples of what an action-theory perspective offers developmental psychology and thus to complement rather than evaluate their presentation.

I stress action-theory *perspective* because, to me, the heuristic function of action theory is more important than specific hypotheses derived from it.

Basic to the perspective is the assumption that *human beings are potentially reflective and act intentionally with reference to the environment* (Eckensberger & Silbereisen, 1980). Development is considered to be initiated by intentional, goal oriented (inter)actions of the developing subjects themselves. Viewed in this way, development is action (Lerner & Busch-Rossnagel, 1981; Silbereisen & Eyferth, in press).

A key to the action-theory perspective is its interest in the *microgenetic interplay* between observable behavior on one hand and covert cognitive and emotional processes on the other. (Chapman and Skinner share this interest although their emphasis on the analysis of actual everyday behavior is less than would seem to be warranted.) A systematic correspondence between covert processes and observable behaviors is required. "Development is action" assumes that the course of self-directed development is a result of a series of coordinated actions and, therefore, is somehow *structurally analogous* to the microgenesis of single actions.

There are particularly appropriate methods for analyzing this microgenesis. Von Cranach, Kalbermatten, Indermühle, and Gugler (1982) lead the field using systematic observation plus what they call the self-confronting interview: While watching a videotape of his/her actions, a subject is asked to describe the cognitions and emotions accompanying action.

An action-theory perspective is particularly useful in understanding the psychosocial development of the adolescent (Silbereisen, in press). Intentional, goal oriented interventions by the individual, and by society at large, play a role in adolescent development.

The *domain* of action theory encompasses all phenomena in which individuals actively attempt to further their own development. The numerous aspects of identity-formation and self-concept development are prominent examples.

In the following section, the principles outlined are illustrated by examples of studies on social cognition. The approach is traced from the redefinition of concepts through alternative methods to, I hope, provocative results.

RESEARCH ON SOCIAL COGNITION IN AN ACTION-THEORY FORMAT

Inherent in the action-theory perspective is a challenge to develop theoretical and methodological concepts that view behavior, cognition, and emotion as connected. Attempts to establish this connection post hoc by correlating empirical data do *not* adequately meet the challenge.

Research on social cognition is a case in point. Although in everyday life a person's attempts to understand another person's "social perspective" (i.e., motives and thoughts) are embedded in social interactions, research on social cognition has nearly always disregarded these natural circumstances. Sociocognitive capabilities have been studied, for the most part, in artificial contexts (e.g., cartoon stories instead of real-life experiences) in which neither personally relevant interaction goals nor realistic means are present. The relationship between both parts—interactional behavior and social cognition—has been established post hoc by statistically correlating the two independently measured variables instead of studying both in a common framework.

Only recently have studies been published that shed light on the interplay between thinking and behavior in natural action contexts:

1. Bar-Tal, Ravis, and Leiser (1980) as well as others (cf. Eisenberg & Silbereisen, 1984) systematically investigated reasons (i.e., the results of sociocognitive processing) for prosocial behavior in differing social contexts.

2. Among the very few studies is Selman's (1980). He investigated whether adolescents in everyday social interaction used those levels of perspective taking appropriate to the competence level of their age group. An example is self-reflective perspective taking—that is, predicting another's action in reaction to one's own prior action. Contrary to what might have been expected based on the

subjects' competence, this level of perspective taking was seldom used, and then only in contexts in which the subject felt attacked by his or her partner.

An action-theory perspective appears to provide research on social cognition with a fresh, unifying framework. Eckensberger and Silbereisen (1980) tried to overcome what we felt was an atheoretical, merely nominal definition of social cognition (cf. Flavell, 1977): "people reading"—that is, the notion that social cognition is *social* because of persons and their relationships as objects of cognition. In contrast to this, we redefined social cognition as *thinking about action*,—that is, cognition about goal directed, intentional behavior of people in their environments. Thus, the conceptual difference between cognition and social cognition lies not in the subject matter of thought (objects versus people) but in the attributed type of activity (mere physical movement versus intentional action); a child's alarmed exclamation, "Mom, the cloud is eating the sun!" could be an instance of social cognition.

Of course, this is a gross differentiation. On the other hand, social cognition seen in an action-theory format permits categorization into several hypothetical processes. Perspective taking (cf. Flavell, 1977; Selman, 1980), the construct on which most earlier research efforts have been concentrated, could be reinterpreted as a compound of several processes aimed at tackling different components of one's own or the other's action: *goal taking* and *means–ends taking*, for example. Interestingly enough, this reinterpretation enables integration of otherwise unconnected research traditions—for example, perspective taking and so-called interpersonal problem-solving skills (Shure & Spivack, 1978). The most advanced of their interpersonal skills exactly corresponds, in the action-theory reinterpretation, to means–ends taking: coordinating means and ends in an ordered sequence of alternative action plans.

In a series of studies, my coworkers and I are evaluating the actual role of thinking about action in three interaction contexts: action accompanying social cognition in children's traffic behavior, in referential communication between parent and child, and in trainer–trainee interaction between adults and adolescents. We are interested in age differences in thinking about goals and action steps, and their strategic coordination. Furthermore, we are analyzing situational cues that call upon one's sociocognitive repertoire.

Action-Accompanying Social Cognition in Traffic Behavior

A study by Baumgardt, Küting, and Silbereisen (1981) on children's goal directed behavior in everyday traffic used both aspects of an action-theory perspective: The variables under scrutiny were conceptualized in an action-theory framework, and the methods were specially designed to reveal the interplay between cognition and behavior.

Twelve children (six from the first and six from the fourth grade) were escorted separately by an interviewer along the route to their school or playground. The children were instructed to consider themselves to be experts explaining to the interviewer how they coped during the outing. Thus, the children reported their spontaneous thoughts regarding their parts in traffic and regarding street events including others' traffic behavior. The interviews were in the form of open dialogues directed largely by the children's utterances. The interviewer's role was to ask those questions necessary to establish which goals, means of action, or possible consequences the children considered when observing their own actions or those of others. The interviews were recorded on cassette tape and transcribed; their average length was 20 minutes. The children's comments on a total of 113 street-traffic episodes were analyzed.

All the episodes were analyzed, first, according to the complexity with which the structural components of actions (i.e., goals, means, ends) were interrelated in the children's thinking, and second, according to the level of social perspective taking implicit in their action plans.

The *complexity of action planning* was divided into three categories: (1) episodes containing a simple mention or enumeration of action steps ("Wait here, look left and right, then cross"); (2) thinking in simple means–ends relationships, and (3) considering alternative means–ends relationships—that is, evaluating the relative merits of alternative actions ("If you're riding your bike and someone is driving beside you, it can very easily happen that somebody opens a car door. That is really dangerous, and then if you swerve to avoid the door, the problem is that there can be another car coming from behind.").

The results of a comparison between the children in the two grades are shown in Table 15.1. There is a clear age trend in the children's action planning. Single-action steps and simple means–ends relationships predominate among the first graders. The fourth graders' thinking is characterized by simple means–ends relationships and alternative means–ends relationships. The relative importance of single-action steps versus alternative means–ends relationships is reversed

TABLE 15.1
Complexity Levels of Action Planning in
First and Fourth Graders' Traffic
Behavior (Percentages)[a]

Complexity	Grade	
	1	*4*
Action steps	45	9
Means–ends relationships	46	61
Alternative means–ends relationships	9	30

[a]N of episodes: 56 (grade 1); 57 (grade 4).

TABLE 15.2
Perspective-Taking Levels of Action
Planning in First and Fourth Graders'
Traffic Behavior (Percentages)[a]

	Grade	
Level of Perspective Taking	1	4
No perspective taking	82	39
Subjective perspective taking	16	44
Self-reflective perspective taking	2	16
Mutual perspective taking	0	2

[a]N of episodes: 56 (grade 1); 57 (grade 4).

between the two groups: only 9% of the first graders' episodes—but 30% of the fourth graders'—show the most elaborate category of action planning. And whereas single-action steps characterize 45% of the first graders' episodes, only 9% of the fourth graders' episodes are so characterized. (Despite the low percentage of single-action steps reported by older children, it would be a misinterpretation of the data to conclude that older children did not think at this level of complexity. Presumably, children report what they feel is important; for the older children, thinking in single-action steps is apparently so routine as not to be worth mentioning.)

The same episodes were then evaluated according to level of *perspective taking* (cf. Selman, 1980). Four categories were used: (1) no perspective taking—simple description; (2) subjective perspective taking—the perspectives of self and other are recognized as potentially different, but another's subjective state is believed to be obvious through simple physical observation; (3) self-reflective perspective taking—the child puts him- or herself into another's shoes and expects the other to do the same; (4) mutual perspective taking—the perspectives of self and other are both viewed from a third-person or generalized other perspective. The data are shown in Table 15.2.

Whereas only 18% of the younger children's remarks took any account of another person's social perspective at any level, 62% of the older children's did. Clearly, the older children more often took into account actions, feelings, or perceptions influencing others' behavior in traffic situations. An 11 year old offered an example of self-reflective perspective taking: "That driver should really be careful, because when he drives so fast (driver is turning right), that woman (riding a bicycle straight ahead) can't see him." Age differences for self-reflective perspective taking are again striking.

In sum, the data show clear age differences in the complexity as well as in the social sensitivity of action planning. Whether a few, or even a noticeable proportion, of the reports may have been, strictly speaking, not action accompanying but rather retrospective interpretations is unimportant for the present argument. The critical point is that the situation required thinking about action—that is, social cognition in a *natural* context.

Comparing the age trends in Table 15.2 with what is known from Selman's competence measurements, there appears to be a striking underrepresentation of the more developed modes of social cognition in the present data. Selman, however, did not use task materials involving traffic behavior. Hence, there is a question as to whether the discrepant results mirror differences between hypothetical competence and performance or situational peculiarities. Fortunately, Günther (1981) also studied perspective taking using traffic situations; his task materials, however, were hypothetical, cartoon-like stories. The children in his study also showed more perspective taking than we found in the natural context of real traffic behavior. Thus, Günther's results lend support to the conclusion that in natural situations children plan and organize their actions below their competence levels. This may occur because everyday interaction in natural situations is so routinized as not to require advanced thinking modes.

In a study designed to cross-validate these results, parents and their children were exposed to a *novel* situation that actually required nonroutine social understanding.

Action-Accompanying Social Cognition in Referential Communication

To communicate effectively, one has to adapt one's message to the listener's situation and dispositional requirements; a sort of tuning is required that can be guided by sociocognitive processes.

If adults are asked to reflect upon why verbal communication between two people has been successful or unsuccessful, they are likely to recognize that a speaker may convey the intended meaning ambiguously or unambiguously, that if a message is ambiguous, the listener may make an incorrect interpretation, and that to guarantee a correct interpretation of an ambiguous message, the listener must be given more information. In contrast, data collected by a number of researchers using a variety of procedures and methods of analysis (cf. Robinson, Silbereisen, & Claar, in press) confirm that 5 year olds do not have such understanding. At that age children do not make accurate analyses of the causes of communication failure, and they do not use their linguistic skills as effectively as they might, either as speakers or as listeners.

Incidental natural observations have led researchers (cf. Robinson & Robinson, 1981) to hypothesize that children remain ignorant of the reasons for their message's ambiguity because of the way their parents or other adults talk with them in everyday settings: The adult's usual *strategy* for dealing with misunderstandings and nonunderstandings presumably does not inform the child that there is a communication problem. Parents relatively seldom give their children explicit information about the causes of misunderstandings.

A direct test of these assumptions requires more than just measuring communication efficiency or observing interaction sequences: Communication strategies are conceived as goal directed, intentional behavior—that is, actions. Thus, attempts at discovering communication strategies have to take into account these goals and intentions and—more generally still—all the action-accompanying social cognitions.

In two studies my colleagues and I investigated parental-communication strategies in an action-theory format.

Study 1. The core of the experimental paradigm was a task of the *referential-communication* type, which is often used in research on communication failures.

The task required the child to select four out of eight dolls and to place them on a toy truck's four seats, which could be described in terms of position (front or back row) and color (brown or white). The dolls differed in only a few details of clothing and hair style. The child was asked to describe these dolls and their position to a female adult listener who was visually separated by a screen. The listener had an identical set of eight dolls and a toy truck on her side of the screen. She attempted to reproduce the child's placement of dolls in the truck by following the child's clues. The task was designed to be difficult enough that 6-year-old nursery school children would not be able to give unambiguous information about the specific doll and seating position. In other words, they were not old enough to be sufficiently aware of the critical referents in the referential communication task. Consequently, the listener had to tell the child repeatedly that she did not know which doll he or she was talking about. The child's mother (in a few cases, the father) took part in the task as a naive observer. The parents were told that they could try to help their children during the task if they wished, and most did.

In the first study, Walper, Mülle, Noack and Silbereisen (1981) used this research paradigm with a group of 17 nursery school children and their mothers. The parents could have intervened in such a way as to maximize the children's learning of advanced referential communication skills, yet most parents failed in their attempts to do so.

Study 2. The following analysis of the action-accompanying cognitions sheds more light on *why* parents missed the chance to help their children develop referential communication skills. The self-confronting interview technique (cf. von Cranach et al., 1982) was used to investigate the reasons: Video recordings of the parent–child interaction were shown to the parents in a series of short clips. Parents were asked to recall their thoughts and feelings in each situation. These comments were then transcribed. A different group of 12 nursery school children and their mothers was used in this study by Claar and Silbereisen (1982).

SILBEREISEN

In all, 278 cognitions were excerpted from the parents' communications. Of these cognitions, 105 had the self as object and 173 were directed toward the child. Only the child directed cognitions were analyzed for both action components and perspective-taking level.

The following *action components* were distinguished: (1) information reception ("She hadn't noticed that two dolls were quite similar"); (2) information processing ("Now, with the second doll, she knows what the point is"); (3) action goals ("And then she wanted to rearrange all the dolls"); (4) action steps ("She took the doll out of the car"); (5) action plans—that is, a more complex coordination of steps and goals of action ("And then I heard her say, 'She's wearing a short skirt,' so it won't happen again that the wrong doll ends up sitting there"); (6) emotional process ("She was a little bit embarrassed then"); (7) motivational process ("I had the impression that he didn't want to continue"); (8) evaluation ("Then she mentioned the tie, which I thought was good, since the other one didn't have one of these ties").

Every cognition was further analyzed for level of *perspective taking*: (1) no perspective taking—the child and his or her actions are viewed exclusively from the parent's perspective; (2) simple perspective taking—the child's view is taken into consideration by the parent; (3) complex perspective taking—any higher level (cf. Selman, 1980). Because only 2% of the cognitions showed a complex level of perspective taking, categories (2) and (3) were combined and called "internal perspective."

The frequencies of the several action components, broken down by perspective-taking level, are depicted in Figure 15.1.

In only 66 out of 173 cases (38%) was the *internal perspective* of the child (i.e., his or her action planning), the target of parents' social cognition. About half of these ($N = 32$; 18%) were directed toward the child's information reception and processing. Emotional processes ($N = 11$; 6%) and evaluation ($N = 11$; 6%) also contributed considerably to these cognitions, which are related to the child's internal perspective.

Parents' cognitions, however, concerned goals and plans in only a few cases ($N = 8$; 5% of all cognitions), regardless of perspective-taking level. They, therefore, lacked insight into the deep structure of the task and the child's problem in identifying his or her own ambiguous statements.

Results. Taking together the results of the two studies on action-accompanying social cognition in referential communication, we can ask what the contribution of the action-theory perspective has been. First, the actual role of social cognition in natural social interaction has been made clearer: Sociocognitive processes of the perspective-taking type can no longer be conceived as *the*, or even *a* dominant, organizational principle of social action. Whether in routine or novel action, elaborate levels of perspective taking occur too rarely to be assigned that role. Even in the few cases in which sociocognitive processes are at

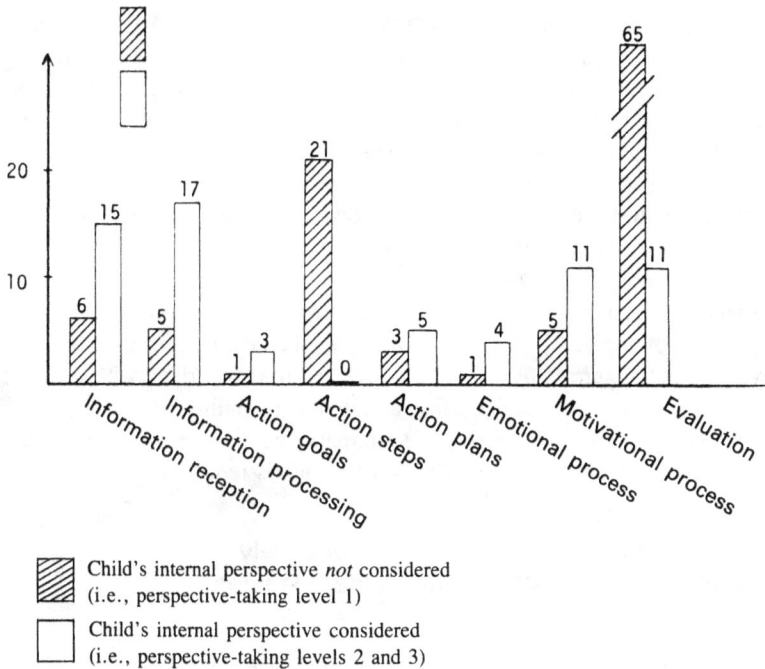

FIG. 15.1. Parent's thinking about child's action: action components broken down by perspective-taking level.

work, they do not so much concern the internal perspective of the interaction partner (i.e., his or her thoughts and feelings), but rather the more peripheral aspects of action planning.

Second, the insight into the dynamics of missed helping opportunity invites speculation about the *mechanisms of development*. Within the framework of cognitive-developmental theories (cf. Turiel, 1974), development is understood to be promoted by inducing *cognitive conflicts* between an individual's expectations on one hand and discrepant experiences on the other. According to Turiel, cognitive conflicts can only be set up when two independent conditions are met: (1) an optimal mismatch (a not too great discrepancy) is established between the child's sociocognitive capabilities and the demand structure of the task; and (2) this mismatch is experienced by the child as contradictory and problematic.

Mugny, Perret-Clermont, and Doise (1981), Lefebvre-Pinard and Reid (1980), Silbereisen (1981), and others have demonstrated the effectiveness of explicit conflict *induction* in training and education settings. These results, however, do *not* confirm the hypothesized role of cognitive conflicts in spontaneous, natural interactions.

To return to the parent–child interaction study: What is the significance of the results for current views of cognitive conflicts seen as mechanisms of development? The parents might have pointed out to their children the discrepancies between the children's efforts to communicate effectively and the failures to do so. The failures were repeatedly evidenced by the experimenter's responses. The question would then have been whether the parents failed to help their children *despite* having induced cognitive conflicts. Yet this connection was never made. In the parents' commentaries to the video clips, in their interventions in the task, and in the open discussions conducted a few weeks after the experimental sessions there was not a single attempt to induce cognitive conflict—either explicitly or without conscious intent.

Analyzing social cognition *during* action provides a more realistic view of the significance of cognitive conflicts. Until now, the peculiarities of action-accompanying social cognition have been emphasized in comparison with results from traditional research approaches. For a full understanding of the specificity of action-accompanying cognitions, a systematic comparison with *retrospective interpretations* of one's own or others' activities is required.

Action-Accompanying versus Retrospectively Interpreted Social Cognition in Trainer–Trainee Interactions

In a therapeutic, vocational training workshop for socially handicapped adolescents, Schuhler (1983) recorded interactions between master craftspeople and their apprentices on cassette tape for 2 hours. In all, 10 master craftspeople took part. From the tape of each training group, those sections were marked in which the master craftspeople had been involved in a personal clash with one or more of the apprentices. A personal clash was defined as a situation in which dispute about sociomotivational problems of the apprentices arose. In all, 36 situations containing personal clashes were recorded.

The marked sections of the tape were then collected and played back to the master craftspeople, who were asked to describe what had happened. These interviews were about 30 minutes long. Analyzing the transcripts, Schuhler (1983) distinguished between what seemed to be mere retrospective interpretation and actual action-accompanying cognitions.

Of a total of 271 reported items, 31 (11%) were found to be action-accompanying cognitions. This particular proportion, of course, should be seen as task specific. Each reported item was assigned to one of three categories: (1) goals ("I wanted him to notice that he was useless"); (2) motivational processes ("I can't say why, but I think it's for their own good to get a proper dressing down"); and (3) strategies ("I wasn't too fussy about the fact that her work was sloppy, even though she wants to be a dressmaker; I didn't want to spoil her satisfaction in it").

Table 15.3 shows the breakdown into retrospective interpretation and action-accompanying cognitions. Retrospective items are further classified as in-

TABLE 15.3
Trainers' Retrospective Interpretations and Action-
Accompanying Cognitions Concerning Goals, Motivational
Processes, and Strategies (Percentages)[a]

	Goals	Motivational Processes	Strategies
Retrospective interpretation			
Own action	25	41	35
Other's action	6	88	5
Action-accompanying cognition	35	20	45

[a]N of cognitions: 153 (own action); 87 (other's action); and 31 (action accompanying).

terpretations of either their own or of their apprentices' interactions. Comparing the two types of retrospective interpretations, a striking difference appears: Whereas the percentages of goals, motivational processes, and strategies are balanced (25%, 41%, and 35%) when the craftspeople are interpreting their own actions, motivational processes heavily dominate (88% for this single category) when they are reporting the apprentices' actions. From the master craftspeople's perspectives, the apprentices' "psychology" is totally different from their own: Apprentices are thought neither to set goals nor to follow strategies; instead they are thought to be driven by motivational processes. In other words, the master craftspeople attribute intentionality and goal directedness only to themselves. (Note that this is not an instance of the fundamental attributional error, because both drives and plans are internal.)

ACTION FOR DEVELOPMENT: A SUMMARY OF POTENTIAL CONTRIBUTIONS

The redefinition of social cognition as thinking about action has consequences for both concepts and methods.

First, *normative models of action organization* acquire a role in structuring the potential content of social cognition. So far, the model has been fairly simple. In all the studies described, it has contained little more than the *structural* components of actions—that is, goals, means, and ends. Certainly, *process* models of action organization will provide further distinctions. It should be mentioned, however, that models of the Miller, Galanter, and Pribram (1960) type are too simple to analyze social interaction adequately. Social interaction is best described by what Kaminski (1983) called the *multiple-action paradigm*, in which two or more action units occur relatively independently of each other at any given time.

The master craftspeople in Schuhler's (1983) study, for example, may be pursuing training goals and egocentric needs simultaneously during a clash with their apprentices. Approaches that elaborate on the basic assumptions of the multiple-action paradigm have been presented by Janis and Mann (1977) and Fuhrer (1982).

Second, the action-theory perspective has led to research on social cognition in *natural interaction contexts*. New methods are needed to uncover thinking about action in the mélange of everyday activities. One of these is the stimulated recall technique using video playback as in Claar and Silbereisen's (1982) and Schuhler's (1983) studies.

What has the action perspective, as realized so far, contributed by way of results on the development and maintenance of social cognition? Clear age differences in thinking about goals, action steps, and their strategic coordination have been established. Baumgardt et al., (1981) reported that action organization becomes more complex as children grow older. On the other hand, people's thinking in natural contexts occurs at simpler levels than their actual competence. This relationship holds for the cognitive organization of children's traffic behavior as well as for adults' attempts to assist their children in potentially instructive situations.

There is no obvious single cause for suboptimal social thinking: On one hand, the circumstances of everyday social interaction are often such that misunderstandings do not lead to catastrophe. For example, traffic regulations "free" the individual from the necessity of taking the perspective of others and predicting their behavior at a street crossing. The reduced sociocognitive complexity in everyday behavior has its costs, however. As Claar and Silbereisen (1982) demonstrated, mothers did not draw on their more complex thinking resources even in situations in which routine attempts had failed.

The question is, *which* situational cues cause a person to call upon the full range of his or her sociocognitive repertoire? Schuhler's (1983) study provides one answer: The actor's understanding of the interpersonal relationship is an important determinant. The master craftspeople attributed much greater action-like behavior complexity to themselves than to their apprentices.

The data are far from conclusive. The number of cases in each study was small, and the situations were entirely different. What does seem clear, however, is that further systematic research using the action-theory perspective can contribute to a fuller understanding of how social action is organized and develops.

ACKNOWLEDGMENTS

An earlier version of this chapter was presented at the Second Planning Conference on Child Development in Life-Span Perspective, held at the Max Planck Institute for Human

Development and Education, Berlin (West Germany), July 9–11, 1981. The studies reported were supported in part by the German Research Council Grant Si 296/1–1,2,3,4 (principal investigator: Silbereisen) and the Federal Highway Research Institute Grant 8011 (principal investigator: Silbereisen). The author wishes to thank Mary Grunwald for her helpful comments.

GOAL DIRECTED BEHAVIOR IN
SOCIAL CONTEXTS

Athay and Darley take up one aspect of action theory in relation to social psychology. One prominent American social-psychological theory that does see people as engaged in intentional action vis-a-vis one another is exchange theory. Exchange theory is the view that social action is essentially the attempt on the part of individuals to trade outcomes with each other—that is, each participant acts so as to maximize his or her gain from interaction while minimizing his or her costs. But Athay and Darley argue that this is a distorted view of the typical kind of social interaction we engage in.

In their view, the standard case of social interaction involves people doing toward one another what each other's position in a social organization demands. Thus, in the standard case of the exercise of power, people in subordinate positions do what is demanded of them without calculating what it is that each participant gets out of the interaction. This is so because for both the subordinate and the person in power, even in a private interaction, there is a third party deriving benefits and imposing costs— namely, the community.

Sabini, Frese, and Kossman take up two points. First, they extend the discussion of the relation of action theory to behavior in the context of institutions, arguing that in the standard case of a person's carrying out a role requirement, only those alternatives consistent with the role are considered in an expectancy-value analysis.

Second, they develop the implications of action theory's commitment to the view that an objective social world is understood through action. This notion is explored in relation to "person perception," collective action, and the person–situation controversy.

16 The Role of Power in Social-Exchange Relationships

Michael Athay
John M. Darley
Princeton University

INTRODUCTION

Our object in this chapter is to show that currently popular conceptions of social exchange do not establish their authors' and advocates' claim to provide an account of the fundamental mode of organization for face-to-face interaction. These conceptions are inadequate because they rely on an overly rationalistic model of social cognition favored by microeconomists (and herein named, following a common usage, *the theory of rational choice*). We argue that even though it has a limited place in ordinary interaction, social exchange conceived in this rationalistic way is not the basic mode of organization because it is only rarely that actors undertake the sort of reflecting, criticizing, evaluating, and calculating moves it ascribes to them. For the most part, ordinary interaction is governed by relations of interpersonal power of a very particular sort, which we analyze in the first half of the chapter. These "positional power" relations exhibit essential features that distinguish them sharply from relations of social exchange, and especially from that subset of the latter that conforms to the rational-choice model. The lesson we draw, however, is *not* that the notion of social exchange lacks theoretical utility. Our project, rather, is to establish the domains of proper application, within the broad range of types of interchange comprising everyday social life, both of social exchange generally and of rationalistic social exchange in particular. The picture of the interaction process we present thus stresses three distinct modes of organization: positional power, routinized social exchange, and rationalistic social exchange; it identifies the different sorts of circumstances under which each is dominant, and it characterizes the socially competent actor as one who is able to operate effectively with all three modes.

SOCIAL ACTION AS A PROCESS OF TREATMENT PRODUCTION

Social interaction is a goal directed process in which people interact with others in order to secure various treatments that they require in order to satisfy specific social-psychological needs. The process is an "economic" one in the sense that actors enter social relations for the purpose of securing a share of their communities' limited resources. When the needs to be satisfied are social psychological, rather than narrowly material, the resources in question include such things as affirmations and confirmations, affection, interest and concern, simple attention, encouragement, support, respect, praise and criticism, as well as more immediately utilitarian behaviors such as professional assistance, instruction, or advice.

Taken as a whole, the patterns of interaction within a community constitute a system for ensuring the production and distribution of the treatments that members require in order to continue functioning as people who are capable of satisfying the community's standards with respect to kind and quality of "legitimate" activity. Parallel to the community's system for producing and distributing material commodities (the "economy" in the narrow sense), and constantly interpenetrating with it, we thus find a second production system, the yield of which is persons—or more strictly, socially competent persons. Every actor is at once a producer and a consumer in this system, demanding from others various particular treatments—*interaction commodities* as we call them—as means to fulfilling his needs and in turn producing particular treatments to satisfy the needs of his alters. As a producer, each actor is possessor of a repertoire of specific skills or capacities (interaction competencies) for constructing the distinctive patterns of action comprising such treatments (Athay & Darley, 1981, 1982).

Actors' attempts to secure needed treatments from particular others are, in effect, efforts to persuade these others to exercise certain of their competencies on the applicants' behalf. An element of manipulation thus enters into all social relations: Actors enter relationships with particular alters because they perceive them as possessing competencies in the production of treatments that they need, and they adopt given behavior strategies for the purpose of placing those alters in the position of wanting, or needing, or having to exercise their competencies to the "manipulators'" benefit. Manipulation is inevitable because actors' interests inevitably conflict in a society that, like ours, has a very complex division of labor, with divergent values, perspectives, and lifestyles attaching to the many different roles actors are compelled to play. In the *standard* case of interaction, a given participant can realize his needs only if others undertake to act for him in ways that, from a narrowly egocentric point of view, are not immediately and fully, and often not at all, in their interests. The actor is thus forever confronted with the strategic problem of so operating on the other as to bring him to see it as worth his while to incur the costs of satisfying the actor's treatment demands.

It is plausible to think that under these conditions, interaction must take the form of social exchange: Every actor depends on receiving specific treatments from others in order to carry out his projects of action, so each naturally will attempt to take advantage of this interdependence by demanding particular needed responses from his alters as a condition of providing the performances they in turn require of him. In the last 25 years, this view of interaction as fundamentally depending on relations of exchange has received considerable attention and development, particularly in the work of Thibaut and Kelley (1959, 1978), Homans (1961), and Blau (1964).

We contend, however, that exchange theorists vitiate this important insight by the two related errors we describe in our introduction: They ground their conceptions of exchange in a rationalistic model of ordinary cognition that has only a very limited application in ordinary social life, and they insist that the resulting account of exchange relations is *the* primary mode of organization for face-to-face interaction.

As a consequence, exchange theory has tended to ignore the extent to which social life depends on the unreflective application of routines of interaction. Even the elements of manipulation it rightly presumes to be fundamental features of the interaction process are most often a matter of actors' exercising interpersonal power in the routine ways we describe later (pp. 237, 240–241). When strategies of manipulation do take on the form of negotiation and exchange, they often still are highly routinized, depending on familiar, taken-for-granted models of instrumentally effective performance (pp. 245–246). To demonstrate this, we first need to articulate the "standard version" of social exchange.

SOCIAL EXCHANGE AND RATIONAL CHOICE

In the form that concerns us, the theory of rational choice is a set of assertions about the determinants of actors' behavior in interaction situations. In particular, it assumes that the actor carries out a complex set of intellectual operations including the following: (1) articulation and survey of the various courses of action available to him as means for realizing his goals in the situation; (2) appraisal of each alternative in terms of its instrumental utility; (3) evaluation of each alternative with respect to the probability of its successful execution; (4) rank ordering of the alternatives by preference, with the "expected utility" of an alternative (its utility weighted by the probability of its occurrence) as the criterion of "more preferred"; and finally (5) the decision, in the form of an explicit mental act, to follow the "most preferred" course of action. (Here, and in the account that follows, we are relying extensively on Heath's excellent [1976] analysis of the basic presumptions of exchange theory, especially as it is formulated by Blau, Homans, and Thibaut and Kelley. Heath's reconstruction is something of an idealization, and we are adapting it in order to make this version of social exchange maximally plausible as a model of social cognition. We do not claim that all exchange theorists subscribe to all of its provisions, but that most accept most of them. Space limitations force us to refer the reader to Heath [1976] for detailed argument in support of this contention.)

Exchange theory appeals to this model in order to explain why two or more actors undertake interchange with each other in a given case—the answer being that each believes, on the basis of the sorts of calculations detailed, that producing a certain treatment in return for certain treatments from the other constitutes the most preferred of the alternative means available to him for realizing some particular project he brings to the situation. Add to this account Homans' (1961) sweeping dictum that " . . . social behavior [is] an exchange of activity, tangible or intangible, and more or less rewarding or costly, between at least two persons" [p. 13]; or Blau's (1964) only slightly more conservative formulation:

> Exchange is here conceived as a social process of central significance in social life . . . [underlying] relations between groups as well as . . . individuals; both differentiation of power and peer group ties; conflicts between opposing forces as well as cooperation; both intimate attachments and connections between distant members of a community without direct social contacts" [p. 4].

Here we have a picture according to which a highly rationalistic form of social exchange constitutes the fundamental organizer of face-to-face interaction, indeed, of social life generally—or in our formulation, of the community's activities of social production.

It is an essential feature of the rational-choice model, hence of this view of exchange, that it ascribes to actors an attitude of critical reflection with respect to their ordinary activities. Their distinguishing and weighing of courses of action proceeds according to well-formulated principles of criticism, involving calculations of relative costs and benefits, consequent assignments of more or less determinate utility factors, calculation and comparison of probabilities of successful execution. Calculation, comparative evaluation, acquisition, and application of rules of criticism are highly rationalistic mental operations that, in the paradigm cases with which we all are familiar (and in which many of us have been trained in our capacities as professional intellectuals), involve reflection, self-monitoring, and a style of thinking that is inferential rather than associative. It is true that exchange theorists sometimes qualify this picture by suggesting that with practice, the steps in the model and the use of its rules of evaluation may become more or less unconscious and automatic (Thibaut & Kelley, 1959). But this move begs the question we address: Does it make sense to assert that cognitive operations of this *sort* are fundamental and pervasive determinants of social action? Or is it rather the case that an adequate model for the majority of social interchanges, including exchange relationships, simply has no place for variables involving such rationalistic processes, be they carried out consciously or unconsciously?

POSITIONAL POWER AND THE ORGANIZATION OF 'SOCIAL PRODUCTION'

According to the alternative model we have in mind, the structure of most interactions is in the first instance determined by a special class of interpersonal power arrangements that, for reasons that become apparent shortly, we term *positional power*. We adapt our notion of positional power from Marx's 1906/1977) brief account of money as comprising the most powerful of material commodities because it has the capacity to attract all other material commodities. By analogy, we speak of the power attaching to a particular type of treatment produced by one actor as consisting of its capacity to "attract" other types of treatment produced by other actors. Extending the analogy further, we take power as attaching primarily to *competencies* in the production of treatments, rather than to the treatments themselves, because competencies are the fundamental unit of social production. Thus, actors who are known to possess particular interaction competencies are able to attract specified treatments from others by virtue of their statuses as recognized proficients in those modes of production. A production competency thus carries powers of attraction over interaction commodities in the sense that possessing particular competencies enables an actor to mobilize on her behalf particular competencies possessed by other actors.

This account yields an analysis of interpersonal power because, from the point of view of social production, an actor's power must consist ultimately in her ability to get alters to provide the treatments that she requires in order to fulfill her projects and satisfy basic psychological needs. We now take this to mean that an actor is powerful to the extent that she possesses production competencies that carry powers of attracting from other members of the community these wanted treatments. Following Weber's (1968) point about the element of compulsion in our intuitive notion of power, it must be added that the powerful actor must be able to get alters to do their producing for her whether or not they would "rationally choose" to provide the performances she demands. It is the specifically *positional* aspect of interpersonal power, we are about to argue, that accounts for this element of compulsion.

We claim that actors come to possess particular competencies, hence powers of attraction, by virtue of their occupying given positions in systems of social positions generated by their communities to organize the production and distribution of interaction commodities. The sorts of community mainly responsible for social production are for the most part highly localized collectivities of persons who regularly interact with each other: friendship groups, neighborhoods, families, on-the-job groups (offices, university departments, production teams in factories), clubs, religious groups, and so on. Some such interaction communities (e.g., job-related groups) have as their primary functions the performance of tasks (e.g., the production of some material commodity) not directly related to members' self-maintenance, whereas other communities (e.g., families, friendship groups) exist primarily as units of social maintenance. But every interaction community has as part of its social function the regulation of its members' activities of producing the treatments they require from each other to reproduce themselves as viable, socially competent personalities. In particular, it must so organize these activities as to ensure each member that he will be able to satisfy basic needs to a degree that will permit him to perform the tasks it requires of him. Communities carry out this organizing function by generating frameworks of interrelated social roles and by compelling members to make their production activities conform to the principles of action defined by these roles. Taken in this way, as a unit of social production, a social role consists of some fairly definite set of interaction competencies, publicly recognized within the community as comprising a cohesive, natural-kind-like collection of capacities and dispositions. Learning the role involves acquiring those production competencies; playing the role involves exercising the competencies by producing the specified treatments in the face of legitimate demands by would-be consumers. Consumption is organized in terms of this same system of roles. As an incumbent of a given role, the well-socialized actor is expected to manifest social-psychological needs, and to aspire to fulfillment of projects of action, which are communally defined as appropriate to an actor in that role.

The point of our definition of positional power in terms of production competencies is to show how power relations are part of this role-based organization of social production. Learning the consumer aspect of a social role involves learning, along with the production competencies defining it, a more or less well-specified set of powers of attraction that each competency exercises over the treatment productions of actors occupying correlated producer roles. Learning the role's producer aspect involves learning that certain competencies possessed by other actors in turn exercise powers of attraction over one's own products—that is, involves learning that certain roles stand to it as legitimate consumer roles. Because role systems are systems of normative principles of action, the point is perhaps best expressed by speaking of "producers' obligations" and "consumers' entitlements" with respect to the provision of interaction commodities. Incumbency in a particular role thus *entitles* the actor to receive certain treatments from incumbents of its correlated producer roles, and at the same time *obligates* him to produce specified treatments for incumbents of its correlated consumer roles. "Socialization" of the actor to fit a role consists of training him to recognize these obligations and entitlements as legitimate principles governing everyone's activities.

Although we rely here on the standard conception of a social role as a set of rights and duties attaching to a position in the community, our interpretation of roles as loci of (in terms of) positional power departs from standard treatments in placing special emphasis on their character as sets of determinate skills in the production of particular kinds of treatment. We see power as consisting ultimately in the ability to command the resources necessary to satisfy needs and fulfill projects, and this, in turn, as the ability to command other actors' exercise of their production competencies. The obligations and entitlements attaching to roles are the instruments of this control, enabling actors to compel appropriately placed others to employ various of their special skills when and where needed. Our conception thus stresses the performance aspects of roles, to the point of identifying incumbency in a role with the acquisition and exercise, socially enforced, of capacities for carrying out specified types of performance under specified conditions. It thereby relegates rights and duties to the status of handles by means of which these performances can be regularly and reliably elicited.

ILLUSTRATIONS: ROLES IN A UNIVERSITY DEPARTMENT

This thesis that social-production activities in general are organized in terms of systems of social position (e.g., roles) commits us to seeing as role governed many types of everyday activity that are not normally thought of as socially structured behavior, but are taken rather as the product of exchange negotiations between actors. The examples of social role that come most readily to mind are relatively formal roles—department chairperson, homemaker, parent—consisting of collections of competencies closely related to the official tasks of the social unit that recognizes them. But many other sorts of activity yield treatments that are so important to members' effective functioning that the community cannot leave it up to the individual to produce them or not, as egocentric interest dictates. In these cases, the community will come to recognize as a cohesive set the particular competencies that are required to produce these treatments, and it will ensure their production by making them subject to obligations and entitlements of the sort we have been describing.

In the academic world, as in any other world, the signals individuals receive concerning how others value their performances are fragmentary and confused. On occasion all of us need to review these signals with a respected other, and devise action implications from them. To do this, we often turn to an individual whom we might call the "sympathetic counselor." There are a number of elements in the set of treatments this individual is to provide; one is a "narrative-facilitating" treatment. The counselor must define the setting so as to make it natural and appropriate for the target person seeking advice to narrate episodes in which she represents herself as exercising particular interaction competencies. (For an account of the importance and prevalence of "personal narratives" in social interaction, see Goffman, 1974.) Some such narratives demonstrate particular competencies—for example, the professional intellectual's account of some part of her work, in which she is given the chance to demonstrate competency in a subject matter by telling about the development or content of her special views. Most, however, are reports of episodes in which the narrator presents herself as having exercised some particular competency—for example, an account of her skillful handling of after-colloquium questions.

Another function of the counselor is to provide the story teller with an opportunity to secure confirmation of herself as possessing the competencies figuring in her story. Once a generalized "agreement" on the story-teller's competencies has been marked, the interaction can turn to advice-giving business. The advice given by the counselor is now contextualized as advice given to a competent other on how to improve some of the "packaging" of her ideas. Suggestions are introduced with competence-preserving disclaimers. Although only an anal-neurotic would care, doing 17 analyses of variance violates certain statistical assumptions. Why don't you use a multivariate analysis instead?" "Here are some obscure references that you can use to show that others are making points similar to yours. Although not, of course, with the sustained force of your ideas. . . ."

Within a given community, quite definite skills are required in order to counsel adequately. In the case of an academic colleague's narrations of professional competency, for example, responses must be made that indicate interest, attention, and a willingness to consider seriously the content of the report. Related to this, the counselor must deliver his advice in a way that does not challenge the competence of the recipient. Finally, the counselor must spend the considerable time it takes to give this sort of advice, must remain alert during the counseling sessions because egos are at risk, and must have the depth of background knowledge in the content fields and the conventional standards prevailing in those fields to give good advice.

Communities of professional academics standardly articulate a role for one or more of their members that consists of providing these sorts of treatments—witness the department member who is invaluable to colleagues as a sympathetic sounding board for ideas, as a walking library of possibly relevant materials, as a source of constructive criticism, as a forestaller of embarrassing mistakes and omissions.

Fulfilling this role is a time-and-effort consuming task. Actors who fill this role are entitled to receive a range of treatments that the community determines are due them both as a kind of social reward for the exercise of their special skills, and because exercising the skills effectively requires they receive those treatments. This second point is important: Counselors can fulfill their functions of providing opportunities for actors to give representations of themselves as possessing given competencies only if the consumers of these treatments accord them appropriate sorts of respect. Telling stories about intellectual work to colleagues whose judgments are little valued is of little use in confirming one's representation of oneself as possessing intellectual skills. Counselors are thus able to carry out their production activities only if the community obligates members to produce for them treatments constituting "intellectual respect." Communities normally assign to certain roles the major part of their "respect-marking" tasks. In academic departments, the production of such treatments is usually assigned to the department chairperson and to certain senior members. Counselors will thus hold powers of attracting from incumbents of these roles the special treatments constituting "communal respect of professional academic work." Moreover, counselors will be entitled to such treatments independently of whether their own work enjoys a high standing in the professional community outside the department. Their entitlements are contingent on their readiness to exercise the competencies comprising their roles when qualified social persons demand narrative-facilitating treatments, but on little else. In particular, they are not required to enter into negotiation-and-exchange relations with the providers of respect markers. They are entitled to these treatments simply by virtue of fulfilling their roles.

The counselors' obligations to exercise their competence for others are similarly independent of any considerations of utility to themselves. The only relevant conditions are the appropriateness of the circumstances and the qualifications of the demanding other: The obligation clearly obtains for "department faculty member," for example, but probably not for "undergraduate major." It obtains for "department graduate students" only at official times and places.

Communities commonly induce members to acquire important roles by rewarding incumbents with entitlements that are not so closely tied to their competencies as in the case we have described. For example, supremely skilled counselors can often secure from the community a willingness to suspend judgments on the dimensions of activity that are central to the community's official tasks. They may be granted more time than is normal to produce concrete evidence of professional competence (degrees, books, papers, etc., in the case of academics); or their services to the community may be so valuable that they are given the usual rewards of promotion, raises, and honors without having to fulfill professional requirements imposed on colleagues who are not thus skilled.

Articulation of the counselor's role is a case of the community's using its positional structure to regularize a type of everyday activity that we usually consider to be a matter of individuals' voluntarily helping each other, from motives of friendship, altruism, or the possibility of gain through the reciprocation of other desirable treatments. Facilitation of intellectual narratives is so important to the self-regard of professional academics that no academic community will succeed in retaining its members' commitments unless it takes definite steps to ensure a sifficient supply of these treatments.

The point applies even more clearly to production activities that are more closely related to the community's official tasks. Consider, for a second example, the importance of special competencies in the business of securing research grants in a social science department. This importance goes beyond the basic need for material support because the standards of professional competence specify that the "scientific value" of a member's work is demonstrated by his or her ability to secure financial support in a process of peer review.

Although the ideology of the research grant asserts that only universalistic criteria determine the fate of particular proposals, it is well known by all practitioners that various more particularistic factors, in fact, figure prominently. These include "packaging" considerations, such as the wording of the proposal, the way the research is related to attention-getting work in the area, the way the grant is slanted toward the most recent "relevance" requirements, and so on. In addition, it is known that the different agencies look with differential favor on research of particular sorts. Success thus depends in some part on applying to the right place at the right time in the right way.

It is in the manipulation of these less-than-universalistic variables that the skills of the expert grant getter—we follow a familiar usage and call this person the "grantsperson"—become relevant. In order to fill the role, an actor must demonstrate competence through success in getting grants herself. Exercise of the competence consists of making available to others her special knowledge. Acquiring this knowledge involves sustaining a network of persons who are knowledgeable about review panels. This grantsperson must keep close track of the priorities of as many agencies as possible in order to form a reasonable judgment about their likely responses to any one sort of proposal. In addition she must keep well informed as to areas that do and do not attract interest currently. Inevitably, much time and effort must go into this business of sustaining contacts throughout the field and forming reasonable summary judgments of the wide range of disorderly information thereby gathered.

The obligations of the grantsperson role, then, include acquisition of this specialized knowledge and a readiness to share it with qualified persons by reviewing their grant proposals and advising them on their packaging and presentation. As with the counselor, she is expected to provide these services on demand, irrespective of whether she believes she will gain thereby. Qualified alters need not negotiate and exchange for these treatments. The principal entitlement of this role is an entitlement to community members' respect of her work as original and important scientific work, irrespective of its evaluation by the larger professional community. Her reputation outside the department may be that of uninspired competence, but within the community she will be entitled to the marks of respect normally reserved for leading practitioners. In part, this is because respect for her own grant-getting ability must be expressed as respect for her scientific abilities, or else the institution of peer review as a standard of evaluation will come into question; in part it is a matter of the collective's acting to reward her for services it cannot do without.

Grantspeople are entitled to receive the described respect-marking treatments from all social persons who are their clients but especially from incumbents of the community's official respect-marking roles. That his entitlements are contingent on his fulfilling the obligations of the role is evidenced by the fact that a skilled grant getter who refuses to make his special knowledge available to the community will not infrequently find it suggested that his success is due to this special expertise and not to the quality of his research. Successful grant getters, unlike the grantsperson, are not entitled to the latter's special respect-marking treatments, but must win such treatments on the basis of straightforward professional competence.

We claim that all social roles, including highly formalized roles with rights and duties defined by statute, are units of social production after the fashion of our two examples. All comprise special production competencies, and all carry treatment obligations and entitlements. Our present point, again, is that activities usually thought to be highly informal and dependent only on the idiosyncratic desires of their producers are structured in basically the same ways—though less formally—as the activities of the community's officers and officials.

POSITIONAL POWER VERSUS RATIONAL CHOICE

Actions governed by positional power diverge from the rational-choice model in two principal respects: (1) they control behavior directly, in a fashion little affected by actors' utility calculations; (2) the application of these regulating principles normally exhibits a routine quality that is inconsistent with the model's picture of actors as calculating strategists.

We argue the first point by suggesting a special status for that small subset of a community's normative principles of action that are genuinely fundamental to its organization of members' activities. These "foundational" principles provide the basis whereby actors make themselves calculable to each other to the degree necessary for smooth, orderly interaction. It is a basic condition of interaction that actors be able to count on there being limits to the variability of the responses they will have to cope with in others. Otherwise, they will be in the impossible position of having to formulate predictive and explanatory principles and correlated performance strategies anew for each new situation. Limitations on time and cognitive-processing capacity alone preclude such constant rethinking of interaction programs. In addition, no actor can sustain either the sense or the appearance of competent, controlled interaction if he must constantly face conditions that alter so rapidly as to be beyond his capacity for coping.

For these reasons, actors must be able to take for granted a set of limits on each others' behaviors. This necessity translates into a basic condition of "social competence" as publicly defined by the interaction community: Actors who are socially competent, hence safe to interact with, must constantly signal this fact by so acting as to present themselves as people whose commitments to foundational principles need never be considered problematic. (Interestingly, the requirement does not rule out instances of noncompliance altogether, but it demands that the malefactor make special remediation moves, showing that exceptional circumstances obtained, that he did not understand the principle's application to such cases, or, more simply, that he is sorry and will not do it again. Neither does it rule out consistent noncompliance, in the face of which remedial moves will not be taken seriously as indicators of future behavior.) Failure to so act, even if it is unwitting (due, e.g., to ignorance or psychopathology), is met with heavy penalties: Interactants begin to suspect the reliability of the actor's normative commitments, and come to feel that interaction with him is risky. They begin to withdraw from interactions that include him until he is cut off completely. This threat of exclusion from essential production relationships provides the community's most effective enforcer of foundational principles. (The point we are making here is an application of Goffman's [1974] discussion of "normative alignment.")

This threat introduces an element of compulsion that is simply inconsistent with the rational-choice model's picture of the actor's freely choosing among critically evaluated alternatives. Obligations for treatment production dictate courses of action outright, irrespective of the utilities that might be realized by their performance. If there is a utility calculation involved, then it will always be the same one: Given the heavy penalty of exclusion from production relationships, noncompliance must be a least-utility option. This, however, is not what the model means by "rational choice." It pictures the actor's evaluating each course of action as one of many options, each carrying a degree of utility, each to be considered on its merits, relative to the others. No real option obtains where the consequences of all but one course of action are disastrous; and there is no genuine evaluation, in the sense of the model, where it is determinable a priori that just one course of action will always have the highest utility.

Of course, the division we describe here between rational choice and positional power depends heavily on the effectiveness of the threat of exclusion from interactive relationships. This dependence suggests that if an actor has available alternative sources of supply that are equally satisfactory to him, then the element of compulsion attaching to positional power norms will be greatly reduced—to the point, perhaps, that it becomes possible for him to treat the question of compliance with the obligations and entitlements obtaining within one set of production relationships as a matter of choice in light of relative utilities. Here, we suggest, is a condition of application for the rational-choice model, hence one marker of the boundary between its domain of application and that of positional power. Notice, however, the final and irrevocable character of whatever specific act reveals the decision to reject the foundational rules of one interaction community. Adoption of a "rational-choice" attitude to these rules is possible *only* to the extent that exclusion can be accepted with impugnity.

The second divergence we see between positional power and the rational-choice model involves a conception of how power operates in ordinary affairs, which is in one respect at odds with the usual Weberian definition of power as the ability to compel the other to comply against his or her will. (Here, and in the sentences following, we adapt a point cogently made by Westergaard & Resler, 1975, Part 3.) The implication of Weber's formulation is that the exercise of interpersonal power consists of explicit acts of will undertaken in the face of acts of opposition by some other individual actors or groups, in order to secure the latter's compliance with some sets of demands.

Such a conception fits well into the rational-choice framework because of the importance attached to individuals' decisions. Certainly, it is true that power ultimately is exercised by actors over actors, and equally true that having power involves having the capacity to enforce compliance whether the other "wants" to give it or not. But the view errs in making the everyday exercise of power into a matter wholly of confrontations, of persons actively exercising their wills against each other. It ignores the fact that power relationships are more often experienced as impersonal states of a taken-for-granted world. Westergaard and Resler (1975) point out that economic power, for example, resides less in positive acts of decision making by powerful groups or individuals, undertaken in the face of resistance by others, than in the everyday, largely unquestioned application of assumptions that sustain private-property relations [pp. 143–144]. Yet these assumptions determine who is and is not capable of realizing their projects of action, whose activities ultimately serve whose ends.

Our claim is that positional power relations control the activities of social production in this same routine, largely impersonalized way that institutionalized economic power governs material production relations. Normally, actors conform to the powers of attraction each commands in an unreflecting, unquestioning, matter-of-course way. Their conformity does not depend on the outcomes of appraisals of the relative utility of compliance or noncompliance, nor on any inference-making acts of applying rules of calculation. In the normal case, they do not *decide* to comply or not comply at all, for the question does not arise. Positional power relations do, of course, break down, and actors do fail, through intention or inadvertence, to conform to them. Confronted with such malfeasance on the part of an alter, the actor may call upon obligations and entitlements in a more explicit way in an effort to compel compliance. If the breakdown is serious enough, or the other resists the routine efforts at remediation with which actors are trained to respond automatically (Goffman, 1974), then it is natural (as we argue shortly) for the actor to resort to something like rational-choice procedures. The model applies, however, only under these emergency conditions, and not to the ordinary operation of positional power relations.

As the foregoing arguments make apparent, most of our objections to exchange theory as it is currently practiced are really objections to the rational-choice model that underlies it. Shortly, we argue that exchange processes need not be conceived in terms of this model. But first we want to point out that positional power relations contrast with social exchange however it is conceived.

The essential feature of any organization of productive activities founded on exchange is the requirement of reciprocity between individual producers: Actors produce treatments demanded by others only if those others offer some return compensation. Such reciprocity is notably missing in the operation of positional power relations. The obligations and entitlements we have been describing dictate that an actor receive specified treatments from qualified others simply by virtue of his or her fulfilling the production requirements of his or her social position. Entitlements rest on his or her status as a social person and not on his or her willingness to serve the needs of the particular actors of whom he or she makes these demands.

DOMAINS OF APPLICATION FOR POSITIONAL POWER
AND SOCIAL EXCHANGE

Positional power relations stabilize interaction by limiting the extent to which the inherent indeterminacies of negotiation and exchange can adversely affect actors' access to necessary treatments, thereby guaranteeing them a minimal ability to calculate their prospects of fulfilling projects and satisfying needs. Positional power thus establishes a sort of base line of rights to treatments that is assured for each actor who is willing to fulfill the production requirements of the roles the community offers. But it does no more than that. Always it is open to actors to negotiate a level of mutual treatment that exceeds that of the base line. Indeed, in most cases, full realization of projects and fully adequate satisfaction of needs will demand that procurement substantially exceed the base line. The basic reason for this, we suggest, is that the base line, like social-welfare benefits in our society, is for functional reasons always placed at a level that is inadequate to sustain a standard of consumption the community deems adequate. The functional requirement operating here has to do with a general need for flexibility in the social-production system. As the needs and tasks of an interaction community change, so do the capacities for performance that it requires of its members. The community must therefore generate mechanisms that will enable it to induce actors to learn new production competencies and to give up their reliance on old ones (a process now appropriately known as *recycling*: the learning of new job skills in the face of collapse of demand for those of "the first career").

Reconstruction in the social-production system thus requires direct communal pressure to acquire new competencies, together with assurances of reward for doing so, which further requires compulsion of other actors to accept new treatment obligations. Orderly reconstruction is therefore possible only if the community has available strong penalties for noncompliance. From the perspective of the position we have been developing, the only really significant penalty must be exclusion from some important set of production and consumption relations, with attendant restriction of the actor's resources for satisfying some important set of needs. This penalty can be effective, clearly, only if there is a scarcity in the community of the sort of treatment normally sought from the relationships from which exclusion is threatened, or else recalcitrants will simply turn to alternative sources of supply. Interaction communities employ various "market" devices for manipulating scarcity by controlling supply (cf. Blau, 1964; Heath, 1976). Whatever the particular mechanisms involved, it is obvious that scarcity can be maintained only if the base line guaranteed by positional power relations is set low enough so that actors are not guaranteed more than a part of what they feel they must have in the way of treatments. In this way, positional power relations provide both a guarantee of functionally necessary minimums of treatment production and distribution, and a basis for communal revision of the production system.

For these reasons, we may expect that actors will seek a level of treatment provision from their interactants that significantly exceeds that of the minimum guaranteed by positional power relations. In this domain of production activities not regulated by the coercive norms of positional power, social-exchange processes normally are the basis of organization. In practice, the division of domains works something like this:

Entering an interaction situation, actors initially rely on positional power relations to fill their needs. They will, in other words, permit the operation of obligations and entitlements to take its normal course. Following the argument just concluded, it is inevitable that at some point in the interaction one or more parties will find themselves requiring treatments not guaranteed by these positional power relations; or alternatively, they will find that others are making such demands on them. The situation will then be redefined as one in which the rule of reciprocity, the scheme of offer and counteroffer, and the processes of negotiation characteristic of social exchange become the basis of actors' efforts to secure treatments from each other. We conceive this "shift" between the "domains" of exchange and positional power on the model as a shift in "interaction frames" (Goffman, 1974). If all parties can satisfy their treatment requirements by relying on a matter-of-course application of positional power, then the situation may be "framed" as a case of participants' seeking to discover and selectively activate each other's production competencies. When demands cannot be satisfied on the basis of position-based obligations and entitlements, then the situation may well have been framed as one of negotiation and exchange. Actors are likely to employ both sorts of frame in the course of any extended interaction situation, and to move frequently, and easily, between them. In the normal case, production and consumption will proceed more or less automatically on the basis of positional obligations, until demands develop that cannot be satisfied on this basis and parties move into a negotiation and exchange frame to settle these; next there is a return to reliance on the positional norms. We suggest an ordering of frames, with actors attaching priority to the positional power frame in the sense that they strive to organize their production relations on the basis of it alone; once they have been forced to abandon it for negotiation and exchange processes, they return to it as quickly as treatment demands permit.

Relations between graduate student and thesis advisor provide one familiar example of actors' shifting between the domains of positional power and social exchange. The obligations and entitlements of their respective roles dictate that the advisor freely give and the thesis student accept contributions to the work that count as criticism of design or interpretation, or advice about the shape and organization of the work. Advisors are obligated to provide this sort of assistance without receiving any formal recognition of their contributions to the final product, beyond that contained in routine markers of the role relation.

But suppose the student cannot come up with an important research question, or produces a text that is incoherent, an argument that is inconsistent, or a set of results that indicates that his or her conceptualization has broken down radically. Completion of the project may then require that the advisor set the research question anew, rewrite the text, or produce a coherent ad hoc interpretation of the results that gives some value to the work completed. This degree of involvement is not generally regarded as an obligation of a thesis advisor and seldom will be provided as a matter of course, without a demand for basic revision of the terms of the relationship.

At this point, there is a dramatic shift in the perspective that defines the relationship from one of positional power to one of explicit social exchange. The advisor will attempt to redefine the relationship as one that properly is subject to negotiations and exchange, with treatment demands *legitimately* judged according to whether the interest of the producer is advanced thereby. In particular, the advisor may demand the formal status of coauthor in exchange for his or her providing the sorts of assistance required to ensure the project's successful completion. Because this is a significant benefit, the student will be able to make further demands himself—for example, for material support from the advisor's stock of equipment and labor resources, whereas before, as advisee rather than coinvestigator, his role forced him to be content with doing his own routine work with whatever instruments he could scrounge. The nature of the relationship changes quite radically for both parties, once a shift of this sort has taken place. Neither can proceed any longer in the unquestioning ways of the old regime, but both have new possibilities for securing benefits from the relationship that were not permitted them by their positional power norms. On the other hand, if the negotiation-and-exchange basis of the relationship proves uncomfortable, then the relationship may be shifted back to the domain of positional power. Or rather, the actors may so attempt to shift it. Success will require that the nature of the work changes so that each can come to perceive the advisor's contribution as once again falling within the limits of the obligations of the advisor role.

MODES OF SOCIAL EXCHANGE

We see social exchange itself dividing further into two distinct modes of situation framing, with correspondingly distinct domains of application: (1) a critical mode in which actors conduct their exchange relations in conformity with the rational-choice model; and (2) a routinized mode, in which the activities of producing and receiving treatments are carried out in an unreflecting, habitual fashion. Again, our objective is to demonstrate that social exchange in its standard, rationalistic conception does have a place in the theory of face-to-face interaction, but that its place is a restricted one.

We claim that most activities of negotiation and exchange are carried out in the routine mode, with actors resorting to the critical and reflective mode only when difficulties in the exchange situation or relationship compel them to do so. The routines can be thought of as script-like in character, following Abelson's (1976) formulation, with each script specifying what appropriately might be said and done in carrying out negotiations and what might be accepted in the way of exchange agreements in such a situation. Because they are routines of exchange, rather than of positional power, the scripts will specify that treatments be produced only on condition of reciprocation by the consumer, with perceived balance of cost and benefit the mark of adequate reciprocation. Most importantly, each script will specify symbolic actions that have *succeeded* in the past in the sense that these negotiations have been found to lead to the accommodations sought, and the resulting exchanges have been found to facilitate the projects involved. Thus the scripts will specify reciprocations of treatments that the actor has found both satisfactory to him- or herself and likely to be accepted by alters.

Because of this basis in successful past experiences, the scripts will consist of implicit situation definitions that the actor feels competent to understand and apply, and performance sequences he feels competent to carry out successfully. Their utility lies in their articulation of ways of managing familiar exchange relationships that feel to the actor to be within his capacity to execute in an unstressed (and eventually, unthinking) fashion. Because they are routinized, these schemes of offer-to-elicit–counteroffer are not recipes for bargaining in the explicit fashion of, say, labor–management or business contract negotiations. They resemble more the rituals of gift exchange in a primitive society, in which the classes of admissible offer and adequate counteroffer are specified in advance. Application of *successful* exchange scripts has the smooth, formal, regularized quality of ritual action, with sequences of offer and counteroffer proceeding rote-like to a highly expectable accommodation (Bourdieu, 1977, Chapter 4). Our claim is that every actor equips himself with a repertoire of these script-like paradigms by routinizing the procedures he has found most effective in the situations in which positional power has failed to supply an adequate mode of coping. Confronted with an apparently new situation, the actor will always attempt to assimilate it to some one of the routines in his repertoire. Unless it fails to fit, the assimilation and the consequent production of performances will all proceed in an unreflecting way—up to the point, if it comes, at which idiosyncratic features of the situation make scripted moves inappropriate. In this case, his initial response will be to amend and adapt the failing routines or else to adapt other routines from his repertoire; if either of these moves proves feasible, the actor may withdraw from the situation altogether. Often, however, withdrawal is too costly to be a viable option. When this is the case, the actor will respond by "shifting frame" from the routine to the critical mode of exchange behavior. If it is the case that the reconstructive task is complicated enough to force the actor to stand back from the situation and reflect in a self-conscious way about what has gone wrong for him and what to do about it, then he will proceed in ways that are fairly accurately represented by the rational-choice model: His performance will be the product of explicit choices from among articulated alternatives; these choices will be determined by evaluation of the relative expected utilities of the alternatives; utility appraisals will involve explicit weighing of costs and benefits, together with evaluation of his or her capacity to carry out each alternative successfully in the circumstances, and so on. The actor and the alters will negotiate explicitly and self-consciously, each offering the least costly terms he thinks he can get by with and demanding the highest benefits he believes the other can be made to accept. Moves and countermoves will take the form of manifestly attempting to manipulate the situation. The interaction will take on some of the quality of the poker game, with bluff and deception and the familiar forms of psychological pressure figuring prominently. The situation will be perceived by all parties as one of conflict and opposition. Under these circumstances, with actors alert to every possibility for securing an advantage, the sequences of offer and counteroffer will exhibit little of the ritual smoothness of interaction routines.

CONCLUDING COMMENTS

At the present time social psychology is dominated by themes and research paradigms that focus on one individual's perception of another individual. All too frequently, Bruner's comment that the purpose of perception is action is forgotten, and individuals are not thought of as acting toward one another. As a consequence, the mutual interplay in which initial perceptions generate actions, these actions and their consequences modify perceptions, and so on, is not studied, and an unrealistically static view of human action results. Social-exchange theory seems to us to be one of the theories least susceptible to these criticisms and thus, from the perspective of an action theorist, one to be developed. We have argued that its development has been blocked by an excessively rationalistic conceptualization of the determinants of actors' goals, with its implausible image of the constantly calculating actor. By introducing the concept of positional power, we hope to sketch the parameters of a more reasonable theory of social exchange. Our purpose in doing so is to facilitate the eventual development of a psychological theory of social functioning that uses a more plausible account of social cognition to assign an appropriately fundamental role to the goal directed characteristic of ordinary interaction.

17

Some Contributions of Action Theory to Social Psychology: Social Action and Actors in the Context of Institutions and an Objective World

John Sabini
Michael Frese
Debra A. Kossman
University of Pennsylvania

INTRODUCTION

Michael Athay and John Darley's chapter raises interesting issues with regard to action theory. Although their critique is more specifically aimed at exchange theory, the points it raises fit well in the context of action theory, and our discussion here first attempts to elaborate the implications of their contribution, as we see them, for action theory. In a second section we point out additional relations between action theory and social psychology.

POSITIONAL POWER AND EXPECTANCY-VALUE THEORY

Both exchange theory and expectancy-value theory suggests that we act so as to maximize our net utilities. The Athay–Darley critique of such views is not so much that such claims are wrong, but rather that they are misleading. They are misleading because they blur distinctions.

Imagine that a graduate student appears at the door to ask for a reference, and a professor spends some time looking for it. On an expectancy-value view, the professor decided that she would maximize her utility by spending the few minutes doing this rather than by listening to the radio, working on a paper, straightening the office, reading a novel, calling a friend on the phone, working on her taxes, and so on. To imagine that she consciously, or for that matter unconsciously, considered all, or even a fraction, of these possibilities strains credulity. It seems to her that what she did was simply to realize that she had an obligation to the student by virtue of the student's being a student and her being a professor. Note that it even strains credulity to imagine that she decided at that moment that being a professor was worth all of the bothers, like this one, that it entails.

The general point of this example is that a precondition for any expectancy-value analysis that relaxes the strain is that it distinguish the behaviors a person might plausibly do from the behaviors she could possibly do. One of the Athay–Darley points is that institutions, through the formal and informal roles they involve, make this distinction. As Berger and Luckmann (1966), following Schutz (1973), point out, the first, and perhaps most important, sense in which roles affect behavior is *not* by providing sanctions for misbehavior, but by limiting the choices that people see themselves as facing.

The power of institutions and roles to constrain people's sense of their behavioral options is shown clearly in the Milgram (1974) experiments on obedience to authority. In this experimental setting, subjects obeyed commands to shock an innocent experimental accomplice well beyond the limits we, as outsiders to the situation, would expect. An expectancy-value analysis of the Milgram experiment suggests that subjects calculated obedience as the most desirable action given their values. This analysis is dead wrong. Rather, it would seem that they obeyed because the possibility of simply disobeying is not one that the subjects took seriously. (See Sabini & Silver, 1982, Chapter 4, for more on this.)

Expectancy-value theory can, no doubt, be fixed up to cover this case. Perhaps we might argue that something about the situation caused people to value obedience more than they do in other circumstances. But even if such a claim can, somehow, be saved from circularity, one probably wouldn't want to make it. If it makes any sense at all to speak of people's having values, it is because values don't change drastically from situation to situation. Once we allow values, as well as opportunities to express them, to vary from situation to situation, then we are preserving a calculational theory without regard for whether that theory sheds any light on the phenomenon to be investigated. Rather than do this, we should limit the scope of expectancy-value theory by using other concepts, like role or positional power, as a framework to constrain the behavioral options over which expectancy-value theory calculates.

Roles and Perspective Taking

Exchange theory suggests that actors must not only keep track of their options, but must also keep track of the options of the people with whom they are interacting. This monitoring involves, however, an impressive cognitive demand—one we sometimes bear, but don't typically. (Cf. Silbereisen, this volume, on perspective taking in naturalistic situations.) Roles again simplify matters. Just as the professor in the preceding example didn't calculate her maximum utility over the list of disparate things she might have done in response to the request for references, neither did the student who came to ask her for the reference. The student's understanding of the professor's understanding of their relative positions within the institution was all the student needed to form a "strategy" to get the reference. Indeed, Athay and Darley claim that interaction involves "manipulation" on the part of both actors to get their ways, but this is probably an unfortunate way to put it: not only because manipulation, in ordinary discourse, refers to illegitimate attempts to get someone to do what you want— students who flatter a professor to get an A are manipulating, those who study hard for the exam sure aren't—but because the term suggests too much work and thinking. The graduate student didn't have to, and knew she didn't have to, do much to get the reference. Roles, then, not only constrain the options we take seriously, but also, because they are shared social knowledge, constrain the options others take us as taking seriously. One offers money to token vendors in the hopes of getting a token because that's what token vendors do, not because one has decided that the token vendor's interest would best be served by offering a token in exchange for the money.

Roles and the TOTE Model

The Athay–Darley critique also bears on the Miller, Galanter, and Pribram (1960) Test–Operate–Test–Exit (TOTE) model. The position one occupies in the social order affects one's actions in a variety of ways, some of which are obvious, and some of which are not so obvious.

The role one occupies affects one's goals and the resources one has to accomplish them; educators have the goal of educating the young, and lecture halls to do this. Hacker (this volume) discusses some of the ways that occupational goals figure in action theory. There are, however, other ways that one's position affects one's TOTEs.

As Athay and Darley point out, interactants occupying complementary social roles are well practiced at managing interactions, and this suggests that *aspects of these interactions* have been automatized. Professors are used to meetings with graduate students, and have, one supposes, automatized techniques for, say, ending those meetings. Indeed, only on reflection, or when these techniques fail, do they even notice their attempts to accomplish this end. Thus, in the standard case, much of interaction can pass without attention or strain. (Cf. Semmer & Frese, this volume, on automatizations.) Other ways that roles affect individual action are more subtle.

Occupants of social roles, as Athay and Darley argue with their example of "personal counselor," must present themselves to their audiences as having certain, typically socially valued, qualities. The requirement that one present oneself is, on occasion, the goal of a person's action: Winning a grant is one way to so present oneself, and an academic might write a grant proposal to just that end. But as Goffman (1959) and Harre and Secord (1972) have pointed out, the requirements of self-presentation typically don't determine the goal of action. Rather, self-presentation typically specifies *how* an act is to achieve a goal. The requirements of self-presentation are standards against which the performance of an act is to be assessed. For example, academics, in some circles at least, are expected to display wit and worldliness; their papers, talks, and comments at faculty meetings are supposed to express these personal qualities. The wrong way to achieve this impression is by performing some acts whose goal is academic accomplishment, and other acts whose goal is the display of wit. Self-presentational requirements are imposed on action not as subgoals, but as concurrent standards imposed on the process of acting (just as speaking grammatically isn't a subgoal of giving a lecture, but a standard to be imposed on the whole of the extended act). To pull this off, the generation of alternatives that meet these standards had better be automatized, something that can be done while one attends to the goal of an act. Thus, one of the ways in which the social order is specialized is in the particular standards that occupants of different positions in the social order must meet, and therefore in the standards that have become "second nature."

This analysis adds complexity to the TOTE model. The test phase of the model must not only compare output against a representation of the goal state, or subgoal state, but it must also compare behavior against an indefinite number of standards it must meet. To take an example: A job applicant may have the goal of impressing the faculty with her knowledge of psychometrics as a subgoal toward the goal of getting hired. As she discusses the advantages of traditional versus avant-garde techniques for doing cluster analysis with her prospective employers over dinner—something that she may well have planned as part of a strategy— she will not only have to keep track of whether she has spontaneously made all of the interesting points she scripted, but she also has to be sure that she isn't talking: too loud, too much, too informally, too formally, too assertively, too retiringly, and so on. Pained expressions on the faces of her interactional partners will tell her that something is awry, but they will not, unfortunately, tell her whether to talk more quietly or informally (or cogently). To be a more realistic model of human behavior, action theory will have to deal focally with just how these concurrent tests are carried out in the test phases.

Professors not only have automatized ways of ending meetings, but they also have automatized ways of dealing with students' remarks at those meetings. They have ways of responding to comments that are wrong, vague, or off the point. These standard techniques are, no doubt, automatized; the standard form of such a technique can be invoked while paying attention to the content of this particular remark. The general point the example is meant to illustrate is that interactants who occupy specific roles are well practiced not only at managing their own self-presentations, but also at assisting the self-presentations of those who occupy complementary roles. One reason that academics, say, might find it easier to interact with other academics than to interact with baseball players is that they have well-practiced ways of sustaining each other's identities even in the face of failure. To use Athay and Darley's example, there will be little occasion, when talking to a third baseman, to suggest that "only an anal-neurotic would care. . ." Thus, for a variety of reasons, interactions with frequent role partners are less effortful, and more graceful, though perhaps less challenging.

ACTION THEORY AND PERSON PERCEPTION: ACTION VERSUS PERCEPTION

Action theory has striking implications for the "person-perception" literature. To see these, we should focus on the origins of this literature. Both Asch (1952) and Heider (1958) were, of course, heavily influenced by Gestalt notions and were writing in the context of an American psychology dominated by S–R thinking. The main thrust of their work was that our thinking about people could not be accommodated by notions of contiguity, because our thinking about a person was "structured." That is, they both argued, and tried to show, that we could not, or not easily, assimilate any and every fact into our conceptions of a particular person. This was surely an important point to be made about our understanding of each other.

Both Heider and Asch also persistently used perceptual language to develop this point; this metaphor has had an impact on future work in the field. In particular, as Neisser (this volume) points out, thinking about perception in their era had a static flavor. Eventually this way of thinking led to a generation of research in perception dominated by the tachistoscope, a device useful for identifying what a person can find out about the world in a single glance when the subject has no particular motive in glancing out at that world. Parallel to all of this in person perception was a generation of research on *impression formation,* research on what we can learn about another person in a single glance when we have no particular reason for wanting to know about that person. Such research, obviously, provides rather limited information about how we understand people. This approach is also out of step with current thinking about perception itself. In particular, Neisser (1976) has introduced the notion of a *perceptual cycle,* the idea that perception is guided by expectations and the feedback that the world provides relative to those expectations. In this view, tachistoscopic glimpses and impression-formation stimuli are quite distant from the heart of perception.

Of late, just as von Hofsten and Neisser (both this volume) have tried to tie perception more directly to action, so have some investigators of social perception tried to tie our understanding of people to action. In particular, C. Cohen (1981) has made the important point that what we learn from observing a person depends, at least in part, on our reason for looking at him or her in the first place.

In a similar vein, McArthur and Baron (1983) have provided an important reconceptualization of the person-perception literature starting with (as does von

Hofsten) J. Gibson's ecological approach to perception. Their review, along with stressing the way perception depends on our motives for looking, also argues for an innate "tuning" of our perceptual systems to certain stimulus features. This recent work is an important step forward in providing a richer framework for our understanding of our understanding of each other. It too, though, is limited, limited by its allegiance to the perception metaphor. It is this limitation that we shall now address.

Action Theory and Person Understanding

In the introduction to their article on the Gibsonian approach to perception as applied to person perception, McArthur and Baron (1983) discuss the things about objects that we pick up directly from observing them in the real world. One thing they suggest we pick up is how heavy a sphere is from observing it roll down an inclined plane. And, they are probably right that we do sense the heaviness of an object from watching it roll down an inclined plane. But this impression is wrong. Actually, holding aside friction and air resistance (typically minimal for objects rolling down an inclined plane), all objects roll at the same rate; their velocity and acceleration are independent of mass and depend solely on the angle of the incline. The point is not that psychologists make mistakes about physics; the point is that our impressions can be mistaken—even about the mass of an object.

Action theory, in the spirit of Dewey, Pierce, and James, allows for the correction of error through action in a way that the passive conceptions of perception embodied in tachistoscopic research don't. Anyone who lifted spheres that they had observed rolling down an inclined plane would, presumably, realize that his impressions of heaviness were wrong. The analogous point is that even though we may "perceive" what people are like, in the sense of form an impression, from a limited exposure to them, this is not all there is to our understanding of people. Impressions we form can be corrected by feedback. Treating our knowledge of each other as if it were perception obscures this point. Neisser's notion of a perceptual cycle suggests that perception is continuously refined, that the results of one glimpse at an object inform our next looks, and so on. Our understanding of people, however, is informed by more than just looking at them; if there is a cycle, it is broader than a perceptual cycle, perhaps we could say a *cognitive cycle,* were that not so infelicitous.

To see this distinction, consider the color of an object. Our first impression may be wrong; we may find that in better light an object we had thought was red was actually orange. But in the case of color, the only information that could correct our impression is *further looking* at the object. That is, for "sensory" features, like color, impressions are formed simply by looking, and they are corrected by more behavior of the same kind—more looking. Although we may form an impression of the mass of an object from watching it roll down an inclined plane, our impression can be corrected by doing something very different from watching it roll down the incline even more. In this sense, our concepts of heaviness are quite different from our concepts of color. Color is a truly (visual) perceptual feature; heaviness isn't. Now what about person perception?

McArthur and Baron (1983) report favorably on the substantial literature that has developed on the perception of emotion. Apparently, people are quite good at reading emotions from facial expressions. But, is this akin to people's inferring mass from the acceleration of an object down an inclined plane? The mere fact that people agree about it doesn't distinguish perceptions of color from perceptions of heaviness. In other words, is there evidence that *could* correct our impressions of a person's emotional state, evidence that is different in kind from what we find out about them by looking at their faces? Presumably we also find out about people from the way they interact with us. And, presumably, this information could be used to correct our impressions gleaned from looking at their faces.

If action can correct impressions triggered by looking at faces, then our concepts of emotional state are *not* like color—that is, they are not perceptual concepts. Our representations of other people's emotional states may be, in some cases, *formed from* our observing their faces but they are not *representations of* their faces nor are facial expressions *criteria about* their emotional states.

The suggestion here is that we replace the person-perception metaphor; it has outlived its usefulness. The question we need to answer is not *On the basis of what do we form impressions?*, but *How do we combine information derived from different sources, especially interaction, to understand each other?*

Action Theory and the Objectivity of the Social World

If one thinks of our understanding of people and situations in terms of the perceptual metaphor for too long, something odd happens. One begins to notice that people form different impressions of other people and situations. This begins to sap one's belief in the objectivity of descriptions of people and situations. But action theory suggests a different view. In the spirit of a pragmatist epistemology, action theory would not use as a test of the objectivity of personality descriptions (or situation descriptions) whether or not people's impressions of that person (or situation) correspond, but whether the representations we have about people (derived from interacting with them) mesh. (Again, about color judgments there is no further test of objectivity aside from shared responses based on looking—though physics gives us ways of producing arbitrary wave lengths, a kind of externalization of the experience of color. Physics, a kind of work, leads to the externalization and, to use Schutz's term, sedimentation of individual experience.) Action theory stresses the ways that our representations of the world are based on our plans, goals, and motives in interacting with it. Thus, we should not expect that two people interacting with the same other person (or in the same situation) would form the same impression of that person (or situation) in so far as their plans, goals, and motives differ. Action theory would expect that the various representations formed about the same object could be brought into agreement.

Consider a lecture hall. There is a way in which a lecture hall is the same situation to the lecturer, students, and the plumbing contractor in charge of the heat. But the way in which it is the same situation is fairly trivial. There is a far more important sense in which, because students come there to learn (or at least to be able to pass as people who have learned), lecturers come there to teach (or at least pass as having taught), and plumbers come there to fix the heat (or . . .), the same hall is a very different situation for these different classes of people. It evokes from these different classes of people different motives, goals, and plans. Nonetheless, the objectivity of the lecture hall as a single place does not depend on all three groups' having the same representation; rather it depends on their being able, at least given enough time, knowledge, and good will, to understand each others' representations.

Collective Action

There are important consequences of the objectivity of the situation. We can act collectively only because there is an objective social world. Let us take the example of a wildcat strike. The collective actions needed to initiate and sustain a wildcat strike are impossible without prior agreement about the social world, agreement about the social interests that are to be defended by the strike, agreement about the fact that strikes can be effective, agreement that it is unfair that the employer's profits are rising but the workers' paychecks aren't, and so on. If an individual were free to define the situation in any way he or she wants, then shared knowledge would appear only through ''suggestion'' or some other irrational social influence. Suggestion, however, does not produce a wildcat strike, as any analysis of social movements shows (Moore, 1978; Schumann, Gerlach, Gschlössl & Milhoffer, 1971). Rather, the effective force behind social movements is a shared understanding of the social situation. Only through shared understanding of the social environment derived from being in a roughly similar position (being a blue-collar worker, being at the same point in the economic cycle, etc.) vis-a-vis this environment, developing roughly similar interests, and developing similar estimates of the success or failure of potential actions, can there be collective actions.

Additional concepts drawn from action theory can be applied to help us understand collective actions. Collective action must be organized. This means that a division of labor (including a hierarchy) has to be developed within the group. It also implies that certain routines, roles, and institutions have to be developed before collective action can be effective—riots are collective actions that are not organized. For example, a detailed study of the German wildcat strikes of 1969 (Schumann et al., 1971) shows that the backbone of the strike was the labor union's structure with its shop stewards, even though the labor union did not officially participate in the strike (and was bound by law to refrain from doing so). The skills and shared understandings needed for collective action may have to be developed over time; for example, many successful revolutions and social movements have been "practiced" (for example, the Russian Revolution was practiced in 1905 and the Polish working class practiced their organization in the 1960s and 1970s before the labor union Solidarity could develop).

Action Theory and the Personality–Situation Dichotomy

Action theory's ability to handle different, but objective, representations of the same situation has implications for the personality–situation controversy. Does the fact that the lecture hall means different things to a plumber than to a lecturer mean that they are different situations for them? Certainly their behavior there will be different. If we agree that a lecture hall is a different situation to these groups, then something funny has happened to the notion of situation: It has entered the head. That is, the nature of the situation has become relative to the motives, plans, and goals that people bring to the (physical) situation. In this sense, situations now differ from person to person. But this means that the "situation" variance is also "individual-difference" variance. The simple dichotomy between the person and the situation is eroded. But it is eroded in a different way from the way Kelly's (1955) personal-construct theory erodes it.

Action theory is consistent with the view that the nature of the situation, in any psychologically interesting sense, varies with the motives of the individuals who enter it. Indeed, action theory would hope to show how, given the motives of an individual and the "affordances" of the situation to particular individuals, we could explain why different people act in different ways in the same (physical) situation. In this way real individual differences (in motives or abilities) can be integrated with shared physical attributes to generate differences in behavior. Kelly's approach suggests that each person can "construe" the situation differently, and then predicts behavior from those construals, but insofar as it fails to explain the genesis of those construals, it lapses into tautology—surely it would be hard to find evidence to refute the claim that people respond to the situation as they understand it! Action theory can allow people to have different understandings of the same (physical) situation without resorting, at least immediately, to tautology. Thus, the situation can enter the head without losing its objective quality.

III APPLICATIONS OF ACTION THEORY

PSYCHOLOGY OF WORK

Hacker has worked to integrate Leontiev's and Miller, Galanter, and Pribram's work on the psychology of action and activities. The application of this theoretical framework to the industrial sphere has been particularly useful. It made it possible to overcome two problems without lapsing into the problems of previously proposed alternatives: behavioristic conceptions—mainly F. W. Taylor's (1911)—and mentalistic-humanistic conceptions. Taylor's system of particularistic movements as the basis of industrial psychology and engineering is not able to deal with the fact that human beings regulate their actions cognitively and are goal oriented in their pursuit of goals. Mentalistic-humanistic conceptions (e.g., in the footsteps of Maslow), on the other hand, have not been able to provide rigorous scientific knowledge and have not been able to describe how knowledge, general representations, and motivations are translated into concrete actions in the workplace. Hacker uses the concept of activity (the only possible but still awkward translation of the German term Taetigkeit) to explain how workers' knowledge and representations regulate their actions at the workplace. Additionally, he shows that the concept of "complete action" can be taken as a starting point for criticisms of work conditions that the humanistic conceptualizations have criticized as well. This critique is now much more concrete and scientifically based.

Broadbent underlines some of these major points: the idea of personality enhancement as a criterion of work psychology and activity as a unit of analysis; however, he points to some major problems in Hacker's approach: the problem of how and under what conditions cognitions regulate actions and the question of personality differences in relation to the workplace. There are dissociations between conscious knowledge and successful actions, and there are differences between declarative and procedural knowledge (cf. Semmer & Frese's contribution to this book, which raises similar issues). Furthermore, there may be differences in personality with regard to how much control and decision latitude people want at their workplaces. Similarly, Broadbent discusses to what degree opportunities to automatize one's actions are valued and at what point they become dysfunctional—a problem related to decision latitude and the work cycle.

261

18 Activity: A Fruitful Concept in Industrial Psychology

Winfried Hacker
Technical University of Dresden

INTRODUCTION: THE ROOTS OF THE CONCEPT

There are distinctions to be drawn between the concepts of activity (*Taetigkeit* in German), action (*Handlung*), and operation. Activities are motivated and regulated by higher-order goals (*Oberziele*) and are realized through actions that are themselves relatively independent components of each activity (Leontiev, 1977/1979). Actions differ from each other with respect to their goals. They are themselves analyzable into their subordinate components: operations; operations are described as subordinate because they do not have goals of their own. Operations can be taken to be complexes of movement patterns or, in the case of mental activities, elementary cognitive operations, following the suggestions in R. B. Miller's (1971) taxonomy. Movements can, in turn, be decomposed into muscle movements. The concept of a psychology of activities has been, for the last 50 years or so, central to the tradition of Marxist psychology. There are many points of agreements with, but also important differences between, the orientations of the leading research groups, particularly around Leontiev (1977/1979)—a student of Vygotski—around Rubinstein (1958), and around Tomaszewski (1981) and Polish Praxeology. The philosophical foundations of Marx, the psychological findings of Lewin (1926b), the psychophysiological results of Bernstein (1967) and Anokhin (1967), the pathophysiological results of Luria, and cybernetic, particularly system-theoretical suggestions have all contributed to the development of this concept. At various times useful summaries have been provided (e.g., Bernstein, 1967; Leontiev, 1972, 1977/1979; Luria, 1971, 1973).

In this article I procede by first pointing out the necessity of developing a

262

concept of activity that includes the cognitive regulation of activity. This regulation is oriented toward something—that is, a goal. The goal orientation of work activities is therefore described next. I concentrate on goal orientation, particularly as it pertains to work activities in contrast to other activities. If goal orientation is removed from work (and if work design does not allow for the development of strategies), the activity is not complete, but rather "partialized". Finally, I discuss the specifics of mental representations of goals and plans.

The concept of activity has been used systematically in the field of industrial psychology for only the last two decades; neither Marxist general psychology nor industrial psychology can claim to have produced a closely knit theoretical system of thought about this notion. Thus, this article can only describe some arbitrarily selected fragments that might eventually help to produce such a theory. The background of this endeavor includes: a specific concept of human nature, a specific picture of humans; clear-cut notions of the relation between so-called basic and applied research; and a specific idea of the societal role of industrial psychology. These ideas are important parts of this chapter, but they are not articulated in it—they silently accompany and guide it. Similarly silent is another guiding thought: Challenging, societally useful, goal oriented activity plays an irreplaceable role in the development and preservation of mental processes and, thus, of physical and mental health.

THE DESIGN OF ACTIVITIES AND THE MENTAL PROCESSES: REGULATING THEM AS THE SUBJECT MATTERS OF INDUSTRIAL PSYCHOLOGY

The subject matter of industrial psychology is activities at work; it involves the working conditions producing those activities and their effects. Work activities are goal oriented, conscious activities that always have, simultaneously, two classes of effects: (1) they produce socially valued products, with greater or lesser effectiveness (their efficacy); (2) they in turn have an influence on the worker and therefore can alter his personality in the long run. They can lead to "deskilling," or they help to enhance personality through demands on the individual to learn and develop his abilities (personality enhancement).

From this point of view, the most prominent task of industral psychology is to design jobs that demand effective and challenging activities. Contributions of psychologists have to be oriented toward the desirable aspects of activities; this is possible only if they design the division of functions between humans and machines (or computers), the division of labor between different people, and the forms of cooperation between different workers, as well as a training method that is conducive both to the goal of training and the personality of the learner. The decisive long-range goal of the psychology of work must be the development of methods that will allow us to design activities, along with their desired characteristics, on the drawing board. At the moment, however, the main task of industrial psychology is to correct characteristics of already-existing activities.

The question is, what has to be corrected? In our analysis of the demands on workers in assembly, machine operating, and control activities in various branches of industry, we have found the following general tendencies: Differences in effectiveness between workers are due largely to differences in cognitive strategies. These strategy differences are, in particular, differences in efficiency in the organization and planning of one's own activities. But this difference holds only when there are degrees of freedom in choosing appropriate actions. The second very important reason for these efficiency differences lies in differences in the use of time—for example, in differences in limiting or overextending breaks. The *least* important source of differences in efficiency is differences in the speed and precision of the sensorimotor skills, which are automatized systems of movement patterns (Rühle, 1979; Schneider, 1977).

Because of these results, we have to refocus the tasks of industrial psychology: The design of activities must focus primarily on those mental components that regulate activities and that thereby decisively influence their efficiency, and, in turn, influence the personalities of workers. This task of industrial psychology has to be performed regardless of whether one is designing from scratch at the drawing board or is correcting structures of existing activities. To put it metaphorically: Designing activities means to design their "deep structure," which produces and regulates their "surface structure."

Work as Goal Oriented Activities

Work cannot adequately be researched in stimulus–response terms. The elements or "building blocks" of even primitive and unchallenging occupational activities are not just passive reactions, but goal oriented actions. Actions are, then, the "building blocks" of work and are consciously oriented toward a goal. If he or she is free to decide, the worker can also determine the goal of his action. Actions are controlled and led by anticipations and further mental representations of the conditions of execution, all of which are products of cognitive processes. This is a different conception of action from the limited notion of mechanisms of motoric control (Harvey & Greer, 1980). As was pointed out in the beginning of this chapter, the term *goal oriented activity* is used as the more comprehensive term. Work activities result from self- or other-determined tasks and are oriented to higher-order goals.

There are five important stages needed to describe the mental regulation of work activities (Tomaczewski, 1981):

1. Redefinition of the task as the individual's goal, derived from his motives in performing the task (goal setting),
2. Orientation toward the conditions of execution in the environment and toward the actor's memory.
3. Construction, or reproduction, of sequences of subgoals, and the action

programs belonging to them. (These are mental operations on mental representations of the conditions of execution.)

4. Decision among particular variants of execution, if there is adequate freedom to choose. (This decision, too, is an operation on mental representations.)

5. Control of the execution, comparing it to the mental representations of the result—the goal—and to plans for execution—the sequence of subgoals and programs.

These feedback mechanisms show the cyclical structure of the regulation of action. We suggest that activity-regulating, functional units have to be represented in working memory, at least for the duration of the execution of the activity. These units consist of goals (conceived of as anticipations and intentions), of programs belonging to these goals, and of feedback mechanisms. In complex activities, one can take these regulating, functional units to be hierarchically interwoven. Miller, Galanter, and Pribram (1960) have described these elementary units as Test–Operate–Test–Exit (TOTE) units, as did von Helmholtz (1856). Critical analysis of the formal structure of TOTE units suggests directions in which this idea must be further developed (cf. the preface to the Russian edition of *Plans and the Structure of Behavior* by Leontiev & Luria, 1965). A more careful analysis is warranted of what has to be compared with what in the testing phase, and of the nature and the development of the content—that is, the goals and programs of the various levels of regulation that serve as standards of comparison.

The Organization of Activities

There are good theoretical reasons to describe the structure of the regulating mental processes and representations as being simultaneously sequentially and hierarchically organized (or more generally heterarchically). Recent reviews of, and the arguments for, this view are presented, for example, by Norman (1981) and Volpert (1982). This concept of hierarchical organization can help to explain the different degrees of consciousness of the mental processes and representations that regulate activities. In work activities one can distinguish among:

1. Unconscious regulating processes and representations that one is normally not able to process consciously.
2. Processes that one is able to regulate consciously, but is not obligated to have in consciousness.
3. Processes that have to be represented in consciousness.

Processing of input information, one part of the regulation of action, goes on to all of these levels of consciousness:

1. The unconscious processing of kinesthetic signals.
2. The sometimes conscious processing involved in perceptual classifications.
3. The conscious intellectual operations of analyzing and synthesizing.

Programs that generate actions in response to information can also be distinguished by these levels of consciousness:

1. Unconscious programs for elementary movement patterns.
2. Sometimes conscious action schemata.
3. Conscious plans, metaplans, and strategies.

Although we certainly do not know enough yet, we think that the differentiation of these levels of mental regulation is heuristically useful, not only to understand effective action, but also to understand personality. The "higher" the level of regulation in the hierarchy, the better are the chances of developing efficient work strategies (Rühle, Matern, & Skell, 1980), given enough degrees of freedom.

We have looked at this question in several different studies (see Rühle et al., 1980). Training programs were used in a variety of occupations; in each, experimental groups of apprentices were compared with matched control groups. In addition to training in specific skills, relatively abstract, general, heuristic rules were provided for the experimental groups. These rules were meant to be intellectual training for the worker in the self-organization and planning of his or her steps in the work process. The control groups were provided with the usual training, mainly in sensorimotor skills and in the necessary technical knowledge. The experimental groups were significantly better than the control groups when compared on performance measures, such as the time required for producing products or the quality of the products. Furthermore, the experimental groups showed superior performance *without increased fatigue*. In several cases, we even found that the systematic acquisition of the mental foundations of work activities reduced experienced monotony and satiation in comparison to the control group. It also led to comprehensive recognition and use of the objective amount of freedom of choice in ways to carry out tasks. Thus, the executed activities became more diverse (had more variety) and challenging for the experimental groups than for the control groups.

Personality and the Organization of Activities

Even more important than this task-specific superiority is a second difference between the experimental and control treatments: "Higher" levels of regulation should also increase workers' opportunities to use, and thereby train and enhance, cognitive abilities—ideally in a more generalizable and flexible way.

In studies on more than 100 assembly, machine-operating, and control activities, the following relationships were found with a semistandardized system of work study (the Job Analysis Survey; Hacker, Richter, & Ivanowa, 1983): Level of regulation is strongly influenced by the range and type of division of labor. It is dependent, for example, on the length of the work cycle and on the degree of participation of the worker in the tasks of organizing and leading his department. Level of regulation clearly correlates with the educational level demanded by the occupation. Furthermore, the degree of psychological automatization of parts of the activities is lower in jobs that demand higher levels of regulation. In such jobs, one must use what one has learned and must learn more.

The task of industrial psychology is to design activities. This means that there are special features of industrial psychology's analysis of activities, features not shared by, for example, cognitive psychology. For one thing, cognitive psychology limits itself to the analysis of existing activities. It very often does not even look at *complete* activities, but, rather, artificially isolates certain components of activities, like perception or deductive reasoning. The analysis of activities within the framework of industrial psychology, on the other hand, is oriented toward *designing* activity. Therefore, it cannot stop with analysis, but it also must evaluate the content and structure of the activities with an eye toward the need for redesigning them. This entails the use of normative, societal values, and it thereby transcends the limits of psychology as "pure science" (cf. Baron, this volume).

WORK AS A SPECIAL CLASS OF GOAL ORIENTED ACTIVITIES

Psychology has traditionally distinguished various classes of behaviors—for example, reflexes, affective responses, and goal oriented actions (volitional actions). The special nature of goal oriented activities is clearest when they are contrasted with the behavior of human beings who are not, or not yet, able to orient their activities to goals: mentally retarded people or those with major injuries of the frontal cortex. Those activities that are not organized toward goals are typically characterized as trial and error, impulsively and unreflectively driven, without direction and orientation, and without examination of the consequences of alternatives, either in terms of an immediate, visual image, or in terms of a verbal, propositional analysis. Goal oriented selection of programs, known or yet to be developed, is lacking. The particular steps of the plan are not oriented toward goal implementation. The steps are neither *integrated parts* of linear sequences of steps nor *subordinated components* of a hierarchical plan. Thus, they are all perceived to be of equal importance for goal implementation. In particular, comparison with a desired end state is not used to determine in advance one's own performance potential, or the expenditure necessary in relation to the immediately obtainable results or subsequent consequences. Furthermore, the comparison between the actual end state and the desired goal state are not *anticipated*. Thus, a prospective evaluation of action consequences is lacking.

The concept of goal oriented activities is a relational one that relates at least five factors:

1. The anticipated result, represented as a goal.
2. The objects of the activities, which typically have their own laws governing how they can be transformed. (In social interaction these laws also include characteristics of a partner, which govern reciprocal behavior.)
3. Transformations of the physical or social world, requiring the expenditure of energy and the use of information (i.e., the *actual change* of the objects without which there is only intention).
4. The acting person, with her ability to have an impact on, and attitudes toward, the processes; these processes, in turn, act back on the person.
5. The means needed for, and the contextual conditions of, the activities.

Research that reduces this complex of relationships among five distinct factors may not adequately represent the characteristics of goal oriented action.

Work activities are *a special type* of goal oriented activity; therefore, generalizations from other classes of goal oriented activities can be made only very cautiously. In work, the satisfaction of needs is mediated by wages and other consequences (instrumentalities, in the sense of Vroom, 1964). This mediation makes work motivationally and cognitively different from other goal oriented activities. Moreover, work activity is different from other goal oriented action because economic forces require efficient procedures. Finally, work activities are distinct because they are often integrated into a larger technical process; remaining work activities are frequently subsidiary parts of mechanized and automatized technical processes and are, therefore, subordinate to the laws governing them. Work activities are very often only possible at certain stages in the technical process; for example, in automatized chemical processes, people can only intervene at certain points in the process. Work activities are also frequently constrained, offering very little in the way of freedom of choice. Figure 18.1 schematically describes some cognitive consequences of work activities' being subordinate to the person–machine system.

The conceptualization of functional units with goals as anticipations (of results strived for), as intentions, and as desired values (with which to compare

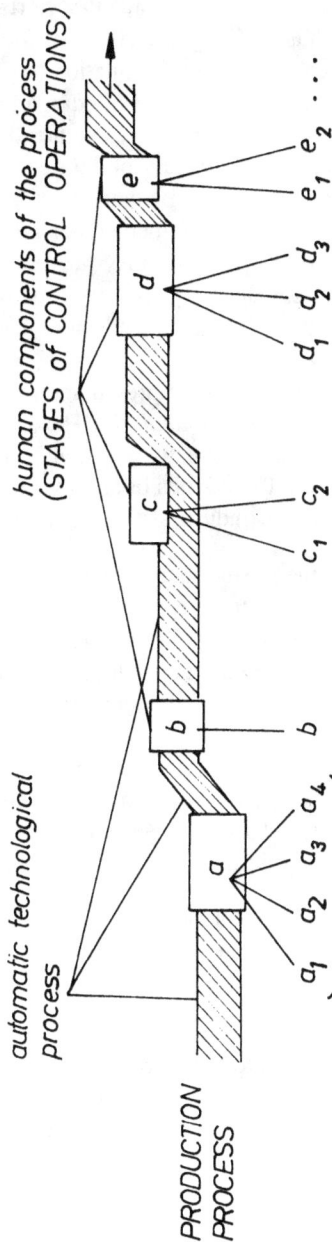

FIG. 18.1. Main sources of cognitive job demands in person–machine systems.

PRODUCTION PROCESS

automatic technological process

human components of the process (STAGES of CONTROL OPERATIONS)

various possibilities of suitable control operations (DEGREES of FREEDOM of ACTION)

a_1 a_2 a_3 a_4

b

c_1 c_2

d_1 d_2 d_3

e_1 e_2 . . . .

sources of cognitive demands:

– Number and sequence of stages of control operations performed by man
– Detectibility of the process state ($\rightarrow$ orienting)
– Number of degrees of freedom ($\updownarrow$ searching range in programming)
– Cognitive processes in the realization of operations
– Assessment of consequences of control operations

269

current values) is theoretically and practically useful for various problems in industrial psychology. This usefulness is especially apparent in the anticipations of feedback accompanying the various effects of activities that are characteristic of work. A clear example from our own research is the integration of the difficult concept of "psychological fatigue" with the idea of the mental regulation of goal oriented activities. Everyday life experience teaches us that skilled workers anticipate fatigue from the very beginning of work, and thus calculate their efforts accordingly. Therefore, it makes sense that indicators of fatigue will consist not only of monotonic deterioration—for example, of parameters of heart activity or of performance. Preventive modification of work methods or reduction of aspiration level may also be indicators of fatigue, and they prevent the monotonic deterioration of psychophysiological parameters with work time (cf. Figure 18.2). Elsewhere we have given a fuller presentation of these ideas (Hacker & Richter, 1983).

It is obvious that our interest in the mental processes and representations that regulate activities has consequences for our *methods of job analysis*. The actual regulating mental processes and representations are not directly observable, nor can they, in all cases, be described by the subject. Three kinds of analyses have to be differentiated in the psychological analysis of industrial work activities:

1. Only the temporal sequence of the movement patterns is directly observable. Time and motion studies describe this surface structure of work.

2. The logical structure of the tasks that are to be carried out is not observable. It divides tasks into subtasks, and takes into account not only the motoric steps but also the mental processes (in the sense of control and operation steps of an algorithmic, descriptive system).

3. The regulating, mental "deep structure," in which we are actually interested, does not have to be identical with the logical structure of the task, however. For example, a person will often use simpler but longer plans, instead of a shorter but more complicated version that would be logically optimal.

To describe the relation between the deep and logical structure schematically, one might represent the subgoals set as the knots at the decision points in a graph (see Figure 18.3). The arrows of Figure 18.3 represent cognitive processes that recode higher-order tasks into smaller units.

> To analyze this last point empirically, we attempted to understand the mental processes and representations regulating work activities, using a systematic combination of diverse hypothesis-testing methods. Each step in our attempt gave us a more specific hypothesis for the next one. These steps are:
>
> 1. The analysis of the task to ascertain the logical gross structure of the task.

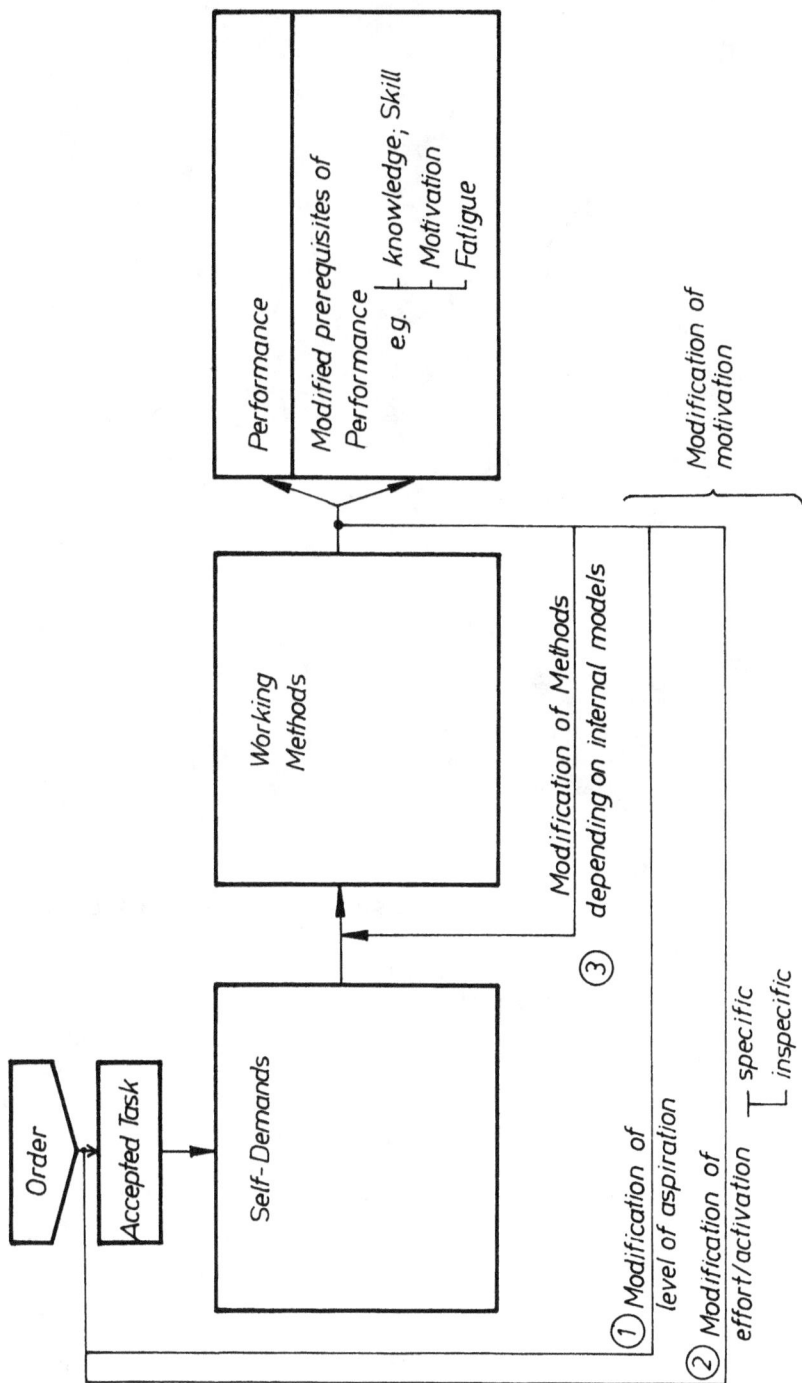

FIG. 18.2. Interrelations between motivation, methods of work, and fatigue.

271

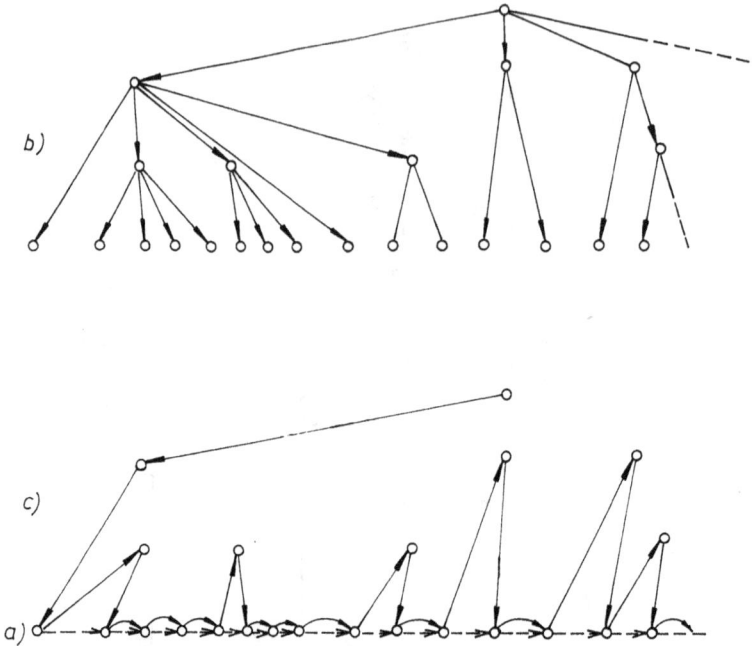

FIG. 18.3.   Aspects of job analysis (example):
   a: Sequence of motor operations (– – →).
   b: Abstract logical job structure.
   c: Hierarchical sequence of cognitive activities: psychological job
      structure (———→).

2. The analysis of the actual process of the activity across a whole work
   day, to get to know the sequence and frequency of those crucial
   component activities that determine performance.
3. Quasi-experimental studies in the style of Cook and Campbell
   (1976; i.e., observations with interviews) of the crucial, component
   activities with regard to their regulating mental processes and representations (for details cf. Matern, 1983).
4. Finally, field experimental steps to identify specific mental processes and representations.

THE CONCEPT OF COMPLETE VERSUS PARTIALIZED STRUCTURE OF ACTIVITY—A USEFUL GUIDE

We have seen that the following components, at least, are needed to describe the
regulating mental processes of work activities: goal setting, orienting, designing
action programs, deciding among different programs, and using feedback in

execution. Some of these processes—orientation, designing the action program, and controlling execution—can be done at various levels of mental regulation. Even individual and isolated work activities are societally determined by factors such as division of labor and their character as working for a wage. The hypothetical concept of "complete activity" enters here (Volpert, 1980): One can designate those structures of activities as complete that include more than routinized execution operations. Complete structures, in addition, leave opportunity for: preparatory mental steps that are developed and realized by the working individual himself; demands on various levels of regulation; and the use of one's potential for productive intellectual processes, at least sometimes. Preparatory mental steps consist of autonomous development of goals on the basis of the amount of freedom to choose subgoals, independent design or modification of action programs that weigh consequences, and autonomous decisions between alternative procedures. In a larger sense, a minimal social context probably belongs to the notion of complete activities too: The goals of work activity should be significant for the individual, in the sense that he should be able to experience the meaning of his own activity and its results for other human beings. Conversely, characteristics of incomplete activities are:

1. Impoverished opportunity for autonomous goal setting because of a lack of freedom (i.e., a lack of transparency of the task and the situation, of predictability, or control of one's own activities).

2. Deficient decision potential with regard to one's own procedures and, therefore, a lack of opportunity to take over responsibility (lacking control).

3. A lack of opportunity to deal with conditions in a cognitive, particularly intellectual, way, using nonalgorithmic and productive intellectual procedures. Such opportunities are often lacking because the activities are thought through, prepared, and layed down in complete detail by other people.

4. A lack of opportunity for cooperation, including social support and communication while acting, because activity is a social and object oriented undertaking.

5. Infrequent demands for action in general—for example, in the control of automated machinery.

Thus, partialized activities can be produced, to varying degrees, by the division of functions between person and machine and the division of labor between different individuals. As the structures of activities become less complete, we should expect them to loose their ability to provide cognitive and motivational development and to contribute to physical well-being. Absenteeism, turnover, fatigue, monotony, satiation, and, in certain combinations, stress, as well as loss of well-being should follow from partialized activity. In another publication, we have reviewed this position (Hacker & Richter, 1983).

Our research has been concerned particularly with the effects of broad or narrow latitude of freedom in goal setting. Using work-study techniques, the Job Analysis Survey (Hacker et al., 1983) includes one scale that indicates the degree and kind of decision latitude (degrees of freedom). An example of the different levels of freedom to set one's own goals in 99 assembly and machine-operating activities is given in Table 18.1. Figure 18.4 describes the results of self-report measures. Workers who work on tasks with a high degree of freedom and with a greater number of different chunks of activities set more goals for themselves and report greater job satisfaction, less fatigue, and less satiation (the last two being measured with the Plath & Richter, 1978, interval scale). Greater decision freedom is associated with fewer anxiety symptoms in older workers, as shown in Figure 18.5. In another study on 100 activities that were representative of the electrical industry of the German Democratic Republic, an agglomerative hierarchical cluster analysis gave four significantly different clusters of the characteristics of activities. For ease of presentation only the two opposite clusters are discussed here. Activities with wide latitude in goal setting, with more challening work than average, with great opportunity to develop one's own plans, and with greater necessity to learn are associated with significantly higher job satisfaction and significantly lower absenteeism than is the opposite cluster with lower-than-average levels of these characteristics. This relationship is not dependent on fatigue and monotony, because these variables did not differentiate between these clusters (Wolff, 1981).

TABLE 18.1

Distribution of the Degrees of Freedom with Respect to Autonomous Goal Setting ("Job Discretion") within a Sample of Assembling Machine-Operating Jobs[a]

Categories of Degrees of Freedom (df) with Respect to Autonomous Goal Setting	Number of Industrial Jobs	Number of Jobs to Be Expected in Case of Normal Distribution
1. Without df with respect to autonomous goal setting	1	5
2. df with respect to goals concerning speed/amount of output (O)	36	25
3. df with respect to O + sequence of steps (S)	32	39
4. df with respect to O + S + procedures/means (P)	22	25
5. df with respect to O + S + P + characteristics of the demanded result	8	5

[a]From Iwanova, 1981.

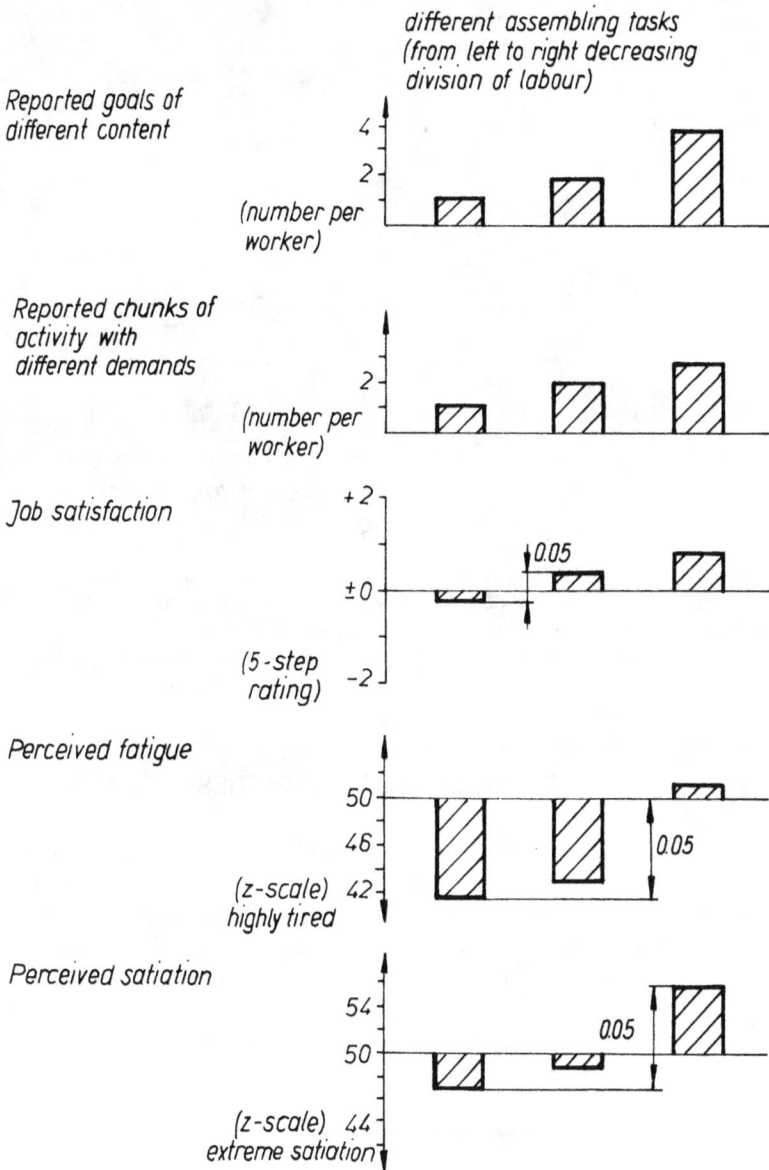

FIG. 18.4. Relations between reported self-set goals, chunks of activity, and some perceived effects of activity (Wolff, 1981).

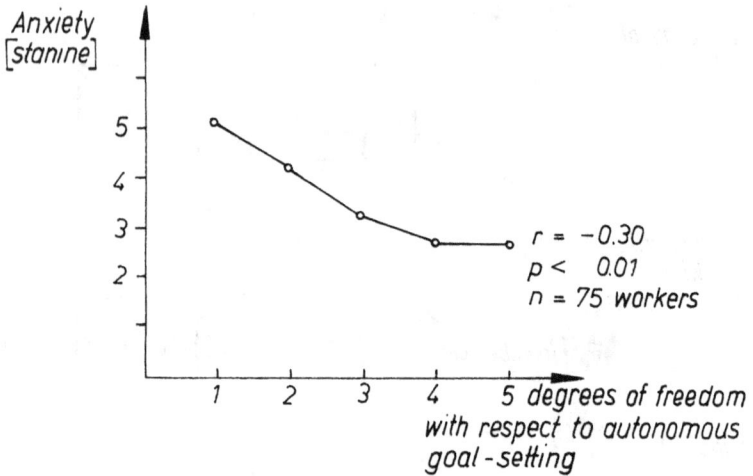

FIG. 18.5.   Relation between the degrees of freedom with respect to autonomous goal setting and perceived anxiety (Richter & Engelmann, 1982). (Assembling and machine-operating tasks in an electronic equipment factory. For scale of "degrees of freedom," compare Table 18.1. $N = 75$ elderly male workers.)

MENTAL REPRESENTATIONS OF GOALS AND PLANS IN THE REGULATION OF ACTIVITIES

Cognitive psychology follows the path from stimulus information to the sense organs through the many transformations necessary for the use of this information in thought (Neisser, 1976). Industrial psychology also raises questions about the path that goes from representations in memory to goal oriented activities that change the environment, and the path back to the changed representations that regulate these activities (Hacker, 1982a).

Three classes of mental representations can be distinguished (cf. Figure 18.6):

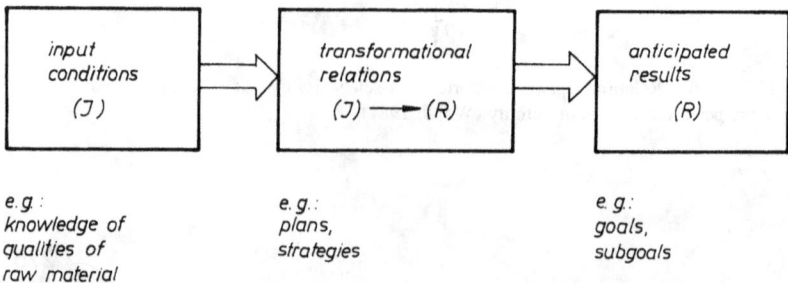

FIG. 18.6.   Possible contents of internal representations.

1. Mental representations about input conditions—for example, ideas about the qualities of raw materials and knowledge about whether and where one can have input into the technical process (input conditions).

2. Mental representations of procedures to transform objects from their input condition to the desired result; this means, for example, representations of plans and strategies, and representations of sensorimotor skills that are components of the plans and strategies (procedures of transformation).

3. Mental representations as anticipations of the future results of activities—for example, goals and subgoals (anticipated results).

Two interconnected questions still have to be pursued. First, how do mental representations regulate activities? Before action is begun, a representation of the anticipated result, the goal, is constructed and stored. These future results determine the necessary steps of activities, their effectiveness, and their reliability. This is relatively noncontroversial; however, many aspects of the processes that are involved here still have to be clarified. For example, which mental processes precede the motoric acts on the environment, and how do they control them: We do not know enough about how such things as goal, intention, and plan bridge the gap between cognition and action (G. A. Miller et al., 1960, p. 10). There are, for example, controversies on the way goals have effects on actions (e.g., Brichin, 1982; Mento, Cartledge, & Locke, 1980).

Second, do mental representations that regulate activities have characteristics that cannot be considered part of their orienting or cognitive function alone but, rather, part of their action-regulating function: Not every mental representation is actually involved in regulating actions. At what point does the representation become action regulating? Is this to be explained, in part, as a function of the specific task demands and the conditions of task implementation?

The mental representations that regulate activities are items in memory that have important functions in all aspects of the regulation of activities mentioned earlier. They also help to explain interindividual differences in performance and in work styles (Broadbent, 1971b). What are the important functions served by these mental representations? Accurate perceptions, images (following Miller et al., 1960), and concepts are mental representations of existing conditions and are essential for the regulation of activities, but they do not suffice. An additional requirement is goals. Their key function is a specific type of representation, one that derives from three components that we have discussed previously:

1. Goals, as *anticipations* of future results, orient an activity toward themselves with the help of sequences or hierarchies of subgoals. Actions and operations are selected and organized toward the goals.

2. Goals are the essential *invariants* that have to exist during a goal oriented process; they function as set points in the feedback between current conditions and desired outcome during the whole execution of the activity (Bernstein, 1967).

3. Goals conceived of as *intentions and* anticipations lead us to see that motivational and cognitive regulation are probably not different processes. Specific emotions, tied to the activities, develop as a result of reaching, or failing to reach, goals. (Cf. Schönpflug, this volume.)

Thus, one can see that the concept of "goal" is objectively full of contradictions. Goals are reflections of a reality that does not yet exist, but has to be created, and thus they connect present with future. They are anticipations and intentions at the same time, and thus they make questionable the status of a dichotomy between motivation and cognition. Goals regulate individual activities, but they are of social origin. Goals pertain neither to an individual, nor to the object of his or her activity, nor to the situation, but they help to relate these factors through object oriented activity.

We have tried to explain various characteristics of goals, and some of their functions in our research. We have found processes in the setting of goals that can be seen as contributing to increased efficacy of behavior. For example, the number of anticipated subgoals seems to be limited to a few, close at hand because it would put too much load on memory otherwise. Differentiation of global goals and a rough outline of actions are made as they become necessary. Furthermore, we found evidence for an efficient form of coding of the anticipated desired result. No matter what kind of information is available in the beginning, representations of the results will develop that minimize the number of transformational cognitive steps needed to regulate the activity.

In an experimentally simulated assembly activity, necessary information about the parts (i.e., chips) and their organization was presented in the same way for two different tasks for two groups of subjects. One group of subjects was to put the parts on a circuit board in columns. The second group had to mount all the parts of one type first, then those of the second type, and so on. For example, they had to mount the rheostats first, then all of the condensers, regardless of where they were located on the board. After multiple repetitions, the mounting was to be done from memory (in the sense of free recall). Here, comparing the two experimental groups, we found evidence for the development of different mental or memory representations in the subjects' performance and in their reports. Figure 18.7 shows that the two groups of subjects became more dissimilar with more trials. These differences can be seen in terms of assembly time and in terms of errors (e.g., mounting the wrong parts, mounting them at the wrong place, and forgetting parts). Thus, the two groups developed in different directions because they were well adjusted to differing tasks.

Furthermore, we are interested in the question of which objective characteristics of activity stimulate independent goal setting and intrinsic motivation.

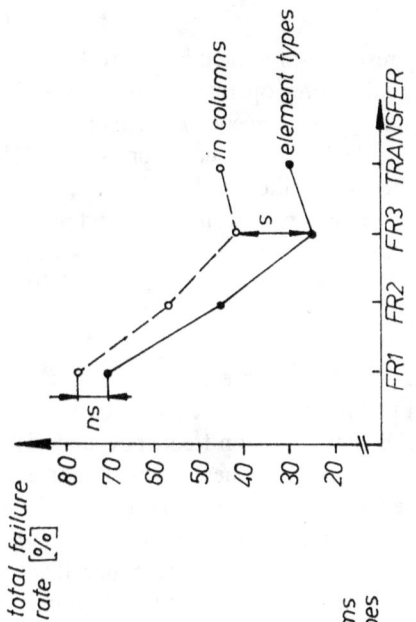

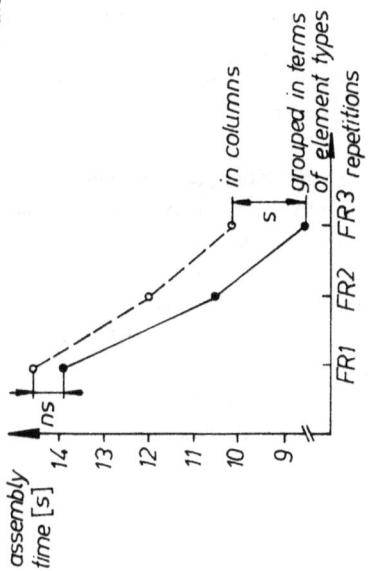

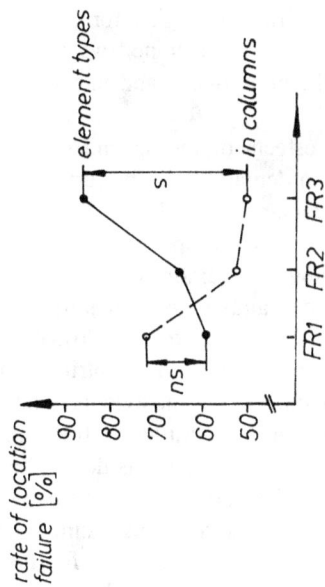

FIG. 18.7. Performance data as functions of demanded mounting procedures and repetitions (before and between test trials with free recall demands) (Cavallo, 1978).

279

We were stimulated to ask this question by results—presented in Figure 18.5—that show that impediments to personal goal setting operate as stressors and reduce health. This result is also suggested by the concept of the motivation potential of activities (Hackman & Oldham, 1975), the concept of task challenges (M. S. Taylor, 1981), and goal theory (Mento et al., 1980). In our studies, the most important determinants of performance, well-being, and motivation were the degree of freedom for autonomous goal setting of one's own activities and variety in task demands (Fritsche, Hacker, Rötschke, & Wolff, 1982).

The following results seem interesting: For a representative sample of about 100 industrial jobs we wanted to find the most frequent configurations of job characteristics. We used the configuration-frequency analysis technique (Krauth & Lienert, 1973). The most frequent configuration is described in terms of degrees of freedom, variety, and type of task demands (e.g., sensorimotor vs. intellectual tasks). We also found a less frequent configuration differing from the first only in the higher-than-normal degrees of freedom to set and implement goals. Job satisfaction is significantly higher for this configuration and absenteeism is lower. This result was sustained when fatigue, monotony, and personality variables like neuroticism and introversion were controlled for.

The effects of the second component of the most frequent configuration, variety in demands, can be further analyzed into three subcomponents: changes in the demands, the degree to which the tasks are structured into meaningful subtasks, and the specific type of demand (e.g., sensorimotor vs. cognitive processing vs. memory demands). We found different effects of cognitive-processing demands (versus operative demands for memory) on performance data and well-being (Hacker, 1982b). With a limited degree of freedom there must be variety in task demands if intrinsic motivation and intrinsic challenge are to be maintained. There is no evidence, however, that variety in demands can compensate for a lack of latitude of freedom to set subgoals.

Personality dispositions do not have a significant influence on the effects of degree of freedom and variety of demands. On the contrary, both are able to influence goal setting and planning behavior. Challenging tasks will produce in the worker the prerequisites for taking advantage of them—that is, only in challenging tasks is one able to develop the ability to make goals and plans on one's own. Thus, goal setting and planning behavior are not necessary prerequisites for the use of enriched or human-centered job design, but this job design in turn may influence goal setting and planning.

Furthermore, it has been shown in the study by Fritsche et al. (1982) that variety in demands and degrees of freedom in setting goals for individual activities are determined by the division or combination of labor and by opportunities to cooperate on the job. Cooperation can enhance the variety and the degrees of freedom of individual activities in addition to affecting social and collective processes (Hacker, 1983; Herrmann, Naumann, & Hacker, 1973).

We saw in the beginning that not only goals, but also other classes of mental representations that regulate activities have an effect. These too can be classed as activity-regulating knowledge. This is not "knowledge in itself" (*Wissen an sich*), but is connected with signals for the execution of programs and is used in the regulation of activities. Parts of this operative knowledge are: knowledge of potential failures and possible preventive measures, knowledge of the degrees of freedom for independent decisions, and knowledge of those sections of the technical processes that allow intervention by the worker in order to increase production. For example, efficient workers in a spinning factory will "see" how long a bobbin will run more precisely than less efficient workers. This foresight enables them, on the one hand, to prepare the change to new, full bobbins in time while, on the other hand, not producing waste by changing them too early (see Figure 18.8). Part of this activity-regulating knowledge is also knowledge of the action programs and abilities of one's coworkers.

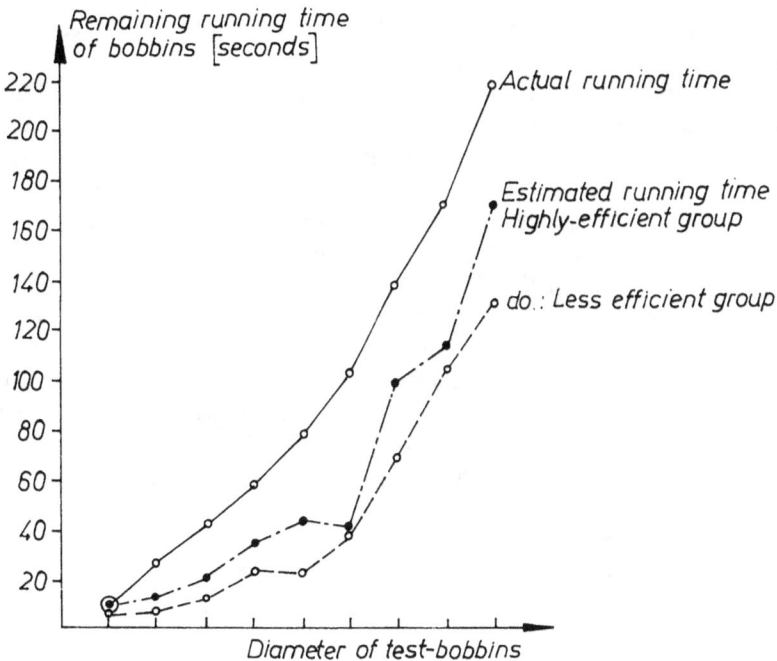

FIG. 18.8. Actual versus estimated remaining running time of bobbins with different diameters. Means for highly versus less efficient workers ($N = 6$ workers/group; $p = .05$) (Rühle, 1979).

Mental representations have an impact on all aspects of preparing an activity. As long as there is enough freedom, these representations impact the generating of sequences of subgoals and programs, the testing of, and decisions on, procedures before they are actually executed (Hacker, 1980). The decision includes an evaluation of the predicted consequences of different procedures and their instrumentalities. These processes of preparation for activities make it seem as if mental representations were the "material" with which the preparatory steps of information processing are done.

Even orientation toward the demands of actions and the conditions of execution are dependent on mental representations. Different representations lead to different hypotheses about conditions of the technical process, thus inducing differing search strategies and the selection of different sources of information. An example is the relation between the actual frequency of failures produced by machines and the failure rate expected by workers. More efficient workers know the actual probabilities of failure better than do less efficient workers; therefore, search time for failures is significantly less in the first group, and workers in this group are better able to prevent failures than workers in the second group. As a result of these and related differences in mental representations, more efficient workers show a higher performance level, but their perceived fatigue at work is not higher (Rühle, 1979; Schneider, 1977; for a review, see Hacker & Richter, 1983).

We expect that the development of efficient activity-regulating mental representations is a multistage and multilevel process. This process should start with a redefinition of the task that allows for a more efficient procedure. Examples of this are: Workers change nonlinear functions to linear ones in the process of learning; hierarchical structures are treated as simple nonhierarchical ones; complex rules are not used; instead, simple rules are learned by heart (Hacker, 1977; Hacker & Matern, 1979; Norros, 1982). This efficient process of redefinition is characterized by a reduction in the number of cognitive operations necessary and a reduction of the memory demands for short- and long-term items (Bruner, Goodnow, & Austin, 1956; Hacker, 1977). Furthermore, the redefined task seems to lead to task-dependent mental representations that reduce the amount of cognitive transformation needed during the execution of the activity. These redefinitions are not constructions in the "constructivist" sense, because they are constrained by task requirements. There are, however, more potential task-setting combinations than the human mind can store as discrete internal representations (e.g., using a stone as weapon, as hammer, as something to play with, etc.). One way to reduce memory load and gain mental capacity is by developing mental representations for the identification of similarities among different tasks. This flexibility would be prerequisite to developing more general, transferable procedures for solving whole classes of tasks.

Thus, there are more questions than before. Progress might lie in being able to ask some questions again and more accurately, given the approach of a psychology of activity. At the same time, it is evident from the ideas sketched in this chapter that an analysis of the mental representations of complex and practical work activities must depend on the results of cognitive psychology. Divisions between basic and applied sciences that do not help this task along must be overcome (Broadbent, 1971).

ACKNOWLEDGMENT

Translated by the editors.

19 Multiple Goals and Flexible Procedures in the Design of Work

Donald E. Broadbent
University of Oxford

THE IMPORTANCE OF ACTIVITY

In the traditional psychological experiment, the person stares into a tachistoscope or presses a reaction key. If the results are to be meaningful, however, the people studied must be trying to follow the instructions they have been given, to achieve in fact a goal, one set by the experimenter. In pursuing this activity the person may look momentarily like a stimulus–response mechanism, and for special purposes it may be legitimate to study his properties as such a mechanism. For example, one may wish to find out how many warning sounds he can discriminate, in order to make use of the findings to design alarms for aircraft cockpits or power stations (Patterson, 1982). Even at this level, however, if we treat experimental subjects as if they were only sound detectors we run the risk of data that are random. Indeed, the results may be worse than random if the goal being pursued is that of retaliation for discourtesy by the experimenter! The laboratory experiment is, in fact, an interaction between highly purposive activities by experimenter and subject. It is successful only if the two mesh cooperatively.

All good experimenters know this caveat, but it is rarely stated in reports of academic studies, because it is so easy to take it for granted. Perhaps the most important of the many excellent points in Hacker's chapter is the emphasis on work as a special class of activity that cannot be adequately studied in stimulus–response terms. In considering real jobs, the purposes of each activity become a central problem. One cannot escape the need to inquire whether the steps in the work process are self-organized or constrained by the social and technical environment of the individual. For this reason, research in this applied field is likely to have salutary effects on theory.

Even at the applied level, however, it is urgent that industrial psychologists follow Hacker's recommendation and consider design of jobs for the future. They should not, as at present, spend most of their time in correcting bad designs that have been put into practice. When the technical environment was simple, a job could be studied and rearranged to produce a worthwhile improvement in perhaps 6 months. As technology becomes more complex it becomes impractical to change one part of the productive process until other parts can be changed, and the process of redesign takes longer. Even with the relatively simple technology (by modern standards) of mechanical sorting of letters, the impact of psychological research from 20 years ago (Conrad, 1960) is only now being put into practice.

Further, there is a danger that new technology may become crystallized into a psychologically undesirable form and change may be almost impossible. For instance, many of us regret the design of the typewriter keyboard or the fact that most calculators have their keys arranged in a way that created maximum confusion with pushbutton telephones. There is little chance now of getting these quite minor points put right; yet the world is moving into an era when the welding or painting of cars will depend heavily on robots and when production and distribution decisions will require the use of electronic "expert systems." If the programming languages, data formats, and interfaces of information technology reduce the level of regulation by human beings of their activities, it will be very difficult to alter a situation once it has become established. Yet, of course, the impact of the new technology could be such as to enhance self-regulation, not hinder it. Hacker's message is of urgent practical importance.

The reason for the urgency lies in another excellent emphasis of the chapter: the intimate link between cognition, on the one hand, and affect or personality on the other. Karasek (1979, 1981) has found that people who differ in the amount of discretion required in their work differ also in leisure activities and in such indicators of emotion as the consumption of tranquillizers. A number of other cross-sectional studies are reported by Broadbent (1982), and one can also show similar effects longitudinally. Nurses going from stressful to unstressful wards in a hospital, or vice versa, show changes in well-validated measures of mental health (Parkes, 1982). In industry, redesign of a job to improve its psychological characteristics has been shown to improve the score of the workers on another measure of mental health (Wall & Clegg, 1981). People who complain in everyday life of an undue incidence of cognitive failures such as distraction or momentary forgetfulness are also often those with a high rate of neurotic symptoms (Broadbent, Cooper, FitzGerald, & Parkes, 1982), particularly in stressful jobs. In giving thought to the regulation of activity that work requires, we are not merely thinking of the "happiness" of the workers, but of changes in them that are damaging to their health. Indeed, our own studies show no difference in satisfaction between paced and unpaced workers (in the same factory, with similar rates of pay, and so on), but a significant difference in anxiety (Broadbent & Gath, 1981a, 1981b).

Thus, the importance of the cognitive aspects of job design is that they have repercussions for personality and mental health; and we need to consider the design of future work, not merely to rectify past disasters. In doing this, we are forced to look at the level of regulation in the job. Yet, as Hacker says, this raises many further questions. Let us consider some problems in empirical results, suggest some changes in conceptual formulation, and raise some directions for future action.

PROBLEMS OF EMPIRICAL FINDINGS

The Question of Cycle Time

One of the features of modern production that has alarmed many observers is that the same actions are repeated at very short intervals. For example, in one study of 90 car-production workers we found that more than half repeated their cycle at intervals of less than 1 minute. In the clothing industry, I have observed substantially shorter times. On the face of it, this kind of work would seem very destructive of autonomous goal setting; yet within groups of production workers in the same plant we have observed no correlation between the shortness of cycle time and any indicator of dissatisfaction or mental health. In a much larger study of female electronic workers, Birchall and Wild (1977) found a positive benefit, in terms of satisfaction, for short cycle time. How can this be?

It is important to note that *all* the men in our correlations were doing work that was repetitive—that is, they all had a cycle, and the question was merely how long it was. If we compare production workers with "tool-room" workers, whose work does not repeat itself, we find a large difference in satisfaction. In repetitive work, we must remember Hacker's concept of efficient procedures developed by redefinition. It has long been known that repeated practice of an unchanging sequence of actions changes the psychological functions involved in some way that reduces interference with other simultaneous activities (Bahrick & Shelley, 1958). An early formulation was that, as the predictability of the events in each cycle increases, they represent less information in the technical sense, and thus require less processing (Broadbent, 1958). A more contemporary concept is that of "automatic processing" (Shiffrin, Dumais, & Schneider, 1981). We need only suppose that, after some months of work at a repetitive task, the actual time occupied by each cycle is irrelevant; or even that shorter cycles may be easier to render automatic. The length of the cycle, therefore, is not important for the impact of the work on the person's autonomous goal setting: only the fact that there is a cycle.

The repetitive nature of the work may indeed make it difficult to achieve the necessary degree of autonomy. In some cases, personal control over distribution of work periods over the day, or the setting and achievement of production targets, may take the place of the nonrepetitive worker's planning of a unique task. Alternatively, the completion of a set number of cycles may act as a subgoal within a general activity of playing a social role.

For example, personal self-respect can be retained through the value of what has been done. This is likely to be the mechanism in the case of the air-traffic controller or the doctor in general practice, each of whom goes through many cycles of activity each day. An acceptable degree of self-regulation can also be gained as the provider for a family (the "instrumental" view of work, depicted for British car workers by Goldthorpe, Lockwood, Beckhofer, & Platt, 1969). Let us return to the conceptual implications later; from an applied point of view, the point is that cycle time may make little difference, if the job is repetitive at all. The problem is to reconcile this fact with the general point of view that Hacker is rightly urging.

Personality and Job Enrichment

Another problem with the general approach is that some individuals appear to desire job enrichment more than others. The classic expression of this view is that of Hulin and Blood (1968), from whose work one might conclude that the requirement for self-actualizing features in the job was dependent on the individual's adhering to the "Protestant ethic" of work and deferred gratification. Job enrichment might thus be of no importance to people with a different set of beliefs.

One may well doubt the sociological side of such a view; it is probably not essential to be a Protestant and live in a small town to desire self-regulation, but there is a great deal of evidence that some individuals find the degree of autonomy in the job relatively unimportant to their satisfaction. Jackson, Paul, and Wall (1981) have provided a particularly good study, and review the earlier literature. They point out that even those who care least about autonomy are still slightly happier in jobs with high discretion, and our own studies certainly confirm that jobs with high discretion are associated with higher average satisfaction in a group taken as a whole. The data on individual differences are not a good argument for rejecting Hacker's case for job enrichment, but it is theoretically puzzling that some people appear not to show the usual increase of happiness when self-regulation is greater (Frese, 1984).

Further, satisfaction is not the same as mental health. In our own studies, jobs of high discretion are more satisfying, but the level of minor psychiatric symptoms in them is the same as in jobs of low discretion. There are effects of discretion on mental health, but they depend on the particular person. Broadbent (1982) quotes the case of depression among electricity workers: Among workers satisfied with their lives outside work, depression is unrelated to available discretion; it increases with low discretion only among those who are unhappy both at home and at work. Further, depression actually *decreases* with low discretion among those who are unhappy at home but happy at work. In unpublished results, we have similarly found that discretion is unrelated to anxiety among workers taken as a whole; however, this conceals the fact that workers with a high level of cognitive failure show higher anxiety in jobs of low discretion, whereas those of low cognitive failure are actually *less* anxious when the job is less autonomous. If jobs are redesigned to increase self-regulation, it is unlikely that anybody will be less satisfied with his or her job as a result—but there is a danger that some individuals may show a decrease in mental health.

To summarize, we have another problem of reconciling the general emphasis on regulation of activity and the existence of individuals who find autonomy unimportant or quite harmful.

The Dissociation of Conscious Knowledge and Successful Action

The third group of problems comes from laboratory studies, in which subjects are asked to control a computer-simulated situation (Berry & Broadbent, in preparation; Broadbent, 1977; Broadbent & Aston, 1978; Broadbent, FitzGerald, & Broadbent, 1983). In some cases they have to make decisions about the size of labor force necessary to achieve target production levels in a sugar factory, in some cases to control the intervals between buses to optimize the traffic situation in a city, in some cases to decide on levels of government expenditure and of tax rate to control inflation and unemployment in a Western-style economy. In a last group of cases they vary the level of intimacy of interaction between themselves and a computer-simulated "person," to try to achieve a satisfactory relationship. One can even undertake combinations, such as managing a factory and a relationship with a person simultaneously, with negative effects on production from interpersonal difficulties, and so on. In all these tasks, the effects of each action alter the problem arising at the next decision point.

The main feature of the results appeared at an early stage of the research (Broadbent, 1977; Broadbent & Aston, 1978) and has since been confirmed with a much wider variety of tasks and subjects (Berry & Broadbent, in preparation; Broadbent et al., 1983). There is a high degree of separation between the ability to act successfully in such tasks and the ability to answer verbal questions about the nature of the system being controlled. It is not merely that people sometimes act correctly without knowing why; they sometimes know what should be done and yet do not do it. Over their entire range of experiments totalling 144 subjects, Berry and Broadbent find a small but significant *negative* correlation between performance and answers to verbal questions. This finding provides objective support for the opinion frequently expressed by practical managers or union leaders in discussions with academics: Knowing the theory is no guarantee that one will do the right thing in practice.

For present purposes, the problem is this: How can the activity be regulated even when the representation cannot be reported consciously? At the very least, if there are key features of the task that cannot be communicated from one person to another, how can the social element in the work, emphasized by Hacker, be properly organized?

SOME CONCEPTUAL SUGGESTIONS

The Importance of Heterarchy of Goals

First, let us develop the point mentioned briefly by Hacker, that the hierarchic tree of goals and subgoals is a special case of heterarchy. In hierarchical classification of goals, a choice low down in the tree implies a more major choice at higher levels. If, for example, I am fitting wheels to a car during assembly, but have discretion about the sequence or tools to be used, the choice of type of spanner is based on the realization that I am indeed going to attach wheels to the car and not to seek to fit the transmission instead. Similarly, the choice of order of operations implies that I have chosen, say, a power spanner rather than an alternative tool that would exclude certain possible orders.

In heterarchic classification, however, choices on one dimension do not determine choices on another. While achieving the goal of fastening wheels to a car, I may also wish to achieve either the goal of saving fuel or that of saving human effort, and this goal might decide whether I should use a manual or power spanner. In either case, the method of operation might be chosen to maximize safety or to maximize speed; again, either goal is consistent with either fuel saving or effort saving and also with either attaching wheels or fitting the transmission. Any individual action thus serves many goals that are not necessarily subordinate to each other but that are equally valid.

The same heterarchic principle applies outside the world of work. In taking a journey, I may serve simultaneous goals of visiting a shop, taking exercise, and experiencing the beauty of a landscape; these goals are not subordinate to each other but may each appear in other combinations. Similarly, in mechanical analogies to human function, one may have not only hierarchic systems such as Test–Operate–Test–Exit (TOTE) units—each controlling behavior until one particular goal is achieved—but also heterarchic ones. The latter may, for example, parse a sentence not simply by routines that seek the goal of assigning a syntactic role to a word, but also by simultaneously seeking the semantic role of that word (Winograd, 1972). The final choice of an output (the "action" of the computer) satisfies both goals.

In terms of industrial psychology, an emphasis on heterarchy makes it easier to understand the apparent exceptions to Hacker's principles. If the achievement of the socially determined goal, for which wages are offered, is only one of the purposes being met by the worker's activity, it becomes understandable why people whose work is highly valued may tolerate apparently repetitive tasks, or why some people with problems of self-regulation outside work find low autonomy at work helpful to mental health. Such a heterarchy of goals also, of course, gives an additional reason for the importance of self-regulation at work, because it may serve not only the goal of more effective work, but also goals on other dimensions.

Declarative and Procedural Knowledge

The second part of Hacker's conceptual approach that we may wish to expand concerns the different kinds of mental representations. I would like to distinguish one type of representation that is, in a sense, a model or reflection of the external world; this representation corresponds to the external world, can be acted upon by internal operations, and can be communicated verbally to other people. Some would call this a *description* within a larger system of possible descriptions called a *representation* (Marr, 1982). I myself prefer to use *representation* only for this kind of internal symbol; I am not sure if Hacker would agree. In any event, the manipulation of this kind of representation is certainly an important part of self-regulation.

I want also to emphasize another form of knowledge: the ability of the person to initiate certain internal processes when a given pattern of internal and external conditions holds. Such an ability can be described as "knowing" a condition-action rule, but persons possessing such knowledge may not be able to communicate it verbally; they differ from those who do not "know" the rule by characteristically carrying out certain mental processes when appropriate, not by possession of a data base embodying a symbolic model of the outer world. A familiar example of such knowledge is the manual skill of the craftsperson; but I regard the experiments mentioned earlier as showing that the same distinction occurs in purely intellectual, as well as manual, operations. In computational analogies of human function, the use of such a set of rules, or "production system" (Newell & Simon 1972), allows very powerful methods for solving intellectual problems. This increase in power arises because a production system need not proceed along a single fixed track of achieving one subgoal before moving to the next. If unpredicted circumstances arise, the system will immediately apply a different condition-action rule rather than continue to try to achieve a subgoal that is no longer appropriate. To return to the example of the car assembler attaching wheels, he should *not* solemnly fix a wheel to an axle in which he can see a serious crack. It is precisely this ability to react sensibly to the unexpected that is lacking in most hierarchically organized mechanical systems, and that failure is responsible for some of the distrust felt by the general public for totally automatic processes.

Notice that until the crack is seen, the worker would have no conscious intention to rectify it. The internal conditions calling a procedure into play are not necessarily representations of the end to be achieved. Thus Newell and Simon's computer programs, in solving a problem in symbolic logic, may follow a rule without a representation of a subgoal; similarly a tennis player may react to an unexpected shot with a stroke that leaves the the opponent unbalanced, without a conscious subgoal of producing imbalance.

There are other advantages for information-processing systems using condition-action rules: They are faster to reach decisions and may produce satisfactory outcomes in cases in which "look-ahead" calculation of the best series of subgoals is mathematically intractable. They have, however, the characteristic that there is no internally symbolized subgoal that can be communicated (Michie, 1980). Thus, for example, chess-playing computer programs working on such principles may be hard for a human being to understand, and similarly the reasons given for their actions by successful medical diagnosticians, industrial decision makers, or statespeople may not be very illuminating to the rest of us.

There has been in cognitive psychology much discussion already of the distinction between *declarative* knowledge that models the world, and *procedural* knowledge that undertakes the correct processes upon the model (e.g., J. R. Anderson, 1976). The distinction clarifies not only the puzzling absence of articulate goals in many people who are clearly self-regulatory, but also the ways in which multiple and heterarchic goals can be served by human actions. Hierarchies of subroutines have difficulty in accommodating multiple goals; condition-action rules do not. Thus, the natural development of Hacker's concepts along these lines can serve to clear up some of the apparent empirical problems.

SOME DIRECTIONS FOR THE FUTURE

There are some obvious immediate implications for application. The first is the need to take into account the role of work in the person's life. Some people, in some parts of their tasks, may appear to reject control and rather to emphasize the use of efficient repeated procedures. Self-regulation may be revealed not only in achieving the main goal of work, but also in opportunities to rectify potential hazards and health risks in the environment. The organization of the work day must also be planned with regard to social context. To be concrete, in the United Kingdom some administrative factors make it easier for organizations to employ fewer people full time, rather than more people part time. For parents, this may mean a choice of little contact with their children, together with a full day of highly repetitive work; or, alternatively, no work at all with a consequent feeling of social isolation and lack of value. Half-time work, for people in this social context, is a highly satisfactory way of meeting multiple goals. Action to change the administrative structure may, in such a case, be more effective than attempts to increase the number of operations performed by each full-time worker.

A second implication is the need for flexibility even when the method of work has been settled. Some of the conditions on which condition-action rules operate are internal, so that the state of the person may change from day to day or even moment to moment the best way in which the job should be done.

Thirdly, it is not always the case that a subgoal can be verbalized successfully; inability to verbalize a structure does not mean that self-regulation has collapsed, because it may be exercised through the possession of a wide range of complex procedures, not operating in a single order but called into play according to circumstances. Training must, therefore, involve the communication of procedures as well as declarative knowledge.

This leads us to a point requiring more long-range research; I do not call it theoretical, because it is of great practical importance. I have emphasized inarticulate action as an equal partner in self-regulation, but I am the first to admit that it should act as a partner and not in isolation. We know very little about the possible relations between declarative representations and procedures, and we need to know how the latter can be transmitted from person to person. Berry and Broadbent (in preparation) show that successful learning can take place through a combination of verbal instruction in the declarative aspects of the task, and of the verbalization of the person during his own procedures when practicing. Each method of instruction alone is ineffective, and this result is a first step toward a theory of training in procedures. A plausible possibility is that procedures can be given verbal labels and can be processed internally and externally in that form. Fancifully, proverbs can be seen as such labels: "Too many cooks spoil the broth." and "Many hands make light work." are not general truths, because they contradict each other. When one proverb is said or thought, however, it calls for one set of procedures for action rather than another, somewhat as the setting of a subgoal introduces one TOTE unit rather than another; but the proverb is not a goal, only a label.

If procedures divide into groups that can be labeled, the system is *modular* (Marr, 1982) and can be explained verbally to human beings. Quite apart from the social benefits of passing on knowledge from one generation to another, an understanding of modularity is going to be needed for one aspect of work that we have not so far considered. Let us conclude by stating that ultimate problem.

Hacker has stated convincingly the need for self-regulation and job enrichment. Because we live socially, however, there is always a final constraint on the autonomy of one person, set by the autonomy of another. In the last resort, self-regulation has to come up against limits. Again, as Hacker says, the division of labor has brought those limits very close; the fitter cannot move the die on which he is working without the cooperation of the crane driver, who may want at that time to have a cup of coffee. Both of them are relying on the efforts of metallurgists and control engineers whose goals and procedures are very different, not only from those of the fitter, but from each others'. Understanding and accepting the reasons for the actions of others is hard enough; but as I indicated earlier, we now have the problem of cooperation with systems that are not human at all. The ultimate problem is this: How do we secure the benefits of mechanical information processing without losing autonomy for the human part of the system?

The ability to regulate actions as part of an activity depends on the ability to predict events in the environment. It is not necessary to know all the detailed causal links that have produced them; but it is necessary to predict the outcome. I do not need to understand all the numerous feedback loops that control the carburation of my car engine; but I do need, when planning driving activities, to take into account the slight hesitation that will occur in speed changes under certain conditions. Similarly, when working with other people I do not (and cannot) know all the internal processes of, for example, the metallurgist or the crane driver. If the work is to be successful, however, I must know enough of their goals to detect any clash with my own, and I must know the broad principles of the condition-action rules that govern their responses to unexpected situations. To echo Hacker, they must not act impulsively or randomly. It is also necessary that I know from experience that they *do* take the right action to achieve their own goals or to implement their condition-action rules; and as a matter of experience, one knows that some people do and others do not. In past years this same assessment of reliability has been used for computers and other mechanical devices, the result often being distrust; nobody will rely on an information system that is out of action half the time. As mechanical reliability increases, though, the importance of the other factors also increases. We must know in general terms what our mechanical devices are doing, if we are to interact with them succesfully: When they are goal seeking, we must know their goals; when they are using rules to launch procedures, we need to know the general nature of the rules. In sum, they need to be constructed in modular fashion; only then can we know when they can be trusted and when they must be overruled. In thinking about such problems, it is, of course, likely that we may clarify our own difficulties in getting along with other people.

My own bias is clearly in favor of activities that are not necessarily made up of repeating sequences of subgoals, but rather of a family of actions that occur in varying sequence, that are flexible and innovative, as the actions of a pilot, a fisherman, or a tennis player may be. This approach is a cultural bias; you will be familiar with the fact that residents of my small island at the West end of a continent are conditioned by centuries of problems in predicting the weather and tend to distrust formal statements of future goals. Similarly, the "silent accompaniment" of these comments is not so much a model of humans, but a trust in a procedure for finding better models. In that process, the achievements of Hacker's group represent an important step forward.

CLINICAL PSYCHOLOGY

Semmer and Frese sketch an action-theoretic approach to psychopathology. First, they criticize theories that underlie cognition oriented therapies because such theories typically do not spell out the relationship between cognition and action. They point out that a plan may be more or less practiced and more or less connected to one's intentions. In this way it is possible to explain why patients sometimes intend to do something but still do not do it. Secondly, psychopathology is discussed in terms of inefficient actions. Inefficiency may occur because general knowledge or higher levels of regulation are insufficiently developed; wrong or unrealistic heuristics, goals, plans, and feedback prevail; behavior is not practiced; or inadequate automatized patterns prevail.

Such a viewpoint has implications for therapy. For example, Semmer and Frese argue that certain therapies (e.g., insight therapies) are more adequate for developing new approaches at higher levels of regulations, whereas others (such as traditional behavior therapies) are more useful when lower levels of regulation (more highly automatized behaviors) are affected.

Klinger argues that this theoretical approach falls short because emotions and motivations are not an integral part of it. Evaluation (and therefore emotion) play a role in each step of the action process. Affect may produce cognitions and may motivate inefficiency. Furthermore, motivational problems sometimes underlie psychopathology (e.g., in the depressive). Finally, he suggests that one therapeutic approach derived from action theory could be guided affective imagery, which is linked to "mental practice"—that is, practice of sensorimotor skills in imagination, a procedure explored by action theorists (e.g., Semmer & Pfäfflin, 1978a).

20 Action Theory in Clinical Psychology

Norbert Semmer
Ministry of Health, Berlin

Michael Frese
University of Pennsylvania

COGNITION AND ACTION

In 1965 when Breger and McGough criticized behavior therapy because its "learning theoretic foundation" was really just an analogy and pleaded for central and cognitive mediators, they could still be dismissed with an arrogant reply (Rachman & Eysenck, 1966). With the impact of the "cognitive revolution," the kind of idea that Breger and McGough suggested has become commonplace in clinical psychology. Most current theoretical and practical proposals in clinical psychology refer to some kind of central mediator. These proposals are usually taken to mean that changing cognitions will by itself lead to changes in other facets of the person (emotion, actions, etc.); but such an idea does not logically follow from the importance of cognition in the regulation of action. The protagonists of the cognitive orientation have missed this important point because they have failed to analyze adequately the relationships between cognitive, emotional, and behavioral processes in detail. Thus, for example, Beck (1976)—one of the most important theoreticians and practitioners of cognitive approaches in clinical psychology—emphasizes the decisive role of cognitive patterns of interpretation and automatic thoughts, yet globally contrasts this approach with the behavioral one. Thus, behavioral approaches are not integrated into cognitions, though Beck takes behavior-therapeutic *techniques* into account. The precise role of cognitions in regulating actions is, then, not worked out to a great enough extent. Apart from a few attempts (e.g., Mahoney, 1974, and Meichenbaum, 1977), researchers are usually satisfied with pointing out the general importance of cognitions. Findings such as those in the area of attitude research—that cognition and behavior often correlate very poorly (Fishbein, 1967)—are overlooked.

In our opinion, psychological action theory, in contrast to cognitive models in general, supplies a point of departure for a more precise analysis of the role of

296

cognition in the regulation of action and, thus, for determining which cognitions will be effective in changing behavior under what conditions.[1] The implications of action theory for understanding psychological disturbances, for the use of therapeutic techniques, and for the analysis of what the therapist is doing in therapy are discussed after a brief presentation of action theory.

Action theory is based on Miller, Galanter, and Pribram's (1960) book and has been extensively applied and developed in German industrial psychology (Hacker, 1980 and this volume; Volpert, 1973). Its central focus is on *how* cognitions regulate (control) behavior by means of an internal model of the path to goals. An internal model includes relevant environmental conditions and the course of action (with its possible variants), as well as its expected results. The regulative function of the internal model can be analyzed into sequential and hierarchical components:

1. *The sequential organization of action:* If the internal model directs actions, then it must contain a representation of the course of that action. Cognitions must run ahead of action in planning its steps. Furthermore, a continuous comparison must take place between the current state of the action, the environmental situation, and the cognitive model. In this way environmental conditions are fed back to the internal model, thus enabling the person to adjust her actions to achieve a given goal. Feedback motivates (a view that was emphasized in the traditional operant version of learning theory) and informs the actor about how far she is from standards (set points); she makes corrections when necessary, and thus masters a particular action.

2. *The hierarchical organization of action:* If actions are regulated by internal models in a sequential way, then models for every action must be stored in memory; however, such an organization would obviously raise unsolvable problems of memory capacity. The solution lies in a hierarchical model. The infinite number of potential concrete operations must be organized and generated by higher levels of regulation (cf. Carver & Scheier, 1982, for a similar point). When needed, they are generated in the action process. Thus, regulation is a matter of a system of hierarchically interlocked units, in which the higher levels have regulative, controlling, and monitoring functions and the lower levels have direct links to muscular activities (cf. Gallistel, this volume). The notion that smaller units can be summarized into larger units has been discussed as chunking (G. A. Miller, 1956) or the development of prototypes (Posner & Keele, 1968).

It is important to emphasize that these units must be *interlocked*—that is, higher units must be able to generate lower ones if needed. The highest unit may then be regarded as a *super code* with which the lower units are combined. For instance, if one has command over the hierarchical system of behaviors that constitute "assertiveness," he or she is able to generate requisite actions merely

---

[1]Meichenbaum (1974) has referred to concepts of sensorimotor learning as being important for the explanation of behavior changes because these concepts put more emphasis on the detailed analysis of the relationship between cognition and behavior.

by "triggering" the highest unit—for example, the strategic decision that in a given situation he or she should not yield but rather should assert him or herself. If, however, this system is not adequately developed, the code "assertiveness" is a mere verbal code. At best it contains lower levels in the form of verbal descriptions, but lacks servicable action plans that entail behavioral skills and the adequate use of feedback. Because its connection to lower units is only vague and global, Volpert (1973) calls this type of higher unit a *global code*. One goal of therapy is to replace global codes with supercodes. Neither the mere cognitive insight (e.g., "I should be more assertive.") nor the mere teaching of specific behavioral skills (e.g., "assertive behaviors") will be sufficient; neither ensures that supercoding will take place. Rather, it is necessary to connect general cognitions with appropriate actions, in such a way that a single command can regulate the entire action sequence. This need for integration leads to the central point of our discussion of action theory: Global insights, internal models, and intentions are frequently not relevant to action, because no action plan is so closely connected with them that the corresponding action can be generated. Environmental disturbances have their full disruptive impact when responses are based only on a global code.

The levels of the postulated hierarchy can be distinguished by their generality (higher levels) and specificity (lower levels) and by whether they involve conscious thought (or problem solving). Actions regulated by higher levels require conscious attention to plan development, decisions, and feedback processing. Actions that are controlled by lower regulatory levels, on the other hand, are relatively automatic—with higher levels used only for occasional monitoring.

This distinction leads us to another source of the dissociation of cognition from action: Highly automatic actions can be consciously regulated only within limits; processing of feedback, in such cases, is delegated to lower levels and is rather limited in nature. Thus, substantial modifications are not possible at this level. Conscious regulation cannot modify such actions; at most, it can stop performance. Thus, actions may assert themselves—contrary to insight—because they have been too well routinized (which in turn can have an influence on insight through dissonance and its reduction). Thus, even the insight that something should be done in a completely different way does not necessarily influence automatic behavior.

Regulation in this hierarchy can be differentiated into four levels (the first three of these are from Hacker, 1980) with many possible shades between them. These levels are meant to be rough categorizations of an actually continuous dimension of low to high levels:

1. *Sensorimotor level:* This is the lowest level of regulation in which stereotypic and automatic movement sequences are organized without conscious attention. An example is well known to the experienced driver who shifts gears (triggered by the internal command "shift") without visual feedback and with few demands on his or her cognitive capacity—that is, he or she can shift while talking to a friend beside him or her without interruption.

2. *Level of flexible action patterns:* At this level there is regulation of general action patterns that are relatively constant in their structure but can be employed flexibly depending on the situation. The experienced driver takes a curve at this level of regulation: she flexibly adapts her action to the particulars of the curve.

3. *Intellectual level:* At this level, complex analyses of situations and of unexpected and unknown disruptions (problems) are regulated. New action plans that do not yet exist as supercodes are generated. Regulation is oriented toward concrete problems, concrete situations, and concrete actions. This level does not include activities such as developing a general heuristic with which to approach problems. Rather, Hacker (1980) sees it as a form of "concrete thinking," which is tied to the action and its concrete features.

4. *Level of abstract thinking:* This is the highest level, the level at which general and abstract thought processes are regulated—that is, this is where logical inconsistencies are tested and abstract heuristics are generated. These heuristics help in developing concrete goals and plans and in using feedback in the action process. Metacognition is related to regulation at this level (Gleitman, in press).

This classification has some empirical basis (Hacker, 1980) and it has heuristic utility. On the other hand, it is still a tentative schema in which it is difficult to separate neatly the boundaries of the different levels of regulation. This ambiguity is not surprising, however, because it is really not a typology but a division at characteristic points on a dimension. The dimension ranges from automatic skills to abstract problem-solving processes. As processes become automatic with practice, they tend to have the following characteristics: (1) they become more situationally specific; (2) they require less effort to be expended in orienting to the right signals; (3) they require less effort for the development of plans; (4) they involve overlap between different operations—for example, one flexes muscles of the foot before releasing the clutch while still shifting the gear; (5) they require fewer decisions to be made; (6) they require less feedback from the environment for the proper execution of the skill; and (7) movements take on a more parsimonious form. When the processes are regulated by higher levels, the opposite of these characteristics is to be expected.

The hierarchy of regulatory levels is changed by learning. The novice regulates most actions on a higher level of regulation; with practice, regulation is delegated to lower levels. Thus, skilled behaviors contain more automatic elements.

We contend that this dimension (and thus the different levels of regulation) applies not only to overt actions but also to covert actions: cognitions. Thus, cognitions can be more or less oriented to conscious problem solving or to automatic processes (because, in contrast to Shiffrin & Dumais, 1981, we assume a dimension, not two categorically different regulatory patterns). We further propose that there are two kinds of automatic cognitions: one related to concrete thoughts and the other oriented to abstract heuristics. The concept of automatic cognition (in Beck's terminology *automatic thoughts*) has far-reaching consequences, particularly if these thoughts are heuristic, and are thus used to develop goals and plans, to decide between different goals and plans, and to use feedback. These heuristics have been called *action styles* (Frese, 1983a) when they determine action processes and when they specifically characterize an individual. Like overt actions, these action styles are used without effort, without much thought, and without many decisions. Like overt actions, they are adaptive as long as the environment is stable, but if the environment changes, automatized responses may become maladaptive. Maladaptive heuristics are especially troublesome because it is difficult to see that one is using them, and even once one detects that one is using them, they are hard to stop.

Automatized cognitions vary in generality: Because they are abstract rules, they can be used in many situations. When an action style is general, it can be called a general personality trait (Bem & Allen, 1974). Examples of such action styles are "Let me think about it once more, before I do it."; "Do I really want the eventual results of this action?"; "Let me do it as quickly as possible."; and "Did I forget anything?" (For details cf. Frese & Stewart, in preparation. Two action styles that have been discussed within a different theoretical framework are action versus state orientation [Heckhausen & Kuhl, this volume; Kuhl, in press] and impulsivity and reflexivity [Messer, 1976].)

ABNORMAL BEHAVIOR AS INEFFECTIVE ACTIONS

An efficient action is (Volpert, 1974): (1) *realistic*—that is, the attainment of the goal must be possible and possible in the available time; (2) *stable–flexible*—that is, one must be able to hold onto the goal (stability) but also to change plans flexibly when the situation requires; (3) *organized*—that is, routine aspects of the task should be delegated to lower levels of regulation so that the upper levels are "free" for anticipatory, preparatory activities.

Many aspects of psychological disturbances can be conceptualized as ineffective actions:[2] unclearly formulated goals, lack of knowledge about general principles of one's own actions and the actions of others, inadequate strategies, failure to convert strategies into actions, automatization of inadequate (though once adequate) actions, insufficient criteria to evaluate feedback, or mistaken perception of that feedback.

Under what conditions does inefficiency occur, and under what conditions is inefficiency maintained? Table 20.1 describes some of the more important rea-

---

[2]This means neither that any kind of inefficient action implies a psychological disturbance nor that a psychological disturbance can be conceptualized in all its aspects as inefficient actions. Gleiss (1978) has objected to such a conceptualization on grounds that suicide can be prepared and executed very efficiently. (On the other hand, one can ask whether the person committing suicide has not failed in reaching other goals.)

TABLE 20.1
Reasons for Inefficiency of Action

	Knowledge Basis of Regulation	Heuristics	Goals	Plans	Feedback
Upper levels affected:					
wrong information unclarity	no knowledge	no heuristics	no goals	no plans	no use of feedback
wrong derivation	inadequate knowledge (e.g., unrealistic)	inadequate heuristics	inadequate goals (e.g., unrealistic)	inadequate plans	inadequate use of feedback
Lower levels affected:					
inadequate no automatization	no automatized signals	no action styles		no automatized plans	no automatized use of feedback
	inadequate automatized signals	inadequate action styles		inadequate automatized plans	inadequate automatized use of feedback

sons for inefficiency. (Table 20.1 serves mainly to clarify the presentation and should not be used as a rigid system with automatic assignments of the fields to any one psychopathology; cf. Schönpflug, this volume, for a similar taxonomy.)

There are some sources of inefficiency at higher levels of regulation and others at lower levels. At the upper levels, inefficiency occurs because one has the wrong information, one derives the wrong steps from an otherwise correct judgment, or one is in a confusing, unpredictable, or uncontrollable situation that does not allow the pursuit of a rational plan of action. These conditions may lead to inadequate and unrealistic knowledge, heuristics, goals, plans, and use of feedback (cf. Schönpflug, this volume, for examples related to faulty regulation on the upper levels). Incorrect regulatory bases and faulty heuristics may be particularly important in sexual disorders (e.g., not understanding the importance of the clitoris to female orgasm) and marital disorders (e.g., believing that praise is a sign of weakness that makes the praised person complacent and lessens his or her motivation). Unrealistic heuristics related to goal development and goal decisions have been posited as the basis for a whole range of behavioral disorders by Ellis (1962). The idea that one should be loved and respected by everyone or that one should be perfect in everything are prime examples of such inadequate heuristics. Incorrect derivations of action programs occur, for example, when someone thinks that to be assertive is to be aggressive. An action program can also be inadequate if it is too flexible or too rigid. Rigidity of action programs has been discussed in the research on sets (Luchins & Luchins, 1959). Rigidity of adherence to a plan is common to obsessive-compulsives. Feedback that is unclear or unpredictable may lead to constant anxiety because there is no safety signal (Seligman, 1975). Such unpredictable feedback may occur simply because one does not understand the processes at hand (a condition that often occurs in accidents, when the operators do not understand the technical processes and thus misinterpret signals).

Automatization is even more important for psychopathology; if very little is automatized, all decisions have to be made in a slow and reflective fashion. This constant reflection leads to overload, taxing cognitive capacity to its limits. Adequate mastery of skills, therefore, requires a certain degree of automatization. Thus, people who are not able to automatize quickly are slow, graceless in their behavior, in disarray because they have to attend to various stimuli and behavioral demands that they have not yet met. Moreover, they have a tendency to fall back on the few automatized behaviors that they have mastered, because these help to reduce the mental load, at least in the short run. Schizophrenic behavior has been described in these terms. (We do not assume that this is an important cause of schizophrenia, only that schizophrenics show a pattern similar to one with few automatized behaviors.)

A different kind of problem occurs with automatized use of signals, heuristics, plans, and feedback that may have been adequate at one time but no longer are. (As goal setting cannot be automatized, this cell is empty.) Action errors

(Norman, 1981) ensue. Although one knows better, one uses automatized patterns, especially when one is not concentrating on the nonautomatized (new) behavior. An example from the industrial sphere may make this point clear. Control of the converter in one steel factory was changed from a purely manual to a hydraulic device. This change meant that the worker operating it no longer had to use great strength to rotate it. This difference in required action led to accidents when the worker rotated the converter too far, splashing the boiling steel out of the container onto the platform. This accident occurred even though the operator had been instructed how to use the new device. The instructors had not realized, however, the power of highly automatized behavior to recur under stress or when attention is directed to other problems. The new behavior had not been trained to the point of automatization. Such an explanation can also, in our view, explain recidivism even after relatively long periods of adequate behavior. The critical period should occur after one has practiced the new behavior long enough to stop attending to it but before it is fully automatized. Inattentiveness to this new behavior contributes to the dominance of the old behavior when circumstances are typical for its occurrence and when the situation demands quick action.

Similar problems occur when signals lead to the wrong conclusions; for example, in social situations there might be a misinterpretation of casual dress as a sexual invitation. When an action has been automatized, its starting point may not be consciously controlled, and it is, therefore, resistant to change once begun. Further, it is difficult to stop using an automatized behavior and to replace it with another one. Thus, there is a tendency to use automatized behaviors even when they are not adequate. To stop using them, one must reintellectualize the plan and think about the information needed to carry it out; such cognitive activity places demands on central processing capacity. If a new plan is constructed, it is likely to be executed awkwardly, at least at first. When time is short or the actor is stressed in other ways, this is a particular handicap. Under these conditions, therefore, there is a tendency to use previously automatized signals and plans (Semmer & Pfäfflin, 1978b). This leads to a maintenance of inadequate automatized behavior that is irrational (as is, for example, the behavior of the phobic). Behavior change in the face of automaticity is, of course, possible, and action theory suggests the factors that are relevant in determining how easy or difficult this change will be. The difficulty involved in change depends on: the availability of alternative behaviors, how much the target behavior has been practiced, and the clarity of the situation as relevant to the new plan. Finally, the difficulty encountered in changing an automaticity also depends on whether a specific behavior or an action style has been automatized. If it is an action style (i.e., heuristics for constructing goals, plans, and the use of feedback that are general and automatized), it relates to relatively abstract rules that can be used in a variety of situations. Specific evidence that a given course of action is inadequate will not necessarily change general heuristics; a whole range of negative evidence might be needed to call an abstract rule into question. Thus, there are further complexities involved in changing an action style.

Automaticity implies that conscious decisions are not necessarily involved in the use of these rules (action styles). Additionally, because consciousness is not involved, interesting paradoxes may creep into their use. For example, the same heuristics used in developing a plan for an action may also be involved in interpreting feedback that results from carrying out this plan. This occurs in the case of a depressive who decides that because nothing can help, even the psychotherapist will be useless. Furthermore, there is a tendency to revert to already-automatized action styles when under stress. Then, too, it is painful to break up automaticities—including action styles: One has to slow down the performance of all operations (to check whether the action style had some effect on the construction of the action process). This reflection interrupts the usual smooth flow of action, and such intellectualization adds a large load to central processing capacity. In this situation one becomes self-evaluative and unsure of oneself (therapeutic advance is, at least initially, often related to a self-evaluative and unsure attitude toward oneself).

Thus, this view suggests that psychological disturbances resulting from inefficient action can arise from four different sources:

1. Higher levels of regulations are not developed at all, and therefore a pure trial-and-error phase produces inefficient action or action completely determined by lower levels of regulation. An example of this is when a depressive gives up all planning and goal setting on a higher level ("because nothing matters"), but still functions somewhat adequately in automatized behaviors in everyday tasks. Senseless behavior such as random aggression similarly falls under this category.

2. Wrong and unrealistic beliefs, heuristics, goals, plans, and use of feedback produce inefficient action. This lack of efficiency is particularly prevalent in social inadequacies.

3. One did not develop automatic behaviors or failed to integrate higher and lower levels of regulation; one is, therefore, confronted with an overload of central processing capacity. The abstract intention of "being assertive," which cannot be put into action because the behavioral elements are lacking, is an example of this (cf. Ajzen & Timko, 1983, for a similar point discussing the relationship between intention and action). Awkwardness in behavior is often an indicator that behavior is regulated by central processing levels.

4. The inadequate use of signals, heuristics, plans, and feedback is automatized; inadequate action styles therefore develop and are stereotypically used in situations in which they do not apply.

How does ineffective action lead to psychopathology? Because of space limitations, we can only give a brief sketch of the argument here. We see a close relationship between psychopathology and stress (see also Lazarus, 1966;

Schönpflug, this volume; Lazarus, this volume). Both involve aversive situations, resulting from the blocking of important goals. Inefficient action may produce such blocks, or it may lead to the wrong type of coping response when stress is present. If there is efficient action to overcome this blocking of goals, the state of stress is transitory; if not, it may become chronic—and we would argue that being psychologically disturbed implies being in a state of chronic stress that one is unable to change (or control). Additionally, inefficient action leads one to blame oneself for the difficulties one is in. Abramson, Seligman, and Teasdale (1978) have suggested that internal, global, and general attributions lead to learned helplessness and depression. We suggest that these attributions develop when one has acted inefficiently for a period of time (in contrast to Peterson & Seligman, 1984, the emphasis of our interpretation is more on realistic perceptions of the person's blaming him or herself rather than on attributional style). Similarly, theories about ulcers have emphasized the role of lack of control—the inability to overcome barriers—in difficult situations (Weiss, 1977).

These conditions, stress and self-blame, coupled with inefficient action may lead to a vicious cycle of stress. Each new attempt to cope with these stress conditions intensifies stress. Stress then becomes chronic because it is experienced frequently and because many important features of one's life are affected. The threshold for triggering stress becomes very low with regard to the intensity of the stimuli and very wide with regard to the types of stimuli that are able to trigger it.

This is, of course, a very general description of how this vicious cycle of stress can lead to psychopathology, and it does not refer to the specific type of psychopathology that will emerge. Which type of psychopathology will develop is another matter and cannot be fully addressed with our kind of analysis (because values, unresolved conflicts, biological determinants, etc., play a role here as well).

THERAPEUTIC IMPLICATIONS OF ACTION THEORY

One important implication of action theory for therapy is that the old argument about *whether* or not therapy has to influence cognitions to be effective is changed in favor of the question: *How* must cognitions be *constituted* in order to regulate actions? As we have tried to show, cognitions might not be able to regulate action because: (1) they are not connected to a plan—that is, they are global codes instead of supercodes; and (2) because the logical implications of an insight are now drawn; instead, automatic cognitions running counter to the insight are triggered in the relevant situation and prove stronger.[3] We now want to point to some consequences that follow from this analysis.

---

[3]Compare Beck's (1976) definition of phobia: ". . . fear of a situation that, by social consensus *and the person's own intellectual appraisal when away from the situation,* is disproportionate to the probability and degree of harm inherent in that situation" [p. 159; italics added].

General Therapeutic Rules that Follow from Action Theory

1. Adequate development of a supercode requires an understanding of general aspects of situations, as well as of specific examples. Clients usually master only one or the other. For example, phobics sometimes list a whole range of situations that they fear but cannot recognize the common principle (heuristics, action style) behind these situations (cf. Beck, 1976). If this common principle is not discussed, and if isolated situations are treated in therapy, there will be little transfer. This specificity is confirmed by Meichenbaum (1975b): Systematic desensitization pertaining to single situations leads to less transfer than the development of coping thoughts that can be applied in a variety of situations.

On the other hand, many clients have only very general cognitions (e.g., "I do not want to argue with my wife.") and are unable to report eliciting conditions, specific cognitions, and alternative behaviors. The connection between individual situations and common principles must be made in the areas of perception (knowledge of typical signals and situations) and behaviors (knowledge and mastery of the appropriate behaviors).

2. Most thoughts and actions are elicited automatically. It is not enough to make them conscious and to discuss them; it is necessary to practice a new behavior to the point of automatization—that is, until it is delegated to lower levels of regulation. "Stress-inoculation-training" by Meichenbaum (1975a) is a good example of this practice. Here, self-instructions that run counter to thoughts that typically occur in stress situations are trained. These instructions encourage the development of action plans that overcome anxiety. The client is trained to use these self-instructions in various situations so that their strategic use is practiced (thereby achieving transfer instead of a rigid bond to one situation).

At the beginning of such training it is necessary to break up the automatism by setting a signal that breaks the chain of behaviors. In our opinion this is the effect achieved by "thought stopping" (e.g., Rimm & Masters, 1974). The stop signal is connected to a specific thought content and interrupts the chain in progress; the client can then orient his attention (higher levels of regulation) to his thoughts and consciously decide to use another strategy. The more the client succeeds, the more he or she can routinize alternative strategies and delegate them to lower levels. Constant monitoring of these behaviors by higher levels is necessary for a long time, however. Still, overlearned behaviors have a tendency to reappear under stress (Semmer & Pfäfflin, 1978b). These recurrences look like spontaneous remission. It is therefore necessary to prepare the client for possible "remission," so that he is not disappointed about the course of events.

3. The internal model that regulates actions must represent not only actual action plans but also common errors and ways to overcome them. This recommendation differs from the traditional learning theory viewpoint; it is useful to present not only positive models who act adequately but also negative models

who present typical action mistakes—something that does not follow from Bandura's (1971) treatment of model learning. Moreover, according to action theory, one must learn strategies to correct action mistakes.[4] Meichenbaum's (1975b) results are in accord with these suggestions in showing that training strategies to cope with one's anxiety work better than mastery strategies that are oriented toward relaxation without the experience of anxiety.

4. The registration and adequate use of feedback are of particular importance. It is astonishing how difficult this is for many clients. A depressive who thinks that he is stammering even though he speaks clearly and intelligibly is an example of this. Many clients do not realize which of their utterances hurt their partners' feelings. Here, it is the obligation of the therapist to give clear and unambiguous feedback. The use of reinforcement, punishment, or extinction alone is a complicated and ineffective strategy. Good feedback not only has to take account of motivational factors, but it also has to transmit information optimally. Such optimal information occurs when the essential aspects are worked out without overwhelming the client with more information than he or she can adequately process. It is also necessary to discuss correct behaviors, as well as errors.

The client must be able to interpret feedback concretely. This does not mean that feedback has to be given in a concrete way *at all times;* when a supercode (instead of a global code) is developed after a series of sessions, it is often enough to give a general cue that the client can concretize herself. Experience shows that clients often create concepts in the course of therapy that characterize a situation or a strategy quite well (e.g., "negative thinking"). They immediately understand once this supercode is mentioned. When this sort of supercode develops, it is a sign that the client is able to use the feedback she receives from the natural everyday situation. As long as the therapist has to give specific feedback to make herself understood and as long as transfer to everyday life is difficult, the client is dependent on the therapist's spelling out the specifics of the feedback.

If the standards against which the success of action is measured are unclear, negative cognitive sets may be sustained even with seemingly different experiences. The depressive who vows to do something "very well" immunizes him or herself against positive experiences; his or her criterion is vague enough so that he can decide, post hoc, that anything was not good enough. Here it is necessary to come to clear agreement on concrete standards. Furthermore, interpretations that come after the fact must be excluded beforehand (e.g., the after-the-fact attribution to chance of an achievement that the patient had already agreed to call "good").

---

[4]The practitioner will often account for such strategies. This is a not infrequent case in which the practice is better than its theory, which in no way implies such an approach.

Different Therapies and the Levels of Regulation

The hierarchical nature of regulatory processes has specific implications for the differential impact of therapies. If the psychological disturbance is in the higher levels of the hierarchy, therapeutic procedures should be more cognitively (in the narrow sense) oriented. This approach is only appropriate if lower levels of regulation are not affected by the psychological disturbance. If there are, for example, adequate tactics of assertiveness available that are simply not used, or are used in the wrong circumstances, a purely cognitive therapy—changing only thinking about events—can do the job of changing the behavior of the client. This is probably the area in which so-called nondirective procedures have their most important function. They redirect the attention of the client to questions such as: Which situations are associated with which emotions? and What is that person thinking? By asking for these aspects and by "forcing" the client to deal with these matters, the client's cognitive field is restructured. It becomes more differentiated; evident contradictions become obvious. This therapy may also be useful for a reintellectualization of automatized cognitions. It does not, however, provide for practice of alternative heuristics and behaviors.

Cognitive restructuring (Ellis, 1962; Goldfried, Decenteco, & Weinberg, 1974) is another cognitive approach in the narrow sense. This framework presupposes that changes in cognitive structure have a direct impact on actions. One would like to question this presupposition, specifically whether cognitive structures are, in fact, so coherent, differentiated, and logical as to be changed in all of their implications when strategies on the highest levels of regulations are changed. It is possible that contradictory cognitions exist (Beck's dual belief system) that have different areas of applications. Thus, the task of therapy is often to reduce or to change areas of application. It is necessary to train the client to see the appropriate signals, particularly signals that appear early enough in the sequence of events that one is able to use alternative strategies. On a practical level, cognitive restructuring approaches clearly use continuous practice of alternative heuristics, thus orienting themselves to changing the action styles of the client.

Cognitive approaches reach their limits when lower levels of regulation of actions are affected. Most actions that are of importance in one's daily routine are regulated by lower levels of regulations—that is, they are automatized. The client will therefore realize that he has done something contrary to his newly won insights only after he or she has already done it or after the action has already proceeded to a point at which it is nearly impossible to stop it. This type of regulation failure occurs often in marital problems. The "ritual of the argument" is already routinized, and minimal cues are enough to release it. The client will be persuaded in therapy that it is not just the partner who is at fault. In the critical situation, however, the client will recognize responsibility only when the sequence of events has already been introduced and they are in the middle of a quarrel. Another reason for the importance of learning to automatize alternative behaviors is that under stress one falls back on one's automatized plans. Finally, the relationship between higher and lower levels of regulation is not necessarily strong enough to make (well-meant) plans operative. Training is often needed to connect upper and lower levels—that is, a global code must be transformed to a supercode.

These are reasons that it is unlikely that cognitive therapy in the narrow sense can by itself lead to success (even when it involves training of new, automatized cognitions). It is necessary to supplement it with behavioral training. Similarly, the oft-used method of learning from a model often can do no more than develop a global code. It is necessary to train the new behavior to the point of routinization so that it is used even under stress. This automatization is particularly important when conflicting automatized behaviors are in the repertoire of the client; it follows from action theory that it is more difficult to break up automatic behaviors than to learn new ones.

Finally, if upper levels are not affected by the disturbance and only lower skill levels are problematic, it may be sufficient to use behavior-therapeutic means in the narrow sense; however, if upper levels of regulation are affected, use of behavior-therapeutic methods (e.g., token-economy programs) means that the client him or herself must find the correct action programs and information for regulation. Mistakes and cognitive detours will appear.

The argument is that different therapeutic approaches will have differential effectiveness depending on whether the disturbance is located in the upper levels or lower levels, is in the relationship between upper and lower levels, or is a matter of automatization of mistaken cognitions. It may be possible to treat mild psychological problems with any kind of therapy (even though sometimes the cost in time and effort will be quite high). If the action programs, goals, action styles, and the knowledge bases for regulation are more or less adequate, it is possible to start at any point, because any change will "radiate" to other parts of the system of action. For example, the patient will change his or her behavior him or herself, after he or she has learned that he or she tends to overestimate negative feedback from others. These ideas can explain the astonishing results that many different therapies have a reasonable and relatively similar rate of success (Glass & Kliegl, 1983; Shapiro & Shapiro, 1982); however, this general rate of success should only be valid for minor disorders in which important parts of the action process are more or less adequate. If these vital components are not intact, therapy must tackle the central problems of the disorder.

SUMMARY AND CONCLUSION

In this chapter we wanted to present the heuristic value of action theory for clinical psychology. Action theory can help to integrate some of the useful aspects of behavioral and cognitive approaches, in which either action is seen as completely determined by outside forces or the human being is seen as a purely cognizing person without orientation toward action. We have shown what *action-regulating* cognitions look like and how cognitions can be made action regulating. The cognitive regulation of action is dependent on plans and the frequent use of these plans. Psychological disturbances can come about because of ineffective action.

Within an action-theoretic approach there is little difference between training and therapy. As in behavior-modification approaches, we assume that therapy is a matter of training adequate skills and cognitions. In contrast to purely cognitive approaches, action theory can explain why certain automatized skills and cognitions are so amazingly difficult to change.

The considerations presented here are of heuristic value and do not (yet) have the status of a complete theory. In any case, heuristic value may be the most important aspect of theories in the applied area. There are no ''new'' techniques that follow an action-theoretic approach. Rather, action theory helps to integrate existing therapeutic approaches and sometimes explains why approaches that have been long used by practitioners (without good theoretical explanation) have been useful. It is the hope of the authors that such an integration helps to overcome eclectic procedures that are used without any coherent framework and at the same time helps to ''salvage'' practical approaches that seem to work (without theoretical explanation).

21 Missing Links in Action Theory

Eric Klinger
University of Minnesota

INTRODUCTION

Semmer and Frese have performed a valuable service in pointing out the missing cognitive links in behavior theory and in applying important concepts of behavioral organization to the domain of clinical psychology. These comments focus first on the adequacy of the theoretical formulation, then on its applications to psychopathology, and finally on its applications to treatment.

AN ACTION THEORY STILL LOST IN THOUGHT

There is no denying the power of the concepts Semmer and Frese present as they relate to cognitive functioning. There is also no denying the importance of cognitive processes in formulating action; however, the formulation presented by Semmer and Frese states that the "central focus" of action theory is on "*how* cognitions regulate (control) behavior by means of an internal model of the path to goals" (p. 297). The formulation then duly proceeds to examine the ways in which goal striving pursuits are organized, including hierarchical organization and automatization. Failures of the kind that lead to psychopathology are construed to result from such things as inappropriate and intractable automatizations, faulty heuristics, incorrect information, an absence of links between strategy and action.

This formulation raises two fundamental questions. One is the question of *the extent to which cognitions regulate behavior*. The second is the *nature of the links between cognition and action*. In regard to both questions, the formulation ignores the roles of motivation and emotion.

311

Cognitions, Goals, and Affect

Cognition plays an essential role in mapping paths toward goals and in assessing progress in traversing the paths. Its role is not, however, an exhaustive one. Cognitions mediate information about what *is* and perhaps about discrepancies between what is and what ought to be, but they do not, in the end, determine what *should* be. That is, they do not, by themselves, assign values. Consider, for example, standing in a traffic lane with a line of trucks bearing down on you. You might form the cognition that if you stay where you are you are likely to be killed by the traffic. Period. The conclusion is drawn, but where does it lead? How should it connect with anything else?

As action theory surely agrees, no cognition about the form an action might take is possible except in relation to one or another goal. *Goal* as used here refers broadly to any desired state of affairs that the individual is committed to bringing about or maintaining. It is not possible to plan, monitor, or correct actions except in relation to goals, and without goals there is little point in perceiving, abstracting, and analyzing. Miller, Galanter, and Pribram's (1960) original Test–Operate–Test–Exit (TOTE) model makes the comparison ("test") between present and desired situations an explicit, central part of the model. Yet, goals are chosen and progress is evaluated through a process that interweaves cognitive operations with affective response.

Cybernetic views of the human organism necessarily reduce psychological processes to series of statements. Thus, there is nothing to prevent such a model from being programmed to assign to certain "perceptual" statements particular evaluative verbalizations. For instance, IF "truck bearing down on me" THEN "frightful situation." IF "frightful situation," THEN whatever the further psychological operations and physical consequences may be (searching for escape routes, increased adrenaline output, etc.). For present purposes, the important point is that in order to turn a plain cognition about a situation into an action, it is first necessary to evaluate the situation in terms of its implications for the individual's goals. In a computer program, the evaluation is bound to be verbal or numeric. In a living organism, however, the evaluation is, in part, affective.

A statement such as "frightful situation" enables a number of different cognitions to converge on it and thereby subsequently to trigger activity in a common action path. By limiting the number of such common action paths, one gains a certain degree of economy and efficiency in the organization of the organism. It is furthermore apparent that a statement such as "frightful situation" serves precisely the role of evaluation. That is, like evaluation, it projects the purely cognitive results onto a broadly applicable standard dimension, one that has immediate implications for action.

How is the step "frightful situation" different from ordinary cognitions? It differs first of all in that it represents more than a construal of either the situation or its likely consequences. It even goes beyond objective comparison between actual and desired states. It contains a kind of imperative: Frightful situations are to be prevented, avoided, or escaped. A second difference is that whereas most cognitions, beyond certain rudimentary perceptual structures, are built up through individual experience with the world, ''frightful situation'' reactions are wired into the organism and are initially also hard-wired to a select group of perceptual events. To put this in other terms, fear—as one kind of evaluative response—is an unconditional response to particular kinds of perceptions. The range of perceptions that elicit it and the range of actions to which it gives rise gradually grow in number and in differentiation as a function of experience.

What is true of fear in this regard is also true of other affects. There is growing reason to believe that affective response forms the core of evaluation (Klinger, 1977; Klinger, Barta, & Maxeiner, 1980; Pervin, 1983). The most fundamental role of cognitions in evaluation, then, is to transform perceptual input into a form that lends itself to evaluation—that is, into a form capable of eliciting in the individual one or another kind of affective response.

Evaluation takes place at a number of different places in goal striving. First, organisms continuously evaluate their own internal states. Second, organisms with more complex goal structures continually evaluate their environments according to opportunities they may offer for advancing toward one or another goal. This goal orientation includes evaluation according to instrumental opportunities or according to the acceptability of various possible goal objects. Third, organisms engaged in goal striving sequences continually evaluate their progress toward the goal.

In each of these kinds of evaluative activities, affective activity is interwoven with cognitive activity. Tennis players, for instance, stay alert for chances to outmaneuver their opponents. When opponents return the ball at a particular speed and angle, players can project the probable landing site and can calculate the likelihood of succeeding with a particular return placement. In all likelihood, the decision regarding how to respond depends partly on an affective calculation—a shifting balance of hope and fear that presumably accompanied the ball on its inbound leg and will continue to evaluate the success of the outbound trajectory. What players say to themselves no doubt has something to do with their affective states, but, if students taking examinations serve as a guide, it is by no means clear that the self-statements determine the affects. It is at least as likely that the self-statements are responses to the affects (Klinger, in press). Thus, in the interweaving of cognition and affect, it is not necessarily cognition that is primary or even prior. Cognitive transformations of perceptual input may determine what combinations of affect are elicited, but much of the affect produced in a situation arises as a relatively automated response to unelaborated perceptions; on the other hand, affect also appears to give rise to additional cognitive processing (Carver, Blaney, & Scheier, 1979). Motivational states, probably through affective mediation, determine what people notice and think about, and thereby determine the very content area of cognitive processing (Klinger, 1978; Klinger et al., 1980).

The inclusion of affective and motivational concepts in an explanatory system makes a considerable difference in the applications of the system in a clinical context. It forces the clinician to recognize that much affect arises independently of the patient's self-statements and requires direct exposure to the affect to produce change efficiently (Marks, 1978). It suggests that tenacious clinging to particular cognitions may sometimes be attributable to affects associated with those cognitions—that the "inefficiency" is motivated. It points in the direction of a wider range of clinical methods, such as imaginal forms of therapy (e.g., Singer & Pope, 1978), that appear to be clinically effective without direct cognitive intervention (Wächter & Pudel, 1980). This is by no means intended to belittle the utility of cognitive therapy, but only to indicate that it has limits and that an action theory that takes affective and motivational factors fully into account is in a position to state where those limits are.

Cognition and Action

The formulation by Semmer and Frese is particularly rich in its treatment of response organization—levels of organization and automatization. That covert responses are organized in these regards like overt responses has already been argued extensively elsewhere (Klinger, 1971). Semmer and Frese's suggestions for clinical treatment, when these are derived from their formulation, are provocative.

Unfortunately, the formulation does not systematically consider the transition from cognition to action. Semmer and Frese indicate that the absence of a usable action plan and of the heuristics necessary to create one will block action. They do not, however, suggest specific mechanisms or a broader range of variables that might determine when a cognitive flow becomes a flow of actions. The concepts of *command* and of *supercode*, or of the linking of an action path to a *general cognition,* fail to do justice to the complexity of the problem.

In real life, an individual at a given point in time has a number of options for action. There is hardly ever a situation in which the choice is to act or not to act. (What does it mean not to act at all?) The choice is among several action alternatives per goal, among several alternative goals, and among various ways to sequence the activities that are addressed to the various goals. The complexity of the problem, as well as the possibility of bringing order to it, is suggested by a model developed by Heckhausen and Kuhl (this volume). The model traces the evolution of an action from the existence of an incentive—attraction without intention of pursuit—through the formation of an intention and hence to the venturing of an action. It not only suggests stages of this evolution but also a variable set—valence, potency, various practicality variables, and so on—that would considerably enrich the possibilities for clinical analysis.

Among the features of the transition from cognition to action—apart from the value considerations described in the previous section and the practicality factors—are the following: First, there must be an innate system for linking perceptions (perhaps via more elaborate cognitions) to action. There is reason to believe that these systems are the larger primitive response patterns of which emotional responses are part (Klinger, 1977; McDougall, 1921). That is, emotional activation leads directly to incipient action, with the nature of the action being left to maturation and experience. Second, the fact that, beyond very early ages, people become less and less subject to emotion-based impulsive activity suggests that the sophisticated behavior of older humans depends on differentiation or inhibition of impulsive behavior, both of which deteriorate under extreme emotional stress. Third, action depends on a prior process of forming a commitment to pursue the particular goal (or an intention, in Heckhausen and Kuhl's terms). The commitment changes response dispositions (Klinger, 1977) and alters the possibilities for subsequent affective response. Thus, actions occur within a framework of previously formed intentions or commitments and are released at appropriate times probably through disinhibition, which is in turn governed by practicality considerations as well as value-based goal and action conflicts.

This is a picture seemingly quite different from that of ''general cognitions'' that (no pun intended) command action hierarchies. It eliminates the risk of implicit homunculi who issue the commands. It also makes clearer why the pedestrian in that traffic lane, with trucks bearing down fast, does not become stuck on the ''frightful situation'' statement. The affect carries avoidance-response tendencies (perhaps partly evolved out of primitive responses to looming, no doubt partly learned through socialization) that are readily disinhibited in the circumstances.

A comprehensive therapeutic approach needs to consider the whole range of this complexity. Thus, failure to act may be attributable to a great variety of problems. Not knowing what to do is certainly one of these, but possessing conflicting values, lacking practical means whose costs stay within an acceptable range, and, in general, dealing with the wider familial and other social consequences of decision making also constitute clinically commonplace problem areas. The possibility that action is at root coordinate with emotional response, in the sense of constituting the actualization of a behavioral tendency of which emotion is part, has clinical implications that have so far not been adequately explored.

APPLICATIONS TO PSYCHOPATHOLOGY

Semmer and Frese suggest interesting therapeutic directions for remedying a variety of psychopathologies and adjustment disorders. They do not, however, distinguish clearly within several pairs of alternatives: response features correlated with psychopathology versus features that cause it, organically based versus psychosocially based psychopathology, and ability versus motivation to perform well. All of these interrelated polarities bear heavily on the recurrent discussion of depression as a target psychopathology.

There may well be personality or response organization features that predispose toward reactive depression. Unfortunately, most of the data in the field that bear on the question are cross-sectional. They reliably demonstrate that depressed individuals are, for instance, less likely than others to exaggerate their control over events (Alloy & Abramson, 1982) and more likely to overgeneralize consequences of failure (Carver & Ganellen, 1983). There is, however, no very good basis for asserting that these qualities predict rather than accompany depression. One rare short-term longitudinal investigation found that cognitive characteristics of depressed patients change markedly as they overcome their depression (Hamilton & Abramson, 1983). This is presumably not attributable to the treatment program. Rather, the presumption is that at least a substantial part of the attributional styles of depressed individuals is associated with the psychopathology rather than constituting a preexisting trait. If this is so, the kinds of interventions deduced from action theory may have an ameliorative effect, perhaps hastening recovery from depression; however, they would get at the factors that produced the depression only insofar as they succeeded in persuading the patient that what had earlier appeared as a personal loss—and had thereby precipitated the depression—was in fact no significant loss at all.

One of the chief difficulties in dealing with depressed individuals is their low level of motivation to pursue supposedly attractive activities. The activities are often not perceived as particularly attractive and are often not enjoyed very much when engaged in. This reduced motivation accounts for the lack of higher-level planning—for the reactive rather than proactive quality of the depressive's life— and it seems unlikely that this motivational impairment will yield to interventions aimed at heuristics or response organization, at least during the early stages of the depression (Klinger, 1977).

It would certainly appear that reactive depression and perhaps other psychopathologies are related to frustration of goals. The action-theory approach may suggest ways of helping patients to encounter less frustration and to process the unavoidable frustration in ways that are less destructive to general functioning. It will also, however, be important to recognize the status of depression as a natural, partly adaptive response to major loss and, rather than assign patients responsibility for the unavoidable depression, assist them in accepting it as a natural reaction whose ill effects they are capable of limiting. That is, it is unnecessary for patients who have sustained genuine losses to consider their depressions as personal defects or failings; instead, they can be led to view them as naturally time-limited phenomena (assuming they are largely reactive), to recognize their pessimism as realistically invalid, and to view their losses in terms no more general than reality dictates. Instructing patients in the natural history of depression is itself often a highly helpful intervention.

APPLICATIONS TO TREATMENT

If I have followed the argument correctly, it appears that the therapeutic implications of action theory overlap those of cognitive approaches in stressing the importance of correct interpretation of feedback, realistic heuristics, and adequate hypothesis testing. Additionally, action theory seems to stress the importance of planning, of rehearsing more desirable cognitive habits to the point of automatization, and of stressing the application of cognitive activities to external situations so as to build bridges to action. Finally, action theory stresses the hierarchical organization of cognition and action and stresses intervention at the highest applicable level of the hierarchy—for instance, at the broadest applicable level of generalization. Generalization is facilitated by making sure that all of the important instances of maladaptive behavior—whether part of the presenting complaint or not—be subjected to scrutiny and modification. This is a phenomenon long known to dynamically oriented therapists as *working through,* but the action-theory formulation systematizes the concept and reemphasizes it.

Semmer and Frese's recommendations imply direct intervention of the kind popularized by behavior therapy and cognitive therapy. That is, the clinician identifies the problem, persuades the patient to modify some cognitive or behavioral practice, and assists the patient in the modification. However, two features of the action-theory approach suggest the likely utility of another approach. One feature is the desire to operate at high levels of generalization; the other is the emphasis on rehearsal. The alternative therapeutic modality is the use of guided imagery.

Imagery has, of course, been harnessed by therapists since the beginning of psychological treatment, and its use was systematized at the beginning of behavioral treatment in the venerable procedure of systematic desensitization. It is, however, both a rather different and a more powerful phenomenon than was at first believed. It is different in that the imagery patients create is probably rather different from what they are instructed to have (M. P. Anderson, 1981), and its power is indicated partly in the finding that, at least in its use with assertiveness training, the therapy is more successful when it provides the opportunity for the patient to elaborate the imagery idiosyncratically (Kazdin, 1979). That is, allowing the patient's fantasy to unfold in its own directions promotes the therapeutic effect. This finding links up with evidence that "Guided Affective Imagery" therapy (e.g., Leuner, 1978), which depends almost entirely on guided imagery with no systematic attempt at interpretation, also produces significant therapeutic effects (Wächter & Pudel, 1980).

Why should guided imagery provide a particularly appealing vehicle for, of all things, an action theory? The reason lies in the manifold links between imagery and the rest of psychological functioning. Not only does visual imagery share portions of the visual perceptual system (Finke, 1980), at least in the sense of functional equivalence, but there is evidence that imagery functionally overlaps other perceptual and motor processes as well, that it is subject to similar motivational influences as overt behavior, and that it is integrated with emotional processes as well (Klinger, 1981). In short, imaginal processes act very much as if they formed a conscious representation of much of an individual's psychic apparatus.

For therapeutic purposes, it is, of course, crucial that imagery be not merely an epiphenomenal reflection of underlying processes but in some sense an integral part of them, a part capable of providing feedback and modifying the underlying structures. Evidence that it performs these critical functions is provided by experimental results showing that mental practice of physical skills is capable of improving the overt performance of those skills (e.g., Rawlings & Rawlings, 1974; Richardson, 1967a, 1967b; Ulich, 1969; K. D. White, Ashton, & Lewis, 1979). The point is also, of course, supported by the therapeutic results already cited. The research with mental practice indicates that vivid imagers benefit more from mental practice than others, that the benefit is modality specific, and that subjects first need to have acquired a minimal degree of skill before mental practice can improve it. The precise mechanism for the improvement—for instance, precise components of cognitive and motor processes that account for the improvement—has yet to be identified.

Taken together, the evidence indicates that imaginal rehearsal provides a way to change overt behavior and that the loosely guided imagery used in Guided Affective Imagery also produces therapeutic change. Because Guided Affective Imagery (and presumably related methods) produces relatively frequent instances of emotionally powerful encounters with problem situations, it would appear to offer a relatively efficient tool, perhaps with some specific modification, for reaching the therapeutic goals of action theory. Furthermore, there is clinical reason to believe (but so far no systematic evidence) that the results of Guided Affective Imagery generalize reasonably widely within an individual's sphere of activity.

SUMMARY

Action theory as presented by Semmer and Frese draws attention to problems of response organization, a topic long overdue for close attention. It also joins other promising approaches in focusing on observational analysis of goal directed activity. It falls short of a comprehensive theory and loses balance in application by omitting emotional and motivational concepts that lie at the heart of behavioral organization. In particular, it lacks explicit mechanisms for evaluation and for the transition from cogitation to action. These gaps are reflected in the implications of action theory for psychopathology and treatment. Straightforward applications of the recommendations—in themselves promising and provocative, if not always original—are likely to overlook important motivational and affective components of the clinical problem. One therapeutic approach that seems a promising tool for implementing action-theory recommendations while incorporating missing elements is guided imagery.

EDUCATIONAL PSYCHOLOGY

Action theory typically begins with a person's goals, but this leads to two problems: first, describing which goals a person will come to have, a topic considered in Chapter 6; and second, deciding which goals a person should *have. Baron attempts to construct a theory of this second sort, a normative theory of goal formation in the context of education, a place where the problem naturally arises, because, as Baron argues, education inculcates motives, and induces "action styles" (i.e., characteristic ways of doing things). To construct a normative theory of goal development Baron starts from Rawls' theory of justice.*

Rawls has proposed, in the Kantian tradition, a normative theory of the just society to which, he argues, one must assent under pain of being irrational. To do this, Rawls works out a theory of rationality that Baron uses as a starting point from which to develop his normative model.

Baron concludes that some aspects of achievement motivation—namely, the desire to develop one's competencies and the desire to act in a socially desirable way—are rational in themselves. That is, Baron argues that to the degree that a person is rational, he or she will want to develop his or her competencies and to act in a socially desirable way. Other aspects of achievement motivation—namely, the desire to compete, the desire to gather information, and the desire to do a task just for the sake of doing it—are only contingently rational. That is, the rationality of such desires depends on the nature of the society in which one lives, or the nature of the task itself. Thus, these desires ought not to be inculcated as ends in themselves.

Schnotz takes issue first with Baron's general approach, and then with specific conclusions Baron draws from that approach. Schnotz is skeptical that Rawls' approach can actually derive conclusions as to what desires it is rational to inculcate; he is skeptical because Rawls' approach is explicitly transcultural and transhistorical. Rawls' concern was to give us criteria of rationality and justice that could be applied to any society, regardless of its particular historical context. Schnotz argues that any theory so divorced from the particularities of sociohistorical facts cannot, in fact, be used to derive the right concrete course of action.

In particular, Schnotz argues, for example, that social desirability is not *a rational goal per se, and that whether it is rational to instill this desire depends on the rationality and morality of the particular culture of which one is a part.*

The debate between those who believe that we do have a concept of justice that is both abstract enough to cover all cultures at all times and, yet, concrete enough to provide real guidance has gone on since Plato's academy. One would not expect to find it solved here. Still, Baron and Schnotz work through these issues in the context of a specific theory of human behavior and a specific pragmatic issue: education. Their discussion articulates the issue in a particularly clear way.

22

Rational Plans, Achievement, and Education

Jonathan Baron
University of Pennsylvania

INTRODUCTION

Education is not just concerned with imparting knowledge and skill, but also with inculcating personality traits, motives, and dispositions. Educators have been particularly concerned with certain styles of action, both as ultimate goals of education and as prerequisites for taking advantage of schooling itself. Good students are those who are conscientious, presistent, and motivated to achieve. Good citizens, as the products of an educational system, are supposed to carry these qualities from school into life. In general, education is concerned with two kinds of action styles, those that affect the success of action, when success is at issue, and those that affect its morality. I concern myself here with those action styles that affect success, which may be classified, following the literature in this field, into those that affect achievement and those that affect persistence. Under "action styles" I include general behavioral dispositions, such as impulsiveness, motives, such as a distaste for uncertainty, or expectations, such as the expectation that further work on a problem will be fruitless.

In this chapter, I assume that education has some legitimate concern with the inculcation of action styles. The proper goals of such inculcation are not obvious, however. There are many aspects of achievement, and it is not clear that all of them should be promoted in all people. Likewise, there is a limit to the amount of persistence that is rational. In order to answer questions about what our educational goals should be, we need two things: a theory of rationality and an analysis of achievement and persistence. In this chapter, I present a theory of rationality, that of Rawls (1971), and I use this theory to argue that certain components of achievement motivation are more rational than others, and hence more worthy of inculcation. I also discuss the current literature on the training of action styles from the point of view of my analysis. First, however, I muse make a more general comment about the kinds of theory we need in psychology and education.[1]

DESCRIPTIVE, NORMATIVE, AND PRESCRIPTIVE MODELS

Those who concern themselves with the relations between psychology and education must ultimately concern themselves with three types of models. Descriptive models are those that try to account for what a person actually does. Most psychological theories are nominally of this type—for example, the theory of achievement motivation. (Many such theories contain an implicit normative component, which may depend on the researcher. Behaviors that promote achievement, for example, may be considered desirable by a student of achievement motivation, and undesirable by a student of behavioral determinants of heart disease.)

Normative models, in contrast, are idealized statements of standards. For example, the theory of expected utility, or utility theory, for short, holds that the relative attractiveness of behavioral choices should be determined by the expected utility for each choice, which is the sum over possible outcomes of the probability of each outcome times its utility (Krantz, Luce, Suppes, & Tversky, 1971, Chap. 8). Utility, in turn, may be decomposed into attributes, which are combined in a simple way. Although models such as this are still disputed (e.g., L. J. Cohen, 1981), it seems to me that there is good reason (e.g., Eells, 1982) to think that some sort of utility theory will survive as a good account of our intuitions, on reflections, about the rules we would want ourselves and others to follow, if we could.

Much research has been devoted to the question of whether such normative models are also descriptive models of human behavior. It frequently turns out

---

[1]My own work on this topic derives from my work on the theory of thinking (Baron, 1981, 1982, in press), which is both a type of action and a means for deciding what action to take. The present chapter is a sketch of a generalization of this kind of theory from the domain of thinking to the domain of action; however, I also touch on the role of thinking in decisions about action.

that the normative models are not good descriptive models (Kahneman, Slovic, & Tversky, 1982; Tversky & Kahneman, 1981). People deviate from them not just because behavior is variable but also because we seem to be systematically biased to act against them. These biases provide an opportunity for education, which should try to find ways to reduce them and their effects. Of course, as we continue the search for biases and for ways to reduce them, we must continually reexamine the normative models themselves.

Normative models are best seen as abstract standards for evaluation, rather than as prescriptions about how to behave. For example (Simon, 1957), in any complex decision, any attempt to imagine all possible consequences of all possible courses of action would take so much time that the cost of the time would not be compensated by the benefits gained from the deliberation. Thus, in addition to normative models, we need prescriptive models, which are, in essence, rules to use as guides for actual behavior. For example, Simon (1957) proposes that it is often sufficient to classify outcomes as acceptable or not, and then choose the first alternative course of action that will invariably lead to an acceptable outcome. The best prescriptive model is the one that is expected to yield the best decisions, as evaluated according to the normative model. The nature of the best prescriptive model might depend on circumstances; for example, Simon's proposal might maximize utility (on the average) in some situations but not in others. In general, it is a safe bet that the best prescriptive model will be based on some sort of simplification of the normative model by which it is evaluated.

My main point is this: A goal of education is to help people follow good prescriptive models, where goodness is defined with reference to normative models. One function of research is to determine where people deviate from normative models, and whether any sort of prescriptions can bring us closer to these norms. This type of research is carried out in the domain of decision theory itself, and I think it can be done in action theory as well.

RAWLS' THEORY AS A NORMATIVE THEORY OF ACTION

It seems to me that a good basis for a normative theory of action has been provided by Rawls (1971, Section VII), in his theory of rational life plans. I sketch this theory here and then try to apply it to prescriptive questions about achievement and persistence. First, let me explain the context in which this theory was developed.

Rawls' main concern was the development of a theory of justice. To develop this theory, Rawls considers what basic principles of morality and government might be acceptable to people in an "original position," in which each person was ignorant of his place in society, in history, or even his own ideals and goals (up to a point). People in the original position are assumed to be rational in a "thin" sense. In the original position, only a rational calculation of self-interest is needed, because moral considerations are taken care of by the need to consider all points of view. Because the thin theory is designed for people who do not fully know their particular ideals, goals, and so on, it must state the mimimal conditions of rationality consistent with a variety of such goals.

Rawls derives two basic principles of just societies by showing that these principles would be acceptable to people who were rational in the thin sense. One principle states, roughly, that people are entitled to equal liberty compatible with everyone else having the same liberty (e.g., freedom of conscience); the other states, roughly, that primary goods such as money should be distributed so as to maximize the welfare of the least advantaged social group in the long run. The two principles of justice, in turn, lead to a more complete theory of a just society. Rawls then develops a "full" theory of rational life plans for people living in such a society. In a just society, people would be taught to respect the social order, and they would have no good reason to rebel, because they would also understand why the principles of the society were fair to all. For example, the poorest people in such a society would have no reason to rebel, because one of the principles ensures that goods will be distributed so as to maximize their welfare. The full theory thus takes into account the effect of moral values concerning the social order on life plans. The full theory plays little further role in the development of Rawls' theory, but it serves as an illustration of how the theory of justice can clarify other issues—in this case, the nature of the good life. Although the full theory is developed under the assumption of a just society, I believe that it may require only small modifications to deal with the more general situation. For example, the theory of self-respect that I describe is quite sensible even for a society that is less than perfectly just.[2]

Rawls' theory is concerned with the rationality of "life plans" rather than of individual acts. In this regard, it contrasts with utility theories, in which rationality of acts or decisions is usually defined in terms of the utilities of expected outcomes. The advantage of Rawls' approach is that it does not assume that our utilities are given; it allows that they may come to exist as part of the process of forming a plan. That is, lasting values can be created by single decisions, which we might call plan-forming decisions, taken at a particular point in time (or gradually). (Irwin, 1971, would describe these as initiations of extended acts.) Most of our values come to exist in this way—for example, a liking for classical music, a desire to be a good provider, or an interest in social reform. Even obviously innate values, such as an interest in food or sex, can be modified one way or another as part of the formation of a plan.

It might be argued that the process of coming to value classical music really involves a discovery that classical music satisfies some value already present

---

within us, so that no new value is created (Williams, 1981, Chapter 8). The main implication of this argument, however, is that we ought to discover and try to satisfy all the values within us. If the argument does not have this implication, the difference between "discovery" and "creation" of values is a matter of terminology. If the argument does have this implication, it seems too strong. If I am satisfied with my life as it is, why should I try to "discover" my latent interest in punk rock? Undoubtedly, there are many values that each of us could discover or invent; decisions about life plans involve a choice among these. Certainly, one effect of education is to encourage the discovery or invention of certain values as opposed to others. Thus, a complete theory of rationality must concern itself with the rationality of the values that are chosen (by the individual as influenced by his education) and with the rationality of the process of planning (or forming values, or discovering them), as well as with the rationality of individual acts, given the values of the moment.

A life plan need not be explicitly formulated. We set precedents for ourselves by making a certain decision for a certain reason (Hare, 1952, Chapter 4). If we do nothing more than act according to the same reason in a subsequent similar situation, we can be said to be following a principle or plan. The term *plan* connotes a complex structure of contingency plans, and so on (Miller, Galanter, & Pribram, 1960). In the sense used here, however, it need not have this connotation. In most cases, the term *policy,* which does not have the connotation, would do as well. Of course, plans and policies may be changed.

The thin theory specifies a number of criteria for rational plans, including life plans. These criteria include a set of basic principles that eliminate certain sets of plans from consideration. Most of these principles are technical, ensuring, for example, that the plan with a higher probability of success is preferable to another plan, other things being equal. One that is not so technical is the principle of inclusiveness (Rawls, 1971): "One (short-term) plan is to be preferred to another if its execution would achieve all the desired aims of the other plan and one or more further aims in addition" [p. 417]. Rawls argues that the principle of inclusiveness should be extended to long-term plans as well as short-term ones. Achievement of additional desired goals ought to raise the level of happiness. In addition, Rawls (1971) assumes an "Aristotelian principle" that "other things equal human beings enjoy the exercise of their realized capacities (their innate or trained abilities)" [p. 426]. More generally, "accepting the Aristotelian principle as a natural fact, it will generally be rational, in view of the other assumptions, to realize and train mature capacities" [p. 428]. Of course, this claim must be balanced against the difficulty of training and the probability of success.

Among the plans consistent with the basic principles, the best ones for an individual are determined by the principle of deliberative rationality (Rawls, 1971, Chapter 64). This principle (Rawls, 1971) "characterizes a person's future good on the whole as what he would now desire and seek if the consequences of all the various courses of conduct open to him were, at the present point of time, accurately foreseen by him and adequately realized in imagination'' [pp. 416–417]. The best plan for a person, then, is the one he would choose under this hypothetical condition. It is important to note that the condition *is* hypothetical, which is why this theory is normative without necessarily being prescriptive—that is, it tells us what the best possible plan would be without providing a rule for finding it. One reason for this is that, as Rawls (1971) points out, ''deliberation is itself an activity like any other, and the extent to which one should engage in it is subject to rational decision. The formal rule is that we should deliberate up to the point where the likely benefits from improving our plans are just worth the time and effort of reflection'' [p. 418].

Actual deliberation about life plans depends on a person's beliefs and his innate and acquired dispositions. Such deliberation is most easily understood as a matter of constructing one's values so as to take the facts of one's past history and expected future into account, although, as I noted, it may also be understood as a process of discovery. For example, when I decide to have a child, I do not do so just because the child will further my current values; in addition, I adopt new values, such as a concern for the child's welfare, and the new values stand alongside my others. In making such a decision, I would like to know whether I would prefer a life with the new values, given the chance of satisfying them as well as my others, to a life without them. Because I do not have the new values yet, I cannot make this decision simply by consulting my values. I can, however, rely on other aids, such as imagination of what the new life would be like, aided by the reports of others, and my knowledge of the effects of my circumstances on the satisfaction of various values. In general, education can play a role in providing such aids (e.g., through literature).

A consequence of following all of the principles of rational plans is that (Rawls, 1971) ''a rational individual is always to act so that he need never blame himself no matter how things finally transpire'' [p.422]. Put another way, ''The person at one time, so to speak, must not be able to complain about actions of the person at another time'' [p. 423]. A plan chosen rationally is the best that can be done. If things do turn out badly, it is either because some turn of events could not have been foreseen, or because it could have been foreseen only as a result of an excessive amount of deliberation, which itself would have been irrational, because it takes too long. Faced with the same decision, we would make it the same way; there is nothing to be learned.

The full theory of rational life plans takes into account the need for individual life plans to be consistent with a just social order. Thus, such plans include the development of (Rawls, 1971) ''features of moral character that it is rational for persons in the original positions to want in one another'' [p. 437]. Paramount among these is a developed sense of justice, an appreciation of and a commitment to the principles of justice on which a just society is based. Rawls assumes that such a sense can be inculcated—by suitable rearing and education—out of natural moral motives.

The sense of justice and the appreciation of the social order lead to the choice of a certain kind of life plan—namely, one that fits into this order. Rawls defines "self-respect" as the personal good that is furthered by carrying out such a plan, and I think this definition does considerable justice to our everyday concept of self-respect. In this sense, self-respect consists of the belief that one is capable of carrying out a plan that fits into a social order, in that the plan will be appreciated by others. This belief is more likely if a person's plan includes the development and exercise of his abilities (the "Aristotelian principle," Rawls, 1971, Chapter 65). (Note that the plan can be appreciated by only a few, perhaps even some abstract community that does not yet exist, as in the case of the nonconformist unappreciated in his own time.) According to the rest of Rawls' (1971) theory, it is possible for everyone to attain some self-respect in a just society. "Putting all these remarks together, the conditions for persons respecting themselves and one another would seem to require that their common plans be both rational and complementary: they call upon their educated endowments and arouse in each a sense of mastery, and they fit together into one scheme of activity that all can appreciate and enjoy" [p. 440–441].[3]

Like most other normative theories, this one is developed by the method of trying to reach "reflective equilibrium." Thus, it succeeds if we find it fits our intuitions, once we have subjected these intuitions to the light of the theory. Like many such normative theories, it is possible to view this one as a way of analyzing situations, so that we may see the theory as always fitting our intuitions, given that we have analyzed the situation in a way that is appropriate. Then the test of the theory's value becomes whether it is easy to apply, whether we find the type of analysis congenial, and whether the theory ends up telling us anything we might not have known without it.

The main advantage of Rawls' theory over other theories—such as hedonism or theories based on particular ends such as economic production—is that it takes into account the diversity of ends that exist, without labeling them as irrational without good reason. What counts as "good reason" to label an end as irrational is conflict with a moral order, or internal conflict. Rawls' theory also can help to show us the sense in which certain motives studied by action theorists are rational ones, such as the motive to "achieve." I now turn to this application of the theory.

THE RATIONALITY OF ACHIEVEMENT RELATED ACTION STYLES

I now discuss the rationality of a number of action styles, where rationality is defined by Rawls' theory—that is, I consider whether, and why, it is rational for a person to adopt each style, assuming he had the choice. I assume that education

---

[3]In an imperfect society, this principle might be modified to include several schemes, each for a different group of people that may not coexist harmoniously with other groups.

should inculcate styles to the extent to which they are rational in this sense. I discuss two sets of styles: those concerned with the decision to undertake a task in which achievement is at issue—that is, a task in which one may succeed or fail—and those concerned with persistence in such tasks, once the decision to do a task is made. This distinction is not a sharp one, for action styles that affect the decision to do a task can surely affect persistence in the task as well, and vice versa. It is, however, a distinction that is useful in analyzing results of two different kinds of experiments: those in which a subject is asked to choose among tasks, or among activities, one of which is a task; and those in which the determinants of persistence are studied. To some extent, the distinction is made in training programs as well.

Motives for Choice of Tasks

The styles that have been studied in connection with choice of tasks are mostly general motives, such as competence or competition, and it is only these I discuss here. I assume that a motive is a goal of a plan, and this goal may be treated as a dimension of utility. I assume that each task has a position on each dimension for each subject. For example, practicing the piano may be high on the competence dimension for two people, but it might be high on the competition dimension only for the one about to enter the Van Cliburn competition. People may differ in the weight they assign to each dimension in their decisions. For example, one person may practice much more before the Van Cliburn competition than another because the first weighs competition more heavily.[4] The question that I try to answer for each dimension is: What is the role of this dimension in rational life plans? Should it be given any weight at all, and, if so, why? If there is no reason to give weight to a dimension, then actual use of this dimension amounts to a kind of fallacy, in the sense that the person might want to reconsider his use of the dimension. Research can be directed at methods to detect and correct such fallacies. I consider five general dimensions of motivation to undertake a task: competence, information, competition, instrumentality, and social desirability. These motives are not the only possible ones; indeed, an entirely different analysis of the dimensions of achievement motivation might be possible. These are, however, the ones most discussed in the psychological literature (e.g., Feather, 1982).

Competence.   Anyone who has ever watched an infant or young child cannot help but feel that the opportunity to exhibit competence is an innately attractive attribute of tasks (Deci, 1975; White, 1959).

---

[4]I assume here that judgments are normalized so that the range of values used is the same for all dimensions. I do not assume that the weights are correlated among the dimensions I discuss—that is, that there is a general factor of achievement motivation.

In the achievement-motivation literature, the fundamental issue idea seems to be that competence is exhibited when "difficult" tasks are performed "successfully." One measure of difficulty is the effort required to do the task—either the maximal effort or the total effort over a sustained period. The function relating utility to this measure may be an inverted U, with too much effort being just as unpleasant as too little. More usually, difficulty is defined in terms of probability of success (assuming that success is all or none), so that the principle of expected utility leads to an inverted U function, in which the task has no value at 0 probability of success, because success is impossible, or at probability 1, because success if worthless, but the task does have value at intermediate probabilities. (It is gratuitous to assume that utility is a linear function of probability; without knowing the exact function, the optimum probability cannot be determined.)

In problem solving, "success" is usually discrete; one either solves the problem or not. In other activities, performance can be measured along a continuous scale—for example, taking a test in which the measure is number of problems solved rather than success on any given problem, solving a difficult problem rather than an easy one, producing a better quality solution, or even getting a grade in a course. These kinds of situations are more typical in research on achievement motivation. Often the simplifying assumption is made that the subject defined for herself a discrete criterion of success. However, a more reasonable assumption is that each level of performance has a certain utility associated with it, so that one would really want to know the entire utility function for each subject. (See Keeney, 1977, and Edwards & Newman, 1982, for practical discussions of measuring such functions.)

It is surely rational for a student to give great weight to tasks that allow the exercise of competence, especially when the performance of such tasks becomes the goal of a long-term policy, so that competent performance becomes the end of a long (instrumental) series of efforts at mastery. (The mere display of competence can become a barrier to education, as in the case of students who lose the desire to learn new things once they become competent in one area.) This conclusion follows from the Aristotelian principle, and, more directly, from the need for the development of competence for self-respect (in Rawls' sense). In the dimension of competence, we have an unambiguous case, it seems to me, of a motive that should be encouraged in students.

It would seem, however, that this dimension is less important for older people. In fact, a high competence motivation in an adult, coupled with irremediably low ability in the domains in which competence is sought, can become a source of frustration, an example of a plan or policy with a low probability of success, and therefore irrational (by the principle of greater likelihood).

It is worthy of note that the position of a given task on a given dimension may be manipulated. For example, if a child does a task for "extrinsic" reward—that is, for an instrumental goal—she will be less prone to continue to do the task when it is no longer instrumental, even though she would have done it out of pure competence (and/or some other) motivation if the reward had not been used (Lepper & Greene, 1978). This effect is probably most easily explained in terms of a change in the placement of the task on the competence dimension. When the task is perceived as instrumental, it is not perceived as a task one does to display competence.

Information. A person may do a task in order to find out how well she does at the task. Trope (1979, and references therein) has pointed out that the desire for such information, as well as the desire for competence, can and often does explain the choice of tasks with an intermediate probability of success, so that the choice of such tasks in the laboratory might not arise from competence motivation.

Seeking information about one's ability may play several roles in rational plans. It may serve to monitor one's progress in learning, and it may provide information needed for planning. In both of these cases, the seeking of information is instrumental to other goals. In other cases, information may be sought for its own value. It seems that some people seek such information as a way of confirming their self-worth in some sense—for example, finishing *The New York Times* crossword puzzle every day in order to assure oneself that one is "smart." Such a motivation is not irrational, because out theory of rationality allows wide variation in the goals people pursue; however, it is perhaps self-deceptive for a person to feel that her worth really does derive from this sort of ability. By Rawls' account, a person's worth and self-respect depend on her fitting into the social order in a helpful way. Reflection on Rawls' arguments (or others) may convince a person who chooses to weigh information value heavily to reduce the importance of this motive. It would be of interest to find out whether the apparently widespread tendency to seek information about competence is rational (by being instrumental) or irrational in just the sense just described. For many people, this tendency may be a "fallacy" that they would give up on reflection.

One motive that has achieved considerable attention in the literature is "fear of failure," a motive to avoid situations in which one might fail by whatever standards one has set. (This dimension works in an exactly opposite way from competence, thus creating the greatest aversiveness for tasks of intermediate probability of success.) It seems to me that this motive may be seen as a negative weight assigned to the dimension of informativeness. A person with such a weight actively avoids information about her ability. Needless to say, there is no rational basis for such avoidance in Rawls' theory. It is also hard to imagine that such a motive would be chosen on reflection. We can thus understand why this sort of avoidance is considered a sign of conflict or confusion.

I noted earlier that performing a task for extrinsic reward can undermine intrinsic (competence) motivation. This appears not to be the case when the feedback consists of information about one's ability at the task (Boggiano &

Ruble, 1979; Ryan, Mims, & Koestner, 1983) rather than reward. At least two explanations of this finding are compatible with my framework: (1) information might normally be instrumental, the primary motive being competence (a rational use of information, as noted earlier); (2) seeing oneself as seeking information is compatible with seeing oneself as seeking to display competence, so that the position of the task on the competence dimension is unchanged.

Competition.   A person may value the opportunity to do a task to the extent that it allows him to show that he does the task better than others. Such a motivation is certainly not required by our theory of rational plans, although it may be required in a certain sort of social organization—roughly, capitalist. A large social group that encourages competitive motives in everyone is likely to create considerable frustration, because everyone cannot be best, and some are bound to be worst. (Competence motives do not have this property.) If everyone incorporates competitive motives into his life plan, the majority will have these motives frustrated; their goals will not be achieved. As a result, they will be unhappy to this extent. Thus, any society that encourages such motives had better have good reason, in the form of compensating benefits for other dimensions of people's plans. On the other hand, in a society that does not encourage such motives in everyone, competitive motives in a few can be relatively benign, especially if the ones with these motives are just those who happen to excel in the areas in which they like to compete.

Competitive motivation can become irrational, by Rawls' full theory, when it takes the form of trying to win the competition by hurting one's competitors. This serves no social order. When efforts to instill achievement motivation have the effect of leading to such behavior (e.g., in people who cheat when playing poker with their children), these efforts have gone awry. This may happen in part as a result of the somewhat loose way we, as a culture, think about ''achievement,'' a looseness that affects our psychological instruments as well as our child rearing. (For example, Boggiano & Ruble, 1979, and other investigators, appear to make no distinction between competition and competence as motives for doing a task.)

Instrumentality.   The simplest and most common reason for undertaking a task is to serve some other end. As pointed out by Raynor (1982), this reason is typically absent in laboratory experiments on choice of tasks, once the subject has made the decision to do the experiment. We must distinguish between two ways in which tasks are undertaken instrumentally. In the first case, the motivation for the task is exactly the motivation to achieve the goal to which the task leads. In the second case, there is an additional motivation to do the task that derives from its instrumentality but is not identical to the motivation to achieve the goal. If I have this motive, I prefer the activity of adding up the numbers in order to analyze the data from an experiment I have done to the activity of adding up other numbers while a computer does *my* adding for me. I conceive of this as a motive to do *tasks* that are instrumental (as distinct from actions done for their own sake). It is this second kind of motivation that falls within the framework I am discussing. This motive would tend to make people choose tasks that were instrumental to other goals of their plans, to a greater extent than what is required by the motives attached to the goals themselves. Such people would tend to choose instrumental activities over activities done for their own sakes. In general, they would probably prefer work over play, and when they played, it would be the kind of play that looked like work (e.g., mountain climbing). Implicit in this kind of motivation is a postponement of gratification; it is not just any tasks that are valued, but those that lead to a desired goal. From the viewpoint of Rawls' full theory, such a motive might seem to promote rational life plans, on the assumption that the performance of tasks is appreciated; however, there is no guarantee that it will. A mountain climber's feats just might not be appreciated at all, and a person might work to achieve ends that he would, on reflection, find irrational (e.g., crime). In sum, instrumentality is not by itself rational, although it may turn out to be part of a plan that is rational as a whole. To the extent that it is rational, it could be replaced by other motives, such as the motive to display skills to others for their appreciation and the motive to develop skills (competence).

Social Desirability.   The utility of a task may be influenced positively or negatively by cultural values concerning that task. In a sense, this is a kind of instrumental motivation for doing a task. For some people, however, the utility of any task may be affected by the value of that task for others, and in this case we would say that social desirability is a general dimension of tasks. This is a fundamentally rational motive, from Rawls' point of view, to the extent that the "others" do not value tasks that some larger group would find undesirable. Also, there may be cases in which the culture values tasks, or ways of doing tasks, that go against other rational goals (as I discuss later).[5]

In sum, we see that some of the motives that can underlie achievement motivation have little or no basis in the theory of rational plans. In particular,

---

[5]Schnotz's critique of my chapter takes issue with my conclusion about social desirability, as well as with the use of Rawls' theory for the present purpose. I agree with many of his specific criticisms, but I disagree with his overall pessimism about the application of "ahistorical" normative theories to action styles. In general, I suspect that "historical" theories will turn out to be either relativistic or simply incomplete, leaving implicit the norms that could be made explicit. Of course, there is much more to be said on both sides than can be said here. With respect to social desirability in particular, one reply to Schnotz would be that we should still encourage this motive in children, despite the dangers he cites, because it is a good bet that they will live in a society that (all things considered) it will be better to support than to reject. Even a rebel can act out of social desirability when he tries to improve things; the one who lacks this motive is the one who is so alienated that he does not even bother to rebel.

competence and social desirability seem to be rational in themselves because they are the sort of motives that we would all want in others or in ourselves, other things being equal (and regardless of what the "other things" are). Education should thus try to promote the development of these motives. Other motives, however, are contingently rational. Competition is rational only within a competitive society; information seeking is rational only in pursuing the development of competence or in planning itself; and instrumentality is rational only when other goals are rational. There is thus no particular reason for an educator to encourage the development of these motives in general (although they should be developed in contexts in which it is rational to have them).

Determinants of Persistence

Persistence can also be treated from a normative point of view. Baron, Badgio, and Gaskins (in press) attempt to do so by analyzing it in terms of expected utility. According to this model, a person should work at a task only when the expected utility of continuing is greater than the cost of doing so. (Janoff-Bulman & Brickman, 1982, make a similar argument, pointing out that unlimited persistence is not always a good thing, even if people generally are less persistent than they ought to be. They quote the American humorist W. C. Fields, who said, "If at first you don't succeed, try, try again. If you still don't succeed, quit. No use being a damn fool about it" [p. 218].) Baron et al. (in press) applied this model specifically to tasks that involve thinking, which they defined (following Baron, 1981, 1982) as an attempt to resolve doubt among a set of possibilities by gathering and weighing evidence (possibly from the thinker's own memory). In general, according to their analysis, thinking should continue until the expected benefit from further thinking becomes less than the expected cost. There will usually be such an optimal stopping point, because the expected benefit usually declines as a function of the time spent so far, as expressed in the phrase "diminishing returns." Although their analysis applied to thinking, it may reasonably be extended to other tasks in which persistence is at issue, such as practicing a skill or learning a body of material. (Note that Rawls' theory plays little role in this analysis, although it can be argued that utility theory is a consequence of Rawls' theory.)

The determinants of the stopping point may be divided into those that affect the expected benefit from continuing and those that affect the cost of doing so. The expected value of continuing is affected by several factors, some of which are beliefs rather than values. In particular, this expected value may be affected by what we might call the belief in efficacy (following Bandura, 1982)—that is, a parameter concerning the value of one's work at the task in question. For example, a student working on a proof in mathematics may persist only if she believes that she is good enough at this sort of problem to finish it in less than a lifetime. The lower the efficacy, the more likely a person is to stop. In fact, individual differences in subjective efficacy seem to affect individual differences in persistence, and manipulations of subjective efficacy have substantial effects on persistence (Bandura, 1982).

Another belief, which might be called confidence, concerns the values of the work that has been done on the task so far. For many tasks, the greater this value is, the less room there is for improvement for further work, so even if subjective efficacy is high, so that the subject believes she is generally efficacious at the task in question, there may be little to gain from continuing. For example, in making a decision or solving a problem, high confidence that the solution one has in mind is correct will make further effort unnecessary (even if, once again, the belief is high that further work would be efficacious in case the solution is not really the best). Overconfidence is, in fact, commonly found in judgments of high confidence (Fischhoff, Slovic, & Lichtenstein, 1977; Lichtenstein, Fischhoff, & Phillips, 1982). Baron et al. (in press) report preliminary findings that overconfidence is correlated with impulsivity (lack of persistence) in a judgment task. In sum, premature stopping can arise either from low subjective efficacy or overconfidence, and both seem to play a role. Later, I discuss some training programs directed at these problems.

The expected value of further work is affected not only by subjective efficacy but also by the value of doing well in the task, the value of "success." This value is affected by all of the dimensions that affect one's decision to initiate a task in the first place, and by the instrumental value of the task as well.

The time spent thinking is also required to have a cost by the Aristotelian principle and by the principle of inclusiveness. The faster one does things, the more one can ultimately hope to do. Thus, the cost of time is the cost of lost opportunities. There are other sources of negative utility as well: The expenditure of effort can be inherently aversive; certain tasks may be associated with negative events, such as failure; and so on. Some tasks—for example, the task of writing this chapter—may be intrinsically interesting at first but less interesting over time. That is, the incentive value of this task declines relative to others (Atkinson & Birch, 1970; Premack, 1962).

One may desire to be accurate or fast for its own sake. There is nothing wrong with this; however, people who think that they want to be fast may be deluding themselves about their real underlying motives. In particular, they may not realize that the real basis of their motivation is just their desire to further their other rational plans, and that they would not really have any interest in speed beyond the point that serves this purpose. The same could be said for excessive concern with accuracy, although there is probably less opportunity to say it.

The utility of thinking can also be affected by cultural values concerning thinking itself, as reflected in the social-desirability dimension described earlier. For example, in some cultures, weighing alternatives before making a decision or adopting a stance on an issue may be considered a sign of indecisiveness; in other cultures, it may be taken as a sign of wisdom. Such culturally transmitted values may be a major source of irrationality from the viewpoint of individual rationality. On reflection, people may decide that their culture's values are not their own; but they are unlikely to discover this fact if they do not reflect.

TRAINING IN ACTION STYLES

So far I have suggested that normative considerations may be used to evaluate individual motives and styles. Such evaluation is relevant primarily in decisions about what sorts of motives and styles educators should encourage. Teachers' attitudes about these questions will surely permeate everything they do. There have, however, been a few proposals for specific programs for the direct teaching of action styles, and these programs may be analyzed and evaluated from the normative point of view as expressed in this chapter.

There are two reasons to attempt to train or inculcate action styles in students. First, action styles will affect a student's life beyond school. If one aim of education is to help people live their lives rationally, then educators must concern themselves at least with the effects of what they do on the rationality of their students' plans and decisions. Second, action styles affect a student's ability to benefit from school itself. It is this second concern that has prompted most of the interest in persistence, achievement striving, and so on, among educators (e.g., Covington & Omelich, 1981; Dweck & Elliott, 1983). Although this second concern is properly part of the first, because school is part of life, there are good reasons for considering it as separate: It may be necessary to inculcate certain action styles earlier in life than would otherwise be required, simply because these styles help a child benefit from schooling.

There are four kinds of training that might be seen as attempts to affect action styles. The first emphasizes the direct inculcation of motives, and it was inspired largely by the work of McClelland (1961) on the training of achievement motivation of those planning careers in business. The second approach is direct training of behavior, and it is illustrated by the work of Meichenbaum (1977). The third emphasizes the retraining of attributions for success and failure, with a view to changing persistence and other traits by influencing expectations, without affecting the underlying motives. The fourth method, which I consider separately from the others, is direct instruction in decision making and planning.

A typical study of the first type of training is that of Kolb (1965; deCharms, 1968, reviews other studies of this sort). The goal was simply to increase the motive for academic achievement in a group of underachieving high school boys. To do this, the trainer lived in a dormitory with the students and served as a role model who was both admirable and high in achievement motivation. He met with the students about twice weekly for 6 weeks. Students were told that the purpose of the program was to increase their school achievement; this statement created an expectation that the students would in fact change. They were told that each student would be taught to take responsibility for his actions, to take moderate risks, and to seek feedback about his actions. Students were taught to score stories for achievement imagery around these themes. They also played games in which they could observe and criticize their own motivations in the context of the game. There was both group discussion and individual counseling concerning the conflict between achievement motives and other motives, such as affiliation. The program resulted in substantial and lasting gains in actual school achievement; a control group whose involvement consisted only of summer school resulted in temporary gains only.

The second approach to training focuses on behavior directly. For example, Meichenbaum (1977) teaches children to instruct themselves to be less impulsive. First, a trainer models verbal self-instruction while solving a problem, saying "Be careful, check each step," and so on. Then the child practices such self-instruction while working on his own problem. The self-instruction is then whispered and finally becomes completely "covert." For all we know, the verbal aspect of the self-instruction may disappear completely, leaving only the intention to be careful and to worry about errors. This kind of training has been successful in many studies designed to reduce impulsiveness (e.g., Egeland, 1974; Meichenbaum, 1977).

The third type of training attempts to influence attributions for success and failure and thus influence behavior without necessarily affecting underlying motivation (weighting of dimensions). The rationale for this approach comes from a series of studies (Andrews & Debus, 1978; Diener & Dweck, 1978, 1980; Dweck & Repucci, 1973); showing that persistence, effort, and, consequently, success in school tasks are correlated with the attributions that subjects make for success and failure. Typically, children who are discouraged by failure, and who do not persist once they see themselves as having failed, tend to attribute their failure to low ability, which they cannot hope to improve with further effort. Children who tend to redouble their efforts following failure tend not to make spontaneous attributions for failure at all, but rather focus their concerns on the next opportunity (Diener & Dweck, 1978). Training studies inspired by these findings follow the work of Dweck (1975), who selected children who were judged to be "helpless" in the sense of being discouraged by failure. Each trial in the training consisted of a set of five arithmetic problems, four of which had to be done correctly in a limited time. In the experimental group, some sets were beyond the children's abilities. After these sets, which the children always failed, subjects were told, "You needed __ and you only got __. That means you should have tried harder." Control subjects received no such sets, and never failed. Experimental subjects not only improved in problem solving (following failure) relative to controls but also changed their attributions so that they were more likely to attribute their failures to lack of effort. Chapin and Dyck (1976) found that the training was successful relative to a control group that experienced an equal amount of failure, although the insertion of failure trials followed by successes had an effect in its own right. Andrews and Debus (1978) found that attribution training increased persistence in tasks other than those in which the training was given, even when the transfer tasks were given 4 months later by a different experimenter. Fowler and Peterson (1981, following Hanel, cited in Heckhausen, 1975) found that they could retrain attributions by teaching children to talk to themselves (e.g., "No, I didn't get that. That means I have to try harder."). This method seems more effective than Dweck's in changing actual attributions for failure. Schunk (1982) found that attribution training ("You've been working hard" following success) was effective in increasing persistence in subtraction among children having difficulty with it; however, a control manipulation directed toward the future ("You need to work hard" following success) was ineffective.

Although each of these types of training was designed with a different end in mind, we cannot really be sure that each of these types works for the intended reason. For example, attribution retraining contains an implicit motivational lesson: It might be the case that "helpless" children tend to be those who weigh too heavily the information dimension, whereas "mastery oriented" children are those who are more concerned with competence. Meichenbaum's self-instruction training might also affect the weighting of competence relative to other dimensions. Conversely, direct training in achievement sometimes contains an attributional component, and both this training and direct behavioral training have an implicit attributional component. In particular, if it is possible to improve performance through greater effort (or carefulness) then, by implication, the lack of such effort must have been partially responsible for previous failures.

Even though we cannot be certain of the exact effects of these methods, we can still evaluate them in terms of the fit of their intended effects to the normative models I have described. From this point of view, one criticism of achievement training is that it is imprecise in the motives it attempts to inculcate. It may, for example, encourage a motivation for information or competition, as well as a motivation for competence. The other two methods seem to me to be on safer ground, provided we assume that the students are initially deficient in the areas in which they are trained. For example, students trained to be more persistent or less impulsive must be nonpersistent or impulsive to begin with, in terms of the model described in the last section. (In a training study designed to affect these styles, Baron et al. [in press], found that all children could be taught to slow down while solving problems, but only certain children had greater accuracy as a result—in particular, those who were rated by their teachers as being extremely impulsive or those with high IQs. We argued that the moderate-IQ subjects were not really impulsive to begin with, but were better described as responding quickly because further thinking would not do them any good.) Likewise, students trained to attribute failure to lack of effort should be able to benefit from greater effort in the task in question.

The fourth method consists of direct training in the making of decisions, including decisions about plans and policies. Because decisions are made through a process of thinking, almost any training in good thinking can be considered as contributing to this end. Elsewhere (Baron, 1982, in press; Baron et al., in press), I discuss various methods of teaching good thinking, such as tutorial dialogue (Blank, 1973; Collins, 1977) and pair problem solving (Whimbey & Lockhead, 1980). The particular methods may not be very important in any case; once we have the goal of teaching our students to think, this goal can and sometimes does permeate the entire curriculum, including our selection of what to teach, our methods of teaching, and even our methods of examination.

One idea that seems particularly relevant here seems to me to have received too little attention from educators. This is the idea of more or less direct training in the use of decision theory in decision making, particularly some of the forms of multiattribute utility theory, or MAUT.

MULTIATTRIBUTE UTILITY THEORY (MAUT)

It seems to be that the topic of decision theory in general, and utility theory in particular, suitably packaged, has at least as much claim to a position in the high school curriculum as does much that is already there—my own pet examples being plane geometry and trigonometry. Some attempts have already been made to write material at this level on certain aspects of decision theory, particularly the practical aspects of probability estimation (Beyth-Marom & Dekel, 1983). Wheeler and Janis (1981) have incorporated a related procedure, the decisional balance sheet, into a course on thinking and decision making for college students. There have also been several efforts to use MAUT as a direct tool for assisting students in making decisions (e.g., Aschenbrenner, Jaus, & Villani, 1980).

The Rationality of MAUT

Before I discuss any further the use of MAUT as a basis for training in decision making, I must describe the theory and ask whether it is, in fact, a rational basis for making decisions. The essence of the theory is that each possible outcome of a decision, such as the decision to do a certain task, may be analyzed into dimensions, such as those I have already discussed, and assigned a value on each dimension. The total utility of the outcome may be calculated by multiplying each value by the weight assigned to that dimension and then adding up these products across dimensions. (The expected utility of an action is determined by multiplying the utility of each outcome by the probability of that outcome and then adding up these products across dimensions, but I do not discuss the role of probabilities here.) Is this consistent with, or required by, Rawls' theory?

To conform to MAUT, a person's choices must conform to certain axioms (Keeney & Raiffa, 1976). For example, a person must be able to say that the difference between *A1* and *A2* on dimension *A* is worth the difference between *B1* and *B2* on *B*, regardless of the levels of other attributes of the situation. Prescriptively, this would seem to involve an effort to ignore some attributes when considering the tradeoffs among others.

It is sometimes hard to make tradeoffs at all—for example, when the dimensions are things like beauty and moral obligation. We resist the idea that such tradeoffs can be rationally made. If we take MAUT as normative, we must explain such resistance. Quite possibly, it stems from the fact that such tradeoffs are simply very difficult to make, so that they cannot be made with much consistency or exactness. Such variation need not be irrational, for it would take too much thinking to avoid it.

Is there any reason we should follow MAUT, or utility theory in general? First, let us assume that there is no cost to deliberation. In this case, it would seem to me that it would always be worthwhile, from the point of view of one trying to satisfy the criterion of deliberative rationality, to have policies and plans that allowed full tradeoffs among different attributes. Assume that we already have formed a set of policies that can be stated in the form of goals, and that outcomes may be analyzed into dimensions corresponding to the expected extent to which each outcome furthers each goal. What we now seek is a principle that allows us to trade off goals against one another. It seems to me that MAUT is the policy we should adopt, because, by assumption, it is not inconsistent with any plans we have adopted so far, and, in addition, it has one advantage of its own.

The one advantage is that it prevents inconsistency of a sort that could sabotage our plans in some (albeit obscure) conditions. For example, consider three dimensions, *A*, *B*, and *C*, with two attributes on each dimension, *A1* and *A2*, *B1* and *B2*, and *C1* and *C2*, respectively. Suppose we prefer *A1* + *B2* + *C1* to *A2* + *B1* + *C1*, yet we prefer *A2* + *B1* + *C2* to *A1* + *B2* + *C2*. In this case, the value on *C* affects the way we trade off dimensions *A* and *B*, so we have violated one of the axioms of MAUT, and it would be impossible to explain our preferences in terms of adding the utilities of the three attributes of each outcome. (In particular, the first set of preferences implies that $U(A1) + U(B2) > U(A2) + U(B1)$, where U is the utility, and the second set implies the reverse inequality.) Further, if we have this set of preferences, and if we are indifferent between *A1* + *B2* + *C1* and *A1* + *B2* + *C2* and between *A2* + *B1* + *C1* and *A2* + *B1* + *C2* (that is, if *C1* versus *C2*, by itself, did not matter), someone could give us A2 + B1 + C1, trade it for *A1* + *B2* + *C1* plus a small sum (which we pay to him or her because of our preference for the latter), trade that for *A1* + *B2* + *C2*, and trade this for *A2* + *B1* + *C2* plus another small sum (which we again pay), then trade that for the original consequence, and so on, thereby turning us into a "money pump." More generally, conformity to the necessary axioms of MAUT not only ensures that our preferences can be accounted for by the sum (or product) of utilities, but also ensures that we can avoid certain kinds of situations that, in principle, could lead to subversion of our own ends (assuming, in this case, that money is one of our ends). Although these situations are surely artificial, I think they illustrate the more general point that conformity to the axioms allows a kind of optimization of behavior that is not otherwise allowed. This is the sort of argument that lies at the heart of all accounts of the normative status of utility theories. If we accept it, as I think we should, we should add these normative theories to our plans, whatever else they might contain. Thus, this kind of consistency is something we should try to get, but not expect to achieve.

In practice, we should be satisfied with something less, for to achieve this ideal would take an irrational amount of deliberation. Thus, a realistically rational plan, as opposed to an ideal plan, might fail to specify a particular trade-off. In a sense, the plan is irrational only because it is incomplete. All the decisions it prescribes either will be consistent with one another or according to MAUT or will simply not be prescribed at all.

In this sense, I believe that utility theory is a consequence of Rawls' theory of deliberative rationality. Of course, simply saying that we should follow MAUT says nothing about the attributes we should use or the utilities we should assign to different levels of each.

Use of MAUT

In application, MAUT can be applied at several levels of meticulousness. Naturally, the more important the decision, the more meticulous one would want to be (L. R. Beach & Mitchell, 1978; Christiansen-Szalanski, 1978). The more complex forms of the theory, which require detailed estimation of tradeoff functions for different pairs of attributes and repeated checking of assumptions, take hours to apply and thus cannot easily be evaluated (e.g., Keeney, 1977). Simpler forms of the theory have been used in large-scale studies of birth planning and decisions about transportation (B. H. Beach & Beach, 1982). The simplest form—so simple that it has not been considered as an application of MAUT—is the decisional balance sheet of Janis and Mann (1977). In this technique—adapted from a suggestion of Benjamin Franklin—a decision maker simply makes a list of costs and benefits of the alternative courses of action open to him or her. These are divided into categories, essentially dimensions defined in advance: utilitarian gains and losses for self, gains and losses for others, self-approval or disapproval, approval or disapproval of others. Costs and benefits are then eliminated from the list in balanced groups until the remaining balance is clear.

It is difficult to evaluate any of these techniques. They are designed to help people make decisions more consistent with each individual's ideal plan, and an outside observer cannot know just what that is without using a similar procedure.

About the only practical criterion one can use is the occurrence of regret following a decision. In fact, use of the balance-sheet procedure in the course of
making a decision (for example, a decision to undertake a program to stop
smoking) does reduce regret measured in various ways (Janis & Mann, 1977).
This reduction, however, may be a consequence of the subjects' belief in the
effectiveness of the balance-sheet procedure, rather than of its real effectiveness.

On the other hand, as Mann and Janis (1982) points out, such techniques as
the decisional balance sheet are bound to make people consider reasons they
would not otherwise have considered. Thus, the technique is bound to be helpful,
to the extent that people are generally prone to make decisions too hastily and on
the basis of too little evidence. More generally, from the point of view of the
theory I have considered, it would seem useful to encourage people to reflect on
their own general motives. Through the effort to evaluate choices in terms of the
dimensions of utility, a person may become aware of what those dimensions are
for him and how he weighs them. He may decide that some of the dimensions of
utility are over- or underweighted for him or her, especially if he or she is
encouraged to question those dimensions that have no justification in terms of a
theory of rational life plans.

CONCLUSION

I have tried to show how a normative theory of action, of some use to psychology
and education, can be based on a general theory of rational plans such as that of
Rawls. I have also discussed a number of dimensions of utility in terms of the
theory, and I have argued that some motives were more easily justified than
others in terms of the general constraints on rational planning. I have discussed
various training techniques, and their bearing on the motives I reviewed before.
Of these techniques, one that seems particularly promising is direct training in
decision making, particularly the use of MAUT, and various related schemes,
which I feel can itself be justified in terms of Rawls' theory.

I conclude with the following recommendation: Research on achievement
motives and action styles can in principle be conducted in the same way as
research in decision making and probability assessment. Rather than pursuing
descriptive models alone, we should seek to discover why people deviate from
normative models, and what kind of prescriptions we can give them to help them
deviate less. In particular, we should ask what reasons students have for choosing particular tasks, courses, and so on, and we should evaluate these reasons in
terms of the theory of rational plans; if we find that some reasons are not easily
justified by this theory, we should seek ways of inducing students to reconsider
their motives. Moreover, in the case of young students, we should look for ways
of inculcating the more rational motives directly, without instilling the less
rational ones, such as desire for information for its own sake, or competition of

the destructive sort. This effort, will, I think, require more careful distinctions among dimensions of motivation than are usually made. Unless this sort of effort is ultimately made, research on action styles cannot be of much use in education, nor, I suspect, in other applications.

ACKNOWLEDGMENT

I thank the editors for helpful discussions and comments on earlier drafts.

23 On Problems of Rationality in Education

Wolfgang Schnotz
Institute for Foreign Studies, Tuebingen

THE PROBLEM OF NORMS IN EDUCATION AND EDUCATIONAL PSYCHOLOGY

Most psychological theories of action presuppose an individual who has already adopted certain goals. In most cases, though, the source and shaping of those goals remain unspecified. An equally important topic is which goals should be adopted and pursued. This problem of setting and justifying norms is one of the central concerns of teaching; it involves the question of which educational goals to pursue and arises at the beginning of every pedagogical activity. This concern is also of great importance in research on educational psychology because an educational psychology that is only a technology risks being indifferent to values and, thus, being applicable to any and every goal. Baron's contribution is very interesting because he is concerned with precisely this problem, the problem of norm setting and justification: What should be our goals in education? More specifically, which components of achievement motivation and achievement oriented action styles should be encouraged? To answer this question Baron uses a theoretical framework that is new to psychology. He brings motivational and educational psychology together with practical philosophy and ethics. He does this by attempting to derive the useful, and not so useful, components of achievement motivation and achievement oriented action styles from a general theory of justice and rationality (Rawls, 1971).

Baron sees the function of education as the shaping of an individual's behavior in the direction of a normative (or prescriptive) model. He sees the task of research as supporting this process by providing appropriate aids and direction. One must agree unconditionally with Baron's claim that decision theory in gener-

345

al, and utility theory in particular, should be made part of the school curriculum. If one has set oneself a goal and this goal is acceptable, one should—ceteris paribus—attempt to achieve this goal with the least effort. This is the instrumental aspect of rationality. Decision theory and utility theory could be helpful in increasing the coherence of individuals' normative and value systems. They force individuals to think about things about which they otherwise would not, by forcing them to explicate their motives, thus making their individual "weights" more apparent. These theories could also help individuals make better thought-out decisions by getting them to contemplate things they otherwise might have ignored. Thus, this type of decision-making training helps optimize behavior. The question of the goals of this behavior and their legitimation must have been answered before, of course.

ON DEDUCTION OF EDUCATIONAL OBJECTIVES FROM NORMATIVE MODELS

For Baron, the question of which educational goals are worthwhile is identical to the question of which goals are rational. Generally, a means–ends analysis is used to examine the rationality of plans, actions, and goals. Plans and their related actions are considered rational to the extent that they are appropriate for achieving specific goals. This definition of rationality is consistent with the basic principles of rational decision making as postulated by Rawls: effectiveness, inclusiveness, and the principle of making decisions with the greatest probability of success. Goals may be more or less rational, too. They are considered rational to the extent that they provide a good starting point for reaching broader goals; they are irrational if they make it impossible to achieve other goals. In short, plans, actions, and goals are judged according to their usefulness for the achievement of other goals. Thus, rationality never exists per se, in isolation, but only with regard to specific goals. The justification of plans, actions, and goals from the point of view of their relation to further goals can lead only to a relative justification, in relation to other (superordinate) goals.

Baron uses Rawls' theory of rational life plans as a basis for determining the rationality of educational goals. Rawls developed his theory as one component of a more encompassing theory of justice. According to the theory, a rational life plan is one free of contradiction and one that fits into (or contributes to) a just social order. The highest goal or basic value is the contribution to a just social order—justice as Rawls defined it. Thus, rationality of educational objectives is determined with regard to this highest goal or basic value.

Is Rawls' theory really an appropriate basis for deciding which goals and motives we should encourage in our children? Is it really possible to derive from it which components of achievement motivation should and should not be furthered? If the goals deduced by Baron really follow necessarily from Rawls' theory, it should be impossible to come to other conclusions from either Rawls' theory or Baron's assumptions. I want to show in the following, however, that it is quite possible to come to some contrary conclusions from these premises. I am not concerned with making better suggestions about educational objectives to pursue. I agree with Baron's claims concerning this question at many points. I am only concerned with this question: Do we really have goals here that can be deduced with logical necessity from Rawls' theory? I try to show that we do not. I start with Baron's thoughts on the rationality of instrumentality. The motive of instrumentality is rational to the extent that the entire plan, which is served by the (instrumental) action, is rational. Thus, instrumentality gets its rationality from the rationality of its higher-order goals. (This is the classic position of purposeful rationality as it was presented earlier.) This consideration can be applied to other aspects of the achievement motive to the extent that they contain an instrumental aspect.

Social Desirability

The motive of social desirability is rational, according to Baron, because it should lead to the choosing of those tasks that are positively valued (by society or its largest groups). On the other hand, he sees this motive as a type of instrumental motivation that is directed toward the fulfillment of cultural norms. The rationality of this motive would, then, depend on the rationality of these values. As Baron indicates at another point, culturally communicated values can also be irrational.

In fact, the cultural values with which an individual is confronted are always the values of her specific peer group. The motive of social desirability is always relevant to an individual's life within social groups. The critical point, however, is to which group she belongs and, thus, which norms she accepts. If the motive of social desirability is unconditionally encouraged it may lead an individual to accept and undertake arbitrary tasks depending on whether they are judged to be appropriate by her peer group. History has shown that this pattern can have very irrational consequences. An extreme example would be the World War II concentration-camp commanders tried at Nuremberg who voluntarily assumed the task of destroying human beings—a task that was seen as correct by their peer groups. In such a case, insisting that the peer-group values should be followed only if they do not contradict the values of a larger group does not suffice as a corrective because this "task" was apparently accepted by the majority of the society. Unconditional encouragement of the motive of social desirability may be appropriate from the standpoint of legal positivism (according to which the behavior of social institutions is, per definition, never unjust); however, Rawls' theory, as a natural-law or contract theory, is opposed, in this fundamental way, to legal positivism. Undifferentiated encouragement of social desirability cannot be brought into agreement with Rawls' theory because such strong adherence to social desirability could also lead to blind obedience and opportunism.

Information

For Baron the information motive is rational only to the extent that self-evaluation is useful to one's plans and actions. Many people, however, seek information for self-evaluation only to increase or stabilize their feeling of self-esteem. Baron comments directly on this tendency by saying that those persons should give less weight to this motive. I agree with this conclusion completely as long as it concerns self-evaluation done only for its own sake: Such a motive does not contribute to the social order and thus is not rational according to Rawls.

Self-evaluation oriented toward increasing or stabilizing self-esteem, however, is not generally irrational for the following reasons: The information motive can also be thought of as instrumental. It is instrumental to take on a task out of the information motive because self-evaluative information becomes available through it. It is also instrumental for the protection of self-esteem because one gains information about the degree of social desirability one has achieved. Seen in this way, the information motive is an instance of the instrumental motive, whose rationality depends on the rationality of the pertinent superordinate goals. According to Rawls, a person's self-esteem comes from (among other things) the integration of her plans into the social order. A self-evaluation that is concerned with self-esteem based on achievement implicitly questions the degree of integration in the social order and is thus potentially functional for an improvement of this integration. As this adjustment is considered to be rational, so must the pertinent self-diagnostic activity be considered rational. Thus, an information-seeking motive, which is oriented toward an individual's feeling of self-esteem, can be quite rational.

There is still more evidence for this claim: In the phylogenesis of humans the motive and evaluation systems were changed by increasing social interweaving of behaviors and social division of labor, such that social aspects acquired motivating power in addition to the already present purely organismic processes. The reflection of the self in the admiration and recognition of others thus became (in terms of natural history) an important source of satisfaction that led to (among other things) a desire to increase self-esteem through efforts that are highly valued socially (Klix, 1980). If this developmental analysis is accurate, it follows that an information motive, which is focused on self-esteem, is functional, as a socially oriented self-diagnosis, for social cooperation. Thus, it is, in Rawlsian terms, just as rational as self-diagnosis that is concerned with acquiring competence.

Competition

Baron is correct in stating that the competition motive is not rational from a social standpoint when it results in injury to the competitors. However, what about the motive of competition in general—without those negative consequences? Baron states that such competition is not required by his normative theory. I think, on the contrary, that a certain variant of this motive can also be quite rational even in Rawls' sense. From Klix' statements mentioned previously that suggest that the desire to increase self-esteem through the admiration and recognition of others became an important source of satisfaction during natural history and led to an increase in efforts that are socially valued, we can also conclude that competition can indeed be helpful to the social order and, thus, be rational. This rationality remains as long as destructive acts are excluded. Thus, I think, we should make a distinction between a constructive and a destructive kind of competition, in which, according to Rawls' premises, the constructive kind would generally be rational and the destructive kind would generally be irrational.

Competence

Baron believes the competence motive to be completely rational because the development of personal abilities serves the social order and permits the individual feelings of self-esteem. This conclusion seems to be too general and—if Rawls' theory is its basis—not convincing. First, it is necessary to ask about the type and content of the abilities to be developed. A bank robber or a car thief may be very competent in his area, but his abilities do not contribute to social order and, thus, are not rational according to Rawls. Secondly, the development of even positive abilities is not rational under every condition, at least if we follow Rawls' theory.

Let us assume that an unemployed young adult has no chance of getting a job for the next several years as a result of a poor economic situation, even if he has good abilities. Baron would nonetheless encourage that person to develop his competence, and I would do the same. Nevertheless, can this advice be derived from Rawls' theory? According to the theory, a plan is rational to the extent that it fits into a just social order. Under the condition just mentioned, however, further development of this person's abilities not only might seem to him to be a useless pursuit, but it would indeed no longer contribute to the social order and, thus, would no longer be rational according to Rawls. Incidentally, I do not think that striving for competence should be less important for older people, as Baron seems to think. Given the increasingly rapid changes in our technical and social environment, educational concepts of "lifelong learning" are becoming increasingly important.

Using a general theory of rational life plans within a general theory of justice is seductive, because it promises to give a general answer to the question of which dimensions of achievement motivation are rational and which are not. As I tried to show, however, it is entirely possible to arrive at different conclusions about the rationality of these motives using Rawls' theory and some of Baron's assumptions. This disparity does not mean that Baron's conclusions have been drawn in an illogical way. It means only that the basis he has chosen—the theory of Rawls—does not unequivocally imply what Baron derived from it. Thus, it means that the motives Baron claims to be rational are not really derived from that basis. This result agrees with Blankertz (1972), who says it is impossible to derive educational goals (and appropriate teaching methods) from superordinate norms of human life. He calls such attempts "normative didactics" and criticizes them as being ahistorical and as oversimplifying the complexity and changeability of objective conditions. These apparently flawless deductions are only illusions. Superordinate norms do not contain everything that is drawn from them didactically. Rawls' theory also contains general superordinate norms of human association. To that extent, Baron's attempt to deduce educational goals from it also falls under the category of "normative didactic." I think his concrete suggestions on that question cannot be seen as a final answer.

Nevertheless, Baron's contribution is very important and useful in several ways. He encourages systematic thinking about a very complex problem that has prompted educators and politicians into vehement discussions. He clearly shows that research on achievement motivation has often distinguished inadequately among the individual dimensions of this motive and also that simple, monolithic encouragement of achievement motivation is not acceptable from an educational standpoint. Even if one can come, to some degree, to conclusions other than Baron's, his contribution shows how discussion in this area can be carried out in a rational way, its structure becoming more transparent, and therefore more accessible to criticism.

HOW CAN WE ACHIEVE MORE RATIONALITY?

Baron is only incidentally concerned with the obstacles we must overcome when we try to achieve greater rationality. On one hand, this lack of attention is quite legitimate, because he is primarily interested in what educational objectives we should pursue. The problem of how to realize these goals and what difficulties must be overcome is, therefore, at a different level of analysis. On the other hand, however, the question of realizability seems to be a central point in evaluating the rationality of these goals: It is irrational to set something as a goal if it is recognized as impossible. An achievable goal can be rational or irrational; a goal that is unachievable from the beginning is always irrational. Without reference to concrete empirical conditions under which specific goals are to be achieved it is, in the final analysis, not possible to determine their rationality.

How can we achieve greater rationality through education? Baron suggests, in several places, the necessity of motivating individuals to reflect on their personal motives. Although reflection is certainly important, I do not think it is the complete solution. We must also attend to the nature of intervening obstacles and we must ask whether a purely cognitive procedure is generally sufficient to overcome them.

For example, why should an individual solve fewer crossword puzzles just because his activity is not rational from a societal standpoint? If we include in the rationality calculation the results of self-evaluation as consequences of action (Heckhausen, 1980; Kelley & Michela, 1980), then the individual's behavior may indeed be rational. As long as a person who is oriented to avoid failure sees no way to experience success other than by doing crossword puzzles, because other "more serious" tasks are at present too "dangerous" for his or her self-esteem, solving crossword puzzles is certainly rational in terms of stabilizing self-esteem. It is not enough to show an individual that a certain educational goal is desirable because it is rational in a social sense. If the individual is to achieve this goal, it must become his or her own goal—that is, the individual must be convinced of its rationality. In trying to convince someone of the rationality of a certain goal, one must also consider the possibility of emotional resistances to that change. Emotions are not only the consequence of cognitions; cognitive processes can also be influenced by emotions (G. H. Bower, 1981; Obuchowski, 1982; Zajonc, 1980). We must also expect "perceptual defense": Sometimes people do not see things because they "do not want to see them" (cf. Eagle, 1983). For example, a person could see the argument that solving crossword puzzles is not socially useful, and is thus irrational, as an indirect threat to his or her self-esteem and thus become defensive. More generally: If our nature coincided with the ideal "rational person," there would be no irrationality. In reality, however, we find irrational behavior, and irrationality is, of course, due to certain causes. I do not think that these causes are to be found solely in the cognitive area or are solely the consequence of deficits in the amount of thinking. If we want to achieve more rationality by means of education, we must also take into account the nature of these causes in order to overcome the corresponding obstacles. I am sure Baron would agree with this comment.

ARE NORMATIVE THEORIES APPROPRIATE FOR DERIVING EDUCATIONAL OBJECTIVES?

As stated previously, rationality never exists per se, but only with regard to specific goals. Baron uses Rawls' theory of justice and of rational life plans as a basis for determining the rationality of educational objectives. An objective is rational to the extent that it fits into a rational life plan, and a rational life plan is one free of contradiction and one that fits into (or contributes to) a just social order. Thus, the highest goal or basic value is contribution to a just social order—a sense of justice as defined by Rawls.

Let us assume for a moment that a satisfactory derivation were really possible: Is Rawls' theory an appropriate basis for the derivation of educational objectives? Let us have a closer look at this theory: Rawls' theory is an alternative to utilitarian ethics. It is in the tradition of natural law. It belongs to a branch of legal and political philosophy that would like to develop an ethical position to be able to evaluate the state, law, and politics. It is in contrast to so-called legal positivism, which rejects such criticism. Using decision-making and game theory, Rawls presents a reformulation of such classic contract theories as Hobbes', Locke's, Rousseau's, and Kant's. Through the use of the fiction of a condition of original equality, in the sense of an information deficit ("veil of ignorance"), individual and public interest coincide. It is thus possible to derive principles of justice from individual interests assuming a free and conscious choice using decision-making and game theory criteria. For Kant, the social contract was not an empirical reality but rather a normative idea of practical reason that is not derived from empirical knowledge of the nature of humans. Rawls' model is also an abstract normative model into whose make-up concrete historical conditions do not enter (cf., Fisk, 1975), and that, as a result, conceives of "justice" as a timeless state.

On one hand, such a general theory is seductive, because it promises to yield a general answer once and for all to the question of what is just. One could accept this idea of justice as a kind of standard that perhaps cannot be fully realized, but that nevertheless serves as a guide, an ideal against which social reality is evaluated. On the other hand, however, there is a danger with such an ahistorical theory, that it settles nothing at all for the following reasons: People at different historical times have had different ideas of justice, different conceptions of what is just and what is unjust. Thus, due to the continuous development of social life, the very concept of justice changes in the long run. Whatever one means specifically by this concept, in order to achieve more justice in a society at any time in history, it is necessary to enlist the support of other people who share the same idea of justice. A theory of justice that is not accepted and supported by a relevant number of people remains ineffective in reality and, thus, is of no help in achieving more justice.

For example, the Rawlsian difference principle (in which societal institutions should maximize the opportunities of the most disadvantaged groups) is unrealistic to the extent that people are not obliged to work for its realization. The difference principle may represent an appropriate choice in the original fictitious situation; it is, however, in reality not acceptable to certain groups once the "veil of ignorance" is lifted (R. Miller, 1974). Historically, representatives of privileged groups have often been unreceptive to arguments that contradicted their interests. The aristocracy, for example, did not dismantle feudal repression on their own, and the capitalists of the Grand Bourgeoisie swore that a reduction in the work day from 16 to 10 or 12 hours was not possible. It is also questionable whether improvement in the position of the most disadvantaged groups in a society is possible solely through appeal to some universal sense of justice. An ahistorical normative model that evaluates the real process of historical development from outside and does not attend to changes in concrete social circumstances and the possibilities resulting from them is unable to take account of the specific ideas people have on justice within that society. Thus, it risks being ineffectual, being a utopian picture that is mounted from the outside and independent of real social development (cf. Dahrendorf, 1967).

A goal that is not immediately accessible is, of course, not irrational for that reason. It would be irrational, however, to pursue a goal that is not even accessible approximately, because one invests energy in an effort that does not lead to success. This relationship does not imply that every ahistorical normative model claims goals that are inaccessible and that they are therefore irrational; it is quite possible that independent of the normative model, real development goes toward this goal. In principle, however, there is this inherent risk with ahistorical theories. Thus, it seems to be doubtful whether Rawls' theory of justice and the theory of rational life plans derived from it are really an appropriate basis for the determination of educational goals.

An alternative to an ahistorical theory of justice would be a theory that acknowledges that people in different epochs had, and will have, different ideas of justice. It could be, for example, a functionalistic theory of justice, which regards these ideas as ideal "concentrates" of requirements that result from humans' living together within the specific social order. In this sense, justice is equivalent to the implicit regulative system that attempts to satisfy the needs of a maximum number of members in the society under their specific historical circumstances (science, techniques, etc.) and is, therefore, accepted by the majority of people within that society. The state's laws may deviate from this implicit regulative system and are then called "unjust" (e.g., many laws during the Nazi epoch in Germany). This theory, which is at first step a descriptive one, becomes prescriptive (i.e., normative) if one decides to act according to this implicit regulative system. Of course, as a prescriptive theory, it also involves certain presuppositions: If one accepts this idea of justice, one implicitly adopts the aim of providing for a smooth coordination of human's activities with the fewest possible disturbances for the sake of satisfying their needs as the highest goal.

If one adopts this position, is it still possible to criticize the practices of a culture? Can one criticize these practices if one rejects taking a position that is outside and independent of the real historical process? I think one can: One can ask which implicit regulative system is most appropriate for fulfilling the needs of coordination that result from humans' living together under their specific historical social circumstances. One can ask what the real needs of development are, what possibilities there are for regulating and influencing the system, and accordingly determine which principles of regulation should be chosen (i.e., what should be seen as just). The difference between this kind of theory and an ahistorical theory of justice is that the concrete society and circumstances of living in it are not left out, and that the criticism of certain practices in it is not derived externally but internally. Reference to concrete social reality cannot be lost. On one hand, one runs a specific risk here—namely of restricting oneself to just those things that are allegedly doable; this restriction implies the danger of being too cautious in estimating what is doable and what is not. On the other hand, however, the chances of really achieving concrete effects seem to be greater because of their stronger ties to reality.

According to this theory, there is no final answer to the question of what the concept of justice means in detail. As long as the circumstances in which a society lives are changing, what is just and what is unjust must be determined again and again. Accordingly, there is no general answer to the question of which goals and values we should encourage by education. This question must also be regularly reanswered with reference to specific social circumstances.

The ongoing dispute between ahistorical theories and historical–relativistic theories of justice, which flourishes in the area of practical philosophy, cannot be resolved in favor of either side within a brief article or discussion. Both theories have their pros and cons. Neither is able to manage its domain without making certain decisions or without presuppositions, which can be questioned again. Baron has asked important questions and made interesting suggestions. His contribution provides the possibility of making the power and the limitations of a rational analysis and derivation of educational objectives more transparent and of formulating the problems within this domain more clearly than has been done so far. We should pursue these questions on the basis Baron provides.

ACKNOWLEDGMENT

Translated by M. Feeley and the editors.

IV POSTSCRIPT

Epilogue

Walter Volpert
Technical University of Berlin

LOOKING THROUGH FACETS TO A WHOLE

Writing an epilogue to this book is no easy task for me. I know only part of the context in which it is written, and my endeavor—a unified theory of action—is too big not to be embarrassed by the fact that almost every author understands a different thing by action and has a different theoretical framework that he may or may not call "action theory."

To recover from this embarrassment, I hypothesize a common reference point of the chapters, which is the Miller, Galanter, and Pribram book *Plans and the Structure of Behavior* (1960), or, at least, some of the central issues of this book. "It is so reasonable," the authors claim, "to insert between the stimulus and the response a little wisdom" [p. 2]. Obviously, modern psychology has dealt a great deal with this "little wisdom." Miller et al. themselves replaced it quickly with the model of a heuristically programmed digital computer, and since then a machine universe has been created consisting of processors and storages, production systems and data bases, programs and networks. Among this Star Wars world some synthetic monsters called "motives" and "emotions" are mingling.

But this whole universe resides in the head. Only some small offshoots descend from a motor processor to something like a limb, a hand, or a finger ready to push a button. It is hard to see what the complicated network is good for, because the system does not act. So—to recite the famous quotation—the rat goes on being "buried in thought," and the "theoretical gap between cognition and action," which Miller et al. (1960) wanted to bridge [p. 9] is not yet bridged; nor are the three gaps the editors of this book frighten us with in the introduction.

The contributions of this book are blueprints, materials, or even suspension bridges to span these gaps. This is what they have in common, and they show a lot of ingenuity and theoretical and empirical work. The chapters are facets, each of them bringing light to a special fragment of the theme. It cannot be my task to put them together, to reconstitute an undivided whole, or to show that this undivided whole is embodied in each facet. It makes more sense to draw some conclusions by pointing to some general lines of, or needs for, development. This is what I try to do.

SYSTEM MODELS AND PROCESS MODELS

A concept often noted in this volume is that of hierarchical structure. Sometimes (e.g., by Broadbent), it is counterpointed by a concept of heterarchy. To deal with this problem, it seems necessary to me to differentiate between *system* models and *process* models. System models assume an organization or an organism that can be divided by analysis into different levels. The units of each level are depicted as enduring structural elements, for instance functional or neurobehavioral units. Conceptualizations like Gallistel's (1980a) or Turvey's (1977) are of this sort. Process models, in contrast, describe the internal logic of an ongoing process. Their units are such transient ''entities'' as planned actions or executed operations. When those actions or operations appear in different processes, they are new units each time, even if they are identical in content and shape. The model of hierarchical-sequential organization of action that is a basis of the deliberations of Hacker and of Semmer and Frese in this volume, and that I tried to describe briefly elsewhere (Volpert, 1982), is a process model in this sense.

The concept of *heterarchy* has a different meaning in the two models. Dealing with a system model, Turvey (1977) assumes different levels or domains of action, but stresses the autonomy of lower-level functional units. Gallistel (1980b, p. 327 ff.) speaks in a similar sense of ''labile hierarchies'' and of the possibility that lower units ''override'' descending commands; the heterarchical elements are here, so to speak, bottom-up. In process models they are top-down. In German action theory some authors accentuate ''multiple actions'' (*Mehrfachhandlungen*), by which different purposes are pursued by the same or parallel actions (Kaminski, 1982), and quick changes in action chains that are due to changing or even oscillating high-level goals (von Cranach & Kalbermatten, 1982a; Dörner, 1984).

I think these are two perspectives on the same matter: In complex organisms and organizations, a multilevel structure exists in which each unit on each level has its own specific and relative autonomy, and the relations between the system and its environment are maintained and developed by cooperation and (sometimes) rivalry between these units (a view that also weakens the distinction between system and environment). This is a well-known model in systems theory, and it reminds us of concepts such as ultrastability (Ashby, 1960) or multistability (Klaus, 1966). Such a model seems to me to be also the general framework of the Turvey group, where the "hierarchically organized heterarchies" have an intermediate—but prominent—place in the order of structures (cf. Turvey, Shaw, & Mace, 1978).

To widen the perspective, it seems to me that the same model appears in modern evolution theories. To build stratified order in which cyclic units of different levels have relative autonomy is, if one follows Jantsch (1980), a central line in evolution and a basic principle of self-organization. Such structures originate when formerly independent organisms amalgamate in a symbiosis or when systems differentiate functional units. Koestler (1969) calls those units in a stratified order "holons;" he believes them to be a synthesis between atomistic and holistic views. It seems fascinating to me that Capra (1982), as a physicist, claims that the universe is such a stratified evolving system. Bohm (1980), another physicist, contrasts the "undivided wholeness in flowing movement" [p. 11] as "implicate order" with our "manifest world" [p. 185] as "explicate order," and then transforms this bilevel model into a multilevel model by introducing "different degrees of implication" [p. 153].

Bohm's concept seems to be an instance of new holistic views that emerge in different sciences. According to Bohm, we mistake the abstraction of the explicate order for reality by elementaristic and mechanistic approaches that assume that the whole is built up by elements that exist separately and independently but are externally related by laws of interaction. This approach is, according to Bohm, valid only in limited cases, the construction of machines being one of them. The preferred view is to "begin with the undivided wholeness of the universe." This "undivided whole" or "holomovement" (as Bohm (1980) calls it, stressing its process character) must be the starting point of analysis: "What is primary, independently existent, and universal has to be expressed in terms of the implicate order" [p. 185]. Its laws are partially recognizable (e.g., in relativity and quantum theory). They "are assumed to be such that from them may be abstracted relatively autonomous sub-totalities of movement" [p. 178] as explicate order. But, to repeat, the main point is to conceive objects as parts of a whole determined by the whole, not as elements whose existence and interaction constitute the whole.

This is not the place, and I am not the person, to discuss whether Bohm's conclusions about modern physics are correct and compelling. It should be noted, however, that such antielementaristic and antimechanistic positions have a mystical appearance only to those who view the world in a Cartesian–Newtonian way. This new holism is just another way to generate scientific conceptions and models—appropriate conceptions and models for modern physics and biology, as some scientists assert.

I hesitate to return to psychology with its rich tradition of holistic views, most pointedly of Gestalt psychology, though I am not able to unfold this tradition here (cf. Metzger, 1968). At least we can learn from this point: that we need neither a system model nor a process model but a model of system-in-process and of system-in-environment. This is exactly the promise of a theory of action.

SCHEMATA—THE INVARIANTS WITH LIMITED VARIABILITY

Does this system have knowledge about its environment and about efficient actions for fulfilling its needs, a knowledge that is persistent but can still be modified and augmented by experience? Cognitive psychologists usually assume a system of internal representations, something like warehouse storage or a giant propositional network. So the human, if not the rat, may have reason to be left buried in thought, traveling in a marvellous internal world and dealing similarly to the cognitivists with the infiniteness of the representational network. In contrast, ecological psychologists like J. J. Gibson (1979) claim that the real world in which we live is this real world that we perceive, a world in which we have bodily experiences and in which we have commerce with subjects and objects— a world that a computer cannot have as it has no body, no situation relative to its experience, and no needs; it cannot, therefore, act in a changing context (cf. Dreyfus, 1979). According to Gibson, perception is direct in this sense, and the invariant features that are transported over time and space are the invariants of external objects and processes. But, as Neisser (1976) stresses, this view leaves unresolved the question of how the subject has consistent but modifiable knowledge of the external objects and ways of dealing with them. Here Pribram's (1977) holographic memory model suggests one concept of perception as both direct and constructional: Neural networks build up a complex wave-like pattern that is tuned to invariants of the environment, echoing and preserving them over time. Coincidence of sensory input and stored pattern leads to an image that is both located in the external world, reflecting an environmental invariance, and constructed by the subject to reflect his or her knowledge and experience.

Regarding what we should call those invariants, I agree with Neisser's proposal in this volume to keep the name *schema* until a better one is found. Since Bartlett (1932) and Piaget (e.g., 1963), *schema* has had two implications: first, an invariant element—a structure maintained over time, but in some sense abstract and stuffless (and thus amodal). Secondly, it has enough variability to define a range of experiences with a prototype in the mean place and some vague or probabilistic definition of boarders; it also has enough variability to be modified by the experiences of the perceiving and acting subject.

It is just this duality of constancy and variability that allows experience to be gained and transported over time, giving Neisser's (1976) perceptual cycle the stable flexibility he emphasizes. This duality holds also for action schemata. It is interesting that most memory and perception psychologists, when introducing the concept of an invariant or of a schema, follow Bartlett (1932) by referring first to the stable basis of action and then generalizing the point.

This gives me the opportunity to recall a research field that is mentioned in this volume by Neisser and by Hacker, but, it seems to me, is a little under-weighted altogether. I mean the work on sensorimotor learning or, as some call it nowadays, *motor control* (cf. Stelmach, 1978; Stelmach & Requin, 1980). I think those approaches are relevant to a theory of action as they try to bridge the gap, or the gaps, between cognition and action—though perhaps from the other bank, so to speak: the analysis of movements and perceptual-motor skills. There the controversy between *open-loop* and *closed-loop* theories is mediated, if not reconciled, by motor schemata concepts, developed especially by Schmidt (1975). We find again the topics of (relative) constancy and (limited) variability (although Schmidt sometimes seems to separate the constant aspect as a "gener-alized motor program"). Here we also have striking examples of the generality and amodality of motor schemata, together with a good deal of interesting experimental work relevant to any action theory.

One of these examples is research on mental practice (mental training). It is very interesting for me to read Neisser's and Klinger's contributions to this volume as this topic of mental practice was one of the springs of German action theory in the 1960s (cf. Ulich, 1967; Volpert, 1969). The use and limits of the effectiveness of such covert rehearsal of actions shed light on the characteristics of a schema as well as on the coherence of perception, imagery, and action.

This leads me back to the close connection between object schema and action schema. This connection seems to me even deeper than Neisser assumes it to be in this volume. It is not only that perception is embedded in the activity of the subject and is itself an active process (Neisser, 1967, 1976), and that action is the criterion for the veridicality of perception (cf. Stadler, Seeger, & Raeithel, 1975) and, ontogenetically, the starting point for perceiving stable things (as Piaget and others showed). But I also think object and action schema are two sides of the same coin: the things in our life space are the bases for our object schemata as well as objectifications (or external stores) of our action schemata. This duality seems to me the main point that J. J. Gibson (1979) makes about *affordances*. German action theory accentuates the relation between action demands and a societal–historical context. This relation traces back to the assertion of Soviet psychologists (especially Leontiev, 1972, and Vygotski, 1978) that human-made things in our world, mainly tools, are materialized action experiences, gener-alized and objectivated goal–means relationships to be transported over genera-tions. (This assertion is expanded to language, a topic not discussed here.) A hammer or a spoon is, to recall Leontiev's examples, a coagulated and externally stored action schema, affording and demanding hammering or spooning. When the individual learns to perform according to these demands and affordances, he or she *appropriates* the action schemata, makes them his or her own. This evolution brings action schema and objects schema into a closer and more cyclic relationship, as Neisser assumes when he speaks of the "alignment" of the two. Within a higher-level action unit, the perception of a demanding and affording object may coincide with the formation of a subgoal and a related lower-level action unit (cf. Volpert, 1982). Within the higher action unit the person may *discover* the object in the environmental context, make it *relevant* (recalling the original sense of the Latin word *relevare: to bring into prominence*), and—to close the cycle—*enact* it, which means to act with it in a way appropriate to the affordance of the objects and the intentions of the subject.

Also relevant to this topic is that the perspective may be broadened by looking to process models of modern evolution theory with similar or identical structure. The concept of *autopoiesis* developed by Maturana and Varela (cf. 1980) and explicated by Jantsch (1980) emphasizes the ability of living systems to build stable internal and external relationships according to their own goals, but in coevolution with their ecological environments. This ability suggests that perception is both direct (an expression of the system–environment relations) and constructional (an expression of the internal coherence of the system) and thus is also deeply embedded in the whole activity of the self-organizing system. To go further, Pribram (1977) points to the structural similarity of his holographic memory model to Bohm's (1980) earlier distinction of implicate and explicate order (mentioned earlier). Indeed, the *abstraction* of isolable objects sounds at least very similar in both frameworks, and this also concerns the action-embeddedness of the procedure: It seems to be one of the most striking results of modern physics that one cannot adequately describe properties of an object of research without referring to the activity and methods (action paths) of the researcher.

SEQUENTIALITY IN PROCESS MODELS: NO ALGORITHM, BUT INTERNAL LOGIC

The third point I want to mention is the problem of how sequences are conceptualized in process models. Obviously, each model of this sort must say something about the temporal order in which things are happening. This sequential order can be conceived, in principle, either as the unfolding of the internal logic of the process, thus being flexible and modifiable, or as a fixed algorithm strongly determining what element must come now and next (though perhaps with a complex, ramifying structure). The algorithm assumption derives from a strongly mechanistic viewpoint, but has the advantage that it can be reproduced by some digital computer software. The former model—of an internal and flexible logic of the process—is in some sense weaker, in that it is not immediately testable by a machine, but it seems to me preferable and empirically more valid from an organismic and evolutionary perspective.

Sequential orders in action theory—like the model of hierarchical-sequential organization or the phase model that Schönpflug presents in this volume—should, in my opinion, be seen as descriptions of internal logic and not as algorithms. I grant that there is some reason for misunderstanding, and I doubt that the approach of Miller, Galanter, and Pribram can be interpreted as a description of internal logic. On the other hand, I think it is possible to conceive of sequential models in action theory in a nonmechanistic way (cf. Volpert, 1984). The top-down unfolding and explication of goals and subgoals and the path from goal setting through strategy finding to execution is then more similar to Gestalt formation (in the framework of Gestalt psychology) or figural synthesis (in the sense of Neisser, 1967). This again points to the close connection between perception and action and to Bohm's concept of building up an explicate order of objects that we can handle.

Perhaps this gives us a chance to insert between the situation and the action a little emotion—one thing some commentators missed so deeply in action theory. When reading about emotions, I find them to be described as global, holistic, and activating evaluations of situations and actions. As Zajonc (1980) points out, there is a duality of *pre-* and *postcognitive* views of emotions. The latter approach asserts that emotions are the results of cognitive analysis. The precognitive view emphasizes emotions as processes of activation and evaluation that precede cognitive analysis—an assumption quite similar to that of Neisser's *preattentive phase* in perception. Zajonc favors this precognitive view, supporting it by significant experimental results. But emotions do not vanish when cognitive analysis starts: It is not a matter of algorithm, but of internal logic. Zajonc speaks of the cooperation of two different evaluation systems with different but complementary qualities.

To continue, one could replace the two linear models of the pre- and postcognitive view with a cyclic or, better, spiral evolutionary model. Emotions are precognitive in the pursuit of action, just as Zajonc puts it. They are quick and global appraisals of action possibilities, of chances and dangers in a given situation (see also Österreich, 1981); but they can be modified by a learning process that involves cognitive analysis (and in this limited sense they are postcognitive). If the same or a similar situation recurs, the appraisals may be more realistic, being just as quick and global as before. A development has taken place not by loosing one's emotions but by making them more profound.

In another text I tried to elaborate this point (Volpert, 1983), showing also that this view has some overlap with models of skill acquisition. What I want to emphasize here is where action theory should be heading. What is needed is not only a model of system-in-environment and system-in-process, but of system-in-evolution: a model that shows how an organism or individual builds up in self-organization (or *autopoiesis*) complex interactions with his environment in which both individual and environment are part of a coevolution process in a larger perspective. Such models are the domain of the new evolution theories (cf.

Bateson, 1979; Jantsch, 1980; von Weizsäcker, 1974). The model must neither give the individual the status of a marionette drawn by external strings, nor leave the individual—perhaps having started with some sensorimotor activities—buried in thought. This, again, is the promise of an action theory—soon to come, I hope.

CONCLUDING COMMENTS

I conclude with three brief comments that may show specific European biases. First, I am astonished that in psychology mechanistic and elementaristic computer- or information-processing models still prevail. More than 20 years ago, Neisser (1963) wrote a small text on this topic, which seems to me still important. Neisser, Turvey, Pribram, and others have offered psychological models beyond an information-processing approach (not completely abandoning it, but giving it its limited place). The research on *artificial intelligence* and *cognitive science* (what strange words!) has made some impressive progress in replacing some experts' knowledge with complex algorithms. But I hardly see progress in cognitive simulation, when it is used to illuminate the processes and structures of human thinking and their evolution. Here the courageous book of Dreyfus (1979) still holds its own. It is curious, though probably not accidental, that mechanistic and machine models hold out in psychology while biologists (some of whom I have cited) developed general system and evolution models much more appropriate for living organisms and while even modern physics has departed from elementaristic and mechanistic viewpoints (cf. Bohm, 1980; Capra, 1982). The prevailing preference for machine models seems to me deeply rooted in our cultural and secular value system, which also seems to have forced *Time* magazine to proclaim the computer *Man of the Year, 1982.*

To return to science, though, it seems striking to me how much models of modern physics, of biological and cultural evolution, and of the perceiving-acting human have in common: the wholeness as *point of departure,* the multi-level order of reality, the cyclic structure of the processing units, and the coincidence of acting subjects and separable objects. It can also be shown that these approaches have a common process model of the system-in-evolution (Volpert, in preparation). I take this to be a strong force to propel us to a unified theory of evolving organisms and subjects, even in a machine-prone world.

My second point is a plea for two forms of continental psychology that seem to me underestimated within and outside action-theoretical framework: Gestalt psychology and the Soviet *psychology of activity.* Even with the problem of different languages (which is sometimes aggravated by translations), those two approaches have the power to offer solutions to real problems of psychology. Gestalt psychology is a synonym for a nonmechanistic view of psychological topics. I referred to some of its assertions in this chapter. Concerning the psychology of Rubinstein, Leontiev, and Vygotski, I mention Hacker's discussion in this volume and add one point: Lazarus is right, I think, when he misses elaborated assumptions within most action theories about emotions and motives and about social impact on individual action. But this, exceptionally, is a gap that can be bridged—especially taking into account the theories and results of Rubinstein, Leontiev, and Vygotski.

Finally, I want to emphasize that the only way to come to a better theory is to formulate this theory. I am very skeptical whether such a goal can be realized by some puzzling with experiments and deriving some faddish conceptualizations. To the contrary, the exertion in building up a coherent theory internally as well as with related sciences should be followed by some deliberate and parsimonious experimentation.

I am afraid that I am not in the mainstream of psychology with that point, but I find consolation in a sentence by Bertrand Russell (1927), which I quote at the end of a book that tried to bring English-speaking and German-speaking psychologists together. I confess to being ethnocentric enough to sympathize with the still-sitting animals:

> Animals studied by Americans rush about frantically, with an incredible display of hustle and pep, and at last achieve the desired result by chance. Animals observed by Germans sit still and think, and at last evolve the solution out of their inner consciousness [p. 33].

ACKNOWLEDGMENT

I thank the editors for helpful discussions and for translating my German English into American English.

References

Abelson, R. P. Script processing in attitude formation and decision making. In J. S. Carroll & J. W. Payne (Eds.), *Cognitive and social behavior.* Hillsdale, NJ: Lawrence Erlbaum Associates, 1976.

Abramson, L. Y., Seligman, M. E. P., & Teasdale, J. D. Learned helplessness in humans: Critique and reformulation. *Journal of Abnormal Psychology,* 1978, *87,* 49–74.

Ach, N. *Ueber den Willensakt und das Temperament: Eine experimentelle Untersuchung.* Leipzig: Quelle und Meyer, 1910.

Adams, J. A. Human tracking behavior. *Psychological Bulletin,* 1961, *58,* 55–79.

Adler, N. T. On the mechanisms of sexual behaviour and their evolutionary constraints. In J. B. Hutchinson (Ed.), *Biological determinants of sexual behaviour.* London: Wiley, 1978.

Ajzen, I., & Timko, C. *Attitudes, perceived control, and the prediction of health behavior.* Manuscript, University of Massachusetts at Amherst, 1983.

Alcock, J. The evolution of the use of tools by feeding animals. *Evolution,* 1972, *26,* 464–474.

Alderson, G. J. K., Sully, D. J., & Sully, H. G. An operational analysis of a one-handed catching task using high speed photography. *Journal of Motor Behavior,* 1974, *6,* 217–226.

Alegria, J., & Noirot, E. Neonate orientation behavior towards human voice. *International Journal of Behavioral Development,* 1978, *1,* 291–312.

Alloy, L. B., & Abramson, L. Y. Learned helplessness, depression, and the illusion of control. *Journal of Personality and Social Psychology,* 1982, *42,* 1114–1126.

Anderson, C. A. Imagination and expectation: The effect of imagining behavioral scripts on personal intentions. *Journal of Personality and Social Psychology,* 1983, *45,* 293–305.

Anderson, J. R. *Learning, memory, and thought.* Hillsdale, NJ: Lawrence Erlbaum Associates, 1976.

Anderson, M. P. Assessment of imaginal processes: Approaches and issues. In T. V. Merluzzi, C. R. Glass, & M. Genest (Eds.), *Cognitive assessment.* New York: Guilford, 1981.

Andrews, G. R., & Debus, R. L. Persistence and the causal perception of failure: Modifying cognitive attributes. *Journal of Educational Psychology,* 1978, *70,* 154–166.

Anokhin, P. K. *Das funktionelle System als Grundlage der physiologischen Architektur des Verhaltensaktes.* Jena: Fischer, 1967. (Original work published 1932)

Anokhin, P. K. Cybernetics and the integrative activity of the brain. In M. Cole & I. Maltzman (Eds.), *A handbook of contemporary Soviet psychology.* New York: Basic Books, 1969.

367

Anokhin, P. K. *Beitraege zur allgemeinen Theorie des funktionellen Systems.* Jena: VEB-Fischer, 1978.

Arbib, M. A. Perceptual structures and distributed motor control. In V. Brooks (Ed.), *Handbook of physiology* (Section 1: The nervous system; Vol. 2, Part 2, Motor Control). Bethesda, Md.: American Physiological Society, 1981.

Asch, S. *Social psychology.* Englewood Cliffs, NJ: Prentice-Hall, 1952.

Aschenbrenner, K. M., Jaus, D., & Villani, C. Hierarchical goal structuring and pupils' job choices: Testing a decision aid in the field. *Acta Psychologica,* 1980, *45,* 35–49.

Ashby, W. R. *Design for a brain.* London: Chapman & Hall, 1960.

Aslin, R. N. Development of binocular fixation in human infants. *Journal of Experimental Child Psychology,* 1977, *23,* 133–150.

Aslin, R. N. Development of smooth pursuit in human infants. In D. F. Fisher, R. A. Monty, & J. W. Senders (Eds.), *Eye movements: Cognition and visual perception.* Hillsdale, NJ: Lawrence Erlbaum Associates, 1981.

Aslin, R. N., & Jackson, R. W. Accommodative-convergence in young infants: Development of a synergistic sensory-motor system. *Canadian Journal of Psychology,* 1979, *33,* 222–231.

Athay, M., & Darley, J. M. Towards an interaction centered theory of personality. In N. Cantor & J. Kihlstrom (Eds.), *Personality, cognition, and social interaction.* Hillsdale, NJ: Lawrence Erlbaum Associates, 1981.

Athay, M., & Darley, J. M. Social roles as interaction competencies. In W. Ickes & E. S. Knowles (Eds.), *Personality roles and social behavior.* New York: Springer, 1982.

Atkinson, J. W. Motivational determinants of risk-taking behavior. *Psychological Review,* 1957, *64,* 359–372.

Atkinson, J. W. Motivation for achievement. In T. Blass (Ed.), *Personality variables in social behavior.* Hillsdale, NJ: Lawrence Erlbaum Associates, 1977.

Atkinson, J. W., & Birch, D. *The dynamics of action.* New York: Wiley, 1970.

Atkinson, J. W., & Birch, D. The dynamics of achievement-oriented activity. In J. W. Atkinson & J. O. Raynor (Eds.), *Motivation and achievement.* Washington, DC: V. H. Winston, 1974.

Atkinson, J. W., & Birch, D. *Introduction to motivation* (2nd ed.). New York: Van Nostrand, 1978.

Austin, J. L. *Philosophical papers.* Oxford: Oxford University Press, 1970.

Baarsma, E. A., & Collewijn, H. Vestibulo-ocular and optokinetic reactions to rotation and their interaction in the rabbit. *Journal of Physiology,* 1974, *238,* 603–625.

Baddeley, A. D., & Hitch, G. Working memory. In G. H. Bower (Ed.), *The psychology of learning and motivation* (Vol. 8). New York: Academic Press, 1974.

Bahrick, L. E. *Infants' perception of properties of objects as specified by amodal information in auditory-visual events.* Unpublished doctoral dissertation, Cornell University, 1980.

Bahrick, H. P., & Shelley, C. Time sharing as an index of automatisation. *Journal of Experimental Psychology,* 1958, *56,* 288–293.

Baltes, P. B., Reese, H. W., & Lipsitt, L. P. Life-span developmental psychology. *Annual Review of Psychology,* 1980, *31,* 65–110.

Baltes, P. B., & Schaie, K. W. On the plasticity of intelligence in adulthood and old age: Where Horn and Donaldson fail. *American Psychologist,* 1976, *31,* 720–725.

Bandura, A. Analysis of modeling processes. In A. Bandura (Ed.), *Psychological modeling: Conflicting theories.* Chicago: Aldine, 1971.

Bandura, A. Self-efficacy: Toward a unified theory of behavioral change. *Psychological Review,* 1977, *84,* 191–215.

Bandura, A. Self-efficacy mechanisms in human agency. *American Psychologist,* 1982, *37,* 122– 147.

Banks, M. S. The development of visual accommodation during early infancy. *Child Development,* 1980, *51,* 646–666.

Bärends, G. P. Fortpflanzungsverhalten und Orientierung der Grabwespe, *Ammophila campestris* Jur. *Zeitschrift fuer Entomologie,* 1941, *84,* 68–275.

Baron, J. Reflective thinking as a goal of education. *Intelligence*, 1981, *5*, 291–309.

Baron, J. Personality and intelligence. In R. J. Sternberg (Ed.), *Handbook of human intelligence*. New York: Cambridge University Press, 1982.

Baron, J. *Rationality and intelligence*. New York: Cambridge University Press, in press.

Baron, J., Badgio, P., & Gaskins, I. W. Cognitive style and its improvement: A normative approach. In R. J. Sternberg (Ed.), *Advances in the psychology of human intelligence* (Vol. 3). Hillsdale, NJ: Lawrence Erlbaum Associates, in press.

Bar-Tal, D., Ravis, A., & Leiser, T. The development of altruistic behavior: Empirical evidence. *Developmental Psychology*, 1984, *16*, 516–525.

Bartlett, F. C. *Remembering. A study in experimental and social psychology*. Cambridge, Eng.: Cambridge University Press, 1932.

Bates, E. *Language and context*. New York: Academic Press, 1976.

Bateson, G. *Mind and nature—A necessary unity*. New York: Bantam, 1979.

Battmann, W. Regulation und Fehlregulation im Verhalten. IX. Belastung und Entlastung durch Planung. *Psychologische Beitraege*, in press.

Baumgardt, C., Küting, H. J., & Silbereisen, R. K. *Social competence as an objective of road safety education in primary schools*. Paper presented at the International Conference on Road Safety, Cardiff, September 7–11, 1981.

Beach, B. H., & Beach, L. R. Expectancy-based decision schemes: Sidesteps toward applications. In N. Feather (Ed.), *Expectancy and actions: Expectancy-value models in psychology*. Hillsdale, NJ: Lawrence Erlbaum Associates, 1982.

Beach, L. R. Decision making: Diagnosis, action selection and implementation. In L. McAlister, *Choice models for buyer behavior*. Greenwich, CT: JAI Press, 1982.

Beach, L. R., & Mitchell, T. R. A contingency model for the selection of decision strategies. *Academy of Management Review*, 1978, *3*, 439–449.

Beatty, H. A note on the behavior of the chimpanzee. *Journal of Mammals*, 1951, *32*, 118.

Beck, A. T. *Cognitive therapy and the emotional disorders*. New York: International Universities Press, 1976.

Beck, A. T. Depression inventory. In A. T. Beck, A. J. Rush, B. F. Shaw, & G. Emery (Eds.), *Cognitive therapy of depression*. New York: Wiley, 1979.

Beckmann, J., & Irle, M. Cognitive dissonance and action control. In J. Kuhl & J. Beckmann (Eds.), *Action control: From cognition to behavior*. New York: Springer, in press.

Bem, D. J., & Allen, A. On predicting some of the people some of the time: The search for cross-situational consistencies in behavior. *Psychological Review*, 1974, *81*, 506–520.

Berger, P. L., & Luckmann, T. *The social construction of reality*. New York: Doubleday, 1966.

Bernstein, N. A. *The coordination and regulation of movement*. London: Pergamon, 1967.

Berry, D., & Broadbent, D. E. *On the relationship between task and performance and associated verbal knowledge*. In preparation.

van Beusekom, G. Some experiments on the optical orientation in *Philanthus triangulum* Fabr. *Behaviour*, 1948, *1*, 195–225.

Beyth-Marom, R., & Dekel, S. *Thinking under uncertainty: A textbook for junior high school students*. Jerusalem: Hebrew University, 1983.

Birch, D., Atkinson, J. W., & Bongort, K. Cognitive control of action. In B. Weiner (Ed.), *Cognitive views of human motivation*. New York: Academic Press, 1974.

Birchall, D., & Wild, R. Job characteristics and the attitudes of female manual workers. *Human Relations*, 1977, *30*, 335–342.

Blank, M. *Teaching learning in the preschool: A dialog approach*. Columbus, Ohio: Merrill, 1973.

Blankenship, V. The relationship between consummatory value of success and achievement-task difficulty. *Journal of Personality and Social Psychology*, 1982, *42*, 901–914.

Blankertz, J. *Theorien und Modelle der Didaktik*. Muenchen: Juventa, 1972.

Blau, P. M. *Exchange power in social life*. New York: Wiley, 1964.

Boesch, C. Nouvelles observations sur les schimpanzes de la forêt de Tai (Côte d'lvoire). *Terre Vie*, 1978, *32*, 195–201.

Boesch, E. The development of affective schemata. In J. Meacham (Chair), *Action theory, control and motivation: Developmental perspectives*. Symposium presented at the meeting of the International Society for the Study of Behavioral Development, Munich, August 1983.

Boesch, E. E. *Psychopathologie des Alltags*. Bern: Huber, 1976.

Boggiano, A. K., & Ruble, D. N. Competence and the overjustification effect: A developmental study. *Journal of Personality and Social Psychology*, 1979, *37*, 1462–1468.

Bohm, D. *Wholeness and the implicate order*. London: Routledge & Kegan Paul, 1980.

Bolles, R. C. On a clear day you can see behavior. *The Behavioral and Brain Sciences*, 1981, *4*, 619–620.

Borjesson, E., & von Hofsten, C. Spacial determinants of depth perception in two-dot motion patterns. *Perception and Psychophysics*, 1972, *11*, 263–268.

Borjesson, E., & von Hofsten, C. Visual perception of motion in depth: Applications of a vector model to three-dot motion patterns. *Perception and Psychophysics*, 1973, *13*, 169–179.

Botwinick, J., & Thompson, L. W. Premotor and motor components of reaction time. *Journal of Experimental Psychology*, 1966, *71*, 9–15.

Bourdieu, P. *Outline of a theory of practice*. Cambridge, Eng.: Cambridge University Press, 1977.

Bower, G. H. Mood and memory. *American Psychologist*, 1981, *36*, 129–148.

Bower, T. G. R. *Development in infancy*. San Francisco: W. H. Freeman, 1974.

Brainerd, C. J. Working memory and the developmental analysis of probability judgement. *Psychological Review*, 1981, *88*, 463–502.

Brandtstädter, J. Action development and development through action. *Human Development*, 1984, *27*, 115–118.

Brandstätter, H., Davis, J. H., & Stocker–Kreichgauer, G. (Eds.). *Group decision making*. London: Academic Press, 1982.

Breger, L., & McGough, J. L. A critique and reformulation of "learning theory" approaches to psychotherapy and neurosis. *Psychological Bulletin*, 1965, *63*, 335–358.

Brehm, J. W., & Cohen, A. R. *Explorations in cognitive disonance*. New York: Wiley, 1962.

Brehm, J. W., & Wicklund, R. A. Regret and dissonance reduction as a function of postdecision, salience of dissonant information. *Journal of Personality and Social Psychology*, 1970, *14*, 1–17.

Breznitz, S. (Ed.). *The denial of stress*. New York: International Universities Press, 1982.

Brichin, M. Goal information and feedback information in the unconscious control of human activity. In W. Hacker, W. Volpert, & M. von Cranach (Eds.), *Cognitive and motivational aspects of goal-directed actions*. Berlin: Deutscher Verlag der Wissenschaften; Amsterdam/New York: Elsevier North-Holland, 1982.

Brinkman, C., & Porter, R. Supplementary motor area in the monkey: Activity of neurons during performance of a learned motor test. *Journal of Neurophysiology*, 1979, *71*, 9–15.

Broadbent, D. E. *Perception and communication*. London: Pergamon, 1958.

Broadbent, D. E. *Decision and stress*. London: Academic Press, 1971. (a)

Broadbent, D. E. Relation between theory and application in psychology. Evening lecture, *Proceedings, XIX Congress of Psychology*, London, 1969, 27–36. London; 1971. (b)

Broadbent, D. E. Levels, hierarchies, and the locus of control. *Quarterly Journal of Experimental Psychology*, 1977, *29*, 181–201.

Broadbent, D. E. *Some relations between clinical and occupational psychology*. Lecture presented at the International Association of Applied Psychology: 20th International Congress, Edinburgh, 1982.

Broadbent, D. E., & Aston, B. Human control of a simulated economic system. *Ergonomics*, 1978, *21*, 1035–1043.

Broadbent, D. E., Cooper, P. F., FitzGerald, P., & Parkes, K. R. The Cognitive Failures Question-
naire (CFQ) and its correlates. *British Journal of Clinical Psychology*, 1982, *21*, 1–16.
Broadbent, D. E., FitzGerald, P., & Broadbent, M. H. P. Conscious and unconscious judgement in
the control of complex systems. Available in electronic form only in the *British Library R&DD
Experimental Electronic Journal "Computer Human Factors,"* Issue 2, 1983.
Broadbent, D. E., & Gath, D. Ill-health on the line: Sorting myth from fact. *Employment Gazett,*
1981, *89*(3). (a)
Broadbent, D. E., & Gath, D. Symptom levels in assembly line workers. In G. Salvendy & M. J.
Smith (Eds.), *Proceedings of International Conference on Machine Pacing and Occupational
Stress* (Purdue University, Indiana). London: Taylor & Francis, 1981. (b)
Brockner, J. Self-esteem, self-consciousness, and task performance: Replications, extensions and
possible explanations. *Journal of Personality and Social Psychology*, 1979, *37*, 447–461.
Bronfenbrenner, U. *The ecology of human development.* Cambridge, MA: Harvard University
Press, 1979.
Brown, T. G. Studies in the reflexes of the guinea pig: II. Scratching movements which occur during
ether anesthesia. *Quarterly Journal of Experimental Physiology*, 1910, *3*, 21–52.
Bruner, J. S., Goodnow, J. J., & Austin, G. A. *A study of thinking.* New York: Wiley, 1956.
Bullinger, A. Orientation de la tête du nouveau-né en présence d'un stimulus visuel. *L'année
Psychologique,* 1977, *2*, 357–364.
Burtis, P. J. Capacity increase and chunking in the development of short-term memory. *Journal of
Experimental Child Psychology*, 1982, *34*, 387–413.
Capra, F. *The turning point.* New York: Simon & Schuster, 1982.
Carver, C. S., Blaney, P. H., & Scheier, M. F. Focus of attention, chronic expectancy, and
responses to a feared stimulus. *Journal of Personality and Social Psychology*, 1979, *37*, 1189–
1195.
Carver, C. S., & Ganellen, R. J. Depression and components of self-punitiveness: High standards,
self-criticism, and overgeneralization. *Journal of Abnormal Psychology*, 1983, *92*, 330–337.
Carver, C. S., & Scheier, M. F. Control theory: A useful conceptual framework for personality-
social, clinical, and health psychology. *Psychological Bulletin*, 1982, *92*, 111–135.
Case, R. Intellectual development from birth to adulthood: A neo-Piagetian interpretation. In R. S.
Siegler (Ed.), *Children's thinking: What develops?* Hillsdale, NJ: Lawrence Erlbaum Associates,
1978.
Case, R., & Globerson, T. Field independence and mental capacity. *Child Development*, 1974, *45*,
772–778.
Cavallo, V. *Leistungs-und belastungsbestimmende Eigenschaften operativer Abbilder.* Mitteilungen
der Technische Universitaet, Dresden, 1978, 22–16–78.
Chapin, M., & Dyck, D. G. Persistence in children's reading behavior as a function of N length and
attribution retraining. *Journal of Abnormal Psychology*, 1976, *85*, 511–515.
Chapman, M. Isolating causal effects through experimental changes in parent–child interaction.
Journal of Abnormal Child Psychology, 1981, *9*, 321–327. (a)
Chapman, M. Pascual-Leone's theory of constructive operators: An introduction. *Human Develop-
ment,* 1981, *24*, 145–155. (b)
Chapman, M. Action and interaction: The study of social cognitive development in Germany and the
United States. *Human Development*, 1982, *25*, 295–302.
Cheng, K., & Gallistel, C. R. Testing the geometric power of an animal's spacial representation. In
H. Roiblat, H. Terrace, & T. Bever (Eds.), *Animal cognition.* Hillsdale, NJ: Lawrence Erlbaum
Associates, 1983.
Chevalier–Skolnikoff, S. A Piagetian model for describing and comparing socialization in monkey,
ape and human infants. In S. Chevalier–Skolnikoff, & F. Poirier (Eds.), *Primate biosocial
development.* New York: Garland Press, 1977.

Christiansen–Szalanski, J. J. J. Problem solving strategies: A selection mechanism, some implications and some data. *Organizational Behavior and Human Performance*, 1978, *22*, 307–323.

Claar, A., & Silbereisen, R. K. *Stimulation of social cognition in parent–child interaction: Do parents make use of appropriate interaction strategies?* Paper presented at the conference on "New Perspectives in the Experimental Study of the Social Development of Intelligence," Université de Genève, June 10–12, 1982.

Cohen, C. Goals and schemata in person perception: Making sense from the stream of behavior. In N. Cantor & J. Kihlstrom (Eds.), *Personality, cognition, and social interaction*. Hillsdale, NJ: Lawrence Erlbaum Associates, 1981.

Cohen, L. J. Can human irrationality be experimentally demonstrated? *The Behavioral and Brain Sciences*, 1981, *4*, 317–331.

Cohen, S. Cognitive processes as determinants of environmental stress. In I. G. Sarason & C. D. Spielberger (Eds.), *Stress and anxiety* (Vol. 7). Washington, D.C.: Hemisphere, 1980.

Collet, T. S., & Cartwright, B. A. Eidetic images in insects: Their role in navigation. *Trends in Neuroscience*, 1983, *6*, 101–105.

Collins, A. Processes in acquiring knowledge. In R. C. Anderson, R. J. Spiro, & W. E. Montague (Eds.), *Schooling and the acquisition of knowledge*. Hillsdale, NJ: Lawrence Erlbaum Associates, 1977.

Conrad, R. Letter sorting machines: Paced, "lagged," or unpaced. *Ergonomics*, 1960, *3*, 149–157.

Cook, T. D., & Campbell, D. T. The design and conduct of quasi-experiments and true experiments in field-settings. In M. D. Dunette (Ed.), *Handbook of industrial and organizational psychology*. Chicago: Rand McNally, 1976.

Corbin, C. B. Mental practice. In W. P. Morgan (Ed.), *Ergogenic aids and muscular performance*. New York: Academic Press, 1972.

Corlett, E. N., & Richardson, J. (Eds.). *Stress, work design, and productivity*. New York: Wiley, 1981.

Covington, M. V., & Omelich, C. L. As failures mount: Affective and cognitive consequences of ability demotion in the classroom. *Journal of Educational Psychology*, 1981, *73*, 796–808.

von Cranach, M. The psychological study of goal-directed action: Basic issues. In M. von Cranach & R. Harre (Eds.), *The analysis of action: Recent theoretical and empirical advances*. Cambridge, Eng.: Cambridge University Press, 1982.

von Cranach, M., & Kalbermatten, U. Ordinary goal-directed action in social interaction. In W. Hacker, W. Volpert, & M. von Cranach (Eds.), *Cognitive and motivational aspects of action*. Berlin: Deutscher Verlag der Wissenschaften; Amsterdam: North-Holland, 1982. (a)

von Cranach, M., & Kalbermatten, U. Ordinary interactive action: Theory, methods, and some empirical findings. In M. von Cranach & R. Harre (Eds.), *The analysis of action: Recent theoretical and empirical advances*. Cambridge, Eng.: Cambridge University Press, 1982. (b)

von Cranach, M., Kalbermatten, U., Indermühle, K., & Gugler, B. *Goal-directed action*. New York: Academic Press, 1982.

Cronbach, L. J. The two disciplines of scientific psychology. *American Psychologist*, 1957, *12*, 671–684.

Csikszentmihalyi, M. *Beyond boredom and anxiety*. San Francisco: Jossey-Bass, 1975.

Cunningham, C. C., & Miffler, P. J. Maturation, development, and mental handicap. In K. Connolly & H. F. R. Prechtl (Eds.), *Maturation and development: Biological and psychological perspectives*. Clinics in Developmental Medicine No. 77/78. London: W. Heinemann, 1981.

Dahrendorf, R. *Pfade aus Utopia*. Muenchen: Piper, 1967.

Darwin, C. *The expression of the emotions in man and animals*. London: Murray, 1872.

Davidson, D. *Essays on actions and events*. Oxford: Clarendon Press, 1980.

Dawkins, R. *The selfish gene*. New York: Oxford University Press, 1976.

de Charms, R. *Personal causation: The internal affective determinants of behavior*. New York: Academic Press, 1968.

Deci, E. L. *Intrinsic motivation.* New York: Plenum Press, 1975.

Deecke, L., & Kornhuber, H. H. An electrical sign of participation of the mesial "supplementary" motor cortex in the human voluntary finger movement. *Brain Research,* 1978, *157,* 473–476.

de Longis, A., Coyne, J. C., Folkman, S. L., & Lazarus, R. S. Relationship of daily hassles, uplifts, and major life events to health status. *Health Psychology,* 1982, *1,* 119–136.

Dembo, T. Untersuchungen zur Handlungs-und Affektpsychologie. X. Der Aerger als dynamisches Problem. *Psychologische Forschung,* 1931, *15,* 1–44.

Dempster, F. N. Memory span: Sources of individual and developmental differences. *Psychological Bulletin,* 1981, *89,* 63–100.

Dennett, D. C. *Brainstorms: Philosophical essays on mind and psychology.* Montgomery, Vt.: Bradford Books, 1978.

Dethier, V. *The hungry fly.* Cambridge, MA: Harvard University Press, 1976.

Dewey, J. The reflex arc concept in psychology. *Psychological Review,* 1896, *3,* 357–370. (Reprinted in W. Dennis [Ed.], *Readings in the history of psychology.* New York: Appleton-Century-Crofts, 1948.)

Diener, C. I., & Dweck, C. S. An analysis of learned helplessness: Continuous changes in performance, strategy, and achievement cognitions following failure. *Journal of Personality and Social Psychology,* 1978, *36,* 451–462.

Diener, C. I., & Dweck, C. S. An analysis of learned helplessness: II. The processing of success. *Journal of Personality and Social Psychology,* 1980, *5,* 940–952.

DiFranco, D., Muir, D. W., & Dodwell, P. C. Reaching in very young infants. *Perception,* 1978, *7,* 385–392.

Dixon, R. A., & Lerner, R. M. A history of systems in developmental psychology. In M. E. Lamb & M. H. Bornstein (Eds.), *Developmental psychology: An advanced textbook.* Hillsdale, NJ: Lawrence Erlbaum Associates, 1983.

Dollard, J., & Miller, N. *Personality and psychotherapy.* New York: McGraw-Hill, 1950.

Dörner, D. *Problemloesen als Informationsverarbeitung.* Stuttgart: Kohlhammer, 1976.

Dörner, D. Heuristic and cognition in complex systems. In R. Groner, M. Groner, & W. F. Bischof (Eds.), *Methods of Heuristics.* Hillsdale, NJ: Lawrence Erlbaum Associates, 1980. (a)

Dörner, D. On the difficulties people have in dealing with complexity. *Simulation and Games,* 1980, *11,* 87–106. (b)

Dörner, D. The ecological conditions of thinking. In D. R. Griffin (Ed.), *Animal Mind—Human Mind* (Dahlem Konferenzen), 1982. Berlin/New York: Springer, 1982.

Dörner, D. The organization of action in time. In E. Frehland (Ed.), *Synergetics: From microscopic to macroscopic order.* Berlin: Springer, 1984.

Dörner, D., Kreuzig, H. W., Reither, F., & Stäudel, T. (Eds.). *Lohhausen: Vom Umgang mit Unbe stimmtheit und Komplexitaet.* Bern: Huber, 1983.

Dörner, D., & Reither, F. Ueber das Problemloesen in sehr komplexen Realitaetsbereichen. *Zeitschrift fuer experimentelle und angewandte Psychologie,* 1978, *25,* 527–551.

Dörner, D., Reither, F., & Stäudel, T. Emotionen und problemloesendes Denken. In H. Mandl & G. L. Huber (Eds.), *Kognition und Emotion.* Muenchen: Urban & Schwarzenberg, 1983.

Dörner, D., & Stäudel, T. *Planning and decision making in very complex fields of reality.* Paper presented at the XXII International Congress of Psychology, Leipzig, 1980.

Dreyfus, H. L. *What computers can't do. The limits of artificial intelligence.* New York: Harper & Row, 1979.

Duncker, K. *Zur Psychologie des produktiven Denkens.* Berlin: Springer, 1935.

Dweck, C. S. The role of expectations and attributions in the alleviation of learned helplessness. *Journal of Personality and Social Psychology,* 1975, *31,* 674–685.

Dweck, C. S., & Elliott, E. S. Achievement motivation. In P. H. Mussen (Ed.), *Charmichael's manual of child psychology* (Vol. 2). New York: Wiley, 1983.

Dweck, C. S., & Repucci, N. D. Learned helplessness and reinforcement responsibility in children. *Journal of Personality and Social Psychology*, 1973, *25*, 109–116.

Eagle, M. N. Emotion und Gedaechtnis. In H. Mandl & G. L. Huber (Eds.), *Emotion und Kognition*. Muenchen: Urban & Schwarzenberg, 1983.

Easterbrook, J. A. The effect of emotion on cue utilization and the organization of behavior. *Psychological Review*, 1959, *6*, 183–201.

Eccles, J. C. The initiation of voluntary movements by the supplementary motor area. *Archives of Psychiatric Neurological Science*, 1982, *231*, 423–441.

Eckensberger, L. H., & Silbereisen, R. K. Handlungstheoretische Perspektiven fuer die Entwicklungspsychologie sozialer Kognitionen. In L. H. Eckensberger & R. K. Silbereisen (Eds.), *Entwicklung sozialer Kognitionen*. Stuttgart: Klett-Cotta. 1980.

Edelstein, W., & Keller, M. Perspektivitaet und Interpretation: Zur Entwicklung des sozialen Verstehens. In W. Edelstein & M. Keller (Eds.), *Perspektivitaet und Interpretation*. Frankfurt am Main: Suhrkamp, 1982.

Edwards, W., & Newman, J. R. *Multiattribute evaluation*. Beverly Hills: Sage Publications, 1982.

Eells, E. *Rational decision and causality*. Cambridge, Eng.: Cambridge University Press, 1982.

Egeland, B. Training impulsive children in the use of more efficient scanning strategies. *Child Development*, 1974, *45*, 165–171.

Eisenberg, N., & Silbereisen, R. K. The development of children's prosocial cognitions: Research, theory, and new perspectives. In H. E. Sypher & J. L. Applegate (Eds.), *Social cognition and communication*. Hillsdale, NJ: Lawrence Erlbaum Associates, in press.

Ellis, A. *Reasons and emotion in psychotherapy*. New York: Lyle Stuart, 1962.

Engels, F. The part played by labour in the transition from ape to man. In F. Engels, *Dialektics of nature* (D. Dutt, ed. and trans.). New York: International Publishers, 1940. (Originally published, 1876.)

Fagan, R. Modelling how and why play works. In J. Bruner, A. Jolly, & K. Sylva (Eds.), *Play: Its role in development and evolution*. New York: Basic Books, 1976.

Feather, N. T. (Ed.). *Expectations and actions: Expectancy-value models in psychology*. Hillsdale, NJ: Lawrence Erlbaum Associates, 1982.

Festinger, L. *Conflict, decision, and dissonance*. Stanford, Calif.: Stanford University Press, 1964.

Field, J., Muir, D., Pilon, R., Sinclair, M., & Dodwell, P. Infants orientation to lateral sounds from birth to three months. *Child Development*, 1980, *51*, 295–298.

Findley, M. J., & Cooper, H. M. Locus of control and academic achievement: A literature review. *Journal of Personality and Social Psychology*, 1983, *44*, 419–427.

Finke, R. A. Levels of equivalence in imagery and perception. *Psychological Review*, 1980, *87*, 113–132.

Fischhoff, B., Slovic, P., & Lichtenstein, S. Knowing with certainty: The appropriateness of extreme confidence. *Journal of Experimental Psychology: Human Perception and Performance*, 1977, *3*, 552–564.

Fishbein, M. Attitude and the prediction of behavior. In M. Fishbein (Ed.), *Readings in attitude theory and measurement*. New York: Wiley, 1967.

Fisk, M. History and reason in Rawls' moral theory. In N. Daniels (Ed.), *Reading Rawls. Critical studies on Rawls' "A theory of justice."* New York: Basic Books, 1975.

Fitch, H. L., Tuller, B., & Turvey, M. T. The Bernstein perspective: III. Tuning of coordinative structures with special reference to perception. In J. A. S. Kelso (Ed.), *Human motor behavior: An introduction*. Hillsdale, NJ: Lawrence Erlbaum Associates, 1982.

Flammer, A. *Toward a theory of asking questions*. Forschungsbericht 22, University of Fribourg, 1980.

Flavell, J. H. *The developmental psychology of Jean Piaget*. New York: Van Nostrand, 1963.

Flavell, J. H. *Cognitive development*. Englewood Cliffs, NJ: Prentice-Hall, 1977.

Folkman, S., & Lazarus, R. S. If it changes it must be a process: A study of emotion and coping during three stages of a college examination. *Journal of Personality and Social Psychology,* in press.

Folkman, S., Schaefer, C., & Lazarus, R. S. Cognitive processes as mediators of stress and coping. In V. Hamilton & D. M. Warburton (Eds.), *Human stress and cognition.* Chichester: Wiley, 1979.

Forssberg, H. S., Grillner, S., & Rossignol, S. Phase dependent reflex reversal during walking in chronic spinal cats. *Brain Research,* 1975, *85,* 103–107.

Forsstrom, A., & von Hofsten, C. Visually directed reaching of children with motor impairments. *Developmental Medicine and Child Neurology,* 1982, *24,* 653–661.

Fowler, J. W., & Peterson, P. L. Increasing reading persistence and altering attributional style of learned helpless children. *Journal of Educational Psychology,* 1981, *73,* 251–260.

Frankenhäuser, M., & Lundberg, U. The influence of cognitive set on performance and arousal under different noise loads. *Motivation and Emotion,* 1977, *1,* 139–149.

Frese, M. Der Einfluss der Arbeit auf die Persoenlichkeit: Zum Konzept des Handungsstils in der beruflichen Sozialisation. *Zeitschrift fuer Sozialisationforschung und Erziehungsoziologie,* 1983, *3,* 11–28.

Frese, M. *Do workers want control at work or don't they: Some results on denial and adjustment.* Institut fuer Human wissenschaft in Arbeit und Ausbildung Bericht 5. Berlin, 1984.

Frese, M., & Stewart, J. Skill learning as a concept in life-span developmental psychology: An action theoretic analysis. *Human Development,* 1984, *27,* 145–162.

Frese, M., & Stewart, J. *Action strategies and action styles.* In preparation.

Freud, S. *Civilization and its discontents* (J. Strachey, ed. and trans.). New York: Norton, 1961.

Fritsche, B., Hacker, W., Rötschke, S., & Wolff, S. *Psychologische Grundlagen der Gestaltung von Arbeitsauftraegen:* W" *:ungsweise von Anforderungsvielfalt und Freiheitsgraden.* Paper presented at 4th Dresdner Symposium zur Arbeitspsychologie, Technische Universitaet Dresden, September 1982.

Fuhrer, U. Defiziente und sub-optimale Strategien des Handelns im Umgang mit hoher Aktivitaetskomplexitet. *Psychologische Beitraege,* 1982, *24,* 583–600.

Gallistel, C. R. From muscles to motivation. *American Psychologist,* 1980, *68,* 398–409. (a)

Gallistel, C. R. *The organization of action: A new synthesis.* Hillsdale, NJ: Lawrence Erlbaum Associates, 1980. (b)

Gallistel, C. R. Precis of Gallistel's organization of action: A new synthesis. *Behavioral and Brain Sciences,* 1981, *4,* 609–619.

Gallup, C. C. Self-recognition in primates. A comparative approach to the bidirectional properties of consciousness. *American Psychologist,* 1977, *32,* 5.

Garber, J., & Hollon, S. D. Universal versus personal helplessness in depression: Belief in uncontrollability or incompetence? *Journal of Abnormal Psychology,* 1980, *89,* 56–66.

Gentile, A. Personal communication, 1981.

Getzels, J. W., & Csikszentmihalyi, M. From problem solving to problem finding. In I. A. Taylor & J. W. Getzels (Eds.), *Perspectives in creativity.* Chicago: Aldine, 1975.

Gibson, E. J. *Principles of perceptual learning and development.* New York: Appleton-Century-Crofts, 1969.

Gibson, E. J., & Rader, N. Attention: The perceiver as performer. In G. A. Hale & M. Lewis (Eds.), *Attention and cognitive development.* New York: Plenum Press, 1979.

Gibson, E. J., & Walker, A. S. Development of knowledge of visual-tactual affordances of substance. *Child Development,* in press.

Gibson, J. J. *The perception of the visual world.* Boston: Houghton Mifflin, 1950.

Gibson, J. J. *The senses considered as perceptual systems.* New York: Houghton Mifflin, 1966.

Gibson, J. J. *The ecological approach to visual perception.* Boston: Houghton Mifflin, 1979.

Glass, G. V., & Kliegl, R. M. An apology for research interpretation in the study of psychotherapy. *Journal of Consulting and Clinical Psychology,* 1983, *51,* 28–41.

Gleiss, I. Pathogene Anforderungsstrukturen der Arbeit-aus der Sicht des Taetigkeitsansatzes. In M. Frese, S. Greif, & N. Semmer (Eds.), *Industrielle Psychopathologie*. Bern: Huber, 1978.

Gleitman, H. Some trends in the study of cognition. In S. Koch & D. E. Leary (Eds.), *A century of psychology as science: Retrospections and assessments*. New York: McGraw–Hill, in press.

Goffman, E. *The presentation of self in everyday life*. New York: Doubleday, 1959.

Goffman, E. *Frame analysis*. New York: Harper & Row, 1974.

Goldfried, M. R., Decenteco, E. T., & Weinberg, L. Systematic rational restructuring as a self-control technique. *Behavior Therapy*, 1974, *5*, 247–254.

Goldman, A. I. *A theory of human action*. Princeton: Princeton University Press, 1970.

Goldthorpe, J. H., Lockwood, D., Beckhofer, F., & Platt, J. *The affluent worker in the class structure*. Cambridge, Eng.: Cambridge University Press, 1969.

Goodall, J. Tool-using and aimed throwing in a community of free-living chimpanzees. *Nature*, 1974, *201*, 1264–1266.

Graybiel, A., Jokl, E., & Trapp, C. Russian studies of vision in relation to physical activity and sports. *Research Quarterly*, 1955, *26*, 480–485.

Greene, D., & Lepper, M. R. (Eds.). *The hidden costs of rewards*. Hillsdale, NJ: Lawrence Erlbaum Associates, 1977.

Günther, R. *Untersuchungen aus drei Bereichen zur Urteilsbildung von Kindern und Erwachsenen*. Unpublished manuscript, Universitaet Tuebingen, 1981.

Gurfinkel, V. S., Kots, Y. M., Krinskiy, V. I., Palstev, Y. I., Feldman, A. G., Tsetlin, M. L., & Shik, M. L. Concerning tuning before movement. In I. M. Gelfand, V. S. Gurfinkel, S. V. Fomin, & M. L. Tsetlin (Eds.), *Models of the structural-functional organization of certain biological systems*. Cambridge, MA: MIT Press, 1971.

Gurin, P., & Brim, O. G., Jr. Change in self in adulthood: The example of sense of control. In P. B. Baltes & O. G. Brim, Jr. (Eds.), *Life span development and behavior* (Vol. 6). New York: Academic Press, 1984, 281–334.

Habermas, J. *Theorie des kommunikativen Handelns*. Frankfurt am Main: Suhrkamp, 1982.

Hacker, W. Anforderungsabhaengigkeit der Nutzung von hierarchischer Ordnung in Sequenzen. *Zeitschrift fuer Psychologie*, 1977, *185*, 1–33.

Hacker, W. *Allgemeine Arbeits-und Ingenieurpsychologie* (3rd ed.). Berlin: Deutscher Verlag der Wissenschaften, 1980; Bern: Huber, 1980.

Hacker, W. Action control: Task-dependent structure of action-controlling internal representations. In W. Hacker, W. Volpert, & M. von Cranach (Eds.), *Cognitive and motivational aspects of goal-directed actions*. Berlin: Deutscher Verlag der Wissenschaften; Amsterdam/New York: Elsevier North-Holland, 1982. (a)

Hacker, W. Beanspruchungskomponenten von geistigen Routinetaetigkeiten. *Zeitschrift fuer Psychologie*, 1982, *3*, 233–258. (b)

Hacker, W. *Verfahren zur objektiven Taetigkeitsanalyse* (tech. rep.). Technische Universitaet Dresden: Sektion Arbeitswissenschaften, 1983.

Hacker, W., & Matern, B. Beschaffenheit und Wirkungsweise mentaler Repraesentationen in der Taetigkeitsregulation. *Zeitschrift fuer Psychologie*, 1979, *187*(2), 141–156.

Hacker, W., & Richter, P. Psychische Fehlbeanspruchung. In *Spezielle Arbeits-und Ingenieurpsychologie: Psychische Fehlbeanspruchung: Psychische Ermuedung, Monotonie, Saettigung und Stress* (2nd ed.). Berlin: VEB Deutscher Verlag der Wissenschaften, 1983.

Hacker, W., Richter, P., & Ivanowa, A. *TBS-L: Taetigkeitsbewertungs-system*—Langform. Technische Universitaet Dresden, Sektion Arbeitswissenschaften; Forschungsbericht, 1983.

Hackman, J. R., & Oldham, G. R. Development of the job diagnostic survey. *Journal of Applied Psychology*, 1975, *60*, 159–170.

Haith, M. *Rules that babies look by*. Hillsdale, NJ: Lawrence Erlbaum Associates, 1980.

Haith, M. M. Visual cognition in early infancy. In R. Kearsley & I. Siegel (Eds.), *Infants at risk: Assessment of cognitive function*. Hillsdale, NJ: Lawrence Erlbaum Associates, 1978.

Hall, K. R. Tool-using performances in indications of behavioral adaptability. *Current Anthropology*, 1966, *7*, 215–216.

Halsey, M. N. (Ed.). *Accident prevention*. New York: McGraw-Hill, 1961.

Hamilton, E. W., & Abramson, L. Y. Cognitive patterns and major depressive disorder: A longitudinal study in a hospital setting. *Journal of Abnormal Psychology*, 1983, *92*, 173–184.

Hamilton, V., & Warburton, D. M. (Eds.). *Human stress and cognition: An information-processing approach*. London: Wiley, 1979.

Hare, R. M. *The language of morals*. London: Clarendon, 1952.

Harre, R., & Secord, P. *The explanation of social behavior*. Oxford: Basil Blackwell, 1972.

Harris, A. *Action theory, language, and the unconscious*. Paper presented at the biennial meeting of the International Society for the Study of Behavioral Development, Munich, 1983.

Harvey, N., & Greer, K. Actions: The mechanisms of motor control. In G. Claxton (Ed.), *Cognitive psychology: New directions*. London: Routledge & Kegan Paul, 1980.

Hasher, L., & Zacks, R. Automatic and effortful processes in memory. *Journal of Experimental Psychology: General*, 1979, *108*, 356–388.

Haugeland, J. The nature and plausibility of cognitivism. *The Behavioral and Brain Sciences*, 1978, *2*, 215–260.

Hay, D., & Oken, S. The psychological stresses of intensive care unit nursing. *Psychosomatic Medicine*, 1972, *34*, 109–118.

Hayes–Roth, B., & Hayes–Roth, F. A cognitive model for planning. *Cognitive Science*, 1979, *3*, 275–310.

Heath, A. *Rational choice and social exchange: A critique of exchange theory*. Cambridge, Eng.: Cambridge University Press, 1976.

Heckhausen, H. Fear of failure as a self-reinforcing motive system. In I. G. Sarason & C. D. Spielberger (Eds.), *Stress and anxiety* (Vol. 2). Washington, DC: Halsted–Wiley, 1975.

Heckhausen, H. Achievement motivation and its constructs: A cognitive model. *Motivation and Emotion*, 1977, *1*, 283–329.

Heckhausen, H. *Motivation und Handeln*. Berlin: Springer, 1980.

Heckhausen, H. Task-irrelevant cognitions during an exam. In H. W. Krohne & L. Laux (Eds.), *Achievement, stress, and anxiety*. Washington, DC: Hemisphere, 1982.

Heckhausen, H. Entwicklungsschritte in der Kausalattribution von Handlungsergebnissen. In D. Görlitz (Ed.), *Kindliche Erklaerungsmuster*. Weinheim and Basel: Beltz, 1984, 49–85.

Heckhausen, H. Achievement and motivation through the life span. In A. Sorensen, F. E. Weinert, & L. Sherrod (Eds.), *Human development—Interdisciplinary perspective*, in press.

Heider, F. *The psychology of interpersonal relations*. New York: Wiley, 1958.

Held, R., & Hein, A. Adaptation of disarranged hand–eye coordination contingent upon re-afferent stimulation. *Perceptual Motor Skills*, 1958, *8*, 87–90.

von Helmholtz, H. L. F. *Handbuch der physiologischen Optik*. Hamburg/Leipzig, 1856.

Von Helmholtz, H. L. F. *Treatise on physiological optics* (J. P. C. Southall, trans.). Rochester, NY: Optical Society of America, 1925.

Henle, M. On the relation between logic and thinking. *Psychological Review*, 1962, *69*, 36–378.

Henle, M. Of the Scholler of nature. *Social Research*, 1971, *38*, 93–107.

Herrmann, G., Naumann, W., & Hacker, W. Studie zur Wirkung unterschiedlicher kognitiver Strategien auf Leistung und Belastung—dargestellt an Bedientaetigkeiten. In W. Hacker, K. P. Timpe, & M. Vorwerg (Eds.), *Arbeitsingenieur-und sozialpsychologische Beitraege zur Rationalisierung*. Berlin: Deutscher Verlag der Wissenschaften, 1973.

Hesse, H. W. *Trainingsinduzierte Veraenderungen in der heuristischen Struktur und ihr Einfluss auf das Problemloesen*. Unpublished doctoral dissertation, RWTH Aachen, 1979.

Hesse, H. W. Effekte des semantischen Kontexts auf die Bearbeitung komplexer Probleme. *Zeitschrift fuer experimentelle und angewandte Psychologie*, 1982, *29*, 62–91.

Heymer, A. *Ethologisches Woerterbuch*. Berlin/Hamburg: Parey, 1977.

Hilgard, E. R. *Theories of learning* (2nd ed.). New York: Appleton-Century-Crofts, 1956.

Hochberg, J. E., & Brooks, V. The perception of motion pictures. In E. C. Carterette & M. P. Friedman (Eds.), *Handbook of perception* (Vol. 10). New York: Academic Press, 1978.

von Hofsten, C. Development of visually guided reaching: The approach phase. *Journal of Human Movement Studies*, 1979, *5*, 160–178.

von Hofsten, C. Predictive reaching for moving objects by human infants. *Journal of Experimental Child Psychology*, 1980, *30*, 369–382.

von Hofsten, C. Eye–hand coordination in the newborn. *Developmental Psychology*, 1982, *18*, 450–467.

von Hofsten, C. Catching skills in infancy. *Journal of Experimental Psychology: Human Perception and Performance*, 1983, *9*, 75–85.

von Hofsten, C., & Lindhagen, K. Observations on the development of reaching for small objects. *Journal of Experimental Child Psychology*, 1979, *28*, 158–173.

Hollerbach, J. M. Effective procedures versus elementary units of behavior. *Behavioral and Brain Sciences*, 1981, *4*, 625–627.

von Holst, E. Relations between the nervous system and the peripheral organs. *British Journal of Animal Behavior*, 1954, *2*, 89–94.

von Holst, E., & Mittelstaedt, H. Das Reafferenzprinzip. Wechselwirkung zwischen Zentralnerven-system und Peripherie. *Naturwissenschaft*, 1950, *37*, 464–476.

Holzkamp, K. *Grundlegung der Psychologie*. Frankfurt: Campus, 1983.

Holtzman, W. H., & Bitterman, M. E. A factorial study of adjustment to stress. *Journal of Abnormal and Social Psychology*, 1956, *52*, 179–185.

Homans, G. *Social behavior: Its elementary forms*. New York: Harcourt Brace, 1961.

Hoppe, F. Untersuchungen zur Handlungs-und Affektpsychologie. IX. Erfolg und Misserfolg. *Psychologische Forschung*, 1931, *14*, 1–62.

Horn, J. Personal communication, October 1982.

Horvath, F. E. Psychological stress: A review of definitions and experimental research. In L. von Bertalanffy & A. Rapaport (Eds.), *General systems* (Vol. 4). Ann Arbor: Society for General Systems Research, 1959.

Hulin, C. L., & Blood, M. K. Job enlargement, individual differences, and worker responses. *Psychological Bulletin*, 1968, *69*, 41–55.

Hull, C. L. Goal attraction and directing ideas conceived as habit phenomena. *Psychological Review*, 1931, *38*, 487–506.

Hull, C. L. *Principles of behavior*. New York: Appleton-Century-Crofts, 1943.

Hunt, E. Mechanics of verbal ability. *Psychological Review*, 1978, *85*, 109–130.

van Iersel, J. J. A. The extension of the orientation system of *Bembix rostrata* as used in the vicinity of the nest. In G. Bärends, C. Beer, & A. Manning (Eds.), *Function and the evolution in behaviour*. Oxford: Clarendon Press, 1975.

Immelmann, K. *Woerterbuch der Verhaltensforschung*. Hamburg/Berlin: Parey, 1982.

Inman, V. T., Ralston, H. J., de Saunders, J. B., Feinstein, B., & Wright, E. W., Jr. Relations of human electromyogram to muscular tension. *EEG Clinical Neurophysiology*, 1952, *4*, 187–194.

Irwin, F. W. *Intentional behavior and motivation: A cognitive theory*. Philadelphia: Lippincott, 1971.

Itani, J., & Suzuki, A. The social unit of chimpanzees. *Primates*, 1967, *8*, 355–381.

Ivanowa, A. *Validierung eines Taetigkeitsbewertungsverfahrens*. Unpublished doctoral dissertation, Technische Universitaet, Dresden, 1981.

Jackson, P. R., Paul, L. J., & Wall, T. D. Individual differences as moderators of reaction to job characteristics. *Journal of Occupational Psychology*, 1981, *54*, 1–8.

James, W. *The principles of psychology* (Vol. 1–2). New York: Holt, 1890.

James, W. *Psychology: Briefer course*. New York: Collier, 1961. (Originally published, 1892.)

Janis, I. L. *Victims of groupthink. A psychological study of foreign policy decisions and fiascoes.* Boston: Houghton Mifflin, 1972.

Janis, I. L., & Mann, L. *Decision making.* New York: Free Press, 1977.

Janoff-Bulman, R., & Brickman, P. Expectations and what people learn from failure. In N. Feather (Ed.), *Expectations and actions: Expectancy-value models in psychology.* Hillsdale, NJ: Lawrence Erlbaum Associates, 1982.

Jantsch, E. *The self-organizing universe.* New York: Pergamon, 1980.

Jantschke, F. *Orang-Utans in Zoologischen Gaerten.* Muenchen: Riper, 1972.

Johansson, G. *Configurations in event perception.* Uppsala: Almvist & Wiksell, 1950.

Johansson, G. Perception of motion and changing form. *Journal of Scandinavian Psychology,* 1964, *5,* 181–208.

Johansson, G. Visual perception of biological motion and model for its analysis. *Perception and Psychophysics,* 1973, *14,* 201–211.

Johansson, G. Visual motion perception. *Scientific American,* 1975, *232*(6), 76–88.

Johansson, G. Spacial constancy and motion in visual perception. In W. Epstein (Ed.), *Stability and constancy in visual perception.* New York: Wiley, 1977. (a)

Johansson, G. Studies on visual perception of locomotion. *Perception,* 1977, *6,* 365–376. (b)

Johansson, G. Visual event perception. In R. Held, H. W. Leibowitz, & H. L. Teuber (Eds.), *Handbook of sensory physiology* (Vol. 8). Berlin/Heidelberg/New York: Springer, 1978.

Johansson, G., von Hofsten, C., & Jansson, G. Event perception. *Annual Review of Psychology,* 1980, *31,* 27–63.

Johnson, M. K., & Raye, C. L. Reality monitoring. *Psychological Review,* 1981, *88,* 67–85.

Kahneman, D. *Attention and effort.* Englewood Cliffs, NJ: Prentice-Hall, 1973.

Kahneman, D., & Beatty, J. Pupil diameter and load on memory. *Science,* 1966, *154,* 1583–1585.

Kahneman, D., Slovic, P., & Tversky, A. (Eds.). *Judgement under uncertainty: Heuristics and biases.* New York: Cambridge University Press, 1982.

Kaminski, G. What beginning skiers can teach us about actions. In M. von Cranach & R. Harre (Eds.), *The analysis of action: Recent theoretical and empirical advances.* Cambridge, Eng.: Cambridge University Press, 1982.

Kaminski, G. Probleme einer oekopsychologischen Handlungstheorie. In L. Montada, K. Reusser, & G. Steiner (Eds.), *Kognition und Handeln.* Stuttgart: Klett-Cotta, 1983.

Kanfer, F. K., & Hagerman, S. The role of self-regulation. In L. P. Rehm (Ed.), *Behavior therapy for depression: Present status and future directions.* New York: Academic Press, 1981.

Kanfer, F. K., Hagerman, S., & Smith, J. R. *Task relevance and depression: Effects of goal setting and performance estimates.* Manuscript submitted for publication 1983.

Karasek, R. A. Job demands, job decision latitude, and mental strain: Implications for job redesign. *Administrative Science Quarterly,* 1979, *24,* 285–308.

Karasek, R. A. Job socialisation and job strain. In B. Gardell & G. Johansson (Eds.), *Working life.* London: Wiley, 1981.

Kay, H. The development of motor skills from birth to adolescence. In E. S. Bilodeau (Ed.), *Principles of skill acquisition.* New York: Academic Press, 1969.

Kazdin, A. E. Imagery elaboration and self-efficacy in the covert modeling treatment of unassertive behavior. *Journal of Consulting and Clinical Psychology,* 1979, *47,* 725–733.

Keeney, R. L. The art of assessing multiattribute utility functions. *Organizational Behavior and Human Performance,* 1977, *19,* 267–310.

Keeney, R. L., & Raifa, H. *Decisions with multiple objectives.* New York: Wiley, 1976.

Kelley, H. H., & Michela, J. L. Attribution theory and research. *Annual Review in Psychology,* 1980, *31,* 457–501.

Kelly, G. *The psychology of personal constructs.* New York: Norton, 1955.

Kerr, N. H. The role of vision in "visual imagery" experiments: Evidence from the congenitally blind. *Journal of Experimental Psychology: General,* 1983, *112,* 265–277.

Kerr, N. H., & Neisser, U. Mental images of concealed objects: New evidence. *Journal of Experimental Psychology: Learning, Memory, and Cognition,* 1983, *9,* 212–221.

Klapp, S. T., Marshburn, E. A., & Lester, P. T. Short-term memory does not involve the "working memory" of information processing: The demise of a common assumption. *Journal of Experimental Psychology: General,* 1983, *112,* 240–264.

Klaus, G. *Kybernetik und Erkenntnistheorie.* Berlin: Deutscher Verlag der Wissenschaften, 1966.

Klein, D. C., Fencil–Morse, E., & Seligman, M. E. P. Learned helplessness, depression and the attribution of failure. *Journal of Personality and Social Psychology,* 1976, *33,* 508–516.

Klinger, E. *Structure and functions of fantasy.* New York: Wiley, 1971.

Klinger, E. *Meaning and void: Inner experience and the incentives in people's lives.* Minneapolis: University of Minnesota Press, 1977.

Klinger, E. Modes of normal conscious flow. In K. S. Pope & J. L. Singer (Eds.), *The stream of consciousness: Scientific investigations into the flow of human experience.* New York: Plenum Press, 1978.

Klinger, E. The central place of imagery in human functioning. In E. Klinger (Ed.). *Imagery* (Vol. 2): *Concepts, results, and applications.* New York: Plenum Press, 1981.

Klinger, E. A consciousness-sampling analysis of test anxiety and performance. (In press) *Journal of Personality and Social Psychology.*

Klinger, E., Barta, S. G., & Maxeiner, M. E. Motivational correlates of thought content frequency and commitment. *Journal of Personality and Social Psychology,* 1980, *39,* 1222–1237.

Klix, F. *Erwachendes Denken. Eine Entwicklungsgeschichte der menschlichen Intelligenz.* Berlin: Deutscher Verlag der Wissenschaften, 1980.

Koestler, A. Beyond atomism and holism—the concept of the holon. In A. Koestler & J. R. Smythies (Eds.), *Beyond reductionism. The Albach symposium.* Boston: Beacon, 1969.

Kohlberg, L. Moral stages and moralization. The cognitive-developmental approach. In T. E. Lickona (Ed.), *Moral development and behavior.* New York: Holt, Rinehart & Winston, 1976.

Köhler, W. *Intelligenzpruefungen an Menschenaffen.* Berlin/Heidelberg: Springer, 1921.

Köhler, W. *Mentality of apes.* London: Routledge & Kegan Paul, 1927.

Kolb, D. A. Achievement motivation training for underachieving high-school boys. *Journal of Personality and Social Psychology,* 1965, *2,* 783–792.

Komorita, S. S., & Moore, D. Theories and processes of coalition formation. *Journal of Personality and Social Psychology,* 1976, *33,* 371–381.

Kortlandt, A. Handgebrauch bei freilebenden Schimpansen. In B. Rensch (Ed.), *Handgebrauch und Verstaendigung bei freilebenden Affen und Fruehmenschen.* Bern/Stuttgart: Huber, 1968.

Krantz, D. H., Luce, R. D., Suppes, P., & Tversky, A. *Foundations of measurement* (Vol. 1). New York: Academic Press, 1971.

Krau, E. Motivational feedback loops in the structure of action. *Journal of Personality and Social Psychology,* 1982, *43,* 1030–1040.

Krauth, J., & Lienert, G. A. *KFA-Konfigurationsfrequenzanalyse und ihre Anwendung in Psychologie und Medizin.* Freiburg/Muenchen: Alber, 1973.

Krenauer, M., & Schönpflug, W. Regulation und Fehlregulation im Verhalten. III. Zielsetzung und Ursachenbeschreibung unter Belastung. *Psychologische Beitraege,* 1980, *22,* 414–431.

Kreshovnikov, A. N. *Studies in physiology of exercise* (in Russian). Moscow, 1951.

Kruse, P., Stadler, M., Vogt, S., & Wehner, T. Raum-zeitliche Integration wahrgenormmener Bewegung durch Frequenzanalyse. *Gestalt theory,* 5, 1983, 83–113.

Kuhl, J. Motivational and functional helplessness: The moderating effect of state versus action orientation. *Journal of Personality and Social Psychology,* 1981, *40,* 155–170.

Kuhl, J. Action versus state-orientation as a mediator between motivation and action. In W. Hacker, W. Volpert, & M. von Cranach (Eds.), *Cognitive and motivational aspects of action.* Berlin: VEB Deutscher Verlag der Wissenschaften, 1982; Amsterdam/New York: North-Holland, 1982.

(a)

Kuhl, J. The expectancy-value approach in the theory of social motivation: Elaborations, extensions, critique. In N. T. Feather (Ed.), *Expectations and action: Expectancy-value models in psychology.* Hillsdale, NJ: Lawrence Erlbaum Associates, 1982 (b)

Kuhl, J. *Motivation, Konflikt und Handlungskontrolle.* Heidelberg: Springer, 1983.

Kuhl, J. Volitional aspects of achievement motivation and learned helplessness: Toward a comprehensive theory of action control. In B. A. Maher (Ed.), *Progress in experimental personality research* (Vol. 13). New York: Academic Press, in press.

Kuhl, J., & Blankenship, V. Behavioral change in a constant environment: Shift of more difficult tasks with constant probability of success. *Journal of Personality and Social Psychology,* 1979, *37,* 551–563. (a)

Kuhl, J., & Blankenship, V. The dynamic theory of achievement motivation: From episodic to dynamic thinking. *Psychological Review,* 1979, *86,* 141–151. (b)

Kuhl, J., & Geiger, E. The dynamic theory of the anxiety-behavior relationship: The champagne-cork effect. In J. Kuhl & J. W. Atkinson (Eds.), *Motivation and action.* New York: Praeger, in preparation.

Kuhl, J., & Helle, P. *Motivation and volitional determinants of depression: The degenerated-intention hypothesis.* Manuscript in preparation.

Kuhl, J., & Weiss, M. *Motivational and functional aspects of learned helplessness: A process-oriented approach.* Manuscript submitted for publication, 1983.

Kukla, A. Foundations of an attributional theory of performance. *Psychological Review,* 1972, *79,* 454–470.

Kummer, H. *Sozialverhalten der Primaten.* Berlin/Heidelberg/New York: Springer, 1975.

Künstler, B., & Zimmer, K. Toward the analysis of motivational influences in coping with mental load. In W. Bachmann & I. Udris (Eds.), *Mental load and stress in activity: European approaches.* Berlin: Deutscher Verlag der Wissenschaften, 1982.

van Lawick–Goodall, J. New discoveries among Africa's chimpanzees. *National Geographic Magazine,* 1965, *125,* 446–453.

van Lawick–Goodall, J. Tool using in primates and other vertebrates. *Advances in the Study of Behavior,* 1970, *3,* 195–249.

Lazarus, R. S. *Psychological stress and the coping process.* New York: McGraw–Hill, 1966.

Lazarus, R. S. Emotion and adaption. Conceptual and empirical relations. In W. Arnold (Ed.), *Nebraska symposium on motivation* (Vol. 10). Lincoln: University of Nebraska Press, 1968.

Lazarus, R. S., Deese, J., & Osler, S. F. The effects of psychological stress upon performance. *Psychological Bulletin,* 1952, *49,* 293–317.

Lazarus, R. S., & DeLongis, A. Psychological stress and coping in aging. *American Psychologist,* 1983, *38,* 245–254.

Lazarus, R. S., & Eriksen, C. W. Effects of failure stress upon skilled performance. *Journal of Experimental Psychology,* 1952, *43,* 100–105.

Lazarus, R. S., & Launier, R. Stress-related transactions between persons and environment. In L. A. Pervin & M. Lewis (Eds.), *Perspectives in interactional psychology.* New York: Plenum Press, 1978.

Lea, S. E. G. The psychology and economics of demand. *Psychological Bulletin,* 1978, *85,* 441–466.

Lee, D. N. Visual information during locomotion. In R. B. MacLeod & H. L. Pick (Eds.), *Perception: Essays in honor of James J. Gibson.* Ithaca, NY/London: Cornell University Press, 1974.

Lee, D. N. A theory of visual control of braking based on information about time–to–collision. *Perception,* 1976, *5,* 437–459.

Lee, D. N. The optic flow field: The foundation of vision. *Philosophical Transactions of the Royal Society, London,* 1980, *B 290,* 169–179.

Lee, D. N., & Lishman, J. R. Visual proprioceptive control of stance. *Journal of Human Movement Studies,* 1975, *1,* 87–95.

Lee, D. N., Lishman, J. R., & Thomson, J. A. Visual regulation of gait in long jumping. *Journal of Experimental Psychology: Human Perception and Performance*, 1982, *8*, 448–459.

Lee, D. N., & Reddish, P. E. Plummeting gannets: A paradigm of ecological optics. *Nature*, 1981, *293*, 293–294.

Lefcourt, H. M. *Locus of control: Current trends in theory and research*. Hillsdale, NJ: Lawrence Erlbaum Associates, 1976.

Lefebvre–Pinard, M., & Reid, L. A comparison of three methods of training communication skills: Social conflict, modeling, and conflict-modeling. *Child Development*, 1980, *51*, 179–187.

Lehrman, D. S. Control of behavior cycles in reproduction. In W. Etkin (Ed.), *Social behavior and organization among vertebrates*. Chicago: University of Chicago Press, 1964.

Leontiev, A. N. *Probleme der Entwicklung des Psychischen*. Berlin: Verlag Volk und Wissen, 1971. (2nd ed., Kronberg/Taunus: Athenaeum, 1980.)

Leontiev, A. N. *On the importance of the notion of "object-activity" for psychology*. Short communication (prepared for the 20th International Congress of Psychology, Tokyo, 1972). Moscow: Academy of Pedagogical Science of the USSR, 146–163, 1972.

Leontiev, A. N. *Taetigkeit, Bewusstsein, Persoenlichkeit*. Stuttgart: Klett-Cotta, 1977; Berlin: Volk und Wissen, 1979.

Leontiev, A. N., & Luria, A. R. Foreword. In G. A. Miller, E. Galanter, & K. H. Pribram, *Plans and the structure of behavior* (Russian ed.; A. N. Leontiev & A. R. Luria, eds.). Moscow: Nauka, 1965.

Lepper, M. R., & Greene, D. (Eds.). *The hidden costs of reward*. Hillsdale, NJ: Lawrence Erlbaum Associates, 1978.

Lerner, R. M., & Busch–Rossnagel, N. A. (Eds.). *Individuals as producers of their development: A life-span perspective*. New York: Academic Press, 1981.

Leuner, H. Basic principles and therapeutic efficacy of Guided Affective Imagery (GAI). In J. L. Singer & K. S. Pope (Eds.), *The power of human imagination: New methods in psychotherapy*. New York: Plenum Press, 1978.

Lewin, K. Untersuchungen zur Handlungs-und Affektpsychologie. II. Vorsatz, Wille und Beduerfnis. *Psychologische Forschung*, 1926, *7*, 330–385. (a)

Lewin, K. *Vorsatz, Wille und Beduerfnis*. Berlin: Deutsche Verlagsanstalt, 1926. (b)

Lewin, K. *A dynamic theory of personality*. New York: McGraw–Hill, 1935.

Lewin, K. *Principles of topological psychology*. New York: McGraw–Hill, 1936.

Lewin, K. *The conceptual representation and the measurement of psychological forces*. Durham, NC: Duke University Press, 1938.

Lewin, K. Defining the "field at a given time." *Psychological Review*, 1943, *50*, 292–310.

Lewin, K. Behavior and development as a function of the total situation. In L. Carmichael (Ed.), *Manual of child psychology*. New York: Wiley, 1946.

Lewin, K. *Field theory in social science*. New York: Harper, 1951.

Lewin, K., Dembo, T., Festinger, L., & Sears, P. S. Level of aspiration. In J. McV. Hunt (Ed.), *Personality and the behavior disorders* (Vol. 1). New York: Ronald Press, 1944.

Lewis, E. R. Dynamic servomechanisms are more fun: A critical look at chapters 6 and 7 of the organization of action. *Behavioral and Brain Sciences*, 1981, *4*, 629–630.

Lichtenstein, S., Fischhoff, B., & Phillips, L. D. Calibration of probabilities: The state of the art to 1980. In D. Kahneman, P. Slovic, & A. Tversky (Eds.), *Judgement under uncertainty: Heuristics and biases*. New York: Cambridge University Press, 1982.

Lishman, J. R., & Lee, D. N. The autonomy of visual kinesthesis. *Perception*, 1973, *2*, 287–294.

Locke, E. A. Toward a theory of task motivation and incentives. *Organizational Behavior and Human Performance*, 1968, *3*, 457–480.

Locke, E. A. Personnel attitudes and motivation. *Annual Review of Psychology*, 1975, *26*, 475–480.

Loizos, C. Play behavior in higher primates: A review. In D. Morris (Ed.), *Primate ethology.* London: Weidenfeld and Nicolson, 1967.

Lomov, B. F. On levels of anticipation. *Proceedings, XXII International Congress on Psychology,* Leipzig, 1980, 154–158.

Luchins, A. S., & Luchins, E. H. *Rigidity of behavior.* Eugene: University of Oregon Press, 1959.

Luria, A. R. The origin and cerebral organization of man's conscious action (Evening lecture). In *Proceedings XIX International Congress of Psychology, London,* 1969, 37–54. London, British Psychological Society, 1971.

Luria, A. R. *The working brain: An introduction to neuropsychology.* Harmondsworth, Eng.: Penguin Modern Psychology Texts, 1973.

MacKay, D. G. The problem of rehearsal or mental practice. *Journal of Motor Behavior,* 1981, *13,* 274–285.

Macmurray, J. *The self as agent.* London: Faber & Faber, 1962.

Maffei, L., & Fiorentini, A. The visual cortex as a spatial frequency analyzer. *Vision Research,* 1973, *13,* 1255–1267.

Mahoney, M. J. *Cognition and behavior modification.* Cambridge, MA: Ballinger, 1974.

Mann, L., & Janis, I. Conflict theory of decision making and the expectancy-value approach. In N. T. Feather (Ed.), *Expectations and actions: Expectancy-value models in psychology.* Hillsdale, NJ: Lawrence Erlbaum Associates, 1982.

Mannarino, A. Friendship patterns and self-concept development in preadolescent males. *Journal of Genetic Psychology,* 1978, *133,* 105–110.

Marks, I. Behavioral psychotherapy of adult neurosis. In S. L. Garfield & A. E. Bergin (Eds.), *Handbook of psychotherapy and behavior change: An empirical analysis.* New York: Wiley, 1978.

Marr, D. *Vision.* San Fransisco: W. H. Freeman, 1982.

Marx, K. *Capital* (Vol. 1). (B. Fowles, trans.) New York: Vintage, 1977. (Originally published, 1906.)

Maslow, A. H. *Motivation and Personality* (2nd ed.). New York: Harper & Row, 1970.

Matarazzo, J. D. *Wechsler's measurement and appraisal of adult intelligence.* Baltimore: Williams and Williams, 1972.

Matern, B. *Psychologische Arbeitsuntersuchung. Spezielle Arbeits-und Ingenieurpsychologie: Psychologische Arbeitsanalyse.* Berlin: VEB Deutscher Verlag der Wissenschaften, 1983.

Mathieu, M. *Piagetian assessment of cognitive development in primates.* Paper presented at the 47th Annual Meeting of the American Anthropological Association, Los Angeles, 1978.

Maturana, H. R., & Varela, F. J. *Autopoiesis and cognition.* Boston: Reichel, 1980.

McArthur, L. Z., & Baron, R. M. Toward an ecological theory of social perception. *Psychological Review,* 1983, *90,* 215–238.

McClelland, D. C. *The achieving society.* Princeton, NJ: Van Nostrand, 1961.

McClelland, D. C., Atkinson, J. W., Clark, R. A., & Lowell, C. L. *The achievement motive.* New York: Appleton-Century-Crofts, 1953.

McDougall, W. *An introduction to social psychology.* London: Methuen, 1921.

McGrew, W. C. Socialization and object manipulation in wild chimpanzees. In S. Chevalier-Skolnikoff & F. Poirier (Eds.), *Primate biosocial development.* New York: Garland Press, 1977.

McGrew, W. C. Recent advances in study of tool-use by nonhuman primates. In A. B. Chiarelli & R. S. Corruccini (Eds.), *Advanced view primate biology.* Berlin/Heidelberg/New York: Springer, 1982.

McGrew, W. C., Tutin, C. E. G., & Midgett, P. S. Tool use in a group of captive chimpanzees. I. Escape. *Zeitschrift fuer Tierpsychologie,* 1975, *37,* 145–162.

Meacham, J. A. Verbal guidance through remembering the goals of action. *Child Development,* 1978, *49,* 188–193.

Meacham, J. A. A note on remembering to execute planned actions. *Journal of Applied Developmental Psychology*, 1982, *3*, 121–133.

Meacham, J. A. The social basis of intentional action. *Human Development*, 1984, *27*, 119–124.

Mechanic, D. Social structure and personal adaptation: Some neglected dimensions. In G. V. Coelho, D. A. Hamburg, & J. E. Adams (Eds.), *Coping and adaptation*. New York: Basic Books, 1974.

Meichenbaum, D. A. *Cognitive behavior modification*. Morristown, NJ: General Learning Press, 1974.

Meichenbaum, D. A. A self-instructional approach to stress management: A proposal for stress inoculation training. In C. D. Spielberger & J. G. Sarason (Eds.), *Stress and anxiety* (Vol. 1). New York: Wiley, 1975. (a)

Meichenbaum, D. A. Self-instructional methods. In F. H. Kanfer & A. P. Goldstein (Eds.), *Helping people change*. New York: Pergamon, 1975. (b)

Meichenbaum, D. A. *Cognitive behavior modification: An integrative approach*. New York: Plenum Press, 1977.

Meichenbaum, D., Henshaw, D., & Himel, N. Coping with stress as a problem-solving process. In W. Krohne & L. Laux (Eds.), *Achievement, stress and anxiety*. Washington, DC: Hemisphere, 1982.

Melden, A. J. *Free action*. London: Routledge & Kegan Paul, 1961.

Meltzoff, A. N., & Moore, M. K. Imitation of facial and manual gestures by human neonates. *Science*, 1977, *198*, 75–78.

Mendelson, M. J., & Haith, M. H. The relation between audition and vision in the human newborn. *Monographs of the Society for Research in Child Development*, 1976, *41*(No. 167).

Mento, A. J., Cartledge, N. D., & Locke, E. A. Maryland vs. Michigan vs. Minnesota: Another look at the relationship of expectancy and goal difficulty to task performance. *Organizational Behavior and Human Performance*, 1980, *25*, 419–440.

Menzel, E. M., Davenport, K. R., & Rogers, C. The development of tool-using in wildborn and restriction-reared chimpanzees. *Folia Primatologica*, 1970, *12*.

Messer, S. B. Reflection-impulsivity: A review. *Psychological Bulletin*, 1976, *83*, 1026–1052.

Metzger, W. *Psychologie*. Darmstadt: Steinkopff, 1968.

Meyer, J. P., & Mulherin, A. From attribution to helping: An analysis of the mediating effects of affect and expectancy. *Journal of Personality and Social Psychology*, 1980, *39*, 201–210.

Meyer, P. *Taschenlexikon der Verhaltenskunde*. Paderborn: Schoening, 1976.

Michaels, C. F., & Carello, C. *Direct perception*. Englewood Cliffs, NJ: Prentice-Hall, 1981.

Michie, D. Problems of the conceptual interface between machine and human problem-solving. *Experimental programming unit report no. 36*. Edinburgh: Machine Intelligence Research Unit, 1980.

Mikula, G. (Ed.). *Gerechtigkeit und soziale Interaktion*. Bern: Huber, 1980.

Milgram, S. *Obedience to authority*. New York: Harper & Row, 1974.

Miller, A. T. *Self-recognitory schemes and achievement behavior: A developmental study*. Unpublished doctoral dissertation, Purdue University, 1982.

Miller, C. E. Coalition formation in characteristic function games: Competitive tests of three theories. *Journal of Experimental Social Psychology*, 1980, *16*, 61–76.

Miller, G. A. The magical number seven, plus or minus two. *Psychological Review*, 1956, *63*, 81–97.

Miller, G. A., Galanter, E., & Pribram, K. H. *Plans and the structure of behavior*. New York: Holt, 1960.

Miller, I. W., & Norman, W. H. Learned helplessness in humans: A review and attribution theory model. *Psychological Bulletin*, 1979, *86*, 93–118.

Miller, R. Rawls and Marxism. *Philosophy and Public Affairs*, 1974, *3*, 167–191.

Miller, R. B. *Development of a taxonomy of human performance: Design of a systems task vocabulary* (tech. rep. 11). Washington, DC: American Institute of Research, 1971.

Miller, S. M. Predictability and human stress: Toward a clarification of evidence and theory. In L. Berkowitz (Ed.), *Advances in experimental social psychology* (Vol. 14). New York: Academic Press, 1981.

Mischel, H. N. From intention to action: The role of rule knowledge in the development of self-regulation. *Human Development*, 1984, *27*, 124–129.

Mischel, H. N., & Mischel, W. The development of children's knowledge of self-control strategies. *Child Development*, 1983, *54*, 603–619.

Mischel, W., & Patterson, C. J. Effective plans for self-control in children. In W. A. Collins (Ed.), *Minnesota symposium on child psychology* (Vol. 11). Hillsdale, NJ: Lawrence Erlbaum Associates, 1978.

Mischel, W., Zeiss, R., & Zeiss, A. Internal–external control and persistence: Validation and implications of the Stanford Pre-School I-E Scale (SPIES). *Journal of Personality and Social Psychology*, 1974, *29*, 265–278.

Moore, B., Jr. *Injustice: The social bases of obedience and revolt.* White Plains, NY: Sharpe, 1978.

Mugny, G., Perret–Clermont, A. N., & Doise, W. Interpersonal coordinations and sociological differences in the construction of the intellect. In G. M. Stephenson & J. M. Davis (Eds.), *Progress in applied social psychology* (Vol. 1). New York: Wiley, 1981.

Mündelein, H., & Schönpflug, W. Regulation und Fehlregulation im Verhalten. VIII. Ueber primaere (unmittelbar zielgerichtete) und sekundaere (auxiliaere und praeventive) Anteile von Taetigkeiten. *Psychologische Beitraege*, 1983, *25*, 71–84.

Neisser, R. The imitation of man by machine. *Science*, 1963, *139*, 193–197.

Neisser, U. *Cognitive psychology.* New York: Appleton-Century-Crofts, 1967.

Neisser, U. *Cognition and reality: Principles and implications of cognitive psychology.* San Francisco: W. H. Freeman, 1976.

Newell, A., & Simon, H. A. *Human problem solving.* Englewood Cliffs, NJ: Prentice-Hall, 1972.

Nicholls, J. G. The development of the concepts of effort and ability, perception of own attainment, and the understanding that difficult tasks require more ability. *Child Development*, 1978, *49*, 800–814.

Nicholls, J. G., & Miller, A. T. Development and its discontents: The differentiation of the concept of ability. In J. G. Nicholls (Ed.), *The development of achievement motivation.* Greenwich, CT: JAI Press, 1983.

Nigro, G. N. *Improvement of skill through observation and mental practice.* Unpublished doctoral dissertation, Cornell University, 1983.

Nisbett, R. E., & Wilson, T. D. Telling more than we can know: Verbal reports on mental process. *Psychological Review*, 1977, *84*, 231–259.

Nissen, H. W. A field study on the chimpanzee. *Comparative Psychology Monthly*, 1931, *8*, 1–122.

Noble, D. *The initiation of the heartbeat.* Oxford: Clarendon Press, 1975.

Norman, D. A. Categorization of action slips. *Psychological Review*, 1981, *88*, 1–15.

Norros, L. *Kodierung, Strategie und Aufwandsregulation beim Erlernen funktioneller Beziehungen.* University of Helsinki: General Psychology Monographs, NO B 3, 1982.

Nuttin, J. *Tâche, réussite et échec. Théorie de la conduite humain.* Louvain: Publications Universitaires, 1953.

Obuchowski, K. *Orientierung und Emotion.* Koeln: Pahl-Rugenstein, 1982.

Oppenheimer, L. Action and (social) cognition: Some developmental curiosities. In L. Oppenheimer (Ed.), *Action theoretical approaches to (developmental) psychology* (Report No. 81–04). Amsterdam: University of Amsterdam Vakgroep Ontwikkelingspsychologie, August, 1981.

Oschanin, D. A. *The operative image of a controlled object in "man-automatic-machine" systems.* XVIII International Congress of Psychology, Moscow, 1966.

Osgood, C. E., May, W. H., & Miron, M. S. *Cross-cultural universals of affective meaning.* Urbana: University of Illinois Press, 1975.

Oesterreich, R. *Handlungsregulation und Kontrolle.* Muenchen: Urban & Schwarzenberg, 1981.

Overton, W. F., & Reese, H. W. Models of development: Methodological implications. In J. R. Nesselroade & H. W. Reese (Eds.), *Life-span developmental psychology: Methodological issues.* New York: Academic Press, 1973.

Parker, S. T., & Gibson, K. R. Object manipulation, tool use, and sensorimotor intelligence as feeding adaptations in cebus monkeys and great apes. *Journal of Human Evolution,* 1977, *6,* 623–641.

Parker, S. T., & Gibson, K. R. A developmental model for the evolution of language and intelligence in early homonids. *Behavioral and Brain Sciences,* 1979, *2,* 364–407.

Parker, S. T., & Gibson, K. R. The importance of theory of reconstructing the evolution of language and intelligence of hominides. In A. B. Chiarelli & R. S. Corruccini (Eds.), *Advanced view primate biology.* Berlin/Heidelberg/New York: Springer, 1982.

Parkes, K. R. Occupational stress among student nurses: A natural experiment. *Journal of Applied Psychology,* 1982, *67,* 784–796.

Pascual–Leone, J. A mathematical model for the transition rule in Piaget's developmental stages. *Acta Psychologica,* 1970, *32,* 301–345.

Patterson, R. D. *Guidelines for auditory warning systems on civil aircarft.* Civil Aviation Authority Paper 82017, 1982.

Pearlin, L. I., & Schooler, C. The structure of coping. *Journal of Health and Social Behavior,* 1978, *19,* 2–21.

Peiper, A. *Cerebral function in infancy and childhood.* New York: Consultants Bureau, 1963.

Perry, R. B. Docility and purposiveness. *Psychological Review,* 1918, *25,* 1–21.

Pervin, L. A. The stasis and flow of behavior: Toward a theory of goals. In M. M. Page (Ed.), *Nebraska symposium on motivation, 1983* (Vol. 30). Lincoln: University of Nebraska Press, 1983.

Peters, R. S. *The concept of motivation.* London: Routledge & Kegan Paul, 1958.

Peterson, C., & Seligman, M. E. P. Causal explanations as a risk factor in depression: Theory and evidence. *Psychological Review,* 1984, *91,* 347–379.

Phares, E. J. *Locus of control in personality.* Morristown, NJ: General Learning Press, 1976.

Piaget, J. *The origins of intelligence in children.* New York: International University Press, 1952.

Piaget, J. *La naissance de l'intellegence chez l'enfant.* Neuchatel: Delachaux & Nestlé, 1963.

Plath, H. E., & Richter, P. Der BMS-I-Erfassungsbogen-Ein Verfahren zur skalierten Erfassung erlebter Beanspruchungsfolgen. *Probleme und Ergebnisse der Psychologie,* 1978, *65,* 45–86.

Plooij, F. Tool-use during chimpanzee bushpig hunt. *Carnivore,* 1978, *1,* 103–106.

Posner, M. I., & Keele, S. W. On the genesis of abstract ideas. *Journal of Experimental Psychology,* 1968, *77,* 353–363.

Posner, M. I., Nissen, M. J., & Klein, R. M. Visual dominance: An information-processing account of its origins and significance. *Psychological Review,* 1976, *83,* 157–171.

Poulton, E. C. Perceptual anticipation in tracking with two-pointer and one-pointer displays. *British Journal of Psychology,* 1952, *43,* 222–229.

Premack, D. Reversibility of the reinforcement relation. *Science,* 1962, *136,* 235–237.

Premack, D. *Intelligence in ape and man.* Hillsdale, NJ: Lawrence Erlbaum Associates, 1976.

Premack, D. Does the chimpanzee have a theory of mind? *Behavioral and Brain Sciences,* 1978, *4,* 515–526.

Pribram, K. H. *Languages of the brain.* Englewood Cliffs, NJ: Prentice-Hall, 1971.

Pribram, K. H. Holonomy and structure in the organization of perception. In J. M. Nicholas (Ed.), *Images, perception, and knowledge.* Dordrecht: Reidel, 1977.

Putz-Osterloh, W. Ueber die Beziehung zwischen Testintelligenz und Problemloeseerfolg. *Zeitschrift fuer Psychologie,* 1981, *189,* 80–100.

Rabbitt, P. M. A. Errors and error correction in choice-responses tasks. *Journal of Experimental Psychology*, 1966, *71*, 264–272.

Rachlin, H., Green, L., Kagel, J. H., & Battalio, R. C. Economic demand theory and psychological studies in choice. In G. H. Bower (Ed.), *The psychology of learning and motivation* (Vol. 10). New York: Academic Press, 1976.

Rachman, S., & Eysenck, H. J. Reply to "a critique and reformulation of behavior therapy." *Psychological Bulletin*, 1966, *65*, 165–169.

Rapport, D. J., & Turner, J. E. Economic models in ecology. *Science*, 1977, *195*, 367–373.

Rawlings, E. I., & Rawlings, I. L. Rotary pursuit tracking following mental rehearsal as a function of voluntary control of visual imagery. *Perceptual and Motor Skills*, 1974, *38*, 302.

Rawls, J. *A theory of justice.* Cambridge, MA: Harvard University Press, 1971.

Raynor, J. O. Self-evaluation and achievement motivation: Use of an expectancy × value theory of personality functioning and change. In N. Feather (Ed.), *Expectations and actions: Expectancy-value models in psychology.* Hillsdale, NJ: Lawrence Erlbaum Associates, 1982.

Reason, J. Actions not as planned: The price of automatization. In G. Underwood & R. Stevens (Eds.), *Aspects of consciousness* (Vol. 1). London: Academic Press, 1979.

Reason, J. T. Skill and error in everyday life. In M. J. A. Howe (Ed.), *Adult learning.* Chichester: Wiley, 1977.

Redshaw, M. Cognitive development in human and gorilla infants. *Journal of Human Evolution*, 1978, *7*, 133–141.

Reed, E. S. An outline of a theory of action systems. *Journal of Motor Behavior*, 1982, *14*, 98–134.

Reed, E. S. Darwin's worms: A case study in evolutionary psychology. *Behaviorism*, in press.

Reese, H. W., & Overton, W. F. Models of development and theories of development. In L. R. Goulet & P. B. Baltes (Eds.), *Life-span developmental psychology: Research and theory.* New York: Academic Press, 1970.

Reither, F. *Self-reflective cognitive processes: Its characteristics and effects.* Paper presented at the 22nd International Congress of Psychology, Leipzig, 1980.

Reither, F. Thinking and acting in complex situations—A study of experts' behavior. *Simulation and Games*, 1981, *12*(2), 125–140.

Reither, F. *Denn sie sagen nicht was sie tun-Diskrepanzen zwischen verbalen Aeusserungen und tatsaechlichen Handlungen beim komplexen Problemloesen.* Paper presented at the "25. Tagung experimentell arbeitender Psychologen," Hamburg, 1983. (a)

Reither, F. *Fehlerresistenz und Trainingsmoeglichkeiten beim Umgang mit komplexen Problemen.* Paper presented at the "25. Tagung experimentell arbeitender Psychologen," Hamburg, 1983. (b)

Rensch, B. Malversuche mit Affen. *Zeitschrift fuer Psychologie*, 1961, *18*, 347–364.

Rensch, B. *Gedaechtnis, Begriffsbildung, Planhandlungen bei Tieren.* Berlin/Hamburg: Parey, 1973.

Rensch, B., & Ducker, G. Manipulierfaehigkeit eines jungen Orang-Utans und eines jungen Gorillas. Mit Anmerkungen ueber das Spielverhalten. *Zeitschrift fuer Tierpsychologie*, 1966, *23*, 847–892.

Reuman, D. Ipsative behavior variability and the quality of thematic apperception measurement of the achievement motive. *Journal of Personality and Social Psychology*, 1982, *43*, 1098–1110.

Revelle, W., & Michaels, E. J. The theory of achievement motivation revisited: The implications of inertial tendencies. *Psychological Review*, 1976, *83*, 394–404.

Reykowski, J. Efficiency of self-regulation and tolerance for stress. *Studia Psychologica*, 1972, *14*, 294–300.

Reynolds, V., & Reynolds, F. Chimpanzees of the Budongo Forest. In I. DeVore (Ed.), *Primate behavior. Field studies of monkeys and apes.* New York: Holt, Rinehart & Winston, 1965.

Rholes, W. S., Blackwell, J., Jordan, C., & Walters, C. A developmental study of learned helplessness. *Developmental Psychology*, 1981, *16*, 616–624.

Richardson, A. Mental practice: A review and discussion, Part I. *Research Quarterly,* 1967, *38,* 95–107. (a)

Richardson, A. Mental practice: A review and discussion, Part II. *Research Quarterly,* 1967, *38,* 263–273. (b)

Richter, P., & Engelmann, P. *Anforderungen und Belastungen bei Altersdisenaire-Patienten.* Unpublished manuscript, Technische Universitaet, Dresden, 1982.

Rimm, D. C., & Masters, J. C. *Behavior therapy: Techniques and empirical findings.* New York: Academic Press, 1974.

Robinson, E. J., & Robinson, W. P. Ways of reacting to communication failure in relation to the development of children's understanding about verbal communication. *European Journal of Social Psychology,* 1981, *11,* 189–208.

Robinson, E. J., Silbereisen, R. K., & Claar, A. La development de la communication. In G. Mugny (Ed.), *Psychologie sociale du development cognitif,* in press.

Rock, J. In defense of unconscious inference. In W. Epstein (Ed.), *Stability and constancy in visual perception.* New York: Wiley, 1977.

Roeder, K. D. *Nerve cells and insect behavior.* Cambridge, MA: Harvard University Press, 1967.

Romanes, G. Y. *Animal intelligence.* London: Kegan Paul, 1882.

Rosenblueth, A., Wiener, W., & Bigelow, J. Behavior, purpose and teleology. *Philosophy of Science,* 1943, *10,* 18–24.

Rothbaum, F., Weisz, G. R., & Snyder, S. S. Changing the world and changing the self: A two process model of perceived control. *Journal of Personality and Social Psychology,* 1982, *42,* 5–37.

Rotter, J. B. Some problems and misconceptions related to the construct of internal versus external control of reinforcement. *Journal of Consulting and Clinical Psychology,* 1975, *43,* 56–67.

Rozin, P. The evolution of intelligence and access to the cognitive unconscious. *Progress in Psychobiology and Physiological Psychology,* 1976, *6,* 245–279.

Rubinstein, S. L. *Grundlagen der Allgemeinen Psychologie.* (2nd Ed.) Berlin: Volk und Wissen, 1958.

Ruff, H. A., & Halton, A. Is there directed reaching in the human neonate? *Developmental Psychology,* 1978, *14,* 425–426.

Rühle, R. *Inhalte, Methoden und Effekte der Analyse und Vermittlung operativer Abbilder bei Bedientaetigkeiten der Mehrstellenarbeit.* Unpublished doctoral dissertation, Technische Universitaet, Dresden (Naturwissenschaftlich-mathematische Fakultaet), 1979.

Rühle, R., Matern, B., & Skell, W. Training kognitiver Regulationsgrundlagen. In W. Hacker & H. Raum (Eds.), *Optimierung kognitiver Regulationsgrundlagen.* Berlin: Deutscher Verlag der Wissenschaften, 1980; Bern: Huber, 1980.

Rumbaugh, D., & Gill, T. Lana's mastery of language skills. In D. M. Rumbaugh (Ed.), *Language learning by a chimpanzee.* New York: Academic Press, 1977.

Russell, B. *The analysis of mind.* New York: Macmillan, 1921.

Russell, B. *An outline of philosophy.* London: Allen & Unwin, 1927.

Ryan, R. M., Mims, V., & Koestner, R. Relation of reward contingency and interpersonal context to intrinsic motivation: A review and test using cognitive evaluation theory. *Journal of Personality and Social Psychology,* 1983, *45,* 736–750.

Ryff, C. D. Self-perceived personality change in adulthood and aging. *Journal of Personality and Social Psychology,* 1982, *42*(1), 108–115.

Sabini, J., & Silver, M. *Moralities of everyday life.* New York: Oxford University Press, 1982.

Salmon, M. Coastal distribution, display and sound production by Florida fiddler crabs (genus *Uca*). *Animal Behavior,* 1967, *15,* 449–459.

Savage, E. S., & Rumbaugh, D. M. Communication, language, and Lana: A perspective. In D. M. Rumbaugh (Ed.), *Language learning by a chimpanzee.* New York: Academic Press, 1977.

Schmidt, R. A. Anticipation and timing in human performance. *Psychological Bulletin*, 1968, *70*, 631–646.

Schmidt, R. A. A schema theory of discrete motor skill learning. *Psychological Review*, 1975, *82*, 225–260.

Schmidt, R. A. More on motor programs. In J. A. S. Kelso (Ed.), *Human motor behavior: An introduction.* Hillsdale, NJ: Lawrence Erlbaum Associates, 1982. (a)

Schmidt, R. A. The schema concept. In J. A. S. Kelso (Ed.), *Human motor behavior: An introduction.* Hillsdale, NJ: Lawrence Erlbaum Associates, 1982. (b)

Schmidt, R. A., & Gordon, G. B. Errors in motor responding, "RAPID" corrections, and false anticipations. *Journal of Motor Behavior*, 1977, *9*, 101–111.

Schneider, N. *Untersuchungen zur Effektivitaet von kognitiven Lehr-und Trainingsmethoden unter industriellen Bedingungen.* Unpublished doctoral dissertation. Technische Universitaet, Dresden (Naturwissenschaftlich-mathematische Fakultaet), 1977.

Schneider, W., & Shiffrin, R. M. Controlled and automatic human information processing. I. Detection, search, and attention. *Psychological Review*, 1977, *84*, 1–66.

Schönpflug, W. Regulation und Fehlregulation im Verhalten. I. Verhaltensstruktur, Effizienz und belastungtheoretische Grundlagen eines Untersuchungsprogramms. *Psychologische Beitraege*, 1979, *21*, 174–202.

Schönpflug, W. Coping and the generation of stress. In W. Bachmann & I. Udris (Eds.), *Mental load and stress in activity: European approaches.* Berlin: Deutscher Verlag der Wissenschaften, 1982.

Schönpflug, W. Coping efficiency and situational demands. In G. R. J. Hockey (Ed.), *Stress and fatigue in human performance.* London: Wiley, 1983.

Schönpflug, W. Regulation und Fehlregulation im Verhalten. X. Entlastung und Belastung durch gesundheitsfoerdernde Massnahmen. *Psychologische Beitraege*, 1984, *26.*

Schuhler, P. *Perspektivenuebernahme im Handlungsvollzug: Konzeption und Evaluation eines Interventionsprogramms.* Unpublished doctoral dissertation, Technische Universitaet Berlin, 1983.

Schulz, P. Regulation und Fehlregulation im Verhalten. II. Stress durch Fehlregulation. *Psychologische Beitraege*, 1979, *21*, 597–621.

Schulz, P. Regulation und Fehlregulation im Verhalten. V. Die wechselseitige Beeinflussung von mentaler und emotionaler Beanspruchung. *Psychologische Beitraege*, 1980, *22*, 597–621.

Schulz, P. Beeintraechtigung von Lernprozessen durch Verkehrslaerm bei unterschiedlich leistungsfaehigen Personen. In A. Schick (Ed.), *Akustik zwischen Physik und Psychologie.* Stuttgart: Klett-Cotta, 1981.

Schulz, P. Regulation und Fehlregulation im Verhalten. VII. Entstehungsbedingungen und Erscheinungsweisen der emotionalen Belastung in Leistungssituationen. *Psychologische Beitraege*, 1982, *24*, 498–522.

Schulz, P., & Schönpflug, W. Regulatory activity during states of stress. In W. Krohne & L. Laux (Eds.), *Achievement, stress and anxiety.* Washington, DC: Hemisphere, 1982.

Schumann, M., Gerlach, F., Gschössl, A., & Milhoffer, P. *Am Beispiel der Septemberstreiks: Anfang der Rekonstruktionsperiode der Arbeiterklasse.* Frankfurt: Europaeische Verlagsanstalt, 1971.

Schunk, D. H. Effects of effort attributional feedback on children's perceived self-efficacy and achievement. *Journal of Educational Psychology*, 1982, *74*, 548–566.

Schurig, V. Experimentelles Bewusstsein bei tierischen Primaten. 2. In P. M. Hejl, W. K. Kock, & G. Roth (Eds.), *Kommunikation und Wahrnehmung.* Frankfurt/Bern/Las Vegas: Lang, 1978.

Schurig, V. Werkzeugverhalten bei Tieren in ethologischer Sicht. In H. Offe & L. M. Stadler (Eds.), *Arbeitsmotivation.* Darmstadt: Steinhoff, 1980.

Schutz, A. *Collected papers* (Vols. 1–2). The Hauge: Martinus Nijhoff, 1973.

Schwartz, S. H. Normative influence on altruism. In L. Berkowitz (Ed.), *Advances in experimental social psychology* (Vol. 10). New York: Academic Press, 1977.

Schwarz, G. Untersuchungen zur Handlungs-und Affektpsychologie. IV. Ueber Rueckfaelligkeit bei Umgewoehnung. 1. Teil. Rueckfalltendenz und Verwechslungsgefahr. *Psychologische Forschung*, 1927, *9*, 86–158.

Schwarz, G. Untersuchungen zur Handlungs-und Affektpsychologie. XVI. Ueber Rueckfaelligkeit bei Umgewoehnung. 2. Teil. Ueber Handlungsganzheiten und ihre Bedeutung fuer die Rueckfaelligkeit. *Psychologische Forschung*, 1933, *18*, 143–190.

Schwarzer, R., Lange, B., & Jerusalem, M. Selbstkonzeptentwicklung nach einem Bezugsgruppenwechsel. *Zeitschrift fuer Entwicklungspsychologie und paedagogische Psychologie*, 1982, *14*, 125–140.

Schwarzer, R., & Schwarzer, C. Achievement anxiety with respect to reference groups in school. *Journal of Educational Research*, 1982, *75*, 305–308.

Scitovsky, T. *The joyless economy*. New York: Oxford University Press, 1976.

Seligman, M. E. P. *Helplessness: On depression, development, and death*. San Francisco: W. H. Freeman, 1975.

Seligman, M. E. P. *Learned helplessness and life-span development*. Paper presented at the International Conference on Life-Course Research on Human Development, Berlin, September 1982.

Selman, R. L. *The growth of interpersonal understanding*. New York: Academic Press, 1980.

Semmer, N. Stress at work, stress in private life, and psychological well-being. In W. Bachmann & I. Udris (Eds.), *Mental load and stress in activity: European approaches*. Berlin: Deutscher Verlag der Wissenschaften, 1982.

Semmer, N., & Pfäfflin, M. *Interaktionstraining*. Weinheim: Beltz, 1978. (a)

Semmer, N., & Pfäfflin, M. Stress und das Training sozialer Kompetenz. In R. Boesel (Ed.), *Stress: Einfuehrung in die psychosomatische Belastungsforschung*. Hamburg: Hoffmann & Campe, 1978. (b)

Shapiro, D. A., & Shapiro, D. Meta-analysis of comparative therapy outcome studies: A replication and refinement. *Psychological Bulletin*, 1982, *92*, 581–604.

Shepard, R. N. Form, formation, and transformation of internal representations. In R. Solso (Ed.), *Information processing and cognition: The Loyola symposium*. Hillsdale, NJ: Lawrence Erlbaum Associates, 1975.

Shiffrin, R. M., & Dumais, S. T. The development of automatism. In J. R. Anderson (Ed.), *Cognitive skills and their acquisition*. Hillsdale, NJ: Lawrence Erlbaum Associates, 1981.

Shiffrin, R. M., Dumais, S. T., & Schneider, W. Characteristics of automatization. In J. Long & A. D. Baddeley (Eds.), *Attention and performance IX*. Hillsdale, NJ: Lawrence Erlbaum Associates, 1981.

Shure, M. B., & Spivack, G. *Problem-solving techniques in child rearing*. San Francisco: Jossey-Bass, 1978.

Silbereisen, R. K. Untersuchungen zur Frage sozial-kognitiv anregender Interaktionsbedingungen. In D. Geulen (Ed.), *Perspektivenwechsel, Rollenuebernahme, Verstehen*. Frankfurt/Mainz: Suhrkamp, 1981.

Silbereisen, R. K. The changing adolescent in a changing world: From segregation to integration of approaches. In R. K. Silbereisen & K. Eyferth (Eds.), *Development as action in context*. New York: Springer, in press.

Silbereisen, R. K., & Eyferth, K. (Eds.). *Development as action in context*. New York: Springer, in press.

Simon, H. *Models of man: Social and rational*. New York: Wiley, 1957.

Singer, J. L., & Pope, K. S. (Eds.). *The power of human imagination: New methods in psychotherapy*. New York: Plenum Press, 1978.

Skell, W. Bemerkungen zur Genese und Realisierung von Plaenen im Arbeitsprozess. In W. Hacker (Ed.), *Psychische Regulation von Arbeitstaetigkeiten*. Berlin: Deutscher Verlag der Wissenschaften, 1976.

Skinner, B. F. *Contingencies of reinforcement: A theoretical analysis.* New York: Appleton-Century-Crofts, 1969.

Skinner, E. A. Action, control judgments, and the structure of control experience. *Psychological Review.* (in press).

Skinner, E. A., & Chapman, M. Control beliefs in an action perspective. *Human Development,* 1984, *27,* 129–133.

Skinner, E. A., Chapman, M., & Baltes, P. B. *The causality, agency, and control interview (CACI).* Max Planck Institute for Human Development and Education, Berlin, 1983.

Slater, A. M., & Findlay, J. M. Binocular fixation in the newborn baby. *Journal of Experimental Child Psychology,* 1975, *20,* 248–273.

Smith, W. J. *The behavior of communicating: An ethological approach.* Cambridge, MA: Harvard University Press, 1977.

Spelke, E. S. Infants' intermodal perception of events. *Cognitive Psychology,* 1976, *8,* 553–560.

Spelke, E. S. Perceiving bimodally specified events in infancy. *Developmental Psychology,* 1979, *15,* 626–636.

Sperandio, J. C. Variations of operator's strategies and regulating effects on work load. *Ergonomics,* 1971, *14,* 571–577.

Stadler, M. Feldtheorie heute—von Wolfgang Köhler zu Karl Pribram. *Gestalt Theory,* 1981, *3,* 185–199.

Stadler, M., Seeger, F., & Raeithel, A. *Psychologie der Wahrnehmung.* Muenchen: Piper, 1975.

Stadler, M., & Wehner, T. Cognitive components in the operative and perceptive anticipation of goal-directed movements. In W. Hacker, W. Volpert, & M. von Cranach (Eds.), *Cognitive and motivational aspects of action.* Amsterdam/New York: North Holland, 1982.

Stadler, M., Wehner, T., & Hübner, H. Ansaetze zur Systemanalyse kognitiver Antizipationsleistungen. In W. Volpert (Ed.), *Beitraege zur psychologischen Handlungstheorie.* Bern: Huber, 1980.

Stankov, L. Attention and intelligence. *Journal of Educational Psychology,* 1983, *75,* 471–490.

Stäudel, T. *Problemloesen und emotionale Verlaeufe.* Paper presented at the meeting der experimentell arbeitenden Psychologen, Trier, 1982.

Stäudel, T. Problemloesen und Emotion. In H. A. Euler & H. Mandl (Eds.), *Emotionspsychologie in Schluesselbegriffen.* Muenchen: Urban & Schwarzenberg, 1983. (a)

Stäudel, T. Die Veraenderung des Problemloeseverhaltens bei emotionaler Belastung. In G. Luer (Ed.), *Bericht ueber den 33. Kongress der DGfPS in Mainz 1982.* Goettingen: Hogrefe, 1983. (b)

Stäudel, T. & Thumser, F. *Problemloesen und Emotionen in Misserfolgssituationen.* Paper presented at the meeting der experimentell arbeitenden Psychologen, Hamburg, 1983.

Steitz, J. A. Locus of control as a life-span developmental process: Revision of the construct. *International Journal of Behavioral Development,* 1982, *5,* 299–316.

Steklis, H. D., & Harnad, S. R. From hand to mouth: Some critical stages in the evolution of language. In S. R. Harnad, H. D. Steklis, & J. Lancaster (Eds.), *Origins and evolution of language and speech.* New York: Annals of the New York Academy of Sciences, Vol. 280, 1976.

Stelmach, G. E. *Information processing in motor control and learning.* New York: Academic Press, 1978.

Stelmach, G. E., & Requin, J. *Tutorials in motor behavior.* Amsterdam: North Holland, 1980.

Stern, D. *The first relationship: Infant and mother.* London: Open Books, 1977.

Stipek, D. J., & Weisz, J. R. Perceived personal control and academic achievement. *Review of Educational Research,* 1981, *51,* 101–137.

Strelau, J. Reactivity and activity style in selected occupations. *Polish Psychological Bulletin,* 1975, *6,* 199–207.

Taylor, F. W. *The principles of scientific management.* New York: Harper, 1911.

Taylor, M. S. The motivational effects of task challenge. *Organizational Behavior and Human Performance*, 1981, *27*, 255–278.

Tembrock, G. *Verhaltensbiologie*. Jena: VEB Gustav Fischer, 1968.

Thibaut, J. W., & Kelley, H. H. *The social psychology of groups*. New York: Wiley, 1959.

Thibaut, J., & Kelley, H. H. *Interpersonal relations: A theory of interdependence*. New York: John Wiley and Sons, 1978.

Thorndike, E. L. Animal intelligence. *Psychological Review Monograph Supplements*, 1898, No. 8. (Reprinted in W. Dennis [Ed.], *Readings in the history of psychology*. New York: Appleton-Century-Crofts, 1948.)

Thorpe, W. H. A note on detour behaviour with *Ammophila pubescens* Curt. *Behaviour*, 1950, *2*, 257–264.

Tinbergen, N., & Kruyt, W. Ueber die Orientierung des Bienenwolfes (*Philanthus tiangulum* Fabr.)— III Die Bevorzugung bestimmter Wegmarken. *Zeitschrift fuer vergleichende Physiologie*, 1938, *25*, 292–334.

Tinklepaugh, O. L. An experimental study of representative factors in monkeys. *Journal of Comparative Psychology*, 1928, *8*, 197–236.

Tolman, E. C. Can instincts be given up in psychology? *Journal of Abnormal Psychology and Social Psychology*, 1922, *17*, 139–152. (a) (Reprinted in E. C. Tolman [Ed.], *Behavior and psychological man*. Berkeley: University of California Press, 1951.)

Tolman, E. C. A new formula for behaviorism. *Psychological Review*, 1922, *29*, 44–53. (b) (Reprinted in E. C. Tolman [Ed.], *Behavior and psychological man*. Berkeley: University of California Press, 1951.)

Tolman, E. C. A behavioristic theory of ideas. *Psychological Review*, 1926, *33*, 352–369. (Reprinted in E. C. Tolman [Ed.], *Behavior and psychological man*. Berkeley: University of California Press, 1951.)

Tolman, E. C. *Purposive behavior in animals and men*. New York: Appleton-Century-Crofts, 1932.

Tolman, E. C. Principles of purposive behavior. In S. Koch (Ed.), *Psychology: A study of a science, II*. New York: McGraw–Hill, 1959.

Tolstoy, L. *Anna Karenina* (C. Garnett, trans.). New York: Random House, 1939.

Tomaszewski, T. Aktywnosc czowieka. In M. Maruszewski, J. Reykowski, & T. Tomaszewski (Eds.), *Psychologia jako nauka o czlowieku*. Warszawa: Ksiazka i Wiedza, 1967.

Tomaszewski, T. (Ed.). *Zur Psychologie der Taetigkeit*. Berlin: Deutscher Verlag der Wissenschaften, 1981.

Trope, Y. Uncertainty-reducing properties of achievement tasks. *Journal of Personality and Social Psychology*, 1979, *9*, 1505–1518.

Turiel, E. Conflict and transition in adolescent moral development. *Child Development*, 1974, *45*, 14–29.

Turvey, M. T. Preliminaries to a theory of action with reference to vision. In R. Shaw & J. Bransford (Eds.), *Perceiving, acting and knowing. Toward an ecological psychology*. Hillsdale, NJ: Lawrence Erlbaum Associates, 1977.

Turvey, M. T., Shaw, R. E., & Mace, W. Issues in the theory of action: Degrees of freedom, coordinative structures and coalitions. In J. Requin (Ed.), *Attention and performance VII*. Hillsdale, NJ: Lawrence Erlbaum Associates, 1978.

Tversky, A., & Kahneman, D. The framing of decisions and the psychology of choice. *Science*, 1981, *211*, 453–458.

Twitchell, T. E. Reflex mechanisms and the development of prehension. In K. Connolly (Ed.), *Mechanisms of motor skill development*. London: Academic Press, 1970.

Tyldesley, D. A., & Whiting, H. T. A. Operational timing. *Journal of Human Movement Studies*, 1975, *1*, 172–177.

Ulich, E. Some experiments on the function of mental training in the acquisition of motor skills. *Ergonomics*, 1967, *10*, 411–419.

Ullman, S. *The interpretation of visual motion.* Cambridge, MA: MIT Press, 1979.

Ullman, S. Against direct perceptions. *The Behavioral and Brain Sciences,* 1980, *3,* 373–415.

Unzner, L., & Schneider, K. Erlebte Schwierigkeit und subjektive Unsicherheit im Leistungshandeln: Ihre Entwicklung im Vorschulalter. *Zeitschrift für Entwicklungspsychologie und Pädagogische Psychologie,* 1984, *16*(4), 323–337.

Vogel, W., Raymond, S., & Lazarus, R. S. Intrinsic motivation and psychological stress. *Journal of Abnormal and Social Psychology,* 1959, *58,* 225–233.

Volpe, J. S. The development of concepts of self: An interpersonal perspective. In J. A. Meacham & N. R. Santilli (Eds.), *Social development in youth: Structure and content.* Basel: Karger, 1981.

Volpert, W. *Untersuchungen ueber den Einsatz des mentalen Trainings beim Erwerb einer sensumotorischen Fertigkeit. Ein Beitrag zur Optimierung von Trainingsprogrammen.* Koeln: Sporthochschule Koeln, 1969.

Volpert, W. *Sensumotorisches Lernen.* Frankfurt: Limpert, 1973.

Volpert, W. *Handlungsstrukturanalyse.* Koeln: Pahl Rugenstein, 1974.

Volpert, W. Ueberlegungen zum Vorgang der Planerzeugung. *Probleme und Ergebnisse der Psychologie,* 1976, *59,* 19–24.

Volpert, W. Zur Erforschung der Entwicklung innerer Modelle. In W. Hacker & H. Raum (Eds.), *Optimierung kognitiver Arbeitsanforderungen.* Berlin: Deutscher Verlag der Wissenschaften, 1980; Bern: Huber, 1980.

Volpert, W. The model of the hierarchical-sequential organization of action. In W. Hacker, W. Volpert, & M. von Cranach (Eds.), *Cognitive and motivational aspects of action.* Berlin: Deutscher Verlag der Wissenschaften, 1982; Amsterdam/New York: Elsevier/North-Holland, 1982.

Volpert, W. Emotionen aus der Sicht der Handlungsregulationstheorie. In J. P. Janssen & E. Hahn (Eds.), *Aktivierung, Motivation, Handlung und Coaching im Sport.* Schorndorf: Hofmann, 1983.

Volpert, W. Maschinen-Handlungen und Handlungs-Modelle—ein Plaedoyer gegen die Normierung des Handelns. *Gestalt Theory, 6,* 1984, 70–100.

Volpert, W. Gestaltbildung im Handeln: Von der Resonanz zur Konsonanz. Gestalt Theory, 1984.

Vroom, V. H. *Work and motivation.* New York: Wiley, 1964.

Vygotski, L. S. *Mind in society. The development of higher psychological processes.* Cambridge, MA: Harvard University Press, 1978.

Wächter, H. M., & Pudel, V. Kurztherapie von 15 Sitzugen mit dem katathymen Bilderleben. In H. Leuner (Ed.), *Katathymes Bilderleben: Ergebnisse in Theorie und Praxis.* Bern: Huber, 1980.

Wall, T. D., & Clegg, C. W. A longitudinal study of group work redesign. *Journal of Occupational Psychology,* 1981, *2,* 31–49.

Walper, S., Mülle, K., Noack, P., & Silbereisen, R. K. *Stimulation of social cognition in children: Do parents use theoretically appropriate interaction strategies?* Paper presented at the Sixth Biennial Meeting of the International Society for the Study of Behavioral Development, Toronto, Ontario, Canada, August 17–21, 1981.

Walster, E. The temporal sequence of post-decision processes. In L. Festinger (Ed.), *Conflict, decision, and dissonance.* Stanford, CA: Stanford University Press, 1964.

Watson, J. B. Psychology as the behaviorist views it. *Psychological Review,* 1913, *20,* 158–177. (Reprinted in W. Dennis [Ed.], *Readings in the history of psychology.* New York: Appleton-Century-Crofts, 1948.)

Watson, J. B. *Psychology from the standpoint of a behaviorist.* Philadelphia: J. B. Lippincott, 1919.

Watson, J. B., & McDougall, W. *The battle of behaviorism.* London: Kegan Paul, Trench, and Trubner, 1928.

Watson, J. S. The development and generalization of "contingency awareness" in early infancy: Some hypotheses. *Merrill-Palmer Quarterly,* 1966, *12,* 123–135.

Watson, J. S. Cognitive-perceptual development in infancy: Setting for the seventies. *Merrill-Palmer Quarterly,* 1971, *17,* 139–152.

Watson, J. S., & Ramey, C. T. Reactions to response-contingent stimulation in early infancy. *Merrill-Palmer Quarterly*, 1972, *18*, 219–227.

Watzlawick, P. *How real is real?* New York: Random House, 1976.

Wazuro, E. B. *Lehre Pawlows von der hoeheren Nerventaetigkeit.* Berlin: Volk und Wisson, 1975.

Weber, M. *Economy and society: An outline of interpretive sociology* (Vol. 1). New York: Bedminster Press, 1968.

Wehner, T., Stadler, M., Kruse, P., & Dahlke, F. Experimental studies on perceptive, mnestic and operative anticipation in sensori-motor learning. *Bremer Beiträge fuer Psychologie*, 1982.

Weiner, B., Russell, D. S., & Lerman, D. Affective consequences of causal ascriptions. In J. H. Harvey, W. J. Ickes, & R. F. Kidd (Eds.), *New directions in attribution research* (Vol. 2). Hillsdale, NJ: Lawrence Erlbaum Associates, 1978.

Weise, P. Werte als Alternativkosten. In H. Stachowiak & T. Ellwein (Eds.), *Beduerfnisse, Werte und Normen im Wandel.* Muenchen/Paderborn: Fink und Schoeningh, 1982.

Weiss, J. M. Psychological and behavioral inferences on gastrointestinal lesions in animal models. In J. D. Maser & M. E. P. Seligman (Eds.), *Psychopathology: Experimental models.* San Francisco: W. H. Freeman, 1977.

Weisz, J. R., & Stipek, D. J. Competence, contingency, and the development of perceived control. *Human Development*, 1982, *25*, 250–281.

von Weizsäcker, E. *Offene Systeme I. Beitraege zur Zeitstruktur von Information, Entropie und Evolution.* Stuttgart: Klett, 1974.

Welford, A. T. Stress and performance. *Ergonomics*, 1973, *16*, 567.

Wertheimer, M. *Productive thinking.* New York: Harper, 1945.

Wertsch, J. V. *The concept of activity in Soviet Psychology.* Armonk, N.Y.: Sharp, Inc. 1981.

Westergaard, J., & Resler, H. *Class in a capitalist society: A study of contemporary Britain.* London: Heinemann Educational Books, 1975.

Wheeler, D., & Janis, I. L. *Making vital decisions: A guidebook.* New York: Free Press, 1981.

Whimbey, A., & Lockhead, J. *Problem solving and comprehension: A short course in analytical reasoning* (2nd ed.). Philadelphia: Franklin Institute Press, 1980.

White, K. D., Ashton, R., & Lewis, S. Learning a complex skill: Effects of mental practice, physical practice, and imagery ability. *International Journal of Sport Psychology*, 1979, *10*, 71–78.

White, R. W. Motivation reconsidered: The concept of competence. *Psychological Review*, 1959, *66*, 297–333.

Wieland, R. *Untersuchung zur Aequivalenz schwankender Schallpegel.* Berlin: Umweltbundesamt, 1982.

Wilensky, H. L. Family life cycle, work and the quality of life: Reflections on the roots of happiness, despair and indifference in modern society. In B. Gardell & G. Johansson (Eds.), *Man and working life.* Chichester: Wiley, 1981.

Williams, B. *Moral luck.* Cambridge, Eng.: Cambridge University Press, 1981.

Winch, P. *The idea of a social science and its relation to philosophy.* London: Routledge & Kegan Paul, 1958.

Winograd, T. *Understanding natural language.* Edinburgh: University Press, 1972.

von Winterfeld, D., & Fischer, G. W. Multiattribute utility theory: Models and assessment procedures. In D. Wendt & C. Vlek (Eds.), *Utility, probability and human decision making.* Dordrecht: Reidel, 1975.

Wolff, S. *Zielsetzungsmoeglichkeiten als Merkmale progressiver Inhalte der Arbeit.* Unpublished doctoral dissertation, Technische Universitaet, Dresden (Naturwissenschaftlich-mathematische Fakultaet), 1981.

Wortman, C. B., & Brehm, J. B. Responses to uncontrollable outcomes: An integration of reactance theory and the learned helplessness model. In L. Berkowitz (Ed.), *Advances in experimental social psychology* (Vol. 8). New York: Academic Press, 1975.

von Wright, G. H. Freedom and determination. *Acta Philosophica Fennica*, 1980, *31*(1).

Wundt, W. *Outlines of psychology*. London/New York: Engelmann, 1907.

Yerkes, R. M., & Dodson, J. D. The relation of strength of stimulus to rapidity of habit-formation. *Journal of Comparative Neurology and Psychology*, 1908, *18*, 459–482.

Young, R. M. *Mind, brain, and adaptation in the nineteenth century*. Oxford: Clarendon Press, 1970.

Youniss, J. *Parents and peers in social development*. Chicago: University of Chicago Press, 1980.

Youniss, J. Single mind and social mind. *Human Development*, 1984, *27*, 133–135.

Zajonc, R. B. Feeling and thinking. Preferences need no inferences. *American Psychologist*, 1980, *35*, 152–175.

Zuckerman, M. *Sensation seeking: Beyond the optimal level of arousal*. Hillsdale, NJ: Lawrence Erlbaum Associates, 1979.

Zuroff, D. C. Learned helplessness in humans: An analysis of learning processes and the roles of individual and situational differences. *Journal of Personality and Social Psychology*, 1980, *39*, 130–146.

Author Index

A

Abelson, R. P., 246
Abramson, L. Y., 205, 206, 207, 305, 316
Adams, J. A., 76
Adler, N. T., 55
Ajzen, I., 304
Alcock, J., 37
Alderson, G. J. K., 88
Alegria, J., 94
Allen, A., 300
Alloy, L. B., 316
Anderson, C. A., 152
Anderson, J. R., 292
Anderson, M. P., 317
Andrews, G. R., 337, 338
Anokhin, P. K., 69, 262
Arbib, M. A., 95
Asch, S. E., 253
Aschenbrenner, K. M., 339
Aslin, R. N., 93, 94
Ashby, W. R., 359
Ashton, D. R., 318
Aston, B., 289
Athay, M., 229, 231, 249
Atkinson, J. W., 134, 137, 141, 151, 161–170, 174, 175, 335
Austin, G., 282
Austin, J. L., 15

B

Baarsma, E. A., 50
Baddeley, A. P., 210
Badgio, P., 334, 335, 339
Bahrick, H. P., 287
Bahrick, L. E., 101, 287
Baltes, P. B., 203, 205
Bandura, A., 206, 307, 334, 335
Banks, M. S., 94
Bärends, G. P., 57
Baron, J., 254, 255, 321, 323, 334, 335, 338, 339, 345–354
Baron, R. M., 253
Barta, S. G., 141, 313
Bar-Tal D., 216
Bartlett, F. C., 360
Bates, E., 44
Bateson, G., 364
Battalio, R. C., 175
Battmann, W., 184
Baumgardt, C., 217, 226
Beach, B. H., 341
Beach, L. R., 123, 131, 341
Beatty, H., 26
Beatty, J., 270
Beck, A. T., 156, 296, 305, 306, 308
Beckhofer, F., 268
Beckmann, J., 153

Bem, D. J., 300
Berger, P., 250
Bernstein, N. A., 85, 262, 277
Berry, D., 289
Beusekom, G., 58
Beyth-Marom, R., 339
Bieglow, J., 15
Birch, D., 134, 137, 141, 161–170, 174, 175
Birchall, D., 287
Bitterman, M. E., 192
Blackwell, J., 208
Blancy, P. H., 313
Blank, M., 339
Blankenship, V., 163, 165, 166, 167
Blankertz, J., 350
Blau, P. M., 232, 233
Blood, M. K., 288
Boesch, C., 26
Boesch, E., 200
Boggiano, A. K., 331, 332
Bohm, D., 359, 363, 364
Bolles, R. C., 68
Bongort, K., 165, 166
Borjesson, E., 82
Botwinick, J., 75
Bourdieu, P., 246
Bower, G. H., 351
Bower, T. G. R., 85
Brainerd, C. J., 211
Branstätter, H., 182
Brandtstädter, J., 200, 203
Breger, L., 296
Brehm, J. B., 186
Brehm, J. W., 136, 153
Breznitz, S., 187
Brichin, M., 277
Brickman, P., 334
Brim, O. G., 205
Brinkman, C., 75
Broadbent, D. E., 192, 261, 277, 286, 287, 288, 289, 358
Brockner, J., 186
Bronfenbrenner, U., 203
Brooks, V., 81
Brown, T. G., 51
Bruner, J. S., 282
Bullinger, A., 93
Burtis, P. J., 211
Busch-Rossnagel, N. A., 215

C

Campbell, D. T., 272
Capra, F., 359, 364
Carello, C., 83
Cartledge, N. D., 277
Cartwright, B. A., 58, 59
Carver, C. S., 297, 313, 316
Case, R., 211
Chapin, M., 337
Chapman, M., 199, 200, 204, 205, 211, 212, 215
Cheng, K., 58
Chevalier-Skolinkoff, S., 42
Christiansen-Szalanski, J. J. J., 341
Claar, A., 220, 226
Clark, R. A., 161
Clegg, C. W., 286
Cohen, A. R., 136
Cohen, L. J., 323
Cohen, S., 188
Collet, T. S., 58, 59
Collewijn, H., 50
Collins, A., 339
Conrad, R., 286
Cook, T. D., 272
Cooper, H. M., 209
Cooper, P. F., 286
Corbin, C. B., 103
Corlett, E. N., 192
Covington, M. V., 336
Coyne, J. C., 177
von Cranach, M., 166, 169, 201, 215, 358
Cronbach, L. J., 190
Csiksaentmihalyi, M., 138, 173
Cunningham, C. C., 88

D

Dahlke, F., 76
Dahrendorf, R., 353
Darley, J. M., 229, 231, 249
Darwin, C., 27, 31, 61, 84, 197
Davenport, K. R., 28
Davidson, D., 17
Davis, J. H., 182
Debus, R. L., 337, 338
Decenteco, E. T., 308
DeCharms, R., 336
Deci, E. L., 368

Deeke, L., 197
Deese, J., 192
Dekel, S., 339
Dembo, T., 135, 185, 186
Dempster, F. N., 210
Dennett, D. C., 10
Dethier, V., 53
Dewey, J., 16, 254
Diener, C. I., 307
DiFranco, D., 94
Dixon, R. A., 203
Dodson, J. D., 191
Dodwell, P., 94
Doise, W., 223
Dolgin, K. G., 19
Dollard, J., 207
Dörner, D., 110–111, 113, 114, 116, 117,
    118, 180, 181, 358
Dreyfus, H. L., 360, 364
Ducker, G., 25
Dumais, S. T., 287, 299
Duncker, K., 180
Dweck, C. S., 207, 208, 209, 336, 337, 338
Dyck, D. G., 337

E

Eagle, M. N., 351
Easterbrook, J. A., 191, 192
Eccles, J. C., 75, 76
Eckensberger, L. H., 200, 201, 202, 215, 217
Edelstein, W. A., 200, 212
Edwards, W., 330
Eells, E., 323
Egeland, B., 337
Elliott, E. S., 336
Ellis, A., 308
Engels, F., 31
Epstein, A., 65
Eriksen, C. W., 192
Eysenck, H. J., 296

F

Fagan, R., 37
Feather, N. T., 326
Feinstein, B., 75
Feldman, A. G., 85
Fencil-Morse, E., 186
Festinger, L., 135, 153

Field, J., 94
Findlay, J. M., 94
Findley, M. J., 209
Finke, R. A., 318
Fiorentini, A., 72
Fishbein, M., 296
Fischer, G. W., 174
Fischhoff, B., 335
Fisk, M., 352
Fitch, H. L., 102
Flavell, J. H., 40
Flammer, A., 113
Folkman, S., 172, 177, 194, 196
Forssberg, H. S., 52
Forsstrom, A., 85
Fowler, J. W., 338
Frankenhauser, M., 181
Franklin, B., 31, 341
Frese, M., 200, 229, 251, 262, 288, 295,
    300, 311, 358
Freud, S., 134, 165, 189
FritzGerald, P., 286, 289
Fuhrer, U., 186, 226
Fritsche, B., 280

G

Galanter, E., 202, 225, 251, 261, 265, 297,
    312, 326, 357, 363
Gallistel, C. R., 47, 48, 58, 67–77, 297, 358
Gallup, C. C., 27
Ganellen, R. J., 316
Garber, J., 205
Garfinkel, V. S., 85
Gaskins, I. W., 338
Gath, D., 287
Geiger, E., 168
Gentile, A., 85
Gerlach, F., 256
Getzels, J. W., 173
Gibson, E. J., 92–95, 100
Gibson, J. J., 81–85, 98–99, 106, 254, 360
Gibson, K. R., 21, 24, 40, 42, 44
Gill, T., 35
Glass, G. V., 309
Gleiss, H., 300
Gleitman, H., 299
Globerson, T., 211
Goffman, E., 236, 242, 244, 251
Goldfried, M. R., 308

Goldman, A. I., 202
Goldthorpe, J. H., 288
Goodall, J., 29, 30
Goodnow, J. J., 282
Gordon, G. B., 77
Graybiel, A., 86
Greene, L., 175
Greene, D., 139, 185, 331
Greer, K., 264
Grillner, S., 52
Gschlössl, A., 256
Gugler, B., 201, 215
Günther, R., 220
Gurin, P., 205

H

Habermas, J., 212
Hacker, W., 72, 172, 180, 183, 184, 267,
  270, 273, 274, 276, 280, 281, 282, 285,
  297, 298, 299, 358
Hackman, J. R., 280
Hagerman, S., 157, 158
Haith, M., 93, 94
Halsey, M. N., 178
Hall, K. R., 25
Halton, A., 94
Hamilton, E. W., 316
Hamilton, V., 192
Harnad, S. R., 42, 44
Harré, R., 251
Harris, A., 169
Hare, R. M., 326
Harvey, N., 64
Hasher, L., 211
Haugeland, J., 193
Hay, D., 196
Hayes-Roth, B., 184
Hayes-Roth, F., 184
Heath, A., 232, 243
Heckhausen, H., 116, 117, 120, 133, 134,
  146, 153, 155, 161–170, 172, 175, 197,
  300, 314, 338, 351
Heider, F., 253
Hein, A., 81
Held, R., 81
Helle, P., 156
von Helmholtz, H. L. F., 80, 265
Henle, M., 194
Herrmann, G., 281

Hesse, H. W., 117
Heshaw, D., 172
Heymer, A., 20
Hilgard, E. R., 12
Himel, N., 172
Hitch, G., 210
Hochberg, J. E., 81
von Hofsten, C., 79, 82, 84, 85, 90, 91, 93,
  94, 97, 253
Hollerbach, J. M., 68
Hollon, S. D., 205
von Holst, E., 69, 81
Holtzman, H. W., 192
Holzkamp, K., 31
Homans, G., 232, 233
Hoppe, F., 181
Horn, J., 211
Horvath, F. E., 192
Hubner, H., 77
Hulin, C. L., 288
Hull, C. L., 17, 20, 189, 191
Hunt, E., 210, 210

I

von Iersel, J. J., 58, 59
Immelmann, K., 20, 35
Indermühle, K., 201, 215
Inman, V. T., 75
Irle, M., 153
Irwin, F. W., 56, 65, 325
Itani, J., 25, 37
Ivanowa, A., 267

J

Jackson, P. R., 288
Jackson, R. W., 94
James, W., 154, 168, 202, 254
Janis, I. L., 182, 195, 226, 339, 341, 342
Janoff-Bulman, R., 334
Jansson, G., 82
Jantsch, E., 359, 362, 364
Jantschke, F., 25
Jerusalem, 213
Jaus, D., 339
Jokl, E., 86
Johansson, G., 82, 86
Johnson, M. K., 179

K

Kagel, J. H., 175
Kahneman, D., 202, 210, 324
Kalbermatten, U., 166, 201, 215, 358
Kaminski, G., 225, 358
Kanfer, S. K., 157, 158
Karasek, R. A., 286
Kay, H., 89
Kazdin, A. E., 317
Keele, S. W., 297
Keeney, R. L., 330, 340, 341
Keller, M., 200, 212
Kelley, H. H., 232, 233, 351
Kelly, G. A., 256
Kerr, N. H., 105
Klapp, S. T., 210
Klaus, 359
Klein, D. C., 186
Klein, R. M., 98
Kliegl, R. M., 309
Klinger, E., 134, 136, 141, 146, 152, 295, 313, 314, 315, 316, 318, 361
Klix, F., 348
Kholberg, L., 175
Koestler, R., 332
Koestner, R., 332
Köhler, W., 20, 27, 28, 38, 43, 73
Kolb, D. A., 336
Komorita, S. S., 187
Kornhuber, H. H., 75
Kortlandt, A., 28, 29
Kossman, D. A., 229
Kots, Y. M., 85
Krantz, D. H., 323
Krau, E., 194
Krautch, J., 280
Kreshovnikov, A. N., 86
Krenauer, M., 181
Kreuzig, H. W., 111, 113, 114, 116, 117, 118, 180
Krinskiy, V. I., 85
Kruse, P., 72, 76
Kuhl, J., 133, 134, 138, 151, 154, 155, 156, 157, 161–170, 184, 186, 300, 314, 315
Kukla, A., 174
Künstler, B., 181
Küting, A. J., 217
Kruse, P., 72, 76
Kruyt, W., 58
Kummer, H., 26

L

Lange, R., 213
Lashley, K. S., 8, 73
Lauria, A. R., 72, 262
Lazarus, R. S., 120, 171, 172, 176, 177, 192, 194, 196, 304, 305, 365
Lawick-Goodall, J., 21, 25, 43
Lea, S. E., 175
Lee, D. N., 81, 88, 89, 100, 107
Lefcourt, H. M., 204, 206, 209
Lefebvre-Pinard, M., 223
Lehrman, D. S., 61
Leiser, T., 216
Leonitiev, A. N., 31, 261, 262, 265, 361, 365
Lepper, M., 139, 185, 331
Lerman, D. S., 175
Lerner, R. M., 203, 215
Lester, P. T., 210
Leuner, H., 317
Lewin, K., 68, 135, 139, 151, 165, 172, 196
Lewis, E. R., 68
Lichtenstein, S., 335
Lienert, G. A., 280
Lindhagen, K., 85, 90
Lipsitt, L. P., 203
Lishman, J. R., 88
Locke, E. A., 151, 277
Lockhead, J., 339
Lockwood, D., 288
Loizos, C., 37
Lomov, B. F., 73, 74
de Longis, A., 177, 194
Lowell, C. L., 161
Luce, R. D., 323
Luchins, A. S., 302
Luchins, E. H., 302
Luckmann, T., 250
Lundberg, U., 181
Luria, A. R., 265

M

Mace, W., 359
MacKay, D. G., 104
Macmurray, J., 202
Maffei, L., 72
Mahoney, M. J., 296
Mann, L., 195, 226, 341, 342
Mannarino, A., 213
Marchburn, E. A., 210

Marks, I., 314
Marr, D., 293
Marx, K., 234, 262
Maslow, A. H., 124, 261
Masters, J. C., 306
Matarazzo, J. D., 211
Matern, B., 266, 272, 282
Mathieu, M., 42
May, W. H., 174
Maxeiner, M. E., 141, 313
McArthur, L. Z., 253, 254, 255
McClelland, D. C., 161, 336
McDougall, W., 5, 315
McGough, J. L., 296
McGrew, W. C., 26, 43
Meacham, J. A., 200, 210, 212
Mechanic, D., 196
Melden, A. J., 17
Melzoff, A. N., 101
Meichenbaum, D. A., 172, 296, 306, 307,
    336, 337
Mendelson, M. J., 94
Mento, A. J., 277, 280
Menzel, E. M., 28
Messer, S. B., 300
Metzger, W., 360
Meyer, J. P., 197
Meyer, P., 24
Michaels, C. F., 83
Michaels, E. J., 163, 166
Michela, J. L., 351
Michie, D., 292
Midgett, P. S., 43
Mikula, G., 174
Milgram, S., 250
Milhoffer, P., 256
Miller, A. T., 208
Miller, G. A., 3, 4, 16, 17, 202, 213, 225,
    251, 261, 265, 277, 297, 312, 326, 357,
    363
Miller, I. W., 206
Miller, L. E., 187
Miller, N., 207
Miller, R., 352
Miller, R. B., 268
Miller, S. M., 187
Mims, V., 332
Miron, M. S., 174
Mischel, H. N., 200, 202
Mischel, W., 200, 206
Mitchell, T. R., 131, 341

Mittler, P. J., 88
Mittelstadt, H., 67
Moore, B., Jr., 256
Moore, D., 187
Moore, M. K., 101
Mugny, G., 223
Muir, D., 94
Mulherin, A., 186
Mulle, K., 221
Mündelein, H., 181, 184

N

Naumann, W., 281
Neisser, U., 72, 79, 92, 106, 107, 144, 253,
    254, 276, 360, 361, 363, 364
Newell, A., 291, 292
Newman, J. R., 330
Nicholls, J. G., 208, 213
Nigro, G. N., 103, 104
Nisbett, R. E., 169
Nissen, M. J., 98
Noack, P., 221
Noble, D., 51
Noirot, E., 98
Norman, D. A., 183, 184, 265, 303
Norman, W. H., 206
Norros, L., 282
Nuttin, J., 172

O

Obuchowski, K., 351
Oken, S., 196
Oldham, G. R., 280
Omelich, C. L., 336
Oppenheimer, L., 200
Oschanin, D. A., 72
Osgood, C. E., 174
Osler, S. F., 192
Österreich, R., 120, 363
Overton, W. F., 203

P

Palstev, Y. I., 85
Parker, S. T., 21, 24, 40, 42, 44
Parkes, K. R., 286
Pascual-Leone, J., 211
Patterson, C. J., 202
Patterson, R. D., 285

Paul, L. J., 288
Pavlov, I., 24
Pearlin, L. I., 196
Peiper, A., 97
Perret-Clermont, A. N., 223
Perry, R. B., 7
Pervin, L. A., 313
Peters, R. S., 135
Peterson, P. L., 338
Pfäfflin, M., 296, 303, 306
Phares, E. J., 206
Phillips, L. D., 335
Piaget, J., 19, 40, 113, 360, 361
Plath, H. E., 274
Plato, 322
Platt, J., 288
Pilon, R., 94
Plato, 13
Plooij, F., 30
Pope, K. S., 314
Porter, R., 75
Posner, M. I., 98, 297
Poulton, E. C., 76
Premack, D., 35, 42, 43, 335
Pribram, K. H., 3, 4, 72, 73, 202, 225, 251,
   261, 265, 297, 312, 326, 357, 360, 362,
   363
Pudel, V., 314, 317
Putz-Osterloh, W., 120

R

Rabbitt, P. M. A., 77
Rachlin, H., 175
Rachman, S., 296
Rader, N., 92, 93
Raeithel, A., 361
Raiffa, H., 340
Ralston, H. J., 75
Rapport, D. J., 173
Ravis, A., 216
Rawlings, E. I., 318
Rawlings, I. L., 318
Rawls, J., 321, 322, 323, 339, 342, 345–354
Raye, C. L., 179
Raymond, S., 192
Raynor, J. L., 332
Reason, J. T., 178, 183, 184
Reddish, P. E., 89
Redshaw, M., 42, 44
Reed, E. S., 83, 84

Reese, H. W., 203
Reid, M., 223
Reither, F., 113, 114, 116, 117, 118, 123–
   131, 180, 181
Remey, C. T., 207
Rensch, B., 20, 25, 28, 31
Repucci, N. D., 337
Requin, J., 361
Resler, H., 241, 242
Reuman, D., 166, 168
Reykowski, J., 181
Reynolds, F., 25
Reynolds, V., 25
Rholes, W. S., 208
Revelle, W., 163
Richardson, A., 103, 318
Richardson, J., 192
Richter, P., 267, 270, 273, 274, 282
Rimm, D. C., 306
Robinson, E. J., 220
Robinson, W. P., 220
Rock, J., 81
Roeder, K. D., 62
Rogers, C., 28
Romanes, G. Y., 27
Rosenblueth, A., 15, 16
Rossignol, S., 52
Rothbaum, F., 186
Rotschke, S., 280
Rotter, J. B., 204
Rozin, P., 95
Rubinstein, S. L., 262, 365
Ruble, D. N., 332
Ruff, H. A., 94
Rumbaugh, D., 35, 43
Ruhle, R., 264, 266, 282
Russell, B., 13–15, 365
Russell, D. S., 175
Ryan, R. M., 332
Ryff, C. D., 205

S

Sabini, J., 17, 229, 250
Salmon, M., 62
de Saunders, J. B., 75
Savage, E. S., 43
Schaefer, C., 172
Schaie, K. W., 203
Scheier, M. F., 297, 313
Schmidt, R. A., 76, 107, 361

V

Villani, C., 339
Vogel, W., 192
Vogt, S., 72
Volpe, J. S., 213
Volpert, W., 265, 297, 298, 258, 361, 362,
  363, 364
Vroom, V. H., 172, 268
Vygotski, L. S., 262, 361, 365

W

Wächter, H. M., 314
Walker, A. S., 101
Wall, T. D., 286, 288
Walper, S., 221
Walster, E., 153
Walters, C., 208
Warburton, D. M., 192
Watson, J. B., 4, 5, 17
Watson, J. S., 207
Watzlawick, P., 197
Wazuro, E. B., 24
Weber, M., 234, 241
Wehner, T., 47, 72, 76, 77
Weib, M., 157
Weinberg, V., 308
Weiner, B., 174
Weiner, W., 15
Weise, P., 174
Weiss, J. M., 305
Weiss, P., 67
Weisy, G. R., 186
Weisz, J. R., 206
Weizsacker, E., 364
Welford, A. T., 192

Wertheimer, M., 73
Westergaard, J., 241, 242
Wheler, D., 339
Whimbey, A., 339
White, K. D., 318
White, R. W., 329
Whiting, H. T. A., 88
Wicklund, R. A., 153
Wieland, R., 177, 180, 181
Wild, R., 287
Wilensky, H. L., 177
Williams, B., 326
Wilson, T. D., 169
Winch, P., 212
Winograd, T., 290
von Winterfeld, D., 174
Wolff, S., 274, 280
Wortman, C. B., 186
Wright Jr., E. W., 75, 212
von Wright, G. H., 212

Y

Yerkes, R. M., 191
Young, R. M., 48
Youniss, J., 212, 213

Z

Zacks, R., 211
Zajonc, R. B., 358, 363
Zeiss, A., 206
Zeiss, R., 206
Zimmer, K., 181
Zuckerman, M., 173
Zuroff, D. C., 204, 207

Subject Index

A

Absenteeism, 273
Acceptor of effect, 71
Achievement behavior, 175
Achievement motivation, 197, 321, 323, 330, 336, 342
  training of, 336–337
Action
  complete, 261
  definition, 84–85
  end phase, 202
  execution phase, 202
  initiation phase, 202
  skillful, 85
Action launching impulse (ALI), 137, 150, 154
Action planning, 114–116
Action slips, 183, 302
Action styles, 300, 303, 306, 322, 328, 333, 336–339, 342
Action tendency, 162–170
Action unit, 124
Activity, 23, 40, 261, 262–283
  and action, 262
  complete, 272–276
  partialized, 272–276
  special nature, 267–268
Activity-regulating knowledge, 281
Adolescents, 216

Advance image, 70
Afferent synthesis, 71
Affordances, 82–84, 99, 102, 361
Agency beliefs, 204–213
Aggression, 26
"Aha" experiences, 118
Algorithm, 362
Anthropology, 31
Anthropomorphism, 10, 21, 23, 31, 33, 39
Anticipation, 68–77, 89, 92, 105, 107
Anxiety, 181, 191, 193, 197
Aristotelian principle, 326, 328, 330, 335
Arousal, 30, 38, 191, 197
Artificial intelligence, 364
Aspiration level, 181
Associationism, 16
Attention, 141, 191
Attributional style, 305, 316
Attributions, 337–338
Australopithecus, 31
Automaticity, 209–210, 232, 251, 287, 295, 298–299, 302–308
Automatic thoughts, 296, 299
Automization, 193, 267

B

Behavior economics, 173–175, 193
Behaviorism
  explanation of purpose, 6–15

molar, 5
molecular, 5
philosophy, 12
physicalism, 12
Behavior therapy, 309
Bipedal locomotion, 32

C

Catching, 87–92
Causality beliefs, 204–213
Chimpanzee, 19–44
Circular reactions, 41–42
Clever Hans, 6
Cognition and action, 296–300, 311
Cognitive-dissonance theory, 153
Cognitive maps, 9, 72, 112
Cognitive therapy, 308
Collective action, 256
Communication, 220–226
Community, 234, 243
Competence, 175, 240, 329–331, 334, 349–
   350
Competencies, 231, 234
Competition, 329, 332, 334, 348–349
Computer stimulation, 111–112
Consciousness, 4, 265, 289
   levels of, 265–267
Control, 201, 266, 286, 288–289, 292
Control beliefs, 204, 206–209
Coping, 171, 192, 193, 196
   collective, 196
Counselors, 237, 251
Current concerns, 136, 141
Cybernetics, 4, 16

D

Decision making, 114–116, 123–131, 198,
   339
   training of, 339–342
Decision theory, 194, 324, 345
Deep structure, 264, 270
Defective want, 142
Degrees of freedom, 269, 274, 280
Deliberative rationality, 326
Depression, 156–157, 305, 316
Depotentiation, 47, 52–55, 64
Desensitization, 306
Deskilling, 263
Digger wasps, 57

Digit-span, 210–211
Disengagement, 171, 186–188, 194
Dynamic of the problem situation, 112

E

Efficiency, 173–185, 193, 195, 264, 281,
   300–305
Effort, 202, 206–209
   mental, 209–213
Effort of attention, 316
Emotion, 47, 48, 61–62, 120, 175, 182, 198,
   222, 351, 363
   display of, 61–62
   having vs. displaying, 62
   and problem solving, 120
Escape, 116
Ethology, 48
Evaluations, 175, 202
Evolution, 5, 19–44, 95, 175, 359
   specialization of perception, 95
Exchange theory, 229–250, 249–252
   critique of, 232–233
Expectancy-value theory, 249–252
Expected utility, 232
Experts, 115
Exploratory actions, 80, 92–95
Extroversion, 120
Eye movements, 94

F

Failure, 173, 175, 193
Fatigue, 266, 270, 273, 274, 282
Fear of failure, 331
Feedback, 15–17, 109, 130, 177, 179, 184–
   185, 254, 265, 301, 302, 307
   detailed, 185
   realistic, 185
   unpredictable, 302
Feed forward, 68
Frustrations, 185, 316, 332
Functional system, 69

G

Gestalt psychologists, 98, 363–364
Goal finding, 112–113
Goals, 16, 20, 22, 26, 27, 28, 33, 35, 40, 41,
   68, 95, 109, 110, 123–124, 127, 137–
   140, 178, 193, 194, 197, 201, 217, 222,

225, 256, 262, 264–265, 268, 275, 277, 278, 290, 301, 312
and anticipation, 268, 277
and aversive tactics, 127–128
clarity, 127
and denial, 268
fatigue, 275
higher order, 262
intentions, 278
and interaction, 268
job satisfaction, 275
longterm, 127–128
satiation, 275
set point, 277
setting, 177, 181–182, 202
social origin, 278
habit formation, 11
Grasping, 28, 94
Group-think, 182
Guided experience, 118

H

Habits, 3, 28
motor, 28
Head-arm coordination, 94
Helplessness, 206–209, 207, 337
Heuristics, 266, 299, 301, 302, 306
Hierarchy, 48, 50, 55, 64, 67–77, 95, 115, 124, 183, 256, 265–266, 272, 297–299, 317, 358
Holistic approach, 359
Holography theory of memory, 72

I

Images, 103–105, 210, 317
Imagination, 74, 101, 296
Implementation skills, 128–129
Impression formation, 253
Inefficiency, 171
Infants, 91, 93–94, 100–101
Information processing, 112–113, 181, 197, 222, 331–334, 348
Initiation phase, 202
Impulsivity, 335
Insight, 20, 27–28, 38, 43, 298
Institutions, 250
Instrumental attitude, 288
Instrumentality, 135, 148–150, 268, 332–333, 347

Insulation, 182
Intellectualization, 303
Intelligence, 20, 28, 120, 211
Intention, 3, 48, 56–61, 70, 134–159, 154, 161, 167, 201, 315
defective, 154–158
dynamics of, 161–170
Interaction competencies, 231
Interdependency of problems, 112
Internal representations, 28–29, 103, 107, 205, 360
Interpersonal problem-solving skills, 217
Intersensory phenomena, 98
Introspection, 5

J

Job Analysis Survey, 267, 274
Job design, 263
Job enrichment, 288–289, 293
Justice, 322, 324–328, 352

K

Knowledge
declarative, 291–293
procedural, 291–293

L

Labor unions, 257
Latent learning, 9
Learned helplessness, 305
Levels of regulation, 298–305, 308
Life plans, 325–326, 346
Long range effects, 115
Lower level inclusion, 139

M

Manipulation, 231
Memory
active, 210–211
short term, 210–211
waking, 210–211
Mental health, 287–288
Mental practice, 80, 103–104, 296, 318, 361
mechanisms, 104
Mental representations, 276–283, 291
Mental retardation, 267
Metacognition, 109

Metavolitions, 153
Misregulation, 177–185
Model construction, 176, 178–181
Monitoring, 126, 127, 130
Monotony, 273, 274
Moral judgment, 175
Motivation, 48, 134–170, 190, 222, 280, 313–315

N

Neanderthals, 32
Need for control, 120
Neonate, 93
Neuroticism, 120
Neurotic symptoms, 286
Noise, 193
Normative models, 323–328

O

Obedience, 250
Objectivity, 255–257
Obsessive-compulsiveness, 302
Obstacles to rationality, 350–351
Orienting reaction, 72
Oscillator, 51, 49–52, 64, 67–77
    heart beat, 51
    rhythm, 51

P

Paced work, 286
Passivity, 186
Perception, 80, 82, 83, 92
    action, 80–108, 97, 99, 102
    direct, 83
    immediacy, 80
    immediacy of, 92
    natural unit of, 83
    of motion, 82–96
    statistic images, 80
Perceptual cycles, 92, 95, 104–107, 253–254, 360
Performance deficits, 207
Persistence, 208, 334
Personality dispositions, 280
Personality-enhancement, 261, 263
Personalistic psychology, 190, 197
Personal narratives, 236
Person perception, 230, 253

Perspective taking, 216–220, 222, 250–252
Phobias, 305
Plans, 109, 184, 197, 201–202, 222, 256, 268, 301, 316–317, 326
Play, 29, 37
Positional power, 230–247
Postdecisional conflict, 153
Potentiation, 47, 52–55, 64
Pragmatism, 255
Predictability, 287
Priority change, 182
Process models, 358
Processing capacity, 240, 303
Problem generation, 173, 175
Problem solving, 20, 28, 172–173
Process orientation, 194
Psychobiological adaptation, 190, 197
Psychologizing, 27
Psychopathology, 295–313, 304, 316–317
Purposes, 4–17, 85

R

Rationality, 321–354
Reafference, 69
Realism, 197, 360
Reflection, 233
Reflexes, 41, 49–52, 53, 64, 67–77
Reflexivity, 201, 337
Rehearsal, 210
Repression, 187
Repressors, 194
Roles, 235–240, 250–252

S

Satiation, 273–274
Satisfaction, 274, 288
Schemas, 72, 92, 103–104, 105, 106–108, 360
Schizophrenia, 302
Scripts, 246
Sedimentation, 255
Self-actualization, 124
Self-assessment, 121
Self-confidence, 120
Self-confronting interview, 216, 221
Self-defense, 47
Self-esteem, 175, 348
Self-instruction, 337, 338
Self-interest, 325

Self-respect, 325, 330
Sensitizers, 194
Sensorimotor intelligence, 40
Sensorimotor behavior, 48
Sensorimotor skills, 296
Sensorimotor theory, 64
Servomechanisms, 16, 49–52, 64, 67–77
  optokinetic reaction, 49
  oscillator, 49–52
  reflex, 49–52
Short cuts, 143
Side effects, 115
Situation analysis, 113–114
Social cognition, 216–226
Social desirability, 333–335, 347
Social exchange, 245
Social interaction, 229
Social order, 327, 346
Social production, 233–240
Social support, 128, 186
Stick use, 28–29, 38
Strategy, 124, 126, 225, 251, 264
Strategy formation, 177, 183–184
Stress, 171–198, 273, 286, 304
Stress-Inoculation-Training, 306
Supercodes, 314
Superstitious behavior, 38
Supplementary Motor Area (SMA), 75–76
Systematic desensitization, 317

T

Tactics, 124–125
Technology, 286
Teleology, 12–17, 20, 27

Test-operate-test-exit (TOTE), 161, 251–252,
  290, 293, 312
Therapy, 305–310, 317–319
Thinking and action, 119–121, 161
Thought stopping, 306
Time and motion studies, 270
Timing, 87–92, 88, 91
Time pressure, 193
Token-economy programs, 309
Tool traditions, 32
Tool use, 21–41
Top spins, 141–146
Trainer-trainee interactions, 224
Trial acting, 74
Turnover, 273

U

Units of behavior, 49
Urgency, 136
Utility
  expected, 232
  instrumental, 232
Utility theory, 339–342, 346

V

Vagabonding, 116
Value-expectancy models, 134–159
  critique, 134
Volition, 150–151
Vulnerability hypothesis, 212

W

Wishes, 134–159

For Product Safety Concerns and Information please contact our EU
representative GPSR@taylorandfrancis.com
Taylor & Francis Verlag GmbH, Kaufingerstraße 24, 80331 München, Germany

www.ingramcontent.com/pod-product-compliance
Lightning Source LLC
Chambersburg PA
CBHW050558270326
41926CB00012B/2098